Philosophy of Justice

Institut International de Philosophie

La philosophie contemporaine

Chroniques nouvelles

par les soins de
GUTTORM FLØISTAD
Université d'Oslo

Tome 12

Philosophie de la Justice

For further volumes:
http://www.springer.com/series/5784

International Institute of Philosophy

Contemporary Philosophy

A New Survey

edited by

GUTTORM FLØISTAD
University of Oslo

Volume 12

Philosophy of Justice

Springer

Editor
Guttorm Fløistad
Institute for the History of Ideas
University of Oslo
Oslo, Norway

Philosophy of Justice/edited by Guttorm Fløistad
p.cm. – (Contemporary Philosophy, A New Survey; v. 12)
English and French
Includes bibliographical references and index.

Published under the auspices of the International Council of Philosophy and Humanistic Studies and of the International Federation of Philosophical Societies, with the support of UNESCO.

Publié sous les auspices du Conseil International de la Philosophie et des Sciences Humaines et de la Fédération Internationale des Sociétés de Philosophie, avec le concours de l'UNESCO.

ISBN 978-94-024-0796-9 ISBN 978-94-017-9175-5 (eBook)
DOI 10.1007/978-94-017-9175-5
Springer Dordrecht Heidelberg New York London

Printed on acid-free paper

Springer is part of Springer Science+Business Media (www.springer.com)

Preface

The present volume is the last of the series *Contemporary Philosophy*. As with the earlier volumes in the series, the present chronicles purport to give a survey of significant trends in contemporary philosophy.

The need for such surveys has, I believe, increased rather than decreased over the years. The philosophical scene appears, for various reasons, more complex than ever before. The continuing process of specialization in most branches, the increasing contact between philosophers from various cultures, the emergence of new schools of thought, particularly in philosophical logic and in the philosophy of language and ethics, and the increasing attention being paid to the history of philosophy in discussions of contemporary problems are the most important contributing factors. Surveys of the present kind are a valuable source of knowledge of this complexity. The surveys may therefore help to strengthen the Socratic element of modern philosophy, the intercultural dialogue or *Kommunikationsgemeinschaft*.

So far, 11 volumes have been published in this series, viz. *Philosophy of Language and Philosophical Logic* (Vol. 1), *Philosophy of Science* (Vol. 2), *Philosophy of Action* (Vol. 3), *Philosophy of Mind* (Vol. 4), *African Philosophy* (Vol. 5), *Medieval Age Philosophy* (Vol. 6/1 and Vol. 6/2), *Asian Philosophy* (Vol. 7), *Philosophy of Latin America* (Vol. 8), *Aesthetics and Philosophy of Art* (Vol. 9), *Philosophy of Religion* (Vol. 10), *Ethics or Moral Philosophy* (Vol. 11).

The volumes are, for various reasons, of unequal length. The obvious shortcomings, especially of Vol. 5 on African and Arab Philosophy, have to some extent been compensated for in the volumes on Aesthetics (Vol. 9) and Religion (Vol. 10).

The present volume on *Philosophy of Justice*, containing 21 surveys, shows different approaches with a variety of interpretations (Greek philosophy, Muslim law, European and American philosophical justice).

The chronicles are as a rule written in English, French and German. In the present volume, 3 surveys are written in French and 18 in English. The bibliographical references, with some exceptions, follow the pattern introduced in earlier volumes. The bibliographies themselves usually follow at the end of each chronicle, arranged in alphabetical order. The bibliographies are selected and arranged by the authors themselves.

I am grateful to a number of persons who in various ways have assisted in the preparation of this new series. My thanks are first of all due to Ms. Kari Horn. Without her help, the volume would have been delayed. I am also most grateful to the Secretariat, especially to Ms. Catherine Champniers and Ms. Grace Frank, at the Institut International de Philosophie in Paris. They have done the final proofreading as well as put up the indices.

My thanks are also due to the Centre National de la Recherche Scientifique (Paris), and to the Conseil International de la Philosophie et des Sciences Humaines (UNESCO), and to the staff at Springer.

Oslo, Norway
January 2014

Guttorm Fløistad

Contents

Introduction

Guttorm Fløistad

With the present Volume 12, *Philosophy of Justice*, the Chronicles Series has come to an end. With this volume we are moving into a sensitive and embarrassing field. The distance between word and action is still violating the basic rights of millions of people. Poverty has, of course, diminished, especially in Africa and Asia. However, in certain parts of the world, the United States and Europe included, the number of poor people have increased. According to the UN, the number of poor in the world has increased by 100 million people between 2008 and 2010. The Aristotelian notion of "distributive justice" has certainly been translated into practice through the centuries. Sometimes, however, it goes the wrong way. (See also f.inst. Fernand Braudel *Les structures du quotidien. Le possible et l'impossible*, Vol. I–III. Paris: Librairie Armand Colin, 1979).

What we have definitely lost is the belief that there are natural rights. This is the view that there are norms that may be regarded as laws, even if they are not authorized by the state or founded in customs. It is commonly agreed among most lawyers that any judgment should be sound and just both by interpreting the laws and by deciding questions of rights that are not solved by laws or prescriptions. These views must not be based on pure evaluation, but have as their source a knowledge of the fact that there exist norms of rights that have a different foundation than positive rights.

What then is the origin of natural rights? Some think that they have a divine origin: natural rights have their origin in religion. Moreover, religion gives natural rights their authority. The phrase "King of God's grace" is well-known. In Sweden the phrase was in use up to 1973, according to Thorsten Eckhoff, professor of law at the University of Oslo, although it was long since an empty phrase. There is a painting of ancient times that shows how the sun-god handed law over to King Hammurabi some 2,000 years before Christ. And we all know the story of how Moses was handed the Ten Commandments on Mount Sinai. Such ideas of how the State and government have a divine origin are called "theocratic".

G. Fløistad (✉)
Institute for the History of Ideas, University of Oslo, Oslo, Norway
e-mail: inst.intern.philo@wanadoo.fr

G. Fløistad (ed.), *Philosophy of Justice*, Contemporary Philosophy: A New Survey 12,
DOI 10.1007/978-94-017-9175-5_1, © Springer Science+Business Media Dordrecht 2015

However, natural rights may also have their origin in reason. Ancient Greeks had no conception of the religious model. Instead, reason studied nature. Both Plato and Aristotle mentioned reason and its interpretation of nature.

The Stoics fully developed the theory of natural laws and natural rights in the year 200 BC. These laws of nature were common to all nations and gave people their rights. The Stoics regarded natural laws and natural rights as having the same origin in nature.

The Stoic view was accepted early on by the Roman Empire. Cicero, among others, took several of his views from the Stoics. They had general validity, applying to people everywhere. The Romans distinguished between their own free citizens and other races. The laws and rights for the free citizens were called *ius civile* and for the last group *ius gentium*. Reflection on natural rights played a central role in the development of *ius gentium* and influenced also *ius civile*.

Quite a few authors of the present volume point to the close relationship between natural rights, and civil rights and morality. This is obviously correct, because in order to obey legal rules you have to obey moral rules in general. It must be difficult to act against the law and be a criminal in one part of life and a saint in the rest. This means, however, that obedience to laws is met with the same difficulty as obedience to moral rules. This is not knowledge of the legal rules, but commitment to them. Commitment or duty is not merely a question of rational argument, but of emotional affection.

Eros and Polis is the title of a book that appeared a dozen years ago (2002, Cambridge University Press). The subtitle is *Desire and Community in Greek Political Theory*. The title gives a new meaning to Eros: It is education to citizenship. It was an honor similar to citizenship in the Roman republic. To be a member of a Greek city and the Roman state was the essential purpose of education, *Senatus Populusque Romanus—S.P.Q.R.* In ancient Greece, this was achieved by handing over the male youth to older men. This was not primarily a case of homophilia, but rather of creating a feeling of love for the city and the Greek community.

This is one of the points emphasized by Bertrand Saint-Sernin in his article "La justice à la lumière des lois". He asks: What is the point of returning to Plato? Do we have something to learn?

We certainly have if we are to abide by history. The commitment to the laws requires, however, primarily a commitment to your community. You have to develop a political Eros in all members of a society, in native-born citizens as well as in members of foreign origin. (The author points, by the way, to the fact that all or most countries have foreigners in their society, just as the Greek and the Romans had). At this point, most countries have a long way to go. Instead of political education, most of us in the West focus on a variety of knowledge in order to cope with demands of our economic system. We seem to be dragging the rest of the world with us instead of focusing first on our political and cultural identity.

Any legal system is part and parcel of the identity of the citizen. In this context, it is, presumably, easier for the "législateur" and the government to point to what is needed for the development of society and to point to the persons needed to fulfill the changes. Saint-Sernin also points to the close relationship between the history of nature and the history of man, between cosmology and anthropology. That is why the two should not be separated. Misuse of nature leads to the destruction of man. Philosophers and psychologists have long since pointed to the *necessary* interdependence of man and nature.

The history of man and nature tends to reduce the Platonic ideas of both man and nature. At the end of the Middle Ages, Kepler developed a mathematical picture of nature and some hundred years later came forward with the mechanical view on the Universe—up to the extinction of man. Man became the victim of biology or the biosphere. Bernard Saint-Sernin, however, does not believe in the products of the brain. Man with his mind and matter is more than can be conceived of in mathematics and sense perception and biology. Mathematics and science have solved some of our problems. Justice is one of the most pressing one worldwide.

Man should not remain inactive in the face of nature, but should apply, perhaps following Plato, his creativity in both science and the humanities to modify his own biosphere. Whether the politicians of today know their *daimon* and are able to fix the "good" for development is doubtful. Plato's *laws (Nomos)* and dialogues are not valid just for a Greek city. The laws and the dialogue carry a general message that conflicts should be solved not by violence, but by a dialogical procedure.

Justice is a main problem in Aristotle's *Politeia*. To participate in politics is natural. It is part of our nature to live and co-operate with others. To participate in government, in the broad sense, is even an honor. Aristotle never mentions the term individuality. This may even be correct. An individual person has never existed. If we follow modern psychology on the theme "attachment", originating in Britain in the 1950s (by Mary Ainsworth and John Bowlby), there can never be an individual. We are all from the very outset necessarily related to our mother, father, sisters, brothers, friends and colleagues in working life. This idea of a necessary relation originates in philosophy, in Aristotle, Augustin, Spinoza and many others. An individual can only be understood through his relations. The problem of the relation between the individual and the community (*polis*), as Eleni Leontsini states, has still not been solved.

Justice is related to equality. There are obvious inequalities, f.inst. between the rich and the poor. If the rich have too much power over the poor, opposition and conflict may easily arise. That is why Aristotle recommends a great majority of the middle class to have a stable and lasting government. Aristotle also discusses oligarchy and democracy. Oligarchy is not a good form of government, for the reasons mentioned. Neither is democracy, because it rests on a false assumption of freedom: Freedom is to do what one wants. It obviously runs counter to the "natural" participation in the *polis*, or political community. Freedom may even destroy a community—and itself—and result in a "lonely crowd" (David Riesman 1950).

Justice is also related to friendship. Friendship is even, in Aristotle, ranked higher than justice. Justice is a good for any community. Friendship is, however, a higher good. A reasonable interpretation is that they belong together. Friendship is a relationship that guarantees the validity of the legal system. It guarantees the commitment to the system.

The thoughts about natural rights in the Middle Ages were influenced both by Christianity and by the ancient Greeks. The most important philosopher of natural rights in this period was Thomas Aquinas. His teaching of natural rights is still valid in the Roman Church. Thomas was a monk of the Dominican order and a deeply religious man. In addition, he had a profound knowledge of ancient Greek philosophy, especially Aristotle. The two sources of natural rights mentioned above, God's Commandments and human reason, joined into a unity in Thomas. God's will was the primary source of rights; God had given man reason which enabled him to acquire an insight into the eternal law of the world (*lex aeterna*). Just as with the Stoics, Thomas regarded the eternal law such that it included both the natural laws as well as the moral and natural rights.

Thomas surely knew Tertullian, the father of the Latin Church, and his work. His well-known phrase runs: *Credo, ut intelligam*, or in English, "I believe, in order to understand". That is, belief in this context opens up for an understanding you otherwise do not have access to. Or, in general: Your attitude is decisive for the kind of knowledge you are able to acquire. Perhaps the Christian belief combined with reason opens up to knowledge of natural laws, that is, laws of the God that created the world.

Thomas had a strong belief in reason, but did not think that it gave us access to the entire eternal law. God therefore gave us the Holy Book to enable us to acknowledge what we cannot achieve by reasoning alone. Nevertheless, Thomas strongly believed in the power of reason in the arrangement of natural rights.

The situation in France in the sixteenth century is difficult although some of the problems (*mutatis mutandem*) are similar. The French humanist and jurist Jean Bodin engaged himself in two major political problems: the concept of sovereignty and the concept of absolutism. In a country divided politically, religiously and socially, this is not an easy task. It was Thomas Hobbes who developed his concept of absolutism and his concept of sovereignty. However, the seeds of the concepts were definitely Bodin's. That is why Thomas Krogh said of his contribution, "The modern state comes into being".

The concept of sovereignty is related to a definition of state power. It is based on the principle "no one above, and no one alongside". If there are two or even more persons who hold the position, conflicts are likely to occur.

In his law studies, Bodin came across Justinian and the Roman legal system. In the beginning, he thought that Roman law was valid also in his own time and asked for extensive translations. After his studies in humanity, especially in history and philosophy, he acknowledged that the authorities and the population were in need of a much more elaborate system of laws. This could only be achieved by interpreting the system of laws in various countries in application to France. In this respect, Bodin was also concerned with the idea of a climate theory of the mentality of nations and peoples, and the question of whether absolutism and state power presupposes a unity of religious belief.

The radical development of science in the following centuries also led to a change in the theory of natural laws and rights. The peak of natural theories was reached in the sixteenth and the seventeenth centuries. The dominant trend, as could be expected, was the rationalistic view on natural rights, liberated from religion. Reason became the final source of natural rights. The founder of this rational trend was the Dutch philosopher Hugo Grotius and the German-Swedish philosopher Samuel Pufendorf. They both lived during the Thirty Years' War and experienced the need to create order among the states. In 1625, the well-known book by Grotius*De iure belli ac pacis* (*On the Law of War and Peace*) was published. Here Grotius explains his views on when it is permitted to us to engage in physical violence, and wage war, and on the foundations for peace. This was in accordance with his view on natural and civil law.

Grotius was an extremely gifted youth. He wrote poems in Latin when he was eight years old and enrolled at the university at eleven, was later appointed historiographer and attorney general by King Henry IV. He was a "miracle", the author, Andreas Harald Aure, quotes in his contribution.

The natural right is the right to self-preservation. However, the best form of self-preservation is to co-operate with others. Man's social behavior with others is a fact. Man is a rational being, wishing a peaceful co-existence with others. To preserve a social order is the real source of natural right, a point of view Grotius also argues for with reference to antique sources. In addition, he draws on the general validity of the Golden Rule: You should not do to others what you do not want others do to you. It also involves that you should respect other people's rights and their properties. The natural rights of the individual are thereby also an anticipation of the later respect for "life, freedom and property". What the individual has a moral right to can in no case be a right to the declaration of war. It follows from the same right that you should pay back your debt.

A warlike situation also occurs at sea. In 1609, Grotius published a chapter from an earlier manuscript entitled *De Mare Liberum (On the Freedomat Sea).* Among other themes, it deals with the right of taking prey at sea. Adam Smith was one of those who greatly learned and further developed his thoughts on natural rights from Grotius.

The principle that agreements should be kept and many others are distinct natural rights—between states as well as between individuals. The rational view on natural rights was the basis of agreements between citizens of a state, usually called *the social contract*. At this point, the social contract could be variously formulated—to the effect that one state could have an authoritarian ruler as in Hobbes with *Leviathan*, as well as in a democracy where you could have a democratically selected ruler, as in Locke. The knowledge of natural laws was gradually changing, from the "laws" of an organic world as in Spinoza, to the laws of a mechanistic world as in Descartes.

One can ask whether the social contract theory was historically founded or just a social construction as in Hobbes: But even as a construction under an authoritarian ruler, it may help individuals not to act "wolfish" toward each other. Samuel Pufendorf, German of origin and for many years professor in Lund in Sweden, worked intensely with natural rights as well as on civil rights in general.

Besides his well-known biographies of the Swedish Kings *Gustaf II Adolph* to *Karl X Gustaf*, Samuel Pufendorf is best known as a moral and legal philosopher,

and included his history of philosophy. His main work, from 1672, shows that he was also engaged with the laws of nature, entitled *De iure naturae et gentium (Om naturen og folkenes rett)* (nearly 1,000 pages).

In moral philosophy, he anticipated the Kantian distinction between the phenomenal and neumenal, pointing to what would later be called the "autonomous moral subject". Kant's critical philosophy is, at the same time, the main reason why Pufendorf largely disappeared from the history of philosophy. He was, as Thor Inge Rørvik says, "written out" of the history of philosophy. This is the reason why several historians of philosophy are trying to bring him back—with some success.

Pufendorf was inspired by some of his contemporaries, like Grotius and Hobbes. But he also criticized them. He was strongly opposed to Grotius' scholastic view on the relation of God to natural laws. The only natural law that existed was the principle of self-preservation. It applied to all living beings, including man. The natural law teaches one "how to conduct oneself to become a useful member of society". Politics and warfare were often related in one way or another to theology. On the basis of his version of the natural law, he desocialized politics, warfare and civil society. Each individual, due to his dignity, has the right to equality and freedom. What modern writers find most attractive in Pufendorf is his theory of moral duties and social being, as opposed to that of rights. With these views, Pufendorf also presupposes later philosophy, while giving critical remarks on liberalism. Freedom is only a moral quality of highest value on the basis of duties. This is similar to the view held by Spinoza and, later, by Hume and Kant.

Spinoza (1632–1672) takes us one step further in his political thinking. He holds to the principle of self-preservation as the primary natural law. He just regards it as an integrated part of God or nature as a whole. Because of his excommunication from the Jewish community in Amsterdam due to his "natural" view on God, he was often accused of being an atheist. He strongly denied this.

Paola De Cuzzani rightly emphasizes *Tractatum theologicus politicus* as Spinoza's key work in his contribution to politics. In the theological part of the book, Spinoza argues against the accusation of being an atheist; in the other part, on the freedom of thought and speech. De Cuzzani has, of course, to draw on Spinoza's work *Ethics (Ethica more geometrica demonstrata)*. This is his main work on the theory of knowledge *and* on moral philosophy. Spinoza belongs to those philosophers who regard moral philosophy not as a separate discipline, but as identical with a theory of knowledge (as, f.inst., Hegel and Heidegger). This is to say that, in order to achieve freedom of thought and speech, you have to move from the first kind of knowledge (gained by opinion and impression) to the second and third kinds of knowledge or those gained by reason and *amor intellectualis erga Deum et naturam* (the intellectual love of God).

From the point of view of natural law, one has of course the right to self-preservation. While being on the first kind of knowledge, to some degree one is subject to external forces. As a member of a civil society, you have to move to the second kind of knowledge. On this type of knowledge, you have even command over external forces. The third kind of knowledge is, according to De Cuzzani, reserved for the sages, although if you dedicate the whole of your life to its pursuit, Spinoza holds, you too may achieve it.

In the following centuries, natural rights' theories met with great resistance. Both Hume and Bentham strongly objected to the idea of natural rights: Natural rights cannot be known objectively; they are subjective, they held. Moreover, moral notions cannot be known. Arguments that there are objective norms for the morally right action they regarded as an illusion. Those who held that natural rights are eternally valid were most easily refuted. In Germany, much of the resistance came from Ranke and the historical school.

As a result of this criticism, the natural rights movement came to ill reputation. In addition, in the present and the former century, the idea of natural rights played a modest role—except within Islam and, after the Second World War, the human rights movement. In Norway, the movement is now fighting for a place in the Parliament. In view of the damage done to nature with pollution all over the world, the human rights movement has become a forceful movement, also supported by the UN. That body has even appointed a commission having meetings in various states around the world.

Islamic leaders hold on to their tradition. They strongly believe in God and human reason. Rational knowledge, according to Lars Gule and Knut Vikør, can unravel how God has construed nature, and thus what natural laws are. It is, however, not possible through reason to determine the normative status of human actions, whether an action is good or bad. This can only be done by God and by his authority alone. Vikør adds that the legal system of the Muslim countries today is basically a secular one, formed on a Western model. There has always been a place of some relevance of the *Sharia* model of law.

This state of affairs was confirmed by my visit to the IKIM Institution in Kuala Lumpur. Their Islamic business procedures were clearly similar to what we do in Europe. The only difference was that they concluded every business transaction by asking for God's approval. It should be added that the Institution deeply regretted some recent developments of their religion.

This volume contains two contributions on Islam, one from the fourteenth century by Lars Gule, and one from our century by Knut S. Vikør.

Ibn Khaldun is an historian and sociologist of the fourteenth century. He left North Africa and settled in Cairo. For over 20 years, he served as a teacher and judge at the school of jurisprudence. Lars Gule points to his cyclical theory of history based on a dialectic between desert and city. The two main forms of organized "habitats" are found in the desert and small villages among the nomads, and in the towns and cities, usually called a dynasty or a state, which is a form of civilization. Law and justice are part of "the semantic" of the state. Within the settlement there are various groups fighting for superior power, resulting in the establishment of a royal family. The dynasty and the royal authority have the same relationship as form has to matter, a notion that has a clear reference to Aristotle. The same applies to the notion of theological causation present in the development.

The moral qualities are most important in the starting point of the dynastic circle. These qualities suffer in the decline of the state. Gule quotes Ibn Khaldun: "Luxurious living, the loss of fighting, spirit, etc., easily lead to corruption".

Khaldun distinguishes between two legal systems, laws of civilization (positive laws), and religious laws or the laws of God, or *Sharia*. The laws of civilization have a rational foundation, taking care of the relation between people. Even the religious laws are subject to learning and education. The society ruled by the laws of God, Ibn Khaldun holds, is the best. In times of crisis, religious laws would take care of the Muslims' strength and just relationships with others.

Based on their knowledge of natural laws, one should perhaps expect that Muslims were more in accord with each other than they really are. We are confronted with a variety of groups, not only Sunni and Shia Muslims, but also different schools of interpretation of *Sharia*. Knut Vikør opens his contribution by pointing to the variety of interpretations of Muslim law. There is no agreement at all. What is of divine origin and what is added by representatives of the legal scholars? Attempts have been made by one caliph to favor one interpretation of the law, only to be immediately refuted.

The purpose of the *Sharia* is human and social welfare. In a sense, the laws are historical; if society changes, rationality may change the interpretation of the laws such that God's intention can be fulfilled in the present situation. This is clearly a reformist view. Modern developments advocated the return to the Quran and Sunna, a description of how Muhammad practiced the laws.

Family policy and the issues of the role of woman and the possibilities of divorce are central. Concerning marriage and divorce, two schools are in opposition to each other, the Hanafi and the Maliki schools. In the first one, "the bride has a strong position in the choice of a marriage partner" without the participation of her father. In the latter school, this is impossible. The bride's father imposes his will on his daughter. On the matter of the wife's access to divorce, the liberal/conservative balance is opposite. The Hanafi School does not allow this at all, even on the permanent absence of the husband. The other school appears almost modern. A wife who "feels the marriage is detrimental to her" can have it dissolved if her argument convinces the judge.

Discussion about various issues in Muslim countries are regularly taking place, including the interpretation of: the political system of Islam, the relation of business to religion and whether women should be allowed to work or not. Political Islam, f.inst., *Sharia*, is heavily suppressed in Syria today. Women may perfectly well go to work in many countries, but should not be a bus or taxi driver. "Muslim feminism" is also in many places a driving force. As many philosophers are saying: What is, is what is happening.

In 2012 there appeared a book on the first centuries of Islam with the title, *Religion fällt nicht vom Himmel. Die ersten Jahrhunderte des Islams* (Darmstadt: Wissenschaftliche Buchgesellschaft). The author, Andreas Goetze, maintains that no religion simply falls from Heaven and gives several linguistic arguments against Islam in its present form (§43). The Arabic language at the time of Muhammad was not as fully developed as we know it. Elements of several languages (Aramaic and Sassanidic and several others) have been taken up later on.

Towards the end of the seventeenth century, the political climate became milder, although the Inquisition of the Roman Church and the conflicts between Protestants and Catholics were still intensive, especially in Europe. British politics split into two parties, the "Whig" and the "Tory" movements. Locke engaged himself in the Whig party, working to establish a constitutional monarchy. The task of the Parliament was to limit the monarch's use of power. The Tories held that the monarch's power came directly from God to the effect that the monarch had absolute power of the subjects. In this situation, Locke published *A Letter concerning toleration* in 1689, and at the same time *An Essay Concerning Human Understanding*.

Helga Varden rightly emphasizes that *Letter* and *Essay* are beautifully written and that Locke's work, especially on politics, greatly influenced later philosophers and economists. His ideas of toleration on labour, the acquisition of private property and religious freedom are just three of them. His *Letter* on toleration points to his later liberal political philosophy, with emphasis on the importance of individual freedom. Participating in a union in Germany, Locke observed that tolerance prevailed between all religious groups, an experience that underlined his view on religious freedom. Individual property should be acquired through the labour you put into an achievement, and influence the amount of property you acquire. Marxists and others have heavily criticized Locke, especially for this statement. What about those who, for various reasons, are not in a position to put labour into any position? What about the class society still prevalent in many or most countries? And what about the poor people and poverty in general?

Freedom is an attractive value—for those who are in a position to use and extend it. Varden points, at the end of her contribution, to the values and criticisms that followed in the wake of John Locke.

In some way or another we all have some experience with the Scottish Enlightenment. We are victims of Adam Smith's fourfold division of freedom. Freedom applied to economic achievement involves competition. One effect is that we have to work as hard as possible. Sometime we lose a competition and have to apply for a new position in a new company. What we do not experience is that hard and fast work in the long run may be contraproductive to moral values. Because moral values, sentiments as Hume calls them, are slow. You cannot, f.inst., be grateful towards or acknowledge a person for good work by rushing along. If you do, the value has no content. While in a hurry, you neither see nor understand the other person, as Gülriz Uygur in her later article, "Seeing injustice", would say.

To blame Adam Smith for this affair is unfair. As a moral philosopher he holds, as Hume does before him, that freedom is dependent on social commitment and cultural values. Freedom on its own may even, in the long run, be destructive to one's "natural" self-preservation. In Europe, The European Union is partly to blame. It focuses mainly on economic development, leaving the national culture to each country. This is understandable. The danger is, however, that the one-sided focus on economy and the variety of products may weaken the cultural and moral commitment of the individual.

Sentiment is the basis of morality, and morality is the basis of justice and rights. Our sentiments and morality do not involve a natural affection for, or love of, mankind. But as members of a political society, we have a "public" interest and sympathies, and these create a need for a legal system.

On quite a few issues, Hume met his opponents. Adam Smith, also inspired by him, argued that justice was not concerned with property alone, but had a much wider validity. He also objected to Hume's view on the artificiality of justice, that is, being a construct upon one's companies' self-preservation. Smith also argued against the view that justice had to do with utility. Another opponent, Thomas Reid, sees a close relationship between justice and rights. He also argued that the Aristotelian view on distributive justice is absent from Hume's philosophy.

Empirism applied to moral values has its limits. Hume, however, connects with the classical problems of *itinerarium mentis* in his use of the term moral improvement.

It is common knowledge that Rousseau took part in the Academy of Dijon's essay competition and won the prize. The question to be answered was, "Has the revolution of Science and Art contributed to the purification of Morals". His answer was negative. In the Age of Enlightenment, when the belief in progress was dominant, this is at least remarkable. The reason might simply be the emergence of the mechanistic world picture, alien to man. The distance between man and nature is obvious. The moral rule of natural rights and natural laws have become civil values only. The same applies to freedom, to which Rousseau is strongly in favor. Man's moral life lies in ruins. It is, however, following Ellen Krefting, perfectly possible to establish a second Nature, physically, morally, and politically, including a society that combines equality and freedom. To Rousseau, it meant another natural law and natural right. In his main work, *The Social Contract* from 1767, Rousseau outlined the community of free citizens, introducing their own laws by means of the idea of "general will". A new political agenda will also help families to educate their children (*Emile* 1761). Social conflicts may be solved, and he even foresees a brotherhood between the nations and "perpetual peace".

Most commentators dwell on the inconsistencies in Rousseau's philosophy. Ernst Cassirer is one of the few who has brought order into his thinking. Ellen Krefting, inspired by Cassirer, does likewise. The creating of new values is the task of the individual and his community.

Kant's philosophy of Right (or Justice) is part of one of his later books, *The Metaphysics of Morals*, that was published in 1797. It appeared nearly 10 years after his main work on ethics, *Theory of Practical Reason* in 1788. The philosophy of Right is closely tied to ethics, although in a way opposite to it. In his practical philosophy, Kant focuses on the necessity of being free. If you choose to follow the moral rule (the categorical imperative) with which you are born, you have to be free. The philosophy of Right deals with freedom, but in the sense of taking care of the freedom of others. It is normative. As Helga Varden emphasizes, you are not allowed to act in a way that violates the freedom of others. Virtue or acting ethically is a much wider concept than right. As long as Robinson Crusoe lived alone on his island, he had no use for rules of rights. In the interactive world, we are all in the domain of the rightful coercion. Moral actions towards the categorical imperative have no limit; they should be universalized and should regard everyone as valuable in himself before regarding him as useful to something. Kant called the standard principle to be applied to the Doctrine of Right "the universable principle of Right".

Freedom involves freedom of speech as well. Speech in itself has no coercive power. Laws that outlaw mere speech represent misunderstanding both of "freedom and force".

Philosophy of Right includes not only general principles, but also views on private life. Kant was inspired by the natural rights theories of Hobbes, Rousseau, and Locke, and he addressed different categories of private rights, such as property rights and rights in family relations. Natural rights are each individual's right in interpersonal relations. Property rights are achieved not in the way of Locke, but simply by taking something into account, like this is my house, this is my daughter. Kant emphasized that all possessions have a normative character. He analyzed the different principles lying behind the various types of possession.

Commentators often heavily disagree on certain parts of Kant's exposition. Robert Nozick, f.inst., does not agree with John Rawls in the interpretation of what is called the principle of redistribution. Helga Varden has, in her interpretation of Kant's philosophy of rights, given an inspiring presentation of a controversial theme.

To produce rational arguments for personal commitment to moral values is perfectly possible although not always easy. In hardly any case is it sufficient to change the emotional attitudes. Kant advocated the personal example. However, an example of moral behavior in a society that, according to most newspapers, abounds with opposite experiences is hardly not enough. To continue talking, in terms of moral advice, may be of no help. That is why the family is important. The family, according to Hegel, is the "primary ethical substance". It just presupposes that children in their first year may be protected against any form of globalization. That may, however, be difficult as the parents (or the parent) in many or even most families leave the home during the daytime. Globalization has long since invaded privacy and destroyed it. That may be one of the strongholds of the Hindu, the Buddhist, and also the Roman Catholic and the Muslim society.

One obvious reason for this dilemma, I think, may lie in our definition of democracy. The social contract theory involves that we all should be committed to each other. This, I take it, is at least a condition for being a society at all. Individual freedom is, of course, a necessary element of a liberal and conservative political system. A major difficulty lies in the combination of these two elements. Herbert Tingsten, the well-known editor of *Dagens Nyheter* (The Daily News) in Sweden, has written a book on the subject, in which he advances his view on the combination of freedom and social responsibilities: They are incompatible. He even says that they contradict each other. This is a very strong assumption. True enough, Isaiah Berlin and John Rawls, for instance, are obviously both adherents of a distinct form of liberalism and individual freedom. Berlin even thought that "negative freedom", that is, freedom from all restraints, is a preferable form of freedom. Positive freedom, he argued, might lead to some form of totalitarianism. Rawls, in his book on justice and on political liberation, spoke often of individual basic rights and liberty, as well as of social and economic benefits for the least advantaged members of society. The development of social commitment is something different. It is rarely achieved by repeatedly saying no, but rather by pointing to opportunities of action and hobbies. That, I would think, is easier achieved. As Hume and Kant both would say on account of their ethic: A sound and self-stimulating freedom is achieved on the basis of social commitment only.

All movements are every now and then in need of renewal. Part of the renewal will always be what has happened before. This applies to the feminist movement as well. For Mary Wollstonecraft and many, or perhaps most, others, feminism is a human or humanisation movement. Both women and men are human beings despite their gender differences. This is the message in Mary Wollstonecraft's well-known book, *A Vindication of the Rights of Woman*. Kjersti Fjørtoft offers a clear outline of what it is about. Both sexes are equally rational and have rights. Consequently, they need education. History in England tells us that men have used their power to deny women education, to the effect that they can neither properly pursue their duties nor demand their rights. John Locke defined freedom, health and property as natural rights. Freedom is the most important right we all are born with. This is the normative value in political theory. Freedom cannot be limited apart from encounters with the freedom of others. Women have too long been the victims of accidental power.

Edmund Burke criticized both the French Revolution and defended rich people's property and honor. For Wollstonecraft, this is the target of criticism. Rich people's property and honor often lead to their neglect of moral education, for which women are suffering. Neither rich people nor women can develop themselves into proper citizens. A woman's primary task is to perform her duty as a mother and wife. The responsibility of a mother is, however, limited in time, in addition to the fact that not all women are mothers. All women should therefore be given the opportunity to work and to take care of themselves. The right to paid work is necessary for all women.

The *Education of Daughters* from 1787 makes the education of women a necessity for forming future societies, each of the sexes in its own way. That is why Wollstonecraft attacks Rousseau's "old-fashioned" view on the education of children, in contrast to her appreciation of his other works. In the education of children at school, she emphasizes the importance of moral education. This is a matter of reason, as was common among many philosophers at that time. Some critics rightly hold that, according to another interpretation of Wollstonecraft, emotion together with reason is the proper solution.

In the mid-1950s, the Marxist Ernst Bloch wrote a book in two volumes called *The Hope as a Principle of Life*. Although you can observe tragedies, both personal and social, nearly all over the world, hope is still a powerful aspect of life. As Nietzsche once said: Life will itself. To deliberately end it is not in accord with life itself, but with external forces. Hope requires freedom. In addition, freedom, as Terje Sparby holds, is a key word in Hegel in his philosophy of right, together with closely related notions like rights and spirit (*Geist*). Rights are based on freedom and spirit. In order to be free, one has to have self-knowledge, and self-knowledge is "to understand oneself as spirit". The body and corporal matter can hardly have any self-knowledge. Self-knowledge is a spiritual matter, although it always includes knowledge of the body.

One way to understand these notions and their relationship is to start at the beginning. And the beginning is the family. The family, according to Hegel, is the primary ethical substance. This is a formation of the personal self and self-understanding as well as the relational capacity. The family is the formation of friendship and love. Self-understanding is part of the relation to others, persons and objects. It just needs a reflexive movement within reason itself. This leads to the understanding of freedom, with the Hegelian phrase, freedom consists in "being with oneself in otherness". Freedom is not negative, in the sense of being freed from all restraints, as Isaiah Berlin holds. It is both determined and undetermined. It needs to be undetermined in others to be free. But it is to some extent determined, due to the experiences the person in question has "suffered" or achieved.

Hegel's concept of freedom is a comprehensive one. It is the expression of the undetermined expression of the mind, or spirit, and right. The system of rights is an expression of the genuine freedom, Hegel says. Freedom is the basis of rights. Moreover, freedom is closely related to ethics. As mentioned earlier, becoming and being a person is in every aspect a moral affair. The realization of freedom is successive in the family, society, and the state.

The various interpretations of Hegel sometimes put an end to history due to "absolute reason". This has several times been refuted. He may be interpreted otherwise: as meaning reason has finally reached itself as a living and reflexive force in the state expressed in freedom in the system of rights. Whether all of us in the world have reached this state of development is a pressing question (cf. Terry Pinkard 2011).

Criticism of capitalism is older than Karl Marx, although he has delivered the most systematic and radical criticism. His viewpoint is, in a way, mentioned already in *The Communist Manifesto* from 1848. "Everything holy has become unholy". Marx distinguishes between political and human liberation. Political liberation in general, through individual rights and liberation, may be achieved in religious societies. However, it is not sufficient for "true" human liberation. What is not sufficient for the human liberation is the individual liberal concept of freedom. The true freedom, as Jørgen Pedersen rightly notes, is freedom within a community with others. The liberal state creates problems for itself.

A central concept in Marx is alienation. This happens in a state with a liberal economy. Frequently after 1850, when new owners took over and focused only on profit, they neglected their employees as human beings. The individual is alienated in several directions, also from other employees. The liberal economy does not contribute to building the community.

Religion is made by man and has no place in the future society. Hegel had already placed religion in the Middle Ages. Reason had taken its place from the nineteenth century onwards. Marx took over his dialectical model, and observed that the economy in a system varied in different ages, and that the various systems contained conflicts that caused the historical change. The main reason for the change of capitalism lies in the reduction of profit. The price of the necessary technology in a competing economy makes it harder to survive.

Time will show whether the improvements in our centuries are sufficient for rescuing our economic system. Charles Handy, a well-known author, wrote a book a few years ago about the need to find the meaning of life beyond capitalism. He is reporting the experience of many people.

Having experienced two world wars, the second bringing huge suffering to her own people, in addition to being a highly reflective person, Hannah Arendt went a short way to become a political thinker. Her credo is *political existentialism*, probably inspired by Martin Heidegger, who was her teacher for some years. The credo is a policy that has relevance for the crisis of "today's globalized and complex world". This means, as Odin Lysaker formulates it, that it should involve "an analysis of the totalitarian ideologies, of the depolitization of democracy and the dehumanization of human dignity".

She explains the sources of globalization and its consequences. Man is basically free, a fact that in the future will counteract any suppressive ideologies in all places. Her main work is *The Human Condition.* She distinguishes between power and violence. Power is based on communication that makes co-operation possible. Violence plays a major part in the depolitization of democracy. This is due to a political crisis because of "privatization and intimatization". It becomes conformist and less meaningful. According to Lysaker, Hannah Arendt advocates the public form, the *agora* of the Greek *polis*, to revive individual freedom and true political communication. The place of the body and bodily dignity are also important notions.

Her radical view on Eichmann after the Second World War is at first surprising. It arose when she observed Eichmann in tribunal. He "subjugated" himself to the Nazi ideology, to the effect that it killed the moral individual. Eichmann was no longer an individual.

Parts of Arendt's viewpoints have been criticized by a number of people. Odin Lysaker mentions Habermas. He objected to her conception of the "social". To Habermas, the social is an important characteristic of man's behavior and communication. In terms of a dialogue, it can make the individual free. To Hanna Arendt, the social is to be privatized. There need, however, to be no inconsequence.

In his *Theory of Justice*, John Rawls draws on the tradition of contract theory and thinks, according to Andreas Follesdal, that each member of a free society will agree on certain principles irrespective of their faith. Justice is deeply situated in everyone. Equal opportunity to achieve different positions is an example. His key theme is "Reflective equilibrism": In periods of economic development, the distribution principle should give decisive weight to the most disadvantaged. This theory is an alternative to utilitarianism—Adam Smith, Jeremy Bentham, John Stuart Mill. The only thing that matters for them is "welfare" in the sense of either happiness or the satisfaction of needs.

The chief problem Rawls tries to solve is the conflict between freedom and equality. A conflict arises when "rights, duties, benefits, and burdens" shall be distributed. The voices defending freedom and even more freedom, undoubtedly at the same time, reduce the value of equality for many people, perhaps the majority. In his attempt to solve the problem, Rawls draws on the traditional social contract theory applied to the social institution as a whole. Rawls' philosophy of justice is a serious attempt to break off veils of ignorance among the political parties.

Rawls is being criticized, f.inst. by Amartya Sen, for ignoring personal differences among people, especially people with some demanding needs, such as disabilities. Justice or fairness is a challenging contribution both for the theoretical discussion—and for the politician.

John Rawls wrote on social justice. According to Dominique Terré, he is moderate and lucid. If one extends the topic, one may ask: What about global justice? This is certainly too ambitious, if not senseless. Dominique Terré also wants to be modest and embark upon discussing two authors and their contributions to justice, Alain Renaut and Alain Supiot. Renaut focuses on human development the ethics, including the global ethics involved in development. At the same time, he focuses on anti-development, which is an idea that comes from the Middle Ages and from the Occident. He suggests a variety of steps to help human development. Alain Supiot accounts for justice from the point of view of a lawyer.

In the discussion, the author draws on prominent names such as Amartya Sen, Martha Nussbaum, Thomas Poppe, and John Rawls. Amartya Sen stresses the normative aspect of development and points to the importance of economy for "justice and fairness" in any society. He may have pointed to the millions of refugees and people imprisoned in various countries for political, religious, and other illogical reasons. The need for a global ethic is doomed to remain a wishful thought. The liberal society may not apply everywhere, or at any rate for the near future. The author asks for a further discussion between Rawls and Sen, the latter questioning Rawls' rigorous defense of the liberal society. Freedom does not take ethics seriously.

Renaut, referring to Amartya Sen, introduces the notion of capability as basic for development. Also Joseph Stiglitz is called upon to assist in human development. His report "Pour une vraie réforme du système monétaire et financier international" is no doubt of great value. What comes out of it and of Renaut's development program, only the future can tell.

Arnold Gehlen defines man as an entity of want. Therefore everyone has to extend its being in order to be what it is. Philosophy has in various ways accounted for these deficiencies. A fairly common definition among philosophers is in terms of care for oneself, or as a struggle for life (f.inst., Augustin, Spinoza, the physicist Erwin Schrödinger and Heidegger). Hegel speaks of "being with oneself in another". Psychologists speak of "attachment" to illustrate the necessity of a relationship. Peter Kemp in his article on Ricœur takes this extension further, in that he like Hegel speaks of love, friendship, charity and praise, all related to justice. The discourse related to praise, f.inst., is "the glorification of charity" in I Cor. 13:4–5.

This procedure is not without an ethical character. Indeed, if you practice the notions of "well-being" with someone else, your move to the highest level of morality and justice is secured.

Another key word in Ricœur is "recognition". He speaks of two types, recognition built on "reciprocity" and recognition of "mutuality". "Reciprocity" refers to

Hobbes, where each man acknowledges the other as equal, especially in court. "Mutuality" refers to Levinas (and before that, Aristotle). With reference to Levinas, Ricœur calls mutuality a counterpart to friendship. And to friendship belongs forgiveness, a rare word in philosophy.

Kemp refers to a French professor of law, Antoine Garapon. He draws a distinction between "reconstructive" justice, which is the mutual recognition that establishes the legal order, the corrective justice, which punishes crime and distributive justice, that "allocates goods and burdens" (Ricœur). The overall value of having a system of law is that there can be no law at all without the recognition of legal equality. Even if no crime is committed, the existing system of law may help in establishing what they in the Renaissance called "the dignity of man".

Hardly anyone discovers the value of someone else (La Bruyère (1645–1696).

This is the problem dealt with by Gülriz Uygur. We often do not really *see* another person. If we follow Emmanuel Levinas, this has much to do with one's moral outlook. We may sometimes be so self-centered that someone who pases by, remains unidentified. We often don't see injustice done to that person either. Uygur distinguishes by categories: justice and injustice, the concept and conception of them. Conception is the wider category, taking into account the entire context of the harm done to somebody. The Nobel laureate Amartya Sen, who also discusses the problem, uses an example: If anyone sees "a big fish devour a small fish", it is a fact and not an injury. In the context of a society, you become conscious of the injustice.

The author quotes Saint-Exupéry: "It is only with the heart that one can see right". What is important is invisible to the eyes.

To see someone and identify him/her requires that you see his/her values. To see those values, you have to know the person. More precisely, you have to know yourself in order to see another. To respect someone and regard him as your equal, you have to have developed those values in yourself. It is not a question of self-perception, but of self-preservation and self-realization. More precisely, it is a question of communal values. In an "age of uncertainty" (Handy), it is no easy matter. The author ends with pointing to some of the difficulties.

A warning is needed. To speak about liberal democracy and the ancient Greek cities as a model for our own development is promising for some of us, but not for all. Jean-Godefroy Bidima points to the challenges nearly all societies have, and refers especially to Africa. For the question of justice "in a world gradually secularized" and having to fight against "the return of racial, ethnic and religious fundamentalism", there are at least three different types of mistrust to the application of a legal system. *First*, the mistrust to the enactment of the legal system through media; *second*, the question of the credibility of a legal system in a world pervaded by mistrust and cynicism; and *third*, the difficulties pertaining to the extension of the international commission for punishment of the accused and the rights of property to the earth.

We all know about the difficulties reported in the media. I shall briefly comment on just two points: that the media does not always convey the rights to the common people, but to the elite is only just one point. However, the author could have mentioned the misuse of media. The misuse of media, which is extensive in most countries, weakens the commitment to moral risks in general and therefore to some extent to legal rights. A mind that always is in a being loses gradually the caring relationship to himself and to others. The same applies to the hectic life in the modern, or as Bidima expresses it, post-modern industrial culture. Even personal relations, if they exist to other people, can turn commercial, and regard people as products that can be bought—and dismissed. "La lumière" (Kant) of the relationship is lost. The pace of the hard-working society often inflicts upon us the inability to genuinely enjoy the slowness of cultural performances. Emphatic, if not to say, love relationships are always a slow happening. Otherwise, they do not exist. No wonder that Bidima turns Ricœur's formula "la sagesse pratique" into "la sagesse tragique".

In the meantime, some of us may comfort ourselves with a word of wisdom picked up in India and the Philippines. Wandering in the poverty-stricken quarters of Calcutta and Manila, close to a bank guarded by a group of police officers with machine guns, I noticed that the doors to the street often were open. Sometimes I was invited in and under refusal was offered their last can of Coca-Cola. During the conversation some of them said, "We are rich, we just don't have any money". This is what the American sociologist David Riesman alluded to in his well-known book *The Lonely Crowd* in 1950 and called the considerable riches transmitted by tradition. The United States from the 1950s and, later on, European countries, according to Riesman, are guided by "external forces". To acquire a rich inner life, despite what has happened, may be the key to commitment to any legal system and to one's community.

La Justice à la Lumière des *Lois*

Bertrand Saint-Sernin

1 Introduction

Il peut sembler inutile de réfléchir à la justice en se référant aux *Lois* de Platon : quels rapports y a-t-il, en effet, entre les cités grecques et la Terre en voie de mondialisation ? La justice a-t-elle le même sens dans des sociétés aux dimensions réduites où les hommes se connaissent et dans des entités politiques immenses où l'individu est anonyme et comme noyé ? Peut-on définir la justice de la même manière quand les moyens de communication étaient la parole, l'écrit et le déplacement des hommes à pied, à dos d'animal, à la rame ou à la voile, et quand l'information devient multiforme et instantanée ? La justice a-t-elle le même sens si l'univers est jugé périodique ou qu'il est en évolution et les vivants en devenir ? Enfin, la justice ne change-t-elle pas de sens et de champ d'application quand la vie, la nature, le cerveau et la conscience deviennent l'objet de modifications, au lieu d'apparaître dotés d'une essence stable ? À première vue, la lecture des *Lois*, loin d'éclairer la notion de justice, égare la réflexion.

Pourtant, les *Lois*, comme le *Timée*, ont traversé les siècles et l'on y trouve des thèmes d'actualité. Ce sont eux sur lesquels nous méditerons.

1. Selon Platon, on ne peut disjoindre l'histoire et la nature de l'homme, d'une part, la nature et les lois de l'univers, de l'autre. Cette conception n'a pas disparu, car on définit toujours l'identité de l'individu et la nature des sociétés en se référant à la nature et aux sciences de la nature : les tentatives pour dissocier l'anthropologie de la cosmologie ne sont pas convaincantes.
2. Le législateur des *Lois* définit les charges qu'une société doit assumer pour se développer ; il sélectionne les individus capables de remplir ces charges. Ce thème conserve son actualité.

B. Saint-Sernin (✉)
Université Paris-Sorbonne (Paris IV), Paris, France
e-mail: b.saint-sernin@sfr.fr

G. Fløistad (ed.), *Philosophy of Justice*, Contemporary Philosophy: A New Survey 12,
DOI 10.1007/978-94-017-9175-5_2, © Springer Science+Business Media Dordrecht 2015

3. Un troisième thème-connexe du précédent-n'a pas vieilli : (1) découvrir quel est le but unique d'une cité : cette découverte étant le seul moyen pour l'entité politique de ne pas errer ; (2) discerner la méthode qui permet d'approcher ce but. L'exigence d'unicité du but que se donnent les sociétés signifie que le politique, pour remplir son office, doit substituer aux opinons ordinaires des opinions vraies ; essayer de transformer en connaissances scientifiques ces opinions vraies ; retourner dans la caverne pour transmettre à ses concitoyens un peu de la « connaissance parfaite » qu'il a entrevue. Ces trois thèmes ont conservé leur actualité à travers les siècles.

Il serait tentant d'en ajouter un quatrième : la différence entre la fondation des cités par essaimage et par rassemblement en un même lieu d'immigrants venus de différentes régions.

2 Cosmologie et Anthropologie

Pour les Anciens, quelle que soit leur école philosophique, la vie juste harmonise l'ordre du monde et l'ordre social. L'astronome Timée, dans le dialogue qui porte son nom, doit élever à l'unité d'une même science cosmologie et anthropologie. Or Platon voit que ce but est lointain, peut-être même inaccessible, puisque, au début du *Timée*, il place le mythe de l'Atlantide, indiquant que la représentation duale de la réalité, par le récit dramatique et les mathématiques, n'est pas près de disparaître.

L'Athénien des *Lois* déclare : « Amis, le dieu qui a dans ses mains, suivant l'antique parole, le commencement, la fin et le milieu de tous les êtres, va droit à son but parmi les révolutions de la nature ; il ne cesse d'avoir à sa suite la Justice, qui venge les infractions à la loi divine *(tou theiou nomou)* et à laquelle, modeste et rangé, celui qui veut le bonheur s'attache pour la suivre… » (716 a). Percevoir les lois de l'univers et s'y ajuster n'est pas, pour Platon, renoncer à sa liberté : « Ainsi changent, dit l'Athénien, son porte-parole, tous les êtres animés, par des changements dont ils ont la cause en eux-mêmes, et, cependant qu'ils changent, ils se déplacent conformément à l'ordre et à la loi du destin » (904 c).

Il évoque ensuite le sort de celui qui reste sourd à la loi divine, « gonflé d'orgueil, exalté par la richesse, les honneurs ou encore la beauté physique associée à la jeunesse et à la folie *(anoia)*, [il] enflamme son âme de démesure ; à l'en croire, il n'a besoin ni de maître ni de chef d'aucune sorte, mais se sent même capable de conduire autrui… ».

Qui se comporte ainsi « reste abandonné de Dieu et, à cause de cet abandon, il s'en adjoint d'autres qui lui ressemblent pour bondir désordonnément et tout bouleverser » (716 b). La démesure exerce un effet d'entraînement. L'homme « abandonné de Dieu » ressemble à l'univers, « quand Dieu en est absent » (*Timée*, 53 b). Dieu n'abandonne pas les hommes, mais les hommes peuvent décider de se séparer de Dieu par un processus que Platon décrit et qui produit non seulement « la mort de Dieu » dans le sujet, mais « la mort [effective] de l'homme ». Le *Timée*, 53 b précise : « Ils demeuraient dans l'état où il est naturel que soit toute chose d'où Dieu est absent ».

Faute d'évidences empiriques et démonstratives, aucune cosmologie ne s'impose : nous devons prendre parti, ou « voter » ; l'inspiration du *Timée* conduit, à l'époque moderne, des savants, admirateurs de Platon comme Kepler, à sacrifier la cosmologie du maître pour ne garder que son style mathématique ; depuis près d'un siècle, il est avéré que notre univers est en devenir. Comment articuler cosmologie et anthropologie, si le réel évolue ? ; enfin, la science n'est plus contemplation *(theoria)* de l'univers : elle agit sur lui au point que se constitue une technosphère qui interagit avec la biosphère et l'ordre physico-chimique.

La justice, dans ces conditions, ne concerne pas l'humanité vue comme une « communauté éthique » (Kant) intemporelle ; elle prend en compte l'inscription du destin collectif dans la nature et dans l'histoire. D'où la réflexion de Cournot dans ses *Considérations sur la marche des idées et des événements dans les temps modernes* (1872) : l'homme est devenu « le concessionnaire d'une planète ». Être juste, c'est donc essayer de bien gérer la Terre.

Qu'est-ce que cela signifie ? À son époque, Cournot trouve comme philosophie de la nature dominante le positivisme, pour qui, note Joseph Fourier dans sa *Théorie analytique de la chaleur* (1822), « les causes primordiales ne nous sont point connues », mais seulement les lois qui expriment certains traits des phénomènes. Cournot a une autre ambition pour la science : qu'elle reconstitue les processus causals d'où résultent les phénomènes observables. La tâche ne lui semble pas irréalisable puisque la synthèse chimique recompose par art les corps naturels et en fabrique que « la nature a oublié de faire ». Le pari du réalisme est donc tenable.

L'espérance chimique de Cournot s'est au cours du dernier demi-siècle étendue à l'ordre vivant : avec le développement des biotechnologies et l'émergence de la biologie de synthèse. L'origine de la vie reste énigmatique et la reconstitution de la vie par l'art, incomplète, mais il n'est pas téméraire de penser que la philosophie des sciences peut revêtir la forme d'une philosophie de la nature.

Reste à discerner ce que pourrait être une telle philosophie de la nature. L'éventail des solutions est large : identifier l'homme avec son cerveau et poser que l'anthropologie se confond avec les sciences cognitives et même avec la biologie ; au contraire, refuser de réduire l'ordre humain à l'ordre biologique, en reprenant, par exemple, la thèse du *Timée*, selon laquelle notre être est fait d'un « génie *(daimôn)* » de facture divine et d'une « âme mortelle » ; croire que tout, dans le comportement humain, peut être amené à la clarté de la raison ; ou, au contraire, penser qu'une opacité irréductible subsiste au cœur des êtres (Platon et Aristote) ; mettre l'accent sur l'intersubjectivité ; ou sur l'atomicité des individus ; considérer la connaissance comme contemplative ou voir en elle le moyen de modifier la nature. Ces divers choix ont une incidence sur notre conception de l'homme.

Pour ma part, je ne crois pas à l'identification de l'individu et de son cerveau ; je souscris à la thèse de Platon, qui refuse d'identifier l'ordre humain à l'ordre biologique. En effet, je crois à l'inséparabilité du *daimôn* et de l'âme mortelle, c'est-à-dire à l'Incarnation ; je ne pense pas non plus que nous puissions dissiper entièrement l'obscurité de notre être ; je crois aussi que nous vivons à travers un réseau d'interactions, de conflits et de certaines formes d'entraide et que la communion des saints en fournit une bonne image.

Et, surtout, je pense que la mission de l'humanité n'est pas de rester passive devant la nature, mais de modifier la biosphère en mettant au service de la justice la créativité de son esprit.

3 Sélection

L'Athénien des *Lois* observe : « il y a deux tâches politiques : la remise des charges à leurs titulaires et les lois que l'on distribue aux diverses charges » (735 a). Le législateur a deux rôles : sélectionner les titulaires les plus compétents pour exercer une charge ; définir les règles du jeu qui sont les plus valables pour l'accomplissement d'une fonction donnée. En effet, « c'est à des hommes que nous nous adressons, et non à des dieux. Or, la nature humaine consiste principalement en plaisirs, en douleurs et en désirs, auxquels tout être est à la lettre comme suspendu et accroché par ses préoccupations les plus profondes » (732 e).

Platon part de l'élevage : « Quiconque a pris en main quelque troupeau, berger, bouvier, éleveur de chevaux ou de tout autre de ce genre, n'entreprendra jamais de le soigner sans l'avoir d'abord épuré par l'espèce d'épuration qui convient à chaque groupement : séparant le sain de ce qui ne l'est pas, les bonnes races et les mauvaises, il renverra celles-ci à d'autres troupeaux et soignera le reste, en considérant quel vain et insatiable labeur imposeraient un corps et des âmes dont le naturel et la mauvaise éducation, après les avoir eux-mêmes gâtés, ruinent en outre ce qu'il y a de sain et d'intact dans les mœurs et les corps de tout le troupeau, le mal passant d'une tête du cheptel à l'autre si on n'y pratique une sélection en l'épurant » (735 b-c).

Le mot « sélection » passe très mal en France, même si l'on y sélectionne officiellement les sportifs et les élèves des grandes Écoles et, sans le dire, les autres étudiants. Max Perutz, dont le laboratoire de Cambridge fut le plus productif en prix Nobel que l'on ait connu, disait que, pour qu'un laboratoire fût créatif, il fallait bien sélectionner les chercheurs ; et les encourager. Il ajoutait qu'il ne fallait pas leur fixer de programme de recherche. « Sélection » se dit *« diakatharsis »* (735 d) : il s'agit de séparer les animaux sains et ceux qui ne le sont pas. Mais Platon dit que, pour le politique, cette opération est plus importante que pour les agriculteurs (735 c). L'Athénien observe que le processus de sélection le meilleur est douloureux *(algeinos)* (735 d).

Les charges pour lesquelles le législateur des *Lois* sélectionne les candidats sont définies par la loi. Ces définitions, quoique précises, sont à présent, dans la plupart des cas, obsolètes. Rester fidèle à l'esprit de Platon, c'est donc utiliser les sciences pour caractériser les charges qu'une société doit remplir pour fonctionner au début du XXIe siècle.

Définir les charges, dans une société, est un acte politique : on le voit aujourd'hui en France où les métiers industriels ont tendance à disparaître, sans qu'on sache si c'est inéluctable, souhaitable ou nuisible. En pratique, les politiques ont besoin, pour remplir cette mission, d'experts, notamment de sociologues. En effet, dans les sociétés en devenir, apparaissent des fonctions inconnues auparavant, par exemple, en matière de recherche, d'enseignement, d'information, de spécialisation des nations, etc. Et, de même, certaines fonctions deviennent marginales ou disparaissent.

D'où l'urgence de discerner ce qui, dans une société, à un moment donné, est utile et acceptable. Par exemple, concevoir de nouveaux métiers ; repousser l'âge de la retraite en fonction de l'allongement de la vie ; modifier la législation relative à la durée du travail hebdomadaire, etc. Pour comprendre comment les métiers se modifient dans une société, du recul historique est souhaitable : il aide à voir le lien entre historicité et créativité, et à discerner ce qui entrave, dans une société, les évolutions nécessaires.

Le tragique de l'Histoire, c'est que les hommes, même quand ils font un choix, ont les yeux bandés. Dans *La Guerre du Péloponnèse* (livre VI), Thucydide élucide ce mécanisme en prenant comme exemple l'expédition de Sicile. Nicias, le général en chef, est hostile à l'entreprise, car il voit les risques d'échec ; Alcibiade, au contraire, arrogant et sûr de lui, pousse ses concitoyens à l'action. Sa séduction opère et, paradoxalement, la circonspection de Nicias va dans le même sens : elle décide les Athéniens à se lancer dans le débarquement en Sicile, car ils ne doutent pas qu'un chef aussi expérimenté et aussi prudent les conduira à la victoire. D'où, pour les Anciens, comme aujourd'hui pour nous, une interrogation majeure : comment éviter que les décisions ne reposent que sur l'opinion ordinaire ? Comment fonder les choix sur une connaissance, si possible, « parfaite » ?

Les sciences sociales éclairent-t-elles ce qui est juste ou injuste dans un changement social ? Se bornent-elles à les décrire et, au mieux, à les expliquer ? Ou peut-elle en outre dire ce qui, dans les changements sociaux, est juste ou injuste ? Max Weber pose ce problème dans *Le savant et le politique*. À ses yeux, le politique ne se trouve pas devant une solution unique : il doit, dit-il, faire le choix de ses dieux, c'est-à-dire des fins de la société. Ainsi, en 1933, l'Allemagne choisit d'élire chancelier Adolf Hitler, sans mesurer, probablement, les conséquences de ce vote.

4 Croyance Ordinaire, Opinion Vraie, Science, Retour à la Caverne

Nous pénétrons dans le cœur de la réflexion de Platon sur la loi : pourquoi le règne de la loi est-il nécessaire ? Comment doter une cité de bonnes lois ? Y a-t-il une méthode pour passer de la diversité empirique des lois à des considérations universelles sur la loi ?

Si les hommes vivaient sous la seule conduite de l'intellect *(noûs)*, ils n'auraient pas besoin de lois, car l'intellect ne reçoit d'ordres de nulle part. Il est libre et souverain. En effet, il est divin, puisqu'il restitue l'ordre de l'univers. La liberté est par essence cosmique : elle ne relève pas seulement de la subjectivité, même si elle doit être assimilée par l'esprit humain. L'Athénien des *Lois* déclare : « Si jamais, en effet, un homme naissait, par faveur divine, naturellement apte à s'approprier ces principes, plus ne serait besoin d'aucune loi pour le commander ; car ni loi ni ordonnance n'est plus forte que la science, et l'intellect ne saurait, sans impiété, être serviteur ou esclave de quoi que ce soit ; il doit être, au contraire, le maître universel, s'il est réellement vrai et libre comme le veut sa nature » (875 c).

Platon évoque un état idéal dont il ne croit pas la réalisation possible. Il imagine, comme le fera Bergson, qu'apparaisse un homme qui échappe aux contraintes de l'âme mortelle, dont, juste avant, il dit : « [...] la nature mortelle le poussera toujours à l'ambition et à l'égoïsme, car elle fuira déraisonnablement la douleur et poursuivra le plaisir, tiendra plus de compte de l'un et de l'autre que du plus juste et du meilleur... » (875 b-c).

Il écarte cette hypothèse : « Mais, en fait, un tel don ne se réalise nulle part ni de nulle façon, que petitement *(kata brakhu)* ; aussi faut-il prendre le second parti, l'ordonnance et la loi, qui ne voient et ne considèrent que la généralité, mais sont impuissantes à saisir le détail » (875 d). Platon fait deux constats : le règne de la loi est nécessaire ; la loi ne saisit que le général, elle est incapable de saisir les cas particuliers. L'art politique ne se soucie que du bien général, et n'entre pas dans les cas particuliers. « Il est difficile de reconnaître que l'art politique véritable ne doit pas s'occuper *(melein)* du particulier *(to idion)* mais du général *(to koinon)* ». On est obligé, quand on légifère, de raboter le particulier.

Le génie *(daimôn)* que l'homme reçoit des dieux est inséparable du corps et du psychisme, c'est-à-dire de l'« âme mortelle ». Or celle-ci ne peut se soustraire à tout un ensemble de passions négatives (ambition, orgueil, envie, haine) dont seule la loi peut la protéger. Comme la loi reste impuissante à saisir les cas particuliers, certaines dispositions légales peuvent heurter ; ce dont le législateur est conscient.

Comment, dès lors, éventer les pièges où risque de tomber le législateur, quand il cherche à doter une entité politique de bonnes lois ? L'Athénien envisage deux modes de fondation des cités : par essaimage ; par rassemblement d'immigrants venus de divers pays. Il note que le second facilite la promulgation de lois nouvelles, mais a du mal à « faire respirer du même souffle *(sumpneusai)* » les citoyens du nouvel État. Faire respirer les citoyens du même souffle ne signifie pas créer seulement une communauté morale à partir d'immigrants initialement étrangers les uns aux autres ; c'est mettre au jour le but *(skopos)* unique en fonction duquel agencer les multiples activités de ladite société. En effet, une société politique qui n'a pas de but, ou qui se donne une multiplicité de buts, est livrée à l'errance et, du même coup, à l'injustice.

Or ni l'opinion ordinaire ni l'opinion vraie ne sont à même de mettre au jour le but unique d'une société : il y faut, dit l'Athénien à la fin des *Lois*, la « connaissance parfaite », connaissance qu'aucun individu ne détient, et dont seul le Conseil nocturne de la cité s'approche. Puisque, dans l'individu, le *daimôn* et l'âme mortelle sont inséparables, une connaissance ne sera « parfaite » que si elle fusionne l'apport de l'intellect *(noûs)* et celui des sensations les plus belles *(kallistai aisthèseis)*.

Que signifie cette expression énigmatique ? *Les Caractères* de La Bruyère et l'œuvre de Joseph Conrad en fournissent l'explication. Selon ces deux grands écrivains, il n'y a qu'une seule manière d'exprimer la vérité d'une situation. La fusion *(krasis)* de l'intelligence et de la sensation produit ce que Whitehead nomme « le sacrement de l'expression », c'est-à-dire place l'esprit dans la perspective unique où le réel apparaît tel qu'il est. Cette prouesse, d'après Platon, n'est pas accessible à l'individu ; elle échoit au Conseil nocturne, collectivité qui opère comme une entité morale détentrice d'intuition, de démonstration, d'expérience et de pouvoir de décision. En un mot, ce Conseil, tout en étant collectif, agit comme s'il possédait tous les caractères d'un individu rationnel et sensible.

En tant que législateur suprême, il jouit d'une liberté souveraine ; mais, comme les hommes ne peuvent faire abstraction de leur psychisme et de leur corps, il instaure le règne de la loi. Le Conseil suprême concrétise un long processus que décrit le *Timée* et qu'illustrent les *Lois*, à savoir l'opération par laquelle le législateur passe de l'opinion ordinaire à l'opinion vraie, de l'opinion vraie à la science, et, après être sorti de la « caverne », retourne vivre au milieu des hommes, dans l'espoir d'en améliorer le comportement et les lois.

5 Conclusion

Les *Lois* se terminent d'une façon étrange : Clinias, le Crétois que ses compatriotes ont chargé de fonder une colonie, a conscience de ne pas avoir en main tous les éléments pour résoudre le problème politique dont on lui a confié la responsabilité. Mégillos, le Spartiate, est du même avis : tous deux demandent à l'Athénien de «participer à la fondation de la cité ». Sans lui, « il faut renoncer à fonder notre cité ». En d'autres termes, l'art politique apparaît, dans ce dernier dialogue, comme un « métier impossible » (Freud).

La 1re leçon qu'on retire des *Lois*, c'est justement la difficulté que l'on éprouve à discerner ce qui fait l'unité d'un système législatif, et le but unique d'une société politique, c'est-à-dire l'*Esprit des lois*.

La 2e leçon qui se dégage de l'œuvre, c'est qu'on ne peut disjoindre la cosmologie et l'anthropologie. Les Anciens, quelle que fût leur école, en étaient convaincus ; cette exigence reste fondamentale aujourd'hui et pour le temps à venir. Or elle n'est pas facile à satisfaire, car la puissance de l'humanité sur la nature extérieure et sur sa nature propre s'est accrue et il n'est pas évident de trier, parmi ces formes de puissance, celles qui augmentent la justice.

La 3e leçon, c'est que, loin d'avoir réalisé le rêve du *Timée* de présenter, dans le même discours scientifique, la cosmologie et l'anthropologie, nous représentons toujours l'action humaine de façon duale, par le récit et par la science. Cela tient au caractère tragique de l'histoire et, peut-être même, de la nature. Or, jusqu'ici, la logique n'a que peu et mal exploré la tragédie.

La 4e leçon, plus visible peut-être dans le *Timée* que dans les *Lois*, c'est que la fidélité à Platon ne consiste pas à l'imiter, mais, plutôt, comme le fit Kepler, à saisir que, pour respecter l'inspiration mathématique de son système du monde, il faut rejeter la forme particulière de son astronomie. Ainsi, comprendre les *Lois*, ce n'est pas chercher à en justifier les dispositions particulières, mais se demander ce que ferait Platon, s'il avait à les récrire au XXIe siècle.

Verrait-il les conditions réunies pour qu'un nouveau Timée donne une forme unifiée à la cosmologie et à l'anthropologie ? Ou continuerait-il à user à la fois de la science et du récit ? Je crois que la seconde solution prévaudrait, car, jusqu'ici, la logique, insistons-y, ne s'est pas hasardée à clarifier l'action tragique.

Maintiendrait-il que la politique est l'art de découvrir et de réaliser le but unique que chaque société se donne ? Je le pense, mais il douterait que les politiques y parviennent, car il verrait dans l'homme un composé instable et indissociable de *daimôn* et d'âme mortelle, qu'on ne peut entièrement soustraire à son obscurité intrinsèque et à ses passions.

La clé des *Lois*, à mon sens, se trouve dans la proposition suivante : « [...] le commencement est un dieu qui, en s'établissant chez les hommes, sauve toutes choses » (775 e). Saint Augustin, dans le *De Civitate Dei* (xii, 21) reprend le thème : « *hoc ergo* [s.e. *initium*] *ut esset, creatus est homo* [pour qu'il y eût du commencement, Dieu a créé l'homme] ». À son tour, Hannah Arendt, dans *Condition de l'homme moderne*, souligne que l'homme n'est pas seulement mortel, mais naissant *(natal)*.

La justice, comme les systèmes de lois, n'est donc pas figée, car les principes universels s'incarnent dans des contextes historiques en devenir. Les *Lois* de Platon ne sont pas à consulter comme un recueil de textes particuliers, relatifs aux cités grecques, mais comme un essai pour discerner, à partir de situations réelles ou imaginaires (historiques ou mythiques), comment le politique cherche à établir une société où règnerait l'équité et où les différends se règleraient par la discussion, non par la violence.

Platon émet, toutefois, deux réserves : le dialogue ne fait pas disparaître tout à fait l'élément tyrannique de la décision ; la raison ne réussit pas à domestiquer entièrement les pulsions : elle ne les élève pas complètement à la transparence et à la mesure.

Justice and Moderation in the State: Aristotle and Beyond

Eleni Leontsini

1 The Centrality of Political Justice

In this chapter I aim to analyze Aristotle's account of political justice (*to politikon dikaion*) in both the *Nicomachean Ethics* and the *Politics*,[1] since it is these accounts that are most relevant to his advocacy of moderation and mixed constitution, and I aim to show how justice (*dikaiosunē*) and equality (*isotēs*) are crucial for the promotion of the common interest (*to koinē symferon*) of the state (*polis*). In addition, I explore the connection made between justice (*dikaiosunē*; *aplōs* or *politikon dikaion*), equality (*isotēs*), democracy (*demokratia*), liberty (*eleutheria*), and friendship (*philia*), and attempt to further excavate Aristotle's conception of political justice (*to politikon dikaion*) and moderation in the *polis*. We will see how this bears on questions in contemporary political philosophy concerning the role of justice as the most fundamental virtue for society, and as an institution that serves to fix the limits of human conduct and to lay down the principles specifying the just distribution of benefits and burdens in a democratic society of equals.

It should be noted that Aristotle's account of justice as presented in both the *Nicomachean Ethics* and the *Politics* is complex and that there are many concepts of justice discussed by Aristotle. Indeed, Aristotle is aware of this complexity in justice, as he makes sure to stress in *NE* II.7.1108b17–19: "With regard to justice, since it has not one simple meaning, we shall, after describing the other states, distinguish its two kinds and say how each of them is a mean". For Aristotle, there are universal

[1] Abbreviations: *NE* (*Nicomachean Ethics*), *EE* (*Eudemian Ethics*), *Pol* (*Politics*), *Rhet* (*Rhetoric*). Translations from Aristotle's *Nicomachean Ethics* and *Politics* are from Ross, D. (1980) *Aristotle Nicomachean Ethics*. Oxford: Oxford University Press, and Stalley, R. F. (1995) *Aristotle. The Politics*. Oxford: Oxford University Press, respectively, and the translations of Aristotle's other works are from Barnes, J. (1984) *The Complete Works of Aristotle*, 2 vols. Princeton: Princeton University Press, with some alterations of my own.

E. Leontsini (✉)
Department of Philosophy, University of Ioannina, Epiros, Greece
e-mail: eleon@uoi.gr

G. Fløistad (ed.), *Philosophy of Justice*, Contemporary Philosophy: A New Survey 12,
DOI 10.1007/978-94-017-9175-5_3,

and particular concepts of justice as well as natural and conventional ones. Especially in the *Nicomachean Ethics*, there are many concepts of justice discussed, and the main distinction made in *NE* V.1–2 is between 'universal' and 'particular' justice.

According to Aristotle, 'universal' or 'general' justice ('the just as the lawful') refers to the whole of virtue:

> This form of justice, then, is complete virtue, although not without qualification, but in relation to our neighbour. And therefore justice is often thought to be the greatest of virtues, and 'neither evening nor morning star' is so wonderful; and proverbially 'in justice is every virtue comprehended'. And it is complete virtue in its fullest sense because it is the actual exercise of complete virtue. It is complete because he who possesses it can exercise his virtue not only in himself but towards his neighbour also; for many people can exercise virtue in their own affairs, but not in their relations to their neighbour (*NE* V.1129b25–35).

This universal or general concept of justice includes all the habits and dispositions of a good citizen and aims at the common advantage (*to koinē symferon*): "The laws in their enactments on all subjects aim at the common advantage either of all or of the best or of those who hold power, or something of the sort; so that in one sense we call those acts just that tend to produce and preserve happiness and its components for the political society" (*NE* V.1129b15–19). As Young succinctly points out, "The identity of universal justice, lawfulness, and virtue as a whole thus brings together two major themes of Aristotle's moral and political philosophy: the moral idea that acting virtuously promotes happiness and the political idea that the political community exists to promote the happiness of its citizens".[2]

'Particular' justice ('the just as the fair and equal') is a character virtue, like the other virtues (for example, courage, temperance, liberality, honesty, loyalty, etc.), and is part of 'universal' justice. Particular justice is divided into two kinds: distributive justice (*dianemētikon dikaion*) and corrective (or rectificatory or commutative) justice (*diorthōtikon dikaion*). Distributive justice operates in a society and allocates benefits and burdens fairly, while rectificatory justice operates between two parties and either maintains or restores a balance (*NE* V.2).[3]

My analysis will mainly focus on the discussion of the Aristotelian conception of political justice which is introduced in *NE* V.6. Having demonstrated that the reciprocal is related to the just, Aristotle points out that "we must not forget that what we are looking for is not only what is just without qualification (*to aplōs dikaion*) but also political justice (*to politikon dikaion*)" (*NE* V.6. 1134a25–26):

> This is found among people who share their life with a view to self-sufficiency, people who are free and either proportionately or arithmetically equal, so that between those who do not fulfil this condition there is no political justice in a special sense or by analogy. For justice exists only between people whose mutual relations are governed by law; and law exists for people between whom there is injustice; for legal justice is the discrimination of the just and the unjust. And between people between whom injustice is done there is also unjust action (although there is not injustice between all between whom there is unjust action), and this

[2] Young, C. M. (2007) "Aristotle's Justice," in Kraut, R. (ed.) *The Blackwell Guide to Aristotle's Nicomachean Ethics*. Oxford: Blackwell, p. 181.

[3] For a clear exposition of the main concepts of justice presented in *NE* V, see Young, C. M. "Aristotle's Justice," *op. cit.*, pp. 179–180.

> is assigning too much to oneself of things good in themselves and too little of things evil in themselves. This is why we do not allow a person to rule, but rational principle, because a person behaves thus in his own interests and becomes a tyrant. The magistrate on the other hand is the guardian of justice, and, if of justice, then of equality also (*NE* V.6. 1134a26–1134b2).

Justice (*dikaiosunē* or *politikon dikaion*) is central to Aristotle's political theory; it is the chief virtue of the *polis* that promotes the common advantage (*to koinē symferon*). As Aristotle points out in *Politics* III, repeating in a way the argument of the first section of the first chapter of *Politics* I[4]:

> In all branches of knowledge and in every kind of craft the end in view is some good. In the most sovereign of these, the capacity for [leadership in] political matters, the end in view is the greatest good and the good which is most to be pursued. The good in the sphere of politics is justice (*dikaion*), and justice consists in what tends to promote the common interest (*to koinē symferon*) (*Pol* III.1282b12–14).

The centrality of justice in Aristotle's political thought is obvious from the very beginning of *Politics* I.2. There, Aristotle defends something we can call 'political naturalism'; the idea is that human beings have the natural impulse to live together and to form political associations.[5] He argues that human beings—being political animals by nature—are uniquely endowed by nature with the ability to form the concept of justice and with the capacity for political co-operation (*Pol* I.1253a7–18): "The city belongs to the class of things that exist by nature, and man is by nature a political animal" (*Pol* 1253a1–3). In addition, Aristotle argues in *Pol* I.1253a31–39 that, although the impulse towards these kinds of associations exists by nature in all people, "the person who first constructed such an association was nonetheless the greatest of all benefactors". This also contains the claim that human beings need law and justice in order to form a political association.[6] Aristotle illustrates this point further by pointing out that:

> Man, when perfected, is the best of animals; but if he be isolated from law and justice he is the worst of all. Injustice is all the graver when it is armed injustice; and man is furnished from birth with weapons which are intended to serve the purposes of wisdom and goodness, but which may be used in preference for opposite ends. That is why, if he be without goodness [of mind and character], he is a most unholy and savage being, and worse than all others in the indulgence of lust and gluttony. The virtue of justice belongs to the city; for justice is an ordering of the political association, and the virtue of justice consists in the determination of what is just. (*Pol* I.1253a29–39)

As we have seen, according to Aristotle, justice is important since its purpose is the common advantage of the *polis* (*to koinē symferon*). It is interesting that he also relates political friendship with the promotion of the common advantage of the

---

[4] Barker, E. (ed.) (1958) *The Politics of Aristotle*. Oxford: Oxford University Press, p. 129.

[5] For an extensive discussion of Aristotle's political naturalism and the relevant bibliography, see Leontsini, E. (2007) *The Appropriation of Aristotle in the Liberal-Communitarian Debate*, with a foreword by R. F. Stalley. Athens: Saripolos Library, pp. 49–92.

[6] See Miller, Fr. D. (1995) *Nature, Justice, and Rights in Aristotle's Politics*. Oxford: Clarendon Press, p. 67.

polis, as we shall see in Sect. 4 of this chapter. In addition, it should be pointed out that the common advantage of the *polis* (*to koinē symferon*) is also associated with both democracy and polity as well as with his constitutional theory in general (*Pol* III.6.1279a17ff.; III.9.1280a10; III.9.1280a22; V.1.1301a36; V.1.1301b36). The best constitution (*politeia*) is the one that aims at the common interest or advantage (*Pol* III.4.1277b7–9 & III.6.1278b6–25). As Aristotle points out, justice is restricted to cities with good rulers, irrespectively of the type of constitution followed:

> Those constitutions which consider the common interest are right constitutions, judged by the standard of absolute justice. Those constitutions which consider only the personal interest of the rulers are all wrong constitutions, or perversions of the right forms. Such perverted forms are despotic; whereas the city is an association of free people (*Pol* III.7. 1279a17–21).

2 Justice and Equality in the *Politics*

In addition, there is an interesting connection, made by Aristotle in various passages, between justice and equality and their relevance to the promotion of moderation in the city.[7] Aristotle's theory of constitutions confirms the centrality of justice for Aristotelian political theory. This is clearly stated in *Politics* III.1282b14–18: "The good in the sphere of politics is justice, and justice consists in what tends to promote the common interest. General opinion makes it consist in some sort of equality". Also, in *EE* VII.1241a13–15: "All constitutions are a form of justice, for a constitution is a community, and everything common is established through justice".[8]

In *Politics* III.3, Aristotle argues that a *polis* cannot be identified by reference to its place or the race of its inhabitants, since it is only the constitution (*nomos*) of a *polis* which unites it:

> If a city is a form of association, and if this form of association is an association of citizens in constitution, it would seem to follow inevitably that when the constitution undergoes a change in form, and becomes a different constitution, the city will likewise cease to be the same city. We say that a chorus which appears at one time as a comic and at another as a

[7] The notion of equality is also discussed at length in *Nicomachean Ethics* (V. 3) where Aristotle presents his theory on distributive justice. It should be pointed out, though, that Aristotle does not put forward the same account of justice in both the *Nicomachean Ethics* and the *Politics*, so one should be careful to first examine these two accounts separately and then try to understand Aristotle's conception of justice as a whole. I will not be discussing the *NE* account of justice here, since my focus is on the *Politics* account. For a discussion of the *NE* account of justice and the relevant bibliography, see Leontsini, E. *The Appropriation of Aristotle in the Liberal-Communitarian Debate*, *op. cit.*, pp. 137–139.

[8] Aristotle's emphasis on equality is also stated in his discussion on community in various passages. A community is, according to Aristotle, a group which co-operates for the sake of some common good. This common good can vary from, for example, meals or property to *eudaimonia*: "There must be some one thing which is common to all the members and identical for them all, though their shares in it may be equal, or unequal. The thing itself may be various food, for instance, or a stretch of territory, or anything else of the kind" (1328a26–b1).

> tragic chorus is not the same—and this in spite of the fact that the members often remain the same. What is true of the chorus is also true of every kind of association, and of all other compounds generally. If the form of its composition is different, the compound becomes a different compound. A scale composed of the same notes will be a different scale depending on whether it is in the Dorian or the Phrygian mode. If this is the case, it is obvious that in determining the identity of the city we must look to the constitution. Whether the same group of people inhabits a city, or a total different group, we are free to call it the same city, or a different city. It is a different question whether it is right to pay debts or to repudiate them when a city changes its constitution into another form (*Pol* III.1276b1–10).

In particular, Aristotle discusses in *Politics* III.9–13 the relation of justice to constitutions, and to wealth. He approaches the classification of the constitutions from the point of view of justice.[9] This account of justice that Aristotle puts forward in *Politics* III gives content to the account of justice by explaining what sorts of equality and inequality are relevant. This was not obvious from the account of justice presented in the *Nicomachean Ethics*. According to Aristotle, the principle of a constitution is its conception of justice. This is stated clearly in *Politics* III.1280a7–9, where he investigates the oligarchic and the democratic conceptions of justice, arguing that "all parties have a hold on a conception of justice; but they both fail to carry it far enough, and do not express the true conception of justice in the whole of its range." According to Aristotle, both oligarchy and democracy rest on a particular social class and have their own distinctive conception of justice concerning the way that offices and honours are distributed, which enables them to justify the predominance of the class they favour.[10] Democrats think that the conception of justice is based on the principle of equality (equality in free birth), while oligarchs base justice on inequality (inequality in wealth). Aristotle's principle of political justice, conversely, is that political offices and honours should be distributed according to virtue. His own view is elaborated through the critique of the respective principles of the oligarchic and democratic constitutions.

Aristotle argues that justice is the political good: "Justice is concerned with people; and a just distribution is one in which there is proportion between the things distributed and those to whom they are distributed, a point which has already been made in the *Ethics*. There is general agreement about what constitutes equality in the thing, but disagreement about what constitutes it in people" (*Pol* III.1280a17–23). But, according to Aristotle, both sides, being misled by the fact that they are professing a sort of conception of justice, and professing it up to the point that they think they are professing one which is absolute and complete, fail to mention the 'real cardinal factor', as he calls it. The cardinal factor in this case is that the end of the city is the common promotion of a good quality of life and not only mere life.

As far as economic and social goods are concerned, Aristotle places the relative proportional equality, desert (*kat' axian*), as the distributive criterion for the person who lives "in the world as we know it" (*Pol* III.1280a33). This applies only to this kind of person, since in a society of exceptional people there is no place for anything

[9] Stalley, R. F. (1995) *Aristotle. The Politics*. Oxford: Oxford University Press, pp. 356–57.

[10] Stalley, R. F. *Aristotle. The Politics*, *op. cit.*, p. 357.

but absolute equality. It should be noted that Aristotle does not define the precise content of this proportional equality, but he simply attempts a formal analysis by leaving the criterion open. In the economic area, proportional equality is determined according to the contribution of each citizen (*Pol* III.1280a25–30). Furthermore, superiority of political rights is not allowed unless in the case of something that contributes to the excellence of performance (*Pol* III.1282b23–1283a1). When laws are said to be 'right', the word must be taken to mean 'equally right', and this means 'right' in regard to the interest of the whole city and in regard to the common welfare of the citizens (*Pol* III.1283b40). In conclusion, seen in the context of the application of his principle of 'mean' and his theory on the best life, Aristotle argues that there should exist for everybody a minimum of social goods and that a maximum of goods should not be exceeded.[11]

3 A Democratic Conception of Justice

This democratic conception of justice that Aristotle presents sounds similar to the liberal definition of freedom. This may suggest that the state should be maximizing freedom, since democrats see freedom as a good. But the democratic conception of freedom should not be confused with the liberal one. If one takes this view to be the ancient conception of freedom that Aristotle is arguing about, then it is a democratic conception, but not a liberal one in the sense that part of its definition at least consists not in exercising freedom of choice but in having a share in rule. In fact, the conception of liberty at play here is that of 'ancient liberty' defined as 'democratic self-government'.[12] Liberty is, for Aristotle, the end of democracy: "Nor should the end of each form of government be neglected, for people choose the things which have reference to the end. Now, the end of democracy is liberty, of oligarchy wealth, of aristocracy things relating to education and what the law prescribes, of tyranny self-protection" (*Rhet* I.1366a).

According to Aristotle, the democratic conception of liberty is defined by two features: (i) the interchange of ruling and being ruled, and (ii) living as you like. Freedom is, thus, the precondition of a democratic state:

> The underlying principle of the democratic type of constitution is liberty. Indeed it is commonly held that liberty can only be enjoyed in this sort of constitution, for this, so they say, is the aim of every democracy. Liberty in one of its forms consists in the interchange of ruling and being ruled. The democratic conception of justice consists in arithmetical equality, rather than proportionate equality on the basis of desert. On this conception of justice

[11] It should be noted that the concept of 'mean' in the case of justice is different from that in the other virtues, because the mean in this case does not refer to the middle between two equally bad habits, but to a mean in relation to things.

[12] Ancient liberty is usually defined as 'self-mastery', but 'self-government' is a wider term including that of self-mastery, describing more precisely the nature of liberty for the ancients in the 'rule and being ruled' elements. See Leontsini, E. *The Appropriation of Aristotle in the Liberal-Communitarian Debate*, *op. cit.*, pp. 220–222.

> the masses must necessarily be sovereign and the will of the majority must be ultimate and must be the expression of justice. The argument is that each citizen should be in a position of equality; and the result which follows in democracies is that the poor are more sovereign than the rich, for they are in a majority, and the will of the majority is sovereign. This then is one mark of liberty, which all democrats agree in making the defining feature of their sort of constitution. Another mark is 'living as you like'. Such a life, they argue, is the function of the free person, just as the function of slaves is not to live as they like. This is the second defining feature of democracy. It results in the view that ideally one should not be ruled by any one, or, at least, that one should [rule and] be ruled in turns. It contributes, in this way, to a general system of liberty based on equality (*Pol* VI. 2. 1317b2–17).

Aristotle's claim about the democrats, that they espouse freedom in the sense of doing what you wish, but nevertheless choose as 'second best' to rule and be ruled in turn, shows exactly that: participation in ruling leads to political liberty. If a person is participating in ruling, that means that he has a say in political decisions, she is able to put forward his views, she is at liberty to choose. Ruling, in turn, is a form of freedom since "it promotes my being able to do what I like".[13] The basic assumption behind this idea is that negative liberty would never be secured unless political participation in government is guaranteed. Without being able to participate in government, negative liberty will almost always be arbitrary and subject to the good will of the occasional 'benevolent' sovereign or sovereign body.

The conflict between liberty and equality that Aristotle finds at the root of democracy is, of course, still unresolved. As he points out in *Politics* 1318a6–10, equality is for the poorer class to have no larger share of power than the rich, and not for the poorer class alone to be supreme but for all to govern equally. In this way, the worst-off would feel that the constitution possessed both equality and liberty. But, as he says in *Politics* VI.1318b39–41, unfortunately, liberty to do whatever one likes cannot guard against the evil that is in every person's character.

Aristotle argues in *Politics* V.1310a26–38 that democracy usually rests on a false conception of liberty. As he says, there are two features which are generally assumed to define democracy: the sovereignty of the majority and the liberty of individuals. Justice is assumed to consist in equality with regards to the will of the masses as sovereign; liberty is assumed to consist in "doing what one likes". But the result of this view is that in extreme democracies each individual lives as she likes and "she chances to desire for any end", as Euripides says. But, according to Aristotle, this is a false conception of liberty, since to live by the rule of the constitution should not be regarded as slavery, but rather as salvation. What is important in the city is for preservation and stability to be ensured, and this will not be achieved if the form of the constitution is based on such a conception of liberty.

For Aristotle, liberty is not a good to be pursued for its own sake; it is not prior to other values, such as justice, since the idea of liberty, on its political side, is ultimately based on the conception of justice. As Aristotle points out in *Politics*

---

[13] Sorabji, R. (1990) "Comments on J. Barnes," in Patzig, G. (ed.) *Aristoteles Politik: Akten des XI. Symposium Aristotelicum*. Göttingen, p. 266.

VII.1324a5, where he examines the question of whether the happiness of the city is the same as that of the individual, or whether it is different:

> Those who believe that the well-being of the individual consists in his wealth, will also believe that the city as a whole is happy when it is wealthy. Those, who rank the life of a tyrant higher than any other, will also rank the city which possesses the largest empire as being the happiest city. Anyone, who grades individuals by their goodness, will also regard the happiness of cities as proportionate to their goodness (*Pol* VII.1324a9–13).

The happiness of the city is the same as that of the individual only in the sense that in the same way that it is important for the individual to be wealthy, good, etc., it is also important for the city to be wealthy, good, etc.

From the above, we can draw the following conclusions regarding Aristotle's conception of liberty. Liberty in one of its forms consists in the interchange of ruling and being ruled (*Pol* VI.1317b2–3). This contributes to a general system of liberty based on equality (*Pol* VI.1317b15–17). But while the democrats adopt arithmetical equality, Aristotle supports proportionate equality. One form of liberty, as he says, is to govern and be governed in turn. This is the conception of liberty that Aristotle accepts; he denies the one form that the extreme democrat advocates, according to which liberty is to do whatever one wants. The idea of liberty, on its political side, is ultimately based on the conception of justice. But justice for Aristotle should consist in proportionate equality on the basis of desert and not in arithmetical equality as in the case of the democratic conception of justice (*Pol* VI.1317b2–11).

Although ideally one should not be ruled by any one, this is not possible since the state would dissolve into anarchy. In order to prevent this, a compromise should be made at the expense of liberty: one should live by the rule of the constitution. Living by the rule of the constitution ought, therefore, not to be regarded as slavery but as salvation (*Pol* VI.1310a33–39). Aristotle argues that it is slavish to live for another with the crucial exception of a friend. If the ideal city rests on an extension of the best type of friendship, the virtuous person's relationship to the city is not slavish.

The greatest of all the means for ensuring stability of constitutions is the education of citizens in the spirit of their constitution. The citizens should be attuned, by the force of habit and the influence of teaching, to the right constitutional temper. It is true that to some extent Aristotle agrees that freedom is living as one wishes; but he denies that living as one wishes requires freedom from the constraints of law or moral education. Therefore, the democratic view is neither an individualist conception of freedom nor of justice. This is further enhanced by Aristotle's criticism of Lycophron's 'libertarian' view (*Pol* III.1280b10–11) and of Hippodamus's view (*Pol* II.1267b37). Aristotle is critical of both the oligarchic and the democratic conception of the state. Nevertheless, his arguments are not undemocratic as such; he is keener to demonstrate the dangers of democracy, than to criticize democracy as such.

Aristotle seems to envisage that a possible role of the state is to promote the good life but not to guarantee just claims. The state's job is not to arbitrate disputes. As he points out at 1280b6–12, if the city does not devote itself to the end of encouraging goodness, a political association sinks into a mere alliance, which only differs in the contiguity of its members from other forms of alliance where the members live at a distance from one another. Thus, "the law becomes a mere covenant, or, in the phrase of the sophist Lycophron, 'a guarantor of just claims', but lacks the capacity to make the citizens good and just" (*Pol* III.1280b10–11).

In order to illustrate this point, Aristotle imagines a hypothetical case where two cities (Megara and Corinth) unite into one, being embraced by a single wall. This union, nevertheless, could not make a single city, since a *polis* is not an association of site (*Pol* III.1280b30) and "this sort of thing is the business of friendship, for the pursuit of a common social life is friendship":

> It is clear, therefore, that a city is not an association for residence in a common site, or for the sake of preventing mutual injustice and easing exchange. These are indeed conditions which must be present before a city can exist; but the presence of all these conditions is not enough, in itself, to constitute a city. What constitutes a city is an association of households and clans in a good life, for the sake of attaining a perfect and self-sufficing existence. This, however, will not come about unless the members inhabit one and the self-same place and practice intermarriage. It was for this reason that the various institutions of a common social life—marriage-connections, kin-groups, religious gatherings, and social pastimes generally—arose in cities. This sort of thing is the business of friendship, for the pursuit of a common social life is friendship. Thus the purpose of a city is the good life, and these institutions are means to that end. A city is constituted by the association of families and villages in a perfect and self-sufficing existence; and such an existence, on our definition, consists in living a happy and truly valuable life (*Pol* III.1280b29–1281a1).

The pursuit of a common social life is, therefore, friendship, but, nevertheless, the purpose of a city is the good life and these institutions are means to an end. Therefore, Aristotle concludes at *Politics* III.1281a2–10 that it is for the sake of actions valuable in themselves, and not for the sake of social life, that political associations must be considered to exist. Those who contribute most to this association have a greater share in the city than those who are equal to them in free birth and descent, but unequal in civic excellence, or than those who surpass them in wealth but are surpassed by them in excellence. This, according to Aristotle, shows that the disputants about constitution profess only a partial conception of justice. It should be noted, nevertheless, that, although Aristotle's conception of the city as promoting virtue plays a part in this context, some of his arguments here are based on the idea that, in the world as we find it, where the ideal is not possible, we may have to choose the kind of constitution which is least prone to *stasis*. These are considerations which do not rest on a concept of desert, do not presuppose a thick theory of the good and could also be recognised by a modern.[14]

Aristotle gives great importance to criticising Lycophron's alternative view because his aim is to emphasise that—when discussing different conceptions of justice, and in particular equality and inequality relevant to the distribution of

[14] For an interesting discussion on relevant criticisms of this Aristotelian argument, see Robinson, R. (ed.) (1995) *Aristotle Politics,* Books III and IV, with a supplementary essay by D. Keyt. Oxford: Clarendon Press, pp. 31–33.

honours—it is important that we have first agreed on the end for which the city exists. The distribution of honours depends ultimately on the purpose for which the association exists. In that sense, Aristotle is able to discriminate between different conceptions of justice, and, also, to demonstrate that each conception of justice contains an element of truth. This is based on the assumption that we have agreed on the end for which the city exists.[15] This criticism of Lycophron is similar to the argument against Hippodamus's theory made by Aristotle at *Politics* II.1267b37. Aristotle's first criticism of Hippodamus's theory concerns the division of the citizen body; all share in the constitution but not all of them bear arms and become, therefore, the slaves of the class in possession of arms.

4 Justice, Moderation, and Political Friendship

As we have seen in Sect. 1 of this chapter, justice, according to Aristotle, is important since its purpose is the common interest of the *polis* (*to koinē symferon*). It is interesting that he also relates political friendship with the promotion of the common interest of the *polis*, regarding it as a special form of 'common advantage friendship' (*to koinē symferon*),[16] as it is obvious in various passages:

> For people journey together with a view to some particular advantage, and to provide something that they need for the purposes of life; and it is for the sake of advantage that the political community too seems both to have come together originally and to endure, for this is what legislators aim at, and they call just that which is to the common advantage (*NE* VIII.1160a11–14).

Aristotle points out that the political community is formed and survives for the sake of the common advantage that its members derive from it. In this sense, it is essential for such a community to aim at securing what is needed by its members to support their lives (*NE* 1160a11–23). All these different small communities, which exist within the larger political association, seem to be subordinate to this political community, because political community aims not at what is immediately useful, but at what is useful for the whole life:

> All these communities, then, seem to be parts of the political community; and the particular kinds of friendship will correspond to the particular kinds of community (*NE* VIII.1160a28–30).

In *EE* IX.1242a6–13, political friendship is also classified as 'common advantage friendship':

> Political friendship on the other hand is constituted in the fullest degree on the principle of utility, for it seems to be the individual's lack of self-sufficiency that makes these unions

[15] Stalley, R. F. (1995), *op.cit.*, p. 358.

[16] For the definition of political friendship as 'common advantage friendship', see Leontsini, E. (2013) "The Motive of Society: Aristotle on Civic Friendship, Justice, and Concord," *Res Publica*, 19, 1 (2013), pp. 25–29.

permanent—since they would have been formed in any case merely for the sake of society. Only civic friendship and the deviation from it are not merely friendships but also partnerships on a friendly footing (*ôs philoi koinônousin*); the others are on a basis of superiority. The justice that underlies a friendship of utility is in the highest degree just, because this is the civic principle of justice.

Aristotle maintained that '*philia* is the motive of society' (*Pol* III.1280b38–39) and argued that friendship is even more important than justice since it generates concord in the city (*NE* VIII.1155b21–27).[17] Indeed, one of the most striking features of Aristotle's account is that he sees an important relation between justice and friendship. In his view, friendship is in some ways as important as justice—if not more—for the prosperity of the state. The city is a partnership for the sake of the good and—in the same sense that justice is the good in the sphere of politics—friendship is also a good and holds the state together. Lawgivers, according to this argument, seem to care more for friendship than for justice, since friendship generates concord (*homonoia*)—i.e., unanimity of the citizens—which is similar to friendship. In that way, friendship can hold the state together—in the same sense that justice does—and can also expel faction. It is in this sense that, when people are friends, they have no need of justice, while when they are just, they need friendship as well, and the highest form of justice seems to be a matter of friendship.[18]

This view is expressed by Aristotle in both the *Nicomachean* and the *Eudemian Ethics* in two central passages, respectively. First, in *NE* VIII.1155a22–28 where he says that

> Friendship seems also to hold states together, and lawgivers to care more for it than for justice; for concord seems to be something like friendship, and this they aim at most of all, and expel faction as their worst enemy; and when people are friends they have no need of justice, while when they are just they need friendship as well, and the truest form of justice is thought to be a friendly quality.

Second, in *EE* III.1234b25–31 where he expresses almost the same view:

> All say that justice and injustice are specially exhibited towards friends; the same person seems both good and a friend, and friendship seems a sort of moral habit; and if one wishes to make people not wrong one another, one should make them friends, for genuine friends do not act unjustly. But neither will people act unjustly if they are just; therefore justice and friendship are either the same or not far different.

Friendship and justice seem to be concerned with the same things and to be found in the same people:

> For there seems to be some kind of justice in every community, and some kind of friendship as well. At any rate, people address as friends their shipmates and fellow soldiers, and similarly those who are members of other kinds of community or association with them. And the extent of their community is the extent of their friendship, since it is also the extent of

---

[17] For the importance of the relation between justice, friendship and concord in Aristotelian political philosophy, see Leontsini, E. "The Motive of Society: Aristotle on Civic Friendship, Justice, and Concord," *op.cit.*, pp. 21–35.

[18] Leontsini, E. "The Motive of Society: Aristotle on Civic Friendship, Justice, and Concord," *op.cit.*, p. 29.

> their justice. The proverb, 'What friends have, they have in common', is correct, since friendship is based on community. But while brothers and comrades have everything in common, what the others whom we have mentioned have in common is more limited—more in some cases, less in others, since friendship too differs in degree (*NE* VIII.1159b25–1160a).

Again, similar examples are also offered by Aristotle in the *Eudemian Ethics*, where he says that:

> Therefore to seek the proper way of associating with a friend is to seek for a particular kind of justice. In fact the whole of justice in general is in relation to a friend, for what is just is just for certain persons; and persons who are partners, and a friend is a partner, either in one's family or in one's life. For man is not only a political but also a house-holding animal, and does not, like the other animals, couple occasionally and with any chance female or male, but man is in a special way not a solitary but a gregarious animal, associating with the persons with whom he has a natural kinship; accordingly there would be partnership; and justice of a sort, even if there were no state (*EE* VII.1242a20–27).

Aristotle's view of political friendship is also closely connected with his advocacy of moderation in the mixed constitution in relation to justice, since equality of means produces the right kind of relationship among the citizens (which is a friendship among equals) and encourages, therefore, not only the right kind of political community but also a secure and stable political regime.[19] Aristotle illustrates this in his discussion on the problems arising from a *polis* in which the distribution of wealth is unequal:

> The result is a city, not of free persons, but only of slaves and masters: a state of envy on the one side and of contempt on the other. Nothing could be further removed from the spirit of friendship or of a political association. An association depends on friendship—after all, people will not even take a journey in common with their enemies. A city aims at being, as far as possible, composed of equals and peers, which is the condition of those in the middle, more than any group (*Pol* IV.1295b20–27).

According to Aristotle, the polity (*politeia*) is bound to have the best constitution, since it is composed of the elements which naturally go to make up a city. The middle classes enjoy a greater security themselves than any other class, since they do not, like the poor, desire the goods of others; nor do others desire their possessions, as the poor covet those of the rich, and since they neither plot against others, nor are plotted against themselves, they live free from danger. The best form of political association is, first, one where power is vested in the middle class, and, second, those cities where good government is attainable because there is a large middle class—large enough, if possible, to be stronger than both of the other classes, but at any rate large enough to be stronger than either of them singly; in that case, its addition to either will suffice to turn the scale, and will prevent either of the opposing extremes from becoming dominant. It is therefore the greatest of blessings for a city that its members should possess a moderate and adequate property. Where some have great possessions, and others have nothing at all, the result is either an extreme democracy or an unmixed oligarchy; or it may even be, as a result of the

[19] Hampton, J. (1997) *Political Philosophy*. New York: Westview Press, p. 154.

excesses of both sides, a tyranny, since tyranny grows out of the most immature type of democracy, or out of oligarchy, but much less frequently out of constitutions of the middle order, or those which approximate them (*Pol* IV.1295b30–1296a12).

5 The Relevance of Aristotelian Justice to Contemporary Political Theory

Aristotle's account of 'polity' seems to be providing a good argument for distributive equality which is of contemporary relevance. The virtues of Aristotle's account can be seen by contrast with some standard contemporary accounts. According to Jean Hampton, "although Aristotle insists that there is such thing as natural slavery, he is even more insistent that the political relationship among people who are equals in their capacity to reason effectively ought to be constructed so that this equality is acknowledged".[20] Indeed, Aristotle is attempting to characterize what constitutes a 'good' political system by relying on a consent-based theory of political authority: "a stable, effective and just political society is one in which the political authority, however it is structured, operates in a way that recognises the equality between the rulers and the ruled".[21] Hampton thinks that Aristotle's theory is even a better alternative to 'welfare egalitarianism' and to Ronald Dworkin's 'resource egalitarianism', since Aristotle does not take for granted that equality is simply part of our conception of what a 'just' distribution is; in that connection, he offers an explanation and he believes that it is both possible and necessary to defend the link between equal distribution and justice by a moral argument. According to Aristotle, "distributive justice is a moral concept whose content we derive rather than discover, and we do so by understanding the way in which some distributions promote certain moral or social values better than others".[22] That is, it serves a purpose rather than being an end in itself, which is, ultimately, mysterious and, thus, intellectually unsatisfying.

The question in contemporary political philosophy concerns the role of justice as an institution intended to fix the limits of human conduct. John Rawls's publication of *A Theory of Justice* in 1971 agitated the then utilitarian dominated field of analytical political philosophy and gave a new turn to political discussion. At a time when some believed political philosophy to be dead, Rawls contributed to its revival

[20] Hampton, J. *ibid*, p. 153.

[21] Hampton, J. *ibid*, pp. 32–33.

[22] Hampton, J. *ibid*, p. 158. It should be noted here that recently there have been many valuable attempts to relate Aristotelian political theory to contemporary political egalitarian theory in general, such as Nussbaum, M. "Nature, Function, and Capability: Aristotle on Political Distribution," *Oxford Studies in Ancient Philosophy*, suppl. vol. (1988), pp. 145–184; "Aristotelian Social Democracy," in Douglass, R. B., Mara, G. & Richardson, H. (eds.) (1990) *Liberalism and the Good*. London: Routledge, pp. 203–252; Sherman, N. (1997) *Making a Necessity of Virtue. Aristotle and Kant on Virtue*. Cambridge: Cambridge University Press, which I did not have space to discuss here.

by abandoning utilitarianism and placing himself in the tradition of social contract theories and Kantian liberalism. Rawls brought forward questions of political obligation and the state, but, most important, he raised the issues of justice and the welfare state. What Rawls actually tried to do was to settle the old quarrel between liberty and equality, and to try to show that liberty could be made compatible with equality. Rawls famously begins his *A Theory of Justice* with the almost axiomatic sentence that "Justice is the first virtue of social institutions, as truth is of systems of thought".[23] Nevertheless, according to John Rawls, Aristotle could never be a liberal because he gives priority to a rational conception of the good rather than to justice. Rawls argues that justice is not prior for Aristotle, since in the definition of the *polis* we can find the good but not the concept of justice.[24]

A similar point, although of course in a very different direction from that of Rawls's, is made by the most notorious neo-Aristotelian communitarian critic of egalitarian liberalism, Alasdair MacIntyre, when he argues that Aristotle offers an instrumentalist conception of the *polis*: namely, that of covering the primary needs of the people (the living as survival), in the sense that the *polis* exists primarily for its members to survive.[25] Aristotle is obviously far from arguing for equality in distribution. But it should be noted that, unlike modern writers on justice, Aristotle is more concerned with distribution of offices than with wealth. His arguments in *Politics* II suggest that he would object to wealth, partly because it is impracticable, but also because it is counter to his conception of virtue. His account of the ideal state suggests that people need a certain minimum of wealth, though this does not seem to be seen as a matter of justice. In addition, it should be pointed out that Aristotle is far from the idea that people have equal rights, or that they should be given equal opportunities.[26]

According to Aristotle, the just is equal as a mean of the inequalities of greed and inferiority, of profit and loss. The just involves persons and objects and is meaningful only in connection with four terms, and is a mean and an equal only in relation to these four terms. The relation of objects must be analogous to the relation of persons; if persons are equal, then they deserve equal shares; if they are not equal, then they will not have equal gain. So, Aristotle says, in the same way that everybody believes that the just is equal, everybody admits that also in distributive justice the just has to be distributed according to worth (*kat' axian*), from the principle of 'assignment by desert'. The dispute lies in the determination of the identity of desert as a criterion of distribution of the parties, because "all agree that justice in distributions must be based on desert of some sort, although they do not all mean the same sort of desert; democrats make the criterion freedom; those of oligarchic sympathies

---

[23] Rawls, J. (1971) *A Theory of Justice*. Oxford: Oxford University Press, p. 3.

[24] Rawls, J. *A Theory of Justice*, *ibid.*, p. 360.

[25] MacIntyre, A. (1985) *After Virtue*, 2nd ed. London: Duckworth.

[26] See on this Vlastos, G. "Justice and Equality," in Waldron, J. (ed.) (1984) *Theories of Rights*. Oxford: Oxford University Press, pp. 41–76 and von Leyden, W. (1985) *Aristotle on Equality and Justice. His Political Argument*. London: Macmillan, pp. 6–10.

wealth; upholders of aristocracy make it virtue".[27] In this way the criterion of distribution is 'proportion', the equality of logical relation, or geometrical equality—as Aristotle calls it—which is qualitative relation as opposed to the arithmetical or numeral equality that applies to corrective law and to friendship. In other domains of law other criteria apply.[28]

Nevertheless, Aristotle's treatment of Lycophron, that we have previously discussed, shows how far his conception is from that of the minimal state. It is also worth noticing that Aristotle does not have any account of procedural justice and, therefore, his accounts of rectificatory justice and of justice in exchange are based on fairness of outcome rather than fairness of procedure. Therefore, one could easily claim that Aristotle could not have much sympathy for Nozickean libertarianism.[29] In addition, democratic justice seems to have much more in common with modern egalitarian liberal theories, since it emphasises freedom, equality of opportunity and equal political rights for citizens. Egalitarian Rawlsian liberal theory assumes (a) that there are many different conceptions of the good, and, (b) that none of these conceptions is preferable on *a priori* grounds. Therefore, the fundamental structure of a just society must be neutral between competing conceptions of the good. Aristotle accepts that there are in practice many competing conceptions of the good, but he does think that one is to be preferred *a priori*. He, therefore, thinks that an account of justice must be founded on that conception of the good. This is related to the question of whether the *polis*, or the state, is a natural entity or an artefact that comes into being naturally.

According to Aristotle, although it is natural for humans to form communities because it is in their nature to be with other people, the *polis* itself is not natural: it is an artefact that came to exist out of this natural need to be with other people. This is the way to reconcile the so-called inconsistency of *Politics* I, when Aristotle says that the person who first constructed the *polis* was the greatest of all benefactors. Unlike the extreme holist, Aristotle did not think that the *polis* is a substance; the *polis* is artificial and not a living organism. But what are we to make of Aristotle's suggestion that man is a political animal, and what bearing does this claim have on his conception of justice? Since it is in our nature to be social and to form associations, it is a necessary feature, and not a contingent one, that we live in a *polis*. Shared conceptions of the good are essential to the Aristotelian view, because otherwise one would not be able to form an association. It should be noted that both of the views that Aristotle examines (oligarchic and democratic) presuppose a conception of the good. The city itself should embody a conception of the good. This conception of the good could well be misguided, and hence a false one, as in the

[27] *NE* 1131a 28–31. This is related to MacIntyre's discussion of the notion of desert (MacIntyre, A. (1985) *After Virtue*. London: Duckworth, 2nd ed., pp. 244–255). In this case, people disagree "because they are bad judges in their own affairs" and also "because both the parties to the argument are speaking of a limited and partial justice, but imagine themselves to be speaking of absolute justice" (*Politics*, 1280a 20–22).

[28] *NE*1131a 2, 1155a 27, 1157b 36, 1158b 29–34, 1132b 21–33, 1134b 8–18, 1161a 20–1161b 1.

[29] Nozick, R. (1974) *Anarchy, State, and Utopia*, Oxford: Blackwell.

cases of democratic and oligarchic constitutions. If the *polis* is natural because it is essential for the good life, then one should know what the good life consists in and would have to be determined by the conception of the good life. The question is whether society is merely a means to achieve our own good, or an essential element in our own good. For Rawls, though, rules of justice are neutral between the different conceptions of the good life. By contrast for Aristotle, rules of justice are determined by the notion of the good life; the notion of desert is determined by our conceptions of the good, and offices and honours have to be distributed in accordance to virtue, or wealth, or equality—according to which conception of the good one holds. In Aristotle's view then, it would seem that, if the state is genuinely neutral between the different conceptions of the good, one could not really have justice, not even rectificatory justice. In conclusion, one should also point out that Aristotle presents kind of a consequentialist argument in defence of the existence of the state; he defends that state on the advantages of that state. There is no individualism explicit in his argument, but neither is the idea of a value-based state; the Aristotelian state is based on a notion of what is the best way to govern.

Acknowledgment I should like to thank Nick Zangwill for his insightful comments on an earlier draft of this chapter.

Jean Bodin: The Modern State Comes into Being

Thomas Krogh

There can be no doubt that in the history of political thought, the French humanist and jurist Jean Bodin (1529–1596) is linked primarily to *two* fundamental concepts: sovereignty and absolutism. They constitute the core in his extremely comprehensive study of the modern state, to which I shall refer in this chapter as *State* (Bodin 1583, 1992).[1] The central topic of this chapter will be the presentation of the two concepts, but without an overview of the challenges that the French monarchy faced in the Renaissance, or (as it is more usually called today) the Early Modern period, in the second half of the sixteenth century, it is hard to grasp either the problems with which Bodin was confronted or his suggestions about how his contemporaries should tackle them.

The concept of sovereignty is linked to a definition of the *state power*, which is the minimum condition for being an autonomous state. It is based on a principle that

English translation: Brian McNeil and Thomas Krogh.

[1] *Les six livres de la république* was published in Paris in 1583. He produced several editions, both in French and in his own Latin translation. There are modern translations into German and Italian that are based on the French edition. A compilation of the first Latin and French editions was published in English in 1606: *The Six Bookes of a Commonweale*, translated by Richard Knolles (reprinted in 1962 in Cambridge, Mass., by Kenneth McRae). Since the book is so extensive and original versions are extremely hard to find, I quote here as far as possible from the following edition: Jean Bodin, *On Sovereignty, Four Chapters from The Six Books of the Commonwealth*, ed. Julian H. Franklin, Cambridge, CUP, 1992. This is drastically abbreviated, but it contains the central portions of the work.—Let me say something about Bodin's terminology. In his period, "republic" did not necessarily denote a form of state that was the opposite of a monarchy. He uses this as the straightforward translation of the Roman *res publica*, which we usually translate as "state"—a term that does not imply any one specific form of state. The English translation "commonweal" points perhaps more in the direction of "society," and the usual French term at that period for the state and the state power was *estat*. But since the main emphasis lies on the concepts of sovereignty and absolute power, which are in any case primarily linked to the state power, I employ the term "state."

T. Krogh (✉)
Department of Philosophy, Classics, History of Art and Ideas,
University of Oslo, Oslo, Norway
e-mail: thomas.krogh@ifikk.uio.no

G. Fløistad (ed.), *Philosophy of Justice*, Contemporary Philosophy: A New Survey 12, DOI 10.1007/978-94-017-9175-5_4, © Springer Science+Business Media Dordrecht 2015

is simple and clear *per se*: "no one above, and no one alongside." The state power must be one, unified, and indivisible; that which cannot be said to possess these characteristics is not a state. And this requirement concerns an institution. We can agree with Quentin Skinner, the English intellectual historian, that Bodin's concept of the state is a very important step on the path toward the modern concept of state, which (according to Skinner) we still hold today. It finds expression in the view of the state as something that is not linked to the personal exercise of power by the citizens or the prince, and that consequently is not identical with one particular territory, but is an impersonal institution (Skinner 1978, 2002).[2] Thomas Hobbes, who developed Bodin's concept of absolutism, may have been the first to elaborate definitively this concept of sovereignty, but we find the basic elements in this theory of the state in the Frenchman. Let us note that for Bodin himself, the unitary character of this institution was perhaps best guaranteed if it had the form of a kingdom. For practical reasons, he goes a long way toward identifying monarchy with the sovereign state, which thus is the only state; but there are also other forms of sovereign states than monarchy. Bodin's doctrine of the state presupposes an apparently total concentration of all legitimate power in the institution of the state. It is, at any rate, possible to identify the probable motives for forming such a theory and accepting such a concentration of power against the background of the catastrophe that France suffered during his lifetime, with struggles between the king and the aristocracy and continuous new civil wars of religion between Catholics and Huguenots.

Bodin was born in 1529. Initially, he joined the Carmelite order, but he was given permission to break off his ecclesiastical career. He studied law in Paris and Toulouse in the 1550s and 1560s; in the France of that period, this entailed thorough studies in history and languages, the subjects that had received the name of humanistic studies in the Italian Renaissance. This found expression in his great work on historical methodology, published in 1566 (1566, 1945), to which we refer hereafter as *Method*.[3] It is here that we also find the first sketch of his political *chef d'œuvre*. He was taken into the royal service in the 1560s, under Charles IX and his brother Henry III, but he fell into disfavor in 1576, at the same time as *State* was published, because he was a representative of the Third Estate at an assembly of the Estates in Blois and refused to support the king's demand for higher taxes. This sheds light on what he understood the expression "absolute kingly power" to mean; we will? return to this below. He was attached for a time to one of the princes of the house of Valois, the Duke of Alençon, who attempted (like so many others) to marry Queen Elizabeth I, but after the duke's death he left the court circles in the 1580s, and held

[2] Skinner, Quentin (1978). See also his "From the state of princes to the person of the state," in Quentin Skinner (2002).—Let me say something about the terminology I employ for periodization. The person and thinker Jean Bodin must be regarded as belonging to the period in France that we can call the Renaissance, and that today is often called the Early Modern period, where new and very ancient ideas mingled with one another. But I agree with Quentin Skinner in seeing his view of the state as modern. In other words, it lays the foundations for the period that begins with the age of Enlightenment, the period to which we ourselves still belong.

[3] Bodin, Jean (1566) *Methodus ad facilem historiarum cognitionem*. Paris. English ed., *Method for the Easy Comprehension of History*, trans. Beatrice Reynolds (1945), New York.

a local administrative post in Laon until his death in 1596. The Catholic party in Laon put pressure on him to support their politics (I shall come back to his own political attitude to the civil wars of religion), but as we shall see, he continued to be intellectually active throughout his life. In addition to his work on the theory of history and the political work that I have already mentioned, I shall discuss in this paper his natural philosophy (Bodin 1596) and his philosophy of religion. He reveals himself as a zealous champion both of witch trials (Bodin 1580) and of a form of religious tolerance that is not easy to define (Bodin 1857, 1975); later generations were to find this remarkably divergent, although it would not have puzzled his contemporaries. We should also mention a work he wrote about the price increases in France in the sixteenth century, which anticipated to a large degree more modern theories about money. And *State* contains a number of speculations about the significance of the climate for the mentality, and hence also the way of life and the constitution, of various peoples, which recall the more famous theories about this topic in Montesquieu.

There are many open questions about his life and his views, especially as regards his relationship to religion. But one thing is certain: Bodin was not only a political philosopher, a person who was interested in theories about the state. He was also, to the highest degree, a political actor in his own age.

This paper explores Bodin's varied activities. First, I shall provide a *Historical context*, in order to show how and why Bodin supported an absolutism of that particular kind. In *The political cosmos*, I extend the context and show how Bodin can have been inspired by his view of the cosmos and of nature, a view that itself was far from modern. He regarded nature as in some sense animate or living, and the kind of forces that are found in nature are, in a strange way, political. In *Universal history*, I take up Bodin's significance for the science of history and show how his political philosophy first emerged as an introduction for historians into this central aspect of their task.

What is a state? then looks at the main substance in Bodin's political philosophy, which is associated with the concepts of *sovereignty* and *absolutism* and the complex relationship between these. In *Between sorcery and tolerance*, we look at the religious and more mystical parts of Bodin's thinking. The new relevance of the question of tolerance has led me to link this part of his writings to the political part. In *History of reception and criticism*, I begin with the more internal criticism of Bodin and then attempt to locate him in the history of political thought.

1 Historical Context

From the late Middle Ages onward, the French kings had fought a long struggle to unite France into one single kingdom (which was to become "France"), that is to say, to impose on all the king's lands a central administration and political leadership, and to bring very independent fiefdoms under this power. In the struggle to create such a state in and out of France, we see the showdown with the Middle Ages, both in practice and in theory. More specifically, this meant that the royal power broke with feudalism, and this in turn entailed the personal and geographical extension of the king's power to regional or local representatives. In one important sense, feudalism, as it had developed in Western Europe in the Middle Ages, had failed as a political and administrative principle. The European Middle Ages, or more correctly, the various states that emerged in this period and that (with hindsight) were to become the various European nations, never resolved the question of how to combine the concentration of political, judicial, and military power with the delegation of power. Feudalism brought with it a regional or geographical division of power: the various vassals or barons were to constitute the political, military, and judicial unity, each in his province, his fiefdom. This never became a system; it was merely a systematic crumbling of power. The task of the kings over many generations was to fight their way out of this situation.

In this context, we must realize that we who live today are easily exposed to a kind of optical illusion when we look at European history. The French Revolution was such a central historical event that we have a tendency to see everything on the basis of it; we perceive the king and the aristocracy as one group—the privileged—whereas in reality, the aristocracy and the king were the great antitheses in large parts of Europe for many centuries. As I have said, the royal power stood for a unified, central government; this came to be called absolutism. The old aristocracy united to fight for its privileges, which were linked to special local arrangements and institutions. The theory behind this is often called constitutionalism, because it wanted to put limits on the royal power.

The French kings in the late Middle Ages and the Early Modern period never succeeded completely in their attempts to centralize and stabilize the central royal power. Their attempts to build up a central seat of power in France were linked in part to the establishing of the so-called "*Parlements*," which were not representative organs like the British *House of Commons*, but courts and institutions for administering the law. It was here that a new aristocracy of civil servants (*noblesse de robe*) emerged alongside the old feudal aristocracy. The usual praxis of selling offices to this group was probably an economic necessity, in order to finance a military power that was independent of the out-of-date obligations that the vassals had to their liege lord. But this helped prevent the development of an administration or a bureaucracy that centralized power, instead of simply spreading the power around again. Privileges and special rights developed on new fields. There were assemblies of the Estates that bore a certain resemblance to what in other places (England) became representative (that is to say, elected) legislative assemblies. But in France, the representation remained in the king's hand, not in the hands of the represented: the members were appointed from above. These assemblies did further cement privileges attached to social rank and to the regions. Besides this, France was divided by factors such as internal customs borders. Also in the economic field, therefore, it was far from constituting a united and centrally governed territory.

We can say that the weapons that the French royal house had forged against the old feudal aristocracy for some generations past now to some extent turned on the kings themselves, and merely cemented the situation they were intended to overcome. The class or stratum of those who were legally or economically privileged in various ways merely grew and became more complex. The kings were driven to concede a form of constitutionalism; the prevalent juridical view was that they had conceded large-scale limitations to their power. (For this overview, see Salmon 1975; Parker 1983; Henschall 1992.)

But the internecine struggle between these two principal adversaries, which had gone on for several centuries, was woven into another conflict in the second half of the sixteenth century. The country had a series of short-lived, weak monarchs, and it was precisely at this time that it became the arena of a lengthy civil war of religion. The fight between the Huguenots (the French Calvinists) and the Catholics split France from top to bottom, and intense military conflicts broke out both within and among the various regions, which threatened to destroy every unitary state power, every central and centralized authority. One event remains especially alive in our memory, the Massacre of Saint Bartholomew's Eve in 1572, when between 4,000 and 5,000 Protestants were murdered in Paris (by comparison: roughly half of those who were killed in the Srebrenica massacre), and then far more were murdered in the rest of the country. Bodin's own biography, with so many details that remains unclear, is (as we have seen) a testimony to this unhappy period; we must remember that civil wars of religion raged in France for most of his lifetime. This meant that both the Christian confessions or churches, which called each other "religions," and the groups of nobles who led them, were a threat to a more modern, effective state power and saw this state power as a threat to their own selves. This led to the emergence of a third current, known as *les politiques*. Bodin was associated with this party—a logical enough choice, if one wanted to give the unitary state priority over all the confessions. *Les politiques* saw the interests of the state, and indeed its survival, as the fundamental element, with the consequence that the religious schools of thought must find a way to live together. They represented the point at which the state (it is still too early to speak of the "nation state," with the possible exception of England), rather than the religious confession, began to be the most important point of orientation, the most important form of identity, in Western Europe. The special element in the ideology of *les politiques* was their breach with one essential and dominant presupposition in earlier political thinking, namely, that the unity of a nation or of a society could be guaranteed, and could in fact be possible, only if there was religious unity. The paradox was that, precisely in order to salvage the strong and unitary state, this school of thought was willing to abandon the requirement of the unity of the religious and the political structure. In other words, unity in less important areas was sacrificed in order to salvage unity in a greater and more essential area. The standpoint of *les politiques* was at any rate easily compatible with Bodin's doctrine of sovereignty, and there is no difficulty in seeing the civil wars of religion as a motive for accepting an absolute state power: everything was better, and every restriction on freedom was preferable to chaos and bloodbath. But there are good reasons to emphasize that while all the French were confronted with these problems, not everyone reacted in a manner similar to Bodin. We cannot simply derive Bodin's view of political problems from the political and philosophical context; all we can do is to present the problems he encountered as a child of his time, and explain why reactions that lead to completely different positions can be understood against the same background.

For Bodin's reaction was, of course, not the only possible reaction to the bloodbath. A considerable amount of Huguenot literature was written that disagreed with Luther's and Calvin's original teaching and defended the right to resist the state power, on the basis of the French people's ancient rights. Here, we must mention at least one book. In the aftermath of Saint Bartholomew's Eve, François Hotman published *Franco-Gallia* (1972), a large-scale historical work in which he claimed that the customs of the French state went back to the free Franks who had moved into the country in the Migration Period, and that ultimately, the king's power was bestowed by the people and could be withdrawn. This entailed a clash between the theory of sovereignty and constitutional theories that wanted to limit the power of the state and of the prince, and that maintained that power lay with the people or, as we have seen, with the aristocratic part of the people.

2 The Political Cosmos

After this historical contextualization, I shall discuss some philosophical positions that may have led Bodin to see the state as an institution with a central government almost like a command center. These positions will thus be more general and more independent of specific historical periods than those we have taken up hitherto. They are found in many of Bodin's contemporaries, but without necessarily leading to the same political theories that we find in him.

Bodin's cosmos can be defined more precisely as marked by what the American intellectual historian Arthur Lovejoy has called *The Great Chain of Being* (Lovejoy 1936).[4] The chain of being is both inclusive and hierarchical. All the phenomena are linked with each other, since they are parts of the same whole and have the same origin; but they are found in various strata of this whole. Individual phenomena have a higher or a lower status, and their mutual relationships involve superiority and subordination. What we encounter here can thus most appropriately be called a political universe: even the mutual relationships between natural phenomena are marked by what we would call political and juridical relationships. For us, this breaks with such obvious distinctions as those between society and nature, or juridical and moral laws on the one hand and the laws of nature on the other—that is to say, between normative and descriptive laws or regularities.

For Bodin, this position had profound effects on political theory. He presupposes ten levels in his cosmos. We start at the bottom with formless matter, and then come ashes. So we ascend to the heavenly bodies, and finally to God. We should note that

[4] Lovejoy, Arthur (1936) *The Great Chain of Being*. Cambridge, Mass.: Harvard University Press. My remarks are also based on Anne Blair (1997) *The Theatre of Nature. Jean Bodin and the Renaissance Science*, Princeton, which is possibly the best recent book about Bodin. She points out that the metaphor of theater includes both nature itself and the book about this theater.

for Bodin, the soul is bodily and belongs to the field of physics. There is something supernatural, but this too is bodily and is precisely the field of demonology, the doctrine of devils, which is built into Bodin's entire version of the cosmos.

Let us look at the part of the universe that is closest to us. God has ordered the universe in such a way that we can go from the heavenly spheres, which determine the orbits of the planets, down to our own planet, where the earth is joined to the stones (by means of clay, which is thus a mediating link between earth and stone), the stones to the plants (here it is corals that are the mediating link), plants to animals, and animals to human beings via apes.

> ...just as the bond of nature...rules over angels, so the angels rule over men, men over beasts, the soul over the body, Heaven rules over the earth, and reasons over the appetites; so that whatever is less fitted to rule may be directed and guided by that which can protest and preserve it, in return for its obedience... (Bodin 1576 A 69, quoted from Lewis 1968: 211)[5]

The entire universe is thus a hierarchy, permeated by relationships of superiority and subordination, by legal regulation and government. The universe is almost a medium for the transfer and the use of power. This is how Bodin sees the link between natural philosophy and political theory.

Bodin's mysticism or Neo-Platonism puts him in opposition both to Aristotle (and hence to Thomas Aquinas) and to a modern thinker like Hobbes. It is indeed true that, for Aristotle, the *polis*, and the human being as a citizen of the *polis*, are something that exists on the basis of nature, in the sense that (in terms of his teleological understanding of nature), the human being, like all natural phenomena, has a tendency and a final goal, and our goal as human beings is achieved by entering into that type of human relationships that we can call the society of the *polis*. But unlike Bodin, Aristotle never claims that everything in nature enters into the same type of quasi-political relationships of superiority and subordination.

And for Hobbes the state is artificial, something created only through actions of the human will. It is only this human product that can provide us with the situation of security and stability that nature on its own cannot give us. But Hobbes's nature, at least in his intention, is completely mechanistic. It is not Neo-Platonic, as Bodin's nature still was.

3 Universal History

Bodin was regarded in his days as one of the most learned men in France. His legal studies became a part of a larger historical study, thereby earning him a place in historiography. And as I have said, it is in this context that Bodin's studies of political theory have their origin. (The following presentation is based largely on Franklin 1963.)

---

[5] *State, op. cit.*, A 69, quoted from Lewis, J. U. "Jean Bodin's 'Logic of Sovereignty'," *Political Studies*, vol. 16 (1968), p. 211.

Much of historiography throughout the Middle Ages and the Renaissance was the history of law, and was thus closely related to jurisprudence, especially studies of ancient Roman law, that is to say, of the collections of legal documents from the Roman republic and empire that were gathered together and edited under Justinian in the eastern Roman empire. These enormous collections are not primarily legal texts, but commentaries and commentaries on commentaries, and so on. In Italy and in southern France—something that was important for Bodin—Roman law had never completely died out, and could still be regarded as valid law. This led in the Middle Ages to an intense work of commenting by the so-called glossators on the original collections, on the explicit presupposition that these were not only valid, but completely consistent and academically perfect juridical works. Another implicit presupposition of this activity of commentating was that mediaeval society stood in an unbroken continuity with the Roman world, so that this law was immediately applicable to the contemporary period. The emergence of Renaissance humanism and of philological and hence also historical studies in Italy in the fourteenth and fifteenth centuries shattered this view in two ways. The growing philological awareness showed that the mediaeval glossators lacked the philological erudition and the appreciation of linguistic development that were absolutely necessary, if the original texts were to be understood. They also lacked an understanding of the enormous historical gulf between the Roman period and the feudal world. This meant the disappearance of the dream of possessing the ideal body of laws. Bodin's place in this humanistic critique of law, or his contribution to a humanistic law, was therefore the replacement of the study of Roman law with a *comparative* study of all the legal systems, including the non-European systems, about which information was available. It is only by seeing what is common to all the legal traditions and to every body of law that one can establish law on a genuinely universal foundation. This means that the search for the universal law is possible only by means of historical investigation.

Bodin saw the body of laws of each nation as a part of its milieu, of its place in the cosmos. To some extent, this makes it possible to see them in the mystical perspective on which I have touched briefly, and opens the door (for example) to the employment of numerology in the description of the various states and of their birth and death. But Bodin was also one of the first to formulate what we today associate mostly with Montesquieu in the eighteenth century, the so-called climate theory about the mentality of nations and peoples. "Climate" here means climatic zones, and Bodin links temperature and the amount of precipitation to the emergence of various character traits, and hence to the body of laws that is appropriate to a country and to its population.

This comparative study took him one step further, to the problem linked to historical science as a whole, history here understood simply as knowledge of the past.

The sixteenth and the beginning of the seventeenth centuries were not a period in which new philosophies arose, but one that saw the revitalization of ancient philosophical schools of thought that had not been prominent in the Middle Ages, such as Stoicism, skepticism, and to some extent atomism. We now for the first time encounter a direct historical skepticism, which was inspired above all by the ancient philosopher Pyrrho, whose name has often been borrowed by modern skepticism. This was an attack on the very possibility of knowledge of the past, and thus also on the literature that had presented itself as true knowledge of the past. These attacks did not lack a certain subtlety. For example, the Italian skeptic Francesco Patrizzi argued that we must concede that the possibility of tenable information about the past is destroyed by the conflict between two pragmatic considerations. Neutral and intentionally objective observers would stand outside the game of politics, while those who knew the game from the inside would be participants and would have every reason to keep silent about what was really going on. Bodin's place in the critique of historical skepticism has its starting point in his comparative method. We are not restricted to the attempt to determine whether this or that presentation is correct (to say nothing of whether it is meant honestly). We can also compare presentations of one and the same topic in order to achieve a balanced view. Bodin also transcended the question whether it is possible to have a good and objective contemporary (eye-)witness. The idea that the good historian is precisely the one who stands outside and who therefore can understand what is happening—that good historiography is linked to a critical distance, *not* to access to direct experience—began to emerge. And good historiography is not linked to moralistic criteria such as honesty and truthfulness, but to insight into law and politics. But if the American intellectual historian Julian Franklin is right, the most important point about Bodin is precisely his intention to investigate a historian's judgment of individual matters, not a person's moral characteristics. He indicates criteria for how one can investigate and determine the degree to which a person is biased in various contexts. We need not be dependent on the rare instance of the honorable historian—or on the fantasy about such a person. Rather, we can know what usually influences people's relationship to the truth.

The historian thus needs knowledge about the government of the state, and the historians on whom we can rely are those who possess this knowledge. This is why *Method* contains an initial sketch of a constitutional theory, of the theory of sovereignty and of what a sovereign is; this is central to Bodin's theory. Here, however, we must point to a further development. Between *Method* and *State* lies Saint Bartholomew's Eve. *Method* still contained a form of constitutionalism, but Bodin rejected this in *State*, because only an absolute government could create peace. According to Quentin Skinner, to whose interpretation I shall return, it was on the basis of this wish that a new and modern concept of the state came to be formulated.

4 What Is a State?

The perspective I have applied to Bodin's political thinking here, and the place I ascribe to him in the history of this thinking, are influenced not only by Skinner, but also to a large extent by Julian Franklin (see Franklin 1973) and his Introduction to Bodin (1992; all the page references below are to Bodin's text in this edition).

Skinner summarizes his view of Bodin's *State* and its modernity as follows: It is here, for the first time, that we find the term "state" used "in a modern way," and that the state's rights and duties are analyzed in a modern way. The princes constitute the highest political will, because their will is the state's will. We all owe obedience to the state. And this state is a purely civil (*civil*) authority that exists for purposes pertaining exclusively to the citizens; the antithesis of "civil" here is, of course, "religious," not "military." Skinner concludes his historical study on just this point:

> with this analysis of the state as an omnipotent yet impersonal power, we may be said to enter the modern world: the modern theory of the State remains to be reconstructed, but its foundation are now complete. (Skinner 1978: 358).

And the place in history of this concept of the state in its turn depends on the concepts of sovereignty and absolutism.

Let us now further expand upon the treatment of these concepts at the beginning of the present chapter. Bodin begins *State* by defining the state in connection with the power that is exercised over families (or households). He sets out what they have in common, but notes that only the state is sovereign. The householder is not sovereign, for otherwise the sovereign could not exercise an absolute and legitimate power in relation to the citizens. Although it is true that there is an important distinction here between the family and the state, depending on the possession or the lack of a sovereign power, I would see a breach with Aristotle already on this point. While Aristotle drew a sharp distinction between the *oikos* and the *polis* and assigned them different goals, Bodin sees the state in continuity with the rule that is exercised over or in families, although this is a rule of a different kind from that which is found within the individual family.

We can now turn to ch. 8 in Book I of Bodin's *State*, where he defines sovereignty. In Bodin's presentation, there are two characteristics of sovereignty or (if we prefer the term) genuine state power: it must be absolute and without limits of time. The latter characteristic is necessary; it differs from the concept "absolute" in that it is possible to give a ruler all power, but only for a limited time. The point is that a power subject to this kind of limitation in time would not be absolute, no matter what it encompassed, since it would still be dependent on the will of another or others. As we now see, sovereignty means the absence of all institutional checks or conditions for the exercise of power. The expression "institutional checks" or "limitations" becomes important at the close of this chapter, but Bodin draws from the very outset a distinction between the king as the one who has the sovereign power, and the king as a private person. If we now, for the sake of simplicity, assume that it is a king who has the sovereign power, this means that the king is above the law. In other words, he is not institutionally bound by the laws established by himself or by his ancestors. This disposes of the idea of a constitutional government, which is incompatible with the very idea of a state.

Bodin's state, like his cosmos, is a medium for the transfer of power, or of commands and instructions, and such a system can function only if it is dependent on one single headquarters, one authority to issue commands, which can of course delegate power, but which can also revoke this delegation at any time.

Here, we must underline two points, the first of which is perhaps more of a quasi-logical nature. Since the sovereign (the king) cannot be bound by other persons or by anything else (at any rate among human beings), what about self-binding? Can he establish laws that he promises not to abrogate? For Bodin, this is impossible. Not even absolute power can abrogate absolute power. (This, of course, recalls the paradoxical question whether it is possible for God to set himself a task that he cannot carry out.) In Roman law, the emperor was said to be *legibus solutus*, freed from, or raised above, the law. Bodin (at least initially) gives the following radical version of this formulation:

> If the sovereign prince is thus exempt from the laws of his predecessors, much less is he bound by the laws and ordinances he has made himself (1992: 12 f.).

The second point is expressed in the distinction between laws and contracts. The king is not bound to the law, but he is bound by the contracts he makes. Here, the king and his subjects are joined together as private persons. Accordingly, the king is obligated only in relation to contracts that he has inherited from his own ancestors, not necessarily from all earlier kings.

> It is essential, therefore not to confuse a law and a contract. Law depends upon he who has the sovereignty, and he can obligate all his subjects (by a law) but he cannot obligate himself. A contract between a prince and his subjects is mutual, it obligates the two parties reciprocally and one party cannot contravene it to the prejudice of the other and without the other's consent (15).

Taken together, this picture of legislating and making contracts shows us something central: it is the institution of the state, which is of course maintained in the person of the king, that is absolute. Absolute power is of an institutional, not of a private nature. This means that the king, as an individual, cannot do whatever he wants. And as we shall see, it means that the subjects, precisely as private persons, have a protection against the state. I shall discuss in the final section of this chapter whether this is an inconsistency on Bodin's part.

Bodin has parted company with the earlier tradition here in two ways. In the Middle Ages, the concept of *legislation* was rather vague. The task was to discover an already existing law and to interpret it in a given situation. Accordingly, the very mark of the king's superior position was that he was the highest judge. Bodin had affirmed this in *Method*, but this changes in *State*, where the king is now primarily the highest legislator, and the various aspects of his judicial function are now subordinated to the activity of legislation.

> We must thus conclude that the first prerogative (*marque*) of a sovereign prince is to give law all in general and each in particular. But this is not sufficient. We have to add "without the consent of any other whether greater, equal or below him" (56).

And *this* power is indivisible. Bodin continues:

> … strictly speaking we can say that there is only this one prerogative of sovereignty, inasmuch as all the other rights are comprehended in it—such as declaring war or making peace… (58).

In Book I, ch. 10, Bodin shows how a number of areas where decisions are to be taken, and which we moderns would allocate partly under the legislative, and partly under the judicial and executive power, are, and must be, united in the activity of legislation. We need not mention these in detail here, but the last example is somewhat distinct from the judicial/administrative picture and points in the direction of the princes' struggle to create culturally unified territory: they can compel their subjects to change their language (86). In this context, Bodin mentions the policies of the Romans as well as the Arabs.

His insistence that only the political organization that has an undivided sovereignty of this kind can be considered a state also breaks with a tradition that goes back to Aristotle and is one of the most long-lived traditions in the history of ideas, namely, the doctrine of the mixed form of state (*politeia*). Aristotle claimed that in practice, the best form of state would be a mixture of the three positive forms with which the Greeks tended to operate, namely, monarchy, aristocracy, and democracy; or somewhat more cynically, a mixture of democracy (which Aristotle regarded as a bad form) and oligarchy. Bodin's position rejects every mixture.

Any of the three traditional forms of rule can be accepted by Bodin as a state, provided that the ruling authority is sovereign. But he cannot accept a mixture. He asks: "If sovereignty is indivisible, as we have shown, how can it be shared by a prince, the nobles and the people at the same time?" (92)

And throughout the whole of Book II, ch. 1, he rains hammer blows on the inheritance from Aristotle, especially as this was mediated by the Greek historian Polybius.

> We shall conclude then that there is not now, and never was, a state compounded of aristocracy and democracy, much less of the three forms of a state, but that there are only three kinds of a state (103).

He states again that the "prerogatives of sovereignty are indivisible" (104) and concludes: "Mixture then is not a state but rather the corruption of a state" (105).

We shall return to this at the close of the next section, in connection with the question of wars of religion.

5 Between Sorcery and Tolerance

As we saw at the beginning of this paper, the commentators disagree widely concerning the nature of Bodin's religious convictions. This uncertainty applies even more strongly to what we may call his religious or religious-philosophical writings. Later commentators have been unable to understand how writings such as Bodin (1580) and (1857) can have been written by one and the same man, since the spiritual horizons they represent appear to be so different. And as we shall see, the standpoint he takes in the second work is the object of much dispute.

The first work, *De la démonomanie*, belongs to the vast literature about sorcery and witches, and the need to combat these with burnings at the stake, that swept over

Europe at that period, and that was to continue to do so in the following century. The second work seems to be associated with the attempts to discover possibilities of religious reconciliation that we find from time to time in the Renaissance and the Early Modern period. But it is the first work that most clearly ties Bodin to his historical period; it was the second book, which appears to report a debate (which is, of course, fictitious) between members of different religions about fundamental aspects of God and of religion, that could not be published. Considerations of space do not allow us to discuss various theories about how the Early Modern belief in witchcraft arose and became so widespread. Let me mention only a few points. The contemporary belief in witchcraft was just as widespread in Catholic as in Protestant countries, and it seems to have been evenly spread between the highest political and intellectual strata on the one hand and the broad masses of the people on the other. And the theory about the witches' Sabbath and the pact between the witch and the devil is not mediaeval, but is typical of the Early Modern period. The fact that the persecutions took the form of a painstaking legal procedure seems to point in this direction: this was something new, something that we might call a new form of superstition that arose in the Early Modern period. And although commentators in the eighteenth and nineteenth centuries saw an almost unsurpassable barrier between the gullible and naïve Bodin who believed in witches, and the learned political philosopher and historian, it is easy to see that Bodin himself regarded his argumentation as completely rational. The most interesting point, historically speaking, is perhaps Bodin's conviction that the basis of his own standpoint, which he shared with most of his contemporaries, was completely rational. If he was exceptional, it was only in his subjective form, in the violence of his expression—not in the fundamental aspects of his conviction. He argued on the basis of common sense, on well-supported testimonies, and on basic scientific principles, that witches existed and that it was necessary for the authorities to unmask and destroy them.

The posthumously published *Colloquium* (Bodin 1857) has a form that was not unknown in the Renaissance, and that was extended by Galileo and others in the seventeenth century from the religious and philosophical field to modern natural sciences. In works of this kind, a number of questions in religion or philosophy are discussed by a group of individuals who represent various views of the subject that were widespread at that time. In Bodin's text, fundamental theological questions, mostly concerning the nature of God, are discussed by seven individuals: a religious skeptic, an adherent of natural religion, a Catholic, two different kinds of Protestants, a Jew, and a newly converted Muslim.

One formal advantage of this genre is that it allows the author to conceal his identity and his own standpoints and to go to considerable lengths in ambushing (so to speak) and ridiculing individualized opponents, rather than engaging in open polemic against particular positions. The strategy of concealment was of course very understandable in the Europe of the civil wars of religion. The form itself tends to suggest a corresponding style of commentary, where the task is to find the author's spokesman. Who is he, and whom among the characters who take part in the debate does most nearly represent him? Commentators in the last 150 years have argued that many various figures in Bodin's work represent the author himself; both the old Jew Solomon and the representative of Catholicism have been suggested.

One can doubtless always find evidence to support such hypothetical ascriptions, but we must ask whether they do not rather express views held antecedently by the commentator. For example, if one is convinced that Bodin actually converted to Judaism, one finds evidence here. I do not wish to deny that I discern a great deal of sympathy in the treatment of Solomon, who is the most learned of the seven. He is allowed to make very ironic or contemptuous remarks about Jesus as a prophet, and so on, and I sense a certain irony in the presentation of the somewhat rigid statements by the two Protestants. We must nevertheless ask whether this interpretative strategy takes the wrong point of departure. Perhaps Bodin does not intend to show us the correct, and still less the most correct religion. His aim may be to exhort us to accept the coexistence of various religious currents.

However, as Quentin Skinner has pointed out (Skinner 1978: 246), this work contains hints of two different models of religious tolerance. And Anne Blair has pointed out that while some dialogues, such as that of Galileo, seek to create unity and to convince the reader of particular standpoints, other dialogues were constructed with the aim of leaving the reader in a state of openness or uncertainty (Blair 1997: 30 ff.). One of the two models that Skinner mentions is relatively well known. We find it in the Neo-Platonic, or perhaps better, the eclectic currents in fifteenth-century Italy, in Pico della Mirandola and Marsilio Ficino. These currents maintained that there is only one true philosophy, and that Plato and Aristotle accordingly held one and the same position. And there is in reality only one religion, and we all, without knowing it, worship one and the same God.

But especially the close of the dialogue points in another direction, toward another model. On the final day, the conversation ends in peace and harmony, but the only result is an agreement that one will *not* continue to discuss the great religious questions. The dialogue thus comes to an end without even the suggestion that there exists a religious unity (no matter how vaguely we might envisage it). Instead, it leaves us with the idea that we will never reach agreement on the fundamental questions. Indeed, it is possible that they have no solution. Perhaps the mistake is even to think of a solution, since in any case, we human beings cannot understand the ultimate mysteries. So let us go on living in peace, let us not bother each other with debates that cannot lead to any positive result. We may call this a relativistic position on religion.

In addition to these two views, we encounter, especially in the seventeenth century, a third solution to the confessional disputes, namely, what we could call a "lowest common denominator" religion, a religion that is to encompass only what everybody could agree on, on the basis of our confessions. The further course of European history shows us that this third standpoint, which rather looks like an invention of philosophers, did not meet with success. Europeans mostly continued to profess allegiance to one of the various confessions.

Nor did Europe accept what I have called a religious relativism. Nevertheless, it was this, the second of the three standpoints I have presented, which sought only to bring the debate to silence, that in practice best corresponded to Bodin's fundamental position as an adherent of *les politiques*: religious questions must not divide the nation, nor must they be allowed to dominate our political life. The thinking of *les politiques* was very realistic. They did not require most people to abandon their confessional membership; all that is required is that this should not be allowed to dominate their political life. As I have said, the unity of religion and politics was abandoned. And this brings us almost to the twentieth century, since religion here becomes a private matter. This is why, despite everything, this solution acquired a practical significance. Europe's citizens continued to belong to one particular religious current. They were still Catholics, Calvinists, or Lutherans, but this did not lead them to kill each other. In the long term, it was perhaps this abandonment of the debate that created a measure of political peace. At this point, we can pick up the threads from both this and the previous sections, since it was in fact only a sovereign state, considered as an impersonal entity, that could and must achieve this. It was necessary to separate the interests of the state from those of the confessions; this is how Skinner sums up Bodin.

> With Bodin's insistence in his Six Books [i.e., *State*, T. Krogh] that it ought to be obvious to any prince that 'wars made for matters of religion' is not in fact 'grounded upon matters directly touching his estate' we hear for the first time the authentic tones of the modern theorist of the State (Skinner 1978: 352, quoting the English version of Bodin's *State* by Richard Knolles and Kenneth McRae (1962), A 14).

6 History of Reception and Criticism

Bodin's theories have encountered much criticism, in his own times and in our own. Later commentators have frequently asserted that although Bodin was one of the most learned legal scholars and historians of his age, the form of his presentation is incoherent and disjointed, and they have emphasized his lack of the ability to concentrate and to set limits to what he writes. Here, we must concentrate on the more substantial charges that are leveled against him. What was the relationship between his concept of sovereignty and the constitutional theories that developed in the seventeenth century? Julian Franklin accuses him of denying too unequivocally the possibility of a state that was constructed on the balance between the state powers. We know this theory best from Montesquieu's tripartite division into the legislative, the judicial, and the execute powers, on which the American constitution is based, but it existed in many versions which did not necessarily include tripartite divisions.[6]

[6] Let me point out here that Aristotle's mixed constitution and the principle of the division of power are not at all the same thing. Aristotle is concerned with the possibility of satisfying legitimate demands for political participation and influence, when these demands clash. In contradistinction to this, the idea of the balance between the state powers is concerned with achieving a balance between differing functions of and in the apparatus of the state. It is generated by fear of a concentration of power (Bodin was afraid of a lack of the concentration of power), and could scarcely have been formulated in the Greek *polis*. In other words, the two theories are not tackling the same problem. But it is possible that ideas about how the mixture could come about "infected" theories

This is the first main question on which Bodin's doctrine has been exposed to severe criticism by later generations. The second question emerges in the frequent assertions that his doctrine of sovereignty, taken as a whole, is self-contradictory and that he in fact prunes this doctrine in a number of ways, so that the result is reminiscent of constitutionalism—a position that is incompatible with absolutism.

Let us take these questions in this order. We begin by asking: Is it our *experience*, on the basis of history, that tells us that states with a mixed constitution are impossible, or does Bodin hold that this conflicts with the very *definition* of a state? Both Quentin Skinner and Julian Franklin affirm that Bodin believes he is presenting an analytic claim, that it is true by definition that sovereignty is indivisible and is the origin of all law, and consequently that there is no right to oppose the state. Divided sovereignty is a square circle (Franklin 1973: 93; Skinner 1978: 287).

It is clear that much of what Bodin says supports such an interpretation. He says that we cannot even imagine any other state (1992: 103). Nevertheless, I am far from sure that Bodin had a concept of the distinction between statements that are true by definition and ordinary empirical statements. And I suspect that Franklin's critique of Bodin on this point actually treats his position as if it were an empirical (and thus untrue) claim. In that case there must be sociological and psychological reasons why such a state would nevertheless collapse as soon as it was formed. It is at least possible to see some of what Bodin says as psychology of this kind. If it is unclear who is entitled to issue commands, the result will be confusion.

Franklin appears to read Bodin as criticizing the possibility of a sovereign state that is constructed upon the division of powers between various state organs or powers. It is, of course, the American constitution that he primarily has in mind—Bodin declared in advance that this was impossible, and now he looks somewhat foolish. Franklin says of Bodin: "… he was primarily responsible for introducing the seductive but erroneous theory that sovereignty is indivisible." (Franklin 1992: xiii) It is of course true that a sovereign state must be constructed on an original authority or rule (examples are USA in 1786 and the Norwegian constitution of 1814), without the implication on one single institution in control of all power.

> He advanced in other words a theory of ruler sovereignty. His celebrated principle that sovereignty is indivisible thus meant that high powers of government could not be shared by separate agents or distributed amongst them, but all had instead to be entirely concentrated in a single individual or group (Franklin 1992: xiii).

He also calls Bodin's doctrine of indivisible sovereignty a "serious confusion" (xx). It is one thing to say that all the prerogatives of the prince must be united, but Bodin's assertion that this united power of prerogatives, which (as we have seen) were located first and foremost in the activity of legislating, could not as a whole be divided among several institutions, did not even correspond to the reality of society at that time. It is this kind of division that Franklin sees in the American constitution, where differing state powers share in the same function, although with varying

---

about the balance between the powers, which found its classical expression in the American phrase "checks and balances." Franklin could have drawn a sharper distinction between Bodin's rejection of Aristotle and his alleged incompatibility with Montesquieu.

weight, just as the American president takes part in the legislation of Congress and is not outside this legislation. Let us sum up: Bodin's mistake was to believe that a concentration of all power necessarily meant that it was concentrated in one group or person. I suspect that Franklin, possibly in agreement with one current in American political thinking, has taken something that, for Bodin, was a question of the organization of political power, and has turned this into a question of law or of the structure of the constitution. As Franklin himself states in several passages, legislation means giving orders and laying down rules. In that case, the simplest way to prevent confusion about the legitimacy of an order is to limit such a power to one empirically identifiable institution, to know that the order comes from the right place—not only to see it as generated by an accepted principle or decision in an original constitutive original assembly.

Franklin is certainly right to say that, in the light of a constitutional setup such as that of the USA, Bodin's theory about how the unitary character of the state must be understood is, at any rate, not necessarily true. But what about states with a parliamentary form of government, where the executive power must have confidence in the legislative power, and the judicial power usually cannot intervene in the legislation (at least, not to the same degree as in the USA)? Paradoxically, the stronger the legislative power becomes in relation to the other state powers, the closer one may be said to come to Bodin's form of absolutism.

After discussing the internal organization of the absolute power, the second question we must examine is connected with the boundaries of absolute power. It must be clear that none of Bodin's contemporaries held that "absolute" meant that the king, as a single individual, could act exclusively on the basis of his private will; we have touched on this in connection with the distinction between laws and contracts. Absolute power certainly did not mean despotism. But how is an absolute power limited? (On what follows, see Skinner 1978: 295 f.).

We must draw a distinction between those laws that are divine (and are also called "natural") and those that are laid down by human beings. As we have said, the king is free to change the latter, but some of these have a special status. These royal laws, as they were called, concerned in particular the order of succession to the throne, which was unshakable. Nor could the king freely sell the property that was his *qua* king; he could only make use of the income from this property.

It also seems clear that the king must respect the citizens' right to property, since the state consists of families. This may imply restrictions on the king's right to set taxes.

Limitations of this kind are due to the existence of another form of laws than those laid down by the king himself. The divine or natural law is binding on the sovereign too, and it is this that guarantees the paterfamilias his unrestricted right to property. In the light of this double body of laws, one cannot simply say that Bodin contradicts himself when he writes about what the sovereign cannot do. A more empirical question, which later theoreticians were to pose, is how much these moral limitations were worth, when one at the same time removed all the constitutional rights to oppose the king. The citizens have no right to resist even if their divinely given rights are infringed. Ultimately, the key to the apparently contradictory tendencies may be that Bodin wanted to ascribe the total unlimited power to an institution, and not to one individual person legal and institutional protection.

Finally, what is Bodin's place in the history of political thinking? Was he really so modern, if he failed to see the possibility of reconciling the principle of the division of power and the concept of sovereignty? Did not his concept of the state reach its zenith in the Versailles of Louis XIV—sovereignty as royal absolutism? The answer is: not necessarily, for does not the concept of the sovereignty of the people likewise derive all power from one single source? This leads to the undeniably tantalizing question of whether the parliamentary system contains a form of absolute power. What is the relationship between Bodin's concepts of sovereignty and absolute power, and what we call the principle of the sovereignty of the people? And how is the parliamentary system linked to the principle of the division of powers? Are they in fact compatible? If the question is put in this way, Bodin becomes once again relevant, and indeed, almost uncomfortably relevant—not because he foresaw the nineteenth-century parliamentary and political forms of organization, but precisely because of the doctrine of the modern state as one unitary power.

Bibliography

Blair, A. (1997). *The theatre of nature. Jean Bodin and the Renaissance science*. Princeton: Princeton University Press.

Bodin, J. (1566). *Methodus ad facilem historiarum cognitionem*. Paris. *Method for the easy comprehension of history* (B. Reynolds, Ed., 1945). New York.

Bodin, J. (1580). *De la démonomanie des sorciers*. Paris. New edition, 1979.

Bodin, J. (1583). *Les six livres de la république*. Paris. In English as Bodin, J. (1992). *On sovereignty, four chapters from the six books of the commonwealth* (J. H. Franklin, Red.). Cambridge: Cambridge University Press.

Bodin, J. (1596). *Universa Naturae Theatrum*. Lyon/Paris.

Bodin, J. (1857). Colloquiuum heptaplomeres de rerum sublimium arcanis abditis, complete edition. Schwerin 1857. In English as *Colloquium of the seven about secrets of the sublime* (1975) (M. Leathets & D. Kuntz, Trans.). Princeton: Princeton University Press.

Bodin J. (1962). *The six books of a commonweale* (R. Knolles & K. McRae Ed., A14). London.

Franklin, J. H. (1963). *Jean Bodin and the sixteenth-century revolution in the methodology of law and history*. New York: Columbia University Press.

Franklin, J. H. (1992). *"Intoduction" to Bodin 1992*. Cambridge: Cambridge University Press.

Franklin, J. H. (1993). *Jean Bodin and the rise of absolutist theory*. Cambridge: Cambridge University Press.

Henschall, N. (1992). *The myth of absolutism, change and continuity in early modern European monarchies*. London: Longman.

Hotman, F. (1972). *Franco-Gallia* (R. Gisey, Ed.). Cambridge: Cambridge University Press.

Lewis, J. U. (1968). Jean Bodin's 'Logic of Sovereignty'. *Political Studies, 16*, 206–222.

Lovejoy, A. J. (1936). *The great chain of being*. Cambridge, MA: Harvard University Press.

Parker, D. (1983). *The making of French absolutism*. London: Arnold.

Salmon, J. H. M. (1975). *Society in crisis, France in the sixteenth century*. London: Methuen.

Skinner, Q. (1978). *The foundation of modern political thought* (Vol. 2). Cambridge: Cambridge University Press.

Skinner, Q. (2002). From the state of princes to the person of the state. In Q. Skinner (Ed.), *Visions of politics* (Vol. 2). Cambridge: Cambridge University Press.

Samuel Pufendorf – Natural Law, Moral Entities and the Civil Foundation of Morality

Thor Inge Rørvik

To make a fair assessment of Samuel Pufendorf (1632–1694), one should perhaps keep in mind that whereas he once was an important and highly influential thinker, widely read and commented upon, he nonetheless seems to have vanished from the history of philosophy at the end of the eighteenth century—i.e., at the very moment when this history underwent the rewriting we continue to acknowledge today. Although the philosopher Christian Garve in 1798 still maintained the view that Pufendorf had elaborated "a new moral principle" and hence brought the whole issue of moral philosophy to a new level, this was only a rearguard skirmish.[1] Garve himself was about to suffer the same fate as Pufendorf: he was relegated to the footnotes, if indeed he was mentioned at all by later philosophers. "The strength of Pufendorf's genius, the clearness of his discernment, the accuracy of his judgment, and the variety and depth of his erudition", lauded by William Enfield in 1797 and repeated in new editions for decades to come, was no longer acknowledged by the philosophers' guild, but was now a mere echo from the mid-eighteen century's great histories of philosophy, translated and adapted to a textbook size by the author without regard for the state of the art.[2]

The rewriting of the history of philosophy, alluded to here, was a result of the Kantian revolution in the 1790s. With the emergence of Kant's critical philosophy, it seemed obvious to many of his followers that the vast reservoir of past thinking had to be organized and presented in a new manner, mainly according to, and regulated by, the following two questions: (1) Which philosophical topics are (from now on) regarded as the most important? and, (2) Who among all the philosophers from

[1] Garve, Christian (1798) *Uebersicht der vornehmsten Principien der Sittenlehre, von dem Zeitalter des Aristoteles bis auf unsre Zeiten*. Breslau, p. 143.

[2] Enfield, William (1819) *The History of Philosophy from the Earliest Times to the Beginning of the Present Century* [1797]. London, Vol. 2, p. 626.

T.I. Rørvik (✉)
Department of Philosophy, Classics, History of Art and Ideas,
Faculty of Humanities, University of Oslo, Oslo, Norway
e-mail: t.i.rorvik@ifikk.uio.no

G. Fløistad (ed.), *Philosophy of Justice*, Contemporary Philosophy: A New Survey 12,
DOI 10.1007/978-94-017-9175-5_5,

the past has treated these very topics in a way that points forward to Kant's own solution? Given these premises, it is no wonder that Pufendorf was immediately written out of what, from then on, became the standard history of philosophy. For this was the history of a more restricted concept of philosophy, in the sense that it reduced much of what until then could be presented as philosophy to unscientific babbling and deemed it obsolete, never to return as viable positions in theoretical or moral discussions. It is all the more interesting then, that a not insignificant share of the renewed interest in Pufendorf during the last 25 years must be understood as attempts to write him *back* into the history of philosophy—or at least into the history of *moral* philosophy. This is obviously the case with J. B. Schneewind's brilliant *The Invention of Autonomy*, one of the best and most comprehensive histories of modern moral philosophy. Although the author concedes that, by holding the view that moral philosophy has a single aim, "we may be overlooking its historical distinctiveness by forcing it into our own molds", and that it is far from likely that all moral philosophers throughout history have been addressing the same questions or focused on solving the same problems, the story that Schneewind tells, and which he integrates Pufendorf into, is still pointing towards Kant.[3] It is a multifaceted story, considering and analyzing philosophers who are not normally mentioned in the histories of moral philosophy. But by fitting them into one particular development, it overlooks the extent to which moral philosophies are time-bound intellectual practices, attempting to address particular contextual issues. The point is not whether Pufendorf fits into the kind of history Schneewind is telling; he obviously does—provided one understands his theory of moral entities as a precursor to the Kantian distinction between the phenomenal and noumenal, or sees his voluntarism as begging for a theory of moral motivation that had to await the concept of an autonomous moral subject that was put forward a hundred years after his death. If this is what it takes to make Pufendorf an interesting figure for current moral philosophy, then so be it. But from an intellectual historian's point of view it might be considered a high price to pay, if the most interesting aspects of a past thinker point towards questions that he himself probably did not consider.

In what follows, the question of Pufendorf's relevance will therefore be addressed with regard to what he himself considered to be the pertinent issues, and the solutions he proposed. This is consistent with another important part of the growing literature on Pufendorf, where the focus is less on trying to fit him into a posterior tradition than on demonstrating to what extent he belongs to a quite different tradition—a tradition to which he deliberately tried to show his adherence.[4] But consider the following quotation from Christine M. Korsgaard's *The Sources of Normativity*:

> Grotius asserted that human beings would have obligations even if God did not exist to give us the laws. Because of that remark, he is often identified as the first modern moral philosopher. But the credit for that should really go to Hobbes and Pufendorf. For they were the

[3] Schneewind, J. B. (1998) *The Invention of Autonomy*. Cambridge, p. 550. His presentation of Pufendorf here (pp. 118–140) is an elaboration of an earlier article: "Pufendorf's Place in the History of Ethics," in *Synthese* 72 (1987), pp. 123–156.

[4] The picture of Pufendorf drawn in the following pages is indebted to the works of Richard Tuck, Ian Hunter and Knud Haakonssen.

> first to identify clearly the special challenge which the Modern Scientific World View presents to ethics, and to construct ethical theories in the face of that challenge.[5]

This is a statement Pufendorf might well have subscribed to, although he would probably have underscored his intellectual kinship with Grotius and, for more or less tactical reasons, clearly distanced himself from Hobbes. In fact, that is exactly what he did, when, at a certain point in his career, he had to publicly defend himself against critiques and elaborate his position by means of a historical argument.[6] For the moment, however, the attention must be paid to the expression "special challenge" from the above quote. With regard to Pufendorf, this points in at least three directions (and none of these is what Korsgaard seems to have in mind), namely: (1) the attempt to break free from the traditional natural law, an attempt initiated by Grotius and further elaborated by Pufendorf; (2) the insistence on a *civil* foundation of morals, detached from religious confession; and (3) the peculiar historical conditions under which Pufendorf's ideas developed.

1 The "Modern" Natural Law

In its broadest sense, the term natural law simply refers to an understanding of morality in legalistic terms, and is a way of thought which can be found, more or less elaborated, as early as the ancient Stoics. But as an elaborated theory, it was mostly associated in the Early Modern period with the theories of Thomas Aquinas, formulated in the late thirteenth century. Following the great Dominican, the Spanish Jesuit Francisco Suarez (1548–1617) understood natural law as simply the way in which God's eternal law applies to human moral nature. On the one hand, it consists entirely in the divine command, proceeding from the will of God; while on the other hand, it dwells within man as the judgment of reason. This was the theory Grotius challenged; an enterprise that for Pufendorf made him "the first person to make our age value the study of natural law".[7] The first of Pufendorf's own works in natural law was likewise, according to the author, heavily indebted to the Grotian enterprise:

> We have drawn much from that marvellous work, *De jure belli ac pacis*, by the incomparable Hugo Grotius. Although appearing to treat merely a part of universal jurisprudence, he has, nevertheless, touched upon most of its parts in such wise that scarcely anything can be written in this field without his name appearing either as authority or as witness.[8]

---

[5] Korsgaard, Christine M. (1998) *The Sources of Normativity*. Cambridge, p. 23.

[6] Hochstrasser, T. J. (2000) *Natural Law Theories in the Early Enlightenment*. Cambridge, pp. 40–72.

[7] Tuck, Richard (1987) "The 'Modern' Theory of Natural Law," in Pagden, Anthony (ed.) *The Language of Political Theory in Early-Modern Europe*. Cambridge, p. 102. The quotation is from the preface to the first edition of Pufendorf's *De iure naturae et gentium* (1672); the preface is not included in the English translation of the work.

[8] *Elementorum jurisprudentia universalis libri duo* (1660), preface, p. 10; hereafter abbreveated ELE. All quotations from this work refers to the translation of W. A. Oldfather, republished as *Two Books of the Elements of Universal Jurisprudence* (Indianapolis, 2009).

There is no doubt that Pufendorf disagreed with Grotius on important issues, but all the same he adhered to the perspectives the Dutchman had put forward in his attempt to address a subject "few have touched upon, and none hitherto treated of universally and methodically".[9] It is also obvious that Grotius exaggerates the novelty of his contribution to the theory of natural law; in fact, he made important use of Scholastic precursors as well as of a revived Stoicism. But this is not the point here; the point is rather that according to himself, as well as to Pufendorf, something decisively new happened with Grotius. The novelty consisted mainly in his attempt to frame the theoretical basis for his work as an answer to moral skepticism. To be able to put forth a convincing theory of man's moral capabilities, based on considerations on the human nature, Grotius had first to rebut the skeptic's argument that such an enterprise was impossible, because a mere observation of the different human societies revealed a fundamental moral disagreement that no account of the material world could resolve. Grotius' answer was that the skeptical posture was but a version of the need for self-preservation that was common to man—and that, given its universality, must be regarded as the foundation of his theory. No society would be able to exist, unless the principle of self-preservation was respected.

Two things have to be stressed here. First, that the scholastic tradition of natural law had paid little attention to the skeptical argument, simply because its main agenda was to harmonize the ethical theories of Aristotle or Aquinas with current moral theology. Grotius, however, in his quest for a universal principle, disregarded these theories simply because they were answers to special circumstances and did not address mankind as such. It was all the more important to him to combat the skeptical conclusion that the kind of moral principle he was seeking could not be found. The second point is that Grotius' own solution must be considered as a kind of minimalism: There *is* a universal morality, albeit a minimal one; namely, the recognition of self-preservation and this, again, presents a kind of lowest common denominator for a universal moral culture.[10]

The Grotian minimalism had crucial consequences for what was to become known as the "modern" theory of natural law. Most conspicuous was its reformulation of the distinction between man's natural state and civil society, whether this was understood in a static manner, as the mere contrast between the universal and the circumstantial, or as two states in a "historical" development centered on the idea of a social contract. The most famous version of the latter was, of course, elaborated by Thomas Hobbes, and while Pufendorf acknowledged Hobbes' version, and therefore seems to be reasoning along the same lines, he also presented another version more akin to the former, where man in civil society is still seen in

---

[9] Grotius, Hugo (1626) *De jure belli ac pacis*, preliminary discourse I., p. 75; quoted from the English translation of Barbeyrac's French edition (1738), republished as *The Rights of War and Peace* (Indianapolis, 2005).

[10] See Tuck "The 'Modern' Theory of Natural Law", p. 113ff for a substantiation of this point.

different relations to the natural state.[11] It would thus be premature to understand him simply as a Hobbesian.[12] The divergences between Pufendorf and Hobbes—or between Pufendorf and Grotius, for that matter—should rather be seen as a distinct trait of the tradition that followed in the wake of Grotius. According to Jean Barbeyrac, the Huguenot writer who later translated both Grotius and Pufendorf into French, and elaborated a comprehensive history of moral philosophy ending with the followers of Grotius, it was obvious

> that Grotius pretended not to give a complete System; which might be easily seen, though he himself had not declar'd it. 'Tis only occasionally that he touches upon even the greatest Part of the principal Subject Matters of natural Right: So that, though his Views had been more extensive, and less imperfect, than they seem in many Things to have been; his Plan did not lead him to a full Discussion of them; it was enough for him to handle 'em so far, as might be sufficient to decide the Question, which concern'd the principal Subject of his Book.

Grotius' work was, therefore, on several accounts,

> very much inferior to that of Mr. Pufendorf; who besides scarce ever borrows any Thoughts from Grotius, but what he improves, and explains more distinctly; and draws from 'em a greater Number of Consequences. In fine, Mr. Pufendorf often refutes Grotius, and that too with Reason ...[13]

Pufendorf was, however, not a "Grotian", because the modern natural law was not considered to be a school of thought. What he did was to continue the attempt to integrate the laws of nature into a system, founded on the principle of self-preservation that Grotius had elaborated. It was an enterprise that did not regard foundational issues as the most important ones, and that therefore allowed for a great deal of disagreement concerning how the system should be interpreted, how the obligatory character of laws should be explained—and whether the system in question was a system of duties or a system of rights.[14] What Grotius left behind was not a scientific theory by which one could attempt another, and better, philosophical justification for ethics. Rather, at least in Pufendorf's case, it must be understood as a set of concepts and perspectives that allowed him to show that moral duties both can and must be acceded to, independently of philosophical justifications.

---

[11] Compare for instance the two different versions of the natural state in *De iure natura et gentium* (1672), book II, chapter 2 and book VII, chapter 1.

[12] The relationship between Pufendorf and Hobbes is, of course, a complicated matter; and far more complicated than Pufendorf himself would admit. See for instance Palladini, Fiammetta (2008) "Pufendorf Disciple of Hobbes. The Nature of Man and the State of Nature," in *History of European Ideas* 34 (2008), pp. 26–60.

[13] Barbeyrac, Jean (1706) *Histoire critique et scientifique de la Science des Mœurs*; quoted from the English translation: *An Historical and Critical Account of the Science of Morality*. London, 1729, p. 84.

[14] Tuck "The 'Modern' Theory of Natural Law", p. 113ff.

2 The Civil Foundation of Morality

Where there is an opening, there is often also a closure. Pufendorf's identification with Grotius was no doubt an attempt to wrestle him away from the old scholastic understanding of natural law, and hence a "Grotian" undertaking in the sense that it aimed at a separation of natural law from theology. All the same, he realized that there were certain elements in Grotius' theories that stuck to the old way of thought, and hence had to be refuted. Prominent among these was the famous *etiamsi daremus*-agument, where Grotius said that the groundwork of his natural law theory would still hold true, even if there was no God, "or that he takes no Care of human Affairs". This argument sustained a moral *realism*, according to which normative claims simply *are there* as part of the framework of the world. According to Grotius, what makes the law of nature differ from positive law is that the actions upon which its dictates are given are

> in themselves either Obligatory or Unlawful, and must, consequently, be understood to be either commanded or forbid by God himself; and this makes the Law of Nature differ not only from Human Right, but from a Voluntary Divine Right; for that does not command or forbid such Things as are in themselves, or in their own Nature, Obligatory and Unlawful; but by forbidding, it renders the one Unlawful, and by commanding, the other Obligatory.[15]

Pufendorf's reply was simply that nothing is noble or base in itself. Moral values are not inherent in nature prior to God's moral legislation; what is inherent, however, is human nature and its capacity to *impose* laws. Prior to this imposition, nothing can be called noble or base—and hence, nothing can serve as objects for natural law.

> For, since Honesty (or moral Necessity) and Turpitude, are Affections of human Deeds, arising from their Agreeableness or Disagreeableness to a Rule, or a Law; and since a Law is the Command of a Superior, it does not appear how we can conceive any Goodness or Turpitude before all Law, and without the Imposition of a Superior.[16]

What begins as a critique of the remnants of scholastic essentialism in Grotius, ends with the conclusion that there is no single (transcendental) point of view from which man can reflect upon himself as a single moral subject. That is not to say that scientific knowledge of morality is impossible; rather, it means that such knowledge cannot be anchored in things considered noble or base in themselves, without reference to the law that makes them good or bad. Moral knowledge is fully possible, but its certainty will be internal to the domain created by the very imposition of laws. This is more than just an epistemological issue, even if Pufendorf's opponents no doubt regarded it as such. It is a way of saying that morality is not anchored in theory at all, but in the web of relations, or moral "entities", that structures civil society.

---

[15] *De jure belli ac pacis*, preliminary discourse XI, p. 89. See also his definition of the law of nature, I.1.10, p. 150ff.

[16] *De iure natura et gentium* (1672), I.ii.6; hereafter abbreviated DJN. All quotations from this work refer to the English translation by Kennett, Basil (1729) *Of the Law of Nature and Nations*. London. See also ELE, I. def XIII.

Furthermore, this also supports another important aspect of Pufendorf's natural law theory, namely that it is duty and not rights-based. When Grotius had considered rights as primary over duties, it was because his moral realism allowed him to regard the transgression against certain rights as inherently wrong. But to Pufendorf, nothing is inherently wrong. Besides, a right is an authority over another in the sense that it is something that the other has a duty to yield to, and there is no such authority before the imposition of a law[17]:

> As to *Grotius's* Definition, where he says the Law obligeth *to that which is right*, we must observe, that he supposeth somewhat to be Just and Right before any Rule or *Law*; whence it must follow that the Law of Nature doth not make what we call *Right*, but only denotes or points it out as a thing already existing.[18]

There have been remarkably few attempts to understand Pufendorf's critique of the scholastic remnants in Grotius, and his attempt to stress the civil foundation of morality, against the background of a broader intellectual scenario in the German states during the seventeenth century.[19] Conversely, most of what has hitherto been written about the development of the political-jurisprudential sphere, or the degree to which the civil sciences in Pufendorf's time contributed to what might be regarded as a "desacralisation of politics",[20] has showed an equal lack of interest in modern natural law. There is no doubt that Pufendorf was a political thinker as well as a moral philosopher, a political adviser as well as a professor, and that his works on natural law should also be understood in the very same political context as his analysis of the German imperial constitution or his history of the principal European states. There is, however, one pure historical context that is often referred to as indispensable to the understanding of Pufendorf.

3 The Westphalian Moment

If moral philosophy is understood as a time-bound intellectual practice, addressing particular or contextual issues, then the Peace of Westphalia (1648) must be regarded as a pivotal event for Pufendorf, not only as creating a situation to which his works seem to be a response, but also as a demarcation between *his* world and the world of thinkers like Grotius and Hobbes. In this regard it is, however, important to

---

[17] For an elaborate version of these issues, see Haakonssen, Knud (1996) *Natural Law and Moral Philosophy*. Cambridge, pp. 40–41.

[18] DJN I.vi.4.

[19] A notable exception is, of course, Hunter, Ian (2001) *Rival Enlightenments. Civil and Metaphysical Philosophy in Early Modern Germany*. Cambridge. Hunter devotes a whole chapter (pp. 63–96) to the relationship between moral thinking and the civil sciences, a relationship he coins "civil philosophy".

[20] The expression itself is coined by J. G. A. Pocock in his essay "Religious Freedom and Desacralization of Politics. From the English Civil War to the Virginia Statute," in Peterson, Merill D. & Vaughan, Robert C. (eds.) (1998) *The Virginia Statute for Religious Freedom*. Cambridge, pp. 43–73. It is frequently employed with regard to Pufendorf in Hunter: *Rival Enlightenments*.

distinguish the historical from the emblematic Westphalia—the language and terms of the treaties from "what they came to signify".[21] The Westphalian moment refers to the establishing of a political order where a system of states agreed to accept constraints on their behavior, based on their own self-interest. What thus emerged was a political order where sovereignty, for the first time, was formally recognized, and war became subordinated to politics. For political and moral philosophers, these arrangements gave birth both to new conceptual issues and to a significant change of perspective. In fact, the settlement also seemed to have solved many of the problems that hitherto had concerned political thinkers.

Grotius and Hobbes both wrote during periods of warfare. As the title indicates, Grotius' *De juri belli ac pacis* (1625) was first and foremost an attempt to regulate and limit the devastation that ruled Europe. Hobbes' *De cive* (1642) and *Leviathan* (1651) appealed for a strong and unified state, capable of putting an end to the rebellions that threatened not only England, but also the weak, internally divided political agglomerations that made up the rest of Europe. Simplifying to a certain extent, it might be said that Grotius and Hobbes had a common orientation: To establish a political society and obedience to this society, or, in short, to make order out of chaos. The problems facing a thinker like Pufendorf, writing in the wake of the peace and stability brought forth at Westphalia, were different. Although he borrowed what he could use from Grotius and Hobbes, this was transformed into a description of, and a reflection upon, the status of political units and the different obligations of the person, both as man and as citizen. In *De officio hominis et civis* (1673), a textbook generated from his larger works but omitting many of the topics discussed there, he formulates his task in a way that clearly illuminates the difference between himself and earlier political thinkers: The natural law teaches one "how to conduct oneself to become a useful member of human society". And with regard both to previous attempts to base natural law upon theology and the religious warfare that had recently come to an end, Pufendorf insists that a science concerned with the education of citizens must desacralize politics by separating transcendent morality from civil authority. To attempt this by way of natural law means that he reconstructs the very discipline that once was designed to hold the two together:

> The scope of the discipline of natural law is confined within the orbit of this life, and so it forms man on the assumption that he is to lead this life in society with others. Moral theology, however, forms a Christian man, who, beyond his duty to pass this life in goodness, has an expectation of reward for piety in the life to come and who therefore has his citizenship in the heavens while here he lives merely as a pilgrim or stranger.[22]

[21] Boucher, David (2001) "Resurrecting Pufendorf and Capturing the Westphalian Moment," in *Review of International Studies* 27, p. 560. See also Tully, James (1991) "Introduction," in Pufendorf, Samuel *On the Duty of Man and Citizen*. Cambridge.—For a critical assessment of the understanding of Westphalia promoted here, see Croxton, Derek (1999) "The Peace of Westphalia of 1648 and the Origins of Sovereignty," in *The International History Review* 21, pp. 569–591.

[22] *De officio hominis et cives*, prol.vi.3 and I.iii.8; hereafter abbreviated DOC. All quotations from this work is from the English edition referred to in note 21.

In his textbook, Pufendorf works the universal rights and duties of man under the natural law into a framework in which they are conceived as both qualified by, and mediated through, the state as itself a "person" possessing rights and duties of its own, and to which its citizens have a set of obligations. The concept of the state as "a composite moral person" is most likely borrowed from Hobbes, and is a clearly modern concept in the sense that it makes the state, as a unified structure of will and power, independent of both its rulers and its subjects.[23] But what is unacceptable to Pufendorf, given the Westphalian situation, is Hobbes' view that the relation between sovereign political communities, or between states and external non-state agents, was akin to the state of nature albeit not in its pure form, but still signifying hostility and warfare. On the one hand, the recent political events had repudiated this view; on the other hand, even if international relations can be seen as aspects of a natural state (and Pufendorf clearly thinks they can), then it is a natural state in the Pufendorfian, not the Hobbesian, sense. According to Pufendorf, the state of nature is a lawless state, in the sense that individuals and societies are bereft of all connections other than those that exist because men are similar by nature, but it is not a state of permanent war. On the contrary, it has a capacity for cooperation and agreement in the same way as international relations, even if the main form of orientation in the latter case is a *raison d'État*, not the legal binding behavior internal to the civil state.[24] The civil state is a moral entity; international relations are not.

4 The Theory of Moral Entities

Whether Pufendorf and Hobbes jointly earn the title of the first modern moral philosopher because they met the special challenge which the modern scientific world view presented to ethics, or if that title should be reserved for Pufendorf alone, since he was the first to conceptualize and elaborate in a systematic form the political world after Westphalia, is an open question. In what follows, his theory of moral entities will be regarded as his most important contribution to both moral and

---

[23] DOC II.vi.10. For the development of this modern conception of the state, see Skinner, Quentin (2002) "From the State of Princes to the Person of the State," in *Visions of Politics II. Renaissance Virtues*. Cambridge, pp. 368–413 and "Hobbes and the purely artificial person of the state", *Visions of Politics III. Hobbes and Civil Science*. Cambridge, pp. 177–208.

[24] In Pufendorf's historical writings the moral content of the natural law often seems almost totally eclipsed by the principles of state necessity and state interests. A good example is his *De statu imperii Germanici* (1667); English translation: *The Present State of Germany* (Indianapolis, 2007), chapter VIII: "Of the German State-Interest" (pp. 210–247). See also the introduction to *Einleitung zu der Historie der vornehmsten Reiche und Staaten so itziger Zeit in Europa sich befinden* (1682–86). For an assessment of Pufendorf in light of the tradition of political realism, see Haslam, Jonathan (2002) *No Virtue like Necessity*. New Haven/London, pp. 62–66; interesting is also the brief portrait of Pufendorf as political adviser in Clark, Christopher (2007) *Iron Kingdom. The Rise and Downfall of Prussia, 1600-1947*. London, pp. 36–37. In the wake of these last works one should perhaps focus less on the lack of natural law in Pufendorf's historical works, and instead look for traces of the political adviser in ELE, DJN or DOC.

political thought. There is likewise no doubt that the theory was put forward as an attempt to give moral science a secure founding, and thus rebut the Aristotelian claim that there can be no certainty in morals.[25] It fills most of Book 1 in Pufendorf's first major work in natural law, *Elementorum jurisprudentiae universalis* (1660), and is carried on into the early chapters of his second major work, *De jure naturae et gentium* (1672), where it is elaborated in a manner that seems to structure the whole work.[26] That means, for instance, that the theory of moral entities precedes the full introduction of the motif of the natural state, which more than suggests that the latter must be understood, and to a certain extent gains meaning, in the light of the former. Pufendorf's theory, and his firm distinction between *entia moralia* and *entia physica*, has, however, been misunderstood as a mere distinction between facts and norms. In one way, this is true, but it still misses the point. It must rather be taken as a means to treat norms as facts, without relapsing into moral realism.

Pufendorf took the concept of moral entity from the somewhat obscure Cartesian Erhard Weigel (1625–1699), his one-time teacher at the University of Jena.[27] Weigel's theory was that physical and moral entities had one important thing in common, namely, that they were products of *imposition*—the physical entities were imposed by God, the moral entities by humans. And this similarity allowed them to be treated from the same metaphysical perspective; hence, the distinction served a *unifying* perspective. Pufendorf radicalized this theory by connecting it to the traditional jurisprudential view that law is the command of a superior will; there can be no law unless there is a legislator with the right to command.[28] And law is an institution used to order and coordinate, without which there is only chaos. God created the world (*entia physica*) by imposition of his will and is thus the supreme Legislator; man created the moral world (*entia moralia*) in accordance with what he *believed* to be in accordance with God's will. Given the voluntaristic theology Pufendorf promotes, however, man bears no *imago Dei* and it is therefore impossible for him to know anything about the supreme Legislator's will, save that he has some reason to *believe* that the will must be good. This is as far as theological voluntarism goes. But the point made is that, from a jurisprudential point of view, a law is compelling if it promotes the good. The problem here is how to identify the precepts without knowing God's will. The only way to do this is by scrutinizing man's own nature with regard to what it takes to live a good life; here it becomes clear that whereas man's primary concern is his own conservation and well-being, his weakness and wretchedness render him incapable of securing either of these concerns by his own efforts. Consequently, he has to join forces with others. Hence, the fundamental law of nature is that man should "cultivate and preserve sociality".[29] And this, in turn, involves a whole range of duties to God, to oneself and to others. While these

[25] Stated in Eth. Nic. 1094b11, and referred to by Pufendorf in ELE, preface, p. 7.

[26] See ELE def. I-XXI and DJN book I.

[27] Röd, Wolfgang (1969) "Erhard Weigels Lehre von den entia moralia," in *Archiv für Geschichte der Philosophie* 51, p. 64.

[28] DJN I.vi.4.

[29] DOH I.iii.9. The different kinds of duties are lined out in DOH I.iv–xiii and DJN II.iii.22.

precepts of natural law are taken from man's own nature and capabilities, the bearer of duties in civil society is *not* an integral moral person with access to a straightforward ground for obligation. Pufendorf employs the concept of moral entities to explain what this means.

Moral entities are imposed by man in accordance with the natural law "for the guiding and tempering the Freedom of voluntary Actions, and for the procuring of decent Regularity in the Method of Life".[30] One way to understand what is at stake here is to realize that *officium* is not the same as "duty" in the sense propagated by modern philosophy in the wake of Kant. In Pufendorf's case, it is obvious that the term also retains the old Stoic connotation of "office." An office is more than just a duty; it is, so to speak, one of the "offices of life" which encompass a whole cluster of duties and rights. To be a member of humanity is not the same as being a member of a family or member of a political society.[31] And moral entities are imposed to order and harmonize the offices of human life in conformity with the will that brought them into being. Pufendorf differentiates the following four types of moral entities[32]:

1. *States* or conditions (*status*) which form the framework or space in which persons actually operate. States are either natural—i.e., the natural state imposed by the divine will (the state of humanity), or adventitious—i.e., special conditions and institutions created by or imposed in accordance with the human will to obey the fundamental law of nature, and hence cultivate and preserve sociality (marriage, civil status, domestic and political society).
2. *Moral persons*—i.e., not just any individual, but also groups of persons (composite persons). By thus separating the concept of moral person from the human (rational) being, Pufendorf is able to show that an individual human being can be the bearer of several moral persons, each with its own duties arising from the purposes for which it was imposed. Obligations are hence derived from multiple ends, which lie outside the individual in the *officia* of civil life.
3. *Moral qualities*—i.e., affective modes, which have an effect on persons at the moral level. Pufendorf draws a distinction here between formal moral qualities (e.g., titles of honor), and what he calls operative moral qualities. Operative moral qualities are in turn divided into passive, i.e., qualities which enable someone lawfully "to do or suffer somewhat, or to admit and receive it",[33] and active, i.e., qualities by which we can morally affect or move others and which hence

[30] DJN I.i.3 and 5.

[31] Haakonssen *Natural Law and Moral Philosophy*, pp. 41–42.

[32] The different kinds of moral entities are elaborated in DJN I.v–xxiii.—In order to provide a brief summary of Pufendorf's own, more complicated style, the following overview is based on Dufour, Alfred (1991) "Pufendorf," in Burns, J. H. & Goldie, M. (eds.) *The Cambridge History of Political Thought, 1450-1700*. Cambridge, pp. 564–566, and Seidler, Michael (2013) "Pufendorf's Moral and Political Philosophy," in *The Stanford Encyclopedia of Philosophy* (Spring 2013 Edition), http://plato.stanford.edu/archives/spr2013/entries/pufendorf-moral/

[33] DJN I.i.20.

makes up the fabric of social life, such as power (*potestas*), obligation (*obligatio*) and right (*ius*).
4. *Moral quantities* or estimative modes—i.e., the valuation of persons, things or actions in terms of their social status or prestige, their price (economic value), or their desert (as in punishment and reward)—all of which are inexact and subject to alterations in the sense that they can be lost or regained.

These different moral entities divide the traditional notion of personhood or moral substantiality into the various roles or agencies that humans can play or assume in civil society, either simply as individuals or as composites. Since we enact multiple, overlapping moral *personae*, it is possible for these to conflict both on an individual and a collective level. It is all the more important therefore to understand the respective obligations and rights of different kinds of moral persons, and to be able to articulate them in terms of their relative priority. Conversely, by dividing the moral personhood, the theory of moral entities rules out the existence of a transcendent moral personality anchored in the nature of man. There is no single *philosophical* foundation of moral; the moral foundation is civil. Hence it is impossible for individuals to unify and rank their offices *from a single point of view*; in fact, such attempts are illegitimate. "Nor must we forget to hint", Pufendorf writes,

> that as one Person may be at the same time engag'd in several States, provided that the Obligations of those States do not interfere with one another, so the Obligations adhering to one particular State, may, according to different Parts, be deriv'd from different Principles. And therefore he that only collects the Obligations flowing from a single Principle, and omits the rest, doth not presently form a distinct State incapable of other Obligations besides those which he hath taken notice of. Thus he that gathers several Parts of the Office of Priests purely from the Holy Scriptures, doth not in the least deny, but that they are likewise bound to such Performances as the Constitutions of particular Governments shall farther enjoyn. So we that profess in this Work to treat only of those Duties of Men, which the Light of Reason shewn to be necessary, do not at all pretend that there ever was, or now is, or ought to be, such a State in which those Obligations only should prevail, exclusive of all others.[34]

It is interesting to notice that this last point is either missed—or simply ignored—by modern philosophers eager to discuss Pufendorf's theory of moral entities. Instead, they seem to focus on the problem of normativity or the connexion between obligation and moral necessity, finding Pufendorf's arguments wanting—which might very well be the case. J. B. Schneewind, for instance, states the problem as follows: "Without the capacity freely to obey or disobey, there can be no obligation. Yet obligation requires moral necessity".[35] And the only kind of necessity Pufendorf seems to be able to provide is the fear of sanctions, i.e., the threat of punishment. For obvious reasons, Pufendorf never considered the Kantian lesson that the only

[34] DJN I.i.11.

[35] *The Invention of Autonomy*, p. 138. For a further assessment of Schneewind's critique, see Bruxvoort Lipscomb, Benjamin J. (2005) "Power and Autonomy in Pufendorf," in *History of Philosophy Quarterly* 22, pp. 201–219.

way one could be obliged to obey a particular law is if one had an antecedent obligation to obey laws of that type. According to him, one simply does not need a prior obligation; obligation is an affective *response* from a properly functioning human being placed in appropriate circumstances (*entia moralia*), and that is all the moral necessity Pufendorf needs. To invoke man as a unified agent standing in the philosophical twilight between moral entities and the physical world is simply not possible for Pufendorf; there is just no space there to gain a foothold. And one of the tasks considered to be of utmost importance by later moral philosophy was to secure such a foothold.

The somewhat sketchy picture of Pufendorf's thought attempted here is of course both limited in scope and one-sided. And it is deliberately so, by highlighting issues that seem to point in another direction than the one taken by modern moral philosophy during the last 300 years or so. However, this is not intended as a critique of current attempts to understand Pufendorf in light of something that he was not trying to do. The fact that moral philosophers still find him an interesting topic is beyond question and signifies his continued relevance. Besides, should it be taken as a critique, this must also be seen as a critique raised against still existing trends in intellectual history that treat him as a member of some monolithic school under the label modern natural law. In Pufendorf's case, the theory in question is not even a theory of rights, but of duties. As such it stands as a contrast to a certain liberal picture, where justice, freedom and toleration appear as rights held by the individual *against* the state. And even if natural law in the century after Pufendorf's death was reformulated into subjective natural rights that, far from being surrendered at the creation of civil society, rather became the definition of current moral and practical claims, "it was not philosophical reason that put an end to religious civil war but, in fact, law and politics, and the forms of reason peculiar to them."[36] In fact, the first liberal rights were achieved when jurists began to understand laws as externally imposed for the sake of peace and tranquility—and, as a consequence, neutral in regard to inner moral truth. Pufendorf was probably not the greatest of moral philosophers, but he played without doubt an important role in molding the "juristic civic consciousness"[37] so vital in this historical process. And whatever his many disciples learned from his books or by attending his lectures, they would never have sided with the Jacobins who during the French Revolution executed "enemies of the human race" for transgressing the laws of nature.[38]

[36] Hunter *Rival Enlightenments*, p. 368.

[37] See Lestition, Steven (1989) "The Teaching and Practice of Jurisprudence in 18th Century East Prussia," in *Ius Commune. Zeitschrift für Europäische Rechtsgeschichte* XVI, pp. 27–80.

[38] See Edelstein, Dan (2009) *The Terror of Natural Right. Republicanism, the Cult of Nature, and the French Revolution.* Chicago.

Hugo Grotius – Individual Rights as the Core of Natural Law

Andreas Harald Aure

Four hundred years ago the Dutchman Hugo Grotius developed his influential theory that man by nature has certain fundamental, enforceable moral rights. The duty to respect these rights is a dictate of right reason, i.e., of natural law, with the principal command to live in peace with other people.[1]

According to Grotius, the state (*civitas*) was formed or should be formed to protect these rights, and is historically and ideally "a complete association of free men, joined together for the enjoyment of rights and for their common interest". The state is thus a result of the individuals it comprises and has basically no greater authority than the individuals have transferred to it. As long as the state protects the individual's rights,[2] citizens are obliged in return to submit to the laws and commands of the authorities.[3]

Grotius was the first central Protestant thinker who redefined the concept of *ius*, subsequently to be understood as individual or subjective rights. This transformation of *ius*, a cornerstone of modern individualism in political theory, has been "obscured from scholarship until recently".[4] For Grotius, the concept of rights

This chapter is an English translation and adaption of "Hugo Grotius: Individuelle rettigheter som naturrettens kjerne," in Pedersen, Jørgen (red.) (2013) *Politisk filosofi fra Platon til Hanna Arendt*. Oslo: Pax.

[1]On natural law and natural right in general, see *inter alia* Passarin d'Entrèves, Alessandro (1970) *Natural Law: An Introduction to Legal Philosophy*, 2nd rev. ed. London: Hutchinson University Library.

[2]Grotius, Hugo *De iure belli ac pacis libri tres: in quibus ius naturae et gentium item iuris publici praecipua explicantur* (IBP), ed. by B. J. Kanter-van Hettinga Tromp (1939), reprinted with additional notes by Robert Feenstra et al. Aalen: Scientia-Verlag. I, i, XIV, 1. Cp. I, ii, I, 5-6 (numbers corresponds to respectively book, chapter, section and paragraph). "[P]rotection of these rights is indeed one of the main tasks of civil government," in van Nifterik, Gustaaf (2011) "Hugo Grotius, Privileges, Fundamental Laws and Rights". *Grotiana* 32 (2011), p. 19.

[3]Grotius explains the limits of the duty of obedience in IBP I, iv.

[4]Haakonssen, Knud (1985) "Hugo Grotius and the History of Political Thought," in *Political Theory*, p. 240.

A.H. Aure (✉)
School of Business and Law, University of Agder, Kristiansand, Norway
e-mail: andreas.h.aure@uia.no

G. Fløistad (ed.), *Philosophy of Justice*, Contemporary Philosophy: A New Survey 12,
DOI 10.1007/978-94-017-9175-5_6, © Springer Science+Business Media Dordrecht 2015

represents a moral quality making it possible "to have or to do something lawfully" and this principle is called *facultas* when it is perfect, and *aptitudo* when it is not perfect (Grotius 1993: I, i, IV). The former part of this division of rights, *facultas*, has historically been understood as "moral claims to freedom of action", "designating a person's legitimate sphere of control", or in Latin his *suum* (one's own). This legitimate sphere of control is a jurisdictional issue, and does not dictate "how a person should conduct herself within that sphere".[5]

Elements of a concept of subjective rights may be said to be implicit in Roman law, which was a key normative source for Grotius.[6] But the Romans did not present a systematic, integrated theory of subjective rights. Indeed, Grotius was inspired by the work of the scholastics, particularly the Spanish neo-Thomists, but Grotius put this concept of *ius* at the core of his natural law theory.

Hugo Grotius, who was born on Easter day 1583 in Delft and deceased in 1645 in Rostock, delivered an extraordinarily diverse and extensive authorship during his lifetime, covering a wide range of literary disciplines. His magnum opus *De iure belli ac pacis*, published in 1625, "broke the ice" for a re-energized legal and political debate in Europe.[7]

In English translation the full title of the work is, "Three books on the law of war and peace, in which the law of nature and the law of nations together with the main constitutional principles are explained." The work contains Grotius' theories on when and in what manner it is permissible to use physical force and wage war, and how *ius naturae et gentium* is indispensable if true peace is the supreme goal.

According to Grotius, it is precisely the infringement of rights (in the notion *facultas* or *suum*) that can deliver a genuinely just basis to start a war. The objective of his magnum opus was to define in detail the necessary limits for the use of physical force in any human relationship within states, between states or outside of states. Not only the law within organized society, but pre-eminently legal norms between states could also, in Grotius' view, be given a systematic form and be labeled a science. The work had great authority and influence in northern Europe and America for more than 150 years, replaced only by Emer de Vattel's (1714–1767) *Le droit de gens* in 1758.[8]

---

[5] Smith, Tara (1995) *Moral Rights and Political Freedom*. Lanham, Md.: Rowman & Littlefield, "Studies in social and political philosophy", p. 18.

[6] Straumann, Benjamin (2009), "Is Modern Liberty Ancient? Roman Remedies and Natural Rights In Hugo Grotius's Early Works on Natural Law," in *Law and History Review*.

[7] Thomasius, Christian (1950) "Vorrede," in Schätzel, Walter (ed.) *Hugo Grotius: Drei Bücher vom Recht des Krieges und des Friedens*, trans. by Walter Schätzel. Tübingen: J.C.B. Mohr, p. 26. I have used the editio maior edition of *De iure belli ac pacis libri tres: in quibus ius naturae et gentium item iuris publici praecipua explicantur*, by B. J. A. De Kanter-van Hettinga Tromp, Leiden 1939. This edition was republished 1993 with additional notes by Robert Feenstra (Aalen: Scientia-Verlag). The 1939-edition is available digitized here: http://www.dbnl.org/tekst/groo001bjad01_01/. The English translation of *De Iure Belli ac Pacis* by Kelsey et al. (*The Law of War and Peace*, Oxford 1925) has been used, but sometimes corrected or changed by myself. There exists also an older English translation by Morrice et al. (*The Rights of War and Peace*, Indianapolis 2005), edited and with an introduction by Richard Tuck.

[8] de Vattel, Emer (1758) *Le droit des gens, ou Principes de la loi naturelle, appliqués à la conduite et aux affaires des Nations et des Souverains*, 2 vols. Londres. A reprint of an English translation came

Grotius lived during a stormy period in European history, caused by the transition to modernity and changes taking place in science, politics and theology. Throughout his life there was war: The 80 Years' War between the Netherlands and Spain ended first 1648 with the Peace of Westphalia. The 30 Years' War lasted from 1618 to that same year, 3 years after Grotius' death.

Grotius was also an important exponent of early modern European thinkers beginning to examine legal and political ideas from a different perspective. In the Middle Ages these ideas were studied on the background of a hierarchical world order, with God and the Pope at the top. Now, some thinkers were beginning to develop legal ideas through a different prism, independent of papal and divine order.

Morality and law were no longer seen primarily as arbitrary commands from above, but rather commands based on the nature and character of the individual and the state. In fact, there was a transition from theological foundations of morality and justice to an increasingly secular law of nature and of nations. During the seventeenth and eighteenth centuries, it became commonplace to highlight individual reason as mankind's principal source of knowledge. This approach to knowledge was its *Zeitgeist.* The present time has more in common with the modern natural law tradition of the 1600s and 1700s than many realize. This tradition handed down to us the fundamental principles of modern government and legal institutions, such as equality before the law, tolerance, fundamental rights and constitutional government. This knowledge is essential to grasp the current outlook on various issues, and the tenets of Western culture.

Note that Grotius' political philosophy is not a theory on how a state must be administered to maintain and preserve power or the status of the prince, as we find in Machiavelli, for instance, and in the doctrines of *ragion di stato* and *arcana.* Grotius' theory is uniquely normative and philosophical, and it is rooted in respectable or honorable morality. His political philosophy was part of, and justified in, ethics, or moral philosophy, though Grotius did not provide us a systematic representation and justification for his moral philosophy.

In the Prolegomena to *De iure belli ac pacis*, Grotius makes it clear that his presentation should be distinguished from practical politics, which can be understood as the guidelines politicians or leaders should follow in specific management of government. These may include guidelines such as the importance of acting wisely, and being useful and appropriate:

> I have refrained from discussing topics which belong to another subject, such as those that teach what may be advantageous in practice. For such topics have their own special field, that of politics, which Aristotle rightly treats by itself, without introducing extraneous matter into it; Bodin[9] on the contrary has confounded it with that which is the subject of this

---

2008: de Vattel, Emer *The Law of Nations or, Principles of the Law of Nature, Applied to the Conduct and Affairs of Nations and Sovereigns, with Three Early Essays on the Origin and Nature of Natural Law and on Luxury*, ed. and with an introduction by Bela Kapossy & Richard Whatmore, trans. Thomas Nugent. Indianapolis, IN: Liberty Fund, "Natural Law and Enlightenment Classics", 2008.

[9] Jean Bodin (1530–1596), French political philosopher who advocated hereditary and absolute royal power, and famous for having shaped the modern concept of sovereignty in *Les Six livres de la République* (first edition 1576). See Chapter "Jean Bodin: The Modern State Comes into Being" for Bodin's political philosophy.

treatise. In some places, nevertheless, I have made mention of that which is expedient, but only in passing, and in order to distinguish it more clearly from what is lawful (Grotius 1993: Proleg. 57).

This chapter contains, beyond the most important element of Grotius' political philosophy—the idea of rights—a short biographical section, a list of the key elements of his legal theory, a section about his method, a section about the source of natural law, a section on the relationship between rights and the supreme power (*summa potestas/summum imperium*), and a section on its reception historically.

1 Biography[10]

Hugo Grotius came from a relatively prosperous family, well connected with Holland's political and intellectual elite. He wrote poems in Latin when he was eight, and he enrolled at the University of Leiden when he was eleven. In 1598, King Henry IV proclaimed Grotius *Le Miracle de Hollande* because of his extraordinary erudition.[11] His bibliography includes more than 100 titles of prose and poetry.[12] At 19, Grotius was appointed the official historiographer of Holland. His membership in the *Respublica litteraria* resulted in a very extensive correspondence, published in recent times in 17 large volumes. He translated works from antiquity and wrote a number of important monographs, especially on theological political-legal topics. In 1621, Grotius in a spectacular fashion managed to escape while hiding in a book chest from his fate as a political prisoner at the fortress Loevestein, near Rotterdam. Under the protection of King Louis XIII he started to write *De iure belli ac pacis* in Paris, and dedicated it to the king. Grotius' early work on natural law, known as *De jure praedae commentarius*,[13] an analysis of right of the victor to capture prize in war, remained unpublished in his lifetime except for the greater part of the 12th chapter, which Grotius in 1609 published under the title *Mare Liberum, The Free Sea.*[14]

Grotius was also a practicing lawyer: He was an attorney at law since he was 16, and he attained the position of attorney general (for Holland) at the age of 25. In 1613, at age 30, he was appointed Rotterdam's chief legal counsel (*pensionaris*); the same year he also served as chief foreign policy adviser to the United Provinces. Between 1635 and 1645 Grotius was ambassador for Sweden in Paris. He died that

---

[10] The most up to date and extensive biography: Nellen, Henk (2007) *Hugo de Groot: een leven in strijd om de vrede 1583-1645*. Amsterdam: Uitgeverij Balans.

[11] Miller, Jon (2011) "Hugo Grotius," in *Stanford Encyclopedia of Philosophy*, p. 2.

[12] For a great bibliography, see: Ter Meulen, Jacob & Jurriaan Diermanse, Pieter Johan (1961) *Bibliographie des écrits sur Hugo Grotius: imprimés au XVIIe siècle*. La Haye: M. Nijhoff.

[13] Grotius, Hugo (2006) *Commentary on the Law of Prize and Booty*. Indianapolis: Liberty Fund, "Natural Law and Enlightenment Classics".

[14] Latin-English edition by Robert Feenstra came 2009: *Mare Liberum 1609-2009: original Latin text (facsimile of the first edition, 1609) and modern English translation*, ed. and ann. by Robert Feenstra, with a general introduction by Jeroen Vervliet, trans. Robert Feenstra. Leiden: Brill.

same year in Rostock from the illness he contracted after the ship that was to bring him home from Stockholm (where he had met with Queen Christina) wrecked off the coast of present-day Poland.

2 Overview of Grotius' Natural Law Theory

With *De iure belli ac pacis*, Grotius became the natural law thinker in the early modern period who most clearly distinguished between divine law given by revelation, and secular natural law based on human nature and defined by reason. He argued that God's existence was no prerequisite for knowing either the natural law order, its precise content, or its binding character. In other words, reason alone is sufficient to realize the obligation to live in accordance with natural law. Nature itself, not the Creator of nature, became the basis of legal order. Grotius turned natural law into a legal discipline independent of *ius divinum* (*voluntarium*), and one that cannot be changed by *ius divinum*. As Grotius says: "The law of nature, again, is unchangeable—even in the sense that it cannot be changed by God" (Grotius 1993: I, i, X, 5). In the famous *etiamsi daremus* passage he dares even to say that natural law would be valid "even if we should concede—which cannot be conceded without the utmost wickedness—that God does not exist" (Grotius 1993: Prolegomena 11).[15] These and other statements expressed an obvious desire to derive legal ideas independent of theology. This is in contrast to such an important precursor to Grotius as Francisco Suarez, who was concerned to show that, for example, the Decalogue (the Ten Commandments) were an expression of natural law.[16] A key objective of Grotius' project was to identify and highlight the existence of a legal system that would apply regardless of faith; indeed, it should have validity even for pagans and infidels.

This approach serves as Grotius' response to all forms of religious and political fanaticism.

Both Grotius' theology and his natural law conception was a call to pluralism. An individual was entitled "to look out for oneself and advance one's interests, provided the rights of others are not infringed" (Grotius 1993: I, II, I, 6). Furthermore, "… there are many ways of living, one being better than another, and out of so many ways of living each is free to select that which he prefers…" (Grotius 1993: I, III, VIII, 2). These were radical and heretical ideas in the seventeenth Century, which was hardly suited to calm already upset tempers, especially in ecclesiastical circles. Unsurprisingly, *De iure belli ac pacis* was immediately put on the papal index of

[15] The statement "Etiamsi daremus … non esse Deum" (… although we would admit … that God does not exist) of Grotius is the most famous expression of the view that natural law does not have to be dependent on theology. Similar ideas were also formulated before Grotius by the scholastics. The earliest and clearest expression is found in Gregory of Rimini, see Suarez 1944, p. 190.

[16] Haakonssen, Knud (1996) *Natural Law and Moral Philosophy: From Grotius to the Scottish Enlightenment*. New York, NY: Cambridge University Press, p. 29.

forbidden books, a ban that was first removed 1900, in order for the Vatican to attend a peace conference at The Hague.[17]

The core of Grotius' secular natural law concept is his belief that people have certain *moral qualities* or *abilities* of legal purport, to have and to do something lawfully, which translate to the rights to life, liberty, contract and rightfully acquired property. It is these rights attached to each individual that underlie law in the proper or strict sense, i.e., legal rights. These legal rights differ from other rights, also attached to the individual, but these are basically, according to Grotius, only of moral or theological purport. These other rights may not (in the state of nature) be upheld by force.

Grotius stood clearly on the shoulders of earlier thinkers, but his way of putting together and developing various ideas were unique. One of his greatest contributions was that he gave the prevalent legal ideas of the time, above all Roman law, an explicit philosophical basis. He identified the underlying philosophical principles that he thought the casuistic and seemingly unsystematic Roman law must have been based on.[18]

Key features of Grotius' natural law theory are:

1. Human beings can grasp natural law by using their reason alone.
2. Natural law can both be grasped and be binding independently of God's will or God's existence.
3. Natural law based on unchangeable rational precepts and volitional law based on arbitrary human or divine will are, by principle, different concepts and should be kept apart. *Ius naturale* can easily be brought into a system, while the norms of *ius voluntarium* are outside the domain of systematic treatment, since they often undergo change and are different in different places (Grotius 1993: 30).
4. The core of natural law is law in the proper sense, based on a moral quality that belongs to every human being. This minimalist, individualized concept of *ius* was epoch-making to political and legal thought in Europe.

3 Grotius' Method

Grotius was a humanist. He was a man of the Renaissance who sought *ad fontes*, a return to the source of knowledge. The learned people of this age rediscovered and refined ancient ideals and ideas, including those of early Christianity. Grotius sought for his natural law theory particular inspiration in Aristotle and Cicero, Stoicism and Roman law. Additionally, he used as sources, and as access to the ancient sources, the works of late-scholastics such as Leonardo Lessius and Francisco Suarez, and the expatriate Italian protestant Alberico Gentili.[19]

---

[17] Hofmann, Hasso (1995) "Hugo Grotius," in Stolleis, Michael (ed.) *Staatsdenker in der frühen Neuzeit*. München: Beck, p. 54.

[18] For the Roman law-influence on Grotius' legal thinking, see Benjamin Straumann works.

[19] On Gentili, see: Kingsbury, Benedict & Straumann, Benjamin (eds.) (2010) *The Roman Foundations of the Law of Nations: Alberico Gentili and the Justice of Empire*. Oxford/New York: Oxford University Press.

Grotius sought to prove natural law either *a priori* or *a posteriori*, i.e., to derive the validity of a statement either from what comes before (*prius est*), or from what comes later (*posterius est*) (see Grotius 1993: I, i, XII). The *a priori* method argues from principles or fundamentals to conclusions or propositions, while *a posteriori* argues from propositions to principles. His understanding of the *a priori* and the *a posteriori* proof of natural law comes from his reception of classic doctrines of rhetoric.[20] These concepts should not be confused with the Kantian notion of a priori and a posteriori. Although Grotius uses both methods in his thinking, the *a posteriori* is dominant.

Those commentators who claim that Grotius' theory represents some sort of methodical analysis of history and literary testimonies are correct.[21] It is, however, important to emphasize the word "methodical", since the analysis of the testimonies is quite "biased". Grotius, before he went through the material, usually had clear notions about which of the testimonies he believed useful to provide evidence for natural law. His aim was to identify legal norms that are non-contradictory, easily understood and acceptable to as many people as possible (Schnepf 1998: 9).

Grotius is clear that statements of ancient authorities do not constitute natural law. Widespread historical evidence does, however, indicate that there is a universal reason behind the conclusions of the legal norms he claims to be valid. But the conclusions of the testimonies qualify only as natural law if one is able to tie them to the principles of nature or reason *certa argumentatione*. Legal norms that cannot by such a certain method be derived from natural principles, yet are recognized everywhere (or at least in most civilized nations), qualify as *ius gentium* (law of nations). The *ius gentium*, or the law of nations, Grotius in *De iure belli ac pacis* defines as: "the law which has received its obligatory force from the will of all nations, or of many nations." (Grotius 1993: I, i, XIV). This type of law represents customs in and among most nations that are recognized by courts in times of peace or war. This type of law may sometimes stand in opposition to natural law—natural law norms are then given the name *ius interna* (inside the *forum internum*), or the law of conscience. Grotius explains the relationship between these customs and the law of conscience in the so-called *temperamenta*-chapters in book III.

He defines certain ideas as unquestionably true, for example, that man is a rational being who wants peaceful relations with his fellow beings (*appetitus societatis*), and that certain other principles follow from this, *a priori*. An *a priori* proof consists in demonstrating "the necessary agreement or disagreement of anything with a rational and social nature" (Grotius 1993: I, i, XII). Grotius argues that the evidence for natural law is built on concepts that are so certain that "no one can

[20] Straumann, Benjamin (2007) *Hugo Grotius und die Antike: römisches Recht und römische Ethik im frühneuzeitlichen Naturrecht*, 1. Aufl. ed. Baden-Baden: Nomos, "Studien zur Geschichte des Völkerrechts". Of particular importance according to Straumann: Quintilian's *Instituto Oratoria.*

[21] Schnepf, Robert (1998) "Naturrecht und Geschichte bei Hugo Grotius. Ein methodologisches Problem rechtsphilosophischer Begründung," in *Zeitschrift für Neuere Rechtsgeschichte*, pp. 1–12.

deny them without doing violence against himself", and that natural law principles are almost as obvious as sense perception (Grotius 1993: Proleg. 39).

Grotius emphasizes the difference between questions of morality and mathematics: "What Aristotle wrote is perfectly true, that certainty is not to be found in moral questions in the same degree as in mathematical science" (Grotius 1993: II, xxiii, I). Grotius thus applied no mathematical method in the sense of building a finely deductive system where all legal questions could be determined from certain axioms, although this has been claimed in studies of his work.[22] Grotius was too eager to connect his thinking with the facts, not to mention with examples and lessons from history.

The overwhelming number of quotes used, especially from ancient philosophers, has been taken as evidence that Grotius was a historicist and not a true natural law thinker. Grotius' interest in ancient sources, however, does not differ significantly from what was common among humanists of the Renaissance. Grotius' method does differ, however, from many of the scholastic predecessors in that citations and practice (*a posteriori* evidence) are given in support of legal ideas which he believed in principle could be proven *a priori*. The sources are used to expand and intensify his own identifications of norms that, he believed, followed from the principles of nature. References to earlier thinkers and historical events thereby have, in regards to the evidence of natural law, only an affirmative function, and not a constitutive or grounding function (Grunert 2000: 70 ff.).[23]

Natural law may therefore be proven through the testimonies of ancient philosophers (*a posteriori*): "In order to prove the existence of this law of nature, I have, furthermore, availed myself of the testimony of philosophers, historians, poets, finally also of orators." But the testimonies have no evidentiary value in themselves. Grotius makes it clear that one should not rely on these authors without discrimination, since they were accustomed to serve their sect, subject or particular cause (Grotius 1993: I, iii, V, 6 and Proleg. 40). Rather, when many at different times and in different places say the same thing, then it appears that a universal cause stands behind the agreed norm in question (Grotius 1993: Proleg. 40 and I, i, XII, 1).

Such a consensus serves firstly as a sort of inductive evidence for Grotius' own reasonable assessment of natural law. Secondly, such a consensus is an indication of a proper understanding of the nature of the problem (or, the universal cause). And, the greater the consensus, the greater is the likelihood that the principle in question is true. In both cases, the use of the classical sources serves only as a confirmation that something can be inferred *ex certis principiis certa argumentatione* (Grotius 1993: Proleg. 40). The content of the testimonies must therefore in principle always "by a sure process of reasoning" be traced back to natural principles in order to qualify as an expression of natural law. Customs and practices that do not stand the test of natural law, yet are recognized as legal norms everywhere, are characterized

---

[22] See e.g. Eikema Hommes, Hendrik van (1983) "Grotius on Natural and International Law," in *Netherlands International Law Review* 30, pp. 67 et seq.

[23] Grunert, Frank (2000) *Normbegründung und politische Legitimität: Zur Rechts- und Staatsphilosophie der deutschen Frühaufklärung*. Tübingen: Max Niemeyer Verlag, p. 70.

as *ius gentium (voluntarium)*.[24] The consensus Grotius identified is not a random reconstruction, but his selection. In this process, Grotius likely learned from, or was influenced by, the sources he found, which meant that he brought this material into his own process of understanding (Grunert 2000: 73).

Some commentators have described Grotius as an eclectic, and believe to have found support for this opinion in *De iure belli ac pacis* (Prolegomena 42). But eclecticism means to systematically borrow other people's thoughts and theories, and presupposes intellectual openness, tolerance, moderation and modesty, qualities that are not very conspicuous (or prominent) to Grotius' method or ideas.[25]

4 View of Humanity and the Source of Natural Law

Grotius searched, in contrast to some Roman lawyers, to define natural law as something distinctively human, relying on the Aristotelian observation that man on essential points is different from other animals. In the Prolegomena of *De belli ac pacis*, he points out that the difference between human beings and every other species is greater than the difference between members of any other species (Grotius 2010: Proleg. 6).

One of these significant points that distinguish man from animals is man's desire to live jointly with others (*appetitus societatis*—Grotius' translation of the Greek term *oikeiosis*), i.e., the inherent desire to live in a peaceful and orderly society with fellow beings.[26] Man alone is weak and needs many things he cannot provide on his own. But even if he should not be lacking anything in his solitude, man would seek community. This desire for society is strengthened by the ability of language that man possesses, and the ability he has to understand general rules and to act upon them. These abilities are unique for man.

Grotius designates the maintenance of a social order consonant with human intelligence as the true source of what is properly called law. As necessary for the maintenance of a social order, Grotius deduces such well-known classical legal norms as abstaining from taking things which belongs to another, restoring that which properly belongs to another, fulfilling promises, making good on a loss incurred to others through one's own fault, and inflicting just punishment (Grotius

[24] See further on this, and with references §§ 70–80, Aure, Andreas Harald (2008) "Der säkularisierte und subjektivierte Naturrechtsbegriff bei Hugo Grotius," in *Forum Historiae Iuris*.

[25] Eclecticism in philosophy has been going through several conceptual mutations since the Enlightenment (though the term originated in ancient times) and is therefore easily prone for anachronistic usage. From having had positive connotations, the word today carries rather negative. The positive meaning during the Enlightenment considered eclecticism as a third way between skepticism and dogmatism. For a *Begriffsgeschichte*: Albrecht, Michael (1994) *Eklektik eine Begriffsgeschichte mit Hinweisen auf die Philosophie- und Wissenschaftsgeschichte*, Quaestiones 5. Stuttgart/Bad Cannstatt: Frommann-Holzboog.

[26] On Grotius' understanding of *oikeiosis*, see Brooke, Christopher (2008) "Grotius, Stoicism and 'Oikeiosis'," in *Grotiana* 29. With further references.

1993: Proleg. 8). Both sociability and rationality are essential characteristics of human nature. The source of natural law is connected with mankind's inherent sociability, which requires the maintenance of a social order. It follows that the nature of man, i.e., his sociability and reason, is to be governed by law or similar rules. Thus, "the mother of the law of nature ... is the very nature of man, which even if we had no lack of anything would lead us into the mutual relations of society" (Grotius 1993: Proleg. 16). Grotius thus argues that natural law only applies to man. Unlike animals, only man has the ability to formulate and act in accordance with general principles (Grotius 1993: Proleg. 7 and I, i, XI, 1). Thus the ancient philosopher Karneades and others were mistaken when they claimed as a universal truth that humans have a natural urge to seek their own advantage at the expense of others. Those who claim this have, according to Grotius, overlooked significant distinctive human characteristics, specifically the human conceptual ability and ability to think and act long range. Grotius emphasizes that it is in one's own direct interest (*utilitas*), as rational and sociable beings, to fulfill our legal obligations:

> [J]ust as the national, who violates the law of his country in order to obtain an immediate advantage, breaks down that by which the advantages of himself and his posterity are for all future time assured, so the state which transgresses the laws of nature and of nations cuts away also the bulwarks which safeguard its own future peace (Grotius 1993: Proleg. 18).

Thus, even if there seems to be no private benefit in sight, it should be considered *prudent* to act in a way that we believe is consistent with our nature. Anticipating objections from those who thought that man is not always a rational and social being, Grotius quoted Aristotle: "In order to find what is natural we must look among those things which according to nature are in a sound condition, not among those that are corrupt" (Grotius 1993: I, i, XII, 2, quoted from Aristotle's *Politica* I, v).

5 The Core of Natural Law

Natural law for Grotius has three meanings: law in the sense of that which is not unjust; law as a moral quality attached to individuals, understood as rights or as law in its proper sense; law as *rectum* or law in the extended sense. The latter sense I will not discuss here, but it includes the obligation to comply with certain positive legal norms that are not in accordance with law in the proper and strict sense.[27]

The first meaning that Grotius discusses is law in the negative sense, as that which is not unjust. He defines unjust as "that which is contrary to the character of a natural community of rational beings" (*iniustum quod naturae societatis ratione utentium repugnat*). The concept *unjust* denotes those actions which put social order and peace at risk. This includes actions such as stealing, breaking agreements and even non-action such as the failure to punish those that violate rights. To Grotius,

[27] The latter sense is explained in Aure 2008 §§ 70–80.

the essence of *unjust* is a violation of *suum* and *dominium* (see below). To allow this would destroy human solidarity and brotherhood (Grotius 1993: I, i, III).

This concept of *ius* is generally understood to mean not undertaking an activity that disturbs community. The Golden Rule of not doing unto others what you do not want them to do unto you inspired Grotius. His concept of law in the negative sense is important to modern liberalism's concept of negative liberty as the absence of coercion: one's liberty exists to the extent that others do not interfere in legal terms.

To further ground the principle of the unjust, i.e., that which is considered to be contrary to a community of rational beings, Grotius goes on to claim that the core or basic idea of *ius* should be seen as a quality or ability directly attached to individuals: "There is another meaning of law viewed as a body of rights, ... which has reference to the person. In this sense a right becomes a moral quality of a person, making it possible to have or to do something lawfully. ... When the moral quality is perfect we call it facultas [faculty], when it is not perfect, aptitudo [aptitude]." (Grotius 1993: I, i, IV).

As previously mentioned, this individual-oriented or subjectivized formulation of natural law builds on the moral quality a person possesses to justly *have* something or *do* something. This moral quality is the product of two different types of justice—attributive and expletive[28] justice. Grotius compared these two types of justice with the Aristotelian terms distributive justice or geometric justice, and restorative or arithmetic justice (Grotius 1993: I, i, VIII). Distributive justice means, for example, that a person who is more worthy or fit for an award or a position has a better claim to it than a less worthy or less suitable person. Restorative justice implies, for example, that interference in the legal sphere of one's own (*suum*—latin for what is "one's own") may be protected and enforced by compensation and punishment.[29]

It was from this individual-oriented meaning of *ius naturale* that Grotius developed his natural law theory and his system of just reasons for war. With a restriction: That which an individual has a "right" to according to his moral quality of suitability, *aptitudo*, and is an expression of *iustitia attributrix* (distributive/attributive justice), cannot serve as just reasons for war. According to Grotius, only a *moral* claim follows from suitability or attributive justice, without any accompanying right to enforcement. From that which the individual himself has a sort of power over, *facultas*, and is an expression of *iustitia expletrix* (restorative justice), however, follows such right to enforcement. *Iustitia expletrix* expresses a so-called perfect moral quality attached to a person, whereas *iustitia attributrix* expresses an imperfect such quality (IBP I, i, IV).

In Grotius' own words: "[T]rue ownership and the consequent necessity for restitution do not arise from aptitude alone, which is not properly called a right and which belongs to attributive justice; for one does not have ownership of that to which is merely appropriate" (Grotius 1993: I, ivii, II).

---

[28] Expletive: Old Greek, perfect or complete.

[29] *Suum* represents that which in John Locke's political theory is expressed with the word *property*, cf. Locke 1988, II, § 87, where "property" is described as "Life Liberty and Estate".

Grotius seeks justification for *iustitia expletrix* by looking back at that which must have been a legitimate sphere of command available to individuals before states were formed.[30] Everyone living then, according to Grotius, would be entitled to protect their life, liberty and their use of unowned natural resources. Communities were formed to protect this original sphere of command:

> For society has in view this object, that through community of resource and effort each individual be safeguarded in the possession, of what belongs to him. … this consideration would hold even if private ownership as we now call it had not been introduced; for life, limbs, and liberty would in that case be the possessions belonging to each, and no attack could be made upon these by another without injustice.

He later adds:

> By nature a man's life is his own, not indeed to destroy, but to safeguard; also his own are his body, limbs, reputation, honor, and the acts of his will (Grotius 1993: I, ii, I, 5 og II, xvii, II, 1).

Ownership (*dominium*) was, according to Grotius, introduced by tacit agreement,[31] as people realized the benefits of this form of life compared to the pre-state life consisting of undefined usage rights (Grotius 1993: II, ii, II, 4). Even if such ownership is introduced by human will, the institution as such is pre-state and enjoys the status and protection of natural law.[32] Grotius argued that men have the same right to their property (*res*) as to their actions (*actiones*) (Grotius 1993: II, xi, I, 3). Law in the legal and strict sense (*ius proprie aut stricte*) thus encompasses, according to Grotius' own enumeration:

- The right over oneself, which is called freedom, or the right over others, as that of the father (*patria potestas*) or that of the master over his *servos*[33];
- Ownership rights, either absolute, or less than absolute, as usufruct and the right of pledge;
- Contractual rights, to which on the opposite side contractual obligations correspond.[34]

By this we testify to an early formulation of the classical liberal rights of life, liberty and property (cf. Miller 2011: 20).

Grotius distinguished between the claim the best flute player has to the best flute under attributive justice (*iustitia attributrix*), and the claim the flute owner has to the

[30] Grotius does not deduce his theory from a hypothetical state of nature consisting of individuals who hypothetically enter into contracts with each other and with appointed regents. There are thus essential differences between Grotius and Thomas Hobbes, see Zagorin 2000. Zagorin still goes too far in writing off Grotius as a conservative and unoriginal thinker.

[31] See further Buckle 1991: 45–48 and *passim*; Haakonssen 1985: 241 and Salter 2001: 546.

[32] Cp. Straumann 2007, p. 172, and Straumann 2009.

[33] On Grotius and *servitus*, see van Nifterik, Gustaaf (2004) "Hugo Grotius on 'slavery'," in Winkel, Laurens & Blom,, Hans (eds) *Grotius and the Stoa*. Assen: Royal Van Gorcum.

[34] Grotius 1993: I, i, V: "… Potestas, tum in se, quae libertas dicitur, tum in alios, ut patria, dominica: Dominium, plenum sive minus pleno, ut ususfructus, ius pignoris: et creditum cui ex adverso respondet debitum." See further Aure 2008: § 61.

flute according to perfect justice (*iustitia expletrix*). Although the best flute player has some kind of right—i.e., that it would be best or most appropriate that the best flute player possesses the best instrument—it is difficult to show that another person may have a specific obligation to ensure that the best player gets the best flute. What is important is that attributive justice in this case will be in conflict with the *suum* or the right of another. The consequence would be that what Grotius calls law in the proper sense would lose its absolute character. A judicial enforcement of attributive justice would be contrary to the terms for the formation of the state, which was precisely the protection of *suum*. Grotius fears that a judicialization of attributive justice would pose a threat to social peace.[35]

Another example that illustrates the point is the consideration of what society could be exposed to if whoever thinks he is, or who really *is*, best suited to become head of state, for example, should have a right to enforce this "privilege". It would give that person a right to this position, regardless of whether others in the community wanted or liked him.

Grotius did not discuss whether *ius attributrix* should or could be partly enforced or implemented. But a full enforcement of *ius attributrix* is impossible, since it would lead to endless conflicts of interest. Instead, this kind of justice serves as a demarcation criterion for his concept of true *ius*: Whether a person deserves a thing or position in accordance with attributive justice falls beyond what could serve as justification for war.

The specific rights and obligations of the individual (*ius proprie*), as described above, are what best promotes life in society. To treat *aptitudo* or moral virtues in the broad sense as legal, i.e., as law in the proper sense, could easily create unrest in society, make things unsafe and pose a real risk for escalation of conflicts. Grotius does not deny that there are other natural rights deriving from *qualitas moralis*, but he refuses them status as law in the proper sense, because these other rights can flourish without this status. He believes, like Aristotle, that virtue requires freedom, and its enemy is coercion.[36] Virtues or rights that adhere to *iustitia attributrix* should, if possible, be realized as moral obligations.

Law in the legal sense is therefore, for Grotius, not any form of virtue or justice, but only the kind of justice *required* for the maintenance of social order. This is what Grotius calls complete (perfect) justice or *ius naturale*. This kind of justice is an attribute, quality, or something a person *possesses* by virtue of being human; the core of natural law is thus no longer something *objective* to be grasped or derived directly from a realm outside human nature. These *moral qualities* are the origin of *ius*; *objective law* is not the source of these moral qualities.[37] Grotius' approach thus represented a significant shift from objective law to a concept of subjective law, or individual rights. This concept must not be understood as the individual himself

[35] Zuckert, Michael P. (1994) *Natural Rights and the New Republicanism*. Princeton, N.J.: Princeton University Press, p. 145.

[36] Cp. e.g. Grotius 1993: II, xx, XX, 1.

[37] Schneewind, J. B. (1998) *The Invention of Autonomy: A History of Modern Moral Philosophy*. Cambridge: Cambridge University Press, p. 80.

deciding what are his rights (which would mean subjectivism), but the *concept* of rights belonging to individuals remains the focal point for that which can be defended with physical force.

For Grotius, law in a political context is primarily about respect for the *legal* rights of others. The right to one's life, limbs and freedom, summarized in the concept *suum*, are certain personal attributes belonging to each and every one prior to and independent of one's affiliation with any kind of community. Grotius' theory ushered in the concept of subjective law in the modern sense. Here, the essence lies in "leaving to another that which belongs to him, or in fulfilling our obligations to him" i.e., *iustitia expletrix* (Grotius 1993: Proleg. 10). Grotius gave form and content to *ius* that later natural law thinkers such as Samuel Pufendorf and, especially, John Locke cultivated, inspiring the American revolutionaries and many European civil rights movements.

6 Supreme Power

I have in this article highlighted liberal markers of Grotius' natural law theory.

How do these relate to the common view of Grotius as an apologist for despotism or absolutism? Grotius is infamous for his statement that people are able to submit to one or more persons and waive fully their right to govern (Grotius 1993: I, III, VIII, 1).

An important reason for this image and seeming contradiction lies in the subject matter of Grotius' *De iure belli ac pacis*. One of its topics is how people may become subjugated to or the subjects of other people, such as when they have been defeated in war. The effects of war may make it necessary for a people to submit to another—so that an independent political entity ceases to be such, as when independent nations in ancient times became Roman provinces.

The question is, therefore, who possesses supreme power (*summa potestas*) in an ordinary existing perfect association, i.e., a state (*perfectus coetus=civitas*). Grotius rejects categorically the widespread idea that *the people* everywhere and without exception are the carriers of supreme power (Grotius 1993: I, III, VIII, 1). At the same time, the research on Grotius has seldom pointed out that the supreme power does not *need to be* in the hand of one or several persons, a *monarchy* or *aristocracy*.

Grotius theorized that *summa potestas* consists of two elements, which are connected: The association as a whole (the state as *coetus perfectus*) is the general carrier or subject of supreme power, while one (monarchy) or more persons (aristocracy), or a combination of the people and one or more persons/government institutions (mixed form of government), is the concrete carrier of state power. He illustrates this by comparing *summa potestas* to sight: The eyes are *subjectum proprium* of sight, while the body as a whole is *subjectum commune* of sight. Likewise, the concrete government institutions are *subjectum proprium* of the *summa potestas*, while the association as such (the *civitas*) is the *subjectum commune* of the *summa potestas*. In accordance with this, the political leaders of a state hold and exercise government authority on behalf of the association as a whole, and in accordance with its legal basis (Grotius 1993: I, III, VII; Haakonssen 1985: 244). The form of government and its legal framework is determined by the choices people are making or have made (Grotius 1993: I, III, VIII, 2). It seems that Grotius held the cherished republican view of the Enlightenment that the people are the proper, primary power source for any state.[38]

Grotius argues that although supreme power (*summum imperium*) by its nature is indivisible, the actual exercise of it is often divided between *partes potentiales* (i.e., different powers that each possesses certain parts of government power) or *partes subjectivas* (i.e., different individuals who possess all government power together) (Grotius 1993: I, III, XVII, 1). Both the possession and exercise of government power can thus be divided into several hands. Grotius was aware of the criticism (particularly by Jean Bodin) against this idea of *divided supreme power*, but replied that in politics (*civilibus*) nothing is entirely without drawbacks; furthermore, "a legal provision is to be judged not by what this or that man considers best, but by what accords with *the will* of him with whom the provision originated" (Grotius 1993: I, III, XVII, 2, emphasis added). In a later chapter, Grotius made it clear that the right to rule emanates from the express (*expresse*) or tacit (*tacite*) will of the people (Grotius 1993: II, IV, X, 2). The theory of shared exercise of government power would become very popular in state practice in the coming centuries.[39]

According to Grotius, a state may be independent even if it is formally ruled by a foreign king (e.g., in a so-called personal union), or has a defense cooperation with another state and, in fact, is a protectorate. Being under protection and being under control are two different things. States entering a defense-cooperation agreement with more powerful states do not lose their independence. "Just as private patronage in the case of individuals does not take away individual liberty, so does not public patronage take away political liberty" (1993: I, III, XXI, 3).[40] These ideas were essential for the defense of Norway's status as an independent state in the union with Sweden from 1814 to 1905.

Grotius was careful to distinguish between individual liberty (*libertas personalis*) and political liberty (*libertas civilis*). The latter kind of freedom is about the independence of the association (*libertas universorum*). To be subject to a king (in a real union) is not consistent with people's liberty (Grotius 1993: I, III, XII, 1), and Grotius assumes that people themselves ought to exercise the highest government power (*summum imperium*) if the people *qua* people shall be deemed free (Grotius 1993: I, III, XXI, 3). But it is perfectly possible for an individual in a state

[38] Reibstein, Ernst (1972) *Volkssouveränität und Freiheitsrechte Texte und Studien zur politischen Theorie des 14.-18. Jahrhunderts*, ed. by Clausdieter Schott. Freiburg [et al.]: Alber, "Orbis academicus Sonderband", pp. 210 *et seq.* Link, Christoph (1983) *Hugo Grotius als Staatsdenker*. Tübingen: Mohr, "Recht und Staat in Geschichte und Gegenwart, vol. 512", p. 25.

[39] Keene, Edward (2002) *Beyond the Anarchical Society: Grotius, Colonialism and Order in World Politics*. Cambridge, UK/New York: Cambridge University Press, "LSE Monographs International Studies", p. 93 and *passim*.

[40] Grotius discusses though, ibid. section 10, how the stronger power can gradually come to usurp government power of the weaker power.

to have his individual liberty intact, even though the people as a whole lack the freedom to govern themselves. The existence of individual liberty is altogether about protection of rights (*suum*), which a government of any kind should provide. In no way need there be a contradiction between an autocratic form of government and individual liberty.[41]

To the contrary, a benevolent reading of Grotius (i.e., a reading he presumably would agree with) assumes that individuals in accordance with the purpose of the formation of the state, which, as stated in the introduction, is to protect their rights and their common interest, should have their rights intact whatever the form of government. People have not joined together in a state to waive their rights, but to get effective protection of them. It may thus be argued that rights as such should not in any state association be restricted beyond that which is required to achieve this purpose (Haakonssen 1985: 246).

7 Historical Reception and Criticism

Posterity has judged Grotius very differently. One of Rousseau's accusations against Grotius in *Du contrat social* was that Grotius built law on fact. This is somehow correct; Grotius built his legal system on that which he perceived to be human nature (e.g. *voluntas*), other empirical data and the sum of human experience. This was not the object of Rousseau's grievance, however. It was Grotius' view that it may be necessary to attach some legality to certain inhuman customs of war, like the arbitrary killings of civilians. But Grotius sanctioned by no means such customs morally. He considered them to be in violation of the law of conscience (*iustitia interna/forum internum*), and he exhorted war parties not to take advantage of or to practice them. Hence the famous *temperamenta*-chapters in (book III, ch. x-xvi) *De iure belli ac pacis*, where he identified laws of war that belligerents in seventeenth- and eighteenth-century Europe ever increasingly began to practice, and which later became an important source of inspiration for international written conventions (the Geneva Hague conventions) that would become important constituents of international humanitarian law.[42]

Kant in *Zum ewigen Frieden* described Grotius along with Pufendorf and Vattel as "sheer sorry comforters" (*lauter leidiger Tröster*), because no head of state cared about their arguments.[43] Hegel said that *De iure belli ac pacis* no longer was read by

[41] A major reason why it has been claimed to exist such a contradiction is probably that many commentators have believed that *libertas civilis* has connotations to *individual liberty* (civil liberty), believing that when the people have transferred *libertas civilis* they have transferred their individual liberty (as well).

[42] Remec, Peter Pavel (1960) *The Position of the Individual in International Law According to Grotius and Vattel*. The Hague: M. Nijhoff, pp. 118 *et seq.*

[43] Kant, Immanuel (1977) *Zum ewigen Frieden: ein philosophischer Entwurf*, ed. by Wilhelm Weischedel in *Werke in zwölf Bänden*. Frankfurt am Main: Suhrkamp, p. 210.

anyone.[44] But long before these great thinkers' negative judgments, Grotius' conceptions of natural law had become commonplace in many parts of Europe. German natural law thinkers and Enlightenment philosophers such as Samuel Pufendorf, Gottfried Wilhelm Leibniz, Christian Thomasius, Jean Barbeyrac and Christian Wolff built to a very large extent on Grotius' theories. Grotius' extensive and detailed system of natural law would prove to act as a source of inspiration and a "Steinbruch aller späteren Naturrechtsgebäude",[45] with great practical-political significance for the drafters of modern constitutions and law codes such as the *Lex regia* in Denmark-Norway in 1665, and the code of the Swedish kingdom from 1734.

In the Anglo-American countries, interest in Grotius was immediate and strong. Some have gone so far as to say that John Locke was not the main spiritual instigator of England's Glorious Revolution in 1688, but Hugo Grotius, "Master of Whig Political Philosophy" (Zuckert 1994: 119). And it is possible to draw connecting lines from the American Revolution to Grotius through his major influence on John Locke and later, the English, Scottish and American natural law and Enlightenment thinkers.

It is claimed that John Locke brought the central substantive content to his idea of natural rights from Grotius (Tuck 1979: 173). At the same time, Hobbes and his natural law and social contract theory formed an important basis for Locke's thinking (Strauss 1953; Syse 2007).[46] What Locke essentially did was to say that the natural rights theory that Grotius primarily had applied to ex-territorial and inter-governmental relationships also should have full validity within states, i.e., that a government has the duty to respect and uphold these same natural rights.

Within the Scottish Enlightenment, Grotius' importance to such thinkers as Adam Smith cannot be overestimated. Smith knew *De iure belli ac pacis* extremely well, developed further Grotius' theory of rights, and considered Grotius to be the greatest of all natural law jurists (Haakonssen 1985: 242 and 251).[47]

In Sweden, the reception to Grotius' ideas began early due to the extensive exchange of scholars between Strasbourg and Uppsala (Lindberg 1976). This reception

---

[44] Quoted in: Grunert, Frank (2003) "The Reception of Hugo Grotius's 'De iure belli ac pacis' in the Early German Enlightenment," in Schröder, Peter & Hochstrasser, Timothy (eds) *Early Modern Natural Law Theories: Contexts and Strategies in the Early Enlightenment*. Dordrecht/Boston/London, "Archives internationales d'histoire des idées/International Archives of the History of Ideas".

[45] Welzel, Hans (1962) *Naturrecht und materiale Gerechtigkeit*. Göttingen: Vandenhoeck & Ruprecht, p. 129.

[46] Strauss, Leo (1953) *Natural Right and History*. Chicago: The University of Chicago Press; Syse, Henrik (2007) *Natural Law, Religion, and Rights: An Exploration of the Relationship Between Natural Law and Natural Rights*, with special emphasis on the teachings of Thomas Hobbes and John Locke. South Bend, Ind.: St. Augustine's Press.

[47] Smith ended his magnum opus *The Theory of Moral Sentiments* (1759) with the following statement about Grotius and his jurisprudence: "Grotius seems to have been the first who attempted to give the world anything like a system of those principles which ought to run through, and be the foundation of the laws of all nations: and his treatise of the laws of war and peace, with all its imperfections, is perhaps at this day the most complete work that has yet been given upon this subject."

increased after Samuel Pufendorf became professor in Lund in 1668, where he published his masterpiece *De iure naturae et gentium libri octo* (The Law of Nature and Nations in Eight Books) in 1672, and in the following year the synopsis and widely used textbook of Enlightenment natural law, *De officio hominis a civis* (On the Duty of Man and Citizen).

In Denmark-Norway, Hugo Grotius' theories (and Pufendorf's) were disseminated by the polymath Ludvig Holberg, who is most famous for his comedies written 1722–1723. His book on natural law and the law of nature, first published in 1716 (5th edition 1751), was for nearly 40 years (after a law exam in order to practice law was instituted in 1736) almost the only law school textbook in Danish, reaching a wide audience.[48]

In the field of international politics, Grotius' ideas experienced a significant renaissance in the late 1800s. It is said that the Hague and Geneva conventions on war mirror his spirit. Along with the scholastic Francisco Suarez, he is probably the main spiritual instigator of the norms today known as international humanitarian law. This has led many intellectual historians to forget the status his ideas, broadly speaking, enjoyed during the Enlightenment for the development of legal and political ideas in general. The symbol of Grotius as a champion of international humanitarian law has thus overshadowed his strong influence on the development of European colonialism.[49] Grotius was far from a pacifist. If you seek to understand Grotius' ideas on legitimate use of force, you must study his concepts of law and his idea of rights.

Grotius' theory of rights as a type of natural attribute of individuals quickly received considerable attention and had a considerable impact on modern European political thought. The appeal of the ideas laid down in the theologically neutral, "minimalist" concept of natural law, with individual rights as its primary characteristic, combined with a large measure of realism, expressed, for example, by the authority Grotius renders *ius gentium* and *ius civile* in his system. Grotius sought here to combine idealism and realism, the theoretical and the practical. Grotius believed this combination would serve his main purpose, namely to prevent and alleviate wars motivated by religion and brute claims for political power. Grotius' emphasis on rationality and individual rights, which he believed were common to all people and applied regardless of religion or denomination, are never obsolete. This concept of law will forever remain a key tool and inspiration for the prevention and resolution of conflicts between people and societies.

[48] Title of the edition 1728 and later editions: *Naturens og folke-rettens kundskab* (The science of the law of nature and nations). The book was translated into German 1748 and into Swedish in 1789. On Holberg, see Langslet, Lars Roar (2012) *Den store ensomme: en biografi om Ludvig Holberg*. Oslo: Press. On Naturens og folke-rettens kundskap, see: Vinje, Eiliv & Sejersted, Jørgen Magnus (2012) *Ludvig Holbergs naturrett*. Oslo: Gyldendal.

[49] Cp. Borschberg, Peter (2010) *Hugo Grotius, the Portuguese, and Free Trade in the East Indies*. Singapore: Singapore University Press.

Bibliography

Albrecht, M. (1994). *Eklektik eine Begriffsgeschichte mit Hinweisen auf die Philosophie- und Wissenschaftsgeschichte*. Quaestiones 5. Stuttgart/Bad Cannstatt: Frommann-Holzboog.

Aure, A. H. (2008). Der säkularisierte und subjektivierte Naturrechtsbegriff bei Hugo Grotius. *Forum Historiae Iuris*, 41.

Borschberg, P. (2010). *Hugo Grotius, the Portuguese, and free trade in the East Indies*. Singapore: Singapore University Press.

Brooke, C. (2008). Grotius, Stoicism and 'Oikeiosis'. *Grotiana, 29*, 25–49.

Buckle, S. (1991). *Natural law and the theory of property*. Oxford: Clarendon.

Grotius, H. (1993). *De iure belli ac pacis libri tres: In quibus ius naturae et gentium item iuris publici praecipua explicantur*, ed. by B. J. Kanter-Van Hettinga Tromp (1939), Reprinted with additional notes by Robert Feenstra et al. Aalen: Scientia-Verlag.

Grotius, H. (2006). *Commentary on the law of prize and booty* (Natural law and enlightenment classics). Indianapolis: Liberty Fund.

Grotius, H. (2009). *Mare Liberum 1609-2009: Original latin text (Facsimile of the First Edition, 1609) and modern english translation,* (ed. and ann. by R. Feenstra, with a general Introduction by J. Vervliet, Trans. by R. Feenstra). Leiden: Brill.

Grunert, F. (2000). *Normbegründung und politische Legitimität: Zur Rechts- und Staatsphilosophie der deutschen Frühaufklärung*. Tübingen: Max Niemeyer Verlag.

Grunert, F. (2003). The reception of Hugo Grotius' 'De Iure Belli Ac Pacis' in the early German enlightenment. In P. Schröder & T. Hochstrasser (Eds.), *Early modern natural law theories: Contexts and strategies in the early enlightenment* (pp. 89–105). Dordrecht/Boston/London: Archives internationales d'histoire des idées/International Archives of the History of Ideas.

Haakonssen, K. (1985). Hugo Grotius and the history of political thought. *Political Theory, 13*, 26.

Haakonssen, K. (1996). *Natural law and moral philosophy: From Grotius to the Scottish enlightenment*. New York: Cambridge University Press.

Hofmann, H. (1995). Hugo Grotius. In M. Stolleis (Ed.), *Staatsdenker in der frühen Neuzeit* (pp. 52–77). München: Beck.

Kant, I. (1977). Zum ewigen Frieden: Ein philosophischer Entwurf. In W. Weischedel (Ed.), *Werke in zwölf Bänden*. Frankfurt-am-Main: Suhrkamp.

Keene, E. (2002). *Beyond the anarchical society: Grotius, colonialism and order in world politics* (LSE monographs in international studies). Cambridge/New York: Cambridge University Press.

Kingsbury, B., & Straumann, B. (Eds.). (2010). *The Roman foundations of the law of nations: Alberico Gentili and the justice of empire*. Oxford/New York: Oxford University Press.

Langslet, L. R. (2001). *Den store Ensomme: En biografi om Ludvig Holberg*. Oslo: Press.

Lindberg, B. (1976). *Naturretten i Uppsala 1655–1720*. Uppsala: Almqvist and Wiksell.

Link, C. (1983). *Hugo Grotius als Staatsdenker* (Recht und Staat in Geschichte und Gegenwart, Vol. 512). Tübingen: Mohr.

Locke, J. (1988). *Two treatises on government*. Cambridge: Cambridge University Press.

Miller, J. (2011). Hugo Grotius. In *Stanford encyclopedia of philosophy*, 18.

Nellen, H. (2007). *Hugo de Groot: Een leven in strijd om de vrede 1583–1645*. Amsterdam: Uitgeverij Balans.

Passarin d'Entrèves, A. (1970). *Natural law: An introduction to legal philosophy* (2nd ed. rev.). London: Hutchinson University Library.

Reibstein, E. (1972). *Volkssouveränität und Freiheitsrechte: Texte und Studien zur politischen Theorie des 14.-18. Jahrhunderts*. Freiburg [et al.]: Alber, Orbis Academicus Sonderband ed. by Clausdieter Schot.

Remec, P. P. (1960). *The position of the individual in international law according to Grotius and Vattel*. The Hague: M. Nijhoff.

Salter, J. (2001). Hugo Grotius: Property and consent. *Political Theory, 29*, 537–555.

Schneewind, J. B. (1998). *The invention of autonomy: A history of modern moral philosophy*. Cambridge: Cambridge University Press.
Schnepf, R. (1998). Naturrecht und Geschichte bei Hugo Grotius. Ein methodologisches Problem rechtsphilosophischer Begründung. *Zeitschrift für neuere Rechtsgeschichte, 20*, 1–14.
Smith, T. (1995). *Moral rights and political freedom* (Studies in social and political philosophy). Lanham: Rowman & Littlefield.
Straumann, B. (2007). *Hugo Grotius und die Antike: Römisches Recht und Römische Ethik im frühneuzeitlichen Naturrecht* (Studien zur Geschichte des Völkerrechts, 1. Aufl.). Baden-Baden: Nomos.
Straumann, B. (2009). Is modern liberty ancient? Roman remedies and natural rights in Hugo Grotius's early works on natural law. *Law and History Review, 27*, 55–86.
Strauss, L. (1953). *Natural right and history*. Chicago: The University of Chicago Press.
Syse, H. (2007). *Natural law, religion, and rights: An exploration of the relationship between natural law and natural rights, with special emphasis on the teachings of Thomas Hobbes and John Locke*. South Bend: St. Augustine's Press.
Ter Meulen, J., & Jurriaan Diermanse, P. J. (1961). *Bibliographie des Écrits sur Hugo Grotius: Imprimés au XVIIe Siècle*. La Haye: M. Nijhoff.
Thomasius, C. (1950). Vorrede. In *Hugo Grotius: Drei Bücher vom Recht des Krieges und des Friedens* (Trans. by W. Schätzel, ed. by W. Schätzel, pp. 1–28). Tübingen: J. C. B. Mohr.
Tuck, R. (1979). *Natural rights theories*. Cambridge: Cambridge University Press.
van Eikema Hommes, H. (1983). Grotius on natural and international law. *Netherlands International Law Review, 30*, 61–71.
van Nifterik, G. (2004). Hugo Grotius on 'Slavery'. In H. Blom & L. Winkel (Eds.), *Grotius and the Stoa* (pp. 233–43). Assen: Royal Van Gorcum.
van Nifterik, G. (2011). Hugo Grotius, privileges, fundamental laws and rights. *Grotiana, 32*, 1–19.
Vinje, E., & Sejersted, J. M. (2012). *Ludvig Holbergs naturrett*. Oslo: Gyldendal.
Welzel, H. (1962). *Naturrecht und materiale Gerechtigkeit*. Göttingen: Vandenhoeck & Ruprecht.
Zagorin, P. (2000). Hobbes without Grotius. *History of Political Thought, 21*, 16–40.
Zuckert, M. P. (1994). *Natural rights and the new republicanism*. Princeton: Princeton University Press.

Baruch Spinoza: Democracy and Freedom of Speech

Paola De Cuzzani

Baruch Spinoza (also known as Benedictus de Spinoza) lived from 1632 to 1677 in the United Provinces of the Netherlands (a federal republic existing during the years 1581–1795, the forerunner of what is today know as the Netherlands). Europe in the mid-1600s was plagued with conflict and strife amongst Lutherans, Calvinists and Catholics. Minorities were persecuted in most countries. The states were developing in an absolutist direction, severely limiting the citizens' freedom of faith. The Dutch Calvinist bourgeoisie of The United Netherlands had amassed considerable social power through extensive international trade, having only recently cast off Spanish and Catholic dominance. The Netherlands had quickly become the richest state in Europe, with Europe's largest merchant fleet, and Amsterdam had established itself as the centre of the European economy. The Dutch bourgeoisie contributed to the building of a more tolerant climate, and the United Netherlands quickly became the country to which persecuted Europeans fled.

Spinoza fought every form of fanaticism and intolerance in and through his works. His struggle formed a great philosophical system, strongly influenced by Descartes' philosophy as well as by ancient Jewish teachings, the Platonism of the Renaissance and the new mechanistic view of nature. His political philosophy builds on Machiavelli's political realism, and Spinoza more than likely studied the work of Thomas Hobbes.

A Romantic tradition shows us Spinoza as a lonely philosopher living a life far removed from worldly interests and passions. Spinoza did, however, participate in civil society with great political as well as theoretical awareness. He enjoyed a certain influence as a member of the circle around one of the great statesmen of the day, the liberal politician Jan de Witt, secretary of state from 1650 to 1672. Spinoza's correspondence suggests that he knew many of the prominent scientists and philosophers of his time.

Spinoza was born in Amsterdam, of Sephardic descent: his Jewish family had fled the Portuguese Inquisition. He attended the local Hebrew school where he

P. De Cuzzani (✉)
Department of Philosophy, University of Bergen, Bergen, Norway
e-mail: paola.de.cuzzani@fof.uib.no

G. Fløistad (ed.), *Philosophy of Justice*, Contemporary Philosophy: A New Survey 12,
DOI 10.1007/978-94-017-9175-5_7,

studied Hebrew, The Old Testament, the Talmud (one of Judaism's most important Scriptures systematising the oral and written tradition and comments on the Torah from the first to the fifth century AD) and the Jewish philosophical tradition: from Moses ben Maimon to Hasdai Crescas to Judah Leon Abravanel (Leo Hebraeus). He learnt Latin from Franciscus van den Enden, a well-known freethinker. An inventory list found after Spinoza's death shows that his library contained several works in Latin, among others Latin translations of Aristotle, works of Horace, Julius Caesar, Virgil, Tacitus, Epictetus, Livy, Pliny, Ovid, Cicero, Martial, Petrarca, Petronius and Sallust. These texts show an interest that was most likely born during his contact with van den Enden. His knowledge of Latin let him read, in addition to ancient classical texts, the Renaissance authors from Machiavelli to Giordano Bruno, more recent philosophical literature from Bacon to Descartes and Thomas Hobbes, and familiarize himself with the whole Scholastic tradition. He gradually expressed his controversial theological ideas more openly, and in response the leaders of the Jewish religious community expelled him from the Jewish synagogue and community of Amsterdam on July 27, 1656. The Protestant as well as the Catholic Church kept up the persecution following his excommunication and expulsion from the Jewish religious community, based on his criticism of Rabbinic truths and the Scriptures of the Old Testament. He subsequently moved from Amsterdam to Leiden (Rijnsburg) and made a living as a lens grinder for optical instruments. In 1661, at the age of 29, Spinoza published *Renati Des Cartes Principiorum philosophiae* (On Descartes' Principles of Philosophy) and *Cogitata metaphysica* (Metaphysical thoughts). These works gave him a reputation as an interpreter of Cartesian philosophy. At this time a circle of friends and disciples had already gathered around him. They later established an extensive correspondence with him, which represents a valuable source on the development of his thinking. He started writing his masterpiece *Ethica more geometrico demonstrata* (*The Ethics*) in Rijnsburg.

The reputation he had gained as an atheist made it necessary, however, to move frequently. He lived in den Haag from 1663, where he became acquainted with the physicist Christian Huygens and Jan de Witt, the leader of the Dutch Republican Party. Stimulated by de Witt's circle, Spinoza systematised his political ideas in *Tractatus Theologico-Politicus* (Treatise on Theology and Politics) published anonymously in Amsterdam in 1670. The publication of *Tractatus Theologico-Politicus* caused consternation in church circles, among Catholics as well as Protestants. His treatise's radical ideas increased the number of his critics and he was characterised as: atheist, *empius* (godless as well as immoral) and materialist. Nevertheless, Spinoza was not a blasphemous thinker. He held an immanent[1] perspective on reality and God, and rejected all traditional theological perspectives.

The political situation had changed as well: Jan de Witt was murdered in 1672 and the monarchical absolutist party of the House of Orange seized political power. One year after de Witt's murder, electoral prince Karl Ludwig of the Palatinate offered Spinoza a chair at the University of Heidelberg. Spinoza declined, however,

[1] The concept "immanent" here implies that God is not distinct from the World.

wishing to preserve his freedom of thought. He calmly continued his work, finished writing the *Ethics* and started writing a new political treatise, *Tractatus Politicus* (Treatise on Politics): he died, however, in den Haag in 1677, before completing his final work. A few months after his death his friends published his collected works, *Opera Posthuma* (1677), which include, in addition to *The Ethics* and the treatises already mentioned, *Tractatus de Intellectus Emendatione* (Treatise on the Correction of the Intellect), *Korte Verhandeling van God, de Mensch en deszelfs Welstand* (Short Treatise on God, Man and his Well-being), correspondence, and a book on Hebrew grammar.

We find Spinoza's political philosophy mainly in *Treatise on Theology and Politics* (TTP) and in *Treatise on Politics* (TP) where he treats very originally subjects such as: the foundations of social life, the individual's fundamental and inalienable rights, the democratic organization of the state, and the freedom of thought.

TTP was published anonymously in 1670 in Amsterdam. The treatise was initiated in 1665 when Spinoza wrote a letter to Oldenburg (EP. XXX), describing his intentions in writing this work. The two primary aims were

1. To argue against the prejudice of theologians and common people, and against the accusation of atheism.
2. A strong desire to defend the freedom of thought and speech.

And so the liberation from prejudice and defence of civil rights are central themes in the book. As Spinoza prepared to write TTP, the fundamental principles of his ontology and anthropology had already been developed, i.e.: his central political tenets built on the theories he had developed in the *Ethics* (E). The theory on natural right, the development of the state, the concept of democracy, the notion that the absolute power of the state may only be upheld if executed rationally, are the fundamental political tenets of Spinoza and involve the solutions to some metaphysical, epistemological and ethical problems; solutions which Spinoza had worked out in *The Ethics*.

In the following paragraphs we will first take a look at Spinoza's fundamental ontological concepts that play such an important role in his political theory. We will then examine his view of human nature, before we turn to the preconditions for political life. Informed by this, we will approach his theory on natural law and democracy. Finally, we will show the central role the freedom of thought and speech plays in Spinoza's political thinking.

1 The New Revolutionary View of God: God or the Infinite Substance, the World and Human Beings

Spinoza rethinks and radically transforms the fundamental theses of Cartesian metaphysics. As we know, Descartes assumed the existence of three kinds of substance: thought (*res cogitans*), extension (*res extensa*), and the infinite substance or God (re. Descartes, *Meditationes de Prima Philosophia*, III, 22). According to

Spinoza, only the latter may truly be considered a substance. When the substance is rigorously defined, it must be one wholly independent reality and it is conceived through itself. I.e., it must be *causa sui* ('self-caused'), and its essence involves its existence. Spinoza brackets all anthropomorphic, personal and volitional aspects of God when he explores the concept of the divine substance on the logical-ontological level. He consequently denies the existence of the personal God and the divine providence. The infinite substance, which Spinoza also calls *God* or *Nature*,[2] consists of infinite "attributes" and each attribute *expresses* the infinite essence of the substance.

Spinoza, who refuses to call himself an atheist, nevertheless denies any form of a transcendent God. God is *ens absolute infinitum* (the absolute infinite being) and all is in God and depends on God (E.I., p. 28, scholium). God is the actualised force or strength *(potentia)*[3] *that* necessarily, eternally and infinitely produces reality. Everything is in God, he is self-caused (*causa sui*), and thereby also the cause—immanent and not transitive—of all that God contains.

Human beings are an expressive part of the substance or reality, but are able to know the substance only through the two attributes in which they participate: thought and extension. Thought and extension, body and mind, are two sides of one and the same reality. Spinoza calls them identical, i.e., that they express the same reality in two different ways. In other words, there is a structure which may be expressed in an infinite number of aspects, and that we human beings know two of these aspects: thought, i.e., the very structure of thought, because we are thought, i.e. mind; and extension, the whole structure of matter, because we are matter, i.e., body.

As a part of substance human beings participate in its productivity or "*potentia*" (actualised force or strength): the essence of human beings is *conatus*, effort or striving for self-preservation and self-realization. This is the case for all things: human beings, animals, rocks, etc. We human beings are part of nature, but only a part: we are a "natural thing", one thing among many other things, and we do not constitute any special domain in nature. This distinguishes Spinoza from other

[2] On *Deus sive Natura* or *Deus seu Natura*: this wording occurs twice in E.IV. Praefatio: "For the eternal and infinite being we call God or Nature acts by the same necessity as that by which it exists" (æternum namque illud et infinitum Ens quod Deum seu Naturam appellamus, eadem qua existit necessitate agit) … "Therefore the reason or cause why God or Nature acts and why it exists is one and the same" (Ratio igitur seu causa cur Deus seu Natura agit et cur existit una eademque est.): this all shows that the wording is used on the productive level. The wording is undoubtedly emblematic for Spinoza's philosophy, but occurs only twice in all of his works and only when he speaks of the "*potentia*"—level.

[3] Translation of the Latin terms *potentia* and *potestas* is difficult to be made in English since the English word power includes two meanings whose difference is essential in the ontology of Spinoza. Martial Gueroult (Spinoza, T.1: Dieu (Ethique, I), 1968) was one of the first which rightly emphasizes this difference. Toni Negri in his "*The savage Anomaly*" from 1981 analyzes deeply this question: "potestas refers to power in its fixed, institutional or 'constituted form', while potentia refers to power in its fluid, dynamic or 'constitutive' form" (Negri 1981, p. xv.) I will therefore make a distinction between potentia and potestas by using power for potentia and actualised force or strength for potentia.

philosophers of the seventeenth century: e.g. Francis Bacon, who wanted to see human beings as the rulers of nature. We find in Spinoza a greater respect for nature, the part cannot dominate the whole. As part of the substance or of the nature, human beings are—each and every human being—at the same time a product of the productive strength of the substance, and also a "producer". Put differently, as part of nature we are ruled by natural laws, and we are consequently determined by external causes, but as part of the productivity of substance, our essence participates in the constitutive process of reality (being). We are thus determined by an external cause, we are passive; and we are also determined by our inner force, we are active and free. But it would be absurd and ridiculous to believe that we may fully overcome our passivity. At best, we can reduce it.

2 View of Human Beings, Freedom and Reason

Spinoza denies that we are free in the sense that the causes of our actions depend solely on us: everything in the world is produced by one or more causes. Being free does not entail evading the laws of nature, but using the laws of nature the way we use the wind—which certainly does not blow because we want it to—when wind fills the sails of a boat. So, according to Spinoza, we should not go against the laws of nature in order to become free in a wider sense; we must, however, bend them to our purposes and our utility (*utilitas*). Being free entails knowing the limits of our freedom and knowing that we can expand our field of intervention only if we are aware of the given conditions for action (these may also be political).

Let us consider a very simple example from Spinoza's own work, from his *Treatise on Theology and Politics.* It is useless to preach to people and admonish them to "be more rational". When human beings are victims of an accident, misfortune, hatred generated by the passions, they will never be rational. Rather, they will become superstitious, and then live in a world of fantasy and passions. A precarious life will make human beings less rational. If a human being wants to become more autonomous,—more able to run his or her own life—he or she must act differently and change his/her life conditions. Only in this way may human beings become more rational. The *Ethics* teaches us how we may control our destiny. According to the *Ethics* we can change all that which throws us into the reign of the passions and partly eliminate it.

How does Spinoza define a human being? We have already seen that a human being is a small "particula", a small part of an infinite order. So what follows from this? From this follows that our emotions, our actions, our behaviour, most of what happens in our lives and in human history, happens as a result of an encounter between us and that which surrounds us. Everything that happens is thus the outcome of an interaction between our essence and the essence of other things. But what is our essence or the essence of a human being? Let us read Spinoza: "Desire (*cupiditas*) is the very essence of man".... "Desire (*cupiditas*) is appetite (*Appetitus*) with the consciousness of itself. And appetite is the essence itself of man, insofar as it is determined to do what is useful for his preservation".[4] Striving is the essence of a human being, i.e., a human being is an animal that desires.

To understand what this definition entails, let us look at some aspects of Spinoza's philosophy of knowledge. Spinoza claims that there are three kinds of, or steps to, knowledge. The first is inadequate and false knowledge. He calls this imagination and it relates only to memory and vague and flighty impressions, when we know things as isolated and arbitrary. The second is rational knowledge, when we learn to see the proper relations between things through their common notions: Reason then, is a "common" domain, and only in this domain may human beings agree.

The third Spinoza calls intuitive knowledge, and this is the knowledge of singular things as a determinate expression of the infinite productive strength of the substance. Intuitive knowledge does not exclude reason, but is simply a form of knowledge that presupposes the two former kinds.

The three forms of knowledge are nothing but three stages of desire: The first is the slavery of the passions, the second is reason, a necessary, but not sufficient level and the last and highest stage, only for the sage, is intellectual love.

The first, inadequate knowledge, leads to vulgar impulses and egoism in a narrow sense. Morally, life is very poor: one's thoughts and actions revolve primarily around oneself. But the passions are not merely chaos; no matter how uncomfortable they may be, they are understandable. Even that which causes suffering has its own explanation. Therefore, the first step we must take is to understand that we are passive, for the passions are signs of our inevitable place in relation to the dominating powers of the universe. However, the passivity may partly be overcome.

Spinoza gives a very clear example: A child is surely more determined by external causes and less autonomous than an adult. But he or she grows up and becomes increasingly more able to rule him or herself, gradually leaving all the fantasies typical of childhood and becomes more rational. According to Spinoza it is thus not to be expected that the passions can be abolished; passions may, however, become transformed into affects, i.e., conditioned by adequate knowledge.

Thus the second level of our way of being and knowing, the second level of our striving or desire: reason. Reason is an instrument that enables us to understand the preconditions for the strengthening of our force to exist. Reason learns to use the most useful passions to strengthen the positive ones, the ones that help a person to express his or her own nature, and to work against the negative ones that imprison a person in loneliness, bitterness and hatred. Reason, in other words, manipulates the passions with a concern for social life. Reason does not limit the passions; reason uses the passions, or as Spinoza says, the affects.

This strategy of the affects has great political implications. However, Spinoza claims variation as being typically human: humans are able to pass from a certain state to a poorer or better state. When I pass into a poorer state, I do this because I am unable to tear myself away from negative passions—sadness, *tristitia*, Spinoza

[4] "appetitum autem esse ipsam hominis essentiam quatenus determinata est ad ea agendum quae ipsius conservationi inserviunt" (Eth.III, Affectum definitiones, Def.1 et explicatio).

calls them—that weaken and oppress me, such as melancholy, hatred, envy. All these emotions imprison me, while I need to be able to grow. The aim of the Spinozistic human being is not just self-preservation—as it is for Hobbes—it is "to grow". A human being (any human individual) is not just a cog in a machine, making itself as one with the machine. According to Spinoza the individual is a particular expression of the eternal substance, and his/her essence is "*potentia*", force, which is part of the strength of nature: "Man, insofar as he is part of nature, constitutes a part of the strength of nature".[5]

Many Spinozistic notions may be comparable to Hobbes' theories, but Spinoza develops other theses: Hobbes has been one of the most rigorous spokesmen for the absolute power of the state, Spinoza has been one of the most eager defenders of freedom of thought and speech and one of the first to claim that democracy is the best form of social and political organization. Behind this great difference lies an alternative view of human nature where "potentia"—strength—plays the most important role.

3 Conditions for Political Life: Conflict and Cooperation

Spinoza states that human beings should avoid negative emotions, individually as well as socially. To handle this problem from a political point of view, Spinoza starts from a critique of theological prejudices.

But why does Spinoza, in one and the same work, treat both theological and political problems? Spinoza recognized that religious and political phenomena have something in common. When he takes religion as his point of departure for his political reflection, Spinoza in a certain sense anticipates what will be the modern sociological problem, developed by Weber in particular: the relationship between the social practices and the religious and ethical ideas that attempted to explain the origin of political power. That is why, when Spinoza examines the conditions for social life, he first and foremost does it as a historian and sociologist. He emphasises that the state and religion both have their historical roots in the primitive and undifferentiated emotion of holiness, as this emerges, e.g. in the history of the Jewish people.

The most obvious and apparent consequence is that politics in modern society play the role that religion played in a traditional archaic society. The understanding of the state, its genesis, its history and its transformations requires a consideration of this crucial fact.

This is why Spinoza opens his political treatise with a focus on the emotions on which theocracy and political oppression are grounded. The most dangerous passions, the theological-political passions par excellence, are fear and hope. We are

[5] Homo quatenus pars est Naturae, eatenus partem potentiae Naturae constituit. (TTP, cap. IV, *Spinoza opera*. Im Auftrag der Heidelberger Akademie der Wissenschaften hrsg. von Carl Gebhardt. 4 vols, Heidelberg, Carl Winter-Verlag, 1925. v.3, p. 58).

used to considering fear as negative and hope as good, as a theological virtue or as a principle to help us survive. For Spinoza, however, fear and hope are just two sides of the same coin: both are passions characterised by future uncertainty. Hope is unstable joy waiting for a future good, fear is unstable sadness waiting for future evil. Hope and fear are characterised by being directed at objects or goods, the acquisition of which is always placed in the future.

This kind of passions causes a weakening of self-awareness and a feeling of insufficiency. Fear as a passion generates a special need for security, and thus plays an important part in the political and social sphere. So from a political point of view fear is the foundation, not just for the absolutism, but for almost every regime: one cannot rule unless one induces fear.

In Hobbes' political thinking fear has a "civilizing role". Fear plays a key role in the establishment of the power of the sovereign. According to Hobbes, individuals understand that if the violence of the state of nature continues, nobody is safe, and that it is better to establish institutions and rules to safeguard the individual. It is the fear of a violent death that drives an individual to accept rational behaviour and social choices (e.g. *pactum unionis* and *subjectionis*, i.e., social contract and contract of subjection).

But even after the social contract is established, fear is not eliminated, for only fear can force people to obey laws. "*Homo homini lupus*", man is a wolf for man; and social peace can only be upheld by a great wolf, the monarch (i.e., with terror and fear).

Spinoza disagrees strongly with all this for he knows that fear weakens human powers. Both philosophers define fear as an affective state like a varying sadness, but Spinoza claims that fear cannot be sublimated through an increase in rationality, neither individually nor politically. Fear—Spinoza continues—effects political relations twice: the fear felt by the masses, and the rulers' constant fear of the masses. In neither case does fear have a stabilising effect, for, even if fear may possibly lead to order and obedience in the short run, it will always lead to discontent and rebellion in the long run. Fear causes a very unstable emotional state that imprisons humans in a world of passing illusions.

From all this follows that human beings are unable to develop in a fear regime that furthers the power of the few, and strangles the life force of the others. Spinoza pits the expression "*Homo hominis Deus*" (Man is a God for man) against the Hobbesian motto. So what does all this mean? It means that the best we can do is to enrich our social life, the most important environment for human development. Spinoza is thus fundamentally in disagreement with "the melancholics", those who retreat into themselves and lead a lonely life, those who do not believe that living in society is worth their while.

So neither fear nor misanthropy will help, but neither will hope or the idea that human beings are able to radically change. The Spinozistic position does not coincide with the modern "homo ideologicus" who uses images and illusions to produce "rational myths" and a series of "industrial" desires unable to steer people in the direction of a "formal" reason. Here we see more clearly than ever the methodological influence from Machiavelli; we must start from the analysis of human nature as it really is: "la verità effettuale della cosa" "the real truth of a matter"[6] stating facts. But what does stating facts imply?

Stating facts implies that in order to understand human nature as it really is, we must also look at what takes place in human beings and that does not just depend on their force. Spinoza designates this area with the classical term of *"fortuna"*. What is *"fortuna"?* This is not the place for a reconstruction of the cultural genesis of the concept—and especially the influence from Quintus Curcius to Niccolò Machiavelli, which is in direct reference to Spinoza. Let us rather see how Spinoza defines the concept: "... by fortune I mean simply God's direction in so far as he directs human affairs through external and unexpected causes".[7] If we remind ourselves that "God's direction" (*Dei directio*) is nothing other than the order of nature, it becomes clear that "fortuna" is the order of external things; i.e., all the events with causes that do not depend on us: *"fortuna"* is, in other words, that which is not in our power, or that "which does not follow from our nature".[8] All that happens around us and in us, all that we experience, but is not in our power to control, this is *"fortuna*": our affects, our actions, our behaviour, most events in our existence and in human history. In front of this unexpected *"fortuna*", this form of necessity which we cannot know nor control in its entirety, and which appears before us as the face of contingency, can we do other than state what has already happened? Spinoza's whole authorship is built up around the purpose of creating a change in human behaviour as well as in the structure of society. The stating of facts becomes the basis for the development of operative strategies.

So stating facts means to take into consideration, simultaneously, human nature, i.e., human *potentia* or force to exist or act, and "fortuna", that which does not follow from our nature.

Human nature, or *conatus*, constitutes natural right. "Each individual thing has the sovereign right to do all that it can do; i.e., the right of the individual is coextensive with its determinate force (potentia)".[9] Everything an individual does is therefore ipso facto valid. And this is so, not just because there are no transcendental norms, but because the norm is in the individual himself and is the justification for everything he does.

Because of all this, a human individual's natural right (*jus naturale*)—disregarding religious and political organizations—is a behavioural rule which does not greatly distinguish itself from the physical laws which all natural things follow with unavoidable necessity. "By the right and established order of Nature I mean simply the rules governing the nature of every individual thing, according to which we conceive it as naturally determined to exist and to act in a definite way. For example, fish are determined by nature to swim, and the big ones to eat the smaller ones. Thus it is by sovereign natural right that fish inhabit water, and the big ones

[6] N. Machiavelli, *Il Principe* in *Tutte le opere, storiche, politiche e letterarie,* a cura di Alessandra Capata. Roma: Newton & Compton editori, 1998, p. 33.

[7] TTP, chap. III, G.3, p. 46.

[8] Eth. II, p. XLIX, sch. G.II, p. 136.

[9] TTP Chap.16, G.3, p 237.

eat the smaller ones. For it is certain that Nature, taken in the absolute sense, has the sovereign right (jus summum) to do all that she can do; that is, Nature's right is coextensive with her strength (potentia). For Nature's strength (potentia) is the very strength (potentia) of God, … But since the universal strength (potentia) of Nature as a whole is nothing but the force (potentia) of all individual things taken together, it follows that each individual thing has the sovereign right (jus summum) to do all that it can do; i.e., the right of the individual is co-extensive with its determinate force (potentia)".[10]

The natural right of the individual is a certain expression of the dynamic aspect of being. Natural right is therefore defined according to the degree of each individual's force (*potentia*) to feel or act in a certain manner, i.e., according to the success or failure of his or her striving for self-preservation. From this follows that an individual follows his or her own right at all times, his or her degree of perfection notwithstanding. Put differently, those who live under the rule of the passions follow the same necessary natural rules as those who live in accordance with the laws of reason, without there being a normative rule to show them another way to live, to convince them or to force them to follow another life norm. The human individual thus has a natural right that corresponds with the physical and intellectual force to exist, feel and act, which in all likelihood will come into conflict with the rights of others.

On the other hand, human beings must necessarily live in a web of relations that represent some sort of community. Spinoza makes this clear in a passage in chapter V of TTP that sums this up more clearly than other texts. Reduced to our own individual resources, we would be in a state of almost complete helplessness. The human body is in fact quite complex and in need of a lot of things in order to sustain itself. All the things we need, a great variety of things, are not immediately accessible in nature. They must be processed in order to be useful to us. One person alone would not have the time and strength to plough, to sow, to harvest, to mill, to cook, to weave, to do all that is necessary to live. In solitude we would be completely incapable to perform all the work life demands: quantitatively it would require much too much time, qualitatively the variation of work needed is much too great, and every human does not possess the necessary skills to perform all the necessary tasks. The most basic survival requires a division of labour, which, even on the poorest level, is a form of mutual cooperation (*mutua opera*).

According to Spinoza, human beings always have the potential for cooperation. The joining of an individual's physical and intellectual strength with that of others, i.e., the joining of an individual's natural rights with that of others, may help each individual to exercise and improve his or her own right.

Conflict and cooperation are preconditions for the political. There are—in human beings—as we stated through facts—negative passions that may lead individuals toward conflict, and positive affects that lead individuals toward cooperation. The whole problem of politics then becomes to unite human beings who are driven by these contradictory principles in such a way that they are best able to

[10] *Ibid.*

cooperate. This entails finding the mechanism that makes it possible to form a political body understood as a harmonious entity, and define forms, structures and rules for a peaceful and free society.

4 From Natural Right to Positive Right and Democracy

In the state of nature human beings thus have a right to all they will and can do. The right is identical with the immanent norms in the exercise of power. Right and reality coincide. But a human being is, in the state of nature, determined by passive emotions and not by active affects: "Thus the natural right of every man is determined not by sound reason, but by his desire and his force".[11] In the supposed state of nature individuals are therefore driven by the passions and this may antagonise them, a tendency which hinders cooperation. In fact, individuals in the state of nature do not live *sui juris* (based on their own rights), but as *alterius juris* (subjected to the power of others). Thus the state of nature is exposed as a state of slavery—a state where the individual's right and power are non-existent. The transition from the state of nature to the state of civil society in history is continuous.[12] This continuous transition consolidates the uniting of human powers and establishes conditions for peace and protection. Human beings are truly able to exercise their rights when living and working together, when they protect their land together so they can live on it and cultivate it. When they are related through mutual dependence, human beings can actively express their individual forces, *ex communi consensus* (by common consent), *una veluti mente* (as one mind).[13] The cooperation between individuals thus forms a *multitudinis potentia* (the strength of multitude)[14] of a social power. The concept of *multitude*, which is at the heart of current debates in political philosophy, has a famous father in Spinoza.

---

[11] "non sana ratione sed cupiditate et potentia determinatur" (TTP XVI, s.378; jfr. TP, II, 5).

[12] Here Spinoza breaks with traditional contract theory, even when using the concept of pact in TTP. The interpretation of Spinoza's relationship to contract theory is quite controversial. Exemplary of an anti-contract theory interpretation is Matheron, A. (1969) *Individu et communauté chez Spinoza*. Paris: Les Éditions de Minuit; Matheron (1990) *Le problème de l'évolution de Spinoza du TTP au TP*, in Edwin Curley & Pierre-François Moreau (red.) *Spinoza. Issues and directions. The Proceedings of the Chicago Spinoza Conference (1986)*. Leiden: E. J. Brill, pp. 258–270; Matheron "The theoretical function of democracy," in Bostrenghi, Daniela (ed.) (1988) *Hobbes e Spinoza: scienza e politica: atti del Convegno internazionale,* Urbino 14–17 ottobre, 1988. Naples: Bibliopolis. Published again in Lloyd, Genevieve (ed.) (2001) *Spinoza – Critical assessments of leading philosophers,* vol. III. London: Routledge. Among those who interpret Spinoza's political theory as contract theory: Giancotti, E. *Individuo e stato nelle prime teorizzazioni dello stato moderno: Hobbes e Spinoza a confronto,* pp. 12–25; (In: *Massa folla individuo,* ed. Alberto Burgio, Gian Mario Cazzaniga, Dominico Losurdo). Urbino: Quattro Venti, pp. 11–25.; Bobbio, Norberto (1979) *Il modello giusnaturalistico*, in Nobbio, N. & Bovero, Mario *Società e stato nella filosofia politica moderna*. Milano: Il Saggiatore.

[13] Ref. T P, II, pp. 13–15.

[14] TP, II, p. 17.

For Spinoza, the concept of the *multitude* means a real entirety of individualities, maintained through a series of positive actions and emotions without reducing this multitude to a unity. It is therefore the foundation of civil rights.

In his explanation of the foundations of civil society Spinoza revises Hobbes and contract theory. The transition from natural rights to civil right is not based on a voluntary decision, but is an *unavoidable necessity*.[15] Further, there is no way, in Spinoza's theory, to rescind power and freedom. Spinoza notes that as he upholds the natural right as it is, his position differs from Hobbes'. Hobbes builds his system on the alienation of natural right: the positive law abolishes natural right. In Spinoza, positive law is upheld to better guarantee natural right and exercise it rationally. Positive law is nothing but natural right which creates the conditions for its own expression.

For Spinoza does not transfer *multitudinis potentia* to a third party, Leviathan, the sovereign authority, through a contract of subjection: "When it comes to politics, the difference between me and Hobbes [...] is that "I continue to hold the natural right complete" and say that "the highest power (*summa potestas*) does not have a greater power over its citizens than that which the authorities have over its subjects".[16] The civil rights, which constitute the state, is the individual right itself exercised collegially: "Such a society's right is called a democracy, which can therefore be defined as the universal assembly of human beings which collegially possesses sovereign right over everything within its power" (coetus universus hominum, qui collegialiter summum jus ad omnia, quae potest, habent)".[17]

And it is this "democracy" which in its turn transfers, not its *potentia*, but the exercise of its power to the representative or representatives in order to express the common will to rule the community as one mind. In a democracy the majority expresses the common will: "...the democratic governance... seemed the most natural and the most closely to the freedom which nature grants to every man. For in a democratic state nobody transfers his natural right to another so completely that thereafter he is not to be consulted; he transfers it to the majority of the entire society of which he is part".[18]

This again distinguishes Spinoza from Hobbes: for Spinoza it is in fact both parties (multitude and power holder) who accept obligations and tasks. Hobbes' Leviathan is rather a perfect machine for obedience, and the subjects can only rebel if the sovereigns are unable to uphold security. Whereas for Spinoza the state has no more right over its citizens than what is given to the state by all citizen's power.

Absolute democratic power, which has yet to be realised in history, is the self-government of the associated and collaborating forces of all individuals, when "all of society, if possible, collegially must exercise power (*Imperium collegialiter*

[15] Ref. ETH. IV sch. II prop. XXXVII.

[16] Ep. 50, G. IV, pp. 238–39.

[17] TTP. XVI, G. 3, p. 241.

[18] TTP, XVI G.3, p. 243.

tenere debet), so that each and every one serves himself and nobody is obligated to serve their like".[19]

In any kind of society, also the most perfect, any sovereign authority will—as soon as it is established—ascertain the conditions for the moral distinction between transgression and obedience to the laws, justice and injustice,[20] and also demand that the pact be kept, with threats of punishment; which shows that transgressions lead to more harm than good.[21] But as we said, above, the transition to the state does not mean an actual loss of individual rights that were only usable in the state of nature. Firstly, the subjects do not transfer their pre-existing power; before the civil state they were not able to exercise their power individually. The natural state was, in fact, a state of powerlessness. Secondly, individuals only rescind what is truly transferable. No one may transfer their power (*potentia*) to others and thus their right in such a way that he or she rescinds being human. No one may transfer the right to judge, or be led to believe the opposite of what he or she thinks. Spinoza therefore insists on freedom of thought and speech, whereas Hobbes not only suggests, but acknowledges, censure of doctrines that may be a threat to the security of the state. According to Spinoza, security is not the only aim to be pursued in order that humans may live together and cooperate in conflict situations. Freedom is, in addition to security, the immanent purpose of a political state. The citizen's obedience to the state is, according to Hobbes, absolute and proportional to the security which the state guarantees. For Spinoza, such obedience requires that the state is rational (and the state is rational because all the citizens have participated in passing the laws) and that the state respects and facilitates the freedom of the citizens. To sum up, both philosophers speak of *multitude*, which is organised and becomes one; while the Hobbesian state *rules* the *multitudo*, the Spinozistic state rules *with* the *multitudo*, for the state and *multitudo* is one and the same.

Spinoza here gives a significant contribution to modern political thinking, as his reflection represents one of the first theoretisations on democracy.

In political life, democracy is the best means available to human beings—the passionate human beings—for winning a form of autonomy, almost in spite of themselves. The association of human beings is realised in a continuous process that expresses the development of reason, reason understood as freedom. Freedom is thus the first condition of and, at the same time, the aim of a democratic state.

5 Democracy and Freedom of Thought and Speech

Spinoza sees democracy as the basis of every form of governance because it is governance of the association of human beings, exercised by the association itself. Democracy is an absolute power because it is governed by a community and entails

[19] TTP, V, G.3, p. 130.

[20] Ref. Ethica, IV, 37 Scholium2 and P.T., pp. 18, 19 and 23.

[21] TTP, V, G.3, p.129 XVI, G.3 pp. 381–382.

common decisions wherein human reason expresses itself. As we said above, reason is a "common" domain for Spinoza: through reason alone may humans reach agreement and strengthen cooperation. Only in this common domain may natural right remain in the civil state.

Reason plays a double role in democracy. On the one hand reason works, as said, positively in social political life. In the democratic order a common reflected decision (*communi consensus decernitus*) and a common determination (*mens una*) are basic elements. But because a common agreement entails *all* people, and a common determination involves *all* parts of society, the capability to use one's judgment becomes a core element. Freedom of thought and freedom of speech, expressed in public open debate, thus have a constitutive role in Spinozistic democracy.

In the Spinozistic democratic state each individual citizen can change the organization of the state only through a process of consensual common decisions.

However, the individual citizen retains his or her own free judgment before and after the common decision, i.e., his/her human essence, which no human being can rescind. This freedom enables citizens to participate extensively in the political debate.

Reason is, on the other hand, a critical instance: Reason is the basis for the change and possible dissolution of the state when the state becomes a machine of oppression.

In fact, under a democratic regime, citizens may enjoy their freedom as long as the state maintains its objective, i.e., the welfare of its citizens, their freedom of thought and speech; in other words, as long as the state preserves its rational essence. When the highest authorities forget the true purpose of the state, they have established the conditions for their own abolition: "For if one abolishes the foundations, the whole building is easily destroyed".[22] Reason, which is an underlying force in the establishment of the free republic, becomes the driving force for change when conflicts arise between the rulers and the ruled.

Spinoza's democracy differs from Rousseau's democratic model, where rights are granted from above, where one says to people by decree "be happy", or "be equal", "be free". This is an important point in the history of culture and in general political philosophy. In Rousseau we see the triumph of the model of natural right, where each citizen transfers his freedom to the general will, to the state, in order to get it back wholly and be as free as before.

Spinoza does not start from such a transfer of the freedom of the citizen. He knows that no state will return freedom wholly to the individual citizen—if he/she does not have power—but will always retain some of this freedom. So the state does not emerge, for Spinoza, from the efforts of a small minority, as with the Jacobeans or the Bolshevik Party. Neither does the state emerge from the idea that individual freedom can come from above, as Robespierre said: "Three men can change the Republic".

We have said that, according to Spinoza, reason is both the foundation of society and a basis for a critique of society. Reason is a constructive force, but not a dominating

[22] TTP, cap XVI, G. 3, p. 194.

force. On the contrary, reason is a subversive force, a basis for change. This dynamic character is typical of Spinoza's concept of reason; the Spinozistic reason thus becomes a critical entity.

One must again emphasise that according to Spinoza a critique of reason is not some sort of lonely anarchist revolt. Reason is developed in a common public debate. In other words, a state is democratic when decisions are made in common, based on free rational debate.

Spinoza himself points to the basic problem inherent to this definition of democracy: only individuals think, where then is a common reason? Where and how may individuals think together? Spinoza was also very much aware of the difference between thinking and feeling! He saw very clearly the inherent danger in all this commonality, i.e., that the individuals, rather than *thinking* together, risk *feeling* together! The unreason at times displayed by people in political decisions may pose some disquieting questions in a democratic society. Is it not often the case that the people prefer dreams to a rational analysis of the true possibilities for social development? Rational analyses are frequently much too difficult and abstract. Very few people are able to walk the steep (*perardua*) path of reason. In other words: the power of reason is less than the power of emotions, and the latter rules most people. The questions which Spinoza poses are the same as Étienne de La Boétie already had asked himself, and that later surprised Jacques Necker: Why do people sacrifice their lives and own interests for the interests and ambitions of other individuals? Why do people accept the authority of others when this harms them more than it helps? Is it possible to develop a political strategy that is based on a reason nurtured by liberating passions and constructive images?

In the Spinozistic project we find the theoretical preconditions for establishing an order where the relation between reason and imagination becomes central, so that one can avoid falling victim to the external order of the passions: an order that otherwise may work on us like a blind force.

We have seen that according to Spinoza the emotions are a necessary and positive part of the structure of the mind. Genuine understanding of the productive force of the emotions thus becomes the starting point for their use as the source of freedom. Spinoza's historical-critical concept of reason is the new rational equipment for working with this structure.

Spinoza knows that prejudices have an almost unlimited influence on the human mind. He consequently spends the first part of TTP examining the most common prejudices with regard to religion as "the remnants of an old slavery" and examines prejudices related to a sovereign power's rights. Spinoza carries out a thorough historical-philological critique of the Bible to show how the Scripture's descriptive form and categorical structure are strongly influenced by the historical situation. Spinoza is not the first to historically-philologically analyze the Bible; this was already done by Lorenzo Valla, Erasmus, and Protestant interpreters of the Scriptures. He was not the first who connected philological criticism to political thought: Hobbes did this in the third part of Leviathan. But it was perhaps the first time that all this was done so consistently. In fact, the biblical text is interpreted in the light of Jewish people's culture, language and mentality: in this way, the Bible became a text like the others and was no longer considered sacred. From this premise, Spinoza shows that the Old Testament is a collection of writings with the purpose of regulating Jewish people's lives. The Bible's purpose is moral and the dogmas through which faith is expressed, have no theoretical significance. These principles are simple and common to all religions, and therefore, this should exclude religious conflicts. According to Spinoza, the meaning of religion is justice and charity, and this coincides with what reason itself investigates. People who are not able to realize their freedom through reason and intellect, can, by obedience to "true religion", produce in practice—in practical life—the same effects that people ruled by reason and intellect produce: a life directed by justice and charity. There is thus no contrast between philosophy and "the true religions": the one is based on truth and is autonomous, the others are based on authority and obedience, and are therefore heteronomous.

To understand the significance of Spinoza's analysis of religion it is necessary to recall the situation in the United Netherlands. This was a country where all faiths, not only Christian, were represented, and the main problem in the regulation of social life was the relation between religious authority and political authority. That is why Spinoza's political reflection focuses on the relation between the State and the religious authorities and on freedom of thought. This analysis has great political consequences. Firstly, this allows free philosophical research: the state should not interpret the Scriptures, only guarantee freedom. Not even the church/churches have authority in the interpretation of the Scriptures. Secondly, it is clear that the state cannot legitimately hinder freedom of thought. We must remember how the subtitle of the theological-political treatise explicitly states its purpose: not only to show that freedom of thought and speech does not disturb the peace of the state, but that they are necessary conditions for peace and order in the state.

May Spinoza's thinking be considered as a philosophy of tolerance? In the history of ideas of tolerance one often finds references to Spinoza as a theorist of tolerance. But there is something strange in the works of Spinoza, the concept of tolerance does not exist, or rather: Spinoza does not use this term when he discusses these problems. The concept of "*tolerantia*" occurs only once in the works[23] of Spinoza in TTP, c. XX, understood in its precise etymological meaning: the ability to bear or endure pain and adversity, the ability to withstand the vagaries of life, ability to withstand. He does not ascribe this ability to the state, but to the citizens. For Spinoza the problem was not what the state decides to permit, because permission is considered a lesser evil than the effects of oppression: that would have been a covert form of despotism. It was important for Spinoza to identify the rights that provide the foundations for the state, not what the state may or may not permit. The concept of tolerance is never used by Spinoza with reference to what the state—in this case the rulers (*Summa potestas*)—may permit, most likely because, from his theoretical point of view, the concept of tolerance was insufficient to express the relation between people and therefore insufficient as a foundation for a civil society

[23] Re. Mignini, F. (1991) "Spinoza oltre l'idea di tolleranza," in Sina, M. (ed.) *La tolleranza religiosa. Indagini storiche e riflessioni filosofiche*. Milan, pp. 163–197.

project. If modes and everything that exists as singular and definite things necessarily follow from the infinite substance, every existing thing has a right to exist simply because it exists. So as all that exists, including human beings, exists not only as body, but also as mind, it is clear that to recognize the right of others to diversity only means to recognize that the other exists, and that his/her existence entails the right to exist just as he or she is. So to be tolerant in relation to the diversity of others' thoughts or the diversity of others' faith has, for Spinoza, the same meaning as being tolerant to the fact that the other has either blue or dark eyes, because the others think and feel as they must think and feel based on the inner necessity of their nature. It is on this basis that Spinoza says that freedom of thought and of speech may not only be permitted, but "must be given".[24]

It is impossible and harmful to proscribe everything by law, Spinoza continues, and all that is not forbidden must necessarily be permitted.

Based on this principle it becomes possible to work out political strategies to establish the external conditions necessary to gain security and exercise freedom. Important in this respect is, as we have already seen, the establishment of the democratic society.

Spinoza's answer to the disquieting question posed to a democratic society is as follows: only in freedom (understood as freedom of speech and thought) may individuals develop their rational abilities and cooperation. Freedom of speech is thus a human right and the basis for a human political life, or, in brief, a human life.

Society is, according to Spinoza, not founded on a fear of death (as in Hobbes), but on reasonable choices in solidarity with others. If the individual wants security and respect for his or her own rights, he or she cannot at the same time deny other people this. In such a society the state cannot be an absolute power oppressing its citizens, but must be an institution to guarantee and defend the freedom of the citizens.

Thus the state has a special responsibility to guarantee and defend freedom of thought, the most important condition for developing the individual's abilities and establishing a society. Freedom of thought and speech is therefore, according to Spinoza, a necessity for the state. Without freedom of thought there is no civil right. Here it is not a matter of tolerance, but of right; freedom of thought and consequently freedom of faith refer to each individual's right, which cannot be rescinded when the social body is built. This freedom is the true purpose of the state.[25]

6 History of Reception and Critique

Spinoza's influence and his reception are very complex, having constituted a continuous, more or less underlying, contrasting leitmotif in the history of thought from his death until today. The history of the reception of Spinoza's thoughts

[24] TTP, XX, G.3, p. 247.

[25] ref. TTP, XX, G. 3, p. 241.

entails historical and theoretical assessments of enlightenment philosophy, idealism, materialism (a.o. Marxist materialism), and, in part, political theory in postmodern thinking.[26] Jonathan Israel's book *Radical Enlightenment* (Oxford University Press 2001) is fairly paradigmatic in this respect. Israel identifies the origin of the radical enlightenment in 1650, when Spinoza cleared the way for theoretical and political enlightenment thinking in all of Europe: radical critique of religion, church, state, interpretation of the Holy Scriptures in the materialistic sense, attacks on European monarchies and acceptance of a radical democracy. Spinoza's thinking is, however, not easily susceptible to "classification", or reduction to a certain tradition. As a result, his political thinking has gone through a long series of partly contrasting interpretations, presenting Spinoza both as a contract theorist and not as a liberal or a proto-revolution theorist, etc. Spinoza's political thinking has not always received the attention it deserves, and he is frequently not included in canons of political doctrines. (See e.g.: George H. Sabine, *A History of Political Theory*, 1937.) However, we must remember the happy exception of Guido Fassò who, in his history of the philosophy of law (Fassò, 1966), devotes a chapter to Spinoza. Only from the second half of the twentieth century did the renewal of the study of Spinoza in France contribute to a focus on his political thinking.

In a discussion about the reception of his political philosophy, it is necessary to remember that for Spinoza politics is closely related to ontology, or as André Tosel said "Ontology becomes politics and politics is revealed as ontology" (Tosel 1984, p. 274), and the reception history of Spinoza's political philosophy is tied up with the interpretation of his ontology.

The reception may roughly be divided into three phases. The first phase is from the publication of his works to the so-called "Spinozismusstreit", a second phase influenced by the need to read his thinking in reliable texts, and finally a new beginning for the study of Spinoza from the end of the First World War up until today.

The first phase is characterised by a—we may say hidden, but nonetheless strong—presence of Spinoza's teachings in philosophical debates. The real problem with this reception is its approach. On the one side, we find the critics of Spinoza who see his doctrine as a threat to Christian thinking; on the other, the ones who make use of his ideas without naming him.

Spinoza's ideas became known during his lifetime in a small cultural circle from the beginning of the 1660s in the United Netherlands. During his own lifetime he developed a reputation for being an atheist and materialist (ref. Spinoza's correspondence).

Opera posthuma, published with only the initials (BdS), and initially widely available, later became a rare bibliographic object, even if the books are found listed in the inventories of some collections in private libraries. The work was never published again until the 1700s, and Boulainvilliers' translation from 1710 had a limited distribution. One may in fact count on one's fingers the authors who show a

[26] We must here give only a very short and somewhat superficial sketch of all this. A good introduction may be found in Garrett (1996).

thorough and accurate knowledge of Spinoza's texts. So how did the teachings of Spinoza spread from his death and to Romanticism? What was Spinoza's thought as referred to by the Spinozistic enlightenment philosophers—the famous radical enlightenment philosophers? Spinozism spread in two ways: on the one hand, thanks to the polemicists who used Pierre Bayle's ambiguous presentation in his *Dictionnaire*: Spinoza as atheist and anti-Christian. An atheistic teacher, the virtuous atheist, all the more dangerous as he was an example of a moral life in no need of Christianity. On the other hand, Spinoza's philosophy spread after his death thanks to a whole set of secret heterodox and illegal literature taking him as a source of inspiration for new ideas on deism or "atheism" (and "pantheism", at that time frequently used as a synonym for atheism) [*La Vie et l'Esprit de Mr. Benoit de Spinoza* (Life and Teachings of Mr Benedict Spinoza, 1719), later published under the title *Traité des Trois imposteurs* and *Symbolum Sapientiae* or *Cymbalum Mundi*].

Polemical texts with refutations are published all over Europe. Spinozistic atheism, materialism and determinism was refuted by S. Clarke (1705–1706) and by the freethinker J. Toland (1704) in Great Britain. In 1731 three works were published in one volume in France: *Réfutation des erreurs de B. de Spinoza.* One of these is the false refutation by Henri de Boulainvilliers. Boulainvilliers does not actually criticize Spinoza but gives an account of Spinoza's text. Boulainvilliers was one of the few who had directly studied the works of the Dutch philosopher. His *Essai de metaphysique* (1731) was, according to P. Vernière, "the breviary of Spinozism of the eighteenth century" and was later used as a source by Voltaire and Diderot. Through these heterodox texts Spinoza's ideas implemented what Margaret Jacob and Jonathan Israel call the radical enlightenment.[27]

In the second half of the eighteenth century the so-called neo-Spinozists found inspiration in some of Spinoza's theses. Faced with new scientific discoveries and new political events, Julien Offray de La Mettrie (1709–1751), Pierre Louis Moreau de Maupertuis (1698–1759), Denis Diderot (1713–1784) and Paul Henri d'Holbach (1723–1789) developed their materialist theories from the conceptual frame of the *Ethics.*

We must nevertheless emphasise that no one (not even those most influenced by Spinoza's thinking) openly acknowledged being Spinozistic, although many were accused of being so.

The refutation of Spinoza's teachings dominated in Germany (see *Scriptorum Anti-Spinozianorum* from 1710 and Trinius, in *Freydenkerlexicon* (1759) which provides an estimate of 129 enemies). According to German enlightenment philosophers such as Leibniz (1646–1716), Christian Wolff (1679–1754), Christian Thomas (1655–1728), Andreas Rüdiger (1673–1731) and Christian August Crusius (1715–1775), Spinoza is a threat due to his atheism, which again is a consequence of his speculative rational method.

---

[27] Jacob, Margaret (1981) *The Radical Enlightenment: Pantheists, Freemasons and Republicans.* London/Boston; Israel, Jonathan (2001) *Radical Enlightenment: Philosophy and the Making of Modernity 1650–1750.* Oxford.

The year 1785 represents a turn in the reception of Spinoza: the first public debate on Spinoza's teachings took place and Friedrich Heinrich Jacobi (1743–1819) publishes *Über die Lehre des Spinoza Briefen an der Herrn Moses Mendelssohn.* The book opened a debate on Spinozism that strengthened the pantheistic tendency that already animated the new post-enlightenment era in Germany, from Schiller and Schleiermacher to Goethe.

It should be noted that even though Spinoza's teachings are finally openly debated, and many acknowledge being Spinozistic, Spinoza's ideas are used to develop a whole new philosophy: The German idealist spirit of nature philosophy. The period from 1780 and the first part of the 1800s is possibly the period with the most intense studies related to the philosophy of Spinoza, as it involves all the great German philosophers, from Hegel to Schelling, from Schopenhauer and Feuerbach to Marx and Nietzsche. In the wake of Hegel, Spinoza is read as a great metaphysician, the philosopher of the infinite and indefinite substance, and the things and variety disappear and become reduced to a state of illusion. However, only the parts of Spinoza's texts that better explained the new philosophy were read, namely parts I and II of *Ethica*. So, more or less consciously, these readers fail to mention the three-quarters of his works devoted to human passions, society and politics. This tendency is even today dominant in some of the secondary literature. We must, however, also remember that the great interpretation problem in relation to Spinoza's ontology is met with strictness and precision. The need for a more correct historical and philological analysis of Spinoza's work subjects his writing to textual criticism. At the end of the nineteenth century *The Short Treatise on God, Man and its wellness* was discovered. This period sees the publication of the two most complete editions of Spinoza's work (van Vloten and Land 1883; Carl Gebhardt 1925). This great historical and concept-analytical work provides the foundations for later studies that again spark the contemporary Spinoza renaissance. The thinkers of the 1900s also engaged with Spinoza's philosophy, thanks to a significant improvement in historical studies: see e.g. Wolfson's *The Philosophy of Spinoza* (1934) and L. Robinson's *Kommentar zur Spinozas Ethik* (1928), P. Vernière, *Spinoza et la pensée française avant la Révolution* (the reception of Spinoza before the French Revolution, 1954), the numerous articles by E. M. Curley, Y. Yovel's *Spinoza and other Heretics* (1989), and *Lexicon Spinozanum* edited by E. Giancotti. New, robust philosophical interpretations emerge in the 1960s, particularly in France. The new reading of Spinoza is developed in the philosophical context of structuralism and its crisis. In 1961, M. Gueroult published his structuralist analysis of the first and second part of the Ethics: *Spinoza Dieu* (1961) and *Spinoza L'Âme* (1974). The book will influence many later works. Even Althusser acknowledges that Spinoza's philosophy played a fundamental role in the development of his later theories, and he participates, with Deleuze, in the great French—Italian new interpretation of Spinoza's philosophy in a Marxist view. Althusser's contribution to the interpretation of Spinoza influenced the works of G. Deleuze: *Spinoza et le problem de l'expression* (1968), A. Matheron's *Individu et communauté chez Spinoza* (1968), E. Balibar's work on the transindividual in Spinoza, and Antonio Negri's *L'anomalia selvaggia*, where the key concept is multitude, to become the principle of a new form of political life.

Bibliography

Recommended Further Reading

The works of Spinoza, translations, encyclopediae and bibliography

Akkerman, F. (1977). *Spinoza's tekort aan woorden: humanistische aspecten van zijn schrijverschap*. Leiden: Brill.
Bartuschat, W. (1977). Neuere Spinoza-Literatur. *Philosophische Rundschau*, 24 (1977), 1–44.
Baruch de Spinoza *Sämtliche Werke*. Hamburg: Felix Meiner Verlag, 1976.
Baruch de Spinoza *Obras Completas*, I-V Prologada por Abraham J. Weiss y Gregorio Winberg. Tradocciones.
Baruch de Spinoza *Opera*. Lateinisch-deutsch. Darmstadt: Wissenschaftliche Buchgesellschaft, 1979 und 1980 (Zweite, unveränderte Auflage: Wissenschaftliche Buchgesellschaft, Darmstadt 1989).
Benedicti de Spinoza. (1802). *Opera Quae Supersunt Omnia* (H. E. G. Paulus, Ed., 2 vols.). Jena.
Benedicti de Spinoza. (1882–1883). *Opera* (J. van Vloten & J. P. N. Land, Eds., 2 vols.). The Hague. (Reprinted 1895, 1914)
Boucher, W. I. (1999). *Spinoza in English: A bibliography from the seventeenth century to the present* (2nd ed.). London, New York: Thoemmes Press.
Bulletin de bibliographie spinoziste, rédigé par le Groupe de Recherches Spinozistes (CNRS/ CERPHI) en collaboration avec l'*Association des Amis de Spinoza depuis 1979.*
Crapulli, G., & Giancotti Boscherini, E. (1969). *Ricerche lessicali su opere di Descartes e Spinoza*. Roma: Ed. dell'Ateneo.
Œuvres de Spinoza Traduit et annoté par Charles Appuhn (4 vols.). Paris: Garnier, 1964.
Fassò, G. (1966). *Storia della filosofia del diritto*. Bari: Laterza.
Giancotti Boscherini, E. (Ed.). (1970). *Lexicon Spinozanum* (2 vols.). La Haye: Nijhoff.
Gueret, M., Robinet, A., & Tombeur, P. (1977). *Spinoza Ethica: Concordances, Index, Listes de fréquences, Tables comparatives*. Louvain-la-Neuve: CETEDOC Université Catholique de Louvain.
Kajanto, I. (2005). *Spinoza's latinity*. Leiden: Brill.
Næss, A. (1970). *Equivalent terms and notions in Spinoza's ethics*. Oslo: Inquiry, Filosofisk Institutt, Universitet i Oslo.
Préposiet, J. (1973). *Bibliographie Spinoziste*. Paris: Belles-Lettres.
Santinelli, C. (1983). *Spinoza in Italia. Bibliografia degli scritti italiani su Spinoza dal 1675 al 1982*. Urbino: Università degli studi di Urbino.
Spinoza. (1999). *Œuvres* (Pierre-François Moreau, Ed., 5 vols.). Paris: Presses Universitaires de France (An excellent bilingual critical edition with French translation).
Spinoza. (2007). *Opere*, a cura e con un saggio introduttivo di Filippo Mignini, trad. e note di Filippo Mignini e Omero Proietti. Milano: Arnoldo Mondadori Editore, I Meridani – Classici dello Spirito.
Spinoza. (2010). *Tutte le opere, testi originali a fronte*, red. A. Sangiacomo. Milano: Bompiani, "Il Pensiero Occidentale".
Spinoza Opera. (1925). Im Auftrag der Heidelberger Akademie der Wissenschaften hrsg. von Carl Gebhardt (4 vols.). Heidelberg: Carl Winter-Verlag.
Spinoza: Complete works (S. Shirley, Trans. and M. Morgan, Ed.). Indianapolis: Hackett, 2002.
The collected writings of Spinoza. Princeton: Princeton University Press, 1985.
Totaro, G., & Veneziani, M. (1993). Indici e concordanze del Tractatus theolocico-politicus di Spinoza. *Lexicon philosophicum, 6*, 51–193.
Wetlesen, J. (1968). *A Spinoza bibliography*. Oslo: Universitetsforlaget.
Wetlesen, J. (1974). *Internal guide to the ethics of Spinoza*. Oslo: University of Oslo.

About Spinoza

Note: There is a huge bibliography on Spinoza in many languages, especially French, Italian, Dutch, English and German. This is a very selective list of books.

Biographies

Dunin-Borkowski, S. (1910). *Der junge De Spinoza. Leben und Werdegang im Lichte der Weltphilosophie*. Münster: Aschendorff. 2. Aufl. 1933.
Freudenthal, F. (1904). *Spinoza, Sein Leben und Seine Lehre*. Stuttgart: F. Fromman.
Nadler, S. (1999). *Spinoza: A life*. Cambridge/New York: Cambridge University Press.
Pollock, F. (1880). *Spinoza, his life and philosophy*. London: C. Kegan Paul.

General works on Spinoza's philosophy – Miscellanies

Althusser, L. (1993). L'unique tradition matérialiste. In J. Baudrillard, L. Altusser, et al. (Eds.), *Logiques du capitalisme*. Paris: Hazan.
Balibar, E., Seidel, E., & Walther, M. (Hrsg./Eds.). (1994). *Freiheit und Notwendigkeit*. Würzburg: Königshausen & Neumann.
Bend, J[ohannes] G[erit] van der (Hrsg./Ed.). (1974). *Spinoza on knowing, being and freedom*. Assen: Van Gorcum.
Garrett, D. (Ed.). (1996). *The Cambridge companion to Spinoza*. Cambridge/New York: Cambridge University Press.
Giancotti Boscherini, E. (a cura di) *Spinoza* I. Agora, n° 2/3-2003.
Montag, W., & Stolze, T. (Eds.). (1997). *The new Spinoza. Theory out of bounds*. Minneapolis: University of Minnesota Press.
Moreau, P. F. (Hrsg./Ed.). (1996). Architectures de la raison. Fontenay/Saint-Cloud: ENS Éditions.
Spinoza nel 350. Centenario della nascita Atti del Congresso internazionale di Urbino 4-8 ottobre 1982, a cura di E. Napoli: Bibliopolis, 1985.
Wetlesen, J. (Ed.). (1978). *Spinoza's philosophy of man*. In Proceeding of the Scandinavian Spinoza symposium (1977). Oslo.

Studies

Deleuze, G. (1968). *Spinoza et le problème de l'expression*. Paris: Les Éditions de Minuit.
Deleuze, G. (1981). *Spinoza – Philosophie pratique*. Paris: Les Éditions de Minuit.
Gueroult, M. (1968). *Spinoza*. I. *Dieu* (Ethique, I). Paris: Aubier-Montaigne.
Gueroult, M. (1974). *Spinoza*. II. *L'âme* (Ethique, II). Paris: Aubier-Montaigne.
Hubbeling, H. G. (1964). *Spinoza's methodology*. Assen: Van Gorcum.
Lloyd, G. (1996). *Spinoza and the ethics*. London: Routledge.
Macherey, P. (1977). *Hegel ou Spinoza*. Paris: Maspero.
Misrahi, R. (1972). *le Désir et la réflexion dans la philosophie de Spinoza*. Paris/London/New York: Gordon & Breach.
Montag, W. (2002). *Bodies, masses, power: Spinoza and his contemporaries*. London: Verso.
Moreau, P. F. (1971). *Spinoza et le spinozisme*. Paris: P. U. F., coll. "Que sais-je ?".
Moreau, P. F. (1975). *Spinoza*. Paris: Éditions du Seuil.
Næss, A. (1999). *Det frie menneske: en innføring i Spinozas filosofi*. Oslo: Kagge.
Scruton, R. (1986). *Spinoza: A very short introduction*. Oxford: Oxford University Press.

Vernière, P. (1954). *Spinoza et la pensée française avant la Révolution* (2 vols.). Paris: P. U. F.
Wetlesen, J. (1979). *The sage and the way: Spinoza's ethics of freedom.* Assen: Van Gorkum.
Wolfson, H. A. (1934). *The philosophy of Spinoza* (2 vols.). Cambridge, MA: Harvard University Press.
Zac, S. (1963). *L'Idée de vie dans la philosophie de Spinoza.* Paris: P. U. F.
Zac, S. (1965). *Spinoza et l'interprétation de l'Écriture.* Paris: P. U. F.
Zac, S. (1996). The relation between life, conatus, and virtue in Spinoza's philosophy. *Graduate Faculty Philosophy Journal, 19*(1), 151–173.

On Spinoza's political thinking

Balibar, E. (1998). *Spinoza and politics.* London: Verso.
Balibar, E., Seidel, H., & Walther, M. (Special Editorial Team). (1993). *Studia Spinozana, Spinoza and modernity: Ethics and politics* (Vol. 9). Würzburg: Königshausen & Neumann.
Bartuschat, W. (1984). *The ontological basis of Spinoza's theory of politics.* Amsterdam: North Holland Publishing Company.
Belaief, G. (1971). *Spinoza's philosophy of law.* The Hague/Paris: Mouton.
Bostrenghi, D. (a cura di). (1992). *Hobbes e Spinoza, Scienza e politica,* Introd. by E. G. Boscherini. Napoli: Bibliopolis.
De Cuzzani, P. (2003). 'Imaginatio' og demokrati hos Spinoza. *Agora,* (2/3).
Den Uyl, D. (1983a). *Power, state and freedom: An interpretation of Spinoza's political philosophy.* Assen: Van Gorcum.
Giancotti, E., Matheron, A., & Walther, M. (Special Editorial Team). (1985). *Studia Spinozana, Spinoza's philosophy of society* (Vol. 1). Alling: Walther & Walther/Verlag Königshausen & Neumann.
Gianini, H., Moreau, P. F., & Vermeren, P. (Hrsg./Eds.). (1997). *Spinoza et la politique.* Paris: L'Harmattan.
Levene, K. N. (2004). *Spinoza's revelation: Religion, democracy, and reason.* Cambridge, MA: Cambridge University Press.
Matheron, A. (1969). *Individu et communauté chez Spinoza.* Paris: Éd. de Minuit.
Matheron, A. (1971). *le Christ et le salut des ignorants chez Spinoza.* Paris: Aubier-Montaigne.
Matheron, A. (1988). The theoretical function of democracy. In D. Bostrenghi (Ed.), *Hobbes e Spinoza, Scienza e politica: Atti del Convegno internazionale,* Urbino 14–17 ottobre, 1988. Napoli: Bibliopolis. New edition in Lloyd Genevieve (Ed.). (2001). *Spinoza – Critical assessments of leading philosophers* (Vol. III). London: Routledge.
McShea, R. J. (1968). *The political philosophy of Spinoza.* New York: Columbia University.
Negri, A. (1981). *L'anomalia selvaggia saggio su potere e potenza in Baruch Spinoza.* Milano: Feltrinelli (english translation: The savage anomaly).
Negri, A. (1998). *Spinoza sovversivo: variazioni (in) attuali,* Introd. by Emilia Giancotti. Roma: A. Pellicani, rist. in "Spinoza"/Derive Approdi.
Tosel, A. (1984). *Spinoza ou le crépuscule de la servitude.* Paris: Aubier.

Literature

In addition to the list of literature in Paola De Cuzzani "Conatus, individuo, modo in Spinoza" (PhD dissertation), University of Genova, Italy, 1982, s.250–270, see:

Balibar, E. (1985). *Jus, pactum, lex in Studia Spinozana I,* republished in Montag, Warren & Stolze, Ted (1997) *The new Spinoza.* Minneapolis: University of Minnesota Press.
Bodei, R. (1991). *Geometria delle passioni. Paura, speranza e felicità: filosofia e uso politico.* Milano: Feltrinelli.

Curley, E. (1996). Kissinger, Spinoza and Gengis Khan. In D. Garrett (Ed.), *The Cambridge companion to Spinoza*. Cambridge: Cambridge University Press.
De Cuzzani, P. (1987). La pace tra *potentia e potestas:* strutture sociali e strutture economiche nel 'Tractatus theologico-politicus' di Spinoza. in: "I filosofi e la pace". In *Atti del V Convegno tra studiosi di Filosofia Morale in memoria di R. Crippa* (Sanremo 15 dicembre 1984). Genova: E.C.I.G.
De Cuzzani, P. (1999). Essence et existence dans la Pensées de Spinoza. In *Actes du Congrès de l'ASPLF*, n° XXVII. Quebec/Paris: Les Presses de l'Université Laval/Librairie philosophique Vrin.
De Cuzzani, P. (2001). Fornufts arbeid i skyggen av kjærlighet. Spinoza og 'amor erga foeminam'. *Norsk filosofisk tidsskrift,* (4).
De Cuzzani, P. (2002). Une anthropologie de l'homme décentré. *Philosophique,* (1).
De Cuzzani, P. (2003). 'Imaginatio' og demokrati hos Spinoza. *Agora,* (2/3).
Den Uyl, D. (1983b). *Power, state and freedom*. Assen: Van Gorcum.
Goetschel, W. (2004). *Mendelssohn, Lessing, and Heine*. Madison: University of Wisconsin Press.
Morfino, V. (2002). *Il tempo e l'occasione. L'incontro Spinoza Machiavelli*. Milano: LED.
Negri, A. (1981). *L'anomalia selvaggia. Saggio su potere e potenza in Baruch Spinoza*. Milano: Feltrinelli.
Negri, A. (1992). *Spinoza sovversivo*. Roma: Pellicani.
Tosel, A. (1984). *Spinoza ou le crepuscule de la servitude*. Paris: Aubier-Montaigne.
Zac, S. (1964). État et nature chez Spinoza. *Revue de Métaphysique et de Morale*, 14–40.

Ibn Khaldun: Law and Justice in the Science of Civilisation

Lars Gule

1 Introduction

Islam and law are inextricably intertwined, and the law is religious law—*shari'a*. Thus, the study of law—*fiqh*—became a theological discipline. The concept of justice within the Islamic tradition is also indivisibly connected to revelation and the religious law. The philosophers within the Islamic tradition who explored justice have started from these premises. Therefore, the major classical divisions of philosophy do not easily fit the way these philosophers approached the subject of law and justice. Nevertheless, it is possible to have a closer look at these concepts from a philosophical perspective. The aim of this paper is to do so through a study of the position(s) of Ibn Khaldun (1332–1406).

Ibn Khaldun should be counted among the important thinkers in historiography and the social sciences. Within his grand theory of the rise and fall of civilisations in his major work, *al-Muqaddima*, there are also a political theory and theories of law and justice. His ideas deserve scrutiny because his work is not yet presented in the standard philosophy and sociology curricula of Western universities. Yet, Ibn Khaldun's ideas are important in the history of philosophy and ideas.

The lack of common knowledge about him justifies a brief presentation here of the main facts of Ibn Khaldun's life. His full name was Wali al-Din 'Abd al-Rahman ibn Muhammad ibn Muhammad ibn Abi Bakr Muhammad ibn al-Hasan ibn Khaldun. His ancestors had settled in Seville in Spain in the ninth century CE. Under threat from the Christian *reconquista*, the family emigrated from that city to North Africa in the thirteenth century and finally settled in Tunis in Ifriqiya where Wali al-Din 'Abd al-Rahman was born in 1332. His grandfather and father both held important posts in the government of the Hafsid dynasty that ruled in the region from 1228 through 1574.

L. Gule (✉)
Department of International Studies and Interpreting, Oslo and Akershus University College of Applied Science, Oslo, Norway
e-mail: lars.gule@hioa.no

G. Fløistad (ed.), *Philosophy of Justice*, Contemporary Philosophy: A New Survey 12,
DOI 10.1007/978-94-017-9175-5_8, © Springer Science+Business Media Dordrecht 2015

Ibn Khaldun had a very comprehensive education in Tunis and later in Fez (in present day Morocco). It included religious sciences, comprising the Qur'an, the traditions (*hadith*) approved by the Maliki school, dialectical theology (*'ilm al-kalam*), jurisprudence (*fiqh*), and mysticism (Sufism); and the philosophical disciplines, comprising logic, mathematics, natural philosophy, metaphysics, and politics, including ethics and rhetoric. In addition, he received practical training for government service.

Ibn Khaldun was early drawn into political life and intrigue. At the age of 25, he was imprisoned for his suspected participation in a plot against the ruler in Fez. Shortly afterward he was on the winning side and this started a long career as a politician and diplomat. He was often used on delicate diplomatic missions and saw the changing fortunes of dynasties and kingdoms from both sides. In 1375, he withdrew from active politics and diplomacy, maybe because he was in a precarious position at the time, and sought refuge in the desert castle Qal'at Ibn Salama (in present-day Algeria). Here he spent the next years writing on his world history, of which *al-Muqaddima*, meaning prolegomena, is the introduction and the first book, and in November 1377, as he wrote in his autobiography, he finished the introduction. We know that it took several more years to complete the whole work and that it underwent numerous revisions and changes throughout the rest of his life.

In 1382, Ibn Khaldun left western North Africa and settled in Cairo, but although he tried to escape the dangers of active politics by leaving the Maghreb and concentrating on research and teaching, he did not manage to stay out of political intrigues. He was appointed grand judge or *Qadi* of the Maliki *madhhab* (school of jurisprudence) in Egypt several times, but also deposed almost as often. Thus, he had a practical experience with the administration of justice even if we cannot see these experiences reflected in the *Muqaddima*. We must also assume that his work as a teacher and judge in Cairo for more than 20 years resulted in some writings, not least *fatwa*s, i.e., theological-juridical opinions. However, these works are not known, but he wrote about his experiences as a judge in his autobiography. Since he did not mention his legal opinions in this book, he might have seen them as not relevant as theoretical works.

Toward the end of his life, he was taken by the Egyptian sultan on a campaign against the invading army of Tamerlane (Timur Lenk) in 1401, but was left in the besieged city of Damascus. He met with Tamerlane and negotiated with him, but was unable to save the city from being sacked. Ibn Khaldun managed to obtain a safe conduct and could return to Egypt where he spent the last years of his life until his death in 1406.

2 *Al-Muqaddima*—Central Concepts

The tumultuous life of Ibn Khaldun, as well as the observable decline of culture in North Africa, was obviously an important source of inspiration for the writing of the *Muqaddima*. The basic cyclical theory of history it contains is "brilliantly simple,"[1]

[1] Flew, Antony (ed.) (1979) *A Dictionary of Philosophy*. London: Pan Books, p. 148.

and based on a dialectic between desert and city. Humankind is divided into two parts: the primitive (i.e., original) and nomadic or Bedouin—*'umran badawi*—on the one hand, and the civilised and settled—*'umran hadari*—on the other. The first precedes and produces the other as the nomads become settled and civilised, and develop to the peak of culture or, rather, civilisation—*'umran*. However, in the process the Bedouin virtues, which established civilisation in the first place, become corrupted by the luxury and power caused by the very same process of civilisation. This weakens the ruling dynasty and the whole civilisation, and thus clears the way for a new dynasty to establish power and a new civilisation.

The word *muqaddima* is a technical term with the meaning "premise", but it is usually translated with "introduction" or "prolegomenon". *Al-Muqaddima* is an introduction to the greater work of world history Ibn Khaldun wrote, *Kitab al-'Ibar*, the Book of History. Ibn Khaldun originally divided *Kitab al-'Ibar* into an introduction and three books. The original introduction together with book one has become known as *al-Muqaddima*, a comprehensive work in its own right.[2]

In *al-Muqaddima*, Ibn Khaldun developed his argument according to a stringent plan and logical structure. Thus, his new science of civilisation relies on the presentation of several basic premises or fundamental principles—*muqaddimat*—from which we can draw knowledge in order to understand the unfolding of history proper, i.e., historical narrations. In his approach, Ibn Khaldun is (also) utilising a method where he is not discussing causes in a modern sense (efficient causes), but borrowing from legal reasoning notions about causes or reasons in his discussion of causes of social change.

Ibn Khaldun recognised only a few of his predecessors as real historians. Many of them were just imitators in the field of universal history, and they have not sought the causes of events. However, he insisted on the originality of his own endeavour:

> I followed an unusual method of arrangement and division into chapters. From the various possibilities, I chose a remarkable and original method. In the work, I commented on civilization, on urbanization, and on the essential characteristics of human social organization, in a way that explains to the reader how and why things are as they are, and shows him how the men who constituted a dynasty first came upon the historical scene. As a result, he will wash his hands of any blind trust in tradition. He will become aware of the conditions of periods and races that were before his time and that will obtain thereafter.[3]

The last sentence gives a clear indication of Ibn Khaldun's belief in the universal nature of the causes that rule history. History as a science is about the principles of politics, the true nature of existing things, and the differences among nations, places, and periods with regard to ways of life, character qualities, customs, sects, schools, and everything else.[4] But most important, the historian "must compare similarities

[2] Many translations into different languages exist. The quotations in this chapter are from Ibn Khaldun, *Al-Muqaddimah* (trans. by Franz Rosenthal, ed. and abridged by N. J. Dawood), Princeton: Princeton University Press, 1969/5th printing 1981.

[3] Ibn Khaldun, *Al-Muqaddimah*, p. 8.

[4] *Ibid*, p. 24.

or differences between present and past conditions. He must know the causes of the similarities in certain cases and of the differences in others."[5]

Ibn Khaldun calls the new science he founded *'ilm al-'umran. 'Ilm* is sciences or knowledge. *'Umran* is translated both as civilisation and culture. "Organised habitation" perhaps best translates the word. The Arabic word derives from a root that means "to build up" or "to develop." Ibn Khaldun even uses the term with the further meaning of "population." "When a social organization grows more populous, a larger and better *'umran* results."[6] In Arabic, the word has a rich etymology and rich associations in lexicography and geography, "all of which can be reducible to the generality of the opposition between emptiness and its antonym, *'umran*."[7] The two main forms of organised habitation are found in the desert and small villages, among the nomads, and in the towns and cities, among the sedentary population. They represent importantly different cultures or forms of civilisation, i.e., *'umran badawi* and *'umran hadari.*

However, according to the Syrian-British philosopher and sociologist Aziz Al-Azmeh, the state is the primary object of study in the *Muqaddima* because, "in order to be meaningful, organized habitation has to be placed within the semantic field of the state."[8] This is also, why law and justice are important. The focus on the dynasty, furthermore, connects Ibn Khaldun's writing to prior Islamic historiographies, whose subject matter was the dynasties. Ibn Khaldun's term, indeed the Arabic term, for state is *dawla*, which also means "dynasty". A state only exists as a dynasty, or the persons that it consists of and that hold it together. When the dynasty disappears, the state also collapses because the two are coextensive.

The central explanatory concept of the *Muqaddima*, however, is *'asabiya*. This is also a concept that is difficult to translate. It has been rendered as 'group feeling'. Others use 'social cohesion'. It is related to *'asaba*, which also means paternal relatives. The content of the concept could then be explained as making common cause with one's (paternal) relatives. The term *'asabiya* had been much used in Muslim literature before Ibn Khaldun's times but in a negative sense. It was usually condemned as the blind support for the cause of one's own group, without regard for the justice of this cause. Therefore, *'asabiya* was seen as a manifestation of a pre-Islamic mentality. Ibn Khaldun was aware of this usage and condemns this form of *'asabiya*. However, in his transformation of the idea to a more descriptive but also positive explanatory concept, Ibn Khaldun seems to connect the term with the related *'isaba* and the Qur'anic *'usaba*, both meaning 'group' in a more general sense.[9] It is this group feeling that provides the motive force that carries ruling groups, i.e., dynasties, to power. This seems so evident to Al-Azmeh that he prefers

---

[5] *Ibid.*

[6] N. J. Dawood, "Introduction", in Ibn Khaldun, *op. cit.*, pp. x–xi; cf. also Ingvar Rydberg, "Översettarens inledning", in Ibn Khaldun, *Prelogomena*, Lund: Alhambra, 1989, p. 12.

[7] Al-Azmeh, Aziz (1990) *Ibn Khaldun*. London/New York: Routledge, p. 135 (note 1).

[8] *Ibid*, p. 27.

[9] Rydberg, Ingvar (1989) "Översettarens inledning," in Ibn Khaldun *Prelogomena*. Lund: Al-hambra, p. 13.

the translation "power group" for *'asabiya*.[10] The central parts of *Muqaddima* are devoted to the analysis of the emergence, growth and decline of *'asabiya* through the complex interplay of what we today would term psychological, sociological, economic, and political factors.

Many commentators want to see Ibn Khaldun as the father of sociology, as a thinker who explicates geographical, climatic, psychological, social-psychological, economic, etc., factors in his approach to history. This can easily become an anachronistic approach to his work, which seems to be the case when commentators without hesitation identify Ibn Khaldun's causes with the modern notion of efficient causes. However, he has to be understood against the background of his times. Thus, his notions of causality were heavily influenced by both Aristotle's four causes and the rejection of natural causality as expounded by the Ash'arite school of theology. Maybe Ibn Khaldun's causes should be understood in the same way as the causes or rather *reasons* (*'illa*) that a judge would base his decision on. Nonetheless, a further discussion of Ibn Khaldun's understanding of causes and causality shall not be pursued here.[11]

3 The Growth of *'Asabiya* and the State

Ibn Khaldun perceived a theory of cyclical history, where dynasties emerge, grow, and inevitably decay. He explicitly states that "dynasties have a natural life span like individuals."[12] This recurring history has a natural beginning in man's social nature, which makes man also political by nature. Thus, "human social organization is something necessary,"[13] Ibn Khaldun states in the opening sentence of chapter one, and continues: "This is what civilization means." Therefore, civilisation is both the beginning and the end of social development and political organisation, because as soon as humankind has achieved social organisation something is needed for the defence against the aggressiveness of man toward each other. This restraint cannot come from outside. "The person who exercises a restraining influence, therefore, must be one of themselves. He must dominate them and have power and authority over them, so that no one of them will be able to attack another. This is the meaning of royal authority."[14] Therefore, royal authority or the state in Ibn Khaldun's view clearly rests on power.

---

[10] Al-Azmeh, *op. cit.*, *passim*.

[11] For an interesting discussion of this theme, see Al-Azmeh, Aziz (1981) *Ibn Khaldun in Modern Scholarship – A Study in Orientalism*. London: Third World Centre for Research and Publishing; a briefer introduction can be found in Gule, Lars (2003) *Social Development and Political Progress in Two Traditions*. Larvik: Ariadne, pp. 172–189 and 240–248.

[12] Ibn Khaldun, *op. cit.*, p. 136.

[13] *Ibid*, p. 45.

[14] *Ibid*, p. 47.

In the social nature of man, some relations are more natural than others are, and in particular, those of the bloodline are not only natural but also important. It is in natural groups like families and tribes that *'asabiya* spontaneously appears. This social cohesion, then, is the basis for political power. It provides the motive force that brings ruling groups to power and allows for the establishments of dynasties. The dynasty (*dawla*) is synonymous with the state, and the state as dynasty is the *form* of civilisation.

Because *al-'asabiya* is the strongest where people are the most dependent on it, in the harsh circumstances of the desert, this is where *'asabiya* results in the genesis of royal authority, that is, the establishment of a dynasty. With a formulation that reflects his Aristotelian teleological essentialism, Ibn Khaldun wrote, "It is thus evident that royal authority is the goal of group feeling."[15] It is this natural goal that leads the focal point of *'asabiya*, the founder of a "house" or dynasty, to increase his power through conquests, by steadily increasing the territory he controls. His success will in turn increase his *'asabiya*, i.e., his power group, because of the increased numbers that will flock around him. In this process, the vanquished will take over the customs and practices of the victors. They will imitate the powerful.

Royal authority, being a noble and enviable position because it gives privileges to the king to enjoy all the pleasures of the world, physical as well as spiritual and intellectual, must be taken by force. "Thus, discord ensues. It leads to war and fighting, and to attempts to gain superiority. Nothing of all this comes about except though group feeling ...".[16] However, "when a dynasty is firmly established, it can dispense with group feeling,"[17] because people forget the beginnings of the dynasty that required a strong *'asabiya*, when successive members of a given family are clearly marked as leaders. Then it becomes "a firmly established article of faith that one must be subservient and submissive to them. People will fight with them in their behalf, as they would fight for their articles of faith."[18] This will even allow members of a royal family to found a dynasty that can dispense with *'asabiya*.[19]

Nevertheless, the dynasties of the greatest power and largest *'asabiya* have their origin in religion based on prophethood or truthful propaganda. This is because royal authority has its roots in that superiority that results from *'asabiya* and "only by God's help in establishing His religion do individual desires come together in agreement to press their claim, and hearts become united,"[20] while jealousy and differences arise when hearts succumb to false desires and are turned towards the world.

Every dynasty, i.e., state, controls a certain territory and the greatness and strength, but also the duration, of the dynasty depends on its numerical strength.[21] Accordingly, a dynasty rarely establishes itself in areas with many tribes and groups

---

[15] *Ibid*, p. 109.

[16] *Ibid*, p. 123.

[17] *Ibid*.

[18] *Ibid*, p. 124.

[19] *Ibid*, p. 125.

[20] *Ibid*.

[21] *Ibid*, p. 128.

because of the differences in opinions and desires this entails. "Behind each opinion and desire, there is a group feeling defending it."[22] This leads to opposition and rebellion against the dynasty, even if it possesses group feeling, "because each group feeling under the control of the ruling dynasty thinks that it has in itself enough strength and power"[23] to establish its own royal authority. When a dynasty has been established, it will claim all glory and honour for itself, exactly because it is based on *'asabiya*. If the dynasty is the result of a coalition, there still need to be a superior group feeling. This highest group feeling can only go to people who have a "house" and therefore leadership in the tribe.

> One of those people must be the leader who has superiority over them. He is singled out as a leader of all the various group feelings, because he is superior to all the others by birth. When he is singled out for (leadership), he is too proud to let others share his leadership and control or to let them participate in it, because the qualities of haughtiness and pride are innate in animal nature. Thus, he develops the quality of egotism, innate in human beings.[24]

Ibn Khaldun adds that politics requires that only one person exercise control because various persons liable to differ among themselves when exercising power, could destroy the whole dynasty.

4 The Decline

In the situation where a dynasty has effective control, it will seek luxury and prefer tranquillity and peace. After having taken possession of the holdings of the predecessors, the prosperity and well-being of a dynasty will grow. "People become accustomed to a great number of things. From the necessities of life and a life of austerity, they progress to the luxuries and a life in comfort and beauty."[25] When royal authority has been established, people no longer do the tiresome chores they had to do to obtain it. All efforts cease, and rest, quiet and tranquillity is preferred. It is in this situation that Ibn Khaldun saw the seeds of decay. The members of the dynasty get used to a luxurious and peaceful life and pass it on to later generations. "When the natural tendencies of royal authority to claim all glory for itself and to acquire luxury and tranquillity have been firmly established, the dynasty approaches senility."[26]

The decline of a glorious dynastic state follows, first, from the monopolisation of glory and honour in the ruler. In the establishment phase of the dynasty, the honour and glory was common to the members of the group and they all made an identical effort. "Now, however, when one of them claims all glory for himself, he treats the others severely and holds them in check. Further, he excludes them from possessing property

[22] *Ibid*, p. 130.

[23] *Ibid*.

[24] *Ibid*, p. 132.

[25] *Ibid*, p. 133.

[26] *Ibid*.

and appropriates it for himself. People, thus, become too lazy to care for fame. They become dispirited and come to love humbleness and servitude."[27] When this condition continues over generations, the dynasty progresses towards weakness and senility.

A second factor in the process of decline is the use of money, again for luxuries. On the one hand, private expectations lead the poor among them to perish and the spendthrifts to squander their incomes. People become too weak to keep their own affairs going. On the other hand, the dynasty's spending of money on luxury depletes the treasury and reduces the army. This will invite attacks from hostile neighbours, "and God permits it [the dynasty] to suffer the destruction that He has destined for His creatures."[28] An important third factor is also that luxury and luxurious living makes the fighting spirit of the desert disappear. All these factors represent a weakening of *'asabiya*.

The whole process leads to the conclusion that dynasties have a natural life span. This, Ibn Khaldun argued, is equivalent to 120 years and covers three human generations. In the fourth generation, its prestige is destroyed. In this process, the transition from desert life to sedentary life is important. These repeated transitions represent the dialectic between the desert and urban life. The first stage of a dynasty, the establishment of the original power group (*'asabiya*), is, as a rule, only possible in connection with desert life. "The first stage of dynasties, therefore, is that of desert life."[29] But when royal authority is acquired, it is accompanied by a life of ease and increased opportunities, and sedentary culture represents this diversification of luxury and refined knowledge of the crafts. Therefore, "the sedentary stage of royal authority follows the stage of desert life. It does so of necessity, as a result of the fact that royal authority is necessarily accompanied by a life of ease."[30] It also follows that when a dynasty decays and crumbles the cities that are the seats of royal authority also crumble "and in this process often suffers complete ruin. There hardly ever is any delay."[31]

Summing up what he saw as the primary and natural reason for this situation, Ibn Khaldun stated that it "is the fact that dynasty and royal authority have the same relationship to civilization as form has to matter."[32] The form is the shape that preserves the existence of matter through the kind of phenomenon it represents, and philosophy has established that the one cannot be separated from the other.

> One cannot imagine a dynasty without civilization, while civilization without dynasty and royal authority is impossible, because human beings must by nature co-operate, and that calls for a restraining influence. Political leadership, based either on religious or royal authority is inevitable. This is what is meant by dynasty. Since the two cannot be separated, the disintegration of one of them must influence the other, just as its nonexistence would entail the nonexistence of the other.[33]

---

[27] *Ibid*, p. 134.

[28] *Ibid*, p. 135.

[29] *Ibid*, p. 138.

[30] *Ibid*.

[31] *Ibid*, p. 289.

[32] *Ibid*, p. 291.

[33] *Ibid*.

Thus, when the form, i.e., the dynasty, that preserves the existence of matter, i.e., civilisation, is separated from matter through the dissipation of the dynasty itself, as will happen when the *'asabiya* dissolves, civilisation also crumbles. Again, Ibn Khaldun utilised Aristotelian concepts in his explanation, establishing both the necessity and dynamic character of the process.

5 A Moral Theory?

A theory of social and political development that is as closely related to notions of not only decay but also decadence as Ibn Khaldun's seems like a moral theory, and there are many references to the effects of moral changes in the cyclical process he described.[34] At the same time, he has been praised for his objectivity and purely descriptive approach to social changes.

The anthropology of Ibn Khaldun must be said to be negative: God created man both good and evil, but without any religious restraint, the evil side would predominate. "Evil is the quality that is closest to man when he fails to improve his customs and when religion is not used as the model to improve him."[35] Evil qualities in man are injustice and mutual aggression. However, Ibn Khaldun also said that "in view of his natural disposition and his power of logical reasoning, man is more inclined toward good qualities than toward bad qualities …,"[36] and these good qualities result in political, i.e. royal, authority. This authority should be used in a just way, which for Ibn Khaldun meant upholding the law.

It seems to be a reasonable interpretation of Ibn Khaldun's position that the naturalness of the human qualities is best expressed in simple circumstances, not least in view of his claim that:

> *Bedouins are closer to being good than sedentary people.*
> The reason for this is that the soul in its first natural state of creation is ready to accept whatever good or evil may arrive and leave an imprint on it. … When customs proper to goodness [i.e., Bedouin customs and practices] have been first to enter the soul of a good person, and his (soul) has thus acquired the habit of (goodness, that person) moves away from evil and finds it difficult to do anything evil.[37]

Man is a product of the customs and the environment in which he lives and not of his natural dispositions.[38] Thus, when sedentary people are much concerned with all kinds of pleasures and preoccupied with luxury and success in worldly occupations,

[34] This is different from a view on moral and immoral forms of authority, cf. Black, Antony (2001) *The History of Islamic Political Thought.* Edinburgh: Edinburgh University Press, pp. 174–177, and below, "The political thought of Ibn Khaldun".

[35] Ibn Khaldun, *op. cit.*, p. 97.

[36] *Ibid*, p. 111.

[37] *Ibid*, p. 94.

[38] *Ibid*, p. 95.

"their souls are coloured with all kinds of blameworthy and evil qualities."[39] In view of the hardy qualities required for the successful establishment of royal authority, that is, a powerful *'asabiya*, the moral qualities of the Bedouins are not only of concern with respect to standards of behaviour based on a sense of right and wrong. Their moral qualities are of paramount importance as the starting point of the dynastic cycle.

The moral aspects of the decline of the state are also clear. Luxurious living, the loss of fighting spirit, etc., easily leads to corruption. "Corruption of the individual inhabitants is the result of painful and trying efforts to satisfy the needs caused by their (luxury) customs; (the result) of the bad qualities they have acquired in the process of satisfying (those needs); and of the damage the soul suffers after it has obtained them."[40] Thus, immoral practices increase and spread moral decadence, which is excused as it is deemed necessary to make a living. People arrives at the point where they only think about money without regard for the means.[41]

In these circumstances, not even his good descent can protect an individual from moral decay. A possible explanation for this is that the profits they acquire is not sufficient to pay for their needs, because of the great number of luxury items desired. "Thus, the affairs of the people are disordered, and if the affairs of the individuals one by one deteriorate, the town becomes disorganized and falls into ruin."[42] The conclusion is the inevitable, as already discussed. Because of the necessary relationship between form and matter, the form of civilisation, i.e., the state, will decline when the matter of civilisation, i.e., its sedentary life, decays.

Although considerations of morals are important in Ibn Khaldun's overall theory, calling it a moral theory would be wrong, but it could be called a sociological theory of morals. Through his description of the effects of social changes on morals and, in turn, the effects of morals on developments, Ibn Khaldun remains within the "empiricist" approach that characterises his work.

6 The Political Thought of Ibn Khaldun

The political thought of Ibn Khaldun is part of his theory of history and of social and political change. It is particularly treated in the chapter of *al-Muqaddima* entitled, "On dynasties, royal authority, the caliphate, government ranks, and all that goes with these things ..." However, since government is the form of culture or civilisation as a whole, we also find extensive discussions of the subject throughout the book. His political theory is in an important sense different from the normative theological-political theory of the classical *'ulama* in its descriptive approach. The ideal

[39] *Ibid*, p. 94.
[40] *Ibid*, p. 286.
[41] *Ibid*.
[42] *Ibid*, p. 287.

Islamic state, based on the ideal *shari'a*, is outside his inquiry.[43] He insists that his treatment of political life is not to be confused with the treatment of political life within the Islamic legal sciences, which aim at determining the legal prescriptions to be followed by adherents to the Islamic Law, with the sayings of popular wisdom, which do not explain the nature of political life. Nor should it be confused with political science or political philosophy, which aims primarily at determining how man ought to conduct himself to achieve happiness and perfection.[44] Thus, Ibn Khaldun was not an explicitly prescriptive reformer and had no concern for the rights of individuals and participation in government as valuable norms in themselves. Nevertheless, Ibn Khaldun saw the importance of law to social order and he recognised the political need to take cognisance of norms. Because royal authority is self-centred, "the decisions of the ruler will therefore, as a rule, deviate from what is right [i.e., just]."[45] This will lead to disobedience and trouble, and could lead to violence.

> Therefore, it is necessary to have reference to ordained political norms, which are accepted by the mass and to whose laws it submits. The Persians and other nations had such norms. The dynasty that does not have a policy based on (such) norms cannot fully succeed in establishing its rule.
>
> If these norms are ordained by the intelligent and leading personalities and minds of the dynasty, the result will be a political (institution) with an intellectual (rational) basis. If they are ordained by God through a lawgiver who establishes them as (religious) laws, the result will be a political (institution) with a religious basis, which will be useful for life in both this and the other world.[46]

Here is also presented two legal systems—a secular based on *qanun* (law) and religious based on the law of God, *shari'a*. This also gives the basis for the exercise of three forms of authority and it explains what the caliphate is. *Natural* royal authority induces the masses to act from purpose and need, while *political* royal authority induce them to act from intellectual and rational insights in their earthly interest, and *caliphal* authority induces "the masses to act as required by religious insight into their interests in the other world as well as in this world."[47]

> (Worldly interests) have a bearing upon (the interests in the other world), since according to Muhammad all worldly conditions are to be considered in their relation to their value for the other world. Thus, (the caliphate) in reality is a substitute for Muhammad in as much as it serves, like him, to protect the religion and to exercise leadership of the world.[48]

---

[43] Rosenthal, Erwin I. J. (1940) "Ibn Khaldun: A North African Muslim Thinker of the fourteenth century," in *Bulletin of the John Rylands Library*, vol. 24, no. 2, p. 309; quoted after the reprint in Rosenthal, *Studia Semitica*, vol. II: Islamic Themes, Cambridge: Cambridge University Press, 1971, p. 5.

[44] See Mahdi, Mushim (2004) "Ibn Khaldun," in Sharif, M. M. (ed.) (2004) *A History of Muslim Philosophy*. Delhi: Low Price Publications, vol. 2, p. 964.

[45] Ibn Khaldun, *op. cit.*, p. 154.

[46] *Ibid.*

[47] *Ibid*, p. 155.

[48] *Ibid*; see also Khadduri, Majid (1984) *The Islamic Conception of Justice*. Baltimore: Johns Hopkins University Press, p. 187.

Accordingly, the ethical point of departure is not neglected by Ibn Khaldun. The best society is that which is ruled in accordance with the law of God but as it is the historical development and its underlying principles that are his main interest, the caliphate becomes only one of several possible state forms. *Within* this state form, the caliphate, Ibn Khaldun's ideas of law and justice seems to be in agreement with the general ideas of the religious scholars—*'ulama*, who were the main explicators of these concepts in the Islamic tradition.

Nevertheless, Ibn Khaldun frames the development of Islamic law within his overall developmental scheme of social and political change. The logical structure of the *Muqaddima* leads to the final chapters where Ibn Khaldun discusses and analyses the various aspects of making a living and the sciences, including the religious disciplines, and the methods of instruction in these sciences. In these chapters, he discusses man's ability to think, which distinguishes human beings from animals and enables them to obtain their livelihood, to cooperate with others to achieve this, and to study the God they worship and the revelations the Prophets have transmitted from Him. Arts and sciences can only prosper within a state and are an integral part of civilisation. Consequently, while states (dynasties) grow and decay within the 120-year framework Ibn Khaldun described, civilisations can "live" longer because the cultural faculties that individuals and societies acquire, enable civilisations, in a larger sense than the dynasty, to survive the political disintegration of a given state.

7 Justice, Law and Civilisation

Ibn Khaldun emphasised the rational foundation of laws, even within the Islamic tradition:

> In connection with the arguments for prophecy, for instance, scholars mention that human beings cooperate with each other for their existence and, therefore, need men to arbitrate among them and exercise a restraining influence. Or, in the science of the principles of jurisprudence, in the chapter of arguments for the necessity of languages, mention is made of the fact that people need means to express their intentions because by their very nature, co-operation and social organization are made easier by proper expressions. Or, in connection with the explanation that laws have their reason in the purposes they are to serve, the jurists mention that adultery confuses pedigrees and destroys the (human) species; that murder, too, destroys the human species; that injustice invites the destruction of civilization with the necessary consequence that the (human) species will be destroyed. Other similar things are stated in connection with the purposes embedded in laws. All (laws) are based upon the effort to preserve civilization. Therefore, (the laws) pay attention to the things that belong to civilization. This is obvious from our references to these problems which are mentioned as representative (of the general situation).[49]

These needs gives the rational legitimation of the various forms of authority already mentioned. Furthermore, Ibn Khaldun reflected on the functions of the law. He boldly stated in a subchapter heading, "The reliance of sedentary people upon

---

[49] *Ibid*, p. 40.

laws destroys their fortitude and power of resistance."[50] In this brief subchapter, he set out his "sociological" ideas on laws.

> Not everyone is master of his own affairs. Chiefs and leaders who are masters of the affairs of men are few in comparison with the rest. As a rule, man must by necessity be dominated by someone else. If the domination is kind and just and the people under it are not oppressed by its laws and restrictions, they are guided by the courage or cowardice that they possess in themselves. They are satisfied with the absence of any restraining power. Self-reliance eventually becomes a quality natural to them. They would not know anything else. If, however, the domination with its laws is one of brute force and intimidation, it breaks their fortitude and deprives them of their power of resistance as a result of the inertness that develops in the souls of the oppressed, as we shall explain.[51]

For Ibn Khaldun all secular laws are expressions of power with oppressive functions, regardless of whether they are harshly implemented or more subtly applied.

> When laws are (enforced) by means of punishment, they completely destroy fortitude, because the use of punishment against someone who cannot defend himself generates in that person a feeling of humiliation that, no doubt, must break his fortitude.
>
> When laws are (intended to serve the purposes of) education and instruction and are applied from childhood on, they have to some degree the same effect, because people then grow up in fear and docility and consequently do not rely on their own fortitude.[52]

It is for this reason, greater fortitude is found among the Arab Bedouins than among people who are subject to laws. Likewise, those who rely on laws and are dominated by them from the very beginning of their education and instruction in the crafts, sciences, and religious matters, are thus deprived of much of their own fortitude.

> They can scarcely defend themselves at all against hostile acts. This is the case with students, whose occupation it is to study and to learn from teachers and religious leaders, and who constantly apply themselves to instruction and education in very dignified gatherings. This situation and the fact that it destroys the power of resistance and fortitude must be understood.[53]

However, not all laws diminish fortitude and self-reliance. Religious law, i.e., the *shari'a*, is different. Ibn Khaldun insisted that it was no argument against the statement just made that the men around Muhammad observed the religious laws, and yet did not experience any diminution of their fortitude, because:

> When the Muslims got their religion from the Lawgiver (Muhammad), the restraining influence came from themselves, as a result of the encouragement and discouragement he gave them in the Qur'an. It was not a result of technical instruction or scientific education. (The laws) were the laws and precepts of the religion, which they received orally and which their firmly rooted (belief in) the truth of the articles of faith caused them to observe. Their fortitude remained unabated, and it was not corroded by education or authority. 'Umar said, "Those who are not educated (disciplined) by the religious law are not educated (disciplined) by God." 'Umar's desire was that everyone should have his restraining influence in himself. His certainty was that the Lawgiver (Muhammad) knew best what is good for mankind.[54]

---

[50] *Ibid*, p. 95.

[51] *Ibid*, pp. 95–96.

[52] *Ibid.*

[53] *Ibid.*

[54] *Ibid.*

After Muhammad and the immediate generations, the influence of religion, i.e., Islam, decreased among men, and they came to use restraining laws. Thus, even the religious law became a branch of learning and a craft to be acquired through instruction and education, and as people turned to sedentary life, they assumed the character trait of submissiveness to law.

> It has thus become clear that governmental and educational laws destroy fortitude, because their restraining influence is something that comes from outside. The religious laws, on the other hand, do not destroy fortitude, because their restraining influence is something inherent. Therefore, governmental and educational laws influence sedentary people, in that they weaken their souls and diminish their stamina, because they have to suffer (their authority) both as children and as adults. The Bedouins, on the other hand, are not in the same position, because they live far away from the laws of government, instruction, and education.[55]

Thus, for Ibn Khaldun laws were a means of social control and exercise of power. While independent Bedouins would keep each other in check because of their individual strength and courage, and therefore preserve some sort of peace among them through a balance of power, sedentary people both had to be ruled by force and would submit to force. Nevertheless, *religious* laws would ensure both that Muslims retained (some of their) fortitude and were ruled justly.

Ibn Khaldun also saw the need for justice in a particular sense as a precondition for social stability, something a ruler needed to achieve. As his ideas on the *content* of law and justice do not seem to vary much from the majority of the *'ulama*, we can look at these concepts from this more generalised point of view.[56] Muslim thinkers—theologians, jurists and philosophers—have all been interested in justice. They have taken as a point of departure the Qur'an and the example of the Prophet. In the Qur'an, the most common terms for justice are *'adl* and *qist* (also meaning fairness and equity). *Qist* is usually accompanied by the word *mizan*, meaning balance and scale; and the scales of justice are mentioned several times in the Qur'an. These terms stand in contradistinction to oppression—*zulm*, the opposite of justice (with the interchangeable meaning of cruelty or unjust acts of exploitation and wrongdoing, whereby a person either deprives others of their rights or does not fulfil his obligations toward them). The God of the Qur'an is thoroughly committed to justice and does not commit any injustice. He urges "social justice" in that He enjoins the believers to assist and support orphans, the needy and the poor (e.g. Qur'an 2:177; 90:8–18). God also urges believers to speak out against oppression, even if it requires going against one's own family (Qur'an 6:152).

A central principle of Islam, which precedes juristic deliberations proper, is that God has commissioned humanity to believe, confess and act in particular ways. The details of this instruction or obligation (*taklif*) were handed down through a line of

---

[55] *Ibid*, pp. 96–97.

[56] For the following, see Calder, Norman (1998) "Islamic philosophy of law," in *Routledge Encyclopedia of Philosophy*, http://www.muslimphilosophy.com/ip/rep/H015.htm; Rahemtulla, Shadaab (2012) "Justice," in Bowering, Gerhard (ed.) *Princeton Encyclopedia of Islamic Political Thought*. Princeton: Princeton University Press; and Mensia, Moqdad Arfa & Mensia, Mongia Arfa (2012) "Islamic Philosophy of Law," in Berry Gray, Christopher (ed.) *The Philosophy of Law. An Encyclopedia*. New York: Routledge.

prophets, culminating in Muhammad. Through Muhammad, the instruction was then embedded in two literary structures that together constitute revelation (*wahy*): the Qur'an, seen as the unadulterated word of God, and the *hadith*, being short narratives of the prophet's doings and sayings that give expression to his (and his community's) ideal practice or *sunna* (the revered tradition). The totality of beliefs and rules that can be derived from these sources, with the assistance of two principles of interpretation, constitutes God's law or *shari'a*.[57] The two principles of interpretation are *ijtihad*—meaning the exertion of one's reason in order to find an answer and *ijma'*—the consensus of the community or the legal scholars.[58]

Jurisprudence in Islam—*fiqh*—is the study of these sources, principles and established precedents, and the legal rules and decisions that can be made on this basis. The juristic literature has generated two major literary genres.

> One, known as *usul al-fiqh* (roots of jurisprudence), deals with hermeneutical principles that can be used for deriving rules from revelation; it represents, in part, something like a philosophy of law. The other, dominant genre, *furu' al-fiqh* (branches of jurisprudence), is an elaboration of rules which govern ritual and social activities. An overall philosophy of law in Islam, not fully articulated in the pre-modern tradition, can only be discovered through consideration of both genres.[59]

Thus, to explicate a philosophy of law in a contemporary sense within Islam would be a somewhat anachronistic exercise. Nevertheless, Ibn Khaldun also discusses *fiqh*.

> Jurisprudence is the knowledge of the classification of the laws of God, which concern the actions of all responsible Muslims, as obligatory, forbidden, recommendable, disliked, or permissible. These (laws) are derived from the Qur'an and the Sunnah (traditions), and from the evidence Muhammad has established. The laws evolved from this evidence are called 'jurisprudence'.[60]

Within the framework of the established interpretations of Islamic law, the caliphate was seen as necessary, as an obligation placed on man by the will of God. The authoritative exposition of the religious necessity and organisation of the caliphate was the work by the jurist Abu al-Hasan al-Mawardi (c. 974–1058), *Al-Ahkam al-Sultaniya w'al-Wilayat al-Diniyya* (The Ordinances of Government). Ibn Khaldun was familiar with this book and referred to it when he described the organisational structure of the caliphal state apparatus. The idea of justice we find in *Ahkam al-Sultaniya*, and in the works of most other Muslim legal and political thinkers, is related to upholding the law and social harmony. This idea is old and can be found in ancient Egyptian notions of justice—*Ma'at*—seen as a cosmic principle of harmony, order, security and equilibrium, i.e. balance.[61] It is also

---

[57] See Calder, *op. cit.*

[58] For a further discussion of these concepts and *usul al-fiqh*, see Calder, *op. cit.*; Vikør, Knut S. "Sharia" from Oxford Islamic Studies Online", December 16, 2013, http://bridgingcultures.neh.gov/muslimjourneys/items/show/226; and Vikør (2005) *Between God and the Sultan: A History of Islamic Law*. London: Hurst.

[59] Calder, *op. cit.*

[60] Ibn Khaldun, *op. cit.*, pp. 344–45.

[61] See Gule, *op. cit.*, p. 411 for a brief discussion.

influenced by Greek notions of justice as balance and social harmony. Thus, justice is about finding one's place in a given social order, but also being given one's due in that order.

The order of things seems important here. It is through upholding the divine law that justice is served, and creating balance and harmony in the process. Thus, it is the law that defines justice, not justice that should determine the content of the law.[62] This also follows from the fact that the law is divine. In the theological voluntaristic position of Islamic orthodoxy, it is God who decides what is right, wrong, just, etc., as it is God who is the ultimate sovereign, not the caliphs, sultans, or kings. This perception of divine sovereignty lay at the foundations of the relationship between the ruling dynasties and the populations they ruled. The imperative of upholding justice as embodied in the *shari'a* therefore had to be reconciled with the demands and expediency of political rule.[63] It was also recognised that "without the sovereign's juridico-political administration ... the Shari'a would also become a hollow system. The Shari'a thus defined the substance and form of legal norms, while the sovereign ensured their enforcement."[64]

In an attempt to overcome the gap between ideals and the contingent demands of rule, the activist jurist Ibn Taymiyya (1263–1328) elaborated what he saw as the conditions for legitimate politics—*siyasa shar'iya*. This was politics that struck a balance between the idealism of *shari'a* as a deduced law from the sources, and the realism of induction from positive sources like precedent and custom. The idea was that the result was in conformity with the *purpose* of *shari'a*.[65] This made the concept of *maslaha*—the common good or general interest—important. This concept gave both flexibility to the interpretation of the law and could prevent the state from degenerating into an unjust and tyrannical entity.

Islamic law had been well established as a legal tradition at the time of Ibn Khaldun. This also meant that this law represented an indispensable source of legitimacy for the rulers.[66] Ibn Khaldun saw this when he, with reference to older Persian wisdom sayings, presented the story of the Mobedhan before Bahram b. Bahram:

> O king, the might of royal authority materializes only through the religious law, obedience toward God, and compliance with His commands and prohibitions. The religious law persists only through royal authority. Mighty royal authority is accomplished only through men. Men persist only with the help of property. The only way to property is

[62] Of course, in the *interpretation* of the law and establishing the right understanding of it in individual cases, ideas of what justice should be will influence the interpretation itself. Thus, the concepts of law and concepts of justice will interact and mutually determine each other in the practical hermeneutical circle of real life activity.

[63] Hallaq, Wael B. (2009) *An Introduction to Islamic Law*. Cambridge: Cambridge University Press, p. 73.

[64] *Ibid.*

[65] Khadduri, *op. cit.*, p. 179.

[66] For a brief but valuable discussion of Islamic law as a source of legitimacy, see Hallaq, *op. cit.*, pp. 42–44.

> through cultivation. The only way to cultivation is through justice. Justice is a balance set up among mankind. The Lord set it up and appointed an overseer for it, and that overseer is the ruler.[67]

Here also is the "circle of justice" introduced. For hundreds of years, ancient and medieval Persian and Arabic rulers invoked sayings known as the "circle of justice" as a model for how to organise their rule. It was also presented as advice to kings in various mirrors for princes. The circle of justice described an ideal relation among classes (i.e., the ruler or political class, tax collectors, the military and the agricultural class). Ibn Khaldun expanded on this by another reference to older Persian experiences:

> There also is a statement by Anosharwan to the same effect: "Royal authority exists through the army, the army through money, money through taxes, taxes through cultivation, cultivation through justice, justice through the improvement of officials, the improvement of officials through the forthrightness of wazirs, and the whole thing in the first place through the ruler's personal supervision of his subjects' condition and his ability to educate them, so that he may rule them, and not they him."[68]

Furthermore, Ibn Khaldun refers to the Book on Politics that was ascribed to Aristotle and had wide circulation.[69] There he found a good deal about the subject under discussion here, but he saw the treatment as not exhaustive. Nevertheless, Ibn Khaldun found the following presentation by the author of particular interest:

> He arranged his statement in a remarkable circle that he discussed at length. It runs as follows: "The world is a garden the fence of which is the dynasty. The dynasty is an authority through which life is given to proper behaviour. Proper behaviour is a policy directed by the ruler. The ruler is an institution supported by the soldiers. The soldiers are helpers who are maintained by money. Money is sustenance brought together by the subjects. The subjects are servants who are protected by justice. Justice is something familiar, and through it, the world persists. The world is a garden ...", and then it begins again from the beginning. These are eight sentences of political wisdom. They are connected with each other, the end of each one leading into the beginning of the next. They are held together in a circle with no definite beginning or end.[70]

Ibn Khaldun agrees with this presentation of the circle of justice and claims that when his discussion in the *Muqaddima* in the section on royal authority and dynasties has been studied and due critical attention given to it, "it will be found to constitute an exhaustive, very clear, fully substantiated interpretation and detailed exposition of these sentences."[71]

---

[67] Ibn Khaldun, *op. cit.*, p. 40; the Mobedh is the title of the Zoroastrian priest and Mobedhan is the Persian plural of the word.

[68] *Ibid.*

[69] This pseudo-Aristotelian book is better known as *Sirr al-asrar* or *Secretum Secretorum* and allegedly translated from Greek, but it appears that the treatise was actually composed originally in Arabic.

[70] *Ibid*, p. 41.

[71] *Ibid.*

8 Ibn Khaldun—The Judge

Ibn Khaldun was not only a theoretical writer but also a teacher and Chief Judge of the Maliki *maddhab* during the last 25 years of his life in Egypt. However, he did not write anything he found worthwhile to mention in his autobiography, but he did write about some if his practical experience as a Maliki judge.[72]

In 1384, the first sultan of the Mamluk Burji dynasty, Al-Malik al-Zahir Sayf al-Din Barquq, who ruled in two periods (1382–1389 and 1390–1399), appointed Ibn Khaldun Chief Maliki *Qadi* of Egypt. The position of Maliki *Qadi* was very powerful and somewhat similar to a Supreme Court Judge in that he heard appeals of sentences from lower Maliki judges. One of the important functions of the Chief *Qadi* was to root out corruption in the lower ranks of the judiciary.[73] Such corruption had become widespread ever since the interpretation of Islamic law and the teaching of Islamic law to students in madrasas had been co-opted by the government. The *Qadi* was also under the influence of government power. A common proverb said, "Of three judges, two are in hell," but Ibn Khaldun seems to have seen himself as that one judge out of three who could rise above the temptations of government corruption.[74]

At the beginning of his career as judge, Ibn Khaldun appears to have assumed the role of reformer—a rather interesting change for a man with his outlook on life, a realist—or even cynic—by both temperament and experience. Nevertheless, he claimed to execute the office of *Qadi* with outmost probity and effort. He was disgusted that lower court judges under his purview did not vigorously root out and sentence influential Mamluk "libertines" and those addicted to luxury. "It was precisely luxury and libertine behaviour that was, for Ibn Khaldun, the root of social decay."[75] In his autobiography, he wrote that "The judges abstained from criticizing their comportment and closed their eyes to misdeeds … in order to be certain they were protected by the powerful."[76]

Ibn Khaldun's calls for reform largely went unheeded. He must also have known that to attempt reforms of long-established customs would make enemies for himself. He must certainly have realised that he could not succeed in introducing reforms in a foreign country without his own *'asabiya*—i.e., power group—to support him in his efforts. So perhaps he was motivated not so much by a conscious plan for reform as by the desire to do his job as *Qadi* well. Maybe this was why he proceeded against corruption and bribery and tried to weed out incompetent *muftis* and ignorant legal advisers. Apart from Ibn Khaldun's efforts

---

[72] For the following, see the biography of Ibn Khaldun by Franz Rosenthal in his three-volume translation of *al-Muqaddima*. Princeton: Princeton University Press, 1958; Khadduri, *op. cit.*, p. 185–189; and Fromherz, Allen James (2010) *Ibn Khaldun, Life and Times*. Edinburgh: Edinburgh University Press.

[73] Fromherz, *op. cit.*, p. 99.

[74] *Ibid.*

[75] *Ibid*, p. 100.

[76] Quoted after Fromherz, *op. cit.*, p. 100.

against corruption and incompetence as described in his autobiography, and which might have been inspired by his cyclical theory of history and its warning as to luxury and libertine behaviour, there is no lasting legacy of Ibn Khaldun as a practical reformer.

In view of his grand theory and its descriptive approach to history, social change and law, it is perhaps not surprising that Ibn Khaldun never became a noted legal and political reformer. It makes sense that he saw himself as an administrator of law—and that he thought that was the best he could do.

9 Conclusion

In *al-Muqaddima*, Ibn Khaldun elaborated a comprehensive science of civilisation. Within this framework, there is also a theory of law and justice. Ibn Khaldun's approach is "sociological" and descriptive. He was concerned with the political function of the law and justice. However, with an eye on these functions, he was also aware of the important differences between secular law and the secular use of even religious law on the one hand, and the different contents of secular and religious law on the other. For Ibn Khaldun, religious laws guaranteed justice when correctly applied, i.e., without corruption or favouritism, and we have reason to believe that he attempted to apply Islamic law in this way when he was practicing as Grand *Qadi* in Egypt.

While Ibn Khaldun was an original thinker when preoccupied with the *function* of law and justice when he described their importance to the development of society, his notions of the *content* of justice and law was comprehensively Islamic. He was, after all, trained in *fiqh* and practiced as Chief *Qadi*. The social function of law and justice is, simply put, to ensure a stable social order, which is necessary for sedentary civilisations to grow. The content of religious, i.e., Islamic, law is there to ensure not only a stable social order, but also to ensure the salvation of the believers and guarantee them a blissful afterlife.

These two aspects of law and justice was interrelated in Ibn Khaldun's thinking. By pointing out the function of law in social and historical processes, Ibn Khaldun also advocated an instrumental approach to be adopted by rulers who need to ensure stability. However, his normative position is also clear in his insistence on the religious law, i.e., *shari'a*, as the only law—when implemented without corruption and favouritism—that will ensure the interests of ruler and subjects alike.

Within Ibn Khaldun's new science of civilisation, his theories on law and justice make up a consistent whole, combining scientific analysis and values or a descriptive method with a normative position, both approaches rooted in his Islamic beliefs.

References and Literature

Al-Azmeh, A. (1981). *Ibn Khaldun in modern scholarship – A study in orientalism*. London: Third World Centre for Research and Publishing.

Al-Azmeh, A. (1990). *Ibn Khaldun*. London/New York: Routledge.

Black, A. (2001). *The history of Islamic political thought*. Edinburgh: Edinburgh University Press.

Calder, N. (1996). Law. In S. H. Nasr & O. Leaman (Eds.), *History of Islamic philosophy*. London: Routledge.

Calder, N. (1998). Islamic philosophy of law. In *Routledge encyclopedia of philosophy*. http://www.muslimphilosophy.com/ip/rep/H015.htm

Crone, P. (2004). *Medieval Islamic political thought*. Edinburgh: Edinburg University Press.

Fakhry, M. (1998). Ethics in Islamic philosophy. In *Routledge encyclopedia of philosophy*. http://www.muslimphilosophy.com/ip/rep/H018.htm

Fromherz, A. J. (2010). *Ibn Khaldun, life and times*. Edinburgh: Edinburgh University Press.

Gule, L. (2003). *Social development and political progress in two traditions*. Larvik: Ariadne.

Gule, L. (2013). Ibn Khaldun og vitenskapen om sivilisasjonene. In J. Pedersen (Ed.), *Politisk filosofi fra Platon til Hannah Arendt*. Oslo: Pax.

Hallaq, W. B. (2009). *An introduction to Islamic law*. Cambridge: Cambridge University Press.

Ibn Khaldun. (1969). *Al-Muqaddimah* (Trans. by F. Rosenthal into English, ed. and abridged by N. J. Dawood). Princeton: Princeton University Press, 1981.

Ibn Khaldun. (1989). *Prelogomena* (Trans. by Ingvar Rydberg into Swedish). Lund: Alhambra.

Ibn Khaldun. (2012). *Al-Muqaddimah* (Trans. by Magid Al-Araki into Norwegian). Oslo: Pax.

Khadduri, M. (1984). *The Islamic conception of justice*. Baltimore: Johns Hopkins University Press.

Lambton, A. K. (1981). *State and government in medieval Islam: An introduction to the study of Islamic political thought: The Jurists*. Oxford: Oxford University Press.

Mahdi, M. (2004). Ibn Khaldun. In M. M. Sharif (ed.), *A history of Muslim philosophy*. Delhi: Low Price Publications. (Originally published: Wiesbaden: Otto Harassowitz, 1963)

Al-Mawardi, Abu al-Hasan. (2000). *Al-Ahkam al-Sultaniya w'al-Wilayat al-Diniyya* [The Ordinances of Government]. Reading: Garnet.

Mensia, M. A., & Mensia, M. A. (2012). Islamic philosophy of law. In C. Berry Gray (Ed.), *The philosophy of law. An encyclopedia*. New York: Routledge.

Rahemtulla, S. (2012). Justice. In G. Bowering (Ed.), *Princeton encyclopedia of Islamic political thought*. Princeton: Princeton University Press.

Rosenthal, E. I. J. (1940). Ibn Khaldun: A North African Muslim thinker of the fourteenth century. *Bulletin of the John Rylands Library, 24*(2), 307–320.

Rydberg, I. (1989). Översettarens inledning. In Ibn Khaldun (ed.), *Prelogomena*. Lund: Alhambra.

Vikør, K. S. (2005). *Between God and sultan. A history of Islamic law*. London: Hurst.

Vikør, K. S. (n.d.). 'Sharia' from Oxford Islamic studies online. http://bridgingcultures.neh.gov/muslimjourneys/items/show/226

Inscrutable Divinity or Social Welfare? The Basis of Islamic Law

Knut S. Vikør

Although controversies about the "Shari'a" are among of the most acute issues of law and politics today, there is little agreement about what it means and what the discussion is really about. It is described as a divine law, but most Muslims agree that its prescriptions are formulated by men. It should belong to religion, but be implemented by a mundane state. And does it have only one correct answer to every problem, or are there a multitude of answers from which scholars are to choose to the best of their ability while only God knows the best and correct (but does not tell us)?

These questions have plagued the discussion of Islamic law since the classical period, and gave rise to divergences both in content and methodology.[1] In the contemporary period, however, the issue of a "real life" implementation of Islamic law has increasingly been conceived both by proponents and critics in a modern way of thinking "law", that of a codified system formulated by a conscious actor and a legislative authority: the state.[2] This is a novelty for the Shari'a, because in its classical form, while the state (the "sultan") was in charge of putting the law into effect through courts, prisons and police, it had no influence whatsoever over the *contents* of the law. The formulation of the Shari'a was the prerogative of an independent body of religious scholars, the *fuqaha* (legal scholars) and *ulama* (religious scholars of Islam).

[1] Weiss, Bernard G. (1998) *The Spirit of Islamic Law*. Athens, GA: The University of Georgia Press; Vikør, Knut S. (2005) *Between God and the Sultan: A History of Islamic Law*. London: Hurst; Hallaq, Wael B. (2009) *Sharî'a. Theory, Practice, Transformations*. Cambridge: Cambridge University Press.

[2] Peters, Rudolph (2002) "'From Jurists' Law to Statute Law or What Happens when the Shari'a is Codified," in *Mediterranean Politics*, VII, 4, pp. 82–95; and Layish, Aharon "'The Transformation of the Shari'a from Jurists' Law to Statutory Law in the Contemporary Muslim World," in *Die Welt des Islams*, XLIV, 1, 2004, pp. 85–113.

K.S. Vikør (✉)
Department of Archaeology, History, Culture Studies and Religion,
University of Bergen, Bergen, Norway
e-mail: knut.vikor@ahkr.uib.no

G. Fløistad (ed.), *Philosophy of Justice*, Contemporary Philosophy: A New Survey 12,
DOI 10.1007/978-94-017-9175-5_9,

These scholars developed the law through a methodology *(ijtihad)* where "proof indications" from individual cases in the Qur'an and the practice of the Prophet Muhammad (the *Sunna*) were transformed into generalized legal principles and rules *(ahkam)*.[3] However, lacking a common religious or legal authority (no pope in Islam), the many competing suggestions of how to formulate such rules were theologically subsumed under the principle of *ikhtilaf*: It is God's bounty that there is a diversity of opinion among the scholars, and each scholar cannot hope to reach more than a relative truth to the best of his ability; only God knows what is best *(Allahu a'lam)*.

The practical need to single out one interpretation as practicable law was solved through the method of a perceived consensus among the scholars *(ijma)*. This is unfortunately a very conservative principle: as long as the body of scholars viewed that a previous generation had reached consensus on a legal issue, it was forever closed and could not be opened again.[4] However, the scholars did, in reality, reach very few such absolute agreements that bound all Muslims. Instead, the consensus principle formed the basis for a number of currents or varieties of the Islamic law known as the *madhhabs*, or "schools of law". The majority Sunni Islam has four such schools, and they became the operative entity within Islamic legal formulation.[5]

Some early caliphs had attempted to favour one interpretation of law over others as a "state law", but were opposed and defeated in this by the united class of *ulama* in the early ninth century. Much later, the Ottoman sultans did impose a sultanic code of law, the *kanunname*, with greater success, but while it was implemented with state power in Ottoman courts, it borrowed its legitimacy from the "divine" law of the Shari'a, of which it was supposedly only a practical implementation.[6]

The sultanic *kanunname* did represent a gradual movement from the classical ideal of seeing the law as the probabilistic result of scholarly, ultimately religious, endeavours of a self-appointed class of scholars, towards the codified singularity of a law code formulated by the state.[7] Nevertheless, the introductions of new Ottoman legal codes in the reformist *tanzimat* period of the mid-nineteenth century constituted a marked shift in this process. The first of these laws, formulated more on the model

---

[3] Schacht, Joseph (1964) *An Introduction to Islamic Law*. Oxford: Clarendon Press; and Kamali, Mohammed Hashim (1991) *Principles of Islamic Jurisprudence*. Cambridge: Islamic Texts Society.

[4] Vikør *Between God and Sultan, op. cit.*, pp. 73–88; and Hasan, Ahmad (1992) *The Doctrine of ijmâ' in Islam: A Study of the Juridical Principle of Consensus*. New Delhi: Kitab Bhavan.

[5] The four Sunni *madhhabs* only differ in rules and rituals, not in theology. Shi'i and other theological currents also each have their own *madhhab*; Schacht, *Introduction, op. cit.*, pp. 28–68; Hallaq, Wael B. (2005) *The Origins and Evolution of Islamic Law*. Cambridge: Cambridge University Press, pp. 150–178; and Bearman, Peri, Peters, Rudolph, Vogel, Frank E. (eds.) (2005) *The Islamic School of Law: Evolution, Devolution and Progress*. Cambridge, MA: Harvard University Press.

[6] Repp, Richard C. (1988) "Qanun and *shari'a* in the Ottoman Context," in al-Azmeh, Aziz (ed.) *Islamic Law: Social and Historical Contexts*. London: Routledge, pp. 24–45; and Gerber, Haim (1994) *State, Society and Law in Islam: Ottoman Law in Comparative Perspective*. Albany: State University of New York Press, pp. 57–78.

[7] Weiss *Spirit of Islamic Law, op. cit.*, pp. 88–112; Gleave, Robert (2000) *Inevitable Doubt: Two Theories of Shî'î Jurisprudence*. Leiden: Brill; and al-Azmeh, Aziz "Islamic Legal Theory and the Appropriation of Reality," in Azmeh (ed.), *Islamic Law, op. cit.*, pp. 250–265.

of European laws than on the revealed sources of the Shari'a, was the *Khatt-i Sharif* of 1839, which for the first time established the principle that its legal principles were equally valid irrespective of religious background, Muslim or non-Muslim.[8] In the following decades, Ottoman legislative assemblies were established, and new criminal and administrative codes were set up. The contents of these laws were still marked by a continuation of the old *kanun*s, and through this the classical Shari'a rules, but the process of formulation was in line with more modern systems. The same was true for the most ambitious of these legal reforms, the *Mecelle-i ahkam-i adliye*, a comprehensive law on contracts, hire, and other economic matters as well as legal administration.[9] Here too, the content was traditional but the form was modernized. New courts were also established to handle the new laws, and legal experts—lawyers and judges—were educated in new institutions.

In the course of the following century, legal reforms continued. While modern Turkey departed from the gradualism of the Ottoman reform model and introduced Western laws wholesale in Atatürk's new republic, the rest of the former empire, now independent Muslim states, continued a slower process, where criminal, economic and administrative laws were eventually Europeanized and secularized, breaking the last bonds to the older Shari'a roots. Only the area of family laws and personal status, including inheritance, was kept as a kind of "preserve" for the Shari'a. Until today most Muslim countries maintain family laws that are based on classical Shari'a ideas.

But even here, most countries have modernized the process of formulation of the laws.[10] The old methods of scholarly *ijtihad* were abandoned for the formulation of structured family laws by a legislator based on state authority. Thus, all countries have in one way or another modified and modernized the classical family laws (almost all countries have, for example, introduced some form of minimum age for marriage). The modernizations, however, have been careful and slow, no doubt due to wariness of how willing the public would be to accept too quick a transformation of these intimately personal areas of life. Thus, no state except Tunisia has outright banned polygamy or give equal access to divorce, but most countries have introduced restrictions in these areas that go far beyond what was known in the classical law.[11] Mostly, these changes go in the direction of requiring the husband—the more

[8] Starr, June (1992) *Law as Metaphor: From Islamic Courts to the Palace of Justice*. Albany: State University of New York Press, pp. 3–42; Vikør *Between God and the Sultan, op. cit.*, pp. 222–253; and Hallaq *Shari'a, op. cit.*, pp. 443–499.

[9] Omar, S. S. (1955) "The Majalla," in Khadduri, Majid & Liebesny, Herbert J. (eds.) *Law in the Middle East: [1:] Origin and Development of Islamic Law*. Washington: The Middle East Institute, pp. 292–308.

[10] Mir-Hosseini, Ziba (1993) *Marriage on Trial: A Study of Islamic Family Law: Iran and Morocco Compared*. London: I.B. Tauris; and Shaham, Ron (1997) *Family and the Courts in Modern Egypt: A Study Based on Decisions by the Sharî'a Courts 1900–1955*. Leiden: Brill.

[11] An-Na'im, Abdullahi A. (ed.) (2002) *Islamic Family Law in a Changing World: A Global Resource Book*. London: Zed Books; Michiel, Otto Jan (ed.) (2010) *Sharia incorporated: A Comparative Overview of the Legal Systems of Twelve Muslim Countries in Past and Present*. Leiden: Leiden University Press; and Jeppie, Shamil & et al. (eds.) (2010) *Muslim Family Law in Sub-Saharan Africa*. Amsterdam: Amsterdam University Press.

powerful party—to register with the courts and to justify his change of status, or have court-imposed monetary penalties imposed on him if he cannot convince the court of the justification for his action. The divorce or remarriage in question will however generally still be considered valid, as both are rights guaranteed in scripture.

Thus, while the legal system in most Muslim countries today is basically a secular one formed on a Western model, there has always been a place and some relevance for the Shari'a model of law, even before the demand in the last quarter century from new Islamist currents to "implement" or "re-implement" the Shari'a.[12] Iran and Sudan are the two Middle Eastern countries that have acceded to such Islamist plans, but both did so by changing the contents of the relevant law codes rather than reintroducing the pre-modern methods of formulation, which thus leaves these laws open to continued contestation and further reform pressures.[13]

1 Shari'a and Fiqh

This insertion of classical Islamic legal thought into modern systems, and the evident disagreements within the Muslim world between those who want to reintroduce legal rules from the classical period (or earlier) and those who want to reform and modernize the Shari'a elements that are already there, have opened up space for more basic discussions of what the Shari'a means and how the religious and divine can relate to the human intellectual efforts. Here, contemporary scholars marshal theories from the medieval controversies and also develop new concepts based on a fresh discussion of what "Islamic law" can mean today.

One issue is how to distinguish the human from the divine. The assumption behind the law is that the all-knowing God is aware of all human actions and situations and has placed each into one of five categories: the required acts which it is a sin not to perform *(fard)* and the forbidden which it is a sin to commit *(haram)*; then, the recommended *(mandub)* and disapproved *(makruh)*, neither of which are considered sins to perform or not; and, finally, the neutral *(mubah)*.[14] These are moral categories, and in the legal practice of the courts only the required *fard* and forbidden *haram* are relevant categories. Nevertheless, God has a will and a meaning

---

[12] Vikør, Knut S. (2000) "The Shari'a and the Nation State: Who can Codify the Divine Law?," in Utvik, Bjørn Olav & Vikør, K. S. (eds.) (2000) *The Middle East in a Globalized World*. Bergen: Nordic Society for Middle Eastern Studies, pp. 220–250.

[13] Schirazi, Asghar (1997) *The Constitution of Iran: Politics and State in the Islamic Republic*. London: I.B. Tauris; and Layish, Aharon & Warburg, Gabriel R. (2002) *The Reinstatement of Islamic law in Sudan under Numayrî*. Leiden: Brill. Pakistan, Afghanistan and parts of Nigeria have also "Islamized" their laws, much in the same fashion; Mehdi, Rubya (1994) *The Islamization of the Law in Pakistan*. London: Curzon Press; and Peters, Rudolph (2003) *Islamic Criminal Law in Nigeria*. Ibadan: Spectrum Books.

[14] Vikør *Between God and Sultan, op. cit.*, pp. 36–37.

for all acts, and he keeps this with him in what we may call the "divine Shari'a", which only he can know fully. What we have on earth is God's indications *(dala'il)* to his divine will in the form of revelation texts which human scholars interpret. But since God's revelation came to a final end with the Prophet Muhammad, this human endeavour, *fiqh* or jurisprudence, is not vetted against God's actual will and cannot itself be divine, and therefore not the results of this *fiqh* either.

All Islamic legal scholars agree on the human limitations of the *fiqh* process, although they of course also emphasize that the aim of any honest scholar is to come as close to discovering the divine will as humanly possible. But this argument is evidently emphasized by those who seek to reform the laws, as removing the divine authority from human *fiqh* means that you can open the law to new developments. The word "Shari'a", however, still resonates strongly with the implication of a "divine law". So it has become common to reserve the name Shari'a for God's divine law as it resides with God and is reflected in the indisputable *(qati)* texts of the Qur'an and Sunna, those few verses and rules which do not require any interpretation or evaluation to discern their legal and moral content. Shari'a can in this way be considered divine and "preserved" from human interference, while *fiqh* is human and open to change and re-evaluation according to accepted legal principles.[15]

This distinction has now become very common, but may cause confusion as "Shari'a" is also often used as the sum total of "Islamic law", that is to say the *ahkam* rules that are the result of jurists' *fiqh*. Therefore, a rule which is based not on a *qati* text of revelation but, for example, on the use of analogical reasoning from another revelation text, can both be called a Shari'a rule and not a Shari'a rule depending on how that name is defined, even when both agree this is a rule Muslims should apply.

It must be added here that in either case, the Shari'a's span is far wider than "law" in Western understandings, as God's code of morality covers every aspect of life. This is recognized by Islamic jurisprudence, which distinguishes between "worship", or man's relation to God *(ibadat)*, and "acts", man's relation to man *(mu'amalat)*. They roughly coincide with rules of religious ritual (prayer, pilgrimage, etc.) against matters that we would consider legal, although the division is not precise: certain crimes considered to have their punishment specified in the revealed texts (the five *hudud* crimes)[16] are part of *ibadat*, as they are for that reason crimes against God, not against men.

---

[15] Vikør *Between God and the Sultan, op. cit.*, pp. 2–3.

[16] These are the Shari'a punishments that are most famous among non-Muslims, for theft (amputation), highway robbery (death), drinking alcohol (whipping) fornication (whipping or death), and false accusation of fornication (whipping). In fact, these five stand alone in the law and were in classical times surrounded by rules meant to limit their application; Peters, Rudolph (2005) *Crime and Punishment in Islamic Law: Theory and Practice from the Sixteenth to the Twenty-First Century*. Cambridge: Cambridge University Press.

2 Legitimacy

As the law thus rests partly on divine revelation and partly on human intellectual efforts, it raises the issue of the relation between God and man in the legitimation of the law. If the Shari'a was a divine law, did that mean that it was also a natural law that could be drawn rationally from human knowledge of nature, or was its divinity delinked from rational discourse? That is to say: was divine law and natural law congruent or separate?[17] Classical Muslim thought considered that it was man's natural disposition *(fitra)* to be a monotheist *(hanif)* and thus a "Muslim" in its most general meaning, but that it is its surroundings (parents or other) that makes the child lose its natural *hanif* state and become Christian, Jew or pagan. In this sense, obedience to God's will is close to a natural state for mankind.

Nevertheless, the general view came to be that while rational thought can unravel how God has constructed nature and thus what his natural laws are, it is not possible through reason to determine the normative status of human actions, whether an act is good or bad. This can only be done by following explicit or implicit commands by God as stated in the revelation and developed from it by *fiqh*. Thus, the laws for mankind are not based on natural law, but on a normative basis provided by God and on his authority alone.

It was, however, possible to formulate some general motivations behind this revelation. Classical thought tended to believe that the purpose of the Shari'a could be summed into "five protections" or "necessities": The aim of God's law was to protect an individual's religion, life, intellect *(aql)*, family *(nasab)* and property.[18]

More controversial was the search for a general divine will behind the law, God's intentions *(maqasid)* with the law. Several medieval legal scholars, in particular Najm al-Din al-Tufi (d. 1316) and Ibrahim ibn Musa al-Shatibi (d. 1388), defined this in a way that has found great favour with modern reformists.[19]

Their understanding is based on the distinction between *ibadat*, the rules for man's relation to God, and the *mu'amalat* rules for interpersonal behaviour. The former rules were created by God simply to be applied as worship to him, and have no other rationality—Muslims pray simply because God has so ordered. Thus the motivation behind them cannot be understood by man and they are not subject to further interpretation or development. Some of them clearly constitute hardship for

---

[17] Griffel, Frank (2007) "The Harmony of Natural Law and Shari'a in Islamist Theology," in Amanat, Abbas & Griffel, Frank (eds.) *Shari'a: Islamic Law in the Contemporary Context*. Stanford: Stanford University Press, pp. 38–61.

[18] Opwis, Felicitas (2007) "Islamic Law and Legal Change: The Concept of *maslaha* in Classical and Contemporary Islamic Legal Theory," in Amanat & Griffel, *Shari'a*, *op. cit.*, p. 66. Other formulations use *ird*, honour, in place of *aql* and soul *(nafs)* for life; Krämer, Gudrun (2007) "Justice in Modern Islamic Thought," in Amanat & Griffel, *Shari'a*, *op. cit.*, p. 23.

[19] Masud, Muhammad Khalid (1995) *Shâtibî's Philosophy of Islamic Law: A Revised and Enlarged Version of Islamic Legal Philosophy*. Islamabad: Islamic Research Institute; and Opwis, Felicitas (2010) *Maslaha and the Purpose of the Law: Islamic Discourse on Legal Change from the 4th/10th to 8th/14th century*. Leiden: Brill.

the believers, such as the annual fasting that can be harsh in the warm weather of the Muslim heartlands. The Shari'a or the Qur'an give no indication of what direct mundane benefit the Muslims should have from it, nor can reason find such benefits. It is a demand God makes and is to be followed for that reason without there being any other motivation that the believers can or should seek to understand.

Not so for the *mu'amalat*. God has clearly stated a purpose for these laws: "God wants ease for you, he does not want hardship"[20]: their purpose is in human and social welfare *(maslaha)*. The ideas of social welfare need not be based on the explicit text of revelation, but can be found independently *(maslaha mursala)*. That is to say, the *mu'amalat* rules are subject to rationality, and scholars can by intellectual efforts fathom why God has made them. That means, the reformers believe, that the key element that Muslims must seek to realize is God's motive of *maslaha*, not necessarily those concrete rules that were developed through *fiqh*.[21] If, for example, society changes so that the Shari'a rules that were formulated at one particular point in time no longer fulfil the divine intention of human welfare, then these rules must change so that God's intentions are fulfilled under today's conditions. In other words, the Shari'a's rules we consider to be legal rules rather than religious ritual—what we call "Islamic law" as law—must be open to change, and in particular those rules that were developed originally through the human and fallible *fiqh* of the early Muslim legal scholars.[22] The important legal activity is to discover the welfare motivation that God sought to impose through the formulations of his revelation, and implement that in the best possible way in the actual social situation of each epoch and society.

Clearly, this is a reformist view, and it was never that of the majority of scholars. In the classical period, a more orthodox understanding of *maslaha*, as expressed by the dominant theoretician Abu Hamid al-Ghazzali (d. 1111), made a distinction between necessity *(darura)*, and need *(haja)*.[23] Only in cases where it was required to ensure the "five protections" of life, religion and so on, and where this necessity was absolutely certain *(qati)* as well as universal for all believers, was it allowed to use the *maslaha* principle to introduce laws that had no textual basis in the revelation. The lower level of "need" was not sufficient for such extensions.

This remained the dominant view, although legal practices accepted a number of legal principles that constituted exceptions to the direct implementation of general rules, in cases where to follow the purely logical extensions of Qur'anic rules would lead to evident unintended hardships. These secondary principles of *fiqh* were variously known as *istislah* (actually "to seek the *maslaha*"), *istihsan*, *rukhsa*, and

---

[20] Qur'an 2:185, similar in several other verses.

[21] Zubaida, Sami (2003) *Law and Power in the Islamic World*. London: I.B. Tauris, pp. 142–146.

[22] Sachedina, Abdulaziz (1999) "The Ideal and Real in Islamic Law," in Khare, Ravindra S. (ed.) *Perspectives on Islamic Law, Justice and Society*. Lanham: Rowan & Littlefield, pp. 15–32; and an-Na'im, Abdullahi Ahmed (2008) *Islam and the Secular State: Negotiating the Future of the Shari'a*. Cambridge, MA: Harvard University Press.

[23] Opwis "Islamic Law and Legal Change," *op. cit*., pp. 66–71.

others, and the motivations were clearly that of seeking general welfare, based on the divine statement that God does not seek to burden the believers unnecessarily, but wishes what eases their life.[24]

3 Modern Developments

There were, however, always voices among legal scholars who favoured a greater role for adaptation and reinterpretation of legal rules, that is, calling for a renewed *ijtihad*.[25] The latter is a controversial and somewhat confusing term, its basic meaning is simply "the elaboration of legal rules", and is technically a prerequisite for any legal scholar of a certain status. However, with the establishment of the four major *madhhab*s from the tenth century onwards, it was considered that completely free *ijtihad* was no longer possible, as all scholars would have to operate within the standards of one of the four schools.[26] Legal developments were thus termed by less absolute concepts, such as *ifta*, basically to formulate how a rule should be applied under specific circumstances, which with other "secondary" legal terms could still give the scholars a fairly wide scope for reinterpretation.[27]

The reform-oriented minority was not satisfied with this level of freedom to formulate rules, and argued that the law cannot be closed. However, for the early reformers until the nineteenth century, *ijtihad* mostly meant to go back to the texts of the revelation, the Qur'an and Sunna, and develop rules that were more in harmony with the actual texts, or by re-evaluating the strength of each verse or Prophetic statement against each other, so that you could achieve an understanding that more correctly represented what God and the Prophet had originally intended.[28]

This was still a self-evident basis for the new generation of reformers that grew from the nineteenth century; *ijtihad* could clearly not be drawn directly from the "whims" of the contemporary scholars. However, such modernist scholars as Muhammad Abduh, Rashid Rida and others looked more and more to *maslaha*

---

[24] Fadel, Mohammad Hossam (2002) "'*Istihsân* is Nine-Tenth of the Law': The Puzzling Relationship of *usûl* to *furû'* in the Mâlikî *madhhab*," in Weiss, B. G. (ed.) *Studies in Islamic Legal Theory*. Leiden: Brill, pp. 161–76; and Vikør *Between God and Sultan, op. cit.*, pp. 65–69.

[25] Peters, Rudolph (1980) "Idjtihâd and taqlîd in 18th and 19th century Islam," in *Die Welt des Islams*, xx, 3–4, pp. 131–145.

[26] Hallaq, Wael B. (1984) "Was the Gate of Ijtihad Closed?," in *International Journal of Middle East Studies*, xvi, 1, pp. 3–41; and *idem*, "Ifta' and Ijtihad in Sunni Legal Theory: A Developmental Account," in Masud, M. K., Messick, B. & Powers, D. S. (eds.) (1996) *Islamic Legal Interpretation: Muftis and their fatwas*. Cambridge, MA: Harvard University Press, pp. 33–43.

[27] Masud, Muhammad Khalid, Messick, Brinkley, Powers, David S. "Muftis, Fatwas and Islamic Legal Interpretation," in Masud & *et al. Islamic Legal Interpretation, op. cit.*, pp. 3–32.

[28] Vikør, Knut S. (2000) "Opening the Maliki School: Muhammad b. 'Ali al-Sanusi's Views on the *madhhab*," in *Journal of Libyan Studies*, i, 1, pp. 5–17.

mursala and the need to draw the changing social and historical conditions into the legal reinterpretation.[29]

In the course of the twentieth century, such reformist thought gained particular ground among legislators who were not necessarily trained in classical *fiqh*, but had to use Islamic legal terminology to justify the changes they wanted to implement within family law and other areas of law where the Shari'a influence was still dominant. Thus, for example, they leaned heavily on the concept of *talfiq*, which had only been accepted in exceptional situations in the classical period.[30] This means to draw a legal rule from *any* of the four schools of law. Classically, any scholar should stay within his chosen *madhhab* and never look over the fence to the other three. While many or even most of the general principles and rules were identical between the schools, each had developed its own jurisprudential principles and methods of deriving the rules, so to "mix and match" would not make sense without a unified methodology for the process.

The modern legislative bodies mostly ignored such methodological niceties, and picked and chose whichever law from any of the four schools that went in the direction they wanted to go. Evident examples are within the areas of marriage and divorce, where the Hanafi and Maliki schools form clear oppositions.[31] In the Hanafi school (dominant in the Muslim north and east, regions earlier dominated by Ottomans or other Turkish rulers), the bride has at least in theory a strong position in the choice of a marriage partner, and can, for example, contract a marriage on her own authority without the participation of her guardian (father).[32] In the Maliki school (North and West Africa), this is impossible: the father has a dominant authority and while the daughter should voluntarily assent to the marriage, she should also (at least in her first, virginal, marriage) accept her father's choice. Modernists clearly favoured the Hanafi system over the Maliki one; in fact, most North African countries have imposed specific laws banning *ijbar*, the father's imposition of his will over his daughter.[33]

On the issue of a wife's access to divorce in the courts, however, the liberal/conservative balance is opposite. The Hanafi school basically does not allow this at all; a court cannot (or only in very exceptional cases) dissolve a marriage against the will or even in the permanent absence of the husband. The Maliki school had, even in the medieval period, a view that sounds almost "modern": a wife who feels the marriage is detrimental to her, be it physically or mentally, can go to the court and

---

[29] Kerr, Malcolm (1966) *Islamic Reform: The Political and Legal Theories of Muhammad 'Abduh and Rashîd Ridâ*. Berkeley: University of California Press.

[30] Kerr *Islamic Reform*; and Qadri, Syed Moinuddin (1983) "Traditions of taqlid and talfiq," in *Islamic Culture*, lvii, 2, pp. 39–61, & lvii, 3, pp. 123–145.

[31] Vikør *Between God and Sultan, op. cit.*, pp. 299–325.

[32] Carroll, Lucy (1996) "Qur'an 2:229: 'A Charter Granted to Wife'? Judicial khul' in Pakistan," in *Islamic Law and Society*, iii, 1, pp. 91–126; and Mitchell, Ruth (1997) "Family Law in Algeria Before and After the 1404/1984 Family Code," in Gleave, R. & Kermeli, E. (ed.) *Islamic Law: Theory and Practice*. London: I.B. Tauris, pp. 194–204.

[33] An-Na'im, *Islamic Family Law, op. cit.*

have it dissolved (if, of course, she can convince the judge of the merit of her argument). It is not modern European liberalism, but it is for women widely preferable to the Hanafi system. Thus, many modern states have simply picked the Hanafi system of marriage and the Maliki system of divorce, notwithstanding that there are divergent *fiqh* methodologies that make the Hanafis and Malikis arrive at their respective rules for both situations.

4 How Wide Is the Possibility of Reform?

This shows that in spite of the apparent immutability of the divine Islamic law, there are differences that can be exploited by reformists today even without stepping outside the reference to classical law, twisting the rules somewhat beyond what some religious scholars may be quite happy with. But how far can such efforts go?

We have today many strands of Islamic reform that can go very far in changing actual rules while maintaining the idea that their views are based on the divine will and the texts of the revelation, in particular the various groups known as "Muslim feminists", many of who deal with legal issues relating to family law.[34] However, it may also be interesting to consider discussions that go on *inside* the class of religious scholars over arguments that may be considered "religiously valid, even if wrong" by opponents who would reject the more strictly feminist interpretations out of hand. This can give an impression of the extent of malleability of Islamic legal thought based on religious premises and established scholarship.

As an illustration, we can look at two works written by two contemporary Syrian scholars on the issue of women's rights, always central to the issue of reform. One of them, Muhammad Habash (b. 1962), is the grandson-in-law of the former mufti of Syria, Ahmad Kuftaro, and thus very much an "acceptable" religious scholar in the country.[35] He is the head of a reformist mosque in the capital, and ran an educational Islamic centre until a few years ago, when his relationship with the authorities hit a rough patch. He is also a politician and was for a period an independent MP in Syria, part of the effort in the 2000s to involve spokesmen for the civil society outside of the Ba'th party.[36]

The other author, Muhammad Said Ramadan al-Buti (1929–2013), was an even more dominant figure in Syrian Islam and one of the most prolific authors on a number of topics, including sharp attacks on the brand of political Islam called

[34] Bøe, Marianne (2012) "Debating Family Law in Contemporary Iran: Continuity and Change in Women's Rights Activists' Conception of Shari'a and Women's Rights," Ph.D. University of Bergen.

[35] Although he came under strong criticism by Kuftaro for the book we discuss here, and later broke with his followers after the mufti's death, allegedly over Habash's statement that the "people of the Book", Christians and Jews, might also aspire to a place in Heaven; Warda, Muhammad Anwar (2003) *Hiwâr … lâ shijâr*, n.p. [Dimashq], pp. 13–14.

[36] Heck, Paul L. (n.d.) *Religious Renewal in Syria: The Case of Muhammad Al-Habash*. Damascus: Dar al-tajdeed, pp. 34 & 74.

Salafism.[37] He was dean of the Faculty of Shari'a at Damascus University, and preached at the prestigious Umayyad mosque there. While he had no direct relationship with the regime, he came out in support of it both in the 1982 crisis and in the current civil war. No doubt for this reason, he was murdered by rebel forces in March 2013.

Thus, both these authors can be placed within the area of "acceptable" legal and social discourse in contemporary Syria,[38] and make, for example, a clear line against the trends of political Islamism, which were of course severely repressed in Syria. The interest in comparing their views lies not there, but in seeing what is the realm of debates that can be and is conducted within what we may call "majority" or at least "official" Islam in a country like Syria. Within this field of sanctioned Islam, Habash could then be seen as a liberal modernist while still a classical scholar, while Buti is perhaps as conservative and traditionalist as it is possible to be in modern Islamic thought. While both are from the fairly secular Syria, similar debates take place in most contemporary Muslim countries.[39]

5 The Role of Women

Habash's views on the position of women are concisely expressed in his book *al-Mar'a bayn al-shari'a wa'l-hayat* [The Woman between the Shari'a and Life][40]; among Buti's many works, his *al-Mar'a bayna tughyan al-nizam al-gharbi wa-lata'if al-tashri' al rabbani* [Women Between the Tyranny of the Western System and the Mercy of Islamic Law][41] indicates already in the title his conclusion on the topic.

Buti's book is clearly an apologia for Islam. It compares the elevated ideal of pious Islamic behaviour with the degraded reality of American society, both virtually presented as caricatures. Nevertheless, there are a few snippets of actual discussion of contemporary Syrian society as well.

Habash presents neither an apologia nor a rejection of contemporary Muslim society, but rather what we may call a "centrist" view. He criticizes both the *mutashaddidun*, "the overly severe", that is of course the Islamist and purist view of

[37] Summed up in his work, *al-Salafiyya: Marhala zamaniyya mubaraka, la-madhhab islami*: "The Time of the Prophet: A Blessed Period of Time, but not an Islamic School of Thought". Damascus: Dar al-fikr, 1988.

[38] That is, the period before the current civil war; all publications here predate this conflict.

[39] Depending, of course, on the political and religious climate of each country, the scope of debate in for example conservative Saudi Arabia and liberal Tunisia is certainly very different!

[40] Damascus: Dar al-tajdid 2005.

[41] Translated into English by Nancy Roberts, 2nd ed., Damascus: Dar al-fikr 2006. Habash is clearly aware of the work of the older and respected scholar, and go out of his way to cite, with apparent approval, ten pages from Buti's book. Buti had no such qualms, and immediately attacked Habash's book for "permitting the forbidden and forbidding the allowed"; Warda, *Hiwâr*, 15.

women, and the “atheist” feminists. The resulting “middle road”, always an ideal in Islamic writings, does open up for a real presentation of changes in the Islamic position.

A crucial legal distinction between them is that Habash here clearly uses *ijtihad* in his discussion of the woman’s question in the law: He draws out Prophetic traditions *(hadith)* that promote tolerance, *tasamuh*, over restrictiveness. Women are, he says, in a “narrow place” because of traditions that have support in *fiqh*, but are far from the spirit of the Shari’a. Buti, on his side, condemns *ijtihad* outright. He says people who promote such reinterpretations of orthodox and established understandings have left Islam and want to empty the text of all content just to make it fit the degraded reality of the Western model; those who follow a Western lifestyle, we cannot even consider them Muslim.[42]

6 The Topics at Issue

Habash approaches various issues that are in current debate on women one by one. We can however group them in two main categories: one arguing that women have a place in the public sphere, the other on the social relations between men and women.

As for the first group, his main arguments are against those who want to restrict women from public life. He supports the views Buti made in his earlier book that a woman must have full access to employment that is compatible with her role as mother and wife. Both scholars reject the idea that women should *have* to work for economic reasons because the husband fails his duty as provider; the onus on providing for the household clearly falls on the man, and he cannot shift that responsibility onto his wife.[43] Also, both agree that there are types of employment that are not suitable for a woman because of her femininity. For Buti, being a bus conductor or taxi driver is not a suitable profession for a woman. Habash, in contrast, includes both the military and police among natural employments for a woman, citing the example from the Prophet’s time where *hadith* tell of women taking direct part in the fighting both areas are completely abhorrent to Buti.[44]

A clear contradiction, and one which has become central in the various recent discussions over Islamic constitutions after the Arab Spring revolutions, is the issue of whether a woman can be head of state. Buti says no, because of the *hadith* about the Prophet saying “No nation led by a women will prosper”, referring to his Persian enemies appointing a female shah.[45] A woman can reach any position in politics, Buti says, apparently including prime minister, but not the specific position of head of state. Buti uses a rather curious reasoning for this; head of state in any Muslim

[42] Buti *Women, op. cit.*, pp. 323–324; and Habash, *al-Mar’a, op. cit.*, p. 182.

[43] Habash *al-Mar’a, op. cit.*, pp. 107–108; and Buti *Women, op. cit.*, pp. 129–132.

[44] Buti *Women, op. cit.*, pp. 89–91; and Habash, *al-Mar’a, op. cit.*, p. 172.

[45] Buti *Women, op. cit.*, pp. 98–101.

country must mean caliph, and among the caliph's duties is to lead prayer. But a woman is exempt from Friday prayer during menstruation, and as she cannot therefore fulfil this duty once every month, she cannot be head of state. The argument is curious because only some Salafists, Buti's ferocious enemies, are anywhere near imagining the caliphate with its religious function as appropriate for a contemporary Muslim state. Certainly no Muslim state today would think of their head of state as a caliph. Thus, the argument seems theoretical and specious.

Habash disagrees and lists all the Muslim countries that now have female leaders as arguments that women certainly can fulfil the highest position in the state.[46] In fact, he says, the Muslim world seems to have a better record in this regard than the West; neither France nor the US has so far had female presidents. But the Muslim female heads of state we have seen were all from Asia. With us in the Arab world, this seems still to be unthinkable, he sighs, so the Arabs must here learn from Asian Muslims.

As for the related issue of whether a woman can lead men and women in prayer (be an *imam*), traditional views have been that a woman may (perhaps) lead other women in prayer, but not men. Habash emphasizes that there is no doubt that a woman in general can be an imam: the Prophet himself asked the woman Umm Waraqa to lead the prayer.[47] And, he says, there were at the time men in the congregation. Indeed, Islam has female prophets like Mary and the Pharaoh's wife, so how can they not be prayer leaders? The *hadith* that is used to prove the contrary is weak, meaning it is unlikely to be a true representation of the Prophet's statement. The traditional commentaries on the Qur'an *(tafsirs)*, written by the best theologians, support the view that a woman may lead the prayer. It was rather the jurists, the specialists in law, who rejected the idea, and we cannot today know why they did so. Is it possible today to change this and allow women to lead prayer? Well, Habash concedes, it would be difficult to implement in the contemporary situation, because of all the bad things that have happened to the woman's situation in the last centuries, as opposed to how it was under the Prophet, but he clearly implies that these hindrances should preferably be removed.

As for social relations between women and men, Habash devotes considerable space to the *hijab*.[48] Besides noting that the Prophet forbade the *niqab* (the veil that covers the face),[49] his main argument is that we should look at the *maqasid*, the intentions behind the rules of clothing, in historical contexts that vary. It is also quite unclear in *fiqh* what exactly is to be covered by the *hijab*, but it must in any case not be seen as a prescription to be enforced, but as a symbol that the Muslim woman

---

[46] Habash *al-Mar'a*, *op. cit.*, pp. 46–49.

[47] Habash *al-Mar'a*, *op. cit.*, pp. 162–165.

[48] Habash *al-Mar'a*, *op. cit.*, pp. 62–104.

[49] Habash *al-Mar'a*, *op. cit.*, pp. 85–86. There is a widely accepted *hadith* that the Prophet was asked about how much a woman should cover, and pointed to the forehead and wrists and said, "here and here is enough", which is thought to indicate that women should not cover more. Reformists consider this a ban on further covering, supporters of the *niqab* only that it is not compulsory to cover more than this.

freely takes on if she so wishes. It is equally as wrong to impose the *hijab* on those who do not wish it, as it is to ban it for those who do; but here again the weight of his argument is against those who try to impose it as a regulation, and he argues for tolerance. It is not so that women cannot be seen in public without the *hijab*. Even in the Prophet's time, some of his wives took part in his military campaigns, helping to nurse the wounded, and they did not wear proper *hijab* at the time.[50] Many other *hadiths* show the same thing; it was not so in the time of the Prophet that wearing the *hijab* was an absolute rule. Indeed, wearing it is a sacrifice for a woman, but she does so to symbolize her adherence to the principle of social propriety. Anyway, in general, the conservative *ulama* give much too much importance to this issue; why, when Muslims were fighting for their lives in Bosnia, some Arab countries sent them boxes of *hijab*s![51]

Social propriety, *afaf ijtima'i*, is a central concept for Habash. The relationship between women and men must be based on the social good, and the family is a cornerstone of society. From this, the woman has a special role in the family, but both men and women must also take responsibility for avoiding the corruption of social relations that we find in the West. Like Buti, Habash criticizes the social dissolution of the family we can find in the Western world. This leads, he claims to have observed in Brazil, to children roaming the streets and being killed by death squads. They are called "human rats", and is it not a human right to be born to two parents?[52]

This is of course a type of argument that Buti goes on about to a great length, with entertaining examples. At a conference on poetry he attended, a woman not wearing a *hijab* got up to give a presentation. When Buti looked around at the audience, he noticed that not a single man paid attention to anything she was saying but only to her "charms"; that is, her hair and appearance.[53] When a presenter wore a *hijab*, however, everyone focused on the content of her thoughts.

In spite of their shared rejection of Western family *mores*, there are clear contradictions between the two authors when it comes to several issues of the Shari'a's family laws. Both do support the Muslim principle of polygamy, in principle. But they use different arguments for why this must be allowed. Buti's reasoning is that polygamy is the only way to avoid adultery; a husband's urges are better settled in a proper way in the form of marriage than in an extramarital affair.[54] Habash explicitly rejects this argument for polygamy as a way to avoid adultery for men only.[55] For him, taking a second wife is only acceptable when there are particular reasons, such as when an illness makes the first wife unable to take care of the children, and the husband would need to remarry to provide them with proper care. It is better that the

[50] Habash *al-Mar'a*, *op. cit.*, p. 172.

[51] Habash *al-Mar'a*, *op. cit.*, pp. 97–98.

[52] Habash *al-Mar'a*, *op. cit.*, pp. 94–95.

[53] Buti *Women*, *op. cit.*, pp. 228–229; playing in Arabic on the words *shi'r* (poetry, her topic) and *sha'r* (hair).

[54] Buti *Women*, *op. cit.*, pp. 172–193.

[55] Habash *al-Mar'a*, *op. cit.*, pp. 123–127.

man is allowed to take a second wife than that he has to divorce the first. He also approves of the restrictions Syria and other countries have made on polygamy,[56] and notes that while the Prophet had many wives, only A'isha had not been married before; the others were all widows or divorced women. As for A'isha's embarrassingly young age at marriage (9), he is a bit doubtful about the truth of that, but anyway, it is certainly to be understood as an example of exceptionalism where the Prophet's example is not to be followed.[57] The Prophet's own daughters were twenty or older when they married, which is a clearly better example.

He brings up the issue of *ijbar*, the rule that a young girl must accept her father's or other male relative's choice of husband, which he disapproves of. This may let a distant relative with little concern for the girl's best interests dictate her future. What is the *maslaha* of this? And in any case, there are *hadith* that the Prophet dissolved marriages because the bride disliked the husband, so such marriages do not have Prophetic authority.[58]

Habash also discusses issues like courtship, arguing that prospective spouses must be allowed to meet and get to know each other before a decision to marry is made, and the case of women travelling alone without a male guardian, where we must take into account the changed conditions of today when it is possible to travel safely alone, unlike in medieval times.

His argumentation on the last point is interesting: He says that the Shari'a rule that women must be accompanied by a relative on travel for more than 3 days is not based on a text of revelation, although there are in fact *hadith* on this topic.[59] But the legal scholars used their own *ijtihad* on these texts so as to make them more restrictive than the actual wording of the revelation. Thus, they ignored opposing *hadith* stating that the Prophet allowed women to travel for more than 3 days. Therefore, there is no problem today with throwing out this rule. What we must do is look at the general tenor of the prophetic *hadith*, which is that of tolerance and practical adaptations.

We must, Habash says, not be caught up in the words of the later (i.e., classical) *fiqh*, but see the basic intention of the Prophet, which is again "social propriety". The atheists are wrong here, in making Islam seem more conservative than it really is. They assume that the restrictive *tashaddud* interpretations of the conservatives and Islamists are the true or only Islam, and that Islam therefore must be discarded. On the contrary, Habash claims, a completely secular society will break down, like in the West. But even more wrong are the conservatives who wish to separate women and men so much that if they had their way, they would have built two Ka'bas, one

[56] Such as demanding that a polygamous marriage has to be registered by court and is only allowed under certain conditions, or that the first wife is allowed a divorce (with compensation) if she does not agree to the second marriage; Vikør *Between God and Sultan*, *op. cit.*, p. 323.

[57] That is implied to be due the special needs for political alliances at the inception of the Muslim state, the most generally cited reason why the Prophet alone of all Muslims was allowed to have nine wives rather than four; Habash, *al-Mar'a*, *op. cit.*, p. 150.

[58] Habash *al-Mar'a*, *op. cit.*, pp. 147–150.

[59] Habash *al-Mar'a*, *op. cit.*, pp. 151–155.

for men and one for women; it is a good thing the rituals of pilgrimage were settled before they got going![60]

These examples give a glimpse of how the social morality of each author informs their legal views. Both the liberal Habash and the conservative Buti assumes a gendered basis for society, and thus also for its laws: Women and men have different roles in society, and this must be reflected in the family laws, such as the rules of polygamy, access to employment, and the like.

For the purpose of understanding how these religious scholars conceive of legal developments, however, the most interesting element is how they view the possibilities for change of the religiously inspired rules, and how it can be brought about. For both scholars, it is important to protect the revealed texts, and thus the religion. The reform-minded sees *ijtihad* as a way to circumvent many undesirable aspects of the revealed text, but within limits. Habash is clearly willing to give much wider space to rejecting established *fiqh* by finding opposing *hadith* that underline the spirit of Islam, which to him is tolerance, including a promotion of women's social role. But he cannot challenge the authority of the texts as such. Instead, he argues like any traditional *fiqh* scholar that the unwanted *hadith* is considered by specialists to be weak (less likely to actually stem from the Prophet) and opposed by contradictory *hadith*. Or he claims that the orthodox scholars have understood the revealed texts incorrectly and base themselves on later interpretations rather than looking at what the Prophet's real example was. This is a manner of argumentation which is in fact similar to that of the Salafist ideologues, only Habash points it in the opposite direction: towards a liberal rather than a more restrictive approach.[61]

Even more interesting is his drawing on *maslaha* or "social propriety" as an independent principle from which to draw rules. When the original Shari'a demanded that women had to be accompanied by a male member of the family when travelling, then we must search for the *maslaha* reason behind this rule, which is that of protecting the women. When the need for such male protection is no longer required, due to the greater security of our time, the original rule becomes an unnecessary burden and must be amended. The original rule is not wrong, but the scholar must discover why it was put into place and see how that intention is best achieved in the circumstances of each era.

[60] Habash *al-Mar'a*, *op. cit*., pp. 88–89. The conservatives claim that men and women must sit in separate sections of the mosque, Habash says, but when God created the Ka'ba in Mecca, he made no separation between the genders! However, when I visited Habash's "Zahra" mosque in Damascus in 2005, women were referred to a gallery with a separate entrance, in a quite normal fashion.

[61] It must be added that many Salafists actually do use similar argumentation to open room for a greater participation of women in for example education, even more so than orthodox like Buti, precisely because they use text-based *ijtihad*, although their general line of interpretation most often is opposite. Thus, the dominant Salafi theorist Nasir al-Din al-Albani came into conflict with his Saudi hosts when he claimed that wearing the *niqab* was not compulsory; Lacroix, Stéphane (2009) "Between Revolution and Apoliticism: Nasir al-Din al-Albani and his Impact on the Shaping of Contemporary Salafism," in Meijer, R. (ed.) *Global Salafism: Islam's New Religious Movement*. New York: Columbia University Press, p. 66.

In the wake of the Arab Spring, the issue of Islam in legislation has become much more contentious than it has been for generations. Earlier demands for "re-implementation" of the Shari'a came from revolutionary groups seeking full control of the state. Today, more moderate and reformist Islamist currents have gained power in agreement with or in parliamentary competition with more liberal currents in important countries like Egypt, Tunisia, Libya, Morocco and others. This opens the way for debates on whether Islamic law, or elements thereof, should have greater say in the legal systems of these countries than they have had in the last century. It is not obvious that this will be the case, but if it happens, we may see more discussions of how such Islamic elements can be integrated into a legal system that, family law apart, is basically secular and Western. Since the Islamist side is divided between moderates and more stringent forces, these issues will also be contentious between the various Islamist currents. It will therefore be important to see the impact of such classical concepts as the distinction between a divine (and transcendent) Shari'a and the human *fiqh* of the scholars; of the role, scope and method of *ijtihad* reinterpretation; and of the possibility to understand the divine rules as the result of the wish for human welfare, *maslaha*, in the social context of today rather than as the application of the fixed rules of *fiqh*. This may change fundamentally what we mean by Shari'a, or it may cause social conflicts in these countries between those who reach opposite conclusions on these legal and methodological issues.

John Locke – Libertarian Anarchism

Helga Varden

1 Introduction

Political philosophers darkly joke that after a revolution they will be among the first to be thrown onto the bonfire. Both those who have political power and those who lack it can find political philosophy threatening, which occasionally makes being a political philosopher a risky affair. John Locke experienced the danger that can accompany the pursuit of political ideas. He engaged with these ideas not only at a philosophical remove, but also intimately, as someone who could be found at the center of volatile political activity. In fact, it seems fair to say that Locke's writings on political philosophy, characterized as they are by passion, courage, and maturity, reflect his first-hand experience with both the significance of political ideas to a society and their perilous nature.

Locke lived from 1632 until 1704. This was an extremely violent period in England's history, and included the English Civil War (1642–1651) which culminated in Charles I's execution for high treason. The unrest with which Locke was directly involved occurred some years after the Civil War ended. To make a long story short, a major cause of that particular unrest was the collision, within British corridors of power, of two different conceptions of what constitutes legitimate state authority. Over time, these two different conceptions organized into the so-called "Whig" and "Tory" movements of the British Parliament. To simplify further, the Whig movement worked for the establishment of a constitutional monarchy, maintaining that the parliament should be authorized to limit the monarch's use of power. Relatedly, the Whigs rejected the ideas that the monarch's power came directly from God, and was thus responsible only to God. The Tories defended the opposite view. They argued that the ruling royal family obtained its power directly from God,

H. Varden (✉)
Departments of Philosophy and of Women and Gender Studies,
University of Illinois at Urbana-Champaign, Champaign, IL, USA
e-mail: hvarden@illinois.edu

G. Fløistad (ed.), *Philosophy of Justice*, Contemporary Philosophy: A New Survey 12, DOI 10.1007/978-94-017-9175-5_10, © Springer Science+Business Media Dordrecht 2015

meaning that the monarch has rightful, absolute power over his or her subjects and is accountable only to God. A second, though lesser, cause of the unrest in which Locke was involved was a certain royal family's—the Stuarts'—possession of the throne. Many of the Stuarts were Catholic, while England was officially Protestant (and had the Church of England). Both the Whigs and the Tories supported the Church of England and were against transforming England into a Catholic country.

Locke became directly involved in these political upheavals due to his close affiliation with the Whig movement. The Whig movement was established and led in the British Parliament by Lord Anthony Ashley Cooper, later the Earl of Shaftesbury. Locke met the Earl of Shaftesbury while the latter was still Lord Cooper and Locke was a young scholar at Oxford. An immediate intellectual and affectionate connection arose between the two when they met, resulting in a lifelong, truly remarkable friendship. For significant periods of his life, Locke lived at the Shaftesbury estate; and in addition to being one of Shaftesbury's closest and dearest friends, Locke was his personal physician and most trusted political interlocutor. Their friendship also resulted in Locke holding various public offices, so the two of them worked together professionally.[1] Consequently, Locke was not only a terrific political philosopher with what were, at the time, relatively radical political ideas, but, due to his close connection with Shaftesbury and the Whig movement, he was positioned at the center of England's political drama.

As noted above, the main reason the political situation surrounding Locke was heating up related to the Whig movement's challenge of the English throne's use of power. Tension along party lines significantly increased when the question arose concerning who would inherit the throne after the childless Charles II (the son of Charles I) died. The Whigs tried to block the Tories' attempt to ensure that James, the Duke of York and the Catholic brother of Charles II, would inherit the throne. The Whigs feared that James would not only make an effort to push England in a Catholic direction, but also try to reinstitute an absolutist reign and demolish Parliament's recently gained political influence over the monarch. The Tories, in contrast, were confident that James would not try to steer England in a Catholic direction. In addition, the Tories held that making James the new king was important for re-establishing the royal family's rightful, absolute power over the people. The Whig movement's effort to prevent James from being crowned as regent failed; James became James II, and many of the Whigs were subsequently persecuted. Shaftesbury himself was jailed twice due to his political involvement in these events, and Locke ultimately had to flee abroad, where he continued to cooperate closely with the Whig movement.

The Whigs were quickly shown to be right in their suspicion that James, once king, would try to exert political power over religious matters. This development entailed that resistance to James II's rule grew stronger, including because many Tories, too, became increasingly critical of him. The Whig victory came with "The Glorious Revolution" of 1688, though Shaftesbury himself died in 1683 and did not get to experience it. The Glorious Revolution culminated in the abdication of James II

[1] For Locke's involvement with various aspects of English colonialism, see Arneil, Barbara (1996) *John Locke and America: The Defense of English Colonialism*. Oxford: Clarendon Press.

and resulted from the cooperation between the Whig movement, important Tories, and William of Orange, among others. After the 1688 revolution, Locke returned to England. He arrived on the same ship as Mary, wife of William of Orange and daughter of James II. William of Orange and Mary, both Protestants, were appointed as the regents William III and Mary II. The "Bill of Rights" became law in 1689, which, among other things, specified limits on the monarch's power, and thus the first important, permanent steps toward a constitutional monarchy in England were made.

After Locke returned to England, he published in quick succession the three works that compose his main, invaluable contribution to Western philosophy: one work on metaphysics and epistemology, *An Essay Concerning Human Understanding* (1689)[2]; and two works on political philosophy, *A Letter Concerning Toleration* (1689) and *Two Treatises of Government* (1690). Locke had been working on the philosophy contained in these three books more or less continuously since his first days as a student at Oxford, so more or less continuously for his entire adult life. As explained below, certain of Locke's developed ideas on toleration were also anticipated in an earlier writing, *An Essay on Toleration,* completed in 1667. Locke chose to publish his political writings anonymously, which is not surprising in light of the drama surrounding his own life and involvement in politics, as well as the relatively radical nature of his ideas on freedom, tolerance, individual rights, and revolution.[3]

The influence of Locke's political ideas can hardly be exaggerated. They continue to inspire political thought from extreme anarchic libertarianism to extreme Marxism. We shall see that Locke's continual influence has been generated especially by three of his major ideas: on toleration; on the individual's so-called natural executive power; and on private property. As I elaborate below, the latter two ideas markedly distinguish Locke's theory from other prominent theories, of his day and ours, in the liberal contractarian tradition. In many ways, in fact, these two ideas account for the fact that his theory can usefully be called "libertarian anarchism."[4]

---

[2] Locke, John (1979) *An Essay Concerning Human Understanding*. Oxford: Oxford University Press. For a work that focuses on the relation between Locke's political philosophy and his main theoretical work, see Grant, Ruth W. (1991) *John Locke's Liberalism*. Chicago: University of Chicago Press.

[3] For more thorough descriptions of Locke's life, see, for example, Ashcraft, Richard (1986) *Revolutionary Politics and Locke's Two Treatises of Government*. Princeton: Princeton University Press; Laslett, Peter (1988) "Introduction" and "Addendum to Introduction," in John Locke's *Two Treatises of Government*, ed. P. Laslett. Cambridge: Cambridge University Press, pp. 1–133; Marshall, John (2006) *John Locke, Toleration, and Early Enlightenment Culture*. Cambridge: Cambridge University Press; Woolhouse, Roger S. (2007) *John Locke: A Biography*. Cambridge: Cambridge University Press. I refer to Locke's *Two Treatises of Government* in this chapter with the abbreviation "TT," I use "I" and "II" to signal which treatise I refer to, and a simple number to indicate which paragraph in the text I cite. I have used John Locke's *Political Essays*. Cambridge: Cambridge University Press, 1997 for "An Essay on Toleration," and *The Political Writings of John Locke*, ed. by D. Wootton. Signet, 1993, for "A Letter Concerning Toleration." I have used Peter Laslett's 1988 edition of Locke's *Two Treatises of Government*.

[4] For an introduction to the contrast between Locke's libertarianism and other historical libertarian conceptions, see Vallentyne, Peter & Steiner, Hillel (2007) *The Origins of Left-Libertarianism: An Anthology of Historical Writings*. New York: Palgrave Macmillan.

Moreover, though controversial as they are, these two ideas have proven tremendously important for liberal legal-political thought and practice. One reason they've been so important for political practice is that Locke justifies both constitutional limitations on the exercise of public power and the value of citizens' actual consent for a legitimate political power by means of these ideas. In other words, these two ideas—on the individual's natural executive right and on private property—serve as the core of Locke's argument in rejection of political absolutism. Therefore, these ideas became significant not only in the Whig movement (which, over time, considered Locke its great philosopher), but in the French and American Revolutions, and in the history of all constitutional, liberal democracies.

This introductory text focuses on the development and core ideas of Locke's political philosophy and outlines a few relevant, current controversies among Locke scholars. After an introduction to Locke's writings on tolerance and their development over time, I shift to his theory of justice as presented in *Two Treatises of Government.* Of particular importance in the latter work are Locke's defense of a so-called "voluntarist understanding" of political legitimacy and the right to revolution, which centrally involves the claim that political power originally belongs to each individual (the individual's natural executive right). To justify this claim, Locke provides us with a theory of laws of nature and individual rights, where he emphasizes private property, which is why special priority is given to understanding these aspects of his theory and contemporary developments of them.

2 Locke's Tolerance Writings[5]

As is the case for most philosophers, it took time for Locke to arrive at his mature political philosophy. In his younger days, he was deeply drawn to more absolutist thoughts concerning justice; he even wrote (though never published) a text that defended the state's right to partially limit persons' freedom of speech, exercise of religion, and other aspects of their personal lives. Locke never believed, however, that the coercive power of the state can reach our convictions or "hearts"—an idea that has been central to all liberal thought since (though it has been developed and defended in different ways). But at this early stage Locke did think that the state could regulate not only our interactions with each other, but also our self-regarding actions, by making laws concerning such issues as whether one must kneel when receiving the sacrament in church. Laws regulating this sort of self-regarding action are clearly illiberal and irreconcilable with any liberal notion of each individual's right to freedom. The reason Locke held such illiberal views in his younger days was due in part, it seems, to his experience with the English Civil War. From this civil war—and its terrifying, destructive, and irrational violence—he initially concluded that harmonious coexistence between different religions was

[5]For an extensive introduction to Locke's writings on tolerance, see Marshall, John (2006): *John Locke, Toleration, and Early Enlightenment Culture*. Cambridge: Cambridge University Press.

impossible, and that the state had a right to make laws that protect us from our own stupidity, thereby enabling a better, more peaceful society. Locke was also skeptical of the Catholics, in light of their regard for the Pope as the foremost leader on earth. More generally, it seems clear that at this time Locke had little faith in religious leaders' and individuals' own abilities to act wisely and virtuously, and that he judged states' leaders better equipped to regulate both religious and personal lives than religious leaders and persons themselves. These convictions led him to conclude that having an absolutist state with a state church was necessary for a harmonious and just society.

Two later events appear to have been especially transformative for Locke, leading him to abandon his pessimistic view of human beings and his related, paternalistic view of the state's authority. First, at a relatively young age (in his early thirties) Locke participated in a diplomatic mission to Germany, acting as a secretary. There he experienced peaceful coexistence between different religious groups, including Catholics. From this he drew the (rather obvious) conclusion that his view of Catholics was, in all likelihood, deeply influenced by his own prejudices and the unfortunate politics of his day—what he had seen of powerful authorities handling religious institutions and questions. Second, not long after he returned from this trip to Germany, Locke met the Earl of Shaftesbury (then Lord Cooper), and their lifelong friendship began. At the time, Locke was considered one of the most promising philosophers in Oxford, and Shaftesbury was not only one of the richest and most powerful people around, but he could match Locke intellectually. Within a year of their first meeting, Locke had accepted Shaftesbury's invitation to come and live with him at his estate in London.

One of the first things Locke did after arriving at the Shaftesbury residence was to write *An Essay on Toleration*. This essay marks a clear maturing of Locke's political thoughts, and points toward his later, liberal political philosophy where the ideas of individuals' rights and freedom take center stage. Part of Locke's motivation in writing this essay was the fact that the establishment of the Anglican Church of England had not led to harmonious religious uniformity, as Locke had earlier thought it would, but instead led to discord and religious persecution, including through the use of state power. Another, and perhaps more important reason for the shift in Locke's thought, were his many discussions with Shaftesbury. In this vein, it is also likely that Shaftesbury's close ties with the current king, Charles II (to whom Shaftesbury was an advisor), had a significant effect on Locke. Like Shaftesbury, Charles II opposed many of the intolerant laws regarding religion that were in place. According to these laws, for example, only Anglicans could fill many public positions, and non-Anglican religious gatherings comprising more than five persons were banned. Locke's "Essay" was a philosophical reflection on the issue of tolerance, and it seems likely that it was written with the thought that the king himself might read it. Whether Shaftesbury merely encouraged or directly asked Locke to write the essay is unclear.

As mentioned above, Locke argued in his earliest, unpublished text that the state's legitimate power could and ought to limit both citizens' actions and interactions. In this newer essay, in contrast, Locke argues that the state should only regulate the citizens' *inter*actions; the state should be the judge of interactions between the citizens and not their actions as such (Locke 1997: 137). In addition, Locke argues that the state should only regulate those interactions that threaten peaceful coexistence, including those that threaten to harm others. Consequently, Locke now treats issues like whether one should kneel or stand when receiving the sacrament in church as not among the issues the state should concern itself with. Establishing a church (or temple or mosque) is of course an interaction (religious institutions are societal institutions established by several people together), but Locke now maintains that one's religious actions in the church have as little effect on societal peace as whether one sits or stands when eating at one's kitchen table (Locke 1997: 138–139).

In the "Essay," Locke still maintains that the state cannot control our convictions or our "hearts"—and he takes the argument one step further. He argues that religion must be a relationship between God and the individual, and that only the individual can be an expert on or assume responsibility for this relationship. Everyone, Locke reiterates, must find one's own way to heaven. In this piece, religion has become a deeply personal affair, and the power of the state is envisioned as secular in nature. Consequently, the state authority should not be mixed into the citizens' religious lives. Correspondingly, the religious authority is limited to the personal or private sphere, because, though it is not secular, it does not have coercive power. Locke concludes, therefore, that the area for religious speculation and worship is the only area where each citizen has unlimited freedom and where absolute and universal toleration must rule (Locke 1997: 136, 140, 150).

Also in the "Essay," Locke raises, yet again, what he takes to be the current "problem" with the Catholics. Liberal thinkers are unconvinced by his description of the phenomenon and proposed solution to the "problem"—and Locke has rightfully received much criticism on this front—but his approach here has become somewhat more reasonable than it was earlier. The problem with the Catholics, Locke now asserts, is that they mix their religious views together with intolerant views concerning interaction among citizens, and consequently Catholics do not have a right to be tolerated (Locke 1997: 146, 151–152). This mixing of religion and politics shows, Locke argues, that the leaders of the Catholic Church have managed to corrupt their own religious institution (Locke 1997: 153, 158). The right to tolerance is not a right to intolerance, and if a group's intolerance takes a practical form that can threaten the state, then the state can and should suppress this group. This means that the state can and should relate to an intolerant group as threatening only if that group becomes powerful enough that it realistically can aspire to treat other people in intolerant and disrespectful ways (Locke 1997: 147–148). In other words, in contrast with other fanatical groups of his day, the problem with the Catholics was that they also composed a powerful social group. The other fanatical groups were split into many factions, and Locke believed that the best way to secure their law-abidingness was to be tolerant toward them, since the use of power would not only fail to convince them of their mistakes (force cannot convince), but it could also lead the various fanatical groups to unite into one actually dangerous group (Locke 1997: 154–157). Finally, in the "Essay," Locke encourages everyone to take seriously the consequences of maintaining (as he himself used to) that having a stable, good state requires one uniform religion. Since the use of force cannot convince our reason or reach our "hearts," anyone seeking religious uniformity must realize that the only means by which to create it involves the massacre of one's own citizens (the killing of everyone with different religious beliefs). And, so, that person must explain how in the world such a massacre could bring about a state characterized by safety and peace (Locke 1997: 157).

Locke published, as noted above, his last and most influential piece on tolerance—*A Letter Concerning Toleration*—after he returned from exile. He published this text anonymously out of concern for his safety. In the "Letter," Locke develops many of the ideas from the earlier "Essay," and the result is a beautifully written, liberal defense of tolerance. Here Locke presents mature versions of the arguments sketched above: he defends both the claims that a just state has religious freedom (since the relationship between God and human is fundamentally private), and that only *inter*actions that threaten to destroy the justice and peace of a society can be regulated by coercive state law.

3 Two Treatises of Government

Along with the "Essay" and the "Letter," Locke's *Two Treatises of Government* is another terrific text in the history of political philosophy. It is divided into two parts: the first treatise largely discusses and rejects various religious arguments in support of absolutism; whereas the second treatise presents Locke's alternative conception of government, and most of the arguments take a secular form (though he sometimes includes religious arguments).[6] The first treatise mainly focuses on the argument that God selects monarchs as our political leaders, hence we must regard the monarch's political authority as inherited and absolute and ourselves as the monarch's proper subjects. In dealing with this argument, Locke's primary opponent is Robert Filmer, who was an influential contemporary thinker of Locke's, and defended the idea of monarchy as divinely authorized patriarchy.[7] Much of the argumentation in this first treatise has, therefore, a theological nature and appeals to close readings of the Bible. It is often explicitly directed at Filmer's contrary position and at his interpretation of the religious text.[8]

[6] For Locke, whether one interprets the Bible or uses one's reason, if done well one will end up at the same conclusions regarding justice. After all, the Bible is supposed to capture God's will and God created human beings along with their rationality. There is no good reason, therefore, to think that the two are ultimately in conflict.

[7] Filmer, Robert (1991) *Patriarcha and Other Writings*, red. Johann P. Sommerville (ed.). Cambridge: Cambridge University Press.

[8] For two works that are especially useful with regard to the religious aspects of Locke's works, see Dunn, John (1969) *The Political Thought of John Locke*. Cambridge: Cambridge University Press, and Waldron, Jeremy (2002) *God, Locke, and Equality: Christian Foundations of Locke's Political Thought*. Cambridge: Cambridge University Press.

The second part of the *Treatise* mainly contains Locke's presentation of and predominantly secular or reason-based argument for his alternative, libertarian theory of justice. Among the ideas he sets out to explain and defend are that all individuals are born free and equal, that the legitimacy of the power of the state depends on citizens' actual (explicit or tacit) consent, and that the social contract (the constitution) citizens agree to, with which all posited laws of the state must be in line, comprises the natural laws concerning individuals' rights. The arguments of the second treatise are often directed against Thomas Hobbes, according to whom (on the standard reading) the political leader ("the leviathan") has absolute political power over his subjects, and everyone else can be forced to enter the civil condition (become subjects of the leviathan).[9] As with the "Essay" and "Letter" on tolerance, it is nearly impossible to read this text without becoming fascinated by the theory presented and Locke as a political philosopher. Locke writes with an inspiring passion, he focuses on many of the absolutely most important questions in political philosophy, and he presents a truly impressive number of arguments worth taking seriously.

Since Locke presents his theory of justice in the second treatise on government, the following discussion attends to that part of his work. The first treatise and the shorter political texts are only mentioned when they can assist in showing the complexity of Locke's argument. Additionally, the second treatise contains Locke's major reflections on the topic of when people have a right to revolution, which, as noted above, was a central question for Locke and his contemporaries. On this subject, the main assumption informing much of Locke's argument is that if there is a right to revolution at all, then it must be the case that political authority (the right to specify, apply, and enforce the laws of nature) originally lies with each individual. Only if political authority originally belongs to each individual can it be the case that the establishment of a legitimate state occurs through each subject's actual consent. To show that we have a right to revolution, Locke maintains, we must demonstrate that every individual has an original, natural political authority, while the state only has a derivative, artificial political authority. This view—that individuals' actual consent is necessary for the state's legitimacy—is often referred to in political philosophy as a "strong voluntarist" conception of political obligations.[10]

How can one show that the individual is the one who possesses original or natural political authority? According to Locke, such a proof requires demonstrating that individuals can, in principle, realize justice in the absence of a state, that is, in

[9] Hobbes, Thomas (1994) *Leviathan*. Indianapolis: Hackett Publishing Company.

[10] A strong voluntarist conception of political obligations maintains, as we have seen, that the legitimacy of the state depends on each subject's *actual* (explicit or implicit/tacit) consent. In contrast, according to a weak voluntarist conception of political obligations, only *hypothetical* consent is necessary for legitimacy. For two excellent discussions of various forms of consent-based accounts of political obligations, see Onora O'Neill's "Kant and the Social Contract Tradition," in *Kant's Political Theory: Interpretations and Applications*, ed. Elizabeth Ellis. University Park, Pennsylvania: The Pennsylvania State University Press, 2012, pp. 25–41, and A. John Simmons' "Justification and Legitimacy," in *Justification and Legitimacy: Essays on Rights and Obligations*. New York: Cambridge University Press, 2001.

a pre-state condition—or what is often called "the state of nature." Establishing this requires arguing for which laws of nature (or principles of justice) the individuals would use, and how they would apply them, to realize justice and regulate their interactions in the state of nature. By revealing which principles individuals would use to realize justice in the state of nature and how they would apply them, Locke argues, one shows not only that such an activity is possible, but also that we have a right to use force to enforce them and to punish those who don't respect these principles of interaction. In this way, exposing the relevant principles and their application justify the claim that every individual has original political authority, that is, that every individual has a natural right to be the legislative, judicial, and executive power or has a so-called "natural executive right." And finally, if this is true, then it is correct to infer that only through each individual's actual consent can a public authority obtain the right to exercise political power on behalf of individuals. On this argument our political obligations to obey the state have a fundamentally strong voluntarist nature; we cannot be forced to become subjects (or citizens) of a state—we cannot be forced to enter the civil condition—we must actually, each and every one of us, consent to enter it. Moreover, if our political obligations to a particular state depend on our actual consent to its authority over us, then the individual has a right to forcibly reclaim from the state her or his political authority if the state abuses the individual's trust by not respecting the laws of nature (the fundamental principles of justice that are constitutive of the social contract) in its use of coercion. This is a defense of the individual's right to revolution.

In what follows, I sketch each of the arguments mentioned above. I begin by discussing Locke's proposal for what the fundamental principle of justice is as well as his theories concerning private property and children's rights, because understanding these elements of his philosophy is necessary for understanding his argument concerning just interaction in the state of nature. After having clarified these aspects of Locke's ideas (through appeal to both his own work and contemporary Lockean developments of it), I return to the questions of political legitimacy and revolution.

4 Locke's Theory of Freedom

Freedom is not, Locke argues, being able to do whatever one wants. Rather, freedom is acting within the framework set by the laws of nature, including when this framework of law is enabled by a legislative power one has consented to (and so entrusted with enforcing these laws on one's behalf):

> The *Natural Liberty* of Man is to be free from any Superior Power on Earth, and not to be under the Will or Legislative Authority of Man, but to have only the Law of Nature for his Rule. The *Liberty of Man, in Society*, is to be under no other Legislative Power, but that established, by consent, in the Common-wealth, nor under the Domination of any Will, or Restrain of any Law, but what the Legislative shall enact, according to the Trust put in it… *Freedom*… is… A Liberty to follow my own Will in all things, where the Rule prescribes

> not; and not to be subject to the inconstant, uncertain, unknown, Arbitrary Will of another Man. As *Freedom of Nature* is to be under no other restraint but the Law of Nature (TT, II: 22).

To understand natural political authority correctly, we must, according to Locke, start from the fundamental assumption that all individuals are free and equal; there is, he argues, no good reason to think that we are not all born free and equal. To be free is to act within the limits set by one's own reason (which are the limits of the laws of nature). As long as one acts within those limits, one can use oneself and one's means to set and pursue ends of one's own without having to ask anyone for permission; to be free and equal is to be independent of subjection to another person's will or power and instead, like everyone else, to be subjected to the laws of nature that limit everyone in the same way (TT II: 4).

Locke continues, claiming that the fundamental moral principle is the individual's right to self-preservation and the preservation of humankind:

> Every one as he is *bound to preserve himself*, and not to quit his Station willfully; so by the like reason when his own Preservation comes not in competition, ought he, as much as he can, *to preserve the rest of Mankind*, and may not unless it be to do Justice on an Offender, take away, or impair the life, or what tends to the Preservation of the Life, the Liberty, Health, Limb or Goods of another (TT, II: 6).

Self-preservation—being able to keep one's life and pursue an existence one finds meaningful (or, exercise liberty)—is only possible if we have the right to possess and use things in the world. It cannot be the case that we must ask others for permission to have and use things, as that would be to live as enslaved and not free. Moreover, since we are equal, no one should buy into the idea that any one person can have or own everything in the world, or has an innate right to have more than others; originally, all the natural resources in the world must be considered common goods (TT, II: 25–30). So how do I make some of the natural resources my own in a way that respects the fact that the resources are originally common goods, and treats everyone in the world as free and equal, *and* does not require me to ask anyone for permission to acquire some of these resources? Locke's answer to this question yields his account of private property right.

5 Locke's Account of Private Property Acquisition

Locke answers the question of how I can make things in the world my own by claiming that every person has an original right to acquire through one's labor a fair share of the world's natural resources, namely a share that is compatible with everyone else being able to do the same:

> Though the Earth, and all inferior Creatures be common to all Men, yet every Man has a *Property* in his own *Person*. This no Body has any Right to but himself. The *Labour* of his Body, and the *Work* of his Hands, we may say, are properly his. Whatsoever then he removes out of the State that Nature hath provided, and left it in, he hath mixed his *Labour*

> with, and joined to it something that is his own, and thereby makes it his *Property*. It being by him removed from the common state Nature placed it in, it hath by this *labour* something annexed to it, that excludes the common right of other Men. For this *Labour* being the unquestionable Property of the Labourer, no Man but he can have a right to what that is once joined to, at least where there is enough, and as good left in common for others" (TT, II: 27).

Later, Locke continues: "The *labour* that was mine, removing them out of that common state they were in, hath *fixed* my *Property* in them" (TT, II: 28). There are, in other words, at least two conditions I must meet in order to acquire something as my own. First, I must labor on the natural resources to make them my own; by mixing my labor with them I add something to them and thereby transform them into *mine*. Second, I must not take too much of the natural resources, but only a fair share, that is, a share that is, in principle, at most as large as and of as good a quality as the share everybody else can make their own. This second point is commonly referred to in the secondary literature as Locke's "proviso," or his "enough-and-as-good proviso," on private property acquisition. This proviso only concerns how we can make natural resources into private property through labor, and it can be understood in terms of the general formula that each of us has a right to appropriate 1/n-th of all the natural resources in the world, where n = the number of human beings in the world.[11]

To illustrate Locke's account of private property acquisition, imagine that you suddenly find yourself on a deserted island with nine other shipwrecked persons. Together, you stand on the beach and try to figure out who will get which of the natural resources on the island. Applying Locke's "enough-and-as-good" proviso, each of you has a right to 1/10th of all the natural resources on the island. For example, if there are a total of 10 coconuts on the island, you each have a right to 1 coconut and you make a coconut yours by climbing up a coconut tree and picking one. Moreover, if someone takes the coconut you have picked, then they steal from you; they steal your rightful share of the coconuts and the labor you invested in it.

The "enough-and-as-good" proviso has received a lot of attention in the secondary literature that accompanies Locke's *Two Treatises on Government*. And for good reason: after all, Locke's argument concerning private property is essential to his claim that justice is possible in the state of nature. Justice can only be possible in the state of nature, and it can only be true that individuals have original or natural political authority, if it is possible for us to make something ours on our own and without having to obtain anyone's permission to take it (so, unilaterally or without anyone's consent to it and without establishing states that have laws concerning private property appropriation). And only if the individual has original political authority can our political obligations to particular states fundamentally rest on

[11] For a critical discussion of the presumption that the notion of a "natural resource" is unproblematic, see my "Lockean Freedom and the Proviso's Appeal to Scientific Knowledge," *Social Theory and Practice*, 2010, 36(1), pp. 1–20.

individuals' actual consent to their establishment (strong voluntarism), and only if this is the case can there be a *right* to revolution.

Despite the clearly attractive qualities of Locke's account of private property, a closer look at the arguments reveals a number of puzzles. For example, we may ask with Robert Nozick[12] why would it be the case that if I climb up a coconut tree and pick a coconut, then I have worked and made the coconut mine, whereas if I pour tomato juice into the ocean, I haven't worked and made the ocean mine? In other words, what is "work" really, and what does it mean to say that we "mix" our work (or labor) with natural resources? Nozick also reformulates a question many others have had, which is, what happens as soon as natural resources become scarce? What happens, for example, if an 11th ship-wrecked person suddenly swims onto the island after the first 10 have divided all the natural resources among themselves?

In response to the issue of scarcity, C. B. Macpherson[13] argues that Locke ultimately defends unlimited, capitalist accumulation, or what Macpherson calls "possessive individualism." On this interpretation, Locke was, regrettably, unmoved by genuine concerns of poverty and quite content to provide a theory that reinforces and further develops the class-based capitalist system (with its distinction between property-owners and laborers). Nozick, who has a more positive response to this aspect of capitalism than Macpherson, presents another take on the issue of scarcity. Applying Nozick's take to the island scenario, he would argue that upon the arrival of the 11th person, it is clear that the last person to take a coconut (number 10), hadn't, after all, left "enough and as good" for the next person. But if this is the case, then it looks like number 9 also didn't leave enough behind for number 10—and so the justness of the appropriations seems to "unzip," as Nozick puts it, all the way back to the first person who appropriated a coconut. In other words, it looks as if the arrival of the newcomer entails that everything that had already been appropriated as private property suddenly isn't private property any longer; the labor employed in accordance with the proviso at the time didn't, as it turns out, "fix" as private property what was appropriated.

Nozick suggests a solution to the "unzipping" problem he articulates. He proposes that the newcomer doesn't have a direct right to land or natural resources, but instead obtains a right to be employed by the owners of the land and natural resources. In this way (through wages and labor markets), the newcomer is secured her or his right to 1/n-th of the total, original value of the natural resources. A. John Simmons[14] challenges this proposal, claiming it cannot be the correct Lockean solution since it entails that those who accidentally arrive earlier have much more (at least for a period of time) with which to create value than those who accidentally arrive later. Such a result, he argues, cannot be in line with the principle expressed by Locke's proviso. It is much more plausible, Simmons continues, to maintain that

[12] Nozick, Robert (1974) *Anarchy, State, and Utopia*. New York: Basic Books.

[13] Macpherson, C. B. (1962) *The Political Theory of Possessive Individualism: Hobbes to Locke*. Oxford: Clarendon Press.

[14] Simmons, A. John (1992) *The Lockean Theory of Rights*. Princeton: Princeton University Press.

as soon as there is a scarcity of resources, everyone has a right to a sufficient amount of resources (or means) with which to sustain themselves and enjoy some conveniences (if the latter is possible, given the total amount of resources and people in the world).

Gopal Sreenivasan,[15] in turn, challenges both Nozick and Simmons, arguing that people do not have to accept that their bad luck (accidentally arriving later than others) means that they do not have a right to land while others (those who accidentally came earlier) enjoy such a right. Sreenivasan argues that if the laws of nature bind all as equals, then one cannot justify the claim that some, but not others, can obtain land for such an arbitrary reason. G. A. Cohen,[16] (a neo-Marxist—Marxists have always been drawn to Locke's labor arguments) and James Tully[17] go further, and argue that when such scarcity arises, the type of private property Locke envisions ceases to exist, and our right to natural resources transforms into a right to *use* them, not "own" them in the strict, liberal sense of the word. Additionally, the secondary literature hosts a continual, on-going debate concerning how the fact that we now live in money economies affects Locke's arguments about private property—a discussion Locke himself started (TT, II: 47–50). Finally, Michael Otsuka[18] asks why only those who can work should be able to obtain private property. What about those unable to work due to physical or psychological conditions beyond their control? Why should they not be able to appropriate private property, also?

6 Private Property and Charity

The question Otsuka raises concerning how the unemployable can appropriate private property is closely connected with another, broader question which many, including Locke, have asked in regard to this theory, namely, the question of how the unemployable are supposed to get their fundamental needs met. What about those who are starving, for example, but whose condition is a result of accident or their own stupidity (perhaps they used up their fair share of the natural resources without creating any further value from their share)? Do they no longer have a right to life? Is their access to the resources they need to survive fundamentally subject to other people's charity? And how can the right that those who labor have to their private property—their right to exclude others from access to their means and to use their means to set and pursue their own ends—be reconcilable with the right, if any, those who are unemployable have to self-preservation? Nozick, in his

[15] Sreenivasan, Gopal (1995) *The Limits of Lockean Rights in Property*. Oxford: Oxford University Press.

[16] Cohen, G. A. (1995) *Self-Ownership, Freedom, and Equality*. Cambridge: Cambridge University Press.

[17] Tully, James (1980) *A Discourse on Property, John Locke and His Adversaries*. Cambridge: Cambridge University Press.

[18] Otsuka, Michael (2003) *Libertarianism without Inequality*. Oxford: Oxford University Press.

characteristically provocative manner, maintains that if the right to charity is enforceable, then there is no right to freedom, since individuals would not then have a right to exclude others from access to their private property (as acquired in ways consistent with the proviso). In other words, if people have a right to access another's private property every time they find themselves in serious distress (have unmet needs), then those whose private property they have access to do not have a right to set and pursue their own ends with their means; that is to say, they are not free.

It is worth noting that Locke's own texts do not clarify this issue. He does not address the issue in the second treatise, and in the texts where he does address it, he seems to hold both that the right to charity is and is not enforceable. More specifically, in the first treatise, Locke argues that *justice* gives everyone a right "... to the product of his honest Industry, and the fair Acquisitions of his Ancestors descended to him; so *Charity* gives every Man a Title to so much out of another's Plenty, as will keep him from extream want, where he has no means to subsist otherwise..." (TT, I: 42). The problem with this argument is, as we have seen, that if the right to charity is enforceable, then it would seem that justice doesn't, after all, give everyone a right to the "product of his honest Industry" (private property); charity can override our right to private property. And Locke seems to endorse precisely this objection to the idea that charity is enforceable in *A Letter Concerning Tolerance*. There Locke argues that charity is the type of moral right or duty that we cannot enforce, since such coercion is irreconcilable with our natural right to the values we have created by honestly laboring on our fair share of the natural resources (Locke 1993: 417, 422).

The concept of an enforceable right to charity therefore seems to give some (poor persons) a right to others' (rich persons') labor and fair share of the resources (their property), which seems to undermine the idea that we have a natural right to our own labor and what we produce by laboring as the proviso instructs. The rich persons' private property rights seem subjected to luck and the poor persons' choices; whether or not her or his property remains untouched depends on which particular rich person's property the poor coincidentally happen to take in order to meet his or her basic needs, which, again, in some cases are unmet because of the poor persons' bad choices. On the other hand, however, without such a right to charity it seems that the poor (including those who are poor because they cannot work) do not have a right to life, since their sustenance would then depend on whether someone wants to take care of them; the poor person's survival would be subject to the rich person's choices (or will). Also on this option, then, choices and luck would determine whether or not someone has rights, here to survive, and this seems inconsistent with Locke's general position that we are free and equal and have a fundamental right to preservation. To solve this problem, we might try to figure out exactly what Locke means when he says that "Every one as he is *bound to preserve himself*... so by the like reason when his own Preservation comes not in competition, ought he, as much as he can, *to preserve the rest of Mankind*..." (TT, II: 6) Perhaps the first part, about preserving oneself, is the principle of *justice* (the enforceable principle), whereas the second part, concerning the preservation of mankind, is merely an *ethical* principle or a principle of *virtue* (an unenforceable principle). But if only the first part is a principle of justice and the second part is an ethical principle—then Locke cannot secure rights for many persons who are poor, sick, or disabled, since their inability to engage in self-preservation through labor means that their right to life is not secured (as they cannot enforce it on their own). Alternatively, perhaps both statements should be understood as two aspects of one (enforceable) principle of justice. Yet if so, then, as we have seen, the principle as a whole becomes inconsistent.

The topic of whether the poor, sick, and disabled have a right to be helped remains a controversial topic in political philosophy, and responses to it mark a distinction between so-called "right-wing" and "left-wing" libertarians, including Lockean libertarians. On the far right, we find Nozick, for example, who argues that charity is only an ethical duty (a duty of virtue), and not a duty of justice. On views like this, being unwilling to engage in charity if one is able reveals a selfish and bad human character, but it is not an unjust act that should be made illegal and for which one should be legally punished. On these views, no one (not even the state) has a right to force anyone to assist the poor, sick, and disabled with their struggle to survive. Rather, this kind of work must result from individuals' virtue and charity (unless some of it can be shown to be required of parents). On the far left, the other side of the spectrum, we find positions like that of Simmons, who argues that charity is a duty of justice in emergency conditions (i.e., extreme poverty) but is otherwise an ethical duty, and Otsuka, who contends that the unemployable have enforceable rights by arguing that their sickness or disability means that they begin with less than their fair share of resources (since they cannot labor) and they should be compensated for this. This is roughly where the discussion between "right-wing" and "left-wing" libertarians stands today.[19]

7 Private Property and Waste

The "enough-and-as-good" proviso is not the only limit Locke places on the just accumulation of natural resources in *Two Treatises on Government*. In addition, he defends what sometimes gets referred to as "the waste restriction." (TT, II: 31–34) This restriction demands that when someone appropriates natural resources in accordance with the "enough-and-as-good" proviso, that person can only take as much as she needs and can productively utilize. If, instead, she takes such a large share that the acquired natural resources go to waste, then these resources automatically transform back into common goods. In other words, if I don't pick the apples off my apple tree, but let them fall to the ground where they will quickly rot, others can take these apples without having thereby stolen from me. In addition, Locke argues, I must use the resources prudently or constructively, as means of realizing

[19] For an argument that none of these proposed solutions to the problem that the issue poses to the Lockean theory work, see Varden, Helga (2012) "The Lockean 'Enough-and-as-Good' Proviso—an Internal Critique," *Journal of Moral Philosophy* 9, pp. 410–422.

my own pursuits or helping others realize theirs; I cannot acquire resources in order simply to destroy them.

Some of the secondary literature, especially from the left-wing, considers this waste argument particularly fruitful for explaining why and how we ought to protect the environment and stop the depletion of the natural resources. More right-wing scholars are unconvinced by the waste argument, and typically contend that it is fundamentally inconsistent with Locke's theory of freedom. If we have a right to freedom—to use our own means to set our ends—then we cannot, they argue, be forced to set only "prudent" or "useful" ends. A right to freedom means a right also to destroy or waste our resources if that is the kind of life we want to live. Here, again, the right-wing libertarians typically maintain that it is entirely possible that such a wasteful life is ethically deplorable, but this is not a type of wrongdoing that should be coercively stopped or punished (including by being made illegal).[20]

8 Locke on Children's Rights

The last set of rights that Locke discusses is children's rights. Children, Locke argues, do not have sufficiently developed reason, so they cannot be free (specify, apply, and enforce the laws of nature on their own) and so they are also not the equals of adults or fully responsible persons (TT, II: 55–58). Instead, children have a right to be taken care of by their parents and a duty to obey them, a right and a duty that corresponds to parents' duties and rights in relation to their children. These sets of rights and duties aim to ensure that children can develop into fully responsible persons. Generally speaking, parents cannot opt to ignore their children's claims on them (the parents) or transfer those claims to others, but if the parents fail to take care of their own children, their rights to their children are forfeited to foster parents. Parents can also demand that children, as they grown older, take on more work in return for their parents' care (TT, II: 64). On Locke's view, the rights and duties that exist between parents and children end once children reach the age of consent (legal responsibility), (TT, II: 55), unless the children are mentally ill or disabled, in which case the rights and duties continue in perpetuity (TT, II: 60). When the children grow up, they owe their parents "respect, reverence, support and compliance" for the care they received when they were children (TT, II: 67).

Among interpreters of Locke, Simmons has discussed the theory of children's rights and duties the most extensively. He argues that on Locke's account, the relationship between parents and children must essentially remain in the state of nature, because children cannot give their actual consent to enter the civil condition (and become citizens) before they reach the age of consent or legal responsibility. Simmons also asserts that Locke's theory does not have the resources to answer many of the difficult questions it raises. For example, Simmons wonders (as did

[20] For a critical engagement with the waste restriction, see Varden, Helga (2006) "Locke's Waste Restriction and His Strong Voluntarism," *Locke Studies* 6, pp. 127–141.

Kant), how children who asked neither to be born nor taken care of can become responsible for showing their parents "respect, reverence, support and compliance" when they grow old. It seems more plausible to maintain, Simmons holds, that children ought to do this if they had good parents, but that would be an ethical duty, not an enforceable duty of justice. In addition, Simmons asks how children, who by definition cannot be morally responsible, can be said to have rights and duties to their parents. Exercising rights and duties appears to presuppose the ability to be morally responsible, but if children were capable of moral responsibility, then there would no need for special rights and duties with regard to them in the first place. In other words, how can it make sense to say that children have rights and duties given the Lockean understanding of rights and duties, when children, due to their immaturity, cannot exercise rights and duties? At the same time, of course, if children cannot be said to have rights and duties, then it is difficult to attribute to them the right to life, which is a problem for Locke's ultimate ambition of capturing every individual's rights.

9 Locke's Strong Voluntarist Conception of Political Obligations and the Right to Revolution

If the Lockeans can solve the problems Locke's various principles of justice, including their application, appear to give us—the problems discussed above—then justice is indeed possible in the state of nature. And if the problems are solvable, the Lockean theory can show us that and how we justly interact in relation to each other and in relation to natural resources, which means interacting in such a way that justice for everyone is realized in the state of nature. But if justice is possible in the state of nature, then the question becomes, why establish states at all, instead of staying in the state of nature? To this, Locke responds that we establish states or enter civil society because various "inconveniences" that characterize the state of nature make it irrational or strategically unwise—"...very unsafe, very unsecure..."—to stay in it (TT, II: 123).

According to Locke, there are three sources of the inconveniences of the state of nature: stupidity (imprudence), bias, and unequal power. And these, in turn, correspond to the fact that in the state of nature the individual is the political authority or the lawgiver, the judge, and the executive power (TT, II, 136). To have a natural executive right is to have the right to specify, apply, and enforce the laws of nature. The main problem in the state of nature, then, issues from the fact that everyone is exercising their natural executive right: everyone is interpreting the laws of nature (the principles of justice), applying them in particular instances, and enforcing them as necessary. Yet because we all have a tendency to think unclearly about the laws of nature, to judge partially and in our own favor, and to use power when we can rather than when it's right, the state of nature is a dangerous place. Hence it is strategically much wiser to leave the state of nature and establish the legal-political institution of a state that specifies, applies, and enforces the laws of nature (the principles of justice). Rather than staying in the unstable state of nature, it is more rational to create the institutional system of a liberal state, whereby the laws of nature are specified by lawgivers, applied by impartial judges when disagreements arise, and upheld by police without regard for the relative weakness or strength of the individuals involved in a dispute. In other words, staying in the state of nature is fundamentally stupid or irrational, as it is a condition where the possibility of justice relies on the virtue and strength of each individual, and, so, the wise choice is to enter the civil condition. But, crucially for Locke's account, being stupid, imprudent, or strategically irrational is not a punishable offense since it does not involve wronging anyone. Consequently, it is unjust to force anyone to leave the state of nature. The state's legal-political institutions are therefore legitimate only if each individual actually agrees—gives her or his actual consent—to leave the state of nature and enter civil society (TT, II: 119). In this way, Locke defends his strong voluntarist conception of political obligations.

Since, on Locke's account, individuals can realize justice in the state of nature by regulating their interactions in accordance with the fundamental principles of justice, each individual's actual consent is necessary for a state's legitimacy. A state's existence and its monopoly on coercion are therefore only justifiable and legitimate if the state both respects the fundamental principles of justice and has the citizens' actual consent.[21] It also follows that the rights of the state are substantially the same as the rights of the individual. The only differences are that the individual originally has political authority whereas the state does not, and certain new laws are needed in order for the state to establish the rule of law (that is, the administrative law constitutive of public legal-political institutions). Moreover, as we have seen, the state becomes authorized to act on behalf of its citizens through individuals' actual consent, which means that by consenting to enter civil society, each citizen entrusts the state authority to uphold the laws of nature on her or his behalf. From this, it follows that if a state doesn't respect the fundamental principles of justice in its use of power, then the citizens have a right to reassert their political authority through a revolution. So, if those in power abuse the citizens' trust by setting aside or misapplying the principles of justice, then the subjects can justly take back their natural political authority. At such a point, they can opt to return to the state of nature, establish a new political authority, or revamp the current political authority.

As discussed, Locke's understanding of a just and legitimate state is bound up with his understanding of the state of nature, the laws of nature, and individual rights.

---

[21] Locke distinguishes between two types of actual consent, namely "explicit" and "implicit" or "tacit" consent. Explicit consent involves clearly stating "yes, I agree" in response to a question posed (here the question of entering civil society), whereas implicit or tacit consent typically involves expressing one's agreement by doing nothing rather than something in certain situations. The argument concerning implicit or tacit consent is important for Locke's account of political obligations in existing states. For a good introduction into this aspect of Locke's theory, see Simmons (1981) *Moral Principles and Political Obligations*. Princeton, New Jersey: Princeton University Press.

This connection is also apparent in his suggestion for the construction of a legal-political authority. His suggestions are roughly in line with Montesquieu's recommendations for the tripartite division of power in a state: the distinction between legislative, judicial, and executive powers. Locke, however, often does not strictly distinguish between the judicial and executive powers, since the executive power frequently applies the law in specific cases. Also for Locke, the laws of nature and the citizens themselves are the highest authority. As a result, he contends that the legislative power has the most authority among the three state powers, that the people must choose the lawgivers, and that where there is disagreement, the majority should decide (there should be democratic majority rule). Nevertheless, Locke's democracy leaves room for the legislative power to be divided among chosen representatives, aristocrats, and a monarch—as it was in England during his lifetime.

The secondary literature contains, of course, many discussions surrounding this account of political obligations and legitimacy. For example, Nozick and Simmons both engage Locke's arguments for the actual consent requirement, and both offer modifications of the arguments. Nozick (1974) has tried to show that the state can force non-citizens to participate in its legal system when interacting with its citizens, and that the state can tax its citizens to enable this use of its legal institutions. Simmons has focused much attention on the implications of the extent to which the planet is now inhabited and of the fact that most of us are born within the jurisdiction of existing states (and, so, Locke's account of so-called "tacit" consent to the political authority). Simmons maintains that the Lockean account must be developed to explain how states can provide the people living within their territory a real option to choose against citizenship, and he has explored some possible directions for this development.[22]

10 Concluding Remarks

Many of Locke's arguments concerning tolerance, citizens' consent, private property, charity, children's rights, state vs. individual rights, the state's institutional structure, etc., are still actively discussed by libertarians generally and Lockeans more specifically. In addition, representatives from other political traditions continuously engage with these arguments, revealing their deep regard for the Lockean tradition as a major voice in legal and political philosophy. For example, Kantian, Rawlsian, Hobbesian, and Marxist theorists frequently challenge Locke's idea of actual consent as necessary for legitimate political power, his argument and conclusion concerning the rights of the state vs. the rights of individuals, and his private property argument. In addition to its presence in ongoing philosophical discussions, Locke's theory is very much

[22] See, for example, Simmons (1981) and his *On The Edge of Anarchy: Locke, Consent, and the Limits of Society*. Princeton: Princeton University Press, 1993.

alive in actual politics. For instance, one need only briefly pay attention to politics in liberal countries before Locke's influence becomes obvious.[23]

Perhaps one of the more surprising spheres of Locke's influence is in a different area of philosophy, namely global justice. His influence there is somewhat peculiar, since Locke himself didn't apply his theory to global justice in any significant way. He quickly notes that a state's executive power is responsible for international relations and must follow the laws of nature in such interactions, but he doesn't expound on this argument. Despite this, many contemporary arguments of the so-called "cosmopolitan" theories of global justice are clearly Lockean in structure. Broadly speaking, these cosmopolitan theories maintain that global justice, like all forms of justice, requires that everyone respect the individuals' human rights. Hence, if a particular state does not respect its citizens' rights or the rights of non-citizens with which it interacts, then no one (neither other states nor any individual) has a duty to respect this state's borders or its use of force. Consequently, in the case of a civil war or a state's oppression of a set of its own citizens, for example, other states, individuals, or international organizations are entitled to intervene, especially if those being subjected to the abuse of power want such intervention (granting that often it is obviously unwise for others to involve themselves in the conflict). Like Locke, these positions maintain that no state has a right to use violence against its citizens that conflicts with individual human rights. If states use illegitimate force—force inconsistent with individuals' human rights—then citizens can reassume their natural political power and exercise it as individuals or in groups (of private individuals, states, or international organizations). Ultimately, the state only justly uses power if it occurs within the framework established by the rights of individuals, and justice demands that everyone, everywhere and at all times, respects individual rights. Various prominent arguments concerning the global (re)distribution of natural resources also take such a basically Lockean form. The most influential account of this kind is found in Thomas Pogge's proposal of a "global resource dividend."[24] Simply put, Pogge argues that all states and individuals must ensure that the amount of resources within their territory is compatible with the right all individuals on the planet have to a fair share of the earth's natural resources. The global resource dividend proposes a way of globally enacting this principle, now that all resources are possessed within the boundaries of de facto states. Locke's influence, in other words, is far from over.

Acknowledgement Thanks to Ingrid Albrecht, Catherine Champniers, Grace Frank, Tone Monkerud, and Jørgen Pedersen for invaluable help with the presentation of ideas in this chapter.

---

[23] For an exploration of feminist interpretations of Locke, see: Hirschmann, Nancy J. & McClure, Kirstie Morna (eds) (2007) *Feminist Interpretations of John Locke*. University Park, PA: Penn State University Press. For a good introduction to some of the related debates in the libertarian tradition, see Vallentyne, Peter & Steiner, Hillel (2001) *Left-Libertarianism and Its Critics: The Contemporary Debate*. New York: Palgrave Macmillan.

[24] Pogge, Thomas (2008) *World Poverty and Human Rights*. 2nd ed., Malden: Polity Press.

Accounts of Justice in the Scottish Enlightenment

Athanasia Glycofrydi-Leontsini

Justice is a complex concept connected with liberty and law, ethics and politics; it is conceived as being beneficial to others when compared to courage, temperance and wisdom, virtues which are thought of as 'self-regarding'. The history of concepts of justice from Antiquity to the Middle Ages and from then to the present helps us to see how this concept developed over time. Justice, one fundamental virtue or ideal among several, is generally considered as the foundation of social and political ethics. In its links with law and jurisprudence and in legal usage, justice has always had an ethical tinge as lawyers, when appealing to principles of 'natural justice', acknowledge that their system of law is meant to serve an ethical purpose and to follow ethically acceptable methods. In law as in social ethics, the concept of justice is acknowledged to have both a conservative and a reforming role. Conservative justice is to maintain the established order of things, taken to be entitlements, and assumes that everyone benefits from a stable social order, however imperfect. Reformative justice tries to remove imperfections in the redistribution of rights redistributing rights in order to make the social order more just or fair. It is linked with changes to the existing pattern of entitlements by taking account of merit and of need and is connected with the ideas of distributive justice.[1] Historically, the concept of justice has had 'Ancient roots' found in the Bible, in ancient drama (especially in Aeschylus' *Oresteia*), in philosophers such as Plato, (whose *Republic* is a treatise on justice, written as a dialogue between Socrates and some of his upper-class Athenian friends), or Aristotle (who in his *Nicomachean Ethics* gives an orderly account of the varieties of justice and analyzes justice as a virtue of character, in an effort to represent justice as "the disposition to give and receive neither too much nor too little"). At the same time, it is seen as a specific virtue. Justice has been widely discussed among jurists and theologians in the Middle Ages, and

[1] Raphael, David Daiches (2001) *Concepts of Justice*. Oxford: Oxford University Press, pp. 1–7.

A. Glycofrydi-Leontsini (✉)
Department of Philosophy, School of Philosophy,
National and Kapodistrian University of Athens, Athens, Greece
e-mail: aleon@ppp.uoa.gr

G. Fløistad (ed.), *Philosophy of Justice*, Contemporary Philosophy: A New Survey 12, DOI 10.1007/978-94-017-9175-5_11, © Springer Science+Business Media Dordrecht 2015

among philosophers of more modern times from Thomas Hobbes to Rawls and Robert Nozick.[2]

In this chapter, I will focus on the concept of justice as it emerges during the Scottish Enlightenment in the social and political ethics developed by such Scottish philosophers of the eighteenth century as David Hume, Adam Smith, Lord Kames and Thomas Reid. As it has been noted by Knud Haakonssen, justice was treated mainly as a characteristic of the individual person within the various Scottish theories of natural jurisprudence.[3] Justice was considered by Scottish philosophers as a personal virtue, virtue meaning "the propensity to a certain type of behaviour and also the ability to appreciate the moral worth of such behaviour both in oneself and in others".[4] In other words, the Scottish theorists dealt with justice as a characteristic of the individual and, paradoxically, they explained that concept as an institutionalized practice. Central to their theories was whether this virtue is an inherent part of human nature or whether it is artificial. Considered as a social or political virtue, bearing on the relations required by the very existence of community in a way that other virtues do not, the Scottish thinkers believed that their task was to explain why justice was distinguished from the other virtues by being the subject of the institutions of justice, namely adjudication, law and legislation.[5] For Hume—whose account of justice was extensive but narrowly interpreted—justice is an artificial virtue in the sense that it is the product of human conventions. Considering selfishness and limited generosity as qualities of the human mind,[6] Hume points out that "self-interest is the original motive to the establishment of justice" but "a sympathy with public interest is the source of the moral approbation which attends that virtue",[7] and observes that justice lies in its utility in maintaining property as a condition of a stable society, a view criticized by other notable Scottish philosophers such as Lord Kames and Thomas Reid. Reid in particular, in criticizing Hume's theory of justice,[8] is considered as developing a rights-based theory arguing that justice's utility is insufficient to distinguish it from natural virtues such as benevolence. On the other hand, Adam Smith, who has accepted many of Hume's ethical doctrines as well as the theories of the Ancients, mainly those of the Stoics and Cicero, developed in his *The Theory of Moral Sentiments* (1759) a richer theory of justice in an endeavor to connect it with the moral needs of individuals, relating

[2] For the developing role of justice, from antiquity till the present, see Raphael, David Daiches *Concepts of Justice*, *op.cit.*

[3] Haakonssen, Knud (2003) "Natural Jurisprudence and the Theory of Justice," in *The Cambridge Companion to the Scottish Enlightenment*, ed. by Alexander Broadie. Cambridge: Cambridge University Press, pp. 205–221, especially p. 205.

[4] *Ibid.*

[5] *Ibid.*, p. 206.

[6] Hume, David (1978) *A Treatise of Human Nature*, ed., with an Analytical Index, by L. A. Selby-Bigge, revised edition by P. H. Nidditch, 2nd ed. Oxford: Clarendon Press, pp. 487ff., 586. All the following quotations will be from this edition.

[7] *Ibid.*, pp. 500, 533.

[8] For an extensive presentation and examination of Hume's theory of justice, see Harrison, Jonathan (1981) *Hume's Theory of Justice*. Oxford: Clarendon Press.

justice to merit and injustice to demerit that consists in good or ill desert. In criticizing Hume's view that justice depends on utility, Smith coupled justice with beneficence as the two virtues directly concerned with our relationship to other people. He also rejected Hume's doctrine of the artificiality of justice, as he believed that justice is a natural virtue, based on the natural feeling of sympathy for the injured party, and it is the duty of man to make it perfect.[9] Although Smith has taken the characteristics of sympathy from Hume (who in the *Treatise* calls Sympathy, and in the *Enquiry* Benevolence, that which leads us to approve or disapprove of moral excellences and defects), he distances himself from him as he calls the sympathy for the person performing the action 'direct sympathy' and that for the person who is acted upon 'indirect'.[10] Hume and Smith differ in a fundamental respect, as it has been noted, because "for Hume placing the observer in an imaginary position in another's situation means sharing the pleasures or advantages of the agent or the recipient of the action, while for Smith it means feeling the passions of the agent or recipient of the action in order to carry out a comparison with the passions that they really display".[11] The above-mentioned Scottish philosophers connect justice with liberty and equality as well as with law, rights, duties and obligations, and develop theories of justice that reflect their concern with moral and political problems of their age, and with empirical studies of human nature and of natural jurisprudence.[12] My purpose in what follows is to approach Hume's and Reid's views on justice in the main as developed in their moral, social and political theories in order to show, explore and explain their differences.

The Scots' moral theory is perhaps the most studied aspect of their thought, and is connected with recent interest in their political and social theory. As empiricists, the Scots thought it necessary to consult experience in order to know about society.[13] Their debate on the foundations of morals started with Francis Hutcheson, David Hume and Adam Smith, while Thomas Reid continued the discussion in a critical way by reflecting on their theories.[14]

Hume's basic claim is that all our knowledge is based on what we experience through the senses, and his ethical theory as a whole can be considered the 'most important example of empiricist moral philosophy'. He exposes his moral theory in the third book of the *Treatise* and the *Enquiry concerning the Principles of Morals,* examining historically and critically moral theories, from antiquity till his age, dealing mainly with the moral philosophy of his predecessors: Hobbes, Locke,

---

[9] Smith, Adam (1976) *The Theory of Moral Sentiments*, ed. by D. D. Raphael & A. L. Macfie. Oxford: Clarendon Press, pp. 75–78.

[10] *Ibid.*, p. 74.

[11] *Ibid.*, pp. 16–23, as noted by Luigi Turco, "Moral Sense and the Foundations of Morals," in *The Cambridge Companion to the Scottish Enlightenment*, p. 147.

[12] Raphael, David Daiches *Concepts of Justice, op.cit.*, pp. 87–103.

[13] Berry, Christopher J. (reprinted 2001) *Social Theory of the Scottish Enlightenment* (1997). Edinburgh: Edinburgh University Press, pp. 156ff.

[14] Turco, Luigi "Moral Sense and the Foundations of Morals," in *The Cambridge Companion to the Scottish Enlightenment*, pp. 136–156.

Grotius, Pufendorf, Mandeville and Hutcheson.[15] In the *Treatise*, Hume approaches in a psychological way the problem of 'how morality is constituted, that is, what forces are capable of forming morality', while in the *Enquiry* he approaches morality 'as a given social fact'.[16] As in his epistemology so in his moral philosophy, Hume tries to explain how a common world is created out of private and subjective elements; for that reason, examining the foundations of morality, he holds that they are, on the one hand, private and subjective, connecting with the principle of 'oughts', which by nature activates forces in our life, such as passions, and on the other hand, public and objective, as they bind people together and make a society possible. In this sense, the latter has a function that is dependent upon the existence of a common moral language, as every language includes, according to him, a set of terms by which we express praise or blame.[17] Hume was critical of the existing 'foundation-theories' of morality and law according to which moral and legal evaluation had an ultimate source in either the reasoning faculty or the moral sense. With his emotivist moral theory, and relying on the experience of sense and feeling, which was the key idea of Hutcheson's ethical theory,[18] Hume was concerned with the origin of evaluation and with trying to show how solid are the moral distinctions 'derived from sentiment': "All morality depends upon our sentiments; and when any action or quality of the mind, pleases us after a certain manner, we say it is virtuous; and when the neglect, or non-performance of it, displeases us after a like manner, we say that we lie under an obligation to perform it".[19] Hutcheson's influence on Hume seems undeniable. Nevertheless, although he seems to argue in the *Treatise* that moral distinctions are derived from a moral sense, he uses in his discussions of Book III the terms 'sentiment' and 'feeling' instead of 'moral sense'. As we know, Hume and Smith were hostile to the idea of a special sense of justice, and both analyzed the moral sentiments in general in terms of the operations of sympathy. Hume explicitly acknowledges the special character of the feeling of approval, and thinks that Hutcheson's description of the moral sense as disinterested approval of the disinterested motive of benevolence, being recognized by him as the whole virtue, is simple and mistaken.[20] Trying to explain the moral sentiments, Hume pursued a historical examination of justice, which Smith did not follow. Hume tried to stress the validity of the evaluations we make within social and historical contexts, especially in his theory of justice which is considered of great importance as it helped Adam Smith to develop a number of proposals included in

[15] Hume, David (1998) *An Enquiry concerning the Principles of Morals*, ed. by Tom L. Beauchamp, with an Introduction. Oxford/New York: Oxford University Press.

[16] Haakonssen, Knud (1989) *The Science of a Legislator. The Natural Jurisprudence of David Hume and Adam Smith* (1981). Cambridge: Cambridge University Press, p. 5.

[17] *Ibid.*, pp. 4 and 12.

[18] Raphael, David Daiches *Concepts of Justice*, p. 92.

[19] *Treatise*, p. 517.

[20] David Daiches Raphael in his *Concepts of Justice* (pp. 91ff.) notes the impact of Hutcheson's *An Inquiry into our Ideas of Beauty and Virtue* (1725) and *An Essay on the Passions and Affections. With Illustrations on the Moral Sense* (1728) on Hume's moral thought.

his own theory of justice and jurisprudence, which in turn gave a new and original answer to the philosophical question of how legal criticism is possible.[21]

Hume developed his ethical theory in Book III of *A Treatise of Human Nature*, published in 1739–1740, addressed to specialists in philosophy, and then in his *An Enquiry concerning the Principles of Morals*, first published in 1751, a book written for an educated general public. His account of justice has a fundamental role in both books, as in the *Treatise* he gives priority to the doctrine that justice is an artificial virtue, while in the *Enquiry* he concentrates on the utility of justice. He makes a distinction between nature and artifice in Book III of the *Treatise*, and in Part III of this Book, he includes his claim that some virtues, such as love of one's children, beneficence, generosity, clemency, moderation, temperance and fragility, are natural, embedded as fundamental propensities of human nature itself, and points out that as individuals we respond to these virtues with approbation. In Part II of this Book, he quotes the traditional definition of justice as "*a constant and perpetual will of giving every one his due*"[22] and contrasts these natural virtues to the artificial virtues, such as justice, fidelity and allegiance. He distinguishes nature and artifice, and divides natural from artificial causes, which are instituted by men conventionally, clarifying as far as justice is concerned that both, nature and artifice, coexist. This aspect of his thought is more apparent when he tries to answer the question, 'Whether justice is a Natural or Artificial Virtue?'[23] He is convinced that the sense of justice arises artificially and necessarily from education and human conventions.[24] Nevertheless, when discussing the moral character of justice, Hume clarifies in the *Treatise* that it is an artificial invention to a certain purpose, but also a natural tendency to protect the good of mankind.[25]

Hume has been criticized because in his system the ideas of justice and of injustice are connected mostly with the idea of property and concern property arrangements.[26] He describes then how the notions of property, promises and governments were

---

[21] Haakonssen, Knud *The Science of a Legislator. The Natural Jurisprudence of David Hume and Adam Smith, op.cit.*

[22] *Treatise*, p. 526. As Mackie observes, Hume interprets this definition "as protecting everyone in the possession and use of what belongs to him and in the right to transfer his property voluntarily to someone else". Mackie, J. L. (2001) *Hume's Moral Theory* (1980). New York: Routledge, p. 77.

[23] In the *Treatise*, p. 484, the clarification of natural and artificial regarding justice is as follows: "I must here observe, that when I deny justice to be a natural virtue, I make use of the word, *natural*, only as oppos'd to *artificial*. In another sense of the word; as no principle of the human mind is more natural than a sense of justice; so no virtue is more natural than justice. Mankind is an inventive species; and where an invention is obvious and absolutely necessary, it may as properly be said to be natural as anything that proceeds immediately from original principles, without the intervention of thought or reflexion. Tho' the rules of justice be *artificial*, they are not *arbitrary*. Nor is the expression improper to call them *Laws of Nature*; if by natural we understand what is common to any species, or even if we confine it to mean what is inseparable from the species."

[24] *Treatise*, p. 483. Mackie believes that Hume's argument that justice is an artificial virtue is complicated and difficult, and gives an outline of it in eight steps. J. L. Mackie, *Hume's Moral Theory*, pp. 76ff.

[25] *Treatise*, pp. 532–533.

[26] *Ibid.*, pp. 490–491.

instituted as social artifices and tries to show why these are taken to have a moral dimension. He takes the approach that justice is not established as a moral virtue by means of a natural motive, as it comes into existence as a social practice or institution: "No virtue is more esteem'd than justice, and no vice more detested than injustice; nor are there any qualities, which go father to the fixing the character, either as amiable or odious. Now justice is a moral virtue, merely because it has that tendency to the good of mankind; and, indeed, is nothing but an artificial invention to that purpose. The same may be said of allegiance, of the laws of nations, of modesty, and of good-manners".[27] Hume, discussing the origin of justice and property, is eager to show how we acquire the proper passion, and thus the moral obligation, to adhere to it and tries to answer to two questions, viz., "*concerning the manner, in which the rules of justice are establish'd by the artifice of men; and concerning the reasons, which determine us to attribute to the observance or neglect of these rules a moral beauty and deformity*".[28] According to him, justice is an absolutely necessary ingredient in any kind of social life, it is a remedy to some and connected with the possession of external goods, and applies primarily to property. To the question 'how the artifices of justice come into being as means for the promotion of our interests, and how our giving moral approbation to those who follow the artifices' restraints', Hume gives the answer that the "moral obligation" is a natural sentiment, and has to be just as a consequence of our sympathizing with the "public interest",[29] or the "interest of the society",[30] the "good of society",[31] the "public good" or 'the good of society'[32] or the "good of mankind".[33] In concluding, he remarks that the artifices of justice are useful to society, like all useful things,[34] and beneficial to the members of society we sympathize with, especially with the fellow-citizens of our nation.[35]

Hume acknowledges the existence of natural moral sentiments that operate through sympathy, an involuntary, physiological reaction towards the joys and sufferings of others. At the same time, he recognizes that sympathy is a partial and unreliable mechanism as it gives way to self-interest or to other emotions, although in his *Enquiry* he agrees with Hutcheson, in this differing from Hobbes, in holding that man is capable of a disinterested regard for others and he seems to describe "the evolution of the artifices of justice as depending on their serving the interests of each person who participates in them".[36] Hume had also discriminated in ethical

[27] *Ibid.*, p. 577.

[28] *Ibid*,, p. 484.

[29] *Ibid.*, p. 500.

[30] *Ibid.*, p. 579.

[31] *Ibid.*, p. 578.

[32] *Ibid.*, pp. 580, 618, 577.

[33] *Ibid.*, p. 577.

[34] *Ibid.*

[35] Ainslie, Donald C. (1995) "The Problem of the National Self in Hume's Theory of Justice," in *Hume Studies*, v. XXI, N° 2, pp. 289–313.

[36] *Ibid.*, p. 289.

experiences between the functions of reason and sentiment, in this making an important advance upon Hutcheson, who did not assign to reason a distinct and special office. Adam Smith agrees with Hume that morality is a matter of sentiment and traces the moral sentiments to an origin in sympathy, but whereas Hume stresses our sympathy with people in general, Smith stresses our sympathy with the person or persons principally involved. For him, to sympathize with the real or supposed sentiments of our fellow-men is to approve them.

Hume's account of justice is characterized as complicated and inconsistent, and it is developed not only in the *Treatise* or the second *Enquiry*, but also in his *Essays*, such as "Of the Original Contract" or "On National Characters", as well as in his *History of England*. It has been noted that he has a narrow idea of justice, as he applies justice primarily to the rights of property; although in the *Treatise* he uses the term 'fidelity' for respecting and keeping promises and contracts, sometimes including this in justice, treating a promise as a voluntary transfer of the right to future goods or services. Hume was certain that justice's artificiality lies in its dependence on the man-made conventions which create property rights; his goal was to defend the stability of property and society as he thought that individual rights are essential to that goal. So he focused his attention on property rights, and his moral theory is classified as rights-based in contrast to theories based on need or some sort of merit or desert,[37] as he disagrees with the common view that restricts 'merit or moral worth' to moral virtues as contrasted with natural abilities.[38] Baier, examining Hume's theory of justice as a whole in all his works, points out that in the *Treatise* he has a narrow notion of justice "as comprising merely honesty in property matters, and fidelity to promises and contracts", while in his *Essays* and *History of England* he treats justice as a subject matter of jurisprudence and expands the concept beyond considerations of property.[39] Hume insists that there is no natural affection for or love of mankind in general, and that self-interest can run against the common interest as our partiality affects not only our actions but also our conceptions of virtue. Nevertheless, he believes that in small or large societies, such as nations, especially "as members of a political society, with which we have a common interest", we can have a concern for the public interest by means of sympathy for those who are harmed by unjust actions, and that we come in this way "to a moral approbation of justice and a disapprobation of injustice".[40] That opinion coincides with his view that justice and fidelity are social virtues, highly useful and absolutely necessary to the well being of mankind.[41]

---

[37] Miller, D. (1976) *Social Justice*. Oxford: Oxford University Press. For recent discussions on the concept of desert, see Sher, George (1989) *Desert,* Studies in Moral, Political, and Legal Philosophy. Princeton: Princeton University Press.

[38] Raphael, David Daiches *Concepts of Justice, op.cit.*, pp. 88–89.

[39] Baier, Annete C. (2010) *The Cautious Jealous Virtue. Hume on Justice*. Cambridge, Mass./ London: Harvard University Press.

[40] *Treatise*, p. 499.

[41] *Enquiry,* Appendix III, pp. 304–306. Rawls, John (1972) *A Theory of Justice*. Oxford: Clarendon Press, pp. 3ff.

Hume's general theory of morals concerns the morally good and bad, virtue and vice. His account of justice is considered as part of a larger account of the moral and political virtues in general. Actually, in the *Treatise*, in the Section "Of the Origin of Justice and Property", he discusses the moral quality of justice and raises the question, "Why we annex the idea of virtue to justice, and of vice to injustice".[42] Nevertheless, his chief concern is to secure social order by the establishment of stable principles, (that is, a reliable legal system) for dealing with property relations and social cooperation in the organization of commerce. Additionally, in his theory of justice, Hume deals with the origin of justice and the moral value of justice, and although he wants to be precise sometimes he is not clear or consistent. According to Haakonssen, regarding the latter part of Hume's theory, that is the moral value and obligation of justice, which was criticized by Smith, his view can be formulated in the following way, including two solutions: "Either moral value and obligation have to be accounted for in terms of sympathy (*Treatise solution*), though that requires a concreteness of object which is just not present in the case of justice in the 'anonymous' society, that is the society beyond the family group; or they are accounted for by means of 'fellow-feeling' (*Enquiry* solution), which avoids this difficulty, but which is so optimistically forward looking, and in that sense rationalistic, that it is not to be found in ordinary men, but is rather a philosophers' speculation".[43] It has been observed that Hume wrote as a philosophical anthropologist, and not as a reformer, unlike Bentham and Mill. Both of the latter wanted to reform our moral outlook rather than merely to explain it. An ethical naturalist, like Hume, was looking to the function of the rules of justice in social life, although he went beyond an analysis of the emotions expressed in judgments of justice.[44]

Hume's theory of justice was criticized by three other eminent Scottish philosophers, Lord Kames and Thomas Reid, both of whom attacked Hume's view that justice is artificial, and by Adam Smith, who having Hume in mind generally criticizes the view that justice depends on utility.[45] In what follows I shall focus on Reid's account of justice, as he was the immediate and most important critic of Hume's philosophy. It is well known that Reid, the "fit representative of the Scottish philosophy",[46] was aroused to philosophical activity by the speculations of Berkeley and Hume, as both had assumed and carried to their logical conclusions the scholastic doctrine of representative perception, that is, perception by means of intermediate ideas. Reid protested in the name of Common Sense against the special principles and inferences of Berkeley and Hume, and against the pronounced skepticism of the latter. He criticized Hume's theory of ideas, first set out by Locke, and insisted that it is not ideas but objects which are immediately present to the mind. Reid therefore tried to examine and undermine the ideal theory of sense-perception and to establish

[42] *Treatise*, p. 498.

[43] Haakonssen, Knud *The Science of a Legislator*, p. 36.

[44] Ryan, Alan (ed.) (1993) *Oxford Readings in Politics and Government*. Oxford: Oxford University Press, *Introduction*, pp. 10–11.

[45] Raphael, David Daiches *Concepts of Justice, op.cit.*, pp. 104ff.

[46] McCosh, James (1966) *The Scottish Philosophy*. Hildesheim: Geog Olms, p. 192.

the doctrine of common sense. In his theory of perception, judgment plays an important role, as it is immanent in every perception, and one could say it is the basis of the Common Sense philosophy. Reid distinguishes between necessary judgments and contingent judgments, and calls the latter natural. Contingent judgments are always connected with perception; for that reason, their subject is not an idea but the external object. For Reid, as well as James Oswald, James Beattie and Dugald Stewart, morality has been understood as a power of judgment, not inherently different from other forms of reasoning.[47] Reid emphatically rejects the doctrines of Hutcheson, Hume and Smith on the nature of virtue as we can understand from the following passage: "The formal nature and essence of that virtue which is the object of moral approbation consists neither in a prudent prosecution of our private interest, nor in benevolent affections towards others, nor in qualities useful or agreeable to ourselves or to others, nor in sympathizing with the passions and affections of others, and in attuning our own conduct to the tone of other men's passions; but it consists in living in all good conscience—that is, in using the best means in our power to know our duty, and acting accordingly".[48] Reid constructs his moral theory according to his theory of knowledge, acknowledging that "by our moral faculty, we have both the original conceptions of right and wrong in conduct, of merit and demerit, and the original judgments that this conduct is right, that is wrong; that this character has worth, that demerit".[49] In his *Essays on the Active Powers of Man*, which appeared in 1788, Reid enlarged on his moral theory which is connected to his epistemology and to his account of will and action as well as to virtue in general. In his moral theory Reid distinguishes the will, which is appropriate to the power and act of determining, from sensations, affections and desires; he states principles of morals connected (a) to virtue in general and (b) to the different branches of virtue. Taking will as the power that affects the acts of the understanding in attention, deliberation, and resolution or purpose, he points out that some acts of will are transient and others permanent and that all acts, virtuous or immoral, are always voluntary. Reid considers that some things in human conduct merit approbation and praise, others blame and punishment, and thinks that involuntary acts deserve neither. According to him, what is necessary cannot be the object of praise or blame, as men are culpable for omitting as well as for performing acts; for that reason we ought to use the best means to learn our duty. It is our duty to fortify ourselves against temptation, to prefer a greater to a lesser good, to follow the intuitions of nature and to act towards another as we should wish him to act towards us; an act that deserves moral approbation must be believed by the agent to be morally good. His ethical theory has a rational basis as it implies judgment as perception does, but in a different way, because in the case of the external senses sensations

[47] Haakonssen, Knud "Natural Jurisprudence and the Theory of Justice," in *The Cambridge Companion to the Scottish Enlightenment*, p. 208.

[48] Reid, Thomas (1967) *Essays on the Active Powers of Man*, in *The Works of Thomas Reid*, ed. by Sir William Hamilton. Hildesheim: Georg Olms Verlagsbuchhandlung, II, p. 650b. All quotations are from this edition.

[49] *Ibid.*, p. 590a–b.

precede judgment, while in moral perception "the feeling is the consequence of the judgment, and is regulated by it". Thus, he adds, "an account of the good conduct of a friend at a distance gives me a very agreeable feeling, and a contrary account would give me a very uneasy feeling; but these feelings depend entirely upon my belief of the report".[50]

Reid was a close friend of Henry Home, Lord Kames, and his criticism on justice is similar to that of Kames. Henry Home, a judge and jurist who had a reputation as a moral philosopher, included in his *Essays on the Principles of Morality and Natural Religion* (1751) a chapter (Essay II, ch. 7) on justice and injustice. He refutes Hume's view that justice is an artificial virtue and shows that man has a variety of principles, such as self-love, benevolence, sympathy and utility, consonant to the divine will; he has also as a separate principle, in his nature and constitution, a moral feeling or conscience by which he judges all his motives to action. Additionally, examining Hume's theory, he shows that it annihilates all real distinction between right and wrong in human actions.[51] Reid describes justice in terms of a distinction between a favour and an injury. Favour and injury are benefits or hurts done intentionally to some other person or persons, and produce naturally gratitude or resentment, respectively. He defines justice and injustice in terms of rights and the violation of rights, and thinks that justice is a positive respect for the rights of others that is connected with charity or favour.[52] Whatever one thinks of Reid's theory of justice as a whole, his classification of rights is helpful in pinpointing the deficiencies of Hume's account. Answering Hume's original question about the nature of this fundamental virtue, he believes that justice is a natural rather than an artificial virtue, and admittedly, consistent with his philosophy, a complex one, involving judgment as well as sentiment: "When a man's natural rights are violated, he perceives intuitively, and he feels that he is injured. The feeling of his heart arises from the judgment of his understanding; for if he did not believe that the hurt was intended, and unjustly intended, he would not have that feeling. He perceives that injury is done to himself, and that he has a right to redress. The natural principle of resentment is roused by the view of its proper object, and excites him to defend his right [...]. These sentiments spring up in the mind of man as naturally as his body grows to its proper stature".[53] By arguing that the utility of justice is insufficient to distinguish it from natural virtues, such as benevolence, which also have utility, Reid produces an alternative to Hume's theory of justice as an artificial virtue.[54] Criticizing Hume's conception of justice as restricted to property and fidelity to contracts, he tried to provide an alternative account through an examination of a more generally accepted notion of justice.[55]

[50] *Ibid.*, p. 672b.

[51] Raphael, David Daiches *Concepts of Justice, op.cit.*, pp. 104–106.

[52] *Active Powers*, p. 654b.

[53] *Ibid.*, p. 656b.

[54] *Ibid.*, pp. 652–653.

[55] *Ibid.*, p. 643ff.

In his *Essays on the Active Powers of Man*, he calls on his knowledge of jurisprudence to list the six respects in which a man may be injured, and indicates six branches of justice or rights: namely, safety of one's person, safety of one's family, liberty, reputation, property and fidelity to engagements. He notes that, "A man may be injured, *first*, in his person, by wounding, maiming or killing him; *secondly*, in his family, by robbing him of his children, or any way injuring those he is bound to protect; *thirdly*, in his liberty, by confinement; f*ourthly*, in his reputation; *fifthly*, in his goods or property; and, *lastly*, in the violation of contracts or engagements made with him".[56] He claims that man has natural rights, in the sense of being "innate" to life, family, friends, liberty and reputation, which, in contrast to property and contractual rights, are "founded upon the constitution of man, and antecedent to all deeds and conventions of society".[57] Of all the rights cited above, the last two are acquired "not grounded upon the constitution of man, but upon his actions". Reid notes that Hume deals in his *Treatise* with property and fidelity to engagements; these are called acquired rights, as they are the result of a preceding act; occupation, labour or transfer, in the case of property; promise, in the case of engagements. In his critique, Reid maintains that these acquired rights depend on natural rights and so are not wholly artificial or conventional.[58] He also argues that distributive justice is absent from Hume's account, and thinks that the right to the acquisition of property of one individual can be restricted by the right to subsistence of another individual, "as justice, as well as charity, requires, that the necessities of those who, by the providence of God, are disabled from supplying themselves, should be supplied from what might otherwise be stored for future wants".[59] Connecting the conception of justice with the sense of duty or obligation,[60] he regards "injustice as the violation of rights and justice as yielding to every man what is his right".[61] Believing that "the direct intention of Morals is to teach the duty of men: that of Natural Jurisprudence to teach the rights of men", he gives the above-mentioned list of rights[62] that are natural in contrast to Hume's property rights that are acquired. Additionally, Reid points out that rights can exist before or outside political society, and he extends justice beyond a concern for property rights linking justice as a fundamental virtue with man's natural rights. In his discussion of property, although he admits that the right of property generally is "not innate, but acquired" and grounded

[56] *Ibid.*, p. 656a.

[57] *Ibid.*, p. 657a.

[58] Raphael, David Daiches *Concepts of Justice, op.cit.*, p. 108.

[59] *Active Powers*, p. 659a.

[60] *Ibid.*, p. 655b: "This very conception of justice implies its obligation. The morality of justice is included in the very idea of it: nor is it possible that the conception of justice can enter into the human mind, without carrying along with it the conception of duty and moral obligation. Its obligation, therefore, is inseparable from its nature, and is not derived solely from its utility, either to ourselves or to society."

[61] *Ibid.*, p. 656b.

[62] *Ibid.*

"not upon the constitution but upon man's actions"[63]; he insists that property can be acquired initially through occupation and labour, in a state of nature, prior to political convention; in another sense, the right of property it is natural as it flows from man's natural right of liberty,[64] which is a freedom "to act in gratifying desires, a positive rather a negative liberty, as it is restricted not simply by what would hurt others but also by the duties of an individual to God and to self".[65] Reid wanted to criticize Hume's neglect of the "natural rights" in his theory of justice and make a distinction between innate or natural rights and adventitious or acquired rights, claiming that the former do not presuppose any human action, whereas acquired rights do.[66]

Reid wanted to refute Hume's view that justice, meaning property rights, is artificial and in his manuscript notes of his lectures on jurisprudence he focus more on the topic of specific rights than on the concept of justice. In his lectures, which clarify his own social, moral and political thought, he defines justice as abstaining from injury and distinguishes between commutative and distributive justice. Dealing briefly with commutative justice that is described in terms of rights and defined as "fair dealing, honesty, integrity", he then turns to a definition of distributive justice, in its strict and proper sense, as "the Justice of a Judge in executing the Laws and distributing Rewards and Punishments".[67] Reid, in his *Lectures on jurisprudence*[68] as in his *Active Powers*, was more preoccupied with Hume's account of property rights than with a general analysis of justice. His central question of whether justice is artificial or natural in his practical ethics was mostly a critique of Hume's attack on the natural law tradition. Reid propounded in the eighteenth century an account of justice stressing the obligation to help the needy as a requirement of justice that was based on theology. Connecting religion and politics, he draws an analogy between a family and mankind as the family of God, and maintains that 'justice as well as charity' makes the same requirement for 'the family of God' as for a conventional family with regard to the necessities of those members who cannot fend for themselves, making this a duty of strict obligation. Reid acknowledges the strict obligations of special relationship to family, friends and close associates, as well as other obligations of keeping faith in promises, contracts and shunning deceit.[69]

---

[63] *Ibid.*, p. 657.

[64] Active *Powers*, p. 658b: "Every man, as a reasonable creature, has a right to gratify his natural and innocent desires, without hurt to others. No desire is more natural, or more reasonable, than that of supplying his wants. When this is done without hurt to any man, to hinder or frustrate his innocent labour, is an unjust violation of his natural liberty."

[65] Cf. Mackinnon, K. (1989) "Thomas Reid on Justice 'a Rights-Based Theory'," in Dalgarno, M. & Matthews, E. (eds.) *The Philosophy of Thomas Reid.* Dordrecht/Boston/London: Kluwer Academic Publishers, "Philosophical Studies Series 42", pp. 355–367, especially p. 360.

[66] Reid, Thomas (1990) *Practical Ethics,* ed. by Knud Haakonssen. Princeton: Princeton University Press, p. 61.

[67] Reid, Thomas *Practical Ethics,* ed. Knud Haakonssen, p. 139, as cited by Raphael, David Daiches *Concepts of Justice., op.cit.*, p. 112.

[68] Reid, Thomas *Practical Ethics,* ed. Knud Haakonssen, p. 204ff.

[69] *Active Powers*, V.5, pp. 651a–663a, and Raphael, David Daiches *Concepts of Justice*, p. 236.

D. D. Raphael, in his valuable book *Concepts of Justice*, when referring to Reid's claim that there is an essential connection between justice and rights, and to Hume's view of justice in terms of property rights, believes that both were mistaken, because there can be justice in the absence of rights and rights in the absence of justice. Raphael himself has accepted a distinction between rights of action and rights of recipiency, that nowadays are described by theorists as liberty-rights and claim-rights, pointing out that both are more closely connected with obligation than with justice. Nevertheless, he concludes that the association of justice with rights chiefly concerns claim-rights, that is, the right to receive equality of opportunity in the sense of moral rights.[70]

It is worth noting that a common factor in the moral theories of both Hume and Reid is linked to the word improvement. Hume concluded his *Treatise* by claiming that as human beings we have a capacity for sharing good and ills through sympathy, acting for the common good, and he believes that a better understanding of our nature can serve to improve our understanding of human morality.[71] Reid, conversely, by focusing on men's rights and mainly on their duties, acknowledges the positive role of the teaching of morals through a system of natural jurisprudence, and accords to the government a role in the improvement of the moral character of the individual.[72] In conclusion, I would like to add that all the Scottish thinkers of the Enlightenment, since the Act of Union with England in 1707, were concerned with the moral dimensions of modernization and the economic improvement of their commercial or civil society; institutions, such as justice, law, rights and obligations were highly valued by them since they wanted a stable society and government in order to secure the future. It is not surprising then that rights and justice were crucial to them and a matter of wide discussion.

---

[70] *Ibid.*, p. 244.

[71] Baier, Annette C. (2011) *The Pursuits of Philosophy. An Introduction to the Life and Thought of David Hume*. Harvard, Mass./London: Harvard University Press, p. 49.

[72] Diamond, Peter J. (1998) *Common Sense and Improvement: Thomas Reid as a Social Theorist*. Germersheim/Frankfurt am Main: Publications of the Scottish Studies of the Johannes Gutenberg Universität Mainz/Peter Lang, "Scottish Studies International, Vol. 24", p. 335.

Rousseau – Equality and Freedom in the Community

Ellen Krefting

Jean-Jacques Rousseau's name is often associated with an irrationalist, pre-Romantic idealization of the wild, untouched human nature and the primitive existence governed by feelings; or he is associated with shocking honesty and with the birth of the modern autobiography. He is seen as the Romantic in the Enlightenment period. More than anything else, however, Rousseau was a deeply sensitive political philosopher who highlighted a particular kind of state, based on fundamental laws, as the presupposition for human freedom within the parameters of the dawning modern society in which he lived. In this article, I shall re-examine Rousseau's unique and complex concepts of political freedom and equality, just laws, popular sovereignty, the general will, and democracy, and I shall show how these can be understood in the light of core problems in his writings as a whole. Unlike the currents in scholarly tradition which have emphasized the unsurpassable contradictions and paradoxes in the totality of Rousseau's activity as author and philosopher, I shall emphasize (in the spirit of Ernst Cassirer) the connections.[1] I shall thus identify a leitmotif in the great variety of his writings so that the political texts can be read as one of many proposed solutions to what Rousseau saw as the fundamental problem: namely, man's dependence within the social relationships on which modern societies are built. This article will thus contribute to the rehabilitation of Rousseau's political thinking that is under way today and that points out (*inter alia*) the relevance of this thinking to contemporary debates about radical democracy—seen as space where common laws and rights remain open to being contested by the members of society.

[1] In his articles "Das Problem Jean-Jacques Rousseau" (1932) and "Kant und Rousseau" (1939), Ernst Cassirer saw Kant's reading of Rousseau as a key to understanding how the "irrationalist" Rousseau could end up as a vigorous defender of universal reason and of the state under the rule of law. The articles are reprinted in Ernst Cassirer, *Über Rousseau*. Berlin: Suhrkamp, 2012.

E. Krefting (✉)
History of Ideas, University of Oslo, Oslo, Norway
e-mail: ellen.krefting@ifikk.uio.no

G. Fløistad (ed.), *Philosophy of Justice*, Contemporary Philosophy: A New Survey 12,
DOI 10.1007/978-94-017-9175-5_12,

It is indisputable that Rousseau's political solution to what I call the problem of dependence soon gave rise to very different interpretations, from the most liberal and democratic to the most terrifyingly totalitarian—as we shall see toward the close of this article. The two distinct trends in the reception history appeared already during the French Revolution, which erupted 11 years after his death. The Revolution also revealed what are still regarded as the greatest challenges in Rousseau's egalitarian, universal and democratic thinking, namely, gender dualism and the concept of freedom. The last part of this article will emphasize these critical aspects of the history of reception, which also concern questions of political justice. In addition, I will indicate how the tensions and paradoxes in Rousseau's political thinking can nourish a deeper reflection on democracy and its challenges even today.

1 Critique of Civilization and Substitutes for Lost Nature

Few of the works from Rousseau's pen belong clearly to one particular tradition in the history of political thought. Early Modern absolutist concepts, the contemporary language of natural law and contractualism, and classic republicanism left their mark on his political ideas. His upbringing in the independent Calvinist city-state of Geneva, where (if we are to believe Rousseau) it was not least the craftsmen who upheld the republican ideals, constitutes an important background. It was in the well-stocked library of his father, a clock-maker, that he encountered the Roman classics (Cicero, Plutarch, and Tacitus), who gave an early impetus to his profound admiration of the great personalities of classical antiquity and of the republican civic virtues, especially the love of freedom and of one's fatherland.[2] Besides this, all his writings are inspired by the "Augustinian" moral psychology and social analysis developed by the "French moralists" of the seventeenth century (Pascal, La Rochefoucault, Nicole). It is this inspiration that makes it possible to identify the investigation of man's problematic embeddedness in social relationships as the leitmotif that runs through Rousseau's writings, where he attempted in various ways to confront a very modern and secular experience of alienation, dependence, inequality and injustice, an experience of lost nature.

His version of the well-known idea of the state of nature tells us what kind of nature has been lost. We shall examine this shortly; but already at this point, we must recall that Rousseau's way of employing the state of nature to establish a political anthropology is different from what we find in Hobbes and Locke. Instead of describing a state of nature in order to be able to define man's nature and natural rights once and for all, it was more important for Rousseau to use the state of nature to understand how the human being had been changed through history, how man had been formed and distorted by various social and economic structures. The individual human being and his or her motivations are determined less by what is given by nature, than by what is caused by history and society. This means that Rousseau

[2] Rousseau, *Confessions,* in *Œuvres complètes* I, Paris: Gallimard 1959, p. 9.

thought in societal terms of phenomena that had long been understood as nature. This is the foundation of his profound critique of society, a way of thinking that points ahead to Hegel, Marx, and historicism.

The critique of civil society, indeed of the entire "state of society," can be seen already in the first essay Rousseau published, with which he won the first prize in the Academy of Dijon's essay competition. The question that the Academy had announced in late 1749 was: "Has the Restoration of the Sciences and Arts Contributed to the Purification of Morals?" Rousseau's fellow Enlightenment thinkers had developed a strong trust in the individual's reason and in the abilities of culture and knowledge to create ever better conditions, materially, socially, and politically. The basic mood was one of optimism and belief in progress. But the essay competition asked whether this optimism was legitimate, and whether it was equally valid in all areas. Rousseau's clear and famous answer in his *Discourse on the Arts and Sciences* (1750) was negative. Progress in science, technology, and art was all very well, but men's moral life lay in ruins. If science, art, and philosophy had made great strides, this was because it served the personal ambitions, the greed, and the vanity of individuals. His conclusion was that, while the sciences and the arts made progress, people's souls were in decay. There was no necessary connection between science and morality, or between art and virtue; there was no spontaneous harmony between individuals' pursuit of private interests and the public good, or between economic progress and political freedom and justice. Rousseau questioned the very idea of knowledge and enlightenment as intrinsically good and of progress as the necessary form of historical development. He insisted that virtue, freedom, justice, and happiness could most successfully unfold in simple and sober communities in which the agricultural economy and civic virtues had not yet been replaced by trade and personal self-interest, in small republics like Sparta in antiquity or the Geneva of his childhood.

It is characteristic of the Enlightenment culture in the mid-eighteenth century that Rousseau, despite this attack on the cult of knowledge, progress, and commerce, shortly afterward became a centrally important contributor to the great French *Encyclopaedia.* He wrote articles about music and an important article on "Political economy," and he positioned himself as an Enlightenment philosopher. However, a new breach with the Enlightenment milieu came in 1755, with the *Discourse on the Origin and the Foundations of Inequality Among Men* (hereafter: *Inequality*), in which Rousseau elaborated a critique of civilization with stronger political and revolutionary perspectives, while at the same time including the moral arguments from the first essay. He sketched his version of the state of nature, which was not used only to explain the original nature of man, how both inequality and political institutions had come into existence, and why and in what form state authority was legitimate: Rousseau employed the state of nature to put a question mark against civil society itself, against social relationships *per se*. He had to begin here in order to approach the question of the form of the state and the kind of government, of correct and legitimate power. Society was the key to understanding most of what was evil, unjust, and bad in the world, as social interdependence was the key to understanding the psychology and moral condition of human beings. It is important to emphasize that Rousseau was deeply anti-Aristotelian, in the sense that he did not see society as a natural reality. The state of nature is not only a pre-political order; it is also pre-civil and pre-moral. And it is irrevocably lost. The complete self-sufficiency and freedom that characterize the human being in the state of nature can only be objects of thought; they cannot be realized. But if we are inextricably bound to society, how can the state of nature serve as a natural norm for civil life? Is it possible to create good substitutes for lost nature?

From an external perspective, this can appear theoretically insoluble, as long as Rousseau insisted that nature and society were mutually exclusive realities. However, there were practical solutions. It must be admitted that Rousseau sometimes cultivated personal escape routes from social relations, for example by means of "solitary wanderings" and "reveries" that put him into unmediated contact with what he imagined as pure nature, either in his surroundings or in his own inner self.[3] But he did also write texts that proposed a number of other, less personal solutions, because he saw reality, in a secular and modern manner, as contingent, not as something given once and for all. While nature is in its deepest sense immutable, man in the state of society is able to change and reshape his surroundings, and not least himself. "A second nature" can be created physically, morally, and politically. It is not possible to recreate the state of nature, but it is possible to establish a rational and moral society on equality and freedom which is also in conformity with what Rousseau defined as "natural law" or rather "natural *right*" (principles being both natural and rational in the sense of securing the common preservation of all human beings). In this reshaping man takes use of the resources that are present in the civil state, in order to overcome its deficiencies and limitations. As in homeopathy, one must use the symptoms of the sickness itself to repair, compensate, and create good substitutes—in this case, for lost nature.[4]

In his novel *Émile, or On Education* (1762), Rousseau experimented with a "natural" education as the solution to the problem of dependence in civil society. If one followed educational principles that took into account the natural stages of development, it would be possible to neutralize society's destructive effects on the individual. Through an education that combined liberty and discipline, natural independence could be reshaped into individual virtue. Rousseau understood "virtue" primarily as the ability to give the public good priority over one's own private interests. This work acquired an immense importance for subsequent generations' sensitivity to children's character and value; but it also acquired importance for the view of the relationship between men and women in the bourgeoning bourgeois model of society. For Rousseau, the two sexes were of essentially different and complementary natures. This required diametrically opposed types of education and sexually conditioned roles in society, and in the state.

---

[3] See the autobiographical part of his writings, with the posthumously published *Reveries of a Solitary Walker* as a high point.

[4] On the "homeopathic model" in Rousseau's thinking, see Starobinski, Jean (1989) *Le remède dans le mal: La pensée de Jean-Jacques Rousseau*. Paris: Gallimard.

The true solution to the fundamental human problem in society could not, however, be individual as in *Émile,* or based on the transparent family economy as in the immensely popular epistolary novel *Julie, or the new Heloise* (1761). The solution—as Rousseau described it in a number of texts from the 1760s—had to be political.[5] It is especially in his *chef d'œuvre, The Social Contract* (1762), that he formulates the idea of a community of equal and free citizens who impose their own laws by means of the "general will." This must be understood as Rousseau's ultimate compensation for the lost natural independence that he had described in *Inequality.* This moral-political solution entailed reshaping alienating commercial societies into national communities, and transforming divided and egoistic individuals into whole and free citizens. On a cosmopolitical level, it entailed transforming the conflictual international society into a peaceful fraternity of national communities united by binding laws. As we shall see, Rousseau sketched this in his posthumous writings about the possibility of "perpetual peace."

2 From the State of Nature to Society and History

We have already identified Rousseau's understanding of how social interdependence corrupts human nature and existence as the basis of his political thinking. But what is there really that is *not* societally determined? What is there that is pure nature? Rousseau addresses these questions in his presentation of the state of nature in *Inequality,* where he believed that he was going deeper than Hobbes, who had erroneously derived his definition of human nature from an analysis of the civil state.[6] In order to avoid such a wrong inference Rousseau insists that the state of nature is an intellectual construction. It has no empirical anchoring. It can only be the object of thought, as the antithesis of society, of the civil state.[7]

Man in Rousseau's state of nature lives like a nomad, or rather like a solitary animal, "sating his hunger beneath an oak, slaking his thirst at the first Stream, finding his bed at the foot of the same tree that supplied his meal, and with that his needs are satisfied."[8] Existence is more peaceful, and definitely more idyllic, than in Hobbes' world of scarce goods. The principal trait of the wild man is independence:

[5] Work on a "political solution" of this kind can be traced far back in Rousseau's writings; it also finds expression in his article on "Political economy" in the great French *Encyclopedia.* After *The Social Contract,* his political thinking is expressed more concretely in the *Constitutional Project for Corsica* (1764, but first published in 1861) and in *Considerations on the Government of Poland* in the 1760s, which was published in his Collected Works in 1782. Rousseau wrote the texts about international relations in parallel to *The Social Contract*: the *Abstract of Monsieur l'Abbé de Saint-Pierre's "Plan for Perpetual Peace,"* which was printed in 1761 (the more critical postscript was not published until after Rousseau's death).

[6] Rousseau 1997, pp. 132 and 151.

[7] Rousseau 1997, pp. 132–133.

[8] Rousseau 1997, p. 134.

he is "self-sufficient," and this self-sufficiency is his primary characteristic.[9] He is not equipped with any innate ideas, or with reason or an ability to reflect. Nor does he have any language. "Savage man" lives in the feeling of existing in the present moment. He is completely in his own presence. Rousseau conceives of a radically atomistic but nevertheless "happy" individualism—although it is not possible to ascribe to man in the state of nature the ability to feel happiness, or any consciousness of justice.

This self-sufficient individual is driven by two fundamental sentiments or impulses: by the love of self (*amour de soi*), which is moderated by the ability to feel pity (*pitié*) with others whom he may chance to meet along his path. Together these two "natural sentiments" contribute to the mutual preservation of the entire species.[10] The love of self is an instinct of self-preservation that must not be confused with the self-love (*amour-propre*) or egoism that emerges in the civil state, when man has become a sociable being and "always outside himself, [...] capable of living only in the opinion of others and, so to speak, derives the sentiment of his own existence solely from their judgment".[11] A solitary, self-sufficient individual can never be egoistic—or morally good. Egoism, like language, reason, and every distinction between good and bad, or between right and wrong, is the result of permanent interaction with other individuals: in other words, of social intercourse. We should note that Rousseau does not see these as gains here, because he is focusing principally on what man loses through social intercourse, namely, independence. He writes that one becomes a "slave," also in a psychological sense. Man becomes dependent on acknowledgment by others. Civil life creates a struggle to satisfy this false need for esteem, for personal advantages, and for power. This generates historical development, but also unhappy and vicious individuals driven by purely private interests. Paradoxically, the civil state is the cause of individuals' uncivilized behaviour.

The reasons why the "happy" independence of the state of nature is shattered must be sought in those qualities that make natural man more than purely an animal, namely, his "capacity as a free agent" and his "perfectibility". The latter term designates man's ability to realize inherent possibilities by the means of his free will, which makes him able to choose against his instincts; in other words, "perfectibility" means self-transcendence. And as soon as man becomes a social being, there is no way back. The secular fall throws men into a corrupting civil game in which the natural drive for self-preservation is transformed into self-assertion, into a continuous struggle to satisfy one's own particular interests.

For Rousseau, the breach with the state of nature represents the beginning of man as a history-making animal. Human history is marked by two things: a lack of freedom and inequality. As Rousseau sees it, the costs of the civil state are relatively low at an early point in the historical development. The period immediately prior to the agricultural revolution is characterized as the happiest and the longest lasting period

[9] Rousseau 1997, p. 157.

[10] Rousseau 1997, pp. 154–155.

[11] Rousseau 1997, p. 187.

in the *de facto* history of humanity, marked by a kind of simple bourgeois family idyll based on self-reliance:

> so long as they applied themselves only to tasks a single individual could perform, and to arts that did not require the collaboration of several hands, they lived free, healthy, good, and happy as far as they could by their Nature be, and continued to enjoy the gentleness of independent dealings with one another.[12]

The real decline begins with the introduction of property, and not least of the right of property. This was the great turning point in human history. According to Rousseau, it is utterly impossible to call property a natural right. It belongs exclusively to the sphere of positive law. Rousseau emphasized that the right of property actually breaks the natural law, which is the principle that secures the preservation of all human kind. Rousseau thereby challenged the very cornerstone in the commercial bourgeois society that was taking shape in a number of European countries in the eighteenth century. He also engaged in a direct polemic against Locke, who had placed the right to property together with the right to life and to freedom at the very centre of modern natural law thinking.

The attack on the right of property was not completely new. It is found already in Plato and in a number of Christian thinkers and French "moralists," including Pascal. But Rousseau's critique was linked to his insight into what was entailed by the urbanization and the emerging industrialization of the new bourgeois society. The problem with the right of property was the same as with the division of labour, or what he called "differentiation": "the moment one man needed the help of another; as soon as it was found to be useful for one to have provisions for two, equality disappeared, property appeared, work became necessary, and the vast forests changed into smiling Fields that had to be watered with the sweat of men, and where slavery and misery were soon seen to sprout and grow together with the harvests."[13] The right of property and the division of labour intensify the inequality and dependence between man and woman, rich and poor, master and servant.

Let me emphasize that this does not mean that Rousseau saw individuals as equal in terms of nature. On the contrary, he underscores that the natural differences between human beings are huge. A self-sufficient, independent life in the pre-civil state of nature, however, leaves the natural inequality without significance. Men are equal because they are free. There is no justice, nor injustice. Natural inequality becomes a problem only when it is exploited socially, for example in the form of division of labour, which increases both physical and psychological dependence through the need for help, and acknowledgment. And this is a relationship of dependence that rules the rich person just as much as the poor, the master just as much as the servant: "Man is born free, and everywhere he is in chains. One believes himself the other's master, and yet is more a slave than they", Rousseau states early in his great political work, *Of the Social Contract*.[14]

[12] Rousseau 1997, p. 167.

[13] Rousseau 1997, p. 167.

[14] Rousseau 2012, p. 41.

3 A Legitimate Civil Order Based on Common Laws

We have now looked at Rousseau's idea of natural man, and of dependence and inequality in the civil state. But what was the role of politics and law in the development of civil society? It is clear that Rousseau ascribed particular responsibility for the wretched condition of the advanced civil state to political institutions and the body of laws. He claimed in *Inequality* that the historical growth of legislation, civil organization, and political institutions had primarily served one goal, namely, to guarantee and strengthen the private interests of the powerful. In the language of the natural-law tradition, he asserted that neither civil society nor the formation of any state had ever yet been founded on the natural law. Nor were they based on any valid contract between the members of society. On the contrary, law and systems of justice were products of relationships of power in society, which "gave the weak new fetters and the strong new forces, irreversibly destroyed natural freedom, forever fixed the Law of property and inequality, transformed a skillful usurpation into an irrevocable right, and for the profit of a few ambitious men henceforth subjugated the whole Mankind to labour, servitude and misery".[15]

As I have mentioned, there was no way back to the pre-civil state of nature. According to Rousseau, there were no obvious civilizing mechanisms in civil society that enabled it to regulate itself with a more or less just and happy outcome. Was there, then, any alternative to "the right of the strongest"? In fact there was. Already in *Inequality,* Rousseau indicates the possibility of a type of social order that can be seen to be both advantageous and just for all its citizens. Here, power is transferred to a state body through a genuine contract made by a community rather than by isolated individuals. Rousseau envisaged a state based on a "true Contract between the People and the Chiefs it chooses for itself; a Contract by which both Parties obligate themselves to observe the Laws stipulated in it and which form the bonds of their union".[16] The idea of such a valid contract between an assembled "people" and "the Body Politic" was further developed in *The Social Contract,* where Rousseau asked whether it is possible to think of a legitimate form of government in civil society, "taking men as they are, and the laws as they can be".[17] In other words, is it possible to create a civil order that unites the private interests of the individual with a binding body of laws for the best of the community, without infringing the moral integrity and freedom of each individual?

It is important to emphasize that Rousseau, unlike the central thinkers in the natural-law tradition, didn't regard nature as an obvious basis for political legitimation. Every social and political order is in direct conflict with natural independence. Is there, then, anything that can give validity and value to the civil state? What can be equal in value to the individual's natural independence?

---

[15] Rousseau 1997, p. 173.

[16] Rousseau 1997, p. 180.

[17] Rousseau 2012, p. 41.

Rousseau's answer was equality and freedom within a political community. The task of such a political community, which must be a state under the rule of law, is to replace the natural, physical inequality among individuals with moral equality, to replace the natural independence with moral freedom, to replace natural right with legal rights.[18] In this state of affairs, no one has any right to issue commands to anyone other than his own self. Absolutely everyone exercises self-determination. In this way, moral equality is not an end in itself for Rousseau, but becomes a condition for freedom. We can therefore claim that Rousseau saw politics as a potential art of social engineering, where equality leads to freedom. Only a sovereign state body can create the type of equality that secures freedom and that matches the self-sufficiency that Rousseau imagined in the state of nature.[19] But what kind of political community and what political mechanism could guarantee such a form of equality and freedom?

In Rousseau's eyes, the core of a legitimate state was that it obligated and protected all the citizens equally by means of laws that have only general objects. A state's power over its members can be justified only if the laws that the citizens are compelled to respect guarantee equally the free choice of each one. It is thus a question of a just power that imposes on the citizens those limitations in their interaction with each other that are necessary, if they are to be reciprocally free. The question is how such a state can be established.

Like Hobbes and Locke, Rousseau held that political institutions receive legitimacy by means of contracts. Unlike them, however, he held that the state under the rule of law was not dependent on only one contract. Since its task is to protect the commonalty and the reciprocal freedom of choice, it cannot be constructed on one single contract that is entered into directly by individuals and the state. Such a state would merely be dominated by negotiations about the private interests of heterogeneous individuals and groups. For Rousseau, the transfer of power to a sovereign state body presupposes that a different type of contract is already established: a contract, or rather a pact, between the individuals, where not only a majority, but absolutely everyone—on an equal basis and voluntarily—agree to join a binding community, a people, a united body. One can say that this "social pact" entails that each one chooses to disregard his natural inclinations in order to become a part of something larger, something general. For Rousseau, the individual's free will is decisive for such a social contract, since even if the natural independence is irrevocably lost one cannot renounce the freedom to choose without renouncing "one's quality as man, the rights of humanity, and even its duties".[20]

Every man has the capacity to choose to thwart one's natural inclinations and become a part of a people of reciprocally free citizens. This entails establishing a state power—"a Sovereign", in Rousseau's vocabulary—in which "the people

---

[18] Rousseau 2012, pp. 53 and 56.

[19] See Schlar, Judith (1998) "Reading the *Social Contract*" and "Jean-Jacques Rousseau and Equality," in *Political Thought and Political Thinkers*. Chicago: UCP. See also Israel, Jonathan 2001 and 2006.

[20] Rousseau 2012, p. 45.

assembled" imposes common laws that everyone must obey. It can, of course, be difficult to understand how the individuals can choose to let themselves be subjected to a social body, obey laws, and at the same time be free. Rousseau concedes that this is a paradox, which he formulates as a practical challenge in the following way: "To find a form of association that will defend and protect the person and goods of each associate with the full common force, and by means of which each, uniting with all, nevertheless obey only himself and remain as free as before."[21] This is possible, conditioned by "the total alienation of each associate with all of his rights to the whole community: For, in the first place, since each gives himself entirely, the condition is equal for all, and since the condition is equal for all, no one has any interest in making it burdensome to the rest".[22] If all give themselves to all, no one is dependent on the will of one particular other person. It is when each single individual freely puts his freedom and his rights in the common pot that freedom can be restored to them again, so that each one remains as free as before. And it is the famous general will that ensures that the individuals within such a binding community work toward their common preservation and at the same time "only obeys themselves".[23]

4 The General Will

The concept of the will is central throughout Rousseau's thinking, and the concept of the general will occupies the central position in *The Social Contract.* It is free will, rather than reason, that distinguishes man from the animals; and it is thanks to man's will that something other than the forces of nature holds sway on earth. Ultimately, it is also the will that makes it possible for the moral and the political to take the place of the natural. But not all types of will are good and right from a moral and political perspective. The only form of will that can exercise legitimate authority on behalf of the community is the general will. But how are we to understand this complex concept, which has been the object of such diverse interpretations?

Although the concept of the general will tends to be attributed to Rousseau, it already had a history and was relatively widespread in contemporary discussions of the "general good" opposed to particular interests.[24] Rousseau employs the general will as a designation of the will of all the citizens. But this will is not "general" in the sense that it is the sum of the arbitrary particular wills of single individuals; nor is it "general" in the sense that it expresses the common interests of a group, such as we can find, for example, among members of one particular professional group, or

[21] Rousseau 2012, pp. 49–50.

[22] Rousseau 2012, p. 50.

[23] Rousseau 2012, Book IV.

[24] See for example Riley, Patrick (1986) *The General Will before Rousseau.* Princeton: PUP.

in a public office-holder in the state administration.[25] Above these two types of wills—the private will of the individual and the "will of political organs"—there stands the will that is shared by all the members of the community, in virtue of the fact that they are equal, free, and solidly united citizens.

There is nothing mysterious about this form of the general will. It designates what the human individual intends when he or she thinks neither as a private person nor as a member of an interest group or of any part of the administration, but on behalf of the entire collective body. Rousseau's concept of the general will designates what the individual intends, when what he intends could also become a law for everyone in the entire community. Accordingly, he does not deny that even in an ideal state there will always be both private wills and group interests, and that a large part of community affairs will concern these; but the point is that, since there are some things that concern absolutely everyone in the community because they concern their common preservation and the general welfare, it is important that the general will, which is that will in the individual that is always directed to the general good, must take priority over the other two. In order for the state to guarantee moral equality and reciprocal freedom, that which unites must take priority over the plurality, the universal over the particular.

Rousseau is—like so many political thinkers—sceptical with regard to associations and political parties that can become large and powerful, and thereby enforce their majority view—which is, in reality, only one particular view. It is better if the individual citizens let their private particular interests form the starting point for disagreement, because in an enlightened people, this disagreement can culminate in a compromise that gives expression to the general will.[26] But what of those who are not enlightened in this sense, and who continue to pursue their own, purely egoistic interests? A number of controversies in the history of interpretation are linked to Rousseau's affirmation that these persons ought to be "compelled" to act in accord with the general will. For Rousseau, the absence of the abuse of power in the community presupposes that absolutely all the citizens are both the origin of the general will (as "sovereign") and subordinate it to it (as "subject"). We obligate ourselves to follow what we ourselves intend when we think on behalf of the community. This is why he says that "whoever refuses to obey the general will shall be constrained to do so by the entire body: which means nothing other than that he shall be forced to be free".[27]

Rousseau claims that to follow the general will is the highest expression of "civil" or "moral freedom." This concept of freedom is completely different from what both Hobbes and Locke had defended; their concept is often called "liberalist". Rousseau's concept of civil and moral freedom is not about the realization of one's own immediate interests. This form of freedom means not being subject to one's own instincts or to the arbitrary private interests of others. It is linked to the community as a whole and its general good, and thus resembles what is often called

[25] Rousseau 2012, Book II, ch. 3.

[26] Rousseau 2012, pp. 57 and 60.

[27] Rousseau 2012, p. 53.

the "republican" concept of freedom.[28] Freedom means that one need not obey any laws other than those one has imposed upon oneself. For Rousseau, this form of freedom "alone makes man truly the master of himself; for the impulsion of mere appetite is slavery, and obedience to the law one has prescribed to oneself is freedom"—to quote one of the celebrated formulations in *The Social Contract*.[29] It is a kind of freedom that makes the civil state preferable to the state of nature:

> [...] when the voice of duty succeeds physical impulsion and right succeeds appetite, does man, who until then had looked only to himself, see himself forced to act on other principles, and to consult his reason before listening to his inclinations. Although in this state he deprives himself of several advantages he has from nature, he gains such great advantages in return, his faculties are exercised and developed, his ideas enlarged, his sentiments ennobled, his entire soul is elevated to such an extent, that if the abuses of this new condition did not often degrade him to beneath the condition he has left, he should ceaselessly bless the happy moment which wrested him from it forever, and out of a stupid and bounded animal made an intelligent being and a man.[30]

It is not difficult to see how Kant came to be influenced by Rousseau, both in his formulations of the categorical imperative and in his concepts of autonomy and duty. These were to form the very heart of his moral philosophy, which however takes the understanding of the general validity of the self-imposed law one step further than in Rousseau, who did not speak of absolute universality, but anchored the general will in delimited communities.[31]

5 Popular Sovereignty, Democracy, and Education in Civil Virtues

Rousseau's definition of freedom as self-legislation indicates that political sovereignty, that is to say, the legitimate foundation of power in a state, cannot come from above, as in the concept of sovereignty that had its origin in the absolutist thinking of Jean Bodin. Nor can sovereignty be delegated to a prince or to particular groups, even if this is done by means of a contract. In a state under the rule of law, the

---

[28] See for example Boucher, David in Kelly and Boucher (eds) (2009) *Political Thinkers from Socrates to the Present*. Oxford: Oxford University Press, ch. 15.

[29] Rousseau 2012, p. 54.

[30] Rousseau 2012, p. 53.

[31] On Kant's development of Rousseau's line of thought and of formulations from *The Social Contract,* see for example the *Grundlegung zur Metaphysik der Sitten* (1785). However, as Helga Varden has shown in her article on Kant in the present volume, Kant draws a much stricter distinction than Rousseau between ethics and politics/philosophy of law. For Kant, ethics is about maxims and moral motivation; it is the internal obligating motivation that can make the individual action morally good. Law, on the other hand, applies only to interaction, and it is based on a legitimate external compulsion rather than on an internal obligation. To act in accordance with the law is thus not the same as to act morally good. The law consists of external demands that the choices of the individual should be compatible with respect for other persons' freedom to choose, in a perspective of interaction.

legislative power must absolutely be identical with the community, with the general will of the people: this is the heart of Rousseau's principle of popular sovereignty, and it can be seen as the unique result of his integration of the republican, rhetorical, and humanistic thinking about civil virtues from Cicero and Machiavelli with the concept of sovereignty that he found in modern absolutist political thinkers such as Bodin and Hobbes. Rousseau's transfer of sovereignty from the monarch to the people meant that the only legitimate form of state must be the republic, which Rousseau defined as a state governed by laws that apply to absolutely everyone and to which everyone (that is to say, the people) has given assent. At the same time, however, Rousseau drew a sharp distinction between the legislative power, which always belongs to the people, and the executive power, which can be delegated in a state under the rule of law to a government or a central administration, without thereby infringing the principle of the sovereignty of the people.[32] A government is an instrument that the sovereign general will requires, generally speaking, because a special work is involved in formulating, implementing, and enforcing the laws that the general will has decided, and which necessarily have an abstract and general character—since these are the laws that apply to absolutely everybody. But a governmental function of this kind can take various forms. Which form does Rousseau regard as the best?

It is not difficult to identify Rousseau as a defender of what in modern conceptual terms would be called a democratic principle of sovereignty; but this does not mean that he always defended democracy as the ideal form of government or rule. This is because he understood a democratic form of government as the immediate democracy of an assembly in the manner of ancient Athens, where the citizens participated actively in both the formulation and the administration of the laws. In his *Project of a Constitution for Corsica* (1765) which he wrote in parallel to *The Social Contract,* Rousseau did indeed envisage the possibility of a democratic form of government on this island, with its naturally given boundaries, an agricultural society that cultivated egalitarian and patriotic virtues. Mostly, however, as in *The Social Contract,* he emphasized that a democratic form of government of that kind would make extremely high demands on the knowledge, commitment, integrity, and, not least, the time of the individual citizen.[33] The ideal democratic form of government of which Rousseau could dream demanded a strong feeling of community and individual civil virtue, and presupposed that each individual genuinely knew the community's general will and followed it. Otherwise, democracy would merely degenerate into the abuse of power or into a struggle between the interests of various groups, as was the case in the English political party system. And if democracy was demanding even in small city-states of the type and size of Geneva (the most ideal framework imaginable for a republic), what would be the case with the really large communities of the size of nation-states? As he writes in *The Social Contract*: "If

[32] Rousseau 2012, Book 3, ch. 1.

[33] Rousseau 2012, Book 3, ch. 4.

there were a people of Gods, they would govern themselves democratically. So perfect a Governments is not suited to men."[34]

In practice, the form of government and the particular systems of legislation would have to be adapted to local conditions and the character of the inhabitants. Rousseau affirmed that it depended on traditions and customs, and not least on the size of the population, whether the government should be led by one person, by a few, or by many. On this point, he agreed with many thinkers of the eighteenth century, with Montesquieu at their head, who had also arrived at a principle of the separation of powers and of a system of "checks and balances" between the legislative, the executive, and the judicial power, in order to prevent concentration of power. Although Rousseau draws a sharp distinction between the legislative and the executive power, we do not find this kind of principle of "checks and balances" in his writings. This can make it difficult to read his political thinking against the background of the concrete democratic forms of government that were established in the nineteenth century, where the principle of the separation of powers was so central. For Rousseau, the people's power could not be bound, not even by the principles of a state under the rule of law that the people itself had laid down. Besides this, the people's power was indivisible: therein lay the sovereignty. However, Rousseau was aware that it would seldom be rational to let the people propose or administer the laws. This had to be the responsibility of the professional executive power, which occupied an intermediary position between the sovereign legislative power and the individual citizens and could therefore ensure that freedom was maintained in practice. In any case, the most important democratic principle was that the state was based on laws ("political" or "fundamental laws" as opposed to "civil laws", according to Rousseau) to which the people had given its sovereign assent through the general will.[35] Accordingly, while the people is constituted through a contract that gives the same people absolute sovereignty *over* the law, a government is constituted *through* the law. This means that the government is valid only until the sovereign people decides something else.[36] The guarantee against the arbitrary abuse of power by any government is the possibility that all the citizens can come together and agree to abrogate the law, if they believe that it is being abused or is unjust.

We have seen that popular sovereignty and the fundamental principles of the state under the rule of law are closely connected in Rousseau to the general will, in which the individuals' will is directed to what is best for the whole community. But how do we know what is generally best, or what the general will consists of? It is easy for the individual to want certain things, such as the protection of life and moral dignity, to apply to everyone. But very many issues that concern what is best for all, such as the payment of taxes, can conflict with purely private interests. Rousseau did not conceal the fact that one of the greatest challenges to the body politic was to get individuals, who are very strongly inclined to follow

[34] Rousseau 2012, p. 92.

[35] Rousseau 2012, p. 80.

[36] Rousseau 2012, Book 3, ch. 18.

their own instincts and personal interests, to follow the general will and to want what is best for all despite their own private interests. Egoistical individuals do not automatically become responsible and virtuous citizens overnight. Civic virtue is not inherent in the individual as a natural impulse, and there is no reason to put one's confidence in the kind of inbuilt, enlightened reason in which Locke trusted. Equal, free, and virtuous citizens—and a virtuous and just state—must be created.

Rousseau's way of meeting this challenge is, naturally enough, one of the most controversial and the most misused elements in his political thinking. For how, and by whom, are the citizens to be educated to follow the general will? In Book II of *The Social Contract,* we find the celebrated section about the necessity of a "great Lawgiver" on the model of Lycurgus in ancient Sparta:[37] a man with particular insight and virtue who can miraculously "foresee" the general will and establish the laws and the mechanisms that direct the habits and attitudes of the individuals toward moral citizenship, and that allow the consciousness of the general will to emerge in each individual.[38] But Rousseau also highlighted a civil religion as a means to educate citizens. A democratically motivated and controlled censorship body was also important, in order to prevent a developed general will from being corrupted. Everything that can promote the development of emotional bonds and the experience of fellowship makes a contribution to the formation of a people of virtuous citizens, where the clash between private interest and that which is best for the community is reduced as far as possible. This is also why patriotism, the love for a suitably large and precisely defined "fatherland" with shared values, is an important point in Rousseau's political thinking. This "communitarian" argumentation finds particularly clear expression in his *Considerations on the Government of Poland,* which he wrote in the 1770s. The important point about the patriotism that was expressed in Poland was its contribution to making the "we" a guideline for individual conduct. Patriotism cultivated the positive rather than the negative aspects of social interaction that Rousseau had described in his critique of civilization. Patriotism made possible a voluntary redirection of private interests and passions towards the community, contributing thereby to the formation of a rational moral order. This rational, moral, and just order was thus not natural, but it could be implemented as a "second nature," as a substitute for the natural self-sufficiency and independence.

[37] Lycurgus was the legendary legislator in Sparta in the seventh century before the Common Era, who is said to have carried out the successful militarization of the Spartan city state. Rousseau wrote admiringly about Lycurgus. He also emphasized the significance of soldiers for the feeling of community in his home city of Geneva, for example at the close of his *Letter to M. D'Alembert on Spectacles* (1758). These factors lend support to those interpretations that point to the soldier as the model for Rousseau's nostalgic concept of civil virtue.

[38] Rousseau 2012, Book II, chs. 6–7.

6 Perpetual Peace

Much of what we have seen up to this point makes Rousseau the thinker of the modern nation-state, but the picture of him as the theoretician of nationalism is not unproblematic. First of all, Rousseau saw the "nation" and the "people"—the sovereign state, so to speak—not as natural, essential realities, but as constructed realities. And secondly, there is also a cosmopolitical element in his thinking, visible in the brief concluding chapter of *The Social Contract.* He made a less well known contribution to the problems connected with international law and lasting peace in what has come to be known as the Geneva manuscript, which is an earlier version of *The Social Contract*, and through a summary and critical commentary on Abbé Saint-Pierre's *Plan for Perpetual Peace* written about half a century earlier.[39] Saint-Pierre was an early radical Enlightenment thinker whose utopian dreams of a European republic inspired the more critical and realistic Rousseau to envisage the possibility of establishing a binding community based on law on a supranational European level. Rousseau thereby took his place in a tradition that can be traced back to the large-scale plans of Emile Crucé and Sully for a European federation in the early seventeenth century.

Rousseau's cautious assent to the idea of lasting peace was based on his conviction that there were shared historical bonds in Europe that made it possible for every nation, every people, to see the general good on a higher level and to acknowledge the shared gain in a supranational league of nations. This, however, presupposed the real existence of peoples who were allowed to speak for themselves and to define that which was best for all. Princes and ministers who ruled in non-republican states were not interested in peace and the common good: on the contrary, war often brought them personal advantages. In this situation, two paths to "perpetual peace" among European states could be imagined, according to Rousseau. Either a statesman with exceptional qualities, a new Henry IV or a Sully, must appear on the scene, a man who is able to enforce what is best for all;[40] or else a democratic revolution must take place throughout Europe. Rousseau indicates in his last political text that this revolution would no doubt be violent. We can see in this focus on republican forms of state as a precondition of international law clear trajectories that lead up to Kant and his writings on international law and the preconditions for perpetual peace. Kant's texts are, however, much better known today than Rousseau's.[41]

---

[39] Rousseau, Jean-Jacques (1917) A Lasting Peace through the Federation of Europe and The State of War, translated by C. E. Vaughan. London: Constable and Co. "The State of War" is also included in *The Social Contract and Other Political Writings*. Cambridge: 2012.

[40] Rousseau, 2010, p. 524.

[41] Kant's knowledge of Saint-Pierre and of Rousseau's summary can be seen clearly already in Kant's *Idea for a Universal History with a Cosmopolitan Aim* (1784). In the third Part of *On the Common Saying*: *"That may be correct in theory, but it is of no use in practice"* (1793), which deals with international law, Kant also refers to Saint-Pierre's and Rousseau's enthusiastic ideas about a European league of states. Kant agrees with these ideas, because we are obliged to accept perpetual peace as a possibility.

7 The History of Reception and Criticism

In the context of the history of ideas, it has often been asked whether Rousseau's thinking contributed to the outbreak of the French Revolution in 1789. The answer can be in the affirmative, if we bear in mind that the veneration of Rousseau as a person was just as important for the revolutionaries as the reading of his political texts. Rousseau was the object of an intense cult in France in the 1780s, especially after the publication of his autobiographical *Confessions* in 1781.[42] His life story, from the modest beginnings in the artisan milieu in Geneva to an admittedly controversial position among the foremost Enlightenment philosophers in fashionable Paris, was held up as a mirror against the existing state of affairs. Thanks to his struggle against the way of life of the aristocracy and their privileges, in favour of the simple and the popular, Rousseau became a symbol of opposition to the superficial and unjust order imposed by the absolute monarchy. He was the foremost defender of the oppressed "people."

After the Revolution had become a reality, Rousseau's concepts were employed in the struggle by the various parties to define the political parameters of the new nation. The Revolution years revealed the interpretative spectrum that found a basis in his political thinking. First, his ideas about the constitutional foundation of the state and his concepts of the general will and popular sovereignty were employed in the elaboration of the Declaration of Human Rights and the various constitutional proposals; after this, Rousseau's concept of democracy was used both by the *sans culottes* to justify a larger popular participation in politics and by Robespierre to argue in favour of dictatorship and terror as instruments to inculcate the patriotic civic virtue and to create a unified community. Unlike the *sans culottes,* who were inspired by Rousseau's preference for the direct democracy of assemblies, Robespierre held that democracy demanded a transfer of power from the people to representatives who already possessed the virtues that the people initially lacked.[43] The freedom and sovereignty of the collective were more important than those of the individual.

It is clear that Rousseau's political thinking nevertheless acquired a lasting significance for the rehabilitation of the ideal of democracy and government by the people, which had generally been looked at askance since classical antiquity. As we have seen, Kant was profoundly inspired by Rousseau, not only in his moral philosophy, but also in his political thinking about the state under the rule of law and about international relations. And although the idea of representation, as this was formulated by Robespierre and others, rapidly prevailed over Rousseau's ideal of direct participation as the core of the democratic state, the principle of popular sovereignty served as an inspiration for most of the democratic thinkers and movements and constitutions in the course of the nineteenth century, including the Norwegian constitution of 1814. At the same time, there are echoes of *The Social Contract* in more revolutionary movements too, and in totalitarian ideologies long

[42] Miller 1984, ch. 6.

[43] Miller 1984.

after the bloodiest years of the French Revolution had passed into history. Lenin, Stalin, Mussolini, Hitler, Mao, and Pol Pot all appealed to elements from Rousseau. In Cuba, Fidel Castro is said to have claimed that he "fought against Batista with a copy of *The Social Contract* in my pocket."[44]

In a similar manner, the more academic interpretations of Rousseau's political thinking have taken divergent paths in the history of reception down to the present day. One group of interpretations emphasizes the collectivist and authoritarian, indeed totalitarian, aspects of Rousseau's ideas of the homogeneous political body, while another group emphasizes his defence of the individual's freedom and autonomy in relation both to the forces that can rule arbitrarily *ab extra* and to those that can rule *ab intra.* A third group has focused on the clearly egalitarian aspects in Rousseau. The varied interpretative traditions bear witness to the difficulty in locating this thinking within any of the great modern political "isms."

In a summary of some of the most important objections that have been leveled against Rousseau's political philosophy after the French Revolution, and that must be said to be still interesting and valid, we cannot omit the feminist critique. It is indeed true that feminist thinkers from Mary Wollstonecraft down to the present day have found inspiration in Rousseau, especially because he made "private concerns" linked to family life, gender, and sexuality objects of political thinking. The problem was that on Rousseau's terms, this meant that he could never grant women the full status of citizens. While he put equality and autonomy at the very heart of political thinking, he was at the same time the most important ideologue of modern gender dualism. Rousseau insisted on the equal dignity of the two essentially different sexes, but his greatest fear was that they might attain genuine equality in society. Despite Wollstonecraft's celebrated criticism of the many paradoxes in the thinking of the theorist of equality on this point, his complementary view of the nature of the sexes and their different roles in society became immensely significant for the arguments against giving women political status that accompanied the democratic wave for a long time, from the last part of the eighteenth century onward.

We must mention another important objection to Rousseau's political thinking. This concerns the concept of freedom. In the aftermath of the English philosopher Isaiah Berlin's celebrated 1957 lecture on "Two concepts of liberty," we tend to speak of Rousseau's concept of freedom as positive, in contradistinction to the liberalists' negative concept of freedom.[45] This distinction can be traced back to Benjamin Constant, who clearly attacked Rousseau in a lecture he gave in 1819 entitled "The liberty of the ancients compared with that of the moderns".[46] Constant, from French-speaking Switzerland, was one of the enthusiastic young revolutionaries

[44] See Bernard Gagnebin's Introduction to Rousseau, *Œuvres complètes*, III. Paris, Gallimard, Pléiade, p. xxvi.

[45] Berlin, I. (1958) *Two Concepts of Liberty*. Oxford. Berlin himself regarded Rousseau as "the most sinister and the most formidable enemy of liberty in the whole history of modern thought" in *Freedom and its Betrayal. Six Enemies of Human Liberty,* ed. Henry Hardy, Princeton University Press, p. 49.

[46] "De la liberté des anciens comparée à celle des modernes", Athénée Royal de Paris, 1819.

who became convinced after the Terror that the French Revolution had taken the wrong path both in its goal and in the means it had employed. One of the lessons to be learned from this was that the power of the state had to be limited. The main problem was the Jacobins' use of an inappropriate concept of freedom that had its origin in Greek thinking about democracy and had been mediated by Rousseau. This concept of freedom was not necessarily illegitimate *per se,* but it belonged to the world of classical antiquity. The republican political freedom to play a continuous and active part in government, legislation, and administration was all very well in the small and homogeneous city-states of antiquity, where slaves did most of the productive work, in order that the citizen could use all his time, his energy, and his moral ability to dedicate himself to the political government of the community. Constant claimed that this was completely out of place in modern reality; first, because the states had become too large to be directly ruled by the citizens, and second, because in a society where war has been replaced by commercial trade, the great majority of people are obliged to earn their daily bread by working. Constant insisted on the distinction between the state and society in the modern world. Modern people are not primarily "citizens" in the state (as Rousseau had dreamed). They are primarily at home in society: it is in the family and by means of work that modern people can realize themselves, their virtue, and their freedom. Modern freedom—to choose one's profession, administer one's property, enjoy equality before the law, express one's opinions, form associations, and practice one's religion—is primarily private. Rousseau had insisted that freedom is primarily political and linked to the community, but Constant emphasized that it is individual.

According to Constant, it is not only inappropriate, but fatal to demand of modern people that they should be willing to exchange their individual rights, their personal freedom in society, for the possibility of participating in the collective state power. The need for personal freedom cannot be suppressed in a modern society in the same way as, for example, in Sparta, the militarized city-state of antiquity, which Rousseau seems to present as a model in his political thinking. This can result in a tyranny, as was the case under Robespierre and the regime of the Committee of Public Safety. Constant blames this on Rousseau's anachronistic concept of freedom: "by transposing into our modern age an amount of social power, of collective sovereignty that belonged to other centuries he provided deadly pretexts for more than one kind of tyranny".[47] He pointed out here the totalitarian potential in Rousseau's thinking, where it was so easy to confuse freedom with authority. In Constant's eyes, the task of the modern nation-state could not be the authoritative education of the citizens for a political life in the collective body. On the contrary, the primary task of the state must be to protect the inhabitants' personal freedom to realize themselves in the pluralistic society. It was immensely important to establish boundaries for the sphere of activity of the state power.

At the same time, Constant also saw the problematic aspect of transferring the day-by-day political government to democratically elected representatives. The price for

[47] Constant, Benjamin *The Liberty of the Ancients compared with that of the Moderns*, translated by Jonathan Bennett, 2010, http://www.earlymoderntexts.com/pdf/conslibe.pdf, p. 7.

enjoying societal freedom can be a total political passivity. This is why he emphasized, at the close of his lecture, that the task of the state institutions includes "influencing public affairs, calling on the people to contribute to the exercise of power through their decisions and their votes, guaranteeing their right of control and supervision through the expression of their opinions, and by shaping them up through the exercise of these high functions, give them both desire and power to perform them".[48] Hence, Rousseau's ideal for citizens was not completely alien to the modern world.

This has also become clear in the recent commentators who have emphasized the advantages of reading Rousseau in the light of the classic republican tradition, which has its roots in Aristotle and in late Roman thinking about the state and which emphasized a freedom that was linked to the community and an active citizenship. It argued for a state constructed on just laws.[49] Commentators such as Merja Kylmakoski, Helena Rosenblatt, and David Rosenfelt have pointed out the significance this tradition had for Rousseau's critique of the citizens' freedom in commercial societies, which was only an apparent freedom not to be confused with civic freedom.[50] In this way, we can say that Rousseau's thinking is an important source of an alternative, non-liberalist concept of freedom that has acquired a new relevance in our own age, not least in connection with communitarian political thinking.

The question, however, is whether these various interpretations take sufficient account of the tensions and ambiguities that will always be found in Rousseau's political thinking. Some of the most interesting contributions to scholarship in recent years have focused on the need to see the inbuilt contradictions in Rousseau's political texts as precisely a part of the way in which he thematizes democracy. For example, Kevin Inston has connected Rousseau's concepts of freedom and equality within the parameters of the community with the theories of Ernesto Laclau and Chantal Mouffe about radical pluralist democracy, which are currently of great interest; this has allowed Inston to demonstrate how the eighteenth-century thinker opened a path to understanding democracy and the construction of fundamental common laws as open political processes.[51] Rousseau was the first to show that society, community, and universally valid laws were not givens, but things that had to be created. This centred attention on the political processes. If we accept that it is impossible to achieve the perfect political system once and for all, a total democracy in which the people directly and immediately govern themselves, democracy itself becomes a perennial project in which those who share in the community must become actively involved, in order to define and guarantee freedom and equality under continually shifting historical circumstances.[52]

---

[48] Constant, 2010, p. 14.

[49] Quentin Skinner and J. G. A. Pocock, historians of political ideas, have recently highlighted the historical role of the republican tradition.

[50] See for example Kylmakoski, Merja (2001) *The Virtue of the Citizen: Jean-Jacques Rousseau's Republicanism in the Eighteenth-Century French Context*. Frankfurt am Main: Peter Lang Pub. Inc.

[51] Inston, Kevin (2010) *Rousseau and Radical Democracy*. London: Continuum.

[52] This is a revised version of an article published in Norwegian in Jørgen Pedersen (ed), *Politisk filosofi fra Platon til Hannah Arendt*. Oslo: Pax, 2013, here translated to English by Brian McNeil and Ellen Krefting.

Bibliography

Boucher, D., & Kelly, P. J. (Eds.). (2009). *Political thinkers from socrates to the present*. Oxford: Oxford University Press.

Cassirer, E. (2012). *Über Rousseau*. Berlin: Suhrkamp.

Cohen, J. (2010). *Rousseau: A free community of equals*. Oxford: Oxford Scholarship Online.

Constant, B. (1819/2010). *The liberty of the ancients compared with that of the moderns* (J. Bennett, Trans.). http://www.earlymoderntexts.com/pdf/conslibe.pdf

Inston, K. (2010). *Rousseau and radical democracy*. London: Continuum.

Kant, I. (1785/2005). *The moral law: Groundwork of the metaphysic of morals* (H. J. Paton, Trans.). London: Routledge.

Kehohane, N. O. (1980). *Philosophy and the state in France: The Renaissance to the Enlightenment*. Princeton: Princeton University Press.

Kylmakoski, M. (2001). *The virtue of the citizen: Jean-Jacques Rousseau's Republicanism in the eighteenth-century French context*. Frankfurt am Main: Peter Lang Pub. Inc.

Lange, L. (Red.). (2002). *Feminist Interpretations of Jean-Jacques Rousseau*. University Park: The Pennsylvania State University Press.

Miller, J. (1984). *Rousseau. Dreamer of democracy*. New Haven/London: Yale University Press.

Orvin, C., & Tarcov, N. (Red.). (1997). *The legacy of Rousseau*. Chicago/London: The University of Chicago Press.

Riley, P. (1986). *The general will before Rousseau: The transformation of the divine into the civic*. Princeton: Princeton University Press.

Rousseau, J.-J. (1917). *A lasting peace through the federation of Europe and the state of war* (C. E. Vaughan, Trans.). London: Constable and Co.

Rousseau, J.-J. (1959). In B. Gagnebin & M. Raymond (Reds.), *Les Confessions, Autres textes autobiographiques I: Oeuvres complètes I*. Paris: Gallimard.

Rousseau, J.-J. (1997). *"The discourses" and other early political writings* (V. Gourevitch, Ed. & Trans.). London: Cambridge University Press.

Rousseau, J.-J. (2012). *"The social contract" and other later political writings* (V. Gourevitch, Ed. & Trans.). London: Cambridge University Press.

Schlar, J. (1998). "Reading the social contract" and "Jean-Jacques Rousseau and equality" I. In *Political thought and political thinkers*. Chicago: University of Chicago Press.

Starobinski, J. (1989). *Le remède dans le mal: La pensée de Jean-Jacques Rousseau*. Paris: Gallimard.

Immanuel Kant – Justice as Freedom

Helga Varden

1 Introduction

Kant's practical philosophy is a philosophy of freedom. For Kant, it is our ability to be free that sets us apart from all other living creatures, and makes it possible for us to act normatively, including be ethically and legally responsible for our actions. The concept of freedom is central to all of Kant's practical works, regardless of whether the work focuses on ethics, religion, politics, right (justice), history, education, or anthropology. Kant is convinced that if we can understand our ability to be free, the appropriate critical standards to apply as we describe and evaluate our actions, interactions, societies, histories, states, and legal-political systems will also become clear.

Kant lived from 1724 to 1804. Despite several interesting early publications, Kant's real philosophical breakthrough occurred relatively late in his life, with the 1781 publication of his main work in theoretical philosophy, the *Critique of Pure Reason*. This work marked the beginning of a formidable period of publication, which lasted for approximately 23 years, until his death. During this period, Kant published works encompassing more or less all areas of philosophy. If we borrow Plato's division between the true, the right, and the beautiful—or between theoretical philosophy, practical philosophy, and aesthetics—then Kant produced in this time one major work (a "critique") for each of these major areas of philosophy: the aforementioned *Critique of Pure Reason* (theoretical philosophy) in 1781; the *Critique of Practical Reason* (practical philosophy) in 1788; and the *Critique of Judgment* (aesthetics) in 1790. These three works concern, in other words, our ability to experience and obtain knowledge about the world (theoretical philosophy), our ability to be morally responsible for our actions (practical philosophy), and our ability to experience beauty (aesthetics). In addition to these comprehensive

H. Varden (✉)
Departments of Philosophy and of Women and Gender Studies,
University of Illinois at Urbana-Champaign, Champaign, IL, USA
e-mail: hvarden@illinois.edu

G. Fløistad (ed.), *Philosophy of Justice*, Contemporary Philosophy: A New Survey 12,
DOI 10.1007/978-94-017-9175-5_13,

critiques, Kant wrote several works of varying lengths within each of these fields, as well as quite a few books and articles dealing with historical, anthropological, educational, and religious themes. Considerably limited means and unreliable health made it impossible for Kant to travel, something he compensated for by reading extensively, especially texts concerning geography, anthropology, different legal-political systems, and important contemporary domestic and international legal-political issues.

Kant's comprehensive knowledge about and genuine concern for the world in which he lived are reflected in his many comments on significant contemporary events in his essays and more minor works, such as his comments on the French Revolution of 1789 and European colonization. His first major work in moral philosophy—the *Groundwork for the Metaphysics of Morals*—was published in 1785, 3 years before the *Critique of Practical Reason* (1788). The *Groundwork* is a short book of about 80 pages, and it concerns moral philosophy in general and first-personal ethics in particular. Kant himself thought that this would be his most "popular" work, explaining that he wrote it with an eye to its content being accessible to any enlightened, interested person, not only philosophers. Given how inaccessible this book actually is, it is ironic that Kant correctly predicted it would be his most popular work. For a long time, and somewhat unfortunately, not only students and the interested public, but also philosophers, took this work as representative of Kant's practical philosophy—supplementing it only occasionally with the *Critique of Practical Reason* and various essays. Not until the 1970s did this problem in Kant interpretation begin to be properly remedied, and not until the 1990s did philosophers all over truly attend to Kant's theory of justice—or what Kant calls "right"—in particular to his main work on justice, "The Doctrine of Right."

"The Doctrine of Right" composes the first half of *The Metaphysics of Morals*, which is one of the last of Kant's published works (1797). This is the only place where Kant systematically outlines the basic structure of his theory of right or justice. All his other published works on right and politics are essays and discuss more limited questions. Among the most important of these essays are: "An answer to the question: What is enlightenment?" (1784); "On the wrongfulness of unauthorized publication of books" (1785); "On the common saying: That may be correct in theory, but it is of no use in practice" (1793); "Toward perpetual peace" (1795); and "On a supposed right to lie from philanthropy" (1797).[1] Although these essays have historically received greater attention than his main work "The Doctrine of Right," it is reasonable to assume that Kant intended his essays to complement the latter, and this introduction to Kant's legal-political philosophy is written under that assumption.

As when reading Kant's work in general, it is also useful to remember that no one engages Kant's texts because they are easy to understand or beautifully written. One must therefore approach the ideas in this introduction with the kind of patience

[1] All these works, including *The Metaphysics of Morals*, can be found in *Immanuel Kant: Practical Philosophy*, trans. and ed. by Mary J. Gregor. New York: Cambridge University Press, 1999. All citations from Kant's work are from this translation. I abbreviate the reference to *The Metaphysics of Morals* as MM in this paper, and I refer to particular pages by means of the Prussian Academy Pagination.

one needs to bring to Kant's own texts, a kind of impatient patience: It is only possible to understand Kant if one actively challenges oneself along the way and accepts that one may have to think through the ideas more than once (maybe ten or a hundred times) before they finally click. Those many people, both Kantians and non-Kantians, who are deeply attracted to Kant's philosophy read Kant only because his arguments are fascinating and challenging, and so they find themselves drawn to them again and again. For that reason, rather than over-simplifying the arguments, this introduction aims to outline them in a way that serve well the reader who engages, alongside the introduction, Kant's own texts and the body of secondary literature he has inspired.

After a short explanation of Kant's distinction between right (justice) and virtue (ethics), I sketch his theory of "private right," which are the rights individuals have in relation to each other. Subsequently, I address the question of why we have states and public legal-political systems, followed by the issue of states' rights (public right), specifically, the question of whether the state has (public) rights that extend beyond the (private) rights individuals have in relation to each other. The final two parts of this introduction focus on the distinction between "active" and "passive citizens," the relation between right (justice) and politics, the issue of global justice, and, briefly, the historical influence of Kant's ideas about justice.

2 Kant's Distinction Between Right and Virtue

Jean-Jacques Rousseau's opening lines in Chapter One from *Of the Social Contract* (1762) are among the most famous ones in the history of philosophy: "Man is born free, and everywhere he is in chains. One believes himself the others' master, and yet is more a slave than they. How did this change come about? I do not know. What can make it legitimate? I believe I can solve this question." (Rousseau 1962: 351)[2] Rousseau's deep influence on Kant's ideas about justice is hardly disputed. Like Rousseau, Kant focuses on the question of what limitations can be forcibly placed on our actions in the name of freedom—and, so, in the name of justice. In fact, it would not be an exaggeration to say that the question concerning which coercive limitations our actions can be subjected to without our freedom being disrespected is a main question of Kant's, not only in all of his shorter legal-political writings but also in "The Doctrine of Right." Time and again Kant emphasizes that the issue of right fundamentally concerns the rightful use of, or, the authority to use coercion, where coercion is, exactly, defined as a hindrance of freedom:

> Resistance that counteracts the hindering of an effect promotes this effect and is consistent with it. Now whatever is wrong is a hindrance to freedom in accordance with universal laws. But coercion is a hindrance or resistance to freedom. Therefore, if a certain use of freedom is itself a hindrance to freedom in accordance with universal laws (i.e., wrong), coercion that is opposed to this (as a *hindering of a hindrance to freedom*) is consistent with

[2]The text reference here uses the standard pagination, but the translation is from *Rousseau': The Social Contract and other later political writings*, ed. Victor Gourevitch. New York: Cambridge University Press, 1997.

> freedom in accordance with universal laws, that is, it is right. Hence there is connected with right by principle of contradiction an authorization to coerce someone who infringes upon it (MM 6: 231).

For Kant, the rightful use of coercion—the "chains" on freedom we can justify—is only that which is necessary for reciprocal, respectful freedom, or reciprocally free choices. The only rightful limitations of freedom, the only legitimate laws are those that are necessary because they make interaction under universal laws of freedom possible for all.

The domain of right is the domain of rightful coercion: those restrictions upon our choices that we can be forced to respect for the sake of freedom when we interact. In this way, Kant sets a high threshold for the rightful use of coercion. Virtue or ethics, in contrast, is properly understood as an analysis of what we *ought* to do as individuals, that is, of the type of action through which we prove our ability to be truly free. The importance of this point to Kant's philosophy of right cannot be emphasized enough, including because it entails that his analysis of virtuous actions in, for example, the *Groundwork for the Metaphysics of Morals* cannot be directly applied to the sphere of right or justice. More generally, one of Kant's major contributions to moral or practical philosophy is his proposal for how virtue (ethics) should be distinguished from right (justice).

Some key arguments from his ethical theory help to illustrate Kant's proposed distinction between right and virtue (or, between justice and ethics). Recall that in the *Groundwork of the Metaphysics of Morals*, Kant maintains that acting virtuously (ethically) involves *both* acting on the basis of maxims (first-personal or subjective rules of action) that can be "universalized" (can pass the test of the "categorical imperative"), *and* doing what is right (so understood) *because* it is right (actions have "moral worth" only when we act "from duty" or from a "moral motivation"). In the *Groundwork*, Kant also emphasizes that we have both perfect ("strict") and imperfect ("wide") ethical duties. Somewhat simplified, we may say that the perfect duties concern our obligation never to act aggressively or destructively against ourselves or others, while the imperfect duties concern our obligation to both develop our own capacities and assist others in their pursuit of their ends (their pursuit of happiness). We have perfect duties not to kill or lie, for instance, while we have imperfect duties to seek knowledge about the world in which we live and to aid others who are struggling. Furthermore, however, if we abstain from killing others only because we are afraid of ending up in jail, then we do not act virtuously, but strategically. Our choice (not to kill) is in agreement with what our reason (morality) demands of us, but it does not have "moral worth" because the moral motivation (duty) is absent; we're not doing what is right *because* it's right. Similarly, Kant argues, if we give money to the poor because we want others to think that we are such wonderful, virtuous people and not because it's the right thing to do, then we are not practicing beneficence (but, for example, pursuing our self-interest).

In the introductions to the *Metaphysics of Morals* and "The Doctrine of Right," Kant highlights some important consequences of the fact that virtue (ethics) essentially concerns maxims and moral motivation. First, Kant argues, this entails that right (justice) and the law cannot "reach" ethics or virtue, because being forced to act in a way consistent with virtue, such as being forced to give money to the poor, is not to be forced to act virtuously (in this case, beneficently). Virtue or ethics, Kant argues, concern "internal" (subjective or first-personal) lawgiving, while right concerns "external" (coercively enforceable) lawgiving. To act virtuously is to act on universalizable maxims from a moral motivation; without both of these elements present, whatever we are doing is not to act virtuously. And, the maxim and the motivation are only accessible from an internal, first-personal perspective; only I can know what I'm doing (which maxim I'm acting on, or which end I'm pursuing) and why I am doing it (whether my motivation is moral—whether I'm doing it simply because it is the right thing to do). Coercion (the use of external force) cannot, therefore, give an action moral worth, or make it an ethical or virtuous action. Coercion can make me act consistent with a certain end, like helping the poor, but it cannot make me set that end (act on that maxim) or do it because it's the right thing to do (act from a moral motivation). At most, coercion can function as a threat that makes me conform to an end (such as by making me part with some of my money). On Kant's account, it follows from this that everything having to do with ethics or virtue (maxims and moral motivation) necessarily lies beyond the scope of right (justice), whereas everything that lies within the domain of right is accessible from the point of view of ethics (i.e., I can and ought to follow just laws *because* following them is the right thing to do). Hence, the sphere of virtue (ethics) is wider than and encompasses the sphere of right, and while duty is the motivation of virtue (ethics), external force is the motivation of right (justice). Although right and virtue are not diametrically opposed, from the point of view of right, an action that falls within the boundaries of the law suffices, while from the point of view of virtue, an action must be done *because* it is the right thing to do in order to have "moral worth" (MM 6: 220).

Kant also emphasizes a second significant consequence of the fact that virtue (ethics) essentially concerns maxims and moral motivation. He argues that because actions that express imperfect duties require a moral motivation to qualify as such actions, any attempt by a legal system to force people to perform imperfect duties will necessarily fail. As indicated above, this implies that the duty of beneficence can only belong to the sphere of virtue and *not* to the sphere of right. Applying the same example, if a person is forced to give a certain amount of money to the poor, this person is not thereby forced to act beneficently. A beneficent action presupposes that someone both chooses to give money to the poor *and* does so *because* it is the right thing to do (acts from duty or with a moral motivation). Since no one can be forced to set a particular end or to act from a moral motivation, no one can be forced to perform beneficent actions. This is true, according to Kant, despite the fact that a person can, of course, be forced to give up money, which can then be given to the poor, and many of us can be threatened into acting in a way consistent with virtuous ends, such as by giving money to the poor.

In the introduction to "The Doctrine of Right," Kant expands upon the implications of this distinction between right and virtue by proposing some principles constitutive of a legal-political theory that conceives of justice in terms of freedom. He starts by emphasizing that though right is inherently normative, and is therefore inherently concerned with questions of how to act morally, it is crucial to note three things about it. First, right only concerns *interaction* in the world, and not all action. Therefore, as long as Robinson Crusoe remained alone on the island the issue of right (justice) did not arise for him; only ethical questions concerning how to take care of and develop himself were relevant to him. There was no interaction until Friday arrived, so only when he did, did right or justice become an issue—the issue of how to interact in such a way that reciprocal freedom under universal laws of freedom was possible.

The second point to notice about right, Kant argues, is that it only concerns the question of whether a person's actions are reconcilable with respecting others' external (or outer) freedom, that is, with others' rights to set and pursue their own ends with their means. Right does not concern itself with whether a person's ends are ethical or virtuous; it does not ask whether or not we set ends or use our means in ways virtue demands. Not only does this entail, as mentioned above, that imperfect duties like beneficence or generosity cannot be duties of right (duties we can be forced to respect), but also, importantly, that the duties of right are not identical to the perfect ethical duties. For example, even if I live in conflict with my perfect duty not to act in self-destructive ways—if I stupidly waste all my money on parties or gambling—I have not done anything wrong from the point of view of right (justice).

Third, a theory of right (justice) that takes freedom seriously cannot predetermine specific ends that everyone must pursue. This is not merely a reiteration of the earlier point that no one can be forced to act on a specific maxim (i.e., set particular ends) because the most anyone can be forced to do is act in conformity with particular ends. Rather, the point is that all people have a right to live their own lives and to set their own ends with their means. In other words, the principles of right (so, any rightful laws) must be universal in the sense of not presupposing any specific ends on behalf of those subject to the laws; right (justice) can only properly demand that every person's choices (ends) respect all others' freedom to choose ends for themselves, too. Right or justice secures reciprocal freedom, or equal freedom for every person interacting under universal laws of freedom, which means that no particular ends are presupposed by the principles involved—they are *universal* laws of *freedom* (Kant MM: 230).

Combining these arguments with Kant's insistence that a rightful state cannot attempt to enforce beneficence, it might appear that Kant rejects both the notions that we can be forced to assist the poor and that states can establish welfare institutions to protect their poor. For a long time, many people drew exactly this conclusion about Kant's theory. Consequently, some scholars tried to develop Kantian theories of justice that overcame this apparent consequence, such as John Rawls in *A Theory of Justice* and Onora O'Neill in *Bounds of Justice*. Others used the arguments they found in Kant to criticize these Kantian developments. The most famous debate of this kind is probably still right-wing libertarian Robert Nozick's criticism of the redistributive principle in John Rawls's *A Theory of Justice*.[3] In *Anarchy, State, and Utopia*,[4] Nozick argues at length that Rawls's theory is not

[3] Rawls, John (1999) *A Theory of Justice*, revised ed. Cambridge, Mass.: Harvard University Press.
[4] Nozick, Robert (1974) *Anarchy, State, and Utopia*. Basic Books.

reconcilable with the normative fact that respecting freedom demands that no one can ever be forced to help others *simply* because they need help; of course, it is ethically wrong not to help if one can, but it ought not be seen as unjust, criminal, or a legally punishable wrong. The failure to help is an ethical, not a legal, wrong in a just (liberal) state; along Kantian lines, Nozick argues that failing to respect others' rights to set their own ends (including selfish ones) with their means is to treat them as mere means and not as ends in themselves. Controversially, Nozick claims it follows from this that a just state cannot tax its citizens in order to provide assistance to the poor (which would be coercive redistribution). Consequently, on his account, the existence of even extreme poverty *as such* is not a sign of injustice in a state.[5] The state should be "minimal," in that it should not tax its population to redistribute resources in response to the needs of the poor. As will become clear in the discussion of states' rights (public right) below, some contemporary libertarian Kantians still maintain this interpretation. Other contemporary Kantians (in the republican interpretive tradition) maintain that even if Nozick correctly interprets Kant as rejecting the idea that the state can tax some citizens *merely* in response to other citizens' needs, Nozick incorrectly concludes from this that Kant rejects all forms of poverty relief by the state. These interpretations of Kant hold that "The Doctrine of Right" convincingly refutes an assumption that Nozick's argument requires, namely, the assumption that (excluding the administrative laws needed for the establishment of a legal-political institutional order) the rights of the state (public right) are, in principle, identical with the rights that private citizens have in relation to each other (private right). As is further discussed below, once we reject this assumption, the conclusion that the state must be "minimal" no longer follows; the state is not only permitted to provide unconditional poverty relief, but required to do so (as it must secure legal access to means for the poor).

It is important to attend to a few further points from the introduction to "The Doctrine of Right" in order to understand Kant's approach to questions of right (justice): Kant's proposal that the Universal Principle of Right (and not the Categorical Imperative) is the fundamental principle of right; Kant's view that each individual has an innate right to freedom; and, finally, his conception of freedom of speech. These points are intimately connected to what has already been discussed above, but let me briefly engage with each one before moving on to Kant's doctrine of private right.

Kant quickly clarifies in the introduction to "The Doctrine of Right" that when it comes to questions of right (justice), the standard or principle we should apply is not the Categorical Imperative (from his ethics), but the Universal Principle of Right. The Universal Principle of Right states: "Any action is *right* if it can coexist with everyone's freedom in accordance with a universal law, or if on its maxim the freedom of choice of each can coexist with everyone's freedom in accordance with a

[5] For Nozick, whether or not an instantiation of extreme poverty is a sign of injustice depends on its history, or how it came about. See the paper on Locke in this volume for more on this issue, as well as on how the rights of the poor remains a live issue in the Lockean tradition, one that separates "right-wing" from "left-wing" Lockeans.

universal law" (MM 6: 230). Kant then emphasizes that the demands that follow from the Universal Principle of Right are, of course, compatible with virtuous (ethical) action (with persons acting on universalizable maxims from duty, or, with the Categorical Imperative), but virtuous action cannot be demanded from the point of view of right (MM 6: 231).

Next, Kant stresses that there is only one innate right, which is each individual's right to freedom: "Freedom (independence from being constrained by another's choice), insofar as it [one's freedom] can coexist with the freedom of every other in accordance with a universal law, is the only original right belonging to every… [human being] by virtue of… [one's] humanity" (MM 6: 237).[6] Freedom is, in other words, understood as independence from subjection to others' choices and reciprocal respect for each other's exercise of freedom under a universal law. Moreover, any restrictions upon freedom must be demanded by freedom itself or respect for each person's right to freedom when interacting, such that any justifiable restrictions are understood in terms of reciprocal freedom under universal laws of freedom, since universal law cannot presuppose any contingent ends. This is a point over which Kant disagrees with earlier, major political philosophers, and it becomes apparent how important this point is for Kant when considering the nature of that disagreement. Thomas Hobbes and John Locke, for instance, assert that the individual's fundamental right (the innate right) is the right to preservation or self-preservation.[7] For Kant, self-preservation (the right to life) is a natural force or drive; it is not the fundamental moral right we have in virtue of our capacity for freedom. Justifiable restrictions on freedom cannot involve appeal to any contingent ends, which means that freedom cannot rightfully be limited by ends we have in virtue of our biological natures (e.g., self-preservation). Kant's theory is a universal theory of freedom that only permits coercive restrictions on interacting persons' external freedom if those restrictions follow from how persons must respect each other's freedom when interacting.

Finally, let me say just a few words about Kant's conception of freedom of speech. Words do not, in themselves, have coercive power. Consequently, Kant argues, right cannot limit the mere use of words as such. Because speech, in itself, does not have coercive power, talking *simpliciter* cannot wrong anyone, and so all just legal systems must recognize the right to freedom of speech. Simply by saying something to me, you do not *thereby* interfere with my external freedom; after all, I can easily choose not to respond and ignore what you are saying, or, at least, choose to do what I want or think I ought to do. Laws that outlaw mere speech

---

[6] I have amended Mary Gregor's translation here, since she pays insufficient attention to how in the original Kant's German is gender neutral. This is not to say that Kant's account of women is unproblematic; he simply doesn't use sexist language here, hence, in fairness, the translation shouldn't either. The original German reads: "Freiheit (Unabhängigkeit von eines Anderen nötigender Willkür), sofern sie mit jedes Anderen Freiheit nach einem allgemeinen Gesetz zusammen bestehen kann, ist dieses einzige, ursprüngliche, jedem Menschen kraft seiner Menschheit zustehende Recht."

[7] For elaboration, see the papers in this volume on Thomas Hobbes and John Locke.

therefore fundamentally misunderstand both freedom and force (power). They presuppose that words have a force or power that they do not have, that is, coercive power. In addition, of course, such laws express a lack of respect for each person's right to freedom, since they limit an individual's freedom even though the individual has wronged no one. To express this point in "Kantianese": such laws hinder freedom rather than hinder hindrances of freedom, which is why these laws are always and necessarily unjust.[8]

3 Private Right

Having clarified fundamental principles his theory of right rests upon, Kant proceeds to outline his account of private right, which is his account of the rights private individuals have in relation to each other. To get a good handle on the account of private right, it is important to be aware that in it Kant engages many ideas at once. For one thing, he relates his theory to the theories of justice that were then prominent, such as the so-called "natural right" theories of Thomas Hobbes, Jean-Jacques Rousseau, and John Locke.[9] He also aims to present a theory that incorporates the different juridical categories of private right, specifically those of private property right, contract right, and what gets referred to in some legal systems as "relations of status," which includes family right. Finally, Kant seeks to situate, where useful, his theory of right within his own overall philosophical system. Once again, the complexity of Kant's theory and the way in which he presents it make it very attractive to many philosophers though challenging to understand. Impatient patience both with Kant and with oneself is a prerequisite.

Natural right theories dominated in Kant's day. These theories are called natural right theories in part because they typically begin their account of right or justice by analyzing which "natural" rights and duties individuals have in relation to each other. To investigate that issue, these theories typically appeal to a thought experiment[10] that involves imagining individuals living together before they establish states, in the so-called "the state of nature" or the "natural condition." The resulting analyses typically reflect upon how human beings ought and are likely to interact prior to the construction of states and legal systems, and they commonly include arguments

[8] For a comprehensive study of Kant's conception of freedom of speech, see Niesen, Peter (2008) *Kants Theorie der Redefreiheit*. Baden-Baden: Nomos. For a shorter engagement in English, see Varden, Helga (2010) "A Kantian Conception of Free Speech," in *Free Speech in a Diverse World*, ed. Deirdre Golash. New York: Springer Publishing, pp. 39–55.

[9] It seems clear that an important source of many of the questions asked and issues attended to by Kant must have been Grotius since so many of the questions Kant addresses or clearly pays attention to are explicitly raised by Grotius. The relationship between Kant and Grotius is mostly unexplored territory in the current secondary literature, however.

[10] Of course, sometimes this involves, at least, an analysis of how people actually did live together before states/legal systems were established.

concerning why and how states and legal systems ought or are likely to be established. Kant's theory is not an exception to this model: he provides an analysis of which principles should regulate individuals' interaction in the state of nature—what he and many legal systems call principles of private right—as well as arguments concerning why and how legitimate states and legal systems are established and should function.

Kant interpreters still disagree extensively over many parts of his analysis of the state of nature and the proper establishment of a state's legal systems—as they do with regard to virtually all aspects of Kant's philosophy—so let us start with the aspects that are not, at least any longer, very controversial. Kant begins his analysis of the state of nature and private right with two important observations. First, he suggests that there are three kinds of things we describe as "our own"—that we think we can possess in some way: objects, other persons' actions, and other persons. For example, we might say, "this is my mug," "you owe me 3 h of work," and "this is my daughter." Second, Kant emphasizes the importance of noticing that the possessive relation expressed in these statements is thoroughly normative and not empirical. In other words, if the mug really is mine, it is not only my mug while I hold it in my hand (and have empirical, or—one of Kant's favorite terms—"phenomenal" possession of it). Rather, it is also mine once I put it on the table and leave it there for a while (I have normative, or—another of Kant's favorites—"noumenal" possession of it). Calling something *mine* is not a fundamentally empirical statement, but a normative one. Hence it describes not a relation between a person and empirical things in the world (since empirical things cannot act normatively), but a normative relation between you and me with regard to something empirical. Empirical and normative possession only coincide, Kant holds, in our possession of our own bodies: from a juridical point of view, my body and my person are one; it is an "analytic" relation, in Kant's terms. In contrast, all other possessive relations are synthetic in nature: they inherently involve seeing a person as normatively related to something distinct from her- or himself (MM 6: 249–250). Because empirical and normative possession are united with regard to our bodies, infringements on someone's bodily integrity are particularly grave wrongdoings; to violate another person's body is to violate another's person.

The normative fact that we can make objects distinct from us—empirical things in the world—our own (make them into what Kant calls "external objects of our choice") is crucial for our freedom. What it means for embodied beings like us to be free is to set and pursue ends in the world, and setting and pursuing ends in the world requires being able to make things our own in order to use them as means by which we pursue our ends. Being able to make things our own is inherent to freedom. Moreover, the kinds of things we can control and thereby make into our means limit the kinds of ends we can choose to set for ourselves. For example, though I wish I could fly like Peter Pan, I cannot choose to fly like Peter Pan since my body doesn't have the function of flight. In order to fly, I have to make an airplane by transforming materials in the world into one. And to do this, I need to be able to make these materials (these means) into my own. Kant's theory of private right outlines the principles he believes we use when we make things in the world our own.

These principles concern property, contract, and status relations. Although the details of Kant's account cannot be fully engaged here, a brief exposition may be helpful.

According to Kant, the three principles of private right are structurally distinct from each other: the first principle (of private property right) is one we apply unilaterally in the state of nature; the second (of contract right) is one we apply bilaterally (together as two); and the third (of status right) omnilaterally (together as many).[11] Regarding the principle of private property, Kant argues that our first step in making something our private property is applying our own power or force to it, so that we can control it. For example, I may take possession of a piece of land on which I plan to grow vegetables and fruit. By taking possession of the land, I make it into a means for myself. This account differs from Locke's, for example, as Locke contends that my *labor* on the natural resources in the world determines how I make something becomes mine through physical action. In contrast, Kant argues that it is taking *control* over things through our physical power that is the first step of possession. These different types of accounts imply different answers to classical questions in the philosophy of right concerning private property, including land ownership. For example, who owns the hare that gets shot if two different hunters, unbeknownst to each other, have chased it? Or, if my bees fly away and settle somewhere else, do I still own them? Alternatively, the famous question of why, as seems to be the case, we cannot own the oceans? To put this question by means of Nozick's famous objection to Locke's labor theory of acquisition: why do I not get to own the ocean when I pour tomato juice into it (mix my labor with it), but I do obtain possession when I, say, to stay with the example above, plough a field and plant my vegetables in it? Kant's answer is: because it is not the mixing that is the clue, but control: you can't control the ocean, whereas you can control the field. All we can control of the oceans, really, is the water close to the shore, that part of the water can be controlled from land, or so "as far as our canons can reach." Hence the oceans cannot be owned, but the waters outside our shores can. In addition to arguing in a way that shows clear awareness of these legal puzzles (whatever we take Kant's actual answers to be), Kant also focuses on another central philosophical question in the discussion of private property right, namely, how the fact that I have taken something under my control can obligate others to abstain from using it. How can, if at all, the fact that I've chosen to subject something, such as a piece of land, to my physical power or force issue a normative obligation to others to stay away from it? I return to this issue shortly.

The second type of private right is contract right. Making a binding contract involves a normative agreement between two parties, Kant maintains, a bilateral agreement about doing something (exercising causality) for each other. For example, you and I may enter a binding agreement, according to which I will paint your car in exchange for a certain amount of money from you. Or, we might agree that you will sell your horse to me at a certain price. Kant's proposed principle for this type of agreement is that ownership is transferred only once something changes hands.

[11] These three principles are, according to Kant, the normative employments of the relational categories of the understanding (substance, causality, and community).

Only once the horse has been delivered, for instance, is it mine; up until the point of its delivery it is not mine. This standard becomes central to the understanding and resolution of disagreements over contracts. As we will see below, however, Kant's analysis of how contract disagreements should be understood and solved is disputed in the secondary literature.

Finally, relations of status concern how two or more people share a home. These relations pertain to a certain kind of claim we can have on other people, that they are "ours" in an important sense and how they become "ours" in a way that is legally binding. Kant presents three categories within relations of status: relations between parents and children; between spouses; and, between families and their servants. Although these types of relations are all omnilateral because they all involve the establishment of a shared private life, they are importantly distinct from each other, too. Children are neither equals with their parents nor free: children do not and cannot consent to be a part of the family; they are born without providing consent, they are as yet incapable of assuming responsibility for their choices, and they are born into their parents' family. Unlike children, two spouses are both free and equal; they both have to choose each other as spouses (say "yes" to marrying each other). And finally, unlike both children and spouses, although both servants and the families they serve are free, they are not equal with each other: within the home, servants are not the equals of the heads of the family (their employers).

All of these types of status relations are, Kant continues, especially vulnerable because they involve a fusion of several people's private lives. For that reason, he treats status relations separately, rather than subsuming them under an analysis of private property or contract right. The special danger in these relations arises because they involve shared private lives. Hence, there is a real possibility for the shared home to become a place where might replaces right, and the weaker become the slaves of the stronger in their own homes. It can easily become the case that the lives and choices of the more vulnerable members of the household are subjected to the decisions of the stronger. Recognizing this, Kant became one of the first philosophers to detail a separate set of private right principles applying to relations in private homes (relations between parents and children, between spouses, and between families and their servants). His private right principles for relations of status recommend a way of realizing right or justice in the home, so that homes do not become unjust spaces where the right becomes identified with the choices of the stronger. I return to the topic of relations of status with a brief discussion of some of the disagreements it has generated in contemporary Kant interpretation.

4 Why Do We Establish States? Three Different Kantian Answers

At this point in Kant's account of the private right principles, the details of both his arguments and the disagreements among the different interpretations of his arguments are becoming a little too complicated for an introductory text such as this one.

At the same time, since there is so much disagreement in the secondary literature concerning the remainder of Kant's account of private right, it is hard for newcomers to the "The Doctrine of Right" to make heads or tails of this secondary body of work. In an effort to provide some help to those readers trying to orient themselves in this literature, I sketch some of the distinctive lines of interpretation below. Informing this categorization of the secondary literature is the idea that some of these become apparent if we focus on how to understand the relationship between Kant and other prominent theories of justice in his time. More specifically, some of the disagreement in the secondary literature may be understood as arising in virtue of whether or not the theories understand (or are fundamentally informed by the assumption that) the structure of Kant's theory as very similar to Hobbes's absolutist legal positivism, Locke's libertarian theory, or a republican development of Rousseau that is also deeply influenced by (at least) Hobbes and Locke. In this section, I consider the question of Kant's relationship to these other theories of justice by examining the different interpretive traditions' understandings of Kant's account of private right, and in particular in relation to the question of why we must establish states (public legal-political institutional systems backed by a monopoly on coercion) at all. In the subsequent section, I outline how the different interpretive traditions answer the question of what the legal-political institutions of a just state look like.

According to Hobbesian lines of interpretation, Kant agrees with Hobbes's claim in the *Leviathan* that it is impossible to realize rights in the state of nature because human beings so often act irrationally, in the sense of acting in strategically unwise ways, or not in ways an enlightened self-interested person would act. Therefore, given human nature and the context of the state of nature (where everyone must fend for themselves), the trust required for peaceful, rightful interaction simply does not exist. Hence Hobbes famously says that life in the state of nature is one characterized by "continuall feare, and danger of violent death;" indeed the "life of man" in this condition is "solitary, poore, nasty, brutish, and short." (Hobbes, *Leviathan*, ch. 13)[12] Since our reason is fundamentally prudential or strategic in nature, Hobbes continues by arguing that we do not have a right to remain in the state of nature. We do not have a right to act as stupidly, irrationally, or imprudently as the choice to stay in the state of nature is. Consequently, we can be forced to leave the state of nature and enter the civil condition by becoming subjects of the Leviathan or a state.

The civil condition, in turn, is understood as characterized by law-regulated stability backed up by overwhelming force (an effective monopoly on coercion). In virtue of the law-governed stability such a legal-political system offers, it is strategically wiser to live within its boundaries even when the actual laws are unfair and oppressive; choosing to live under bad laws is more rational, strategically speaking, than choosing to stay in the brutal condition of the state of nature, where all lives are miserable and end in premature, violent deaths. Those who read Kant in this kind of way do not, of course, agree with Hobbes that human beings have only strategic rationality. Rather, they emphasize the places where Kant describes human beings

---

[12] Hobbes, Thomas (1996) *Leviathan*, revised student edition, ed. Richard Tuck. Cambridge: Cambridge University Press, p. 89.

as both good and bad—such as Kant's claim that we are made out of so very crooked timber, "aus so krummem Holze"—and maintain that it is this view of Kant's that leads him to argue that we cannot realize right or justice in the state of nature. Because of our unreliable characters (our liability to vice), we are incapable of interacting rightfully on our own (in the state of nature), and this is why we can be forced into the civil condition. In the civil condition, our propensity to act wrongly is tamed by the real threat of punishment from the state. This Hobbesian approach to Kant's theory entails that we can be obliged to obey a public authority even if we have not consented to its establishment or existence.[13]

A second prominent interpretation of Kant's theory views it as structurally similar to libertarian theories. On these lines of interpretation, Kant is seen as arguing that we can realize justice in the state of nature as long as every individual respects everyone else's bodily integrity, and conscientiously and correctly regulates her or his interactions by all three principles of private right. Those who read Kant in this way agree with the Hobbesian interpreters' claim that our frequently unwise (stupid), ignorant, imprudent, biased, and evil actions are the main impediment to the realization of justice in the state of nature. Hence, they agree that the establishment of the state more effectively realizes justice. Creating a set of laws that are posited by legislators, applied by impartial judges, and enforced by the police is much smarter than leaving it to individuals to do all of that on their own. Moreover, they continue, because we are obliged to deal with our innate badness (our propensity to act in wrongful ways), we can be forced to enter the state since it provides everyone with security against everyone's badness. At this point, though, libertarian-style interpretations clearly diverge from Hobbesian ones. They argue against the Hobbesians' legal positivism, the legal positivist claim that any law-governed monopoly on coercion can issue political obligations. Libertarian-type interpreters argue that since we have knowledge of the laws of nature and how to apply them in the state of nature, and since the laws of nature are laws of freedom, the only rightful state we can establish is the liberal state, a state composed of these same laws of freedom that individuals in the state of nature ought to use to regulate their interactions. Hence, only liberal states can issue political obligations, according to libertarian interpretations of Kant.[14]

The third line of interpretation can be understood as a republican tradition.[15] Republican interpreters maintain that Kant challenges a presupposition shared by

[13] See, for example, Onora O'Neill (2000) and Howard L. Williams's (1986) *Kant's Political Philosophy*. New York: Palgrave Macmillan, for interpretations along these lines.

[14] Most recently, Sharon B. Byrd & Joachim Hruschka (2010) presented an interpretation along these lines in their *Kant's Doctrine of Right: A Commentary*. New York: Cambridge University Press.

[15] Of course, the nature of these republican interpretations of Kant's private right argument vary greatly. Contrast the following, for example: Ebbinghaus, Julius (1953) "The Law of Humanity and the Limits of State Power." *The Philosophical Quarterly*, Vol. 3, No 10, pp. 14–22; Flikshuh, Katrin (2008) "Reason, Right, and Revolution: Kant and Locke," in *Philosophy and Public Affairs*, Vol. 36:1, pp. 375–404; Kersting, Wolfgang *Wohlgeordnete Freiheit. Immanuel Kants Rechts- und Staatsphilosophie*. Berlin: de Gruyter, 1984/Frankfurt: Suhrkamp 2nd ed. 1993; Ripstein, Arthur

both the Hobbesian and the libertarian strands of interpretations; namely, the idea that only our irrationality prevents the realization of justice in the state of nature. Republicans contend, in contrast, that Kant provides ideal reasons for why the realization of justice requires the civil condition (the establishment of a rightful state or a public authority). Hence, even on the assumption that we never act imprudently or unwisely, justice remains impossible in the state of nature; the state is seen as ideally constitutive of the realization of justice. These interpretations argue that it is impossible in the state of nature rightfully to use coercion or establish a coercive power that can normatively obligate everyone to obey it. This is because all use of power in the state of nature is thoroughly private, which means it expresses some set of individuals' choices, whereas rightful coercion is the subjection of interaction only to universal law. No one can be obliged to subject themselves to or obey another private person's choices, since everyone has an innate right to be free—to be subject only to universal law and independent of subjection to another's arbitrary choices. Hence justice requires a public authority: a rightful, institutional public "us" with a monopoly on coercion. To realize justice, we need to establish a forceful "us," which can be understood as a public representation of what Rousseau usefully called a "general will". Only if we establish such a common representative "us" through which we can specify, apply, and enforce laws will it be the case that we can transform the threat and use of physical power or force from wrongful violence to rightful coercion. We establish rightful states or public authorities, therefore, not only because our typical lack of prudence or virtue, but because only in this way can we establish and secure rightful interaction, including the possibility of a rightful, authoritative use of coercion.

Since this republican strand of interpretation is slightly harder to understand than the other two, let me illustrate a common line of reasoning by focusing on what is sometimes called the "indeterminacy argument." As mentioned, on this approach to the "Doctrine of Right," Kant argues that our frequent imprudent and evil actions are not the only or most important reason why we cannot rightfully specify, apply, and enforce the principles of private right in the state of nature. Rather the most important reason why justice, which requires rightful use of coercion, is impossible in the state of nature issues from the fact that there are many reasonable ways to specify and apply the principles of private right in specific situations. Because there are many such reasonable ways, a person cannot rightfully use coercion to enforce her own choice of specification without thereby forcing those with whom she interacts to her arbitrary choice (rather than subjecting their interactions to universal

(2009) *Force and Freedom – Kant's Legal and Political Philosophy*. Cambridge, Mass.: Harvard University Press; Pogge, Thomas (1988) "Kant's Theory of Justice." *Kant-Studien* 79, pp. 407–433; Varden, Helga (2008) "Kant's Non-Voluntarist Conception of Political Obligations: Why Justice Is Impossible in the State of Nature," in *Kantian Review*, vol. 13–2, pp. 1–45; Waldron, Jeremy: "Kant's Theory of the State," in Kleingeld, P. (2006) *Toward Perpetual Peace and Other Writings on Politics, Peace, and History*. New York: Yale University Press, 2006, pp. 179–200; Weinrib, Ernest (1995) *The Idea of Private Law*. Cambridge, Mass.: Harvard University Press.

laws, as the Universal Principle of Right and respecting the others' innate right to freedom requires).[16]

To illustrate this argument, consider Locke's theory of private property appropriation. According to Locke, all individuals have a right to a fair share of the world's natural resources ("the enough-and-as-good proviso"), and they have a right to use coercion to take and defend their fair share. According to Kant, however, even if we accept this as the correct principle of private property appropriation (which, as we saw above, he doesn't do), it is impossible to figure out exactly which particular parts of the world's resources are, objectively speaking, mine. After all, no one is in a position to decide how much any specific part is objectively worth. There is no objective value that attaches to objects in the world, like specific coconuts, trees, pieces of land, lakes, etc. Alternatively, if we go with Kant's general rule of first possession, the fact that I have chosen to take something as mine cannot, in itself, issue an unproblematic, normative obligation on all others to stay away from it: I cannot subject their freedom to my choices in this way. Therefore, regardless of which principle of private property appropriation we choose (Locke's or Kant's own), Kant's argument holds: my decision to make something mine remains normatively problematic, since it renders our interactions, including how we distinguish between what is yours and mine, irreducibly subject to my choice (rather than simply to universal laws of freedom).

At this point, one might, of course, object by pointing to the scenario in which we all happen to agree on the value of each specific thing or who gets to possess each thing, so that we never need to use coercion to settle any disagreement. But there is no reason to think this must happen, Kant is seen as arguing, since the type of disagreement under discussion does not track unreasonableness. Moreover, even if we do happen never to disagree on anything in the state of nature, what we have is not a condition of justice or injustice, but rather a condition "devoid of justice" (MM 6: 312). In such a scenario, it is mere chance that no one disagrees, and though this may tempt us to think that we do not need to establish a state, this is mistaken.

[16]The indeterminacy argument is, in my view, best viewed as referring to both the problem of specifying the abstract or universal principles of right as general laws or rules for interaction and the problem of specifying how to apply these laws in particular situations. In turn, the first problem of specification is, again in my view, best seen as linked to why we need a public, legislative authority, whereas the second problem of specification can usefully be seen as linked to why we need a public, judiciary authority. Another, separate kind of argument is sometimes referred to as the "assurance" argument, which usefully can be seen as a sophisticated development of Hobbes' security argument. For reasons of simplicity, I am not outlining this argument here. Again, my suggestion is that this problem of assurance is linked to why we need a public executive power. Hence, solving the three problems explain why we need a tripartite public authority: the two problems of specification (specifying how which general laws captures best the abstract principles of right and specifying how these general laws should be applied in particular situations) explain why we need the legislative and judiciary authorities, whereas the problem of assurance (a problem of securing rightful trust through power) explains why we need a public executive power with a monopoly on coercion. To what extent the various republican interpreters defend both types of indeterminacy arguments as well as the assurance argument varies. In addition, as mentioned above, the exact way in which these scholars understand these arguments differ quite a lot too.

Such a peace would rest on contingent facts (our chance agreement), and there is still no possibility of rightful use of coercion in this condition. And an account of justice must be able to explain how we can use coercion rightfully, and as this is only possible in the civil condition, the fact that there can be peaceful times (de facto agreement) in the state of nature is insufficient to show that we have an enforceable right to remain in the state of nature. Because justice is impossible in the state of nature, the establishment of civil society is viewed as constitutive of justice, and we do not have a right to stay in the state of nature. Since rightful coercion is only possible through the public, legal-political institutions of the state, we have, instead, an enforceable duty to enter civil society. This is why, these interpretations maintain, Kant says that choosing to stay in the state of nature is to do "wrong in the highest degree" (MM 6: 307).

5 The Rightful (Just) State: Three Kantian Answers

These interpretive disagreements about why we have states at all are also reflected in interpretive approaches to Kant's conception of the rightful or (minimally) just state, which includes the issue of whether we have a right to revolution. After a brief sketch of those issues, I return to Kant's views on the responsibilities the state has to address poverty among its citizens. These disagreements in the literature illustrate well the different ways the three types of approaches read the first of three chapters on public right in "The Doctrine of Right," the one Kant entitles "The Right of a State" (MM 6: 311). I return to the other two chapters on public right, which deal with global (international and cosmopolitan) justice, in the final section below.

Simply put, the absolutist (Hobbesian) interpretations maintain that according to Kant, any stable system of law that is enforced by a sufficiently powerful state is legitimate. If one considers the civil condition as the solution to an extremely dangerous state of nature, this is of course the view that follows, because almost all states will be more capable of preserving life than individuals on their own in the state of nature. And it is easy to find support for such an interpretation in Kant's texts. For example, this reading fits quite well with Kant's claim that we do not have a right to revolution, not even under very unjust conditions (MM 6: 318ff). It also accords with some of Kant's remarks about the French Revolution, especially those in which he seems to say that even if no one had a right to participate in it, it took humankind in the right direction.[17] Those Kantians who promote this reading of Kant are also typically frustrated with his theory of right and its apparent implication

[17] Generally, those who read Kant's "Doctrine of Right" in this absolutist way are likely to emphasize: the so-called assurance or security arguments one finds in the first chapter of the private right part (MM 6: 245–257); Kant's arguments in support of the claim that citizens do not have a right to use coercion against the public authority (MM 6: 339–340, 370–372); and Kant's conclusion of the private right discussion (MM 6: 305–308) as well as his opening paragraphs of the public right discussion (MM 6: 311–313).

that one is politically obliged to obey even the most oppressive and unjust states, including Hitler's Nazi-Germany. Consequently, these interpreters often attempt to develop (what they see as) revised Kantian theories of justice that can explain why one is not politically obliged to obey just any gruesome regime with a monopoly on coercion.

Libertarian (Lockean) interpretations, in contrast, typically hold that a just and legitimate state is one that establishes a legal-political system to specify, apply, and enforce all the private right principles that individuals (ideally) utilize in the state of nature to regulate (justly) their interactions. The major difference between the rights of the state (public right) and the rights of individuals (private right) is that the state has certain additional rights in consequence of it having to establish a legal-political institutional system. For example, the state has to establish laws of public administration, something individuals obviously have no need of in the state of nature. On the libertarian reading, Kant's idea of a rightful state is a "minimal" one. It is minimal because, beyond the laws it needs to fulfil its administrative tasks (public law), the state creates no new types of rights and laws, but only posits those laws needed to secure the rights individuals already possess in the state of nature (private law). Moreover, once established, if a state doesn't respect the rights of individuals in its use of power, then, on these interpretations, there ceases to be a civil condition. Since, in such circumstances, individuals find themselves thrown back into the state of nature, they have to defend their rights against violations as best as they can. Hence, on this interpretive line, when individuals in these circumstances resist "state officials," they are actually not engaging in revolution (strictly speaking) but find themselves in the state of nature where they are, yet again, enforcing their rights by their own means (individually).[18]

The third strand of interpretation considers, as mentioned, Kant's state a (Rousseauean) republican alternative to (Hobbesian) absolutism and (Lockean) libertarianism.[19] Republican interpretations object to the absolutist claim that all stable, law-regulated uses of power qualify as civil conditions. A Kantian republic, they argue, must establish "freedom as independence," where this independence is enabled by the establishment of a representative, public authority comprising a certain institutional structure. The precise meaning of this latter claim, however, is a highly contentious issue. Some republican interpretations, characterized as more liberal, hold that Kant's distinction between "barbarian" and "civil" conditions hinges on whether or not the laws of the state *represent* the people, which means securing certain private and public principles of right for all citizens, thereby

[18] Naturally, these interpretations also pay careful attention to Kant's arguments about assurance or security, but they also emphasize that individual rights are what must be secured. Especially important parts of Kant's text, for these scholars, tend to be chapter 2 in "The Doctrine of Right," which concerns the private right principles (especially the principles concerning private property and contract right, pp. MM 6: 258–280. 284–286), and the concluding arguments and claims in the private right section (MM 6: 256–257, 305–308).

[19] To defend their position, republican interpreters often point to what Kant says in the beginning of the "public right" section (MM 6: 311–313), in addition to challenging the readings of the text absolutist and libertarian interpretations highlight.

guaranteeing their status as free, equal, and independent.[20] Other republican interpreters contend that with the term "representation," Kant firmly commitments himself to democracy as the only just form of government.[21] Finally, yet other republican interpretations downplay certain aspects of Kant's text that seem to espouse liberal rights, and argue instead for normative, non-absolutist, yet legal positivist interpretations of Kant. According to these interpretations, a state is legitimate as long as there is a condition of stability enabled by its citizens' normative (and not merely de facto) recognition of the state's authority over them.[22] Despite these internal disagreements concerning the importance of liberal rights and democracy, all republican interpreters agree with the libertarian interpreters that not any form of rule-governed use of power constitutes a legitimate state, in Kant's view. But, they argue against the libertarian claim that the Kantian position can recognize a *right* to realize justice on their own if they find themselves subjected to an illegitimate state. Hence, it does not matter, they argue, whether or not we call such use of coercion the exercise of a right to revolution; what matters is that we cannot call such use of coercion *rightful*. Since justice is impossible in the state of nature, we cannot have a *right* to reassume our natural rights or we cannot describe what we are doing as re-establishing rightful relations (since rightful relations are only possible in civil society). This is why Kant says, they maintain, that we do not have a *right* to revolution. The republicans also typically deny the libertarians' view that the rights of the state (public right) are, with the exception of the additional laws necessary for public administration, coextensive with the rights of individuals (private right).

Let me conclude this section by returning to the issue of what responsibilities the state has, if any, with regard to poverty among its citizens, which illustrates some of the key differences between what I have called the absolutist, libertarian, and republican interpretations. According to both the Hobbesian absolutist interpretations and the legal positivist republican interpretations, this issue is (or at least should be) quite simple. Presupposing, as these interpretations do, that on Kant's view most stable and rule-governed states are legitimate, then such states may redistribute resources or not without this affecting their political legitimacy one way or the other. On the absolutists' reading, the will of the sovereign authority properly determines how the state responds to citizens' poverty, whereas according to the legal positivist republicans, the "normativity" of the people (whether linked to a democratic will or otherwise) determines the state's proper response. Problematically,

[20] In my view, Arthur Ripstein (2009), Helga Varden ("Kant's Non-Absolutist Conception of Political Legitimacy: How Public Right 'Concludes' Private Right in the 'Doctrine of Right'," *Kant-Studien*, Heft 3: 331–351, 2010), and Jeremy Waldron (2006) fall within this camp of interpreters.

[21] Both Pauline Kleingeld (*Kant and Cosmopolitanism: The Philosophical Ideal of World Citizenship*. New York: Cambridge University Press, 2010) and Ingeborg Maus (*Zur Aufklärung der Demokratietheorie. Rechts- und demokratietheoretische Überlegungen im Anschluss an Kant*. Frankfurt: Suhrkamp, 1992) defend such democratic interpretations of Kant.

[22] Prominent interpreters who take such a legal positivist line are Ingeborg Maus and Peter Niesen. The main difference between them concerns the way in which Maus sees normativity as resting on the people's democratic affirmation of the public authority.

however, these absolutist and republican interpretations require (insofar as they stay consistent with their own basic philosophical commitments) us to disregard most of what Kant says directly about the issue of poverty, including in "The Doctrine of Right," and treating it as somewhat irrelevant to understanding the legal-political structure of Kant's theory. This is a puzzling move, though, since poverty and distribution of resources seem to be important issues for Kant (also) in this work.

An apparent advantage of the remaining interpretations is that they account for or do not (need to) downplay the importance of what Kant says about poverty, although they disagree over how to understand these passages. Recall that on the libertarian interpretations the rights of the state (public right) are coextensive with the rights of individuals (private right) when we exclude public administrative rights. As a result, in order for the state to have a right to redistribute resources to the poor, individuals (in the state of nature) must have such a right in relation to each other too. But, as discussed above, Nozick rejects the possibility of just that sort of individual right in his famous libertarian Kantian objection to Rawls's Kantian position. Individuals cannot, Nozick argues, have an enforceable obligation to redistribute goods in response to the needs of the poor, since that would be irreconcilable with each person's right to set her or his own ends with her or his means (each individual's right to freedom). Consequently, the state cannot have such a right either; all the state has a right to do is to ensure that everyone has a fair starting point, and Nozick revises Locke's "enough-and-as-good" argument to how this can be done. (Obviously, if we go with Kant's first-come-first-served principle of private property acquisition instead, the newcomers get even less than they do on Nozick's Lockean "enough-and-as-good" principle, maybe even nothing.) Notice, however, that even if one can refute Nozick's objection to Rawls, to make the case successfully for state's rights to enforce redistribution of means in response to problems of poverty, the Kantian argument must show that forced redistribution of resources in response to need amounts to something other than failed attempts at beneficence; otherwise, Kant's objection that forced beneficence is impossible becomes relevant. In my assessment, no libertarian Kantians have yet been able successfully to refute these two objections (that is, without giving up something essential to the libertarian account). Therefore, it appears libertarian interpretations of Kant must ascribe to him a minimal state view. The problem with such a view, however, is that it cannot justify the use of public provisions to ensure that the poor's legal access to means are not subjected to other private persons' arbitrary choices (choices to provide them with charity or employment).

Broadly speaking, the liberal rights-oriented republican interpreters reject (or ought to reject for consistency's sake) all of these approaches to the issue of the state's responsibility to deal with poverty among its citizens. On the one hand, they can and should reject any absolutist or legal positivist claim that a legitimate state has the option of engaging in poverty relief or not, and on the other hand, they can and should reject the libertarians' claim that the rights of the state are co-extensive with those of the individuals. In my view, the most promising liberal, yet republican, line of argument proceeds in the following way: a state can rightfully establish a monopoly on coercion only if it also ensures that the legal system as a whole is reconcilable with each citizen's fundamental right to freedom. The only way to do this is by securing everyone's right to freedom (which includes a right to independence) by guaranteeing or securing each citizen's legal access to means. In other words, if some citizen doesn't own anything at all and everything already belongs to someone else, then this destitute citizen can only obtain access to means either by committing a crime (stealing from the rich) *or* by benefiting from the choice of the rich to give her or him charity or employment. In this latter situation, the poor citizen's possibility of freedom is subjected to rich persons' choices (to provide her or him with charity or employment, or not)—and this is irreconcilable with the poor citizen's right to freedom, which is a right that secures independence from having one's freedom subjected to another person's private choice in this way (and instead subjected to universal laws). For this reason, the minimally just or legitimate state must guarantee all its citizens legal access to means, as part of public right—as one of the claims citizens have on their own public authority (and not with regard to each other as private citizens). The right to poverty relief should therefore be understood as a public right (part of public law), and not a private right (part of private law). On this approach, then, poverty is a systemic problem related to the state's establishment of a monopoly on coercion, and it is a problem the state must assume responsibility for by unconditionally guaranteeing or securing all citizens' legal access to means. It should be noted that the state can address this systemic problem of poverty either by regulating private charitable organizations entrusted with fulfilling this function (by legally committing to give all people equal access to them without having to declare allegiance to a particular religion, for example) *or* by establishing public shelters (what used to be called "poor houses"). The main point remains that the state must assume responsibility for ensuring that all poor citizens' have legal access to shelter and food, an access that is not subjected to rich citizens' choices (to exercise charity or employ them).

In my view, one strength of this republican line of interpretation is that it accords with Kant's claim that such public welfare institutions (what he calls "poor houses") should not be considered forced charity or beneficence; that is because poverty relief of this kind provides the necessary institutional solution to a systemic problem. Poverty relief is necessary in order to reconcile the state's monopoly on coercion (and the actual institution of private property) with each citizen's innate right to freedom.[23] Another strength of this republican line of interpretation is that it avoids Nozick's criticism of Rawls, since that objection presupposes that the rights of the state (public right) are co-extensive with the rights of individuals (private right). In contrast, this republican argument, if it holds up under further scrutiny, shows that citizens have certain claims against their public authority (public right) that they do not have against each other (private right).[24] Consequently, liberal states

[23] For an excellent account of how this type of account is also consistent with what Kant says about poverty in his ethical works, see Lucy Allais (forthcoming): "What Properly Belongs to Me: Kant' on Giving to Beggars," *Journal of Moral Philosophy*.

[24] Interestingly, Nozick himself makes one similar move in his account of why what he calls the "ultraminimal state" must be transformed into a "minimal state." Basically, he argues that once a

have a right and a duty to provide welfare institutions that address problems of poverty, which involves coercive redistribution, despite the fact that private individuals do not have a corresponding legal right and duty against each other.[25]

Another disagreement within the secondary literature concerns how to interpret Kant's distinction between so-called "passive" and "active" citizens in "The Doctrine of Right" (MM 6: 314–315). Kant draws this distinction between those who can (in principle) vote and those who cannot. Kant himself situates all children, servants, apprentices, and women in the category of "passive citizens," while placing all "independent" men in the category of "active citizens." Some of the interpretive controversies arise not only because Kant draws this distinction, but because he claims, a few sentences later, that it must be possible for "anyone" to work one's "way up from this passive condition to an active one" (MM 6: 315). The problem, then, is how to reconcile the distinction he draws between active and passive citizens with his claim that all people must be able to work themselves out of a passive condition and into an active one.[26] This controversial issue in Kantian scholarship has been particularly important for those working on women's and children's rights, and there is significant and increasing engagement with Kant's account of passive and active citizens both in feminist and Kantian literature.[27]

---

so-called private protection agency has established a de facto monopoly on coercion, it can force the independents (those who are not cutsomters of this protection agency) to use its legal system, but only if it secures the independents with means with which to do so. If necessary, these means will be obtained by the state taxing its members—a consequence of his own argument that puzzles Nozick. An advantage of Kant's account is that similar features of his account are not similarly puzzling on these liberal, republican interpretations since they simply follow (conceptually) from an account of justice consistent with its own starting point; the innate right to freedom.

[25] Five works that highlight the complexity of the Rawls-Kant discussions are, in my view: Katrin Flikshuh's *Kant and modern political philosophy* (Cambridge: Cambridge University Press, 2000); Jean Hampton's "Should Political Philosophy be Done without Metaphysics?" (*Ethics* 99, 1989, pp. 791–814); Thomas Pogge's "Is Kant's *Rechtslehre* Comprehensive?" (*The Southern Journal of Philosophy* (Supplement), 36 (1997), pp. 161–188; Arthur Ripstein's "Private Order and Public Justice: Kant and Rawls," *Virginia Law Review* 92, pp. 1391–1432; Helga Varden's "A Kantian Critique of the Care Tradition: Family Law and Systemic Justice," *Kantian Review*, 2012, 17:2 pp. 327–356. The accounts of public right that are the closest to the one described in this paragraph are those of Ripstin and myself. The best account of how to view this type of Kantian approach to poverty relief to Kant's ethics is found in Lucy Allais' "What properly belongs to me: Kant on giving to beggars," *Journal of Moral Philosophy*, forthcoming 2014.

[26] For brief introductions and proposed solutions to some of these textual controversies, see: Holtman, Sarah W. "Kantian Justice and Poverty Relief," in *Kant-Studien*. 95, pp. 86–106; and Varden, Helga (2006) "Kant and Dependency Relations: Kant on the State's Right to Redistribute Resources to Protect the Rights of Dependents," *Dialogue – Canadian Philosophical Review*, XLV, pp. 257–284. In my view, the current best overview of the Kantian literature on this issue (as well as many other issues) can be found in Elizabeth Ellis (ed.) (2012) *Kant's Political Theory: Interpretations and Applications*. University Park: The Pennsylvania State University Press, but see also the bibliographies of Lara Denis (ed.) (2010) *Kant's Metaphysics of Morals*. New York: Cambridge University Press, and Oliver Sensen (ed.) (2013) *Kant on Moral Autonomy*. New York: Cambridge University Press.

[27] For a relatively comprehensive overview of the relevant literature, see Hay, Carol *Kantianism, Liberalism, and Feminism: Resisting Oppression*; Herman, Barbara (2002) "Could It Be Worth

6 Global Justice: International and Cosmopolitan Right

Kant follows his public right discussion of legitimate states (in "The Right of a State" chapter) with two short chapters on public right. The first of those, entitled "The Right of Nations", addresses international or interstate justice (MM 6: 343–351), whereas the second concerns "cosmopolitan right," which concern interactions between states and aliens (citizens of other states and stateless persons, including refugees) (MM 6: 352–353). The conclusion of these chapters—and of the entire "Doctrine of Right," for that matter—is the same as that of Kant's perhaps most popular legal-political essay: "Perpetual Peace" is the highest political good (MM 6: 355). Perpetual peace is rightful peace and the goal toward which we should strive. Perpetual peace is not merely the absence of coercion, but requires rightful interaction within states, between states (international right), and between states and aliens (cosmopolitan right). Perpetual peace therefore requires rightful relations on the entire planet. For this reason, Kant is uncompromising, for example, in his criticism of European colonialism. It also seems fair to point out, however, that Kant is not confident of our ability to establish perpetual peace, something that is quite clear in his more historical essays. Therefore, in the legal-political texts he aims to show not that there will in fact be perpetual peace, but rather to establish which principles and legal-political institutions are needed for reaching perpetual peace in principle. After all, if we haven't even clarified the ideals we ought to strive for, then we cannot, except perhaps by chance, move in the right direction. And, of course, if Kant can show the ideals and how we might reach them, then he has shown that perpetual peace is possible. In fact, it seems reasonable to maintain that if Kant can show the possibility of perpetual peace, then he has done all he can as a philosopher; the rest—the actual realization of perpetual peace—is up to each and every one of us, as individuals and together.

The interpretive controversies between the absolutist, libertarian, and republican interpretations concerning the necessity and structure of a public authority and legal system at the national level are paralleled at the international and cosmopolitan level. Indeed, it seems fair to say that the disagreements at those levels are even greater than they are at the domestic levels or regarding Kant's theory of rightful states. In the case of global justice, one reason for the heightened disagreement among interpretations is the fact that on Kant's analysis, states already exist once we arrive on the global stage—that is, before we can think about establishing rightful international institutions, we must already have established rightful states. This normative fact complicates the arguments. Regardless of this, many other interpretive

---

Thinking About Kant on Sex and Marriage?" in *A Mind of One's Own*, edited by L. M. Antony & C. E. Witt (ed.), pp. 53–72. Boulder: Westview; La-Vaque-Manty, Mika (2006) "Kant's Children," *Social Theory and Practice* 32, No 3, pp. 365–388; Schott, Robin M. (1997) *Feminist Interpretations of Immanuel Kant*. Pennsylvania: Pennsylvania State University Press; Varden, Helga (2012) "A Kantian Critique of the Care Tradition: Family Law and Systemic Justice," *Kantian Review*, 17:2, pp. 327–356. Hay, Herman, and Varden all propose their own, somewhat different Kantian interpretations of many of these issues.

controversies concern whether or not Kant is defending the claim that worldwide perpetual peace requires the establishment of some kind of global, public authority with or without its own coercive power. For example, there is significant disagreement over: the question of what Kant's assessment of the United Nations would be (was it a (necessary) step in the right direction or not?); the question of whether our aims in global justice should be (more or less) the same as they are in domestic justice, including as concerns poverty and redistribution of resources; and, the question of which rights and duties existing states have given the absence of a well-functioning, global public authority. In this context, there is still as little agreement between Kant interpreters as there is between theorists about global justice more generally. As Thomas Nagel (2009) observes, however, this may very well be a reflection of how philosophical thinking concerning the establishment of global institutions is at a very early stage of development.[28]

7 Concluding Remarks

As we have seen, the history of Kant's legal-political philosophy has taken a peculiar trajectory, since most philosophers, even Kantians, did not until quite recently read Kant's main legal-political work carefully. Instead, they focused most of their attention on his moral-ethical works, especially the *Groundwork for the Metaphysics of Morals*, although some also attended to the *Critique of Practical Reason* and some of his shorter political essays, like "Perpetual Peace." This is not to say that Kant's ideas concerning respect for human dignity, freedom, and perpetual peace haven't had a tremendous influence in the public culture of modern, liberal democracies, for

[28]To see some of these disagreements, compare, for example: Carson, Thomas (1988) "Perpetual Peace: What Kant Should Have Said," *Social Theory and Practice*, Vol. 14, 2, pp. 173–214; Cavallar, George (1999) *Kant and the Theory and Practice of International Right*. University of Wales Press; Dodson, Kevin E. (1993) "Kant's Perpetual Peace: Universal Civil Society or League of States," *Southwest Philosophical Studies*, 15, pp. 1–9; Doyle, Michael W. (1983) "Kant, liberal legacies, and foreign affairs" (Part 1 and 2), *Philosophy and Public Affairs*, 11/12 (3/4), pp. 205–235/326–353; Habermas, Jürgen "Kant's Idea of Perpetual Peace, with the Benefit of Two Hundred Years Hindsight," in J. Bohman, M. Lutz-Bachman (eds.) (1997) *Perpetual Peace: Essays on Kant's Cosmopolitan Ideal*. MIT, pp. 113–153; Hodgson, Louis-Philippe (2012) "Realizing External Freedom: The Kantian Argument for a World State," in *Kant's Political Theory: Interpretations and Applications*, ed. E. Ellis. University Park: The Pennsylvania State University Press; Kleingeld, Pauline (2012) *Kant and Cosmopolitanism*. Cambridge: Cambridge University Press; Mikalsen, Kjartan K. "In Defense of Kant's League of States," *Law and Philosophy* 30 (3), pp. 291–317; Nagel, Thomas (2005) "The Problem of Global Justice," *Philosophy and Public Affairs*, 33(2), pp. 113–148; Pogge, Thomas "Kant's Vision of a Just World Order," in T. E. Hill (ed.) (2009) *The Blackwell Guide to Kant's Ethics*. Blackwell Publishing Ltd, pp. 196–208; Ripstein, Arthur (2009) *Force and Freedom – Kant's Legal and Political Philosophy*. Cambridge, Mass.: Harvard University Press; Rawls, John (1999) *The Law of Peoples*. Cambridge, Mass.: Harvard University Press; "A Kantian Conception of Global Justice," *Review of International Studies*, 2011, Vol. 37, Issue 05, pp. 2043–2057; Williams, Howard L. (2012) *Kant and the End of War: A Critique of Just War Theory*. New York: Palgrave Macmillan.

they surely have. Rather, it is to say that for a long time there was relatively little interest in and much confusion around his main work in legal-political philosophy, namely "The Doctrine of Right" in *The Metaphysics of Morals*. In addition, of course, reading Kant means reading "Kantianese," that particular type of highly technical philosophical language that not only requires a special kind of patience, but also invites controversy and disagreement. Consequently, many different types of legal-political theories, both at the national and the global levels, have been attributed to Kant. But Kant's theory has received increasing attention in recent decades. And, although there is still much disagreement among Kant interpreters, there is little doubt that this disagreement now occurs at a much more constructive and interesting level than it did only a decade ago. There is little doubt, also, that philosophers of all stripes agree that Kant's theory is well worth exploring, and that it is establishing itself as one of the main philosophical resources for thinking about justice.

Acknowledgement Thanks to Ingrid Albrecht, Lucy Allais, Catherine Champniers, Grace Frank, Tone Monkerud, Arnt Myrstad, and Jørgen Pedersen for invaluable help with the writing of this text.

Hegel and the Foundation of Right

Terje Sparby

For Hegel, right is inextricably tied to free will, which he sees as an expression of spirit. His *Philosophy of Right*[1] locates the foundation of right exactly in freedom and spirit. Many have viewed this coupling of right and freedom with spirit as problematic. Hegel has for a long time—at least since Isaiah Berlin's "Two Concepts of Liberty"—been interpreted as a representative of *positive freedom* (being directed by a "true self") and linked to a totalitarian idea of the state. Recent contributions have to a large extent freed Hegel from such charges, focusing on how the freedom of the individual is not only compatible with participation in society, but also realized through it. The state is not understood as the "march" of some god external to human history.[2] Terry Pinkard's recent *Hegel's Naturalism* is an example of such a view: "Spirit" is not an independent, supersensible being directing history from the beyond,[3] but is the collective and individual agency of self-interpreting organisms.[4] Axel Honneth goes further in his *Das Recht der Freiheit*, a reconstruction of Hegel's *Philosophy of Right* in a way suitable for the contemporary mind: Honneth throws the idealist, monist concept of spirit

[1] Hegel, G. W. F (1986) *Grundlinien der Philosophie des Rechts oder Naturrecht und Staatswissenschaft im Grundrisse*, vol. 7. Frankfurt am Main: Suhrkamp. Hereafter references to the Suhrkamp-edition of Hegel's works will be given as TWA followed by volume number and page.

[2] Though some have read Hegel in this way, it is a reading that is based on a misleading translation. See Franco, Paul (1999) *Hegel's Philosophy of Spirit*. New Haven: Yale University Press, p. 288. In § 258Z TWA 7, 403), Hegel states: "Es ist der Gang Gottes in der Welt, dass der Staat ist". "Der Gang Gottes" can be translated as "the way of God in the world" (as Avineri does in Avineri, Shlomo (1972) *Hegel's Theory of the Modern State*. Cambridge: Cambridge University Press, p. 176–177) rather than as the less neutral "the march of God in the world".

[3] Pinkard, Terry (2012) *Hegel's Naturalism. Mind, Nature, and the Final End of Life*. Oxford: Oxford University Press, p. 194.

[4] *Ibid.*, p. 105.

T. Sparby (✉)
Institute of Philosophy, Humbolt Universität of Berlin, Berlin, Germany
e-mail: terje.sparby@gmai.com

G. Fløistad (ed.), *Philosophy of Justice*, Contemporary Philosophy: A New Survey 12, DOI 10.1007/978-94-017-9175-5_14, © Springer Science+Business Media Dordrecht 2015

completely overboard.[5] Why was Hegel so concerned with spirit and why are we so concerned with distancing ourselves from it?

Again, for Hegel, right is grounded in freedom, and in order to be free, one has to have *self-knowledge*. Furthermore, having self-knowledge ultimately means understanding oneself as *spirit*. So the ultimate foundation right is spirit. But spirit is not only the foundation of right, it also has its own right that is *above* all other forms of right. It is this last point that has worried so many who encounter Hegel's philosophy of right. I think this worry is not justified. On the contrary, I think Hegel presents a much-needed depth of thought to the investigation into the foundation of right and rather than being inherently totalitarian, Hegel's doctrine of spirit points a way to a future, more complete, realization of it.

Here I will first outline how Hegel's views on rights are based on his the concept of freedom and how freedom is realized in the state (parts I and II). Then, by presenting Charles Taylor's critique of Isaiah Berlin, I will construct an argument for why the Hegelian view is not inherently anti-pluralist and totalitarian (part III). Taylor ends with the (Hegelian) view that self-knowledge is essential to freedom, but is mute about what self-knowledge consists of more concretely. Finally (part IV), I will outline how Hegel sees right founded in spirit and how spirit has an "absolute right" over the realization of freedom and right in the state. Hegel's philosophy of spirit provides a concrete doctrine of what self-knowledge is. Self-knowledge is essentially spirit's knowing of itself. Furthermore, I do not think the options of naturalizing Hegel (Pinkard) or ignoring Hegel's monist doctrine (Honneth) are attractive. Rather, Hegel poses the strongest challenge when he is read in a way that does not try to make him compatible with the current widespread mentality of denying spirit. And this is a challenge I think we need to address if we want to investigate the deeper foundation of right and the ways in which it is realized.

Before we begin, it might be helpful to note what the concept of "right" means in Hegel's *Philosophy of Right*: It is not only a philosophy of what it means to have rights and what the most basic rights of a human being are, but also a philosophy of "what is right", e.g., what it means to act morally. Hegel calls the rights of a person, insofar as they are considered without their moral foundation, "abstract right". However, Hegel also examines the kind of society that embodies what is right and ensures that rights are upheld. Hegel's philosophy of right thus has three parts: Abstract right, morality and ethical life (which includes the state).

---

[5] Honneth, Axel (2011) *Das Recht der Freiheit*. Berlin: Suhrkamp, p. 17: "Die Voraussetzung eines idealistischen Monismus, in den er [Hegel] seinen dialektischen Begriff des Geistes verankert hat, ist für uns, die Kinder eines materialistisch augeklärten Zeitalters, nicht mehr recht vorstellbar, so daß auch für seine Idee eines objektiven, in den sozialen Instutitionen vewirklichten Geistes eine andere Grundlage gesucht werden muß."

1 The Free Will as the Foundation of Right

In § 4 of *Philosophy of Right*, Hegel gives a concise statement about foundation and realization of "right":

> Der Boden des Rechts ist überhaupt das *Geistige* und seine nähere Stelle und Ausgangspunkt der *Wille*, welcher *frei* ist, so daß die Freiheit seine Substanz und Bestimmung ausmacht und das Rechtssystem das Reich der verwirklichten Freiheit, die Welt des Geistes aus ihm selbst hervorgebracht, als eine zweite Natur, ist.[6]

The foundation of right is spirit as *free will*. Free will, which is basically a capacity, must also be realized: it must be objectified, find a certain way of existing in the world. Or rather, it must find and give shape to its *own world*, which then in effect is "a second birth" of the human being. The human being is a physical organism in possession of a will that in principle is free, but only insofar as another world is set up by the human being, a world that works according to its own rules, can the human being really be called free.

We see then that Hegel's concept of freedom is a *comprehensive* one. The capacity of free will must also be put into practice and be codified into laws. All that is involved in having free will as a capacity (being a practically deliberating, living organism) is what Hegel calls *subjective spirit*, while *objective spirit* is identical to the content exhibited in the *Philosophy of Right* and concerns the way that free will is realized in abstract right, morality and ethical life. However, it is misleading to say that Hegel thinks it is impossible to be free outside of a concrete community (such as a tribe, a family or, in the modern world, the state). In fact, as I will try to show later on, free will *cannot* be fully realized in a particular community. It has to go beyond the particularity of community and find embodiment in a comprehensive, universal standpoint. This is part of the spiritualization of free will. Still, it is true that Hegel not only thinks that it is possible for the modern, free individual to live in harmony with a community, but also that being part of a community is a *part* of the realization of free will.

For Hegel, free will contains a *universal, particular* and *individual* element (outlined in *Philosophy of Right* § 5–7). I will consider each of these in turn.

The human being exists concretely. It has a set of properties that are more or less easy to specify precisely: It has a body with a certain height, it has certain interests, identifies with a nationality, has certain aims in life, and so on. As a *thinking* being, the human can *abstract* from such determinate qualities and still consider itself as a *substance* that has such properties or simply as *existing*. I *happen* to be of a certain height, but I *could* be any other height and still be myself. I can, in fact, consider myself as a being who is nothing other than the pure thought of myself as a singular being. This is what it means to be a thinking I in the most extreme form: *I am only that I am.* Free will as *universality* is this thinking abstraction, the removal of all determinate properties, which leaves nothing but the bare existence of a spiritual substance, the I.

[6] TWA 4: 80.

One can have consciousness of this form of abstract freedom insofar as something is destroyed.[7] Concrete existence presents limits that have to be removed if there is to be any truth to the abstract will. This is the basis of Hegel's analysis of the French Revolution. Everyone was supposed to be free and equal, but as soon as any social order came into existence, there would be differentiation whereby particular human beings took on particular roles. This is not acceptable for the free will that is *fixated* on universality.

The will in its particular element takes a concrete existence as its own. It identifies with this or that, it *commits* to a certain way of being. Identifying with a concrete existence of course means to limit oneself ("I am *this* rather than *that*"), and consequently Hegel does not see *limitation* as such as necessarily opposed to freedom. Actually, Hegel sees the self-limiting of free will, its taking on a particular existence, as something that is rooted in and naturally follows from free will in its universality. The universally free will that sets itself up against any concrete existence as the pure I is not really universal, it is not really indeterminate and free: It *one-sidedly* sets itself up as opposed to something (or everything), which means that it is determined (limited). It is dependent on removing itself from concrete existence and therefore is not universal at all. In other words, the universal will is particular. This particularity can, however, not be sustained—it is an empty abstraction that is only experienced in removal—and it is therefore realized only as it takes on a concrete existence.

In Hegel's view, this way of following the immanent development of a concept—in this case, free will—is what distinguishes the original contribution of his philosophy. His own example is that of Fichte,[8] which, as a dualist, simply starts with the abstract I and then introduces an opposite from outside. In contrast, for Hegel, the task of philosophy is to show that opposites do not really exclude each other, but rather are interrelated. Hence, in the *Philosophy of Right*, the task is to give an exhibition of how the will of the person is interrelated with society, how both are flowing into each other, and how they are nothing on their own.

One has, however, also to set limits to limitation in order to be free. Though free will can and must identify with a given existence, this identification brings the will into conflict with itself. It still is a being that can exist in abstraction as a pure being. It would be absurd to say that I identify with the height of my body and take this as the pinnacle of my existence. Free will seeks certain forms of particular existence that are capable of uniting universality and particularity, forms of existence in which it can exist in a particular way *as a thinking being* capable both of abstraction and identification.

This brings us to the specifically Hegelian formulation of what freedom consists of: Being with oneself in otherness.[9] There are certain ways of limiting myself through which I am not really limited at all, but rather through which I become realized as what I am in myself. This, according to Hegel, is what full freedom of the

[7] TWA 7: 50.

[8] TWA 7: 53.

[9] TWA 7: 54, 57.

will really consists of.[10] Though he claims that this will be hard to get a grip on philosophically, at least for the philosophical intellect, he thinks that most humans have an immediate access to this in their lives in the form of friendship and love.[11] The task of philosophy is to give expression to such feelings of daily life in the form of thought.

This analysis gives Hegel a perhaps unfamiliar place within contemporary debates about freedom. Hegel states explicitly that freedom neither consists of being determined, nor of indeterminacy,[12] but he accepts that both must be part of comprehensive freedom. Free will in its universality is about indeterminacy, but indeterminacy is insufficient for freedom; being determined is also insufficient insofar as free will does not find itself in the way it is determined. Along the same lines, Hegel thinks that the power of choice *(Willkür)* is necessary for freedom, but that identifying freedom *solely* with the power of choice is wrongheaded. Choice is the *form* of freedom, but the content of what we choose between is, in most cases, not determined by free will: We are born with certain desires, brought up in a certain culture, are subjected to natural and rational laws—we have not chosen the way the world is and the specific limits it poses on us. If I choose to follow *one* desire, I often end up frustrating another. If I choose to follow both, none are really satisfied. Not choosing is also not an option, since it would mean a retreat into the one-sided universality of free will.

The key point for Hegel is that in order to be free the content that is given to us, such as the content of what is desired, has to be shaped by reason. This is the notion of purification and education *(Bildung)* of desires, which is vital to Hegel.[13] But reason is not fundamentally inimical to emotions and desires. Desires are in themselves an expression of reason, an expression that the living being is more than bare, physical existence. However, raw desires do not satisfy the human being as a being of reason, desires have to be educated. Or, in other words, being human means being in a process of having one's desires educated. The aim is to find a form of unity of reason and desire in which free will wills itself as free will. This may sound like cryptic *Hegelese*, but the point is simple: The free human being longs to find itself in a world that it wants to be in, a world that accords to itself *as* a free being. When this is the case, the world exhibits right, it *is* right. In Hegel's words: "Dies, daß ein Dasein überhaupt *Dasein des freien Willens* ist, ist das *Recht.*

Hegel thinks that such a world is the *ethical life (Sittlichkeit)*, the modern nation state, though the human being does not find the *highest satisfaction* within the state, as I have already indicated. This is a point that I will return to, after I have more concretely shown how Hegel thinks that freedom is realized in ethical life.

---

[10] TWA 7: 54.

[11] TWA 7: 57.

[12] TWA 7: 57.

[13] TWA 7: 70–71.

2 The Realization of Freedom in the State

As already mentioned, Hegel's *Philosophy of Right* consists of three main parts: *Abstract right* (subdivided into property, contract and wrong), *morality* (purpose and guilt, intention and happiness, the good and conscience), and *ethical life* (family, civil society, state). Hegel's vision is that ethical life in the state brings unity and wholeness; abstract right has the fault that it lacks subjectivity (for instance, the inwardness of personality that can rise up against unjust laws), while morality has the fault that it lacks objectivity: It has no standard against which it can measure its moral intuitions—"anything goes", as long as you follow your own conviction, which means that there is no essential difference between a criminal and a law-abiding citizen. Both take their own inwardness as the standard.[14] Ethical life amends these lacks by giving an external standard, a community, which is such that the subject can find its own deeper nature in it.

Abstract right begins with *the personality*. A personality is the unity of the purely abstract I and concrete, bodily existence. Furthermore, the personality is the fundamental entity that can have rights and is itself subject to the basic command of right: "[S]ei eine Person und respektiere die anderen als Personen." It is the right of the person to have property. How much property a person should have is not a matter for philosophy to discuss, but Hegel does believe that having property is part of the realization of free will. Having property signals the arrival of "second nature". Property is an extension of the person into a realm that is not given to it by nature.

A person with property relates to other persons with property, and the relation is regulated by the *contract*. Having property, which is a condition for being a person, limits what others can take possession of (though property *began* when someone simply claimed it as its own). In practice, one only has property insofar as it is recognized by others. Through the contract the person objectifies this recognition and, furthermore, can transfer its property to others. The person thus realizes its freedom by taking and giving away without losing itself.

But rights can come into conflict with each other without there being a way to decide which right should be given priority, and persons may be subjected to fraud *(Betrug)* and felony *(Verbrechen)*. This shows how abstract right is not a full realization of freedom. Punishment is, for Hegel, a way to respond in a way that recognizes the will of the criminal, but punishment alone cannot be the only thing that holds together and regulates human interaction. The contractual law comes to the human being from the outside; only when supplemented by the "inner law" of morality can the human being realize itself more fully as a particular will in relation to the will of others.

What can be good for particular human beings can come in conflict with the rights of others. What is rightfully yours can be exactly what I need, and although taking it would be theft, it would still do me good. Hegel thinks that it should not at all be considered theft to take something that is not yours if it will save your life

[14] TWA 7: 291.

at that moment. The right to one's own life—to save oneself in a particular moment and situation—is above the right others have to the particular good that will save your life.[15] In contrast, stealing leather to make shoes for the poor may be a *moral* act, but it conflicts with abstract right, and is therefore invalid.[16] Such conflicts between what is moral and what is right can find a resolution in *Sittlichkeit* (for instance, through persons regularly giving up goods so that a community can take care of its poor), but first we will consider what Hegel means by morality.

Morality concerns the subjectivity of the morally acting agent. The subjectivity of the moral agent presents itself in the *purpose* of the act. In its most immediate form, the moral standpoint does not consider the result of an action so that, although the purpose may be good, the result may very well be bad. How much, for instance, should we require with regard to someone's knowledge of the world when it comes to judging the morality of an action? On the one hand, we only want to call someone guilty of something that they had a purpose for doing, but on the other hand, guilt cannot be separated completely from the consequences an action has regardless of the purpose (someone may be "just following orders" but still be guilty of atrocities).[17]

This conflict is resolved through the demand that one acts with an *intention* that is based on a knowledge of how the action relates to happiness. In Hegel's mind, the subject of the modern age has the right to happiness ("sich befriedigt zu finden").[18] But the subject cannot simply will itself into happiness. It must seek to find happiness through action and by bringing its own happiness into harmony with that of others. However, there is no necessary connection between action and happiness, and the happiness of others can come into conflict with my own.

Moral action can, however, detach itself from the contingencies of life and act for the universal good. The pleasure of happiness is from this standpoint less important than doing one's duty for the sake of duty, of finding the good in dutiful action itself.[19] But what is duty? Duty is to *do what is right and seek the happiness of all* ("*Recht* zu tun und für das *Wohl*, sein eigenes Wohl und das Wohl in allgemeiner Bestimmung, das Wohl anderer, zu sorgen."[20]) But, as Hegel infamously has claimed, duty as such is formal and empty: One cannot find an intellectual formula that can serve as a way to measure if an action is dutiful or not. According to Kant, an action that undermines itself through being contradictory cannot be a duty (we have a duty not to lie, because if all would lie, lying would be impossible). But Hegel points out that there is no contradiction in claiming that there should be no property, or that this or that people or family should exist, when these are considered in themselves.[21] That something—like theft and murder—is contradictory, can only

[15] TWA 7: 240–241.
[16] TWA 7: 239.
[17] TWA 7: 218.
[18] TWA 7: 233.
[19] TWA 7: 250.
[20] TWA 7: 251.
[21] TWA 7: 253.

be decided on the grounds of a concrete content that is presupposed. For duty, however, the point is to will the good regardless of what it is. This can be amended by taking the individual *conscience* as the foundation of deciding what is good and what is not. Each and everyone only have to look into themselves in order to know what is good and bad. When there is a conflict between a concrete law and what my conscience immediately knows to be good, then it is right to follow one's conscience. Conscience is the final arbiter.

But conscience is also continuously *on the verge of evil.*[22] Both the conscientious and the evil act take the subject as the only source for knowing what is right: I do it because *I* know it be right. For Hegel, the root of evil is the separate existence of the subject in relation to everything else.[23] But at the same time, this separation is the condition for the realization of freedom, of being one in otherness. If there is no separate, singular existence, there would also be no experience of freedom, there would be nothing to give up and find again in the relationship of love. Both separation and unification are necessary as the foundation of freedom and right. Hence, no clear line can be drawn between a conscientious act and a criminal one when these are views in abstraction from concrete, ethical life.

Here we return to the previous claim that abstract right and morality are one-sided, both having either too much objectivity or too little subjectivity. The moral subject sought an objective standard in following the form of duty, but duty lacks content. The same goes for conscience; it knows that the good is both universal and particular, that there is no absolute separation between the common good and its own will, but it lacks a concrete existence in which it can *live* this insight. This is provided by *ethical life (Sittlichkeit).*

The first form of ethical life is that of the *family.* In the family each member immediately *feels* itself as a part of a greater unity. The family is an immediate existence in which the person realizes itself as a free will; each member gives itself over to each other and sees itself primarily as a family: "Die Familie hat als die *unmittelbare Substantialität* des Geistes seine sich *empfindende* Einheit, die *Liebe* [...]."[24] The foundation of the family is for Hegel marriage, and the family itself forms a person[25] that has its own property, which must be regulated by law. An important function of the family is the education of children to be part of society as independent persons, something that cannot be done remaining within the family. The family is therefore a limited moment of ethical life.

The grown-up realizes its own aims as an independent human being in *civil society.* But it seeks the satisfaction of its own aims and desires in civil society in relation to the satisfaction of others. The person takes part in a *system of needs*, e.g., the production and exchange of goods. For Hegel, it is the nature of civil society that in aiming to satisfy oneself one also takes part in the satisfaction of others.[26] On the

22 TWA 7: 261.

23 TWA 7: 262.

24 TWA 7: 307.

25 TWA 7: 310, 338.

26 TWA 7: 353.

one hand, civil society is the playing field where the particular differences of each human being comes to the forefront—each has different talents, interests, property and so on—and each can seek to improve upon one's own life. On the other hand, Hegel divides society into three classes: the agricultural, business and universal class (civil servants, scientists, etc.),[27] and thinks that without belonging to a class one is *merely* a private person. A private person who does not belong to a class does not particularize its free will; it is a sort of bystander.[28] When the person finds a place within a class, however, civil society becomes a realm of the concrete realization of freedom.

Furthermore, Hegel divides civil society into the *practice of justice (Die Rechtspflege), the police* and *corporations*. Civil society is the area where the life of justice is carried out through clearly formulated laws, courts and legal procedure. But this only takes care of the *abstract* right of the person within civil society. The police take care of the security of persons and their property. As a member of a corporation the person can consciously take part in the satisfaction of the needs of the citizens,[29] it becomes a member of a *second family*[30] and achieves the *honor of a profession (Standesehre)*,[31] which is another significant step in the realization of concrete freedom.

The corporation, however, still stands within the sphere of *particularity*; there are *many corporations*, all of which serve particular interests. In contrast, the state is *one* and is explicitly concerned with the interest of all. Therefore it is a higher expression of the right of free will.

That state consists of inner and outer relations. The inner relations are divided into three areas of power: the legislature, executive power and the monarchy. Though Hegel sees monarchy as a realization of concrete freedom, this is mainly in the sense of having one person be the focus point of the singularity of the state. The ruler in the monarchy only has the power of "saying yes."[32] Furthermore, Hegel is not a democrat in the contemporary sense of the word. The persons of the state do not have the right to vote as individuals, but rather as members of a corporation.[33] The outer relations of the state concerns the relation the state has to *other states*. Each state is sovereign and there is no higher power to guarantee that treaties are respected.[34]

States, as separate existences, are finite and not the full realization of freedom. The right of spirit is above the rights of the state,[35] and this right consists in the

---

[27] If the military class is counted, there are four. The military class, however, is not concerned with the inner life of the state.

[28] TWA 7: 360.

[29] Cf. TWA 7: 397.

[30] TWA 7: 396.

[31] TWA 7: 395.

[32] TWA 7: 451.

[33] TWA 7: 476–479.

[34] TWA 7: 499–500.

[35] TWA 7: 503.

liberation of spirit from the sphere of finitude.[36] This liberation is meditated by world history, and Hegel's claim that the state is the march of God in history can give the impression that spirit stands above everything and simply uses the state and its individuals as a vehicle for its own realization. When individuals—such as Hegel—claim to have insight into this process, the question of totalitarianism arises. Who can claim insight into what is right for others? Is this not the first step towards a totalitarian state, where the individual is forced to sacrifice itself for a greater good beyond itself?

3 Berlin and Taylor on Freedom, Totalitarianism and Self-Knowledge

As we have seen, Hegel grounds right in freedom, and freedom is a complex and concrete interrelation of abstract right, morality and ethical life. One important point that has emerged is that the right of spirit stands above the right of the state. This is a point that is bound to seem strange, perhaps even offensive, to the contemporary mind. Nonetheless it is vital to Hegel's overall project. The typical approach to this issue is to disregard everything that has to do with spirit and adapt Hegel's thinking to the more down-to-earth attitude of current philosophy. Not only is this itself indicative of the *spirit* of our times, but this *self-denial* can also be seen as a grave shortcoming of self-knowledge. This, I think, is a perspective inherent in Hegel's philosophy that is important and almost unexplored when it comes to the understanding of the foundation of right.

In order to argue this, I will examine Isaiah Berlin's distinction between positive and negative freedom, and Charles Taylor's response to it. Berlin favors negative freedom, and although he sees value in positive freedom, to him the danger is that it may deteriorate into totalitarianism, especially when it is granted that some may have an insight into the "true self" of other human beings. Taylor argues that negative freedom is a very limited conception of freedom and wants to defend the notion of positive freedom against Berlin's charge that totalitarianism is lurking in it. Taylor, however, leaves the issue quite open with regard to what the content of a "true self" might be. This is where I think there is a need to introduce something like Hegel's concept of spirit.

According to Berlin, negative freedom has to do with the extent to which someone interferes with someone else.[37] In principle, then, you are ultimately (negatively) free if no one interferes with what you do or what you are.[38] One would be

[36] TWA 10: 35.

[37] Berlin; Isaiah (2002) "Two Concepts of Liberty," in Harding, Henry (ed.) *Liberty*. Oxford: Oxford University Press, p. 170: "By being free in this sense I mean not being interfered with by others. The wider the area of non-interference the wider my freedom."

[38] Cf. *ibid*., p. 169: "What is the area within which the subject – a person or a group of persons – is or should be left to do or be what he is able to do or be, without interference by other persons?"

perfectly negatively free in a world where one is completely left to oneself. Any interaction between human beings implies a mutual interference. As soon as there is interaction—for instance, I enter into your field of vision—then I determine you in a certain way. You (your sensory system) enters into a certain state because of me. Although this may not be experienced as a problem, as a limitation of my freedom, one could also imagine instances where someone simply cannot stand the sight of someone else. What counts as a limitation on my freedom is therefore *up to me* to decide. If I, for some reason, decide to take the way that someone else influences me as an unacceptable breach of my freedom, the other may exclaim that I have no right to interfere with the interference. From an impartial point of view, therefore, it is not possible to draw a clear line between what counts as unacceptable interference and what does not.

Theorists in the tradition of negative liberty tend to base their discussion on a fundamental separation between private and public life (the state), mainly being concerned with limits to the interference of the state in private life. As Berlin says, however, where to draw the line "is a matter of argument, indeed of haggling. Men are largely interdependent, and no man's activity is so completely private as never to obstruct the lives of others in any way. […] [T]he liberty of some must depend on the restraint of others."[39] Consequently the debate is about how much and what kind of interference is allowed without "offending against the essence of […] human nature."[40] However, talk about "human nature" already signals that one has crossed over into the area of positive freedom. Strictly speaking, representatives of negative freedom seem to hold only that non-interference is a good thing,[41] but it seems hard to argue why this is the case without bringing claims about human nature into the picture. This indeed points to the limits of the negative conception of liberty.

Positive freedom or liberty means that one rules over oneself, or has self-mastery.[42] This implies that there is a split in the subject, either in the sense that there is one part that rules and another part that is ruled over, or that the human being as a whole takes the shape of a true self. According to Berlin, this corresponds to the two distinct forms of what it means to be directed by oneself or the true self: Either one *denies* an aspect of oneself (such as one's desires) in order to attain independence or one realizes oneself through becoming identified with a specific principle or ideal.[43] These need not be mutually exclusive. Self-denial may be required in order to become identified with an ideal (though Berlin is skeptical of self-denial insofar as it expresses an attitude of life-denial).[44]

[39] *Ibid.*, p. 171.

[40] *Ibid.*, p. 173.

[41] *Ibid.*, p. 175.

[42] *Ibid.*, p. 178.

[43] *Ibid.*, p. 181.

[44] *Ibid.*, p. 186.

Being free in the fullest, positive sense is to be "a liberated, self-directed actor in the cosmic drama"[45] and "is at the heart of the demands for national and social self-direction which animate the most powerful and morally just public movements of our time".[46] It means to have a will that is permeated by thought[47]:

> I am free if, and only if, I plan my life in accordance with my own will; plans entail rules; a rule does not oppress me or enslave me if I impose it on myself consciously, or accept it freely, having understood it, whether it was invented by me or by others, provided that it is rational, that is to say, conforms to the necessities of things.[48]

Furthermore, Berlin quotes Rousseau as a typical example of a representative of positive freedom: "He is truly free who desires what he can perform, and does what he desires."[49] Another representative is Spinoza, who claims that children are not slaves even when they are coerced, since they adhere to rules that are in their own interest, and that anyone who subjects oneself to a common good cannot possibly be a slave, since the common good includes everyone.[50]

Although Berlin clearly sees the importance of positive freedom in the history of philosophy, as a factor in social change and the self-conception of the human being as a rational agent, he sees a danger involved in positive freedom that negative freedom is exempt from: The threat of totalitarianism, where a particular conception of what makes the true self becomes identified with a certain class, state or moment in world history.[51] The problem is the utopian idea that is involved in such conceptions. The claim to know what is the best for others violates negative freedom based on some form of mystical insight into the true nature of things. Utopians believe that there can exist a form of society where there are no conflicts between the desires and ideals of human beings. Berlin identifies the belief in utopia with the rationalist tradition: The rationalist believes that it is possible to find "a final harmony in which all riddles are solved, all contradictions reconciled",[52] while Berlin thinks that "the possibility of conflict—and of tragedy—can never wholly be eliminated from human life, either personal or social."[53] Because of this, Berlin adheres to pluralism, and favors negative liberty over positive.[54] Human ideals conflict and it is impossible to provide an impartial, rational measure of what ideals are the best (which could make

---

[45] *Ibid.*, p. 193.

[46] *Ibid.*, p. 214.

[47] Cf. *ibid.*, p. 72: "Das Selbstbewußtsein, das seinen Gegenstand, Inhalt und Zweck bis zu dieser Allgemeinheit reinigt und erhebt, tut dies als das im Willen sich *durchsetzende Denken*. Hier ist der *Punkt*, *auf welchem es erhellt*, daß der Wille nur als *denkende* Intelligenz wahrhafter, freier Wille ist."

[48] *Ibid.*, p. 193.

[49] *Ibid.*, p. 185.

[50] *Ibid.*, p. 193.

[51] *Ibid.*, p. 181.

[52] *Ibid.*, p. 213.

[53] *Ibid.*, p. 214.

[54] *Ibid.*, p. 216.

the choice mechanical). "[M]en choose between ultimate values"[55] and this is a basic condition of the freedom of the human being in modern society.

As Berlin himself notes, the idea of freedom as non-interference is often accompanied by the notion that people should be allowed to develop themselves, their character and personality, including their love of truth, independence, imagination and so on.[56] But such human development can coexist with, and perhaps even be supported by, people interfering in the lives of other, for instance, through enforcing strict rules of discipline.

Nonetheless Berlin insists on distinguishing between positive and negative freedom. One gets to the source of negative freedom if one asks, "How far does the government interfere with me?" and positive freedom if one asks, "Who governs me?"[57] However, the contrast only works if it is presupposed that I have a specific nature that can be interfered with. If I do not have a specific nature, if I am fully ruled by the state, it makes no sense to say that I am interfered with by the state. Negative and positive freedom becomes identical in such a case.

One also needs to have an idea of what "me" means, if the question of the extent of government interference is to make any sense. Berlin seems to be aware of this, and the core of his favoring of negative freedom seems dependent on the threat of totalitarianism, where it is taken for granted that there is a clearly defined "me" that the state can interfere with. Berlin's main concern for putting negative freedom first is to secure that all can decide for themselves what the content of their freedom should consist of (what ideals they choose to live by and identify with).

This has been rightly pointed out by Charles Taylor. However, Taylor thinks that Berlin's standpoint is flawed: Negative freedom is too limited as a conception of freedom and positive freedom is not inherently totalitarian.

Taylor basically agrees with Berlin that there is a distinction between positive and negative liberty. Like Berlin, Taylor defines negative liberty as the absence of interference, while positive freedom for Taylor "resides at least in part in collective control over common life",[58] though he also recognizes that positive freedom might mean ruling over oneself.[59] Taylor notes that the proponents of negative freedom often defend the extreme variant of their stance (freedom is exclusively about non-interference, not about self-realization of the individual), while the proponents of positive freedom usually defend a *less* extreme variant of their view (for instance, arguing in favor of individualized self-realization with only some interference of the state). The reason for this, Taylor claims, is "the fear of the Totalitarian Menace" that manifests itself so strongly in philosophers like Berlin.[60]

---

[55] *Ibid.*, p. 217.

[56] *Ibid.*, p. 175.

[57] *Ibid.*, p. 177.

[58] Taylor, Charles (1985) "What's Wrong With Negative Liberty," in *Philosophy and the Human Sciences. Philosophical Papers 2*. Cambridge: Cambridge University Press, p. 211.

[59] *Ibid.*, p. 212.

[60] *Ibid.*, p. 215.

The extreme variant of negative freedom understands freedom as the absence of obstacles to the realization of the desires that someone identifies with.[61] Taylor distinguishes between internal and external obstacles to freedom. One internal obstacle is fear.[62] If I act out of fear I might feel that I am acting according to what I desire (e.g., security), but human beings in many cases also value the overcoming of fear and see such overcoming as a real act of freedom. We make distinctions between desires we should act upon and desires we should not act upon. This is not a matter of *feeling* which desire is stronger, but of making a rational evaluation about what desires really are desirable in the sense of fitting into an overall view of how one wants to live one's life, i.e., what Taylor calls strong evaluations.[63] As soon as we recognize this, we must also admit that we can be *wrong* about what we take to be the rational way to act; we can be wrong about how we evaluate the merits of our feelings. Consequently:

> [...] freedom now involves my being able to recognize adequately my more important purposes, and my being able to overcome or at least neutralize my motivational fetters [such as fear], as well as my way of being free of external obstacles. But clearly the first condition (and, I would argue, also the second) require me to have become something, to have achieved a certain condition of self-clairvoyance and self-understanding. I must be actually exercising self-understanding in order to be truly or fully free.[64]

So Taylor presents a comprehensive theory of freedom that involves both the positive and negative formulation. Negative liberty alone is not adequate as a formulation of freedom, and having self-knowledge is a necessary condition for the full realization of freedom.

Taylor claims that this in no way leads to totalitarianism. If someone may have a wrong self-understanding, this also means that others may be equally wrong when they claim that another self-understanding is right. This, however, does not seem to bring us further than Berlin's pluralism other than, perhaps, that there should be a discourse on what is the ultimate aim of human existence. Only through such a discourse can we come closer to the realization of freedom. A pluralist stance does not think such a discourse has rational appeal and it should not have an impact on how people choose to live their lives. Though Hegel believes that the pluralist standpoint is vital, it is not final, in the sense that it is not adequate for full freedom.

4 The Right of Spirit

Hegel, like Taylor, thinks that negative freedom is flawed. Man, as a being of freedom, seeks not only to be separate from the world, but also to be connected with it. This is an extension of the basic nature of man as a living being, as it expresses itself in desire

[61] *Ibid.*, p. 216.
[62] *Ibid.*, p. 216.
[63] *Ibid.*, p. 220.
[64] *Ibid.*, pp. 228–229.

and rationality. Having no external limits is not identical to being free, and though the absence of limits may be an important component of comprehensive freedom, some forms of limitation serve to realize rather than limit freedom. The highest forms of freedom are such that limitation is not separate from realization. The prime example of this as an immediate feeling is love. As an intellectual activity, the highest freedom consists in the self-knowledge of spirit, where spirit finds itself in what initially was opposed to it (any unconnected material in nature, society, history, etc.). However, before we go further into the issue of the relationship between freedom, self-knowledge, spirit and right, we must first provide a clear case for why such a view should not evoke any suspicion that it is implicitly totalitarian.

Berlin's argument against rationalist utopianism is superficial, at least insofar as it is directed at Hegel. Hegel integrates pluralism into his *Philosophy of Right* and thinks that it comes to its right in civil society. One needs to present an argument for why Hegel's conception of civil society does not do enough justice to the pluralist (particular) aspect of freedom and essentially subordinates the will of the individual to the particular will of a ruling entity (totalitarianism).

However, Hegel believes that it is possible to conceive of a rational order for the whole of society. This raises the question of totalitarianism: Is not the idea of a "rational order" for society inherently totalitarian, seeing as it involves one human having insight into "the truth", which is then used to justify imposing "a true way of being" on others? As we have seen, a claim to *know* that there is "a true way of being" is not by itself inherently totalitarian. It depends on what this way of being is and how one thinks that it should be embodied. Berlin is skeptical about the idea that there is a way of being where all conflict is thought to be resolved once and for all, and that such a view is taken as a reason for putting massive restrictions on negative freedom through state interference.

Hegel cannot be charged with believing that the state provides a realm of final reconciliation and of wanting to force a true way of being upon the subjects of a state. The rational order he believes in gives expression to the highest realization of freedom and essentially involves citizens deciding for themselves how they want to live. Insofar as the individuals of a society experience that some aspect of their freedom is not taken care of or violated by the state means that the state is no longer legitimate (i.e., right).

In fact, Berlin admits in a footnote that he has a limited understanding of what "rationality" means: "The authority of reason and of the duties it lays upon men is identified with individual freedom, on the assumption that only rational ends can be the 'true' objects of a 'free' man's 'real' nature. I have never, I must own, understood what 'reason' means in this context".[65] Rationality, for Hegel, is not a matter of coming up with an abstract idea where all conflicts are resolved. Rather, two opposed ideals can command equal rational consent. Hegel's interest is in thinking through what such conflicts do to us, how we can think about them without succumbing to pessimism, and discover positive significance in the negative.

---

[65] Berlin, Isaiah (2002) "Two Concepts of Liberty," in Harding, Henry (ed.) *Liberty*. Oxford: Oxford University Press, p. 199, n. 1 f.

So not only is there not, as Taylor has shown, a necessary connection between rationalism and totalitarianism, but the notion of rationality that Berlin considers isn't the one that Hegel represents. This should be enough to free Hegel of the charge of totalitarianism. Now we can turn to the issue of how Hegelian understanding of rationality contributes to an understanding of freedom and rights as grounded in spirit.

The topic of Hegelian rationality is in itself immense, but is essential to understanding his conception of spirit and right. By now we have only scratched the surface of it. As I have indicated, real rationality for Hegel does not shy away from conflict, but seeks to resolve it in a way that both goes beyond conflict and includes it in a higher form. In the same vein, spirit has a right over finite existence (e.g., states) because it is a whole that both exists in and rises above finitude.[66] I will try to clarify what Hegel means by this by highlighting certain aspects of his idea of rationality.

One main characteristic of Hegel's conception of rationality in relation to earlier forms of rationalism is that of *processuality*. Ideas are not static, but exist as moving, pulsating wholes. They are synthetic, rather than abstract, universals. Understanding one thing means understanding the whole within which it is embedded. The most comprehensive idea, the *idea* itself, is such that it contains its objectivity within itself. Transferring this to a more commonsensical perspective, we could say that the thinking conception of reality is not separate from reality itself. Rather, the separation of idea and reality, of thinking and thing, takes place *within* reality and is an expression of it: Spirit separates itself from itself in order to come to know itself.

This gives rise to a three-step process of knowledge. First, there is an abstract beginning, where everything is undifferentiated, while still containing a prefiguration of what is to come in it itself. Then a differentiation or separation takes place, before finally a comprehensive whole arises that contains the previous two moments in it and which therefore is also a return to the beginning (this is exemplified in Hegel's concept of freedom as described above). There is no final end to such a process, no final stage where everything enters into an infinite calm. Though there can be relative rest, in the end all things dissolve and give rise to a new beginning. The only infinite is this process itself as a complete self-externalization (nature as space and time) and re-establishment as spirit, and only insofar as something is related to this overall process does it count as real knowledge.

Ethical life (including the state) is a part of this process, but as it exists in a finite realm the moments of freedom (which correspond to the moments of knowledge) exist in relative separation. The family, civil society and the state are areas of society in which the individual can realize all aspects of its freedom. But only to a limited degree. There are contradictions between the finite realm and the infinite that spirit is as a thinking being. This can be seen clearly in the case of pluralism. Pluralism states that all ways of living should be given equal recognition and individuals should decide for themselves what kind of life they want to live. But the forms of

[66] TWA 7: 83 f.

life are in conflict with pluralism (such as totalitarianism) and the pluralist does not want to allow such forms of life. Therefore there is an implicit hierarchy of forms of life inherent in the pluralist view: Those life forms that agree with pluralism are more highly valued than those which do not. Pluralism is a sort of meta-life form with which all have to agree. One can introduce some standard to argue why pluralism is better than other meta-life forms (such as totalitarianism), but again that means to claim insight into an objective good above the single life forms that the individual chooses to adhere to.

The pluralist can claim that this is not a problem; pluralism as such *is* better than other meta-life forms since it allows for as many as possible to live according to ideals of their choosing. This is not sensitive to the point that people want their choices to be *significant*, to be an expression of their true selves as well as something that connects with the world, something beyond themselves. Such significance can often be found in anti-pluralist life forms, which can explain some of their attractiveness. However, anti-pluralism is clearly *regressive*. The true self that is found in anti-pluralism is indeed either a totalitarian state, a particular people, or some sectarian group. Pluralism contains the insight that freedom has to be particularized and therefore, if it is opposed to totalitarianism, is indeed the higher standpoint.

But, the Hegelian claims there is an even higher standpoint, which can be called the standpoint of *comprehensive individuality* (or synthetic universality). For the historical Hegel, the state, as containing the family and civil society, represents a comprehensive individuality. The state is the real existence and guarantee for the rights of the family and the agents of civil society. This guarantee means, for instance, that of a collective defense against other nations. This shows the limit of the state as a realization of freedom. Freedom in the fullest sense was defined as being with oneself in otherness and as finding a way of life where all elements of freedom can be enjoyed. This clearly is not realized in the world as Hegel saw it, but is also the reason why he subordinated the right of the state to the right of spirit. Spirit, through world history, frees itself from its contingent embodiment of states and enters into the realm of universal spirit, ready for self-contemplation as a being both *in* history and *above* it.[67]

Understanding spirit as being both in and above history captures the specifically Hegelian understanding of history. A typical theological standpoint would be that spirit stands above history and guides it from outside. For an atheist, spirit (minimally, human mindedness) is *only in* history. It emerges from nature, but is nothing over and beyond nature. Remove nature and you remove spirit, the atheist would say. The Hegelian standpoint is that the process of the becoming of spirit is the process of history itself, in such a way that spirit at first slumbers in nature, and then rises out of it and understands nature as both a foundation and a part of itself. This process as lived experience and contemplation is the final right of spirit and that which is opposed to it will, due to its own inherent finitude, cease to be. But again, spirit is so intertwined with the process of its own becoming that the ceasing of its

[67] TWA 10: 352.

finite existence is not separate from its own revelation. The self-denial of man of itself could very well be understood as part of the process of self-revelation, the estrangement some feel in relationship to nature and to technology as well. The attempt of the modern individual to live fully according to its own set of particular ideals tests the limits of particularized existence and may very well open up new avenues of community.

The infinite perspective of spirit is always available in principle, but can be hard to reach in practice. It is easy to see the limits of freedom both in the actual world of the nineteenth century as well as in the ideal of a free state that Hegel proposed. It is more difficult to see how our own freedom may be limited. But, perhaps surprisingly, the old Hegelian perspective can reveal our limits. Hegel's claim is that we are not free if we do not see the whole cosmos and what it contains as the process of our own becoming. If we do not desire such a perspective, it may very well point to limits in our own being. We are satisfied with *less*, we are satisfied with living according to the needs of our finite nature, but not the needs of our deeper, infinite nature. Though these two natures quite likely cannot be ultimately separated, there comes a time when *Bildung* requires that one consciously takes over the responsibility for oneself and the development of one's deeper nature. This deeper nature is the one that contemplates the becoming of the world from a point of view that is interested only in the disinterested view[68]; impartial in the sense that both the finite and infinite human nature come fully to their right. From such a viewpoint, I believe, it is easy to see that a fuller realization of freedom would be the creation of a loving bond between nations, a global civil society and a single world government. This would be *right* in the sense of being a *fuller realization* and *embodiment* of freedom. But such a bond and such a global society, a *global ethical life*, must have as its ground, if Hegel is right, in a common religious life, common narratives, and a common, comprehensive science of the becoming of spirit.

[68]TWA 7: 347–352.

Mary Wollstonecraft – The Call for a Revolution of Female Manners

Kjersti Fjørtoft

1 Introduction

Mary Wollstonecraft is best known as the author of *A Vindication of the Rights of Women* published in 1792. In this text, she is arguing against those who justify the suppression of women on the grounds that women are less rational and more impulsive and emotional than men. Wollstonecraft argues that all human beings, regardless of sex, are born as rational beings, and therefore have equal capabilities for rational thinking and acting. Wollstonecraft is a religious thinker and believes that God has created all humans with reason. To develop and cultivate one's reason is therefore a duty everyone has to God. Women are not irrational by nature, but if they are denied education and basic political rights, they will become irrational and ignorant. This is precisely what happens in a society where women are oppressed. To keep women in a state of ignorance means to obstruct their opportunity to fulfill their duty to God and thereby achieve salvation. An equal right to education is Wollstonecraft's main concern.

Knowledge and education are the keys to women's liberation. Wollstonecraft was inspired by John Locke's model of consciousness as a *tabula rasa* (a blank blackboard) and argues that, because human consciousness is formed by experience and expectations, gender has to be a social construction (MacKenzie 1993: 39; Gatens 1986: 10). She was also inspired by early modern theories of natural rights. She claims that every individual has some birthrights independent of any government. Locke defines life, liberty, health and property as birthrights; for Wollstonecraft, liberty is the most important birthright. Therefore, she is most often thought of as a pioneer for liberal feminist political theory (Holst 2009). According to Wollstonecraft, equality requires legal reforms, but legal reforms are not enough. She calls for a "revolution in female manners" which requires that women reconsider their

K. Fjørtoft (✉)
Department of Philosophy, The Artic University of Norway, University of Tromsø, Tromsø
e-mail: kjersti.fjortoft@uit.no

G. Fløistad (ed.), *Philosophy of Justice*, Contemporary Philosophy: A New Survey 12, 257
DOI 10.1007/978-94-017-9175-5_15, © Springer Science+Business Media Dordrecht 2015

identities and self-perceptions. Without a revolution in female manners, women are giving up their birthrights (Wollstonecraft 2003b).

Wollstonecraft was part of a group of intellectuals in London who stressed the importance of the Enlightenment ideals of freedom and equality. They celebrated reason and fought against prejudice and superstition. They believed that rational thinking and scientific activity would lead to more democratic political and legal reforms (Nagel 1999: 129).

Wollstonecraft was born in London in 1759 as the second child in a family of seven. Because her grandfather left behind a fortune, the family was originally relatively wealthy. However, due to her father's bad allocations, the family ended up relatively poor. Her father is described as a brutal alcoholic, while her mother is characterized as a downtrodden person, not able to take sufficient care of her children. From a young age, Wollstonecraft had to support herself and take responsibility for her younger siblings. At the age of 25, she established a school together with her sisters and her close friend Fanny Blood.

Because of Fanny's poor health, and subsequent death, the school was closed down. After this, Wollstonecraft worked as a governess for an aristocratic family in Ireland. Later she went to London where she worked for the publisher Joseph Johnson and established herself as an author. She first published the novel, *Mary, A Fiction*. In 1791 *A Vindication of the Rights of Men,* a criticism of Edmund Burke's attack on the French Revolution, was published. Her most famous work, *A Vindication of the Rights of Women*, was published in 1792.

Wollstonecraft supported the French Revolution, at least in its early stage. She also went to Paris to observe and report on the happenings. In Paris, she meet an American, Gilbert Imlay, who became the father of her first daughter. In 1796, she married William Goodwin. She died of puerperal fever 10 days after her second daughter was born. In the years after her death, Wollstonecraft's reputation was relatively bad. This is caused both by the biography *Memoirs of the Author of a Vindication of the Rights of Women* written by her husband, and because of her support for the French Revolution (Janes 1978: 279).

Goodwin used Wollstonecraft's life story to promote his own radical ideas. In the biography, he revealed that she had an affair with a married man, had a child out of wedlock and that their sexual relationship started before they were married. He also said that she had tried to commit suicide twice (Taylor 1992: 203). It was known that Wollstonecraft had supported the French Revolution, a revolution that in the end became a reign of terror. Opponents of the revolutionary ideas marginalized her political and philosophical ideas with reference to her support for the revolution and her supposed immoral conduct in life (Janes 1978: 299).

Wollstonecraft did not acquire much formal education, but she still became one of the most important intellectuals in England of her time. She has written philosophy, novels and several letters from her travels (Aasen 2010: 61).

The focus in this paper is Wollstonecraft's argument for equal rights for men and women, including the notion of full citizenship for women's and her claim for a right to education. Wollstonecraft's critique of Jean-Jacques Rousseau's ideas of education is important to understand the context of her own ideas on education. Wollstonecraft's ideas on education and women's rights are introduced by her attack on the English philosopher Edmund Burke's harsh criticism of the French Revolution.

2 Wollstonecraft and the French Revolution

The French Revolution and the fall of the Bastille in 1789 have become symbols of the end of absolute monarchy and the development of democratic conceptions of citizenship. Several British intellectuals embraced the revolution and its promises of equality, freedom and brotherhood, in particular, Richard Price, a leading intellectual at that time and a minister in the church many of whose members were rational dissenters. As a woman, Wollstonecraft could identify with the dissenters. Like women, the dissenters were denied public office under the English crown; they were also denied the right to study at English universities (Taylor 2006: 108). Wollstonecraft became acquainted with Price while she worked for Johnson. Price had developed a political theory based on the idea that individual autonomy is the most basic of human capabilities. The normative consequence of his idea is that every human being has the right to act in accordance with his own rational convictions. From this it follows that states, or nations, also have the right to self-government. Appealing to the freedom of both individuals and nations, he defended the American and French revolutions.

Price's concept of freedom is defined in his best read and most influential publication, *Observations on the Nature of Civil Liberty* (1776). In this text, he distinguishes between four kinds of liberty: physical, moral, civic and religious. Physical liberty corresponds to the classic understanding of negative liberty, i.e., freedom from external coercion, or affection. Moral and religious liberty refers to the right to act in accordance with it owns conscience and religious beliefs. As a dissenter, Price's main concern was to defend religious tolerance and the freedom of religion. Moral liberty refers to the ability and right to act in accordance with reason, and not to be led by irrational emotions and impulses. Civic liberty is defined as political liberty, both for individual and states. The civic liberty for the society is sovereignty; the civic liberty of the individual is the freedom to influence the laws they are subjected to (Price 1776).

Like Wollstonecraft, Price claims that individual and political freedom is an unconditional necessity for the individual to be able to develop the capability for rational and critical thinking, and thereby be able to act as a morally responsible actor. The exercise of moral autonomy is a basic human right, and every government is therefore committed to organize society so that people are able to act as morally responsible citizens. He praises democracy, and envisions a society without a king or aristocracy and bishops. Inspired by Rousseau, he argues that the primary task of the government is to promote the will of the people (Thomas 1959: 313). In his publication *A Discourse on the Love of Our Country*, he argues that far from all in England are considered to be free; it was for this reason he praised the French Revolution, and hoped that the same would happened in England in order to fulfill the promise of the Glorious Revolution (Furniss 2006: 58–59). In line with the contract theoretical tradition, he claims that a condition for political liberty is that the citizens themselves are the authors of the laws that they are supposed to obey (Thomas 1959: 318). The exercise of political power is legitimate by virtue of consensus from the citizens.

Wollstonecraft was excited about the French Revolution, at least in its first phase where absolutism was replaced with the assembly of the people. But, when she went to Paris to write about the situation, she was disappointed by the brutality coupled to the implementation of republicanism.

A Vindication of the Rights of Men (1791) was first published anonymously, but as soon as the second edition was published with her own name on the title page she became instantly famous. The book is primarily a reply to Edmund Burke's *Reflections on the Revolution in France* (1790), but also a defense of the ideas of Price. Burke had no confidence in a democratic republic. He thought that most people did not have knowledge and virtues necessary to rule for the best of the society. He also thought that Price was reducing questions concerning political responsibility to questions of personal development and self-realization (Thomas 1959: 321). However, at that time, Wollstonecraft knew more about Burke's writing than the French Revolution (Furniss 2006: 60). Burke is often referred to as the father of modern conservatism. He praises traditions, monarchy, clergy and aristocracy. Monarchy is supposed to be essential because the monarch appears to be in possession of a supernatural and mythical power that forces people to control themselves. Aristocracy and clergy are important to uphold and maintain people's knowledge and morality (Burke 2007: 93). Burke's criticism of the French Revolution is based on the conviction that the Enlightenment's ideal of liberty will eventually lead to a society characterized by individualism and egoism. According to Burke, freedom without tradition will create people whose actions are primarily motivated by their own egoistic preferences (Engster 2001: 579). The danger with revolution is dissolution of traditional norms, which leads to a situation where people no longer have guidelines for right and wrong, good and evil, proper and not proper (Malnes 2007: 15). The women's march on Versailles in October 1789 that forced the royal back to Paris is, according to Burke, the day when general moral conceptions of right and wrong disintegrated (Burke 2007: 95).

Burke is also attacking the rationalization project of the Enlightenment. He believes that it is as equally impossible to conceptualize nature in virtue of clearly defined ideals of beauty, as it is impossible to organize political and social institutions in accordance with rational principles (Malnes 2007). He mocked the national assembly in France and its idea of a constitution based on abstract and universal principles of equality and liberty. While Burke is arguing that the English people already enjoy liberty, a liberty they have inherent from their ancestors, Wollstonecraft is referring to another kind of liberty: namely, the liberty given at birth, which is not institutionalized by any government (Furniss 2006: 60–61). According to

Wollstonecraft, liberty is a birthright arising from the fact that all individuals are rational beings. Liberty is defined as follows:

> The birthright of man … is such a degree of liberty, civic and religious, as is compatible with the liberty of every other individual with whom he is united in a social compact, and the continued existence of that compact (Wollstonecraft 1996: 16–17).

Wollstonecraft is criticizing arbitrary use of power. Individual liberty can only be restricted in order to protect other people's liberty. According to her, Burke's celebration of English liberty is actually a protection of the property rights of the privileged elite. According to Wollstonecraft, inherited property and honorary titles are hindering social progress (Wollstonecraft 2003a: 117). "The demon of property has ever been at hand to encroach on the sacred rights of men and to fence round with awful pomp laws that war with justice" (Wollstonecraft 1996: 17).

Wollstonecraft dreams about a society which is upheld by friendship and equality. She claims that "true happiness arose from the friendship and intimacy which can only be enjoyed by equals; and that charity is not a condescending distribution of alms, but an intercourse of good offices and mutual benefits, founded on respect for justice and humanity" (Wollstonecraft 1996: 19). The French Revolution was, for Wollstonecraft, the event where radical ideas of liberty and equality could be applied in practice. But, when she actually went to Paris she was disappointed. She was not prepared for the terror and carnage. She was threatened because foreigners were persecuted in the continuous search for enemies of the republic. But her relationship to the revolution is ambivalent. In *An Historical and Moral View of the Origin and Progress of the French revolution and the Effect it has Produced in Europe* (1794) she condemned the terror, but at the same time she indicates that violence might be necessary to create an egalitarian society (Furniss 2006).

3 A Vindication of the Rights of Women

A Vindication of the Rights of Women (1792) places the question of gender equality on the philosophical agenda. The early face of the French Revolution resulted in the French declaration of human rights (1798). But, despite such slogans as liberty and equality, civic and political rights were reserved for men. According to Wollstonecraft, this was a betrayal of what she describes as "the glorious principles" that had inspired the revolution. It has been claimed that *A Vindication of the Rights of Women* was written as an attempt to lead the development in France in a more feminist direction (Furniss 2006; Taylor 1992). But, even if Wollstonecraft was inspired by the ideas of liberty, equality and brotherhood, the book is not about the French Revolution. It is an analysis of how being without rights affects the legal and political situation of women. She is also concerned about women's family situation and women's self-esteem and self-perception. One of her main points is that lack of education and lack of opportunities when in comes to political and economic participation prevent women from developing as responsible citizens. In other words, women do not have the opportunity to develop the virtues necessary to exercise their citizenship in a socially responsible way.

However, Wollstonecraft was not the only one who argued for justice for women. Her visions were shared by, for instance, Thomas Paine (1737–1809) and William Goodwin (Taylor 1992: 2). In the well-known *Rights of Men* (1791–1792), Paine argues that men and women should have equal rights and that all citizens should be equal in order to be able to elect the government. This text was published about the same time as the *Vindication of the Rights of Men.* Both Wollstonecraft and Paine argued from the premises that liberty is a human birthright. Different from other revolutionaries at that time, Paine was not an intellectual. He was raised by Quakers, and grew up in a family where people had no, or little, education (Kuklick 1989). He wrote for ordinary people, not to the intellectual elite. *Rights of Men* is, however, considered to be one of the most crucial texts for the development of democratic thought. Paine lived in England, France and America. He experienced both the French and the American revolutions, and he inspired thinkers such as Thomas Jefferson. He criticized monarchy, aristocracy and all kinds of inherited power for reducing the possibility for democracy and the development of a civilized society (Merriam 1899; Walker 2000). He was also cosmopolitan thinker. According to Paine, the two revolutions are necessary tools for a global process of democratization, which in turn leads to less war and more peace on a global level. Democratic societies are more economically effective, and will pave the way for international trade and increased communication and understanding across national borders (Walker 2000: 52, 59).

Wollstonecraft is criticizing both class differences and traditional conceptions of gender roles. She defines both social classes and gender as artificial arrangements that prevent people from achieving moral virtues and that hinder the development of a democratic civilized society. Like Paine and Price, she attacks aristocracy and its inherited conceptions of honor (Wollstonecraft 2003a: 214–217). However, Wollstonecraft claims that inherent fortune and rank create more restrictions for women than for men. Men can at least climb the social ladder by being soldiers or civil servants (Wollstonecraft 2003a: 215). Men without inborn privileges can acquire education that gives them access to professions associated with social status.

Mary Hays, Wollstonecraft's friend and a member of a group of intellectuals associated with Goodwin, published several essays and novels that also argued for women's rights. In *Appeal to the Men of Great Britain on Behalf of Women* (1798), she claims that without education, women are condemned to a life of oppression and dependence. She describes the women's condition as "perpetual babyish" (Mellor 2006: 144). Hays was also an advocate for prostitutes, and states that prostitution was not caused by women's vice, but by men's inclination to seduce naive women (Mellor 2006: 145). The discourse about education was, so to speak, well-established by her time. The debate was initiated by authors Mary Astel, Judith Drake and "Sophia" in the sixteenth century (Rønning Hansen: 1994).

In *A Vindication of the Rights of Women*, much of the space is used to criticize how other authors write about women. Her contemporaries often believed that women were more emotional and less rational than men. Women were therefore, by nature, subordinate to men. Wollstonecraft in particular criticizes Jean-Jacques

Rousseau's ideas of gender-divided education. However, she agrees that women appear more emotional, immature and ignorant than men. But this is caused by culture, not nature. If women and men were given equal rights and opportunities, both sexes would contribute to social and political development. Women would appear as rational and responsible citizens, not only as subjects of men's sexual desires (Rønning and Hansen 1994: 45). Ignorant and emotional women are the products of political, legal and social structures that do not allow them to develop their capabilities, and to make rational and systematic reflections. She claims that women should be educated for responsible citizenship, not only to make them attractive for marriage. Female education has contributed to "render women more artificial, weak characters, than they would otherwise have been: and consequently, more useless members of society" (Wollstonecraft 1988: 22).

Wollstonecraft's vindication of the rights of women is based on both utilitarian and moral psychological arguments. She does not use the concept utilitarianism herself, but she argues that the elimination of female subordination will, in the end, benefit the whole society. The utilitarian argument is that patriarchal social structures prevent the development of a good and civilized society, organized in accordance with rational principles. John Stuart Mill later used the same line of reasoning. In *On the Subjection of Women,* his defense of equality is clearly utilitarian. According to Mill, there is no empirical evidence that a society in which women are oppressed is more beneficial for the community than a society where men and women are equal (Mill 2006). The moral psychological argument is related to the psychological consequences of oppression. According to Wollstonecraft, unjust social relations have created a society of monstrous and unfeeling characters, and people with heartless and artificial emotions (Engster 2001: 581). If women do not have access to formal channels of power, they will instead try to reach their aims through cynical manipulation. Young girls are early taught that power and influence can be achieved by invoking men's appetite (Wollstonecraft 2003a: 99–101). For women, this is both cynical and humiliating, and also risky. Women have power over men only insofar as men find them attractive (Wollstonecraft 2003a). Women need responsibility and empowerment to strengthen their moral character. Increased equality will, in turn, contribute to develop relationships in which men and women respect each other in a new and improved way.

Wollstonecraft's criticism is primarily directed to the wealthiest members of the society. Wealth and inactivity prevent both men and women from developing a moral character. "The comparison with the rich still occurs to me; for when men neglect the duties of humanity, women will follow their example; a common steam hurries them both along with thoughtless celerity" (Wollstonecraft 1988: 64). The working class tends to be idealized because moral character is formed by hard work and struggle. "Happy is it when people have the cares of life to struggle with; for the struggles prevent their becoming a prey to enervating vices, merely from idleness!" (Wollstonecraft 1988: 54). However, Wollstonecraft is surprisingly silent when it comes to the emancipation of working-class women. Nor does she analyze how the oppression of working-class women differs from the oppression of women from the middle-class or upper-class.

4 The Citizenship of Women

As mention in the introduction, Wollstonecraft calls for a revolution in female manners. The kind of revolution she has in mind is primarily a moral revolution which is driven by education, enlightenment and claims of rights, justice and liberty. "Moralists have unanimously agreed that unless virtue be nurtured by liberty, it will never attain due strength" (Wollstonecraft 1988: 191). The revolutions in female manners will necessarily lead to political consequences because it will become apparent that women can make both political and economic contributions in society. Wollstonecraft is however also defending traditional gender roles. She emphasizes that the first duty of all human beings is to develop as rational beings. But after this, the duties of women are primarily related to their roles as mothers and wives.

> Speaking of women at large, their first duty is to themselves as rational creatures, and the next, in point of importance, as citizens, is that, which includes so many, of mother. The rank in life which dispenses with their fulfilling this duty, necessary degrades them by making them mere dolls (Wollstonecraft 1988: 145).

The point is then, if women should be able to educate their children and to take care of the household in a proper way, they need access to a different kind of knowledge (Wollstonecraft 2003a: 102). She asks, how can a woman who does not think be able to take care of her children? (Wollstonecraft 2003a: 121). Women and men have different civic duties, at least for some periods in life, but they are of equal importance for the society (Wollstonecraft 2003a: 95). It is therefore crucial that women are given the opportunity to achieve the knowledge necessary to exercise their citizenship. The most interesting part of her discussion is that she defines domestic work as a civic duty, and that she defines domestic work as equally important as work related to the public sphere. At this point, she seems to be ahead of her time. Later, the feminist movement made recognition of unpaid domestic work one of their most essential claims.

Wollstonecraft is criticizing a society in which women are encouraged to develop vices as cynicism and vanity, instead of reason. She dreams of a society in which both men and women are respected for doing their tasks in a responsible and proper way. She hopes that: "Society will some time or other be so constituted, that man must necessarily fulfill the duties of a citizen, or be despised, and that while he was employed of any of the department of civil life, his wife, also an active citizen, should be equally intent to manage her family, educate her children, and assist her neighbors" (Wollstonecraft 1988: 146).

Women's duties are thereby related to their roles as mothers and wives. But, not every woman is a mother and wife. The responsibility as a mother is also time-limited. Wollstonecraft therefore claims that women should be able to support themselves economically. Economic dependence is a fundamental reason for the oppression of women. The right to participation in the labor market is therefore of crucial importance in order to save women from prostitution (Wollstonecraft 2003a: 222). Since men and women are equal when it comes to mental capacities, there is no reason to exclude women from the professional life: "Women may certainly study the art of healing, and be physicians as well as nurses" (Wollstonecraft 1988: 148).

We have seen that Wollstonecraft's claims for women's rights are based both on moral and political arguments. The point is that rights are necessary in order to make women able to exercise their citizenship in a morally responsible way. This applies both to the public and private sphere. The society should be organized so that all are given opportunities to refine their sense of duty, and contribute to healthy and reasonable social development. According to Wollstonecraft, women will not develop a sense of duty if they are not given any rights (Wollstonecraft 2003a: 217). She is also claiming that women should have access to public offices: "I really think that women ought to have representatives, instead of being arbitrarily governed without having any direct share allowed them in the deliberations of government" (Wollstonecraft 1988: 147).

Wollstonecraft often refers to liberty as the absence of arbitrary power. Within normative political theory it is common to make a distinction between negative and positive liberty. Positive liberty refers to sovereignty and the freedom to self-realization in accordance with a person's rational convictions. Negative liberty is defined as the absence of external force or interference. While positive liberty most often is associated with the republican tradition in normative political theory, negative liberty is associated with the liberal tradition. But as Quentin Skinner points out, a lot was written about liberty in Britain before liberalism was recognized as a common theoretical approach. He is arguing for a third concept of liberty, which was developed by critics of the monarchy under the English civil war (1642–1651). These critics defined liberty as the absence of arbitrary power, a definition that can be traced back to the Roman law and the distinction between a slave (*cervant*) and a free man (*liberi homines*) (Skinner 2009: 86). A free citizen is entitled to act in accordance with his own decisions. A slave is entirely subject to the will of another (Skinner 2002: 249). In the English monarchy, people were forced pay taxes for random reasons, people were arrested without any reason and people were sentenced without a trial. The citizens were not free, but subject to the king's arbitrary use of power (Skinner 2002: 251). According to Skinner, liberty as the absence of arbitrary power is the republican alternative to the classical definition of negative liberty. The classical definition of negative liberty is based on an assumed contradiction between the state and the individual. In the republican tradition, liberty implies free institutions and unhindered public discussions. People are free when they are entitled to participate in the processes of political decision-making (Nilsen 2009: IX). When people are able to make their own laws, there are no contradictions between liberty and a legislative authority (Skinner 2009: 202). But most important, government officials cannot make the law its sole discretion. To be a slave is to be subject to other person's arbitrary will and decisions. Price has formulated a similar definition of liberty. A citizen is free by virtue of not being governed by the arbitrary decisions of another (Walker 2012).

To defend the American colonists' rejection of the British throne, Price claimed that liberty is to live in a self-governed association not subject to decisions made by another over which one has no control (Skinner 2009: 204). It is not unlikely that

Wollstonecraft was inspired by such a pre-liberal conception of liberty. Liberty is referred to as independence from arbitrary decisions and resolutions (Wollstonecraft 2003b: 220). She calls for a society in which women have the right to influence decisions that are of their concern. Women are not only subject to arbitrary power exercised by the government, but also to arbitrary power exercised by their husbands' arbitrary and cultural structures that maintains their dependence. The claim for autonomy applies both to the public life and the family.

5 Wollstonecraft on Education

Wollstonecraft is often referred to as a philosopher of education. But she could have been defined as a moral philosopher or political philosopher as well. Some suggest that she would be better known if she had not been labeled a philosopher of education (Rustad 2003: xiii). Anyway, there is no doubt that her philosophy is driven and motivated by her ideas of education. Enlightenment, knowledge and education are the key to social and political reforms. After she finished her job as a governess with an Irish aristocratic family, she wrote *Thoughts on the Education of Daughters* (1787). In this book, she is inspired by John Locke's *Some Thoughts Concerning Education* (1734). Following the thoughts from Locke, she is arguing for the importance of public education, supported by supervision by the parents. Wollstonecraft warns against both schooling at home and private boarding schools. Children educated at home will often "acquire to high opinion of their own importance, from being allowed to tyrannize over servants, and from the anxiety expressed by most mothers, on the score of manners, who eager to teach the accomplishments of a gentleman, stifle, in their birth, the virtue of a man" (Wollstonecraft 1988: 158). In boarding schools, the children will suffer from lack of care from their parents and the children will use their off-hours in dirty tricks and rottenness (Wollstonecraft 1988: 159). According to Wollstonecraft, the responsibility for education and upbringing should be shared between public day schools and the families. Children should be brought up at home, because home is the place to learn to be caring and to provide tenderness and concern for other people. This is crucial for children to acquire capabilities for friendship and love in their adult lives (Wollstonecraft 2003a: 244). Since Wollstonecraft constantly refers to how harmful it is to be brought up by ignorant, emotional or tyrannical mothers, it's peculiar how she emphasizes the importance of supervising by the parents. I suppose that the family she has in mind is the ideal family, based on friendship and mutual respect.

As we have seen, Wollstonecraft is advocating public day schools, before boarding schools. At public schools, children will learn to recognize each other as equals. Because boarding schools are dependent on the parent's willingness to pay, teachers will work hard to secure children of the richest families admission to the university. Boarding schools will therefore contribute to reproduce and reinforce existing social differences (Wollstonecraft 2003a: 245). Private boarding schools are based on elitism, and prioritize to educate a few bright students at the cost of the many.

This is not to the benefit of the society as a whole (Wollstonecraft 2003a: 244). Wollstonecraft also thinks that girls and boys should study together, so they can learn decencies "which produce modesty, without those sexual distinctions that taint the mind" (Wollstonecraft 1988: 165). The main argument for not having a segregated school is that children should learn to respect each other. The mixing of genders will hopefully make boys less selfish and forceful, and girls less weak and vain. This will make them better prepared for a marriage based on equality and friendship.

Wollstonecraft gives a fairly detailed description of how education should be organized. Elementary school, for children from 5 to 9 years of age, should be free and open to all classes (Wollstonecraft 1988: 168). From the age of nine, those who are intended for domestic employment or mechanical trades should be removed to more practical-oriented schools. Youth with superior abilities should be taught language, natural science, history and politics (Wollstonecraft 1988: 168). The most important point is that also girls need to be taught theoretical knowledge. Those who do not recognize this do not recognize the value of the work women, in fact, are doing. "In public schools, women, to guard against the error of ignorance should be taught the element of anatomy and medicine, not only to enable them to take care of their own health, but to make them rational nurses of their infants, parents, and husbands" (Wollstonecraft 1988: 177).

Wollstonecraft stresses the idea that school is an institution of formation in which the children should be taught virtues that are important to exercising moral good citizenship. Her ideas on education are as much about politics as pedagogy. Her discussion of education should be understood as a premise in an argument for the necessity of social and political reforms which provide women access to the professional life and rights to political participation.

6 Wollstonecraft and Rousseau on Education

In the first parts of *A Vindication of the Rights of Women,* Wollstonecraft is arguing against characteristics of women given by other authors. Much of the discussion is devoted to Jean-Jacques Rousseau's ideas on education. Wollstonecraft respects many of his philosophical ideas. She is an admirer of his anti-elitism and egalitarianism. However, she does not share his skeptical approach to the ideals that characterizes the Age of Enlightenment.

Rousseau claimed that women by nature are weak and passive. Conversely, the nature of men is to be rational, active and creative. Men and women are created different to complement each other in their respective roles. The relationship between the sexes is, so to speak, complementary, but far from egalitarian. In *Emile* (1762), or *Education*, the differences between the sexes is described as the following:

> In the union of the sexes each alike contributes to the common end, but in different ways. From this diversity springs the first difference which may be observed between man and woman in their moral relations. The man should be strong and active; the woman should be

> weak and passive; the one must have both the power and the will; it is enough that the other should offer little resistance. When this principle is admitted, it follows that woman is specially made for man's delight. If man in his turn ought to be pleasing in her eyes, the necessity is less urgent (Rousseau 1921: 353).

According to Rousseau, masculinity is associated with transcendence, reason and development. Women should bring out the best in men by help and support. The difference between men and women is, according to Rousseau, neither a human invention or based on prejudices, but completely rational (Rousseau 1994: 176). The aim of the education of children is to cultivate the natural differences between the sexes. Boys and girls should be prepared to fulfill their different roles later in life. Boys should be educated to become free and independent citizens. They should be encouraged to autonomous thinking and not to become slaves of habits and prejudices. The education of boys should therefore be as unrestricted as possible (Nagel 1999: 132). In contrast to boys, girls should, from early childhood, learn that their duties as women are to please, comfort and obey their husbands.

Wollstonecraft agrees that education should be aimed at cultivating natural capacities. However, since the mental capabilities of human beings are equal, this is rather an argument for the education of both sexes together. She claims that the aim of education should be to give back to women the ability for rational reasoning that the culture has taken away from them. Furthermore, if Rousseau is right that education should prepare women for their role as wives and mothers, his own ideas of education would not do the job. Wollstonecraft cannot understand why girls should be taught the mistresses' art of seduction, if the aim of education should be to prepare them for the role as a mother and a wife (Wollstonecraft 1988: 91). She thinks Rousseau's flawed logic has to do with his sensibility for the charm of women and his inclination to appeal to the emotions of his readers. He is a seducer who does not call for reflection. "And thus making us feel whilst dreaming that we reason, erroneous conclusions are left in the mind" (Wollstonecraft 1988: 91).

Rousseau is known for his skepticism toward the Enlightenment ideals of reason and progress. Human beings are not by definition rational beings. He thinks that reflection is contrary to nature and compares the thinking human being with a perverse animal (Rousseau 1984: 37). Like Hobbes and Locke, Rousseau has developed a theory of how human societies would look like without a state. Unlike Hobbes and Locke, however, Rousseau's state of nature is not characterized by battles and competition. Rather, the opposite: The state of nature is a condition of peace in which people are happy because there is no shortage of goods, and because those who live there do not know how to speak and think. Wollstonecraft is highly critical of his celebration of the pre-cognitive condition.

> I say unsound; for to assert that a state of nature is preferable to civilization, in all its possible perfection, is, in other words, to arraign supreme wisdom; and the paradoxical exclamation, that God has made all things right, and error has been introduced by the creature, whom he formed knowing what he formed, is as philosophical as impious (Wollstonecraft 1988: 14).

Wollstonecraft believes that humans are given the capability to rational thinking in order to be able to create something good. Then it becomes both absurd and impious to downgrade the importance of reason. Reason is a gift that gives human beings a capacity to rise above the state of limited sensation. Keeping women in a condition of ignorance, and encouraging them to cultivate sensuality and emotions are against the order of nature.

7 The Religious Foundation of Wollstonecraft's Feminism

In the feminist reception, the religious dimension in Wollstonecraft's works is often underestimated. *A Vindication of the Rights of Women* is most often interpreted in the humanist tradition of the Enlightenment, and not as a religious text. But her ideas are deeply rooted in her religious convictions. The call for a revolution in female manners is first and foremost an appeal that women should reconcile with the creator (Taylor 2006: 77). She claims that human rights should apply to both sexes because every human being has the right to develop as a rational being. All human beings have a duty to God to develop the ability to rational thinking and to improve one's moral character. This is also a condition for achieving eternal salvation in paradise. Oppression of women is inconsistent with God's command. Enslaving women on earth means denying them access to heavenly paradise.

Wollstonecraft's arguments for equality are also based on her religious convictions. There is reason to believe that she was inspired by the rational dissenters and their liberal, rational and individualistic interpretations of religious beliefs. The dissenters were opponents of the church of England and defended a kind of Protestantism mixed with psychological ideas from Locke, Newtonian cosmology, rational moral philosophy, and ideas of social and political reforms (Taylor 2006: 108). They rejected the idea of original sin. They also believed that humans are good by nature and that all humans can develop toward faultlessness. Liberal values as autonomy and tolerance were given a religious foundation. They argued, for instance, that tolerance follows from the fact that the individual is his or her own authority when it comes to questions of faith. With Price and the dissenters, Wollstonecraft argued that every human should have the right to act in accordance with his or her own convictions. This is the only way humans can act honorably and from virtue (Taylor 2006: 109).

As already mentioned, Wollstonecraft believed that an equal right to education is the first step toward emancipation and legal reforms amendment that will give women access to paid work and public offices. However, education is not only a mean to emancipation, but also is necessary for salvation (Wollstonecraft 2003a: 81).

If both men and women have been given a soul to develop, to encourage women to cultivate their emotions before their reason is not in accordance with the plan of nature. Wollstonecraft upholds that since a women have an immortal soul, she also have an intellect to be developed (Wollstonecraft 2003a: 95).

8 Reception and Criticism

The work of Wollstonecraft has been subject of different interpretations. Because of her definition of liberty as the absence of arbitrary power, her work can be associated with what Skinner defines as the pre-liberal British republican tradition in political theory. But, because of her politicization of family and class and her criticism of private property, she is also characterized as a pioneer of radical socialism (Taylor 1992). Wollstonecraft's politicization of class and family contradicts traditional liberal thought where the market and the family are considered as belonging to the private sphere of the society, in other words, spheres for individual actions that should be protected from political interference. However, Susan Ferguson claims that Wollstonecraft's critique of private property cannot be explained within the framework of socialist ideology. What she it fact is criticizing is the aristocracy, a social structure in which property and privileges are inherited. But she is not arguing for the elimination of private property as such. Ferguson argues that Wollstonecraft is more aligned with Paine, who claimed that aristocratic privileges "stood in the way of a family-based economy of artisans and farmers with relatively equal holdings of private property" (Ferguson 1999: 434). Wollstonecraft, for instance, advises that large farmlands should be divided into smaller farms (Ferguson 1999: 438). This is fairly consistent with Adam Smith's *Wealth of Nations* (Ferguson 1999: 434).

Scholars also disagree on whether Wollstonecraft's work contributes to a politicizing of the family. As mention, within classic liberal thought, the family is regarded as a private institution. The family should therefore be protected from the exercise of political power. Locke is arguing that political power should be distinguished from natural power, which is exemplified by the power of the father over his child, the power of the husband over his wife and the power of the master over his servant (Locke 1993: 115). Wollstonecraft is, however, known for being a pioneer when it comes to the feminist critique of the division between the private and the public spheres of society. It's obvious that she challenges this distinction in some ways, for example, when she emphasizes that unpaid domestic work is useful to society. She also claims the "contract" that regulates social relations in the public sphere should apply to the private sphere as well (MacKenzie 1993: 48). Consequently, principles of liberty and equality should apply to all areas of social life, to the family as well to public life. According to Wollstonecraft, the family is like the state in miniature.

But not all agree that Wollstonecraft challenges the structural distinction between public and private realms. For example, she never denies that women's duties are associated with the care of children and the running of a household. Even though she argues that liberty and equality should apply for the private sphere, she does not discard the existence of a natural sexual distinction of labor (Ferguson 1999: 48). She is not analyzing how the liberal division between the public sphere and private sphere has been used to maintain traditional dualistic conceptions of what is naturally feminine and masculine. Feminists have pointed out that Wollstonecraft ignores that the division of sexes according to duties derives from the division between the public and the private that is the root of women's subordination (MacKenzie 1993: 37). The claim that families should be governed by the same principles as public life is based on ideas of what makes women better mothers and wives.

However, what is obvious is that Wollstonecraft has inspired later thinking on the relationship between private and public, as well as on justice within the family. Her reasoning is reflected in John Stuart Mill's *On the Subjection of Women* (1869) which is a harsh criticism of the legal oppression of women of his time. According to Mill, the family is a school in tyranny and male egotism that contribute to the reproduction of male domination from one generation to the next. Like Wollstonecraft, he attacks political structures and social cultures where women can exercise power only by flattery and seduction. This is a situation that makes women incapable of claiming their rights (Mill 2006: 85–86). Mill argues that if the family should be a school in virtues adapted to a modern society based on equality and justice, then spouses must be entitled to equality before the law (Mill 2006: 91–92). It is possible to assume that Mill's reasoning is influenced by Wollstonecraft's *A Vindication of the Rights of Women.*

Wollstonecraft ends her main work by saying: "Let women share the rights and she will emulate the virtues of man" (Wollstonecraft 2003a: 292). It has therefore been stated that her ideas do not appeal to contemporary feminist political theory. She is criticized, for instance, for not doing anything else than simply adding women to the liberal classic tradition and claiming that women should be treated as men, or as they were men (Engster 2001: 578). Catriona MacKenzie exemplifies this line of criticism by a reference to Moira Gatens, who claims that Wollstonecraft uncritically assumes that the liberal notion of equality and the reasons that ground it are sex-neutral. With this, she ignores that the idea of the equal citizen is constituted in opposition to those affective virtues associated with women. According to Gatens, Wollstonecraft's attempt to apply gender-neutral notions both on private and public relations, in fact, underestimates the ethical significance of virtues traditionally associated with women (Mackenzie 1993: 37). This kind of criticism is conducted within the framework of discussions between liberal feminists and feminist-care theorists (Holst 2009: 93). The early feminist movement was founded on values associated with Enlightenment ideals of liberty and equality. Some contemporary feminists are, however, critical of these values, because liberal values are supposed to be modeled by experiences and activities traditionally associated with male citizens and relations within the public sphere of society. Liberal values are defined in opposition to moral virtues associated with female experience and activities, which are mainly virtues embedded in the activities of care.

Care theorists have constructed ethical theories based on the moral significance of the virtues and modes of reflection embedded in relations of care.

Unlike liberal theories of justice which are based on universal and abstract principles, the ethics of care is taking contextual and situated moral thinking into account (Gilligan 1992; Held 1995). The philosopher Virginia Held argues that the ethics of care makes people better able to protect the vulnerable, reduce poverty and to take future generation into account than liberal theories of justice (Held 1995). Like Burke, she argues that liberal values encourage egoism and individualism.

Wollstonecraft is also critizised for treating emotions as fleeting and unstable and therefore unqualified as the foundation of moral reflections. It has been claimed that she is simply repeating traditional philosophical approaches on emotions. She is arguing that society should be based on reason, and discards Burke's analysis of the ideal of the Enlightenment as individualistic and selfish (Engster 2001: 579). There are, however, those who claim that to interpret Wollstonecraft's ideas as a rejection of the moral significance of emotion is mistaken (Engster 2001; MacKenzie 1993). As Daniel Engster points out, her ideas can enrich current debates on the relationship between care and justice. He argues that Wollstonecraft does not discharge the moral importance of emotion per se, but the unnatural and unhealthy which develop from unjust social relations (Engster 2001: 581). According to Engster, Wollstonecraft's ideas should be used to bridge the ethics of care and the ethics of justice. She argues that relations of care have to grow out of mutual respect and sympathy, which cannot be developed without political and social equality (Engster 2001: 584).

According to Wollstonecraft, social and political inequality is the seedbed of pathological social relations which make women unable to take care of their children and loved ones. A just society will lead to more care both in the public and private sphere. As Catriona MacKenzie points out, Wollstonecraft stresses the importance of a conception of morality which not only recognize women's ability to rational thinking, but also their right to develop healthy moral relations, based on friendship and mutual respect, to those close to them (MacKenzie 1993: 36).

References

Aasen, E. (2010). *Opplysningstidens kvinner*. Oslo: Pax forlag A/S.

Burke, E. (2007). *Betraktinger over revolusjonen I Frankrike*. Oslo: Pax forlag A/S.

Engster, D. (2001). Mary Wollstonecraft's nurturing liberalism: Between an ethic of justice and care. *The American Political Science Review, 95*(3), 577–588.

Ferguson, S. (1999). The radical ideas of Mary Wollstonecraft. *Canadian Journal of Political Science, 32*(3), 427–450.

Furniss, T. (2006). Mary Wollstonecraft's French Revolution. In *Cambridge companion to Mary Wollstonecraft*. Cambridge Online, Cambridge University Press.

Gatens, M. (1986). Rousseau and Wollstonecraft: Natur vs. reason. *The Australian Journal of Philosophy, 64*(1), 1–15.

Gilligan, C. (1992). *In a different voice, psychological theory and women's development*. Cambridge, MA: Harvard University Press.

Held, V. (1995). Non-Contractual Society. In P. Weiss & M. Friedman (Eds.), *Feminism and community*. Philadelphia: Temple University Press.

Holst, C. (2009). *Hva er Feminisme?* Oslo: Universitetsforlaget.

Janes, R. M. (1978). On the reception of Mary Wollstonecraft's: A vindication of the rights of women. *Journal of the History of Ideas, 39*(2), 293–302.

Jones, C. (2006). Mary Wollstonecraft's *Vindications* and their political tradition. In *Cambridge companion to Wollstonecraft*. Cambridge Online, Cambridge University Press.

Kuklick, B. (1989). *Paine. Political writings, Cambridge texts in the history of political thought*. Cambridge: Cambridge University Press.

Locke, J. (1993). *Two treatise of government* [1689] (M. Goldie, Ed.). London: Everyman.
MacKenzie, C. (1993). Reason and sensibility: The ideal of women's self-governance in the writing of Mary Wollstonecraft. *Hypatia, 8*(4), 35–55.
Malnes, R. (2007). *Innledning I Edmund Burke, Betrakninger over revolusjonen I Frankrike*. Oslo: Pax forlag A/S.
Mellor, A. (2006). Mary Wollstonecraft's *A Vindication of the Rights of Woman* and the women writers of her day. In *Cambridge companion to Mary Wollstonecraft*. Cambridge Online, Cambridge University Press.
Merriam, C. E., Jr. (1899). Thomas Paine's political theories. *Political Science Quarterly, 14*(3), 389–403.
Mill, J. S. (2006). *Kvinneundertrykkelsen*. Oslo: Pax forlag A/S.
Nagel, A. H. (1999). Mary Wollstonecraft (1759–1797) – Rettighetsforsvareren. In *Kjønnsperspektiver i filosofihistorien*. Oslo: Pax forlag A/S.
Nilsen, H. (2009). Quentin Skinner og politikken. In Q. Skinner (Ed.), *Vilkårlig makt. Essays om politisk frihet*. Oslo: Res Publica.
Price. R. (1776). Observation on the nature of civil liberty. http://www.constitution.org/price/price_3.htm
Rønning, A. H., & Hanssen, T. (1994). *Feminismens klassikere*. Oslo: Pax forlag.
Rousseau, J. J. (1921). *Emile, or on education*. (trans: Barbara, Foxley). London/Toronto/New York: J.M Dent and Sons. http://oll.Libertyfund.org/titles/2256
Rousseau, J. J. (1984). *Om ulikheten mellom menneskene – dens opprinnelse og grunnlag*. Oslo: Aschehaug Forlag.
Rousseau, J. J. (1994). Fra Emile, eller om oppdragelsen. In A. H. Rønning & T. Hanssen (Eds.), *Feminismens klassikere*. Oslo: Pax forlag.
Richardson, A. (2006). Mary Wollstonecraft on education. In *Cambridge companion to Mary Wollstonecraft*. Cambridge Online, Cambridge University Press.
Rustad, L. (2003). Innledende essay. In *Mary Wollstonecraft, Et forsvar for kvinners rettigheter*. Oslo: Bokklubbens kulturbibliotek.
Skinner, Q. (2002). A third concept of liberty. In *Proceedings of the British Academy* (Vol. 117, pp. 237–268). Oxford: The British Academy.
Skinner, Q. (2009). *Vilkårlig makt. Essays om politisk frihet*. Oslo: Res Publica.
Svendsen, L. (2009). Mary Wollstonecraft. In S. Lars (Red.), *Liberalisme*. Oslo: Universitetsforlaget.
Taylor, B. (2006). The religious foundation of Mary Wollstonecraft's Feminism. In *Cambridge companion to Mary Wollstonecraft*. Cambridge Online, Cambridge University Press.
Taylor, B., & Taylor, B. (1992). Mary Wollstonecraft and the wild wish of early feminism. *History Workshop, 33*, 197–219.
Thomas, D. O. (1959). Richard price and Edmund Burke: The duty to participate in government. *Philosophy, 34*(131), 303–322.
Walker, T. C. (2000). The forgotten prophet: Tom Paine's cosmopolitanism and international relations. *International Studies Quarterly, 44*, 51–72.
Wollstonecraft, M. (1988). In P. Carol (Ed.), *A vindication of the rights of women* (2nd ed.). New York/London: W. W. Norton & Co.
Wollstonecraft, M. (1996). *The vindication of the rights of men*. Cambridge: Cambridge University Press.
Wollstonecraft, M. (2003a). *Et forsvar for kvinners rettigheter* (T. Hansen, Trans.). Oslo: Bokklubbens kulturbibliotek.
Wollstonecraft, M. (2003b). Et forsvar for menneskerettighetene. In S. Lars (Red.), *Liberalisme*. Oslo: Universitetsforlaget.

Karl Marx – A Utopian Socialist?

Jørgen Pedersen

> In one way or the other, the most important events of our times lead back to one man – Karl Marx. (Leopold Schwarzschild, Marx-biographer)

Karl Marx (1818–1883) was a politician, philosopher, economist and journalist.[1] He wrote *The Manifesto of the Communist Party,* one of the most influential political works in history; *Economic and Philosophic Manuscripts,* an inspiration to left-wing philosophers through much of the twentieth century; and *Capital,* a critique of modern economic thinking. He also wrote a great number of newspaper articles published on the continent and in the USA. In various ways these writings formulate a radical critique of capitalism and central liberal institutions.

Marx shaped his critique at a time when the consequences of the industrial revolution were starting to emerge: first in England, later on the continent. In rural areas the population grew at a faster rate than agricultural production, leaving many people with no work. At the same time, the great estates were being taken over by a new type of owners. Capitalist citizens, focusing on profit, replaced the patriarchal aristocrats, who had felt a certain sense of responsibility for their subjects. The factories that gradually emerged were only able to absorb some of the poor and homeless. This created frustration on two fronts: The years between 1800 and 1850 were prone to frequent farmers' rebellions, and in the urban areas the negative consequences of work in the factories—monotonous, strenuous labour, oftentimes in 12–14 h shifts—gradually became evident. The result was social unrest, in the form of an increase in crime and social instability.

In England these developments resulted in the establishment of labour unions and cooperatives fighting for, among other things, universal suffrage and secret elections. The necessary basis for an organised workers' movement was not yet

---

Translated from Norwegian by Linn Elise Kjerland.

[1] I thank Nils Gilje and Jonas Jakobsen for comments on this paper.

J. Pedersen (✉)
Department of Philosophy, University of Bergen, Bergen, Norway
e-mail: Jorgen.Pedersen@svt.uib.no

G. Fløistad (ed.), *Philosophy of Justice*, Contemporary Philosophy: A New Survey 12, 275
DOI 10.1007/978-94-017-9175-5_16, © Springer Science+Business Media Dordrecht 2015

present on the continent. France, however, had its revolutionary tradition, still fighting for power to free the working classes. In Germany revolutionary societies were established in accordance with the French models.

Marx did not become acquainted with the revolutionary movements until the 1840s. After studying law and philosophy in Bonn and Berlin, he received his doctorate degree in philosophy in 1841. Due to his involvement with a group of left-wing radical philosophers who were deeply influenced by Hegel, Marx found it impossible to get a job as an academic. He started to work as a journalist and his interest in the living conditions of the growing working class increased. This interest became more evident when Marx in 1844 started his collaboration with Friedrich Engels (1820–1895), who, to a much greater extent, had seen the consequences of capitalism up close. Engels was the son of a textiles manufacturer and factory owner, and had in-depth knowledge of social economics.

Marx had an ambivalent attitude towards the revolutionary movements and the thoughts these were based on. He was especially interested in thinkers like Henri de Saint-Simon (1760–1825), Charles Fourier (1772–1837) and Robert Owen (1772–1856), all quite influential in the early development of socialism. Marx credits these thinkers with having pointed out the contradictions between the social classes, and for having played an important part in the enlightenment of workers. They did, however, represent a return to a way of thinking that Hegel had left for dead. According to Hegel, philosophy cannot teach how the world *ought* to be, philosophy's contribution relates to revealing how the world *is* (Hegel 2006: 36). Marx made this motive his own, and used it to distance himself from what he called utopian socialism and its attempt to come up with a new way to organise society (Marx 2008a).

Marx's aim thus was not to tell the working class how it *ought* to act, but rather to describe the sort of force it *is*. The basis for changing the world is not subjective or moral, but realistic and scientific.[2] This was undoubtedly Marx's ambition. Whether he succeeded with this or not I shall discuss briefly in conclusion.

Marx's sharp criticism of the utopian socialists notwithstanding, they remained an important resource for his reflections. With German philosophy and political economy, the utopian socialists represent the three sources of Marxism (Lenin 1913: 8).[3] Marx's way of combining these sources was an important reason for why his theory received such great following. He created a socialism that was revolutionary, historical and scientifically founded.

In what follows I will assume a chronological approach and first discuss Marx's earlier writings, that is, all the texts that were written until and including 1846. Of particular importance here is the critique of liberal political rights as presented in *On the Jewish Question*, as well as the critique of estranged labour which Marx discusses in *Economic and Philosophic Manuscripts,* a text written in 1844, but not

[2] In *The German Ideology* Marx writes: "Communism is for us not a *state of affairs* which is to be established, an *ideal* to which reality [will] have to adjust itself. We call communism the *real* movement which abolishes the present state of things. The conditions of this movement result from the premises now in existence (marxist.org/german-ideology)."

[3] For a more extensive analysis of how Marx combines the three sources see Cohen (2000).

published until 1932. I will then discuss Marx's theory of historical materialism. The early beginnings of this part of Marx's authorship we find in *The German Ideology* from 1845 to 1846. However, the *Preface to a Contribution to the Critique of Political Economy* from 1859 gives the best vantage point for understanding the theory. During the final phase of his life, Marx's interests turn to social economics. *Capital* is the seminal work from this period and is seen by many as his main work. Against the backdrop of this discussion of some of his most important writings, I briefly introduce Marx's concept of communism. In conclusion, I sketch a *real-historical* and intellectual history of reception, before I discuss the most important criticisms of Marx's position.[4]

1 On the Jewish Question

After receiving his doctorate, Marx attempted to define his own philosophical position in relation to Hegel and the other left-wing Hegelians he came to know in Berlin. The left-wing Hegelians had gained influence with their critique of religion, but Marx claimed that they did not draw the proper conclusions from this criticism. Rather than limiting themselves to a critique of religion, a critique of capitalist society was necessary; such a society, Marx claimed, keeps human beings from realising their potential.

In *On the Jewish Question* (1843), Marx polemicises against Bruno Bauer, a radical liberal Young Hegelian, who had addressed the question of how the Jews could become politically liberated and gain political freedom. Prussia had passed a law in 1816 that greatly limited the rights of Jews in relation to Christians. This sparked an angered debate on the Jewish question. Bauer claimed that the Jews could only gain their freedom through renouncing their religion. Bauer considered any and all religion to represent an obstacle to liberation, and in his version of the secular state there was no room for religious practice.

In his answer to Bauer, Marx introduces a distinction between political and human liberation (Marx (a)). Political freedom is gained through giving individuals rights and liberties. Based on this distinction Marx claims, against Bauer, that political liberation may be achieved in societies where religion is strong, and he points to the USA as a relevant example. Political liberation is not, however, in any way sufficient for achieving human liberation, according to Marx. It may even become an obstacle to genuine human liberation. The argument goes as follows: The premise for liberal views on justice based on individual rights is that human beings are in need of protection against other individuals. Freedom is understood as freedom from others interfering in one's own private affairs. "The limits within which anyone can act *without harming* someone else are defined by law, just as the boundary between two fields are determined by a boundary post" (Marx (a): 12).

[4] The historical-biographical account in this introduction is based on Wheen (2001).

According to Marx, however, such an understanding of freedom does not take into consideration that true freedom is positively realised in community with others. Thinking of freedom as freedom from interference by others entails the risk of overlooking that true human liberation may only be realised through genuine community with others (Wolff 2006: 128–129). Marx claims that Bauer is not radical enough by far. Bauer simply makes the religion-based state the aim of his criticism, he does not criticise the state as such (Marx (a)). Marx considers it necessary to criticise the very nature of the state, and thus to pose a different question from the one Bauer poses: the question of the conditions for human liberation (Marx (a)).

Marx does not say, however, that political liberation is not a good thing. He writes:

> Political emancipation is, of course, a big step forward. True, it is not the final form of human emancipation in general, but it is the final form of human emancipation within the hitherto existing world order (Marx (a): 7).

Marx's liberal critics have often overlooked this amplification and claimed that Marx rejects liberal rights, but this is based on a misunderstanding. As G. A. Cohen has pointed out, one might rather say that Marx does not consider the declaration and enforcement of individual rights as necessary or sufficient conditions for the realisation of a good society. They are not necessary as it is possible to realise a good society without declaring and enforcing such rights. And they are not sufficient; we know of societies where such rights are declared and enforced but which are, nevertheless, not good (Cohen and Matravers 2009).

Marx does not clarify systematically what he means by human liberation. There are, however, suggestions: To work for human liberation is to attack "the expression of man's *separation* from … himself and from other men" (Marx (a): 7), a theme which Marx was to pursue in his coming works.

2 Alienation in the Economic and Philosophic Manuscripts

Alienation is the most important concept in the *Economic and Philosophic Manuscripts*. Marx thus builds on a theme that was initially discussed within theology and later in the tradition of contract theory, before being given a more systematic significance by Hegel (Schacht 1970: 7–17). By alienation, Hegel means quite generally that something that is a part of a human being becomes alien to it. Feuerbach's critique of religion in *Das Wesen des Christentums* (1841) builds on Hegel and echoes the position we have seen Bauer taking in *On the Jewish Question*. Feuerbach, however, goes deeper, and his critique gains far greater significance. Feuerbach considers God to be a human creation inasmuch as He has been given human characteristics such as kindness, wisdom and love, characteristics that consequently become alien to humans. The greater the kindness, wisdom and love God is imbued with, the lesser the human being. Thus is shaped the particular understanding of alienation that Marx picks up: Something that ought to be in correspondence with the individual is projected out as alien, and the alienated object (God in Feuerbach's version) turns against the individual with oppressive force.

Marx takes over this model, but uses it in a different way as he claims that Feuerbach does not see the underlying cause as to why religion plays an alienating role in human lives. Thus Marx develops his perspective of alienation and, in addition to religious alienation, talks about political and economic alienation (Langslet 1963: 29). Marx writes:

> Man makes religion, religion does not make man. Religion is, indeed, the self-consciousness and self-esteem of man who has either not yet won through to himself, or has already lost himself again. But *man* is no abstract being squatting outside the world. Man is *the world of man*—state, society. This state and this society produce religion, which is an inverted consciousness of the world, because they are an inverted world (Marx (f)).

So the state and, in the last instance, society, create the need for religion. In *A Contribution to the Critique of Hegel's Philosophy of Right* from 1843, Marx pointed out that religion is only an expression of the real misery that is found in economic conditions. Religion becomes "the opium of the people" because people live under unworthy social conditions (Marx (f)). Religion soothes the pain inflicted on individuals by the social and economic conditions, and keeps people from rising up and rebelling against their unworthy living conditions. These conditions are perpetuated by a state apparatus. The state thus becomes an expression of the alienation that may only be done away with through changing the economic conditions.

Marx starts out using the basic model of alienation: The state, which should correspond with the individual, becomes an abstract idea that turns against the individual who experiences this as oppression. Herein also lies a critique of Hegel. Hegel distinguished between civil society and the state. In civil society the individual may, according to Hegel, legitimately pursue his or her self-interest, while the state represents the sphere in which the interests of the community are realised. The problem is that the state as community remains an illusion. Rather than facilitating a true community, the state remains alien to the individual (Marx (e)). Marx is, however, not quite as clear with regard to why the state appears as alien. It seems, however, reasonable to relate this to the social class conditions and thus to the notion that the state is controlled by the landowning classes. We have thus arrived at a form of alienation that may explain the other two forms of alienation: Economic alienation as concretely expressed through estranged labour.

In the most famous chapter in *Economic and Philosophic Manuscripts*, Marx discusses estranged labour. Again the basic model of alienation is pursued, on a general level as well as when it comes to the more concrete results of alienation. Labour is in fact an integral part of human nature, and under capitalism it is made into something external which turns against the individual and becomes alienating.

More concretely, Marx talks about the worker as alienated in four ways. The worker is alienated from the product of his labour, from the act of producing, from himself as a species-being and from his fellow beings. He is alienated from the product in that the product he processes through his work immediately is taken from him and given to the owner of the means of production. When this product—initially a part of the worker because he works on it—is taken from him, it turns against him and becomes alien to him. "The object which labour produces—labour's product—confronts it as *something alien,* as a *power independent* of the producer" (Marx (c)). Marx is not only interested in the objects being produced. He is primarily concerned that the worker under capitalism creates a whole world of objects that do not belong to him, but to the capitalist. This is why Marx points out that "the more the worker spends himself, the more powerful becomes the alien world of objects which he creates over and against himself, the poorer he himself—his inner world—becomes, the less belongs to him as his own" (Marx (d)).

Next, the worker is alienated from the act of producing. Imagine a worker standing along the assembly line, performing purely mechanical work. The work he performs is alien to him because the product is estranged from him, but he also becomes alienated in the very production process as he has the capacity for much more creative forms of work. The work itself becomes external to the worker, it gives him no challenge or pleasure, he "does not feel content but unhappy, … he mortifies his body and ruins his mind" (Marx (d)).

As a species, human beings have, according to Marx in *Economic and Philosophic Manuscripts,* an essence. And the way to realise this human essence is through labour. Labour is the key to human realisation of essence as a species-being, and labour consists of processing nature. Through processing nature man can realise himself. However, the way society is constructed may destroy this possibility of self-realisation through processing nature. And this is what happens in capitalism. The way work is organised alienates human beings from the product and from the act of producing, and thus from themselves as species-beings. "In tearing away from man the object of his production, therefore, estranged labour tears from him his species-life" (Marx (d)).

It follows from the first three forms of alienation that the individual is also alienated from his fellow beings. "One man is estranged from the other, as each of them is from man's essential nature," Marx writes (Marx (d)), and points to how the fundamental conditions related to the organisation of labour also influence interhuman relations. Because labour is so central to human lives, it is impossible to maintain a good relation to one's self and other human beings in a society where labour has become estranged.

The fundamental cause of alienation in a religious, political and economic sense is private property, and Marx is concerned with private ownership of means of production.[5] When private capitalists own the means of production, these means will be used to exploit the workers. Here we see the rough outlines of Marx's theory of social classes. The class that owns the means of production exploits the class that is forced to sell its labour. Marx does not, however, have—as opposed to the utopian socialists—much to say about the alternative to capitalism in his early works. It is clear that Marx uses the concept of communism as the kind of society which will replace capitalism, and that a communist society is a society without alienation. But Marx is very concerned with not drawing a detailed picture of what such a society would look like. The workers must accomplish the transition from capitalism to communism, the transition must come about through a revolution, and the working class must shape the post-capitalist society.

[5] An important new thinking of the concept of alienation may be found in Jaeggi (2005). The book will be published in English in 2014.

3 Historical Materialism[6]

Historical materialism is a theory about historical change. Marx builds on Hegel and assumes that this change will happen dialectically. This entails that all that happens will do so through unfolding its inner nature in an outer form, and when the inner nature is wholly unfolded, it will be transformed and becomes something new (Cohen 2000: 48). According to Hegel the consciousness of freedom is what changes. Historical development is a development towards an ever greater consciousness of freedom.

Marx finds the dialectical method convincing, unlike the assumption that history is a process towards greater consciousness of freedom. History is not, according to Marx, primarily about how we think or what ideas we have, but about how we produce what we need to survive. "It is not the consciousness of men that determines their existence, but their social existence that determines their consciousness (Marx (c))".[7] Marx distinguishes between five basic modes of production throughout the history of humanity: The Asiatic, the ancient, the feudal, the capitalist/bourgeois, and the communist. With the exception of the latter, all these modes of production have built-in oppositions that make them destined to be replaced by new modes of production (Marx (c)).

The modes of production are characterised by how the profits from the production is shared by the producers. In the Asian mode the profits belonged to the despot and were collected through taxes and forced labour. The entire population was enslaved by the despot. In the ancient mode of production there was also a class of slave owners, so that the slaves could be bought and sold, and the profits from production belonged to the slave owner. In the feudal mode of production the worker was bound to the land and could not be sold or bought. The profits belonged to the feudal lord, who, through his ownership of the land, had a right to a share of the harvest. In capitalism the worker is for the first time free to sell his own labour, but the capital owner takes the surplus value created by the workers. A characteristic of all these modes of production is that they are marred by exploitation, and that there is an internal oppositional relation between the exploiter and the exploited. This relation is what towards the end of a given mode of production will lead to the sharpening of these oppositions, and the current production mode will have to give way to a new mode of production.

[6] Marx uses the notion of materialist conception of history, but in keeping with the secondary literature I have been using in this study I will use the concept of historical materialism. In addition to *The German Ideology* and *Preface to a Critique of Political Economy*, the historical chapters in *Capital, The Communist Manifesto* and Marx' writings on French politics are the best sources for an understanding of historical materialism.

[7] In the afterword of the second edition of *Capital* Marx praises Hegel for having developed the principles of dialectics before pointing out that "With [Hegel] it is standing on its head. It must be turned right side up again, if you would discover the rational kernel within the mystical shell" (Marx 2008b: 11).

In order to better understand the dynamics of this process of development, Marx uses the concepts of productive forces and relations of production. The productive forces are used in a production process. These are partly tools, machines, and raw materials, but also labour power, including the worker's physical power, knowledge and skills. The relations of production are economic power relations and include the power, or lack thereof, that people possess over production means and labour power (Cohen 1986: 12–13). The decisive factor here is Marx's claim that conflicts will arise between the productive forces and the relations of production which will lead to a new mode of production. Marx writes:

> At a certain stage of development, the material productive forces of society come into conflict with the existing relations of production or—this merely expresses the same thing in legal terms—with the property relations within the framework of which they have operated hitherto. From forms of development of the productive forces these relations turn into their fetters. Then begins an era of social revolution, the changes in the economic foundation lead sooner or later to the transformation of the whole immense superstructure (Marx (g)).

Marx claims that the productive forces grow continuously, and that they are the driving forces, or what creates the dynamics of history. The productive forces not only include technology, but also the workers' skills. These skills include, among other things, the organisation of the work process and will lead to ever better and closer cooperation between the workers (Marx (e)). As the productive forces develop, ownership becomes increasingly expensive. The number of capitalists gradually decreases, and capital will accumulate in a few hands. As production increases and the exploitation of workers worsens, cooperation between workers improves. Development becomes marked by increased exploitation and greater concentration of capital on the one hand, and improved cooperation between the exploited workers on the other. So we keep getting fewer, but richer, capitalists and increasing cohesiveness among workers. At one point the oppositions will become so strong that the workers will rebel against the current production conditions.

Capitalism thus creates the conditions for the transition to a new mode of production. The development of the productive forces leads to increases in production, and thus is created the material foundation on which the communist society may build. Capitalism also causes the emergence of the working class and thereby creates the class that will enable the transition to a new mode of production. With the coming of the communist mode of production, the oppositions cancel each other and a society without exploitation may become a reality (Marx (g)).

The last quote above ends with a concept of which we have said nothing so far: the superstructure. Marx includes the legal and political institutions, as well as the religious and ideological convictions in a society, in what he calls the superstructure. The institutions are the nation's laws, its legal system and its parliamentary procedures. The superstructure is thus determined by the economic foundation. That is, the legal and political institutions in a society protect the interests of the ruling class.

With historical materialism as a point of departure I shall briefly say something about Marx's understanding of politics.[8] Marx operates with two perspectives on politics. He, as mentioned, understands politics as part of the superstructure, where the task of politics is to secure the preservation of current production conditions. Politics is, however, also a means of revolution. Political struggle is the means to effect the transition to a new mode of production as the current mode hinders the development of the productive forces. Politics does not create the conditions for change, but when such conditions exist, political action is necessary to effect a transition.[9]

In the transition phase from one mode of production to another, politics, or more precisely, the political movement, plays a progressive role. The movement later becomes part of the establishment and obtains a reactionary role. "It is progressive as long as the production conditions remain optimal for the productive forces, it becomes reactionary when new superior conditions appear on the horizon" (Elster 1988: 162). According to Marx these general principles are valid for all modes of production, with the exception of communism. Under communism politics no longer becomes reactionary, but dissolves and disappears, as class conflicts no longer exist.

However, to Marx, the analysis of the capitalist state is of the greatest importance. According to Elster's reconstruction, there is not one but three theories of the capitalist state in Marx's work. The *instrumental* theory sees the state as a tool for the common interests of the bourgeoisie. Marx defended this theory until 1848, but historical development made him discard it later. The bourgeoisie in England and France, the point of departure for Marx's analysis, showed no interest in political power; it rather failed to take it. Marx then developed what Elster calls a *theory of abdication* of the capitalist state. This attempts to explain why the bourgeoisie failed to seize power and left the state apparatus to the aristocracy. Marx's point of departure is that the bourgeoisie did not seize power because it was in their interest not to do so. If the bourgeoisie seized power, capital and political power would have accumulated in a great power centre. This would have given the working class a common goal and a common enemy, and increased the risk of revolution.[10] The last and, according to Elster, the best approach rests on a reconstruction of Marx's abdication theory of the state. This theory sees the state as an independent actor, but emphasises that the interests of the capital class serve as a limitation to the state's possibilities for action. It thus departs from the instrumentalist theory in severing the capitalist state from the objectives of the capital class.

[8] Here I draw support from Elster 1985 and 1988.

[9] Cohen has pointed to the analogy of a pregnant woman to explain the role political practice plays in realising the revolution. The pregnant woman knows that she will be giving birth, she will nevertheless need a midwife when the time comes. Capitalism is similarly pregnant with socialism, but the need is still there for proper politics in order to carry out a revolution (Cohen 2000: 43).

[10] This reflection makes it clear that Marx's concept of classes is more complex than so far described. I have noted above that Marx distinguishes between the owners of the means of production and those who are forced to sell their labour power. This is the most commonly used definition of classes. But here, as we have seen, Marx distinguishes between the aristocracy, the bourgeoisie and the working class. So Marx does not have a univocal definition of class. For a discussion of the concept of class see Elster (1988, chapter 7).

4 Capital

In *Capital*[11] Marx examines the capitalist mode of production, and does this through building on and developing further the teachings of Adam Smith and David Ricardo, established under the designation of political economy. This is the third of the three sources of Marxism. Smith and Ricardo opened up for a whole new form of understanding of the relation between economics and politics. They challenged a view of economics that in a certain sense was influenced by Aristotle. Aristotle saw the household as the foundation of the Polis. He developed a virtue ethics with an emphasis on the head of the family running the household and its material production wisely. But the household remained ruled by the political, and the life of the Polis was seen as an aim in itself with the household subordinate to it. "The economic" appeared thus not as a particular area for theoretical reflection, but was understood based on the dispositions of the head of the family in the Polis (Sieferle 2007: 11).

The classical economists, however, did see the economy as an independent field that one should try to understand. And they claimed that political economy constituted an order that was not created by intentional choices directed at establishing such an order, but rather was the result of spontaneous actions in concrete situations. Thus arises something entirely new. In addition to an ethical sphere for normative action framed by the political, the political economists emphasised an independent economical sphere: the market. In this sphere, individuals were able to act based on self-interest and at the same time contribute to the common good.

The market appeared as extremely efficient because it was based on *division of labour*. By dividing the production process into a number of separate operations and ensuring that each individual worker became specialised in performing his or her work as efficiently as possible, efficiency increased dramatically. Adam Smith opens his *Wealth of Nations* by describing how a traditional pin-maker could produce a few pins a day by personally performing all the necessary work operations. Ten people dividing the work and working simple machines in a "simple manufactory" were, conversely, able to produce some 48 000 pins in a day (Smith 1999: 109). The division of labour led to a further increase in efficiency in each individual task as new machines were developed for various operations. The result was a dramatic increase in production.

This raised the question as to how the market in this unprecedented economic situation should be coordinated. The political economists claimed that there was no need for any detailed regulation of the market by the state; the market would take care of itself. The producers would produce and exchange goods, and leave it to supply and demand to regulate the prices of their products. In the market each individual actor could legitimately operate from self-interest to increase personal wealth. This stood in sharp contrast to the earlier dominant view that a striving for personal riches would result in a form of egoism that would tear asunder the ties that had held society together.

---

[11]The work, with the important subtitle of *A Critique of Political Economy* consists of three volumes, whereof only the first was published during Marx's lifetime (1863). The second volume was published in 1885, while the third appeared in 1894. Engels edited the two last volumes.

The political economists whom Marx took his inspiration from made the market an object of study and analysed how this new order worked. The purpose was to reveal the laws that governed this domain. A new science was thus established, a social science. Hegel's and Marx's positions must be understood on the basis of this new science. Hegel included the new insights by emphasising how modern societies were divided into three institutional spheres: the family, bourgeois society and the state. To a greater extent than Smith and Ricardo, Hegel claimed that bourgeois society, which corresponded to the market, created problems that could only be solved with the help of the state (taking care of the poor, etc.). Marx found this analysis wholly unacceptable, and in the surplus value theory, which he called "the heaviest rock ever thrown at capitalism", he attempts to uncover the exploitation which is built into a capitalist system based on the division of labour. He did this in a radical critique of the insufficiency of political economy.

Marx's most fundamental critique of Smith and Ricardo is that they do not think dialectically. Rather than considering capitalism as an era with a beginning and an end, classical social economics built on a view that history was a gradual process towards the modern capitalist society. The political economists had—according to Marx—failed to see that capitalism had created the conditions for its own demise.

When Marx in *Capital* presents an alternative, he does this by first distinguishing between exchange-value and use-value. An object has a use-value if it satisfies a human need. The exchange-value, however, is the value the object has when exchanged for another object. But what determines the exchange-value of an object? This is a more difficult question, as different commodities must have something in common in order to be compared so as to establish their value. Marx's answer is that the labour invested in the processing of a commodity is what determines its exchange value (Marx 2008b: 23). More precisely, he claims that the socially necessary labour-time determines the value of a commodity; that is, the value of a commodity is determined by the time it takes to produce the commodity, assuming average productivity.

In a capitalist society labour-power also constitutes a commodity. The value of this commodity is determined in the same way as for other commodities, i.e., based on the socially necessary labour-time needed to reproduce the labour-power. The value of one month's labour is consequently the same as the value of the commodities needed for a worker to survive for one month. Marx calls this necessary labour, while the labour over and above the labour needed for the worker's survival is called surplus labour. Let us assume that a month has 30 workdays, and that a worker needs to work 10 days in order to reproduce the labour-power. During the remaining 20 days the worker produces what Marx calls *surplus value* through his surplus labour, and in capitalist society this surplus value belongs to the owner of the means of production, the capitalist.

According to Marx, this system creates the basis for exploitation. The theory of surplus value and surplus labour is the scientific basis for a theory of exploitation, or for understanding what exploitation is. The capitalist exploits the worker by taking out as profit the surplus value created by labour. If we follow the example above, the capitalist will get the value of 20 days of work. This surplus value is the basis of the capitalist's profit. And contrary to earlier historical periods, this exploitation is hidden. During feudalism and the earlier modes of production, it was obvious to all that some sort of exploitation was taking place. This, however, is not the way of capitalism, which depends on the existence of apparently free wage labourers. Marx's point is that capitalism is fundamentally built on exploitation despite the apparent freedom of the paid wage labourer.

This illustrates an important aspect of Marx's critique. Capitalism is built on erroneous assumptions that contribute to maintaining the status quo. A critique of the ideology on which capitalism is built is thus needed. The critique must penetrate the surface and reveal how the institutions of capitalism contribute to the creation of a false consciousness and erroneous assumptions regarding the factual conditions. In capitalism, Marx writes, surplus labour and necessary labour flow into each other. What is surplus labour is not directly visible, and the workers are consequently not aware of the ongoing exploitation (Marx 2008b: 146).[12]

A controversial aspect of *Capital* is the thesis of the end of capitalism, built on the theory of the falling profit rate. In this Marx builds on a distinction between constant capital and variable capital. Constant capital is the capital represented by machines and raw materials, while he calls the capital represented by labour-power variable capital (Marx 2008b: 139–140). As the productive forces develop, more constant capital is required. The constant capital must be taken from the profit the capitalist gains from the surplus value of labour. Thus the rate of profit, or the profit available to the capitalist, will fall. The law of the falling profit rate states that the capitalist must, in order to be competitive in relation to other capitalists, continuously increase constant capital (Marx 2008b: 451). To avoid the fall in the profit rate the capitalist may, however, extend the workday, decrease wages or in other ways increase the exploitation of the wage-labourer. But this will lead to overproduction, and the absence of demand will cause crises that will finally lead to capitalism's demise.

5 Communism

So Marx had no fully developed theory that in detail described an alternative to capitalism. The philosopher was never to develop "an ideal for reality to adhere to". Rather, Marx pointed out that it was the responsibility of the working classes to carry out the revolution. Despite this unwillingness to say anything about communism, there are several references in Marx's writings that may tell us something about how he expected a communist society to be. Let us look at the most important ones.[13]

[12] Ideology is for Marx a false doctrine that serves the interests of the ruling classes. The aim of the critique of ideology is to reveal false doctrines. I do not have the space to treat this theme properly here. For an introduction see Elster (1988, chapter 9). For a historical and critical analysis of ideology critique see Rosen (1996).

[13] I am indebted to Wolff (2002) in my exposition here.

According to Marx, capitalist societies are, as we have seen, alienated societies. It seems reasonable to assume that there would be no alienation under communism, and that the individual would no longer be oppressed and exploited. We also know from Marx's historical materialism that the revolution will arrive only when the means of production are highly developed. We may therefore assume that there will be no more material want; everyone will, in other words, have the possibility to satisfy primary needs. Since material want is abolished under communism, Marx claimed that the way the individual thinks and acts will change. People's attitudes will no longer, as under capitalism, be characterised by narrow-minded self-interest. Individuals will rather see themselves as belonging to a community and work for the good of this community.

A passage from *The German Ideology* is perhaps the most famous, and most ridiculed, reference Marx gives to his idea of a communist society. Marx writes:

> In communist society, where nobody has one exclusive sphere of activity but each can become accomplished in any branch he wishes, society regulates the general production and thus makes it possible for me to do one thing today and another tomorrow, to hunt in the morning, fish in the afternoon, rear cattle in the evening, criticise after dinner, just as I have a mind, without ever becoming hunter, fisherman, shepherd or critic (Marx et al. 2004: 53)

Marx here points out how the labour-divided capitalist society is replaced by a communism with a less thorough division of labour, and thereby a real possibility for self-realisation through a variety of tasks. When this passage is used to ridicule Marx it is because his critics here have found an example of a form of utopian socialism. In passages like this, Marx forgets that high productivity presupposes a highly developed division of labour.

There may be no reason, however, for being so sharply critical of Marx on this point. *The German Ideology* was never published, and we do not find any similar descriptions in later texts by Marx. In one of his later works Marx distinguishes between a transition phase still marred by remnants of the old society, a phase also known as *the revolutionary dictatorship of the proletariat,* and fully developed communism. A passage which accurately sums up Marx's view, and ends in one of his famous quotes, states:

> In a higher phase of communist society, after the enslaving subordination of the individual to the division of labour, and with it also the antithesis between mental and physical labour, has vanished; after labour has become not only a means of life but itself life's prime want; after the productive forces have also increased with the all-round development of the individual, and all the springs of cooperative wealth flow more abundantly—only then can the narrow horizon of bourgeois right be crossed in its entirety and society inscribe on its banners: From each according to his ability, to each according to his needs! (Marx (b): 17)

6 Reception History and Critique

Marx did not manage to complete *Capital* before his death in 1883. Major parts of his early works remained unknown until their first publication around 1930. During the 1880s, the theoretician Marx was first and foremost known for *The Communist*

Manifesto and for the first volume of *Capital,* while he as a politician was known for his work in the First International, an international workers' organisation established in 1864 and dissolved in 1876. Much of Marx's reputation consequently depended on how his unpublished manuscripts were interpreted and which of his published work were emphasised.

Friedrich Engels (1820–1895) naturally has a special place among Marx's interpreters.[14] Through his long and close cooperation with Marx, he enjoyed a natural authority both as an interpreter of unpublished texts and as a central figure in the socialist movement. The time after Marx's death was characterised by great enthusiasm for Darwin's discoveries and a positivistic climate with regard to science in general. Engels had, while Marx was alive, been more interested in natural science than Marx. Afterwards, Engels became known for taking the first step in the direction of constructing a science of Marxism. In the work *Anti-Dühring*, Engels developed three universal dialectical laws that he claimed characterised all developmental processes, in nature as well as in society. Where Marx's works contained a wealth of ingenious, but at times contradictory, insights, Engels contributed to the creation of a rigid and closed system which should answer all possible questions. He contributed to, in Jon Elster's words, the creation of a "Marxism cast in concrete" (Elster 1988: 23).

Engels' final works contain some suggestions that the socialist struggle did not necessarily have to be won through revolutionary means. The success of the Sozialistische Partei Deutschlands (SPD) among voters made Engels ambivalent as to the nature of the future struggle. Thus Engels may be considered as supporting both sides in the future battle that would be known as the Revisionist Debate, a debate which first took place within the SPD, but which later had pronounced consequences in socialist parties in other countries as well (McLellan 2007: 16).

As early as at the SPD party congress in 1890 two fronts emerged. One front went on to work theoretically, the other more practically; the first under the leadership of Karl Kautsky (1854–1938), the other led by Eduard Bernstein (1850–1932). Kautsky's group became defenders of an orthodox form of Marxism. They repeated Marx's predictions of a smaller middle class, the increasing poverty of the proletariat and the coming revolution. Bernstein wanted a revision of Marx's theories and demanded universal suffrage, freedom of speech, free schooling for all and progressive taxation (McLellan 2007: 24). Bernstein criticised the theory of value and of cyclical crises, and consequently rejected revolution as a means: Socialist goals should be accomplished peacefully, through democratic struggle.

A similar split occurred in Russia. The revolutionary Bolsheviks, lead by Vladimir Iljitsj Lenin (1870–1924), were the driving force in the October Revolution of 1917. The revisionist Mensheviks were side-lined, and the Bolsheviks established the Communist International (Komintern). Lenin was one of the most important critics of revisionism (with Rosa Luxembourg (1871–1919)). Lenin claimed, against revisionism, that the improvements that could be won without revolution would prove transient, and, at the same time, they would weaken the fighting spirit

[14]There is no agreement between researchers regarding the relationship between Marx and Engels. Jon Elster finds it unacceptable to use statements from Engels in the interpretation of Marx, whereas Jonathan Wolff explicitly reads Marx through Engels.

of the working class. Lenin developed a *democratic centralism* and argued for the revolutionary party taking the lead and becoming the vanguard of the proletariat. The theoretically trained party elite must lead the masses through the revolutionary battle. After the revolution the elite would hand over power to the people. Lenin did, however, live long enough to become disillusioned with the elite and dismayed at the bureaucracy's capacity for survival.

Lenin complemented Marxist theory with his own theory of imperialism. He claimed that the whole world was affected by capitalism. The industrialised nations were exploiting the non-industrial nations that function as suppliers of raw materials. Mao Zedong (1893–1976) took this idea and developed it further. In Mao's China the industrial proletariat was small; in order to realise socialism, he posited, the country would have to be conquered from the rural areas, with a basis in a great farmers' movement. In a similar way, the whole world must be conquered from the countryside or from the periphery, not from the centre of capitalism. Mao's thoughts greatly inspired a series of Marxist movements in Third World countries like Cuba, Vietnam and parts of South America and Africa (Liedman 1993: 196–219).

It has been said that at a certain moment in history more than half of the world's population lived under regimes adhering to Marxist ideology. And Kautsky, Bernstein, Lenin and Mao are undoubtedly some of the most important Marxist-oriented political leaders. To what extent they truly pass on Marx's thought has, however, been debated. Even during Marx's lifetime forms of Marxism were established which clearly strayed from his fundamental insights. "All I know is that I am not a Marxist", Marx once exclaimed, deeply disappointed over the further development of his thinking by others (MEW vol. 35, s 388, here quoted from McLelland 2007: 22).

Marx's influence has also been (and is) great within academia. A series of historians have worked within the framework of historical materialism (Perry Anderson, C. P. Thompson and Eric Hobsbawm). Marx has been greatly influential in the social sciences as well. Bourdieu's original thinking around the concept of class is an important example, Sverre Lysgård's studies of the workers' collective another. Here I must, due to a lack of space, limit myself to a summary listing of some of the most important philosophers. Georg Lukacs, Antonio Gramsci and Karl Korsh were important representatives of what later became known as western Marxism. They all influenced the Frankfurter School, of which thinkers like Max Horkheimer, Theodor Adorno, Herbert Marcuse, Jürgen Habermas and Axel Honneth are the most important representatives. Common to these thinkers is that they reject the positivistic Marxism of Engels and Kautsky, and read Marx through Hegel. Marxism was not first and foremost about uncovering the laws for historical development, but rather about the possibilities for action in a given historical context.

The most important philosopher of structuralist Marxism is Louis Althusser. Althusser became famous for his thesis describing an epistemological break in Marx's thinking: a break between the early Marx who claimed that humans have an (super-historical) essence, and the later Marx who develops a critique of capital, but who is clear on the point that this is a critique which does not have access to any measures outside this historical mode of production. The late Marx, however, according to Althusser, regards the notion that humans have a super-historical essence as completely unscientific (Althusser 2010).

The most important representatives of analytical Marxism are G. A. Cohen, Jon Elster and John Roemer. They attempted to use tools from analytical philosophy to clarify unclear elements in Marxist thinking. They were also critical to Hegel's influence on Marx and defended a form of scientific Marxism that drew heavily on more recent techniques and theories developed within the social sciences.

In conclusion, I will briefly say something about the most important critique Marx's works have encountered, and discuss a question which has frequently been posed in the research literature: What is the value of Marx's thinking today?

In the earlier writings we saw two primary aspects of Marx's thinking: the critique of the liberal view of rights and the theory of alienation. The first, which is presented in *On the Jewish Question*, has been declared one of the most important works of political theory (Wolff 2002: 3–4). Marx's critique states, as we have seen, that rights cannot secure a sufficiently humane society. They can at worst supply an image of individuals as threats to each other, and thus become an obstacle to a positive realisation of genuine community. Liberal critics have denounced Marx for having rejected the form of freedom that may be attained through ascribing rights, and that Marx's understanding of human liberation is unclear and utopian. I have rebuked the first claim as untenable. The validity of the other depends on whether one is of the opinion that a critique must supply a clear and realistic alternative to what one criticises. I believe that it is important to consider the type of critique Marx raises, even though a less utopian alternative would be preferable. I will return to this.[15]

The theory of alienation has inspired a series of theoreticians from the philosophers of the Frankfurter School to existentialists like Heidegger and Sartre. But will not any society, also a communist one, in some way alienate its members? Is not a mechanisation of the production process necessary for any society that does not want to experience a shortage of goods? And if we answer yes to this question, is not (a certain degree of) alienation something we have to accept (Ottmann 2008: 161)? The critics claim that Marx's theory of alienation is problematic because a society without estranged labour is unattainable, and they claim that Marx in this phase of his theory development based his critique on an essentialist, and thereby not an ahistorical, understanding of human nature. There are, however, profound insights in Marx's theory of alienation, despite the fact that the critique does have something going for it.

Historical materialism has also been subject to thorough criticism. Marx claimed that fundamentally history is about the development of the productive forces, and that whether different forms of society will thrive or decline depends on whether they promote or hinder such development. The deterministic variety of historical materialism claimed, with this as its basis, that historical development could be reconstructed as the development of various modes of production, and that it would be possible to predict what the future would bring. But the theory lacks arguments to support the notion that history actually follows—and will follow—such a pattern of development.

[15] Many of the most interesting attempts at using Marx in modern political philosophy are nevertheless clear that rights must be given a less ambiguous position than what Marx seems to open up for. See for instance Roemer (1994) and Bobbio (1987).

The economic theory developed in *Capital* has been subject to particularly harsh criticism. Marx defended an objective theory of value. The price of a commodity could be objectively determined by calculating how much labour was necessary to produce it. The most important critique was formulated by the Austrian Eugen Böhm-Bawerk, who proposed that the value of the commodity was determined by supply and demand. Böhm-Bawerk pointed out what he called an insurmountable contradiction between volume 1 and 3 of *Capital.* In volume 3, Marx writes about the production price of a commodity, and determines this based on labour and the cost of capital. According to Böhm-Bawerk, Marx thus suggested that the exchange value of the commodity depended on more factors than the labour-time spent in producing it (Ottmann 2008: 179). Böhm-Bawerk's works became an important inspiration for Bernstein's critique of Marx.

The most important critique of *Capital* is, nevertheless, about the way Marx understands his own project. We have seen that Marx does not want to develop an ideal for "reality to adhere to". He claims that he does not defend a specific theory of justice. For Marx there is no super-historical concept of justice, only views of justice relative to a given mode of production. At the same time, his writings, including *Capital*, are permeated by an ideal which does seem to be just that: super-historical and non-relativist. This comes out in his writings about communism, and in *Capital* where he talks about capitalism as a necessary "transitional phase towards the reconversion of capital into the property of producers, although no longer as the private property of individual producers, but rather as the property of associated producers, as outright social property" (Marx (h) 27 III 3).[16]

Taken as a whole, the works of Marx nevertheless constitute an excellent point of departure for reflections on a series of central political questions: Do existing institutions open for individual self-realisation and a well-functioning community? May these institutions be understood as autonomous, or are they governed by an economic logic? What kind of ideals should any change to the structure of society be built upon? Marx gives highly problematic answers to these and a series of other questions. But he did ask them, and his profound insights and gross mistakes represent important resources when we ask these questions again.

References

Althusser, L. (2010). Humanismekontroversen. *Ágora, 1–2*, 294–322.

Bobbio, N. (1987). *Which socialism?: Marxism, socialism and democracy*. Oxford: Polity Press.

Cohen, G. A. (1986). Forces and relations of production. In J. Roemer (Ed.), *Analytical Marxism*. Cambridge: Cambridge University Press.

Cohen, G. A. (2000). The development of socialism from Utopia to science. In G. A. Cohen (Ed.), *If you're an Egalitarian, how come you're so rich*. Cambridge: Harvard University Press.

[16] I am grateful to Nils Gilje for the reference to this quote. For an elaboration of this criticism, see Rawls (2007), pp. 354–372 and Elster (1988), pp. 109–119.

Cohen, G. A. & Matavers, D. (2009). *On the German ideology*, interview with Cohen available at: http://itunes.apple.com/us/itunes-u/reading-political-philosophy/id380223603
Elster, J. (1985). *Making sense of Marx*. Cambridge: Cambridge University Press.
Elster, J. (1988). *Hva er igjen av Marx?* Oslo: Universitetsforlaget.
Hegel Georg Wilhelm, F. (2006). *Rettsfilosofien*. Oslo: Vidar-forlaget.
Jaeggi, R. (2005). *Entfremdung: zur Aktualität eines Sozialphilo-sophischen Problems*. Campus: Frankfurt am Main.
Langslet, L. R. (1963). *Den unge Karl Marx og menneskets "fremmed-gjørelse"*. Oslo: Johan Grundt Tanum Forlag.
Lenin, V. I. (1913). *The three sources and the three component parts of Marxism*. Moskva: Foreign Languages Publishing House. Also available at http://www.marxists.org/archive/lenin/works/1913/mar/x01.htm
Liedman, S.-E. (1993). *Fra Platon til kommunismens fall*. Oslo: Cappelen.
Marx, K. (2008a). *The communist manifesto*. New York: Oxford University Press.
Marx, K. (2008b). *Capital. Critique of political economy*. New York: Oxford University Press.
Marx, K. (a). *On the Jewish question* at http://www.marxists.org/archive/marx/works/1844/jewish-question/
Marx, K. (b). https://archive.org/details/CritiqueOfTheGothaProgramme
Marx, K. (c). *Economic & philosophic manuscripts of 1844* at http://www.marxists.org/archive/marx/works/download/pdf/Economic-Philosophic-Manuscripts-1844.pdf
Marx, K. (d). *Estranged labour* at http://www.marxists.org/archive/marx/works/1844/manuscripts/labour.htm
Marx, K. (e). *A critique of the German ideology* at http://www.marxists.org/archive/marx/works/download/Marx_The_German_Ideology.pdf
Marx, K. (f). *A critique of Hegel's philosophy of right* at http://www.marxists.org/archive/marx/works/download/Marx_Critique_of_Hegels_Philosophy_of_Right.pdf
Marx, K. (g). *A contribution to the critique of political economy* at http://www.marxists.org/archive/marx/works/1859/critique-pol-economy/preface.htm
Marx, K. (h). *Capital* at http://www.marxists.org/archive/marx/works/download/Marx_Capital_Vol_3.pdf
Marx, K., & Engels, F. (2004). In C. J. Arthur (Ed.), *German ideology*. New York: International Publishers.
McLellan, D. (2007). *Marxism after Marx. An introduction*. Basingstoke: Macmillian.
Ottmann, H. (2008). *Geschichte des politischen Denkens. Die Neuzeit*. Stuttgart: Metzler Verlag.
Rawls, J. (2007). *Lectures on the history of political philosophy*. Cambridge, MA: Belknap Press of Harvard University Press.
Roemer, J. E. (1994). *A future for socialism*. Cambridge, MA: Harvard University Press.
Rosen, M. (1996). *On voluntary servitude. False consciousness and the theory of ideology*. Cambridge: Polity Press.
Schacht, R. (1970). *Alienation*. Garden City: Doubleday.
Schwarzschild, L. (1948). *Den røde prøysser. Karl Marx. Legende og virkelighet*. Bergen: John Griegs Forlag.
Sieferle, R. P. (2007). *Karl Marx*. Hamburg: Junius.
Smith, A. (1999). *The wealth of nations. Book I–III*. London: Penguin Classics.
Wheen, F. (2001). *Karl Marx*. Oslo: Pax forlag.
Wolff, J. (2002). *Why read Marx today*. Oxford: Oxford University Press.
Wolff, J. (2006). *An introduction to political philosophy*. Oxford: Oxford University Press.

Humanity in Times of Crisis

Hannah Arendt's Political Existentialism

Odin Lysaker

1 Introduction

Even in times of crisis, Hannah Arendt writes, all human beings have the right to a humane politics (Arendt 1968: ix). Such politics should be based on what she refers to as existential conditions, such as natality, plurality, and freedom. This is the core of Arendt's political existentialism, something which has made her one of the most significant, but also controversial, political thinkers of the twentieth Century (Benhabib 2003: xxiii). If the requirement found in Arendt's political existentialism concerning a humane politics is to have relevance for crises also in today's globalised and complex world, it must still contribute to an analysis of totalitarian ideologies, the depoliticisation of democracy, and the dehumanisation of human dignity.

In the following, I will explore the framework of Arendt's political existentialism, understood as humanity even in times of crisis, through three steps. In the first step (Sect. 2) I will, taking Martin Heidegger's influence as a basis for my reading, address the above-mentioned human conditions and how she understands them as the existential foundation of politics. In the second step (Sect. 3) I will look at three central issues from Arendt's work by focusing on some of her most important publications: ideological totalitarianism in *The Origins of Totalitarianism* (1951), the public sphere's depoliticisation in *The Human Condition* (1958), and the dehumanisation of human dignity in *Eichmann in Jerusalem* (1963). In the third and final step (Sect. 4) I will address in further detail the critique of Arendt made by Giorgio Agamben, Jürgen Habermas, and Seyla Benhabib. Moreover, I will look more closely at how a response to this critique can be found in Arendt's political existentialism. Here I am seeking to demonstrate how Arendt thinks that even in dark times—such as in the case of the above-mentioned totalitarianism, depoliticisation, or dehumanisation—a human being's bodily existence can be the establishment of a new political freedom.

O. Lysaker (✉)
Department of Religion, Philosophy, and History, University of Agder, Kristiansand, Norway
e-mail: odin.lysaker@uia.no

G. Fløistad (ed.), *Philosophy of Justice*, Contemporary Philosophy: A New Survey 12, 293
DOI 10.1007/978-94-017-9175-5_17,

2 The Existential Conditions of Politics

Arendt's political existentialism is closely affiliated with her 'intellectual biography'. Heidegger (1889–1976) and his existential philosophy also play a key role here (Benhabib 2003: 51–56). She was born in Germany in 1906, and grew up in an assimilated Jewish, middle-class family in Königsberg (today Kaliningrad in Russia) (Young-Bruehl 1982). In the years 1924–1926, Arendt studied under Heidegger at the University of Marburg, a short time before the publication of his modern classic *Being and Time* in 1927. In the course of her studies she also became acquainted with several of Heidegger's students, including Hans Jonas. Both would later—albeit in different ways—expand upon Heidegger's existential philosophy. For a short period of time Arendt also studied under the 'founding father' of phenomenology, Edmund Husserl, at the University of Freiburg. In 1929 she submitted her doctoral dissertation on Augustin's concept of love under the guidance of the existential philosopher and her lifelong friend, Karl Jaspers, at the University of Heidelberg. Throughout the entire period of her studies Arendt's work was apolitical. This changed, however, due to Germany's political situation in the 1930s (Benhabib 2003: 35, 118). Because she was Jewish, Arendt lost her political rights and was made stateless. She therefore fled from Germany, and later emigrated to the USA. Arendt spent the rest of her life there, and became an American citizen in 1950. During these years she held professorships at a number of prestigious universities, including Princeton University and Yale University. From 1967 Arendt was a professor at The New School for Social Research, and remained there until the time of her death in New York in 1975.

There are in particular three key concepts in Arendt's political existentialism that draw from Heidegger's existential philosophy: 'natality', 'plurality', and 'action' (Benhabib 2003: xiv, 107–108). According to Arendt these concepts constitute the human condition and thereby also the preconditions of politics (Arendt 1998: 6). What are the contents of these existential conditions for Arendt? With *natality*, Arendt is referring to something she holds to be an ontological fact that each and every human being represents the birth of a new life in the world (Arendt 1998: 177–178). All human beings thereby have in common the fact that their lives are unique. She emphasises also that natality makes possible each individual's spontaneity. With spontaneity, Arendt means the capacity to implement a new beginning, and thereby do something new and unexpected. But natality is also about human beings as *bodily* (Hull 2002: 169; Thorgeirsdottir 2010: 195; Butler 2012: 176–177). According to Arendt, by virtue of this bodily state each and every human being is vulnerable (Arendt 1998: 191) and thereby also dependent upon the recognition of others. She also holds that since natality implies that new life is a new beginning, it is possible for human beings to act freely, against the grain of prevailing social conditions. One has thereby the possibility to criticise in public discourses (Arendt 1998: 9, 25, 200, 246–247), something which in its own right can serve to establish a new and more humane politics (Arendt 1998: 177, 243).

With the concept of *plurality*, Arendt is thinking of the diversity of uniqueness that is brought into the world every time another human being is born (Arendt 1998: 7). Plurality explains the connection between equality and diversity: by recognising one another's existential condition as newborn and unique, the individual's equal and shared human condition of freedom and self-actualisation is simultaneously recognised (Arendt 1998: 178). This human diversity establishes and further develops a public space—or rather, a shared world. This world—or more precisely, the concept of being together with others in the world—revolves around a shared space in which one cooperates with other human beings (Arendt 1998: 52). The shared space is thereby the origin of shared experiences, which makes it possible for the differences between people to emerge. Human beings do not solely act on the basis of their own motivation and own interests; their political cooperation also has a consensus-orientation. This shared human space thereby constitutes a public sphere enabling self-expression and the expression of uniqueness. The world is also based on both equality and difference: equality in the sense of a shared world, and difference in the sense of a space for self-expression. According to Arendt, it is within this shared space that the human diversity of society's unique voices can find expression. The existential conditions of the political are thereby human in the sense of being communicative, which implies having the capacity for language and action. And this structuring of the individual's actions through language is in turn an existential condition for being able to achieve a shared understanding and cooperation (Arendt 1998: 178ff.). This is something she holds to be a prerequisite for a democratic society (Arendt 1998: 7), and thereby the implementation of a more humane politics.

And with the concept of *action*, Arendt is referring to the human freedom that is based on natality and plurality. Every time another human being is born, a new action is made possible. And through participation in the public space that all human beings share, the human being as citizen can thereby utilise his/her freedom and spontaneity to criticise and change the development of society. By acting on the basis of his/her uniqueness in the public space composed of a multitude of opinions, what Arendt calls a 'grammar of action' is established (Arendt 1963b: 175). This grammar is an ontological and normative framework for human judgment and cooperation. The core of this normative grammar is the recognition of others' equality in uniqueness. Action is for Arendt also connected to power, which means the cititzens' ability to act politically through communication. Communicative power is dependent upon language, which means that citizens articulate grounds for their own actions in the public space with the help of intersubjective, acceptable reasoning (Arendt 1998: 178–179, 184–186, 199–200). The objective of political action as communicative power, according to Arendt, is action in a shared space where one can express oneself and one's uniqueness and thereby achieve consensus across society's diversity (Arendt 1998: 200). For only by being recognised, in other words, by achieving visibility for one's shared human equality and uniqueness, vulnerability and dependency, can one emerge in the public space to cooperate and achieve consensus through the use of judgment and deliberation, as well as expression and responsibility. A democracy—in spite of, or possibly, precisely on the basis of dissent—can contribute to a more humane politics.

3 Times of Crisis: Totalitarianism, Depoliticisation, and Dehumanisation

Arendt called herself a political theorist rather than a 'political philosopher' (Villa 1999: 3). The grounds for this statement lie in the fact that she views political philosophy as remote from the world because it is unable to raise and answer questions of current and social relevance. She can, moreover, be understood as a non-systematic thinker. This finds expression in how Arendt does not employ an overriding theoretical framework in her analyses (Benhabib 2003: 232). The claim can also be made that she lacks an explicit normative basis for democracy and human rights (Benhabib 2003: 193–198). Although her works are often empirically informed, Arendt is not interested in developing a methodology, or a specific procedure for political analysis (Benhabib 2003: 63). The reason for this is that political philosophy, in her opinion, is typically abstract and hypothetical, and thereby not equipped to recognise man's existential, and thereby political, conditions. And since natality, plurality, and action, according to Arendt, require the analysis of politics based on the recognition of individuals' uniqueness rather than a generalisation, she is thus sceptical of such standard approaches to the political. Nonetheless, through use of the concepts of life (natality), diversity (plurality), and freedom (action), three issues are highlighted that are of particular importance in her political thought: ideological totalitarianism, the depoliticisation of the public sphere, and the dehumanisation of human dignity, respectively. And at the very least *via negativa* these concepts can be understood as constituting a constructive proposal for how one can establish and further develop a society founded on a humane politics.

3.1 A New Political Principle

How does Arendt define the concept of totalitarianism? In 1951 her book *The Origins of Totalitarianism* (Arendt 1973a) was published, which was her international breakthrough and first publication in English. Here, Arendt investigates the background of the moral and political catastrophes that took place in the first half of the twentieth Century.

In this book Arendt introduces one of her most influential expressions, namely, the *right to have rights* (Arendt 1973a: 295–296). With this concept she makes reference to a right to belong to an organised community, where one is evaluated according to one's opinions and actions. But, Arendt claims, human beings recognise this right only after millions of people have lost—and can no longer recuperate—this right, due to a new global political situation that is contingent upon transgressions such as war crimes, genocide, and crimes against humanity (Arendt 1973a: 177). She distinguishes between ordinary political rights and human rights on the one hand, and what she calls the right to have rights on the other. Rights are something one is given either as a citizen or on the force of the UN's universal declaration of human rights. 'The right' to have such rights in this sense, however, is a reference to a moral—or, more precisely, existential—foundation, specifically, the above-mentioned conditions of natality, plurality, and action. It is by virtue of being born as a bodily vulnerable and unique individual that each human being, according to Arendt, is entitled to the protection of these rights. In this context, Arendt is making a case for a 'new political principle', specifically, humanity or human dignity (Arendt 1973a: ix).

Further, she criticises what she calls a Western nation-state approach to politics—or what one today often calls a methodological nationalism—that uncritically equates a population with a state and its territory (Arendt 1973a: 232). This leads to an interaction between inclusion and exclusion based on one's affiliation—where one lives—and the institutional system of one's affiliation. Arendt holds that there is no empirical basis for such a union of state and nation. This connection also results in a nationalism that excludes those who are not citizens, and—in particular—is not equipped to protect the stateless from human rights violations. Instead, she continues, the stateless, refugees, and others exposed to this type of offense are left without any rights. In addition, they become carriers of solely their naked and violable bodies (Arendt 1973a: 300). To the extent that individuals are excluded from the international human rights system, they must, Arendt maintains, be guaranteed a moral rather than a legal or political right to have rights. And this right must be founded on the one thing nobody can take from another human being, specifically, their inherent bodily vulnerability.

Further, Arendt makes the argument that concentration camps are the defining space in a totalitarian ideology (Arendt 1973a: 438). Accordingly, she is interested in how the camps disclose totalitarianism's psychological and ideological conditions for the execution of power. All the same, she holds that the camps do not perform an instrumental function, but instead are living laboratories where the dividing line between life and death is indeterminate. According to Arendt, totalitarianism is meaningful within the framework of its self-created perception of reality, which does not allow criticism from others, and thereby contributes to undermining a democratic society through the elimination of any distribution of power, equal treatment, and shared political space (Arendt 1973a: 466). Natality, plurality, and political cooperation are thereby replaced by an ideological uniformity, and the naked and vulnerable body is made superfluous.

In *The Origins of Totalitarianism* a distinction between three types of totalitarianism can be discerned (Benhabib 2003: 72–73). First, totalitarianism is understood as a form of *rule*, in other words, a set of principles for a specific means of organising and executing authority in a state. These principles are in turn based on a political ideology. A totalitarian form of rule thereby entails an ideology that uses illegitimate means such as terror and emergency legislation. Second, there is *social* totalitarianism, meaning social movements. The term social movement means informal networks or formal organisations in civil society that are based on and intended to promote a specific totalitarian ideology. Such a social movement contributes thus to supporting the state's totalitarian ideology through mass mobilisation on the part of the members of civil society. And third, there is *institutional* totalitarianism, which refers to the way the state imposes uniformity on the society through its totalitarian ideology and form of rule. Such an institutional totalitarianising entails that the state's objective is for its totalitarian ideology to permeate all areas of society.

According to Arendt's approach, these dehumanising dimensions of totalitarianism—ideological, social, and institutional uniformity—have a three-fold purpose (Benhabib 2003: 65). The first is to make the *legal* status of the individual superfluous, and thereby also the individual's right to citizenship and basic rights. As a result of this, the public sphere is also undermined. Arendt holds that since the public space is a prerequisite for the democratic society, the consequences of making individuals' legal status superfluous are catastrophic (Arendt 1973a: 460–467). In times of crisis, she claims, this is possible because the population accepts that the democratic public sphere is being dismantled and that they are being deprived of their civil rights so as to resolve critical social problems (Arendt 1973a: 460–467).

In an extension of this specification, Arendt also looks at what she calls the paradoxical situation of human rights. This paradox is about how universal rights are based on an abstract conception of man, something which entails that the only concrete addressees are citizens. Human rights therefore do not *de facto* protect all human beings, but solely those who possess membership to a state. This in turn results in the opposite of the objective of human rights, namely, the equal protection of all human beings from violation of their inherent dignity (Arendt 1973a: 291). Arendt's solution to this problem is cosmopolitan in nature, which implies the recognition of each and every individual as being in possession of what I have above called the right to have rights. She thus connects this membership to neither a legal nor political status, but rather to human life and its shared and irrevocable bodily vulnerability.

Second, in addition to making superfluous a person's legal status, totalitarianism aims to degrade the individual's *moral* status, so that the individual ceases to be a member of humanity and is without any entitlement to a life of human dignity. And finally, the totalitarian ideology aims to eradicate the individual's *psychological* status by destroying his or her personality and bodily capacity for free action and feelings of affiliation with a shared world. On the basis of this, Arendt criticises human rights and its legal definition of human dignity, which she maintains is a normative standard that breaks down when viewed in light of the world wars and genocides of the twentieth Century. Moreover, she views the torture and terrorism of the concentration camps as an expression of a humanity that has been alienated and is thereby alone in the world, and by virtue of this no longer experiences any type of meaningful affiliation. It is on the basis of this totalitarian eradication of meaning and shared humanity that Arendt introduces the concept of 'radical evil', in reference to the making superfluous and the destruction of human life through mass murder, war crimes and crimes against humanity (Arendt 1973a: 443).

In her analysis, Arendt is critical of an historical approach that seeks continuity between the past, present, and future in order to explain the sources of totalitarian ideologies and movements. The reason for this is that such an approach will make the recognition of what actually took place difficult. Arendt holds as well that the historically contingent conditions that have made the violations possible—such as the mass production of weapons or new technology for propaganda—can be overlooked. In addition, she makes the existential condition of natality the basis for her political analysis, thereby disclosing how a historical interpretation can obscure both the fact that human beings are radically free and spontaneous and how the future is thereby open for a development in a more humane direction than the violations would imply.

3.2 Freedom's Space of Appearance

What is 'the political'? In Arendt's original and most influential work, *The Human Condition* from 1958, she is seeking democracy's existential conditions (Arendt 1998: 22ff.), something Arendt finds in what she refers to as the active life or life of action *(vita activa)*, specifically, in the public space as a shared human space for both interaction and resistance.

The public space is the core impulse informing Arendt's view of the political. And this, which she calls the space 'in between', is located within each and every interpersonal relation where both speech and discussion as action and interaction arise. This space of appearance must be understood in the broadest sense, as meaning all places where human beings can express themselves (Arendt 1998: 179, 198–199). Such a shared political space is thereby constitutive of the establishment, development, and improvement of the society as a democratic community. Arendt holds that this best occurs through the public formation of opinion and will, based on free communication where everyone's unique voice is expressed and heard (Arendt 1963b: 227–229). The safeguarding of the public sphere is thus dependent upon fellow citizens' active participation in and redefinition of the political community. The democratic public sphere is thereby a shared arena for both consensus and dissent.

In addition to the existential condition of action, in *The Human Condition* Arendt also focuses on labour and work (Arendt 1998: 7). In Arendt's terminology, *labour* means the bodily reproduction and caring function of human life. The bodily is here connected to things such as personal values, family life and the household, love and sexuality. With the term *work*, Arendt is referring to an individual's socialisation and personality development in daily life through cultural and social relations and internalisation, economic interests and consumption. For Arendt, *action* corresponds with—as I touched upon above—her concepts of natality and plurality, and in particular implies the human capacity for communication and cooperation.

In her political thinking Arendt also distinguishes between power and violence (Arendt 1973b: 143–155). The term *power* implies—as explained above—a kind of action that is based on communication and is thereby a reference to what Arendt perceives as being a shared human characteristic which makes cooperation possible (Arendt 1970: 44). The execution of power is accordingly intersubjective and not intra-subjective—in spite of the fact that unique individuals must cooperate in order to execute such a communicative power. Power is also a condition for ensuring that a democracy will be able to function as an infrastructure for the public formation of opinion and will, which in turn provides the foundation for the achievement of consensus among active fellow citizens (Arendt 1998: 200). This entails that the democracy is given legitimacy to the extent that citizens participate actively in its cooperative processes (Arendt 1973b: 140, 151). In contradistinction to power defined as unrestrained and non-violent, Arendt defines *violence*—like Max Weber's classical definition of power—as the opportunity to make others to do something they otherwise would not have done, even if they should put up resistance. Violence is, in other words, an instrumental approach to others and reduces their human dignity to something not entitled to respect (Arendt 1970: 53).

The concept of violence appears to be one of the fundamental principles for Arendt's analysis of that which is called democracy's depoliticisation politics that reduces citizens to means rather than ends in their own right. This is connected with Arendt's distinction between the political and the social. The *political* refers to the democratic public sphere, and to political power as the public formation of opinion and will. In the political sphere all human beings are free to act and cooperate, while the *social* refers to that which is normally defined as the private, in other words, both bodily and material conditions. According to Arendt, what human beings' bodily and material needs have in common is that they are necessary and result in reproduction. These needs are thus not optional. Further, the social sphere can be understood in three ways (Benhabib 2003: 23f.): Firstly, the social can be understood as *capitalism*, or—in an extension of Karl Marx's social analysis—the historical emergence of a society organised on the basis of a market economy (Arendt 1998: 46). Secondly, the social sphere for Arendt refers to a *mass society*, the society's need as such for its members to cooperate according to social roles rather than freedom (natality) and authenticity (plurality) (Arendt 1998: 40). The reason for this is that to find a balance between considerations for freedom and control, complex societies require a form of normative order. And thirdly, the social can encompass *civil society*, specifically the cooperation of citizens through shared values, social networks, and volunteer organisations, which constitute a separate social sphere alongside the private and the state (Arendt 1998: 41).

Although the social for Arendt can be understood in different ways, she maintains that these conceptions have a common characteristic when it comes to the depoliticisation of the public sphere. According to her distinction between the political (i.e., the public) and the social (i.e., the private) she analyses the depoliticisation of democracy as a political crisis. This crisis is due to the fact that the political in modern democracies is privatised and intimatised by the social (Arendt 1998: 49). A rationalisation of the private and the intimate is sought through their deliberation in the public sphere, and the public sphere is exposed to an affiliated privatisation and intimatisation. This has the effect of flattening out the political debate so that rather than being based on plurality it becomes conformist and meaningless. The public sphere is thereby at risk of decaying as a shared space for freedom of expression and societal criticism. This in turn calls for a shared struggle for a more humane politics in which members of society respect one another's arguments rather than allowing themselves to be misled by emotions and intimacy.

3.3 Judgment's Ethical Responsibility

What does the dehumanisation of an individual imply? In 1961 the trial of the Nazi war criminal Adolf Eichmann took place. Eichmann was in particular famous for having been the 'architect' behind what was called 'the final solution': Nazi Germany's plan to exterminate all of the Jews during the Second World War. Here Arendt ran into a type of evil that differed from the evil she had studied previously, namely the abovementioned 'radical evil'. This resulted in her book *Eichmann in Jerusalem*, with the subtitle *A Report on the Banality of Evil*, from 1963 (Arendt 1963a). This work contributed to a paradigm shift within international studies of evil (Vetlesen 2005: 226). In *The Origins of Totalitarianism*, published a decade before, Arendt defined evil as radical. By 'radical evil' she means an act that degrades, makes superfluous, and destroys another human being (Arendt and Jaspers 1993: 166). Moreover, this act is motivated by an evil personality, in other words, an individual who acts with the intention of inflicting pain upon others or having them killed. The relevance of such studies of evil for political philosophy entailed allowing political latitude for historical and current political actions that result in crimes against humanity, war crimes, and genocide. This in turn provided the background for the establishment of such cosmopolitan institutions as the UN, with its founding declaration of human rights, and the Council of Europe's Court of Human Rights in Strasbourg.

But when Arendt attended the trial, her expectations regarding the type of person Eichmann would be were challenged. Based on her original concept of evil, she had an expectation that Eichmann would represent a radical evil due to the genocide of the Jews during the Second World War. But Arendt was unable to find any expression of a personal and profoundly felt hate in Eichmann. Nor did she detect a lack of intelligence, fanaticism, or psychopathology. Eichmann simply did not appear to be the monster one would believe him to be. Instead Eichmann came across as a normal human being, yes, virtually mediocre. There was thus, as Arendt explains it, an asymmetry between what Eichmann had done and his personality. What this meant was that there was no trace of any reflection upon the act's consequences in the form of the murder of millions of people. Instead, in Arendt's eyes, Eichmann seemed to represent what she in her subsequent work calls a particular form of both cognitive and ethical 'thoughtlessness' (Arendt 1978a: 4). What was it then that motivated Eichmann, and what Arendt refers to as 'banal evil'? The Eichmann case is a key to understanding how the Holocaust could have taken place, she holds. Normally Eichmann's actions would have been perceived as radically evil. Arendt, however, maintains that his evil was the result of the political regime in which he was working, rather than any special personality traits. In other words, he did not act through an evil will, but rather something banal, specifically, as a bureaucrat who was merely following rules and orders.

On the basis of this analysis, in *Eichmann in Jerusalem* Arendt replaces her original understanding of evil as radical with the banal. With the term *banal* evil she is referring to cases in which a person acts in extreme compliance with the law or out of a sense of the fulfilment of an ethical duty (Arendt 1963a: 135). Instead of promoting a specific totalitarian ideology, the individual characterised by banal evil is only interested in advancing their career. Banal evil implies that the person in question is simply suffering from being ordinary (Arendt 1963a: 25–26). Arendt wants to explain what had motivated Eichmann in his efforts to ensure that millions of Jews were exterminated in concentration camps during the Second World War. Her answer is that Eichmann lacked judgment, in other words, the ability to put himself in another's place.

The consequences of banal evil are dehumanisation, which implies the negation of human dignity or what Arendt thus terms humanity. The term *dehumanisation* can be understood here in a double sense (Vetlesen 1994: 91). First, dehumanisation entails *degradation*, which means when an offender—in this case Eichmann—reduces the status of human beings as individuals to something purely instrumental. And second, dehumanisation is for Arendt about a type of *self-instrumentalisation*, in other words, when the offender personally degrades his or her own status as an acting and responsible individual. In the case of Eichmann, this latter form of dehumanisation is a matter of acting in a manner that reduces the self to nothing more than a tool for something else. Eichmann subjugated himself to the Nazi ideology and followed orders without questioning. The transgressor thereby killed the moral individual, both in the victim, and in himself. This making superfluous and eliminating a person as a moral being works thereby counter to her or his existential conditions. Because if a person is converted into a non-human and a human being is understood as being dependent upon natality, plurality, and action, then this moral capacity will be destroyed. Moreover, the transgressor's self-dehumanisation can serve as justification for the person's not assuming moral responsibility for his or her actions, even for crimes against humanity. This is due not solely to the offender's dehumanisation, but also to an understanding of both the misdeed and rhetoric used to defend it as being rational, Arendt holds, according to a specific form of bureaucratic logic. This was something that was highlighted when Eichmann depicted himself as a duty-bound ethicist and that he had acted in line with Immanuel Kant's deontological ethics.

For Arendt, Eichmann's lack of judgment is accordingly the same as thoughtlessness. The Eichmann case thus demonstrates the important role of judgment for human cooperation. With *judgment* Arendt is thinking about a form of expanded thought which takes into account the positions of others (Arendt 1961: 220–221). This is a way of making visible for oneself the opinions of others, and whether one might be able to agree with them. But one shall not blindly accept others' opinions and actions, but rather carry out a critical assessment. When one uses judgment, one is then thinking, not feeling, together with others. For Arendt, judgment is something cognitive rather than emotional. Moreover, it is based on the existential condition that Arendt refers to as being in a shared world with others, where one cooperates with and cares about one another (Benhabib 2003: 191). This in turn both recognises as well as respects human diversity and the uniqueness of each and every human being. This kind of judgment was, according to Arendt, lacking in Eichmann, since he never acknowledged what he did. In the work of Kant however, Arendt finds resources for the establishment of a standard for judgment that can be used to assess whether or not an action is ethical (Benhabib 2003: 188). Arendt borrowed this term from Kant's concept of reflexive judgment, which can be understood as an intersubjective procedure for the attainment of public consensus (Benhabib 2003: 189). If it is to be possible to replace the banal form of evil with a humane politics, human judgment appears to be crucial.

4 Ways Out of Arendt: Agonism, Republicanism, and Universalism

Arendt's political thought is, as stated, influential but controversial. This has resulted in her being read in highly divergent ways. Many of these interpretations can be situated along a continuum with agonism and universalism at respective and opposing ends, and with republicanism in the middle. At the one extreme one finds the *agonistic* readings, or readings from the perspective of political realism. These focus on Arendt's critique of both citizenship and national democracy as human rights. The Italian philosopher Giorgio Agamben is an important representative of this approach. And at the other extreme one finds *universal*, or liberal, positions. These maintain, in contradistinction to the agonists, that Arendt is promoting a cosmopolitism based on both human dignity and human rights. Here one finds philosophers such as the American feminist Seyla Benhabib. And in the middle, between agonism and universalism, there is a third opinion, namely a *republican* position. Those who read Arendt from a republican perspective—such as Jürgen Habermas can be held to do—are interested in her analyses of the democratic public sphere as a shared arena for the formation of opinion- and will-formation.

Based on the role the terms natality, plurality, and action play in Arendt's political thought, her intellectual affinity with Heidegger's existential philosophy would appear to be indisputable (Benhabib 2003: xiii ff., 230; Villa 1996: 113–143). Nonetheless, the definition of the term 'political existentialism', as a basis for my analysis, is controversial. This entails that a distinction can be drawn—much like the continuum I just made reference to—between three different and competing definitions of this term, specifically an agonistic, a republican, and a universalist. These three readings appear—as I will return to below—to fall under the three themes I addressed in the first section here: ideological totalitarianism, the depoliticisation of the public sphere, and the dehumanisation of human dignity. In the following I will therefore present three critiques of Arendt's political existentialism, submitted by Agamben, Benhabib, and Habermas, respectively. What these critics have in common is that they think with Arendt against Arendt, which implies that they are both inspired by and in disagreement with her political analyses.

4.1 Democratic Agonism

The agonistic reading claims that Arendt's political thought is anti-democratic due to her seemingly reactionary, elitist, and hierarchical view of the political (Wolin 1994: 289–290; Wolin 2001: 5, 67–69; Jay 1986). The point of reference for this approach is the legal philosopher of law Carl Schmitt, who defines the political as a violent struggle between friend and foe. In extension of Schmitt's political thought it is common to distinguish between 'agonism' and 'antagonism'. While agonism understands politics as conflict and disagreement between adversaries, antagonism implies that agonism passes over into violence (Mouffe 2005: 20–21). Although Arendt's political existentialism can be read in light of the political realist Schmitt, she can simultaneously be said to represent a democratic agonism (Villa 1999: Ch. 5). It is a matter of understanding political conflict as based on Arendt's normative grammar—as I explained above regarding her concept of action—through which a struggle takes place for recognition, inclusion, and equal participation in a society characterised by inequality and exclusion. Such an understanding of Arendt's political existentialism entails her working on the basis of the idea that society is full of conflict, but that parties which are in conflict with one another can nonetheless be reconciled and thereby establish a more democratic and humane political order. This can thereby be called a 'democracy of disagreement'.

Agamben is positioned in this agnostic tradition from Schmitt. Nonetheless, his political thought does not end up in pure political realism. Instead, Agamben attempts to further develop Arendt's double view of the political by maintaining that through violations of human beings' bodily vulnerability, a potential foundation for a new humanity can be found. According to Agamben, one of Arendt's most important contributions in this context is the analysis of violence and biological life. In her investigation of totalitarian ideologies in *The Origins of Totalitarianism*, Arendt addresses in further detail the victims of violations of human rights. Here it is held that not even the human being's nakedness remains inviolable (Arendt 1973a, b: 299).

In his work *Homo Sacer*, Agamben addresses the human being precisely as 'naked life'. This pertains to when a person *qua* bodily life has the characteristics as a fully valid human being reduced to a minimum as a result of totalitarianism (Agamben 1998: 71–86). Here Agamben draws from Arendt's analysis of totalitarian ideologies' degrading and inhuman treatment of other human beings' naked bodies. Arendt is read here through Michel Foucault's concept of biopolitics, which can be understood as a phenomenon that "brought life and its mechanisms into the realm of explicit calculations and made knowledge-power an agent of transformation of human life" (Foucault 1979: 143). In short: Politics as society's control of individuals is not only over but also *in* as well as *through* the body.

In spite of the fact that Agamben further develops a series of Arendt's original insights, he is critical of what he appears to understand as a *biopolitical deficit* (Agamben 1998: 3–4, 120). Not even the fact that Arendt's political existentialism is about precisely the connection between the body and power makes him less critical. In his extension of the concept of biopolitics, Agamben makes reference to how inclusion of the naked life in the political sphere establishes the origin of sovereign power (Agamben 1998: 6). And it is this reversed intellectual construct that he criticises Arendt's interconnection of power and life of having overlooked. According to Agamben, her political existentialism does not allow for the possibility that life in itself is neither original nor neutral, but rather always already a biopolitical product.

Here Arendt and Agamben part company. While Arendt follows Heidegger's enunciation of man's original and existential condition, Agamben adheres to the poststructuralist perspective of Foucault whereby there is no 'original'. Arendt maintains, however, that this does not correspond with human existence in the world as something more fundamental. Each and every human being is *qua* existential conditions born bodily and vulnerable, and this is neither a choice nor optional. If biopolitics is understood as a kind of power, this entails—as in the understanding of the tradition from Weber explained above—that there is an asymmetry between human beings. This type of biopolitical power can to a large degree be said to be incorporated in Arendt's concept of violence, and as I explained earlier, implies an instrumentalisation of human relations. An Arendtian approach, however, will enable a critique of Agamben for not accepting another form of asymmetry, specifically with respect to human beings' existential conditions. Although she is more interested in natality, plurality, and freedom of action, Arendt also highlights 'mortality' as an existential condition (Arendt 1998: 8). Here Arendt is referring to another and non-biopolitical form of asymmetry: the non-chosen and non-optional aspect of the continuum between natality and mortality. If this is a reasonable reading, these existential as well as political conditions constitute an asymmetry in life that lies beyond the scope of human freedom of action, but which is nonetheless one of its conditions. This must thereby be recognised in order for it to be possible to create a more humane politics—even, or possibly precisely, on the basis of a human being's existential condition and bodily nakedness.

4.2 *The Newcomer's Critique*

The republican interpretation of the concept of political existentialism situates Arendt in the tradition from Aristotle instead of Schmitt (Canovan 1992: Ch. 6, 15). This is due to her focus on the public sphere as politics' space of interaction, as in the agora of Antiquity. Here private individuals meet as citizens, in the sense of active and equal participants in society's political processes. The purpose of such a public space is for all affected parties, through the formation of opinion and will, to be able to influence the societal processes that encompass and influence their daily lives. In this way they will be able to reach a consensus about common concerns. This model can to a large degree resemble what I previously called democratic agonism. Nonetheless, the republican reading appears to be less conflict-oriented than the agonistic. It highlights instead the political as a democracy based on value cohesion. The republican reading is also built upon Arendt's understanding of freedom as a type of public freedom (Villa 2008: Ch. 4). For Arendt, freedom here is about the attainment of consensus and execution of power on the part of equal and cooperating fellow citizens (Arendt 1973a: 24).

In 1962, just 4 years after the publication of Arendt's *The Human Condition*, Habermas' modern classic *The Structural Transformation of the Public Sphere* was published. Here Habermas was very much inspired by Arendt's focus on the public sphere as a common sphere for the democratic formation of opinion and will. Nonetheless, their approaches to the democratic public sphere diverge on some important points: Although Habermas in his analysis of what he calls 'refeudalisation' to a large extent seems to share Arendt's perception that the public sphere is in the process of being depoliticised, he holds that a new form of public sphere is emerging. Furthermore, Habermas' concept of both communicative power and the democratic public sphere are clearly indebted to Arendt's distinction between, respectively, power and violence, and the political and the social (Habermas 1996: 119, 170).

But although Habermas expands upon the concept of power in Arendt's political existentialism, he criticises her for what can be called an *institutional deficit* (Habermas 1985: 175; Habermas 1996: 147–151). With the expression institutional deficit, I am referring to what Habermas holds to be a fact of the democratic society, specifically that an institutionalisation of the democracy's communicative power takes place. Here Habermas criticises Arendt's distinction between the political and the social, the public and the private spheres, and the state and the economy for not being applicable to a modern, complex society (Habermas 1985: 219). According to Habermas, Arendt is lacking an understanding of the political that provides for what he terms the 'circulation of political power' (Habermas 1996: Ch. 8.2). The idea that it is possible to describe a democratic society as a circulation of political power implies a multidimensional model of democracy, which highlights that the public sphere, the media, civil society, and state institutions (e.g. parliament, the legal system, and bureaucracy) constitute democracy's different but nonetheless fully interconnected social spheres.

Furthermore, Habermas criticises Arendt's distinction between communicative power and strategic violence, which results in an understanding of democracy in which violence is not a part of politics. Based on his concept of strategic action, Habermas holds that even though it must be possible to describe certain actions as strategic, they are all the same a part of politics. Habermas claims, in other words, that Arendt's political existentialism is not framed by a comprehensive social theory that could have demonstrated a connection between politics and other social spheres as an institutional whole. This would have potentially reflected structural violence as an aspect of her analysis of democracy.

How can Arendt respond to Habermas' critique? Arendt does indeed make a distinction between ethics and politics, between truth and judgment, and can thereby be said to lack a normative standard for politics (Benhabib 2003: 193–198). However, Habermas appears to overlook here Arendt's emphasis on political verbalisation and ethical judgment. It can seem as if her analysis of democracy's depoliticisation is not followed up by any constructive proposals for a solution. But at the same time, Arendt is interested in the existential conditions, on the basis of which she also maintains that every newcomer implies a new start, and thereby new actions and a new critique of the prevailing social conditions. Although she lacks an explanation for democratic legitimisation, as found with Habermas, Arendt is at the very least interested in how citizens, through natality, plurality, and action, over and over again contribute to the establishment, redefinition, and improvement of society as a democratic community, and thereby take part in a struggle for a political existentialism—in other words, a humane politics—which even in times of crisis can result in a repoliticisation of the democratic public sphere.

4.3 Bodily Dignity

The last understanding of the concept of political existentialism claims that Arendt represents a political universalism (Benhabib 2004: 194, 2003: xii; Hayden 2009: 57; Passerin d'Entrèves 2001: 85–90). Arendt's political universalism contains both a moral and a legal dimension. The *moral* dimension refers to Arendt's preoccupation with human beings' existential conditions, through their bodily vulnerability and dependency. This in turn calls for recognition of each individual's given-as-bodily dignity (humanity) or what she refers to as a shared human bodily vulnerability (Arendt 1973a: 299–300; Arendt 1982: 76; Arendt and Jaspers 1993: 413, 423, 431).

While its *legal* dimension is to be found in the UN's universal declaration of human rights, Arendt is admittedly critical of whether what she perceives as abstract human rights and an institutional deficit at a transnational level can mitigate the situation for stateless and other groups without any kind of true protection of human rights. But nonetheless, this reading of her political existentialism holds that Arendt never abandons her faith in a political universalism. She represents instead a kind of justice thinking, which places her in the tradition stemming from Kant's cosmopolitism rather than Schmitt's political realism or Aristotle's politics of the public.

In her cosmopolitan theory of justice, Benhabib builds upon Arendt's concept of the right to have rights (Benhabib 2004: Ch. 2). With this expression Arendt is referring, as stated, to an ontologically based right to have rights. The necessity of understanding rights ontologically is connected with Arendt's political existentialism, which stems from the above-explained existential conditions. Benhabib further develops this train of thought as the normative basis for a cosmopolitan justice, in other words, a theory of justice wherein the stakeholder is a world citizen rather than a national citizen. But although Arendt is one her most important sources of inspiration, Benhabib criticises her of failing to see the need for international rights development instead of connecting the normative requirement regarding the right to have rights to national citizenship in a state. According to Benhabib, Arendt should have considered the connection between the right to have rights and the recognition of individuals' moral status independent of their citizenship (Benhabib 2004: 68). The reason for this is that she would then have been able to avoid that which can be called a human rights deficit.

Benhabib consequently calls for a multilevel legitimation, in other words, a multidimensional understanding of legitimacy, that distinguishes between three different, but connected levels, for legitimising. Multilevel legitimation, according to Benhabib, implies a practical division of labour between, respectively, moral, legal, and political legitimation (Benhabib 2004: 16). Although the right to have rights in a fundamental sense can be said to be morally grounded, it must also be legitimised both through democratic processes among citizens, internally in a state, and in terms of human rights through an institutionalisation process by a transnational legal system. The absence of such a systematic consideration of the relation between morality, justice, and politics results in what can be called Arendt's human rights deficit.

Nonetheless, Arendt's perspective, by virtue of the existential conditions—natality, plurality, and action—contains a dimension that is more existential than what Benhabib would appear to think. Arendt through these conditions establishes a normative basis for human dignity, democracy, and human rights that is shared by and irrevocable to all humans, while Benhabib's Habermas-inspired and discourse-theoretical approach to normative reasoning does not appear to be wholly suitable for Arendt's political existentialism. Although Arendt and Benhabib appear to share many ideas in their political thinking, Arendt's human conditions can be said to contain a more fundamental-ontological character (in a Heideggerian sense), than that permitted by Benhabib's intersubjective and socio-ontological approach (in a Habermasian sense). This entails that Arendt's view of the existential foundation for a more humane politics is more relevant for those who do not have actual protection on the basis of universal human rights than that which Benhabib would suggest.

5 Conclusion

Arendt is a critic of state-bound democracies and universal human rights. Simultaneously, she supports a democratic public sphere and the right to have rights. This double view of the political has the effect of making her a reluctant contributor to the Enlightenment tradition from Kant via G. W. F. Hegel and Karl Marx to Habermas. Still, her own conceptual toolbox—which includes the distinction between the social and the political, between work and labour, and between violence and power—is problematic (Benhabib 2003: xxxvii, xxxix, 137, 198). What relevance, then, does Arendt's political existentialism have in today's globalised and complex world?

In the essay *We Refugees* from 1943 Arendt maintains that refugees who do not have a homeland, but instead float around in a transnational space, constitute a political avant-garde (Arendt 1978b). Arendt is interested in what she calls 'paria', in other words, a person who belongs to a marginalised or excluded group by virtue of having been degraded to 'the others'. While the Jews were such a group of paria in Arendt's day, undocumented migrants can be said to be a corresponding 'avant-garde' group today. The reason for this is two-fold. Firstly, they are exposed to violation, in the form of mis-recognition, something which can establish a sense of 'consciousness of injustice' that is based on experiences of disrespect. Secondly, and more importantly, society is unjust as long as such groups are exposed to violation. According to Arendt it is therefore crucial for the political that such groups are recognised and thereby free to take part on equal standing with other citizens in public life on the basis of their shared human uniqueness.

In spite of her double view regarding the political, Arendt accordingly maintains that even in times of crisis human beings are free to act on the basis of a humane politics. The political must as such be grounded existentially in the struggle for recognition of human beings' shared and irrevocable bodily vulnerability and dependency. In particular, Arendt's original insight about the affinity between the existential conditions and political action can thus be said to be important, also in today's globalised and complex world. It thereby also represents a force in opposition to all politics that degrade human beings so they are treated as illegal or superfluous. Only then will the politics not solely be about a shared humanity, but also about an actual recognition of a life of equal dignity.

Acknowledgments I would like to thank Arne Johan Vetlesen for comments.

References

Agamben, G. (1998/1995). *Homo sacer: Sovereign power and bare life*. Stanford: Stanford University Press.

Arendt, H. (1961). *Between past and future: Eight exercises in political thought*. London: Faber and Faber.

Arendt, H. (1963a). *Eichmann in Jerusalem: A report on the banality of Evil*. New York: Viking Press.

Arendt, H. (1963b). *On revolution*. London: Faber and Faber.

Arendt, H. (1968). *Men in dark times*. New York: Harcourt, Brace and World.

Arendt, H. (1970). *On violence*. New York: Harcourt, Brace and World.

Arendt, H. (1973a/1951). *The origins of totalitarianism*. New York: Harcourt Brace Jovanovich.

Arendt, H. (1973b). *Crises of the republic*. Harmondsworth: Penguin.

Arendt, H. (1978a). *The life of the mind*. New York: Harcourt Brace Jovanovich.

Arendt, H. (1978b/1948). *The Jew as pariah: Jewish identity and politics in the modern age*. New York: Grove Press.

Arendt, H. (1982). *Lectures on Kant's political philosophy*. Chicago: University of Chicago Press.

Arendt, H. (1998/1958). *The human condition*. Chicago: University of Chicago Press.

Arendt, H., & Karl, J. (1993/1985). *Hannah Arendt-Karl Jaspers correspondence 1926–1969*. San Diego/New York: Harcourt Brace/Harcourt Brace.

Benhabib, S. (2003/1996). *The reluctant modernism of Hannah Arendt*. Thousand Oaks: Sage.

Benhabib, S. (2004). *The rights of others: Aliens, residents, and citizens*. Cambridge: Cambridge University Press.

Butler, J. (2012). *Parting ways: Jewishness and the critique of Zionism*. New York: Columbia University Press.

Canovan, M. (1992). *Hannah Arendt: A reinterpretation of her political thought*. Cambridge: Cambridge University Press.

Foucault, M. (1979/1976). *The history of sexuality* (Vol. 1). London: Allen Lane.

Habermas, J. (1985/1976). Hannah Arendt: on the concept of power. In *Philosophical-political profiles*. Cambridge, MA: MIT Press.

Habermas, J. (1996/1992). *Between facts and norms: Contributions to a discourse theory of law and democracy*. Cambridge, MA: MIT Press.
Hayden, P. (2009). *Political Evil in a global age: Hannah Arendt and international theory*. London: Routledge.
Hull, M. B. (2002). *The Hidden philosophy of Hannah Arendt*. London: Routledge.
Jay, M. (1986). *Permanent exiles: Essays on the intellectual migration from Germany to America*. New York: Columbia University Press.
Mouffe, C. (2005). *On the political*. Abingdon: Routledge.
Passerin d'Entrèves, M. (2001). *The political philosophy of Hannah Arendt*. London/New York: Routledge.
Thorgeirsdottir, S. (2010). The Natal self. In R. M. Schott & H. Sara (Eds.), *Birth, death, and femininity: Philosophies of embodiment* (pp. 186–210). Bloomington: Indiana University Press.
Vetlesen, A. J. (1994). *Perception, empathy, and judgement: An inquiry into the preconditions of moral performance*. University Park: Pennsylvania State University Press.
Vetlesen, A. J. (2005). *Evil and human agency: Understanding collective evildoing*. Cambridge: Cambridge University Press.
Villa, D. R. (1996). *Arendt and Heidegger: The fate of the political*. Princeton: Princeton University Press.
Villa, D. R. (1999). *Politics, philosophy, terror: Essays on the thought of Hannah Arendt*. Princeton: Princeton University Press.
Villa, D. R. (2008). *Public freedom*. Princeton: Princeton University Press.
Wolin, S. (1994). Hannah Arendt: democracy and the political. In L. P. Hinchman & S. K. Hinchman (Eds.), *Hannah Arendt: Critical essays*. Albany: State University of New York Press.
Wolin, R. (2001). *Heidegger's children: Hannah Arendt, Karl Löwith, Hans Jonas, and Herbert Marcuse*. Princeton: Princeton University Press.
Young-Bruehl, E. (1982). *Hannah Arendt: For love of the world*. New Haven: Yale University Press.

John Rawls' Theory of Justice as Fairness

Andreas Follesdal

When do citizens have a moral duty to obey the government and support the institutions of society?[1] This question is central to political philosophy. One of the twenty century's main response was John Rawls' theory of justice, "Justice as Fairness", in the book *A Theory of Justice,* published 1971. The book *Justice as Fairness* was an improved and shorter presentation of Rawls' theory, published 2001 with editorial support by Erin Kelly, one of his former students.

When asked how rights, duties, benefits and burdens should be distributed, the ideals of freedom and equality often conflict with each other. In domestic politics we often see such conflicts between calls for more individual freedoms and schemes for universal, egalitarian welfare arrangements. It is such conflict between liberty and equality that Rawls attempts to reconcile with his theory of justice.

There are three main steps in Rawls' theory of justice. Firstly, he assumes certain features characteristic of free societies, as well as some specific ideas about how society and people should be understood. Rawls believes that even people with different beliefs can agree with some principles to resolve basic conflicts over the distributional effects of social institutions. Secondly, he draws on the contract theory tradition in political philosophy, arguing that consent in some sense is necessary for the legitimate exercise of state power. Based on the requirement of consent, in a third step Rawls presents certain principles for a just society that citizens should be expected to support. The main idea of these principles is that political and civil rights must be protected, and that all individuals with the same abilities and efforts must be guaranteed equal opportunity to

[1] An original version of this article appeared as an introduction to *John Rawls: Rettferdighet som rimelighet* [Erin Kelly (ed.) (2003) *Justice as Fairness*] translated by Kai Swensen. Oslo: Pax, pp. 11–36. The present version was developed under the auspices of MultiRights—an ERC Advanced Grant (269841) on the Legitimacy of Multi-Level Human Rights (223274) Judiciary—www.MultiRights.net; and PluriCourts, a Research Council of Norway Centre of Excellence—www.PluriCourts.net.

A. Follesdal (✉)
PluriCourts, Faculty of Law, University of Oslo, Oslo, Norway
e-mail: andreas.follesdal@jus.uio.no

G. Fløistad (ed.), *Philosophy of Justice*, Contemporary Philosophy: A New Survey 12, 311
DOI 10.1007/978-94-017-9175-5_18, © Springer Science+Business Media Dordrecht 2015

achieve different positions. Within this framework, those social groups which are most disadvantaged are given decisive weight in the distribution of economic benefits.

Rawls' theory is an alternative to *utilitarianism,* which had been dominant among philosophers and political thinkers since the mid-eighteenth century. Notable politicians, economists and moral philosophers such as Adam Smith, Jeremy Bentham, John Stuart Mill and Henry Sidgwick had all advocated utilitarianism in one form or another. This tradition asserts the principle of welfare maximization: One should act so as to achieve the greatest expected utility possible, considering all stakeholders. Welfare, understood either as happiness or satisfaction of interests, is the only thing that matters to utilitarianism, and the distribution of welfare between the parties concerned has no essential meaning. Utilitarianism thus claims that it may be appropriate to let someone suffer if necessary to promote the overall welfare. Rawls denies this, claiming instead that each individual has certain rights that can not be sacrificed simply for others to obtain more benefits.

A Theory of Justice is perhaps that contribution in political philosophy that attracted the most attention in the twentieth century. The book revolutionized moral philosophy, and Rawls' critics declared quickly that political philosophers now must either work within his theory or explain why they chose not to do so. Although the book is long and difficult to read, it has had a major influence far beyond the philosophers' series, in law, psychology, political science and economics. Yet *A Theory of Justice* was challenged on many issues, and Rawls continued responding to critics ever since the book appeared.

On some issues he adjusted his views in the light of objections and suggestions, and he often modified and explicated the theory to get a better account than he originally presented. Sometimes he has refuted criticism. In the end, Rawls chose not to revise *A Theory of Justice,* but rather noted changes in articles, as well as in the book *Political Liberalism,* where he developed his thoughts further. The book *Justice as Fairness* is a shorter and updated presentation to a large extent on Rawls' written lecture notes from the 1980s.

This introduction to Rawls falls into eight parts. After a brief biographical introduction, Part 2 presents the allocation principles he advocated. Part 3 presents Rawls' conception of society and the individual, as an introduction to the rest of the argument presented in Part 4. Section 5 takes up his theory of justification, and Part 6 points to three areas where the more recent book *Justice as Fairness* differs somewhat from *A Theory of Justice.* Section 7 presents some of the criticisms that have been raised, and Section 8 points to some lasting contributions of Rawls' theory.

1 Social and Historical Context

John Rawls was born in the state of Maryland in the United States in 1921. With the exception of 3 years of military service during the 2nd World War he devoted his working life to philosophy. He received his Ph.D. in philosophy at Princeton University in 1950 and taught briefly there and at Cornell University in 1962 before he was offered a professorship in philosophy at Harvard University. When *A Theory of Justice* was published, he had worked on the book for 20 years.

A Theory of Justice is characterized by the analytical philosophy's emphasis on conceptual analysis and detailed argument. Why did *A Theory of Justice* cause such attention?

Political philosophy seeks to increase our understanding of how society is and how it should be. John Rawls emphasized that this understanding has an important practical goal, namely to help resolve deep conflicts between community members. Rawls, born and raised in the South of the US, felt strongly that American society suffered from the lack of a well thought out response to the question of how a just society should regulate the distribution of benefits and burdens of cooperation among members. This is the issue he devoted his life to answer.

One of the reasons that *A Theory of Justice* has had such an impact is undoubtedly that Rawls took the views of others seriously, and sought to benefit from the insights of earlier thinkers. Rawls often emphasized that if we are to learn from others, we must interpret them in the best light. It thus leads astray to believe that political philosophers throughout world history have given different answers to exactly the same questions. To the contrary, they often wrote with current political conflicts in mind. Historical insight is therefore necessary to put the theories in a fair light and to harvest others' insights. When earlier thinkers sound naive, it is thus often because our interpretation of them is wrong. This attitude led Rawls to ask: What is the historical context for this author's writing, and what questions concern him—or her? What options do they perceive as possible? Many of the critics of *A Theory of Justice* failed to ask such questions about Rawls' own contributions—though such background helps us to understand why the book caused such a stir due to the political and philosophical conflicts of Rawls' time.

In the middle of the twentieth century the United States was marked by deep political conflicts. The Civil Rights movement in the 1950s and 1960s posed fundamental questions about social life and governance in the US. The country's role in the Vietnam War further focused public attention on governmental legitimacy: By what moral right may the political authorities require that community members obey society's rules and regulations?

Rawls argues that legitimacy is primarily a question of fairness: how rights and benefits are distributed among people. In a democracy, the public legal and political order must ensure political equality. But the situation of African Americans made clear that formally equal civil rights is insufficient to prevent racial discrimination. Inadequate legal protections and limited economic and political opportunities kept this minority oppressed. At the same time, their demand for greater economic and social equality threatened the majority's prosperity and freedom.

2 Rawls' *Theory of Justice*: Justice as Fairness

On the question of when citizens have a moral obligation to obey the social institutions that are maintained with state authorities, Rawls responds that this is primarily a question of justice, and particularly about the effects of the basic institutions when it comes to the distribution of "social primary goods" among individuals.

2.1 Principles of Distributive Justice

The theory justifies specific distribution requirements for the basic institutions of society, as a whole, on the assumption that they are generally complied with (Rawls 1993a: 5):

1. *Principle of Liberty*
   Everyone has the same inalienable right to a satisfying set of equal basic rights, which is consistent with everyone else's corresponding set of rights. They include civil and political rights, such as voting rights, freedom of speech and religion, and the right to equal protection under the law.
2. *The Principle of Social and Economic Inequalities*
   The second principle consists of two conditions for the kind of social and economic differences that can occur over time. Rawls often refers to these two conditions as two different principles:
   2a The Principle of Equal Opportunity
   The social and economic disparities that exist must be linked to social positions—jobs and careers—which are equally accessible to all with the same ability and willingness to use those abilities.
   2b Difference Principle
   Social and economic inequalities are justifiable only if and insofar as they benefit the least advantaged members of society. The smallest piece of the social pie must be as large as possible.

In a society in accordance with these principles, the principle of liberty has priority: the social institutions as a whole must not promote equal opportunity or allow economic inequality in ways that violate others' basic rights and liberties. Similarly, the principle of equality of opportunity prevails over the Difference Principle: Equality of opportunity cannot be sacrificed in order to improve the worst off's income and wealth. The Difference Principle may allow economic inequality between people in different positions, for example, if the reward of extra effort raises productivity and thus contributes to increase the minimum wage in society. But this is justified only as long as the difference in wages is consistent with the other principles: Economic inequality may not translate into unequal political power and the opportunities for education and career choices for the next generation should not be affected. These principles cannot easily be taken to justify neither economic liberalization policies, nor all social democratic policies. Rawls' theory is, in principle, open to allow large or small tax transfers, more or less use of market mechanisms, and means-tested or universal support arrangements. Such choices must depend on the socio-economic conditions and the impact of economic incentives.

These principles are primarily intended for institutions that exist over time, and that thus shape the population's preferences and aspirations. There is no claim on Rawls' part that these principles also apply to strategies to improve existing unjust arrangements. For example, it is not given that it is more important, or more urgent, to ensure political rights than to remove severe economic inequality in a society that is deeply unjust. Similarly, measures such as affirmative action or gender quotas can be normatively justifiable or necessary in some societies for a limited time to remedy existing injustices, even if such measures might conflict with the priority of the principle of equality of opportunity over the Difference Principle. Such important questions about the proper improvement of unjust arrangements fall outside the scope of these principles, since they are intended to apply to arrangements that are already in place.

3 Conceptions of Society and of the Individual

How can the theory of justice as fairness justify such detailed criteria for fair social institutions? Rawls does not attempt to *derive* these principles from a more fundamental principle. Instead, he argues that these principles are *more reasonable* than the utilitarian principle of utility maximization. When we think carefully about our perceptions, we see that many immediate arguments for or against different policies are unsatisfactory. That a certain fairness principle will favour a particular social group may easily be regarded as an unfair argument—the role of principles of distributive justice is indeed instead precisely to assess whether such discrimination is fair. The religious and normative diversity in society also prevents some arguments for proposed principles, such as to promote a certain belief, or to foster certain attitudes or certain capabilities. The argument cannot simply be that this particular view of life, or these attitudes or abilities, are correct or that they have intrinsic value. Individuals with other views concerning what has value have no reason to accept *such* reasoning.

The first step in Rawls' theory of justice consists of two basic beliefs that he believes are central to democratic societies: a particular understanding of community and a conception of community members. He suggests that society should be understood as a system of cooperation between free and equal members of generations. Rawls distinguishes himself from utilitarians, who see society as a mechanism to promote overall well-being, and from many moral philosophers who argue that society should promote one specific human ideal. He believes that his basis is particularly suitable because of two important insights that history and research have given us about the community: the impact of social institutions, and ethical diversity.

Justice as fairness focuses on a limited subject matter: the distributive consequences of basic social institutions such as law, the economic structure, tax arrangements and family structure. The theory is exclusively concerned with a specific theme: how such institutions, considered as a whole, should affect the distribution of certain benefits and burdens among ourselves. Rawls believes that this question is practically relevant, important—and extremely difficult to answer. In order to clarify and understand Rawls' theory, we must look at his views on society and the individual, and the relationship between these two.

Rawls chooses to focus on how the basic institutions of society should influence the distribution of benefits and burdens among ourselves. Two aspects of society make it difficult to agree on criteria for this distribution: We are shaped by the institutions, and we have different beliefs of value.

Social institutions affect our living conditions and values in far-reaching ways. Social institutions are man-made, not natural: they are not uniquely determined by our natural needs, and they could have been different. This is not a new insight: David Hume remarks about "social artifices" that they are carried out with a certain plan and purpose. And these institutions are under human control, in the sense that they can be changed, e.g., by legislation (Hume 1960: 475, 528). Planned institutional change is difficult, and often fails (Elster 1991). But given opportunities for appropriate changes, it still makes sense to ask how social institutions *should* be. Political philosophy has been concerned with such issues at least since Plato.

Rawls tries to answer a particular variant of this question, and is particularly concerned with what he calls "the basic social structure."

We are drastically affected by our social environment, and in this sense we are *social beings*. The legal system, market economy, taxation and family structure creates rights and obligations tied to different roles. These arrangements reward certain abilities and types of work, and provide guidelines for how the fruits of cooperation should be distributed. The institutions affect us in fundamental ways, so that we are not left with many independent indicators to discuss how institutions should distribute such benefits and burdens among us. Institutions exerts influence in three ways: through the distribution of benefits, through the expectations they create among us for future benefits, and by affecting the value we attach to such benefits and burdens.

Institutions firstly affect the distribution of benefits and burdens. We are born into specific places in society, and our opportunities in life are determined largely by the basic social institutions that affect our ability to achieve different social positions.

Secondly, we form expectations in light of these institutions. They reward certain abilities, and some types of work, and provide guidelines for how the fruits of cooperation should be distributed. Under stable arrangements, those who hold certain jobs or social positions are rewarded accordingly, and everyone gets rewarded by what they have earned according to these rules. Thus to "give to all according to merit or effort" provides no answer to the question of what criteria should apply to such institutions which determine the expectations of citizens, which in turn determine what individuals will deserve (Hume 1975). Alternative institutions, such as other legislation for admission to study or for retirement pension, will give rise to different expectations. Existing expectations about the socially defined roles can thus not be the basis for claims of how social institutions should distribute benefits and burdens.

Thirdly, the institutions deeply affect our expectations and values. We are malleable: Institutions characterize even our assessment of the benefits and burdens that such institutions provide (March and Simon 1993; Elster 1983; March and Olsen 1989). Institutions shape us so early and profoundly that it is hard to imagine that we have an 'original' or 'really' complete set of values or interests, which is distorted or developed in the face of institutions. The question is not how such value socialization can be avoided, but rather the values and norms that institutions should nurture among citizens. This is one reason why the question of normative legitimacy is important: that is, how social institutions should distribute benefits and burdens, including how allocation, expectations, and socialization values should happen.

Paradoxically, since the institutions have such massive impact on citizens it becomes difficult to find a well-founded answer to the question of how this power should be exercised. Because of our malleability social institutions' role cannot simply be to give us what we subjectively expect. Such correspondence between expectations and distribution can be achieved by ensuring that institutions reduce the level of ambition of some groups. Many will argue that a fair distribution must satisfy additional requirements: A skewed distribution is not fair simply by making sure that the disadvantaged come to terms with the situation. But if we are not able to argue on the basis of our subjective expectations, there are few other clues to determine how benefits and burdens should be distributed among ourselves. One possibility would be to build on a conception of the good life, but this becomes problematic because of the plurality of conceptions of the good life.

Rawls assumes that a society with freedom of religion and freedom of expression will entertain a diversity of beliefs. Many current normative beliefs may be inconsistent or incompatible with what else we know about biology, psychology, economics and how society can survive over time. But Rawls assumes that unless state power is used to suppress certain beliefs, reflective and moral members of society will not completely agree about human nature and about what the good life consists of. So we cannot use disputed parts of such beliefs as the basis for evaluating our common institutions by their effects on 'the good life' in general. That would mean that someone's beliefs are unduly influential, to the detriment of others'. Rawls believes instead that the rationale for standards of normative legitimacy must be neutral between these values. It does not mean that the reasons must be "value free," or that principles should not benefit any such beliefs, but citizens must be able to support the principles even though they do not agree on such deeper premises.

An additional challenge with this assumption of diversity of conceptions of the good is that a well-ordered society should be stable: Although citizens may hold otherwise incompatible beliefs, the members' sense of justice should be developed and maintained so that they want to conform to the social institutions.

4 Argument Strategy

Rawls draws on the social contract tradition in political philosophy. This tradition regards societal rules as rules one should be able to expect agreement to among all involved parties.[2] This tradition emphasizes the consent of all in some sense—at

[2] Presentations of the social contract tradition include Hampton (1993) and Freeman (1990). Early classic sources include Jean-Jacques Rousseau (1978), John Locke (1963), Immanuel Kant (1980 and 1965). Thomas Hobbes (1968) is also in the social contract tradition, but appears to justify moral norms from non-normative premises; cf. David Gauthier (1986). Among recent contributors to the tradition are Ronald Dworkin (1981a, b, 1987); Brian Barry (1989, 1995); Joshua Cohen (1989), Cohen and Rogers (1995) and T. M. Scanlon (1998).

least among those whose primary goal is to act in accordance with such rules. A satisfactory or appropriate set of rules is one that everyone concerned can expect to agree to, thus regardless of which party to the contract that you happen to be.

Government forces us to follow the laws of the land; we are in practice bound to obey. Can institutions still be said to respect individual freedom and equality? Yes, argued John Locke, Jean-Jacques Rousseau and Immanuel Kant. Under certain conditions, we can regard these rules as respecting us as free and equal, and we are therefore morally bound by the norms—even if we do not actually consent to them. The basic social structure respects individual freedom and equality if this scheme *could be* made the subject of voluntary consent of all parties concerned. However, arrangements are *illegitimate* if a person is worse off than she would have been under specified alternatives—for Locke, this base line was a natural state without social institutions. Locke thus argued that absolute autocracy was worse than such a state of nature, and that this arrangement therefore did not have the moral right to be obeyed.

This tradition interprets the norm of the equality of all human beings in a certain way. All interested parties count, and count equally in the sense that the rules and institutions of society must be defensible toward all. A satisfactory or appropriate set of rules is one that everyone concerned can be expected to join—i.e., that you would accept them regardless of which of the parties concerned you.

Rawls choose such a social contract-inspired approach. He proposed that a just society must meet the distribution criteria that would have been selected by parties on a free and equal footing. When criteria are such that they encounter no great objection to them—when they can therefore be said to be *reasonable*—we relate to each other as free and equal even when we are forced to surrender to our social institutions. This is the idea behind Rawls' suggestion that we should understand *justice as fairness.*

For Rawls, the theme is not, as it was for some earlier social contract thinkers, isolated social institutions, but the social institutions considered as a whole. And the basis of comparison to assess the person's advantage or disadvantage is not for Rawls a natural state. Even though social institutions are "artificial" it is not sensible to try to assess ourselves as "really" existing outside the norms, ties and roles we are born into in. Instead, Rawls seeks to compare alternative principles for assessing basic social structures.

Rawls proposes a tool to make it easier to see how we can justify and rank such proposals for principles of justice. We envisage an initial negotiating "Original Position" in which all parties need to agree on principles for assessing whether social institutions are fair. This corresponds to a social-contract interpretation of equality and freedom as general consent. Furthermore, Rawls asks us to think that the parties are not aware of facts that could entice them to come by unfair or improper arguments. The parties argue thus behind *a veil of ignorance* in the choice of principles of justice.

In this original position the parties know that social institutions affect their lives in crucial ways as indicated above. Although everyone has a philosophy of life that they want to promote, they do not know what particular such beliefs they have.

Therefore no one will advocate a particular distribution of benefits simply because it promotes a certain belief. Nor would anyone argue that social institutions should necessarily favour certain talents such as learning ability, entrepreneurship or bravery, since no one knows whether they have such characteristics. They may still agree that institutions can reward some such character traits, but then for certain reasons, for example, to increase the amount of wealth that all will eventually have a share of. Rawls argues that the most disadvantaged social position will be given decisive weight in the choice of principles of justice. This is expressed by the idea that parties would think of the worst that could happen to them. In ignorance of how each will end up on the social ladder, they will ensure that the worst off are as well off as possible. Rawls' principles would be preferable over utilitarianism's principle of utility maximization, since the latter allows that some can be sacrificed for the benefit of others.

Rawls argues that this hypothetical choice in this original position is relevant to determine the principles of justice because this choice situation reflects the considerations we believe are appropriate when discussing these issues. In this position, the parties would prefer Rawls' principles over utilitarianism. Rawls' principles ensures that everyone, even the most disadvantaged, receive a portion of social goods. Choice in the original position reflects that we are trying to find principles that can be generally consented to, and that we wish to avoid policies that some will have great objections against. Such complaints will typically come from the very ones who are the worst off. Those who get less social primary goods than others will often have weighty objections against such unequal distribution, especially when we take into account that these goods are created through collaboration, and when we realize the huge impact an unequal distribution has on the living standards of the disadvantaged.

For this approach to work it is critical to be able to choose among competing principles on the basis of reasonable objections to any rules, with regard to the effects such rules have on the individuals concerned. Such normative arguments in this tradition require comparability between individuals in terms of the relevant consequences of such rules—i.e., those that define the practices of social institutions. Yet the factors mentioned above make it difficult to agree on such principles of justice: the topic concerns social institutions that affect life plans; the plurality of conceptions of the good, and the malleability of our preferences. These factors limit the effects on individuals that can provide the basis for arguments for and against such principles of justice. Now various theories of distributive justice will have different perceptions about the *benefits* that should be regulated, the *interests of* the parties that matter, and how these interests should be taken into account. Rawls must clarify the benefits and burdens that principles of justice should regulate. This choice must be made in light of the various constraints mentioned above, and based on our need to be able to argue for and against such principles. Thus it is only detectable effects caused by social institutions that can count for or against the assessment of different principles for institutions. In addition, the benefits and burdens have roughly the same effects for all subjects. Rawls also need a theory of relevant interests that can be expected to command general agreement. The size of the benefits and burdens incurred by the various parties concerned must also be comparable.

To compare Rawls' theory with other contributions it will be important to look at these premises about interests, benefits, and equality as they appear in Rawls' argument.

4.1 Interests: Reasonableness and Rationality

Justice as fairness suggests that two interests are paramount (Rawls 1971: 505). When it comes to this issue of distributive justice, he believes that we can expect agreement that an individual for such purposes has two important capabilities—even if we disagree on these important skills in other contexts. Firstly, we all have a *sense of justice.* We have the ability to understand, apply, and submit to the principles and rules we perceive as fair. This sense of justice means that we do not give ourselves unjust objectives contrary to the principles of justice we deem appropriate. Note that this premise is clearly normative. The theory thus does not attempt to justify moral considerations out of self-interest alone.

Secondly, we are *rational,* in a certain sense: Each of us has the ability to form an opinion about the good life within the possibilities envisaged. We try to promote or achieve this goal, alone or in collaboration with others.

In Rawls' theory it is only the consequences for these two interests that are considered as relevant bases for arguments about the principles of justice. Of course, we have many other important skills and interests, and many of these may be more important for each of us. But only arguments that pertain to the distributive effects on these two capabilities are such that Rawls believes we can expect consensus.

4.2 Social Primary Goods

Given our malleability and the plurality of conceptions of the good, it is difficult to find a suitable set of benefits and burdens whose distribution is to be assessed. Rawls introduces "social primary goods" as a creative response to these challenges (Rawls 1971: 62, 1999c). These benefits are political and civil rights and liberties, powers and formal positions and occupations, income and wealth, and the social basis of self-respect.

These benefits are partly of *intrinsic* and partly of *instrumental* value for the two relevant capabilities. Social primary goods are social conditions and assets under institutional control that are usually required in order to develop and use these skills, and to promote the particular conception of the good life one might have. The distribution of these goods emerge as a justified claim. They are even more so suited because we can understand the social primary goods as institutionalized authority. These benefits—income, for instance, in the form of money—give people the legal power to determine the actions of others in specific areas. But such benefits—money—exists only to the extent that the pieces of paper are accepted as legal tender by other social actors. This means that these benefits only exist if the rules are followed and the prescribed outcomes thus actually follow. It is therefore in a sense the citizens' common practices that constitute the social primary goods. The distribution of these social primary goods through the basic institutions of society as a whole, in accordance with the incentives and expectations created, must therefore be such that as a base line, all get equal shares of these goods over time. This is reflected in the principles of distributive justice, justice as fairness.

5 Rawls' Theory of Justification: Reflective Equilibrium

In normative ethics one argues for specific answers to questions about how we should act, what the good life is, or what kind of society we should have. Rawls' book is primarily a contribution to this branch of moral philosophy. In this way *A Theory of Justice* marks a break with much other philosophy that had become common in the West. Few philosophers, either in Europe or in the English-speaking world, had contributed much to answer normative questions. Proponents of logical positivism, for example, worked almost exclusively in clarifying concepts and in reflecting on how we can justify our beliefs and have certain knowledge. Moral philosophers in the analytic tradition thus tended to take no position on the normative questions, but instead discussed important *meta-ethical* issues. They analyzed ethical expression, and discussed whether the ethical claims can be said to be true or false, or whether they just express feelings. *A Theory of Justice* also helped to answer some of these important and interesting questions.

Philosophers have often thought that our beliefs about what is right and wrong in certain situations are only based on more general moral principles about what is good and right, for example, that it is wrong to lie, or to abuse or exploit others. But how can these principles in turn be justified? Rawls proposed that the various allegations and perceptions of the normative theory mutually justify each other when we organize them as premises and conclusions in a systematic and clear way. Premises and conclusions justify each other in "reflective equilibrium". The considered judgements we have about specific situations help justify more general principles 'from below': Slavery is wrong because it violates principles of fairness and equal dignity. And the general principles we adhere to in turn justify particular judgements "from above" by showing that these principles fit well with the many individual perceptions and ethical reactions we have.

Consider Rawls' strategy to clarify the conditions under which people have a moral obligation to support the society's institutions. He sought to ascertain whether the institutions are in accordance with the values and ideals the people have reason to support. To find answers, he sought the justification of the various norms and rules we experience as binding: abstract values such as "freedom, equality and solidarity", specific commands and prohibitions from the government, and our assessments of what we think of as untimely or relevant considerations. He then tried to explicate these norms and values and put them together as coherent chains of premises and conclusions. Thus he sought to determine whether they are justified, or whether they need to be adjusted in light of their premises or consequences.

For example: The civil and political rights in a state respecting the rule of law gives content to the ideals of *freedom* from violations and arbitrary exercise of power. These rights limit legal power, and insist that government must be authorized by law.

Equality is expressed in requirements of due process, and in equal and democratic decision-making procedures. Welfare schemes express *solidarity:* that no one should be left completely without support. Social institutions must, among other things, ensure decent living conditions for the most disadvantaged.

Thus we seek to specify norms and values in different areas of life, at more concrete and abstract levels, and try to tie them together as a theory, as a consistent whole of premises and conclusions. Normative theory has this as its field of research.

This way of understanding the grounds of ethics is not new with Rawls: we find elements in earlier philosophers, as far back as Aristotle. Rawls' contribution was mainly to organize and advocate this form of justification.

W. V. Quine (1908–2000), Rawls' colleague at Harvard, has claimed a more general point of view: that *all* our perceptions, not only in ethics, can *only* be justified by the fact that they are part of a systematic whole that fits with our experience. Rawls himself took no position on this, and would not even argue that his theory of justice is true. He would only say that the theory is an *acceptable* theory in political philosophy, and that it better explains our moral beliefs than does utilitarianism.

6 What's New?

In the more recent book *Justice as Fairness* Rawls addressed some areas where he had changed his views, and clarified some details which he thought critics had misunderstood—such as the use of a 'maximin' principle and whether the theory can criticize oppressive gender roles. Three other aspects may also be mentioned briefly.

In his book *Political Liberalism* (1993b) Rawls discussed in particular how a society with ethical diversity can be fair and maintain support over time—that is, so that it can have both *normative* and *social legitimacy.* Is there reason to believe that citizens with different conceptions of the good will support Rawls' principles of justice and an existing just basic social structure over time? Rawls argues that philosophical reflection of the kind he contributes is important precisely to ensure such stability or sustainability. A common and public explanation of why institutions deserve our support can give everyone reason to support the fair arrangements, and assure each citizen that most others think and do likewise—regardless of their other disagreements. Such justification must be based on assumptions on which we must expect consensus, based on an *overlapping consensus* across a range of beliefs that otherwise disagree on many points.

In late articles Rawls emphasized that the theory is "political" in certain ways. It is not intended as a comprehensive moral theory or a comprehensive philosophical theory of man and society in general. Instead, the theory is only applicable to certain social institutions, where the principles and assumptions are not claimed to be true, but rather pragmatically useful to achieve consensus.

In the book *Justice as Fairness* Rawls made it very clear that the theory is justified by reflective equilibrium. Not only did he refrain from asserting that the premises are self-evident or true definitions of the terms 'justice', 'person', etc. He also stressed that the theory draws on certain conceptions of all persons as equals and on society as a system of cooperation between such free and equal citizens, two beliefs he found confirmed in Western political culture. He let it thus open whether these conceptions also exist and are widely shared in the rest of the world, and in what sense this would matter for the application of the theory. He started to explore some international implications of this theory in *The Law of Peoples* (Rawls 1999b), with regard to the principles such as international human rights that should govern the foreign policies of liberal states.

It is also evident that Rawls did not hold that U.S. institutions were in compliance with the principles of justice he defended. The theory is thus not to be understood as a defense of the existing American social order. He carefully explained that the freedoms his theory gives primacy to do not include private ownership of the means of production. He also argued in favour of two other social systems than the U.S. capitalist welfare system: both what he calls corporate democracy and a liberal, democratic, socialist regime could satisfy his principles. He also noted that the U.S. had moved away from the principles of justice as fairness over time, partly because political parties can use private resources in campaign so that the real value of political rights is reduced.

7 Criticism

Rawls' theory is part of the analytic tradition in philosophy that emphasizes careful argumentation and justification for claims. A strength of the analytic tradition is that the theories are thus more open to criticism: it is easier to identify disputed premises, weaknesses and mistakes. Rawls' theory has certainly not been left unchallenged—an annotated bibliography of critical articles appeared as early as 1982 (Wellbank et al. 1982), and five volumes of critical papers were published in 1999 (Richardson and Weithman 1999). Let us conclude by looking at some objections to the theory of justice as fairness.

Many of the critics have not noted that Rawls addressed a very limited question. Rawls' theory is obviously not responding to all the ethical and political challenges we face. The principles he proposed are intended to apply to the set of basic institutions of society, and they are not necessarily valid for other distribution issues—such as the distribution of health services, the distribution of wealth between generations, or distributive justice across borders. Our responsibility towards the developing world remained largely unanswered by Rawls' side until he discussed the norms of foreign policy in his book *The Law of Peoples* in 1999. The theory of human rights he presented there has also been widely criticized.

Furthermore, principles of justice cannot be applied directly when we decide how we should act in certain situations. Also, the principles were intended by him to apply primarily to a well-ordered society. How social institutions should remedy injustices of the past, and what we should do when we live under unjust arrangements, are important issues that Rawls barely addressed, e.g., in a discussion about civil disobedience. The theory cannot easily answer these questions without further development. Rawls also restricted the scope of application of the principles to communities under "favorable conditions"—That is, he assumed among other things that there is enough of an economic basis to ensure political and civil liberties, and enough to meet basic needs (Rawls 1999c). The priorities among benefits and among social primary goods in poorer countries is an open question.

That his theory does not provide answers to all questions is of course not a weighty objection, especially because parts of the approach may still be fruitful for such topics. But the topic of Rawls' own writings is thus quite narrow.

Even within its intended scope, numerous thoughtful objections are directed to the theory. Rawls takes as given that a fair distribution of benefits is necessary for a legitimate state. Conflicts of interest are therefore the focus of Rawls' view of society. Some critics have argued that this is based on a wrong conception of human nature, since the good society should instead be based on people's love and self-sacrifice (Sandel 1982; cf. Gutmann 1985; Buchanan 1989; Mulhall and Swift 1996; Rasmussen 1990; Follesdal 1998).

One can also criticize the theory for focusing on social institutions, and ignoring other practices. There are at least three problems with this choice. Firstly, it is not clear where to draw the line—for example, Douglass North argues that there is a smooth transition to 'culture' understood as informal institutional rules (North 1990). Here, the above discussion may be helpful: The institutions in question are those that affect individuals in fundamental and inescapable ways and that constitute benefits and burdens. Secondly, it can be argued that social institutions can allow a multitude of different practices with very different distributional effects. This diversity of practices should not be overlooked. Among the many studies on this Robert Putnam's research on Italy is interesting (Putnam 1993). Similar democratic and economic arrangements seem to work much better in the northern than in the southern regions of Italy. Putnam shows that this is due to the number of local networks of NGOs, which supposedly increases citizens' ability to think about the common good and not just on their own welfare. This attitude leads to increased confidence, and consequently to better social institutions. To a certain extent, these findings are consistent with Rawls' theory even if the findings point to obvious limitations in the application of the theory. For instance, one can ask whether it is reasonable to believe that justice as fairness can be stabilizing in the way Rawls imagined—regardless of the interpersonal networks that exist.

Thirdly, several critics argued that Rawls' approach ignores abuses going on in the so-called "private" sphere, shielded from the "public" state. His theory has been interpreted to mean that the division of labor within the family or in a segregated labor market is not a question of justice (Okin 1989; Kymlicka 1991). Rawls and others have argued against this interpretation of justice as fairness (Rawls 1997, 1999a) but there is no guarantee that the theory distinguishes between the private and the public sphere in a convincing manner.

Other political theorists disagree with some of Rawls' terms, or criticize the way they are put together in his theory. Equality and freedom can be expressed in ways other than through the social contract perspective. And even if the contract theory is kept, it is not certain that the ideal of equality requires that the state should be neutral between conceptions of the good in the way Rawls argues. Some may argue that social institutions should take into account the differing opinions about what is good, and promote the view that the majority of members share, and resolve conflicts between the parties in the light of that vision. Others, including those who believe that political activity has an intrinsic value, argue that the ideal of the politically active person can be justified as a premise for a theory of a just society.

One might also submit objections within Rawls' framework, by claiming that other factors must be considered relevant as reasons for principles of justice. This can be presented as a disagreement about what the ignorance veil should cover as to what the parties know about themselves and the society they live in.

Still other critics accept Rawls' formulation of the original position, but argue that participants would prefer other principles than Rawls': either enhanced versions of utilitarian principles or other principles. Alternative normative theories will give different answers on which of a person's *interests* should be emphasized, what *benefits* must be ensured, and/or the *allocation principles* for these goods that institutions should satisfy over time. Arguments for various policies indicate the value of such goods for certain interests. A major challenge for these options is to deal with the fact that social institutions also affect our preferences and values (Sen 1992).

Rawls' assumptions about citizens' interests are criticized from the view that other abilities and attitudes should be decisive in the choice of principles of justice. For example, minorities claim group rights to protect their own culture. An interesting development of the liberal political tradition has been to determine how such interest shall be expressed and weighted in ways that draw on Rawls' insights (Kymlicka 1995; see Follesdal 1996 for further references).

Amartya Sen has criticized Rawls' theory for ignoring personal differences in the metabolism of goods. Some "demanding" citizens, such as people with disabilities or special health needs (Sen 1980), must have more benefits to achieve the same opportunities to act. In addition needs vary with longevity, climate, employment, etc., in ways Rawls' theory does not capture. Therefore Sen criticizes a focus on social primary goods as *fetishistic*. They are understood as expressing benefits, but ignore that a benefit is essentially a relationship between individuals and goods. Social primary goods are considered as means to achieve something. Rather than focus on the equal distribution of these funds Sen believes that one should focus on equal distribution of what these means are means for, namely *functions and possibilities* (Sen 1992, 1993).

Sen argued that individuals' claims should not be evaluated based on what resources or primary goods they use, but on the basis of what features and freedoms they actually have to choose lives they have reason to value. Such interests captures the personal variations in leveraging resources, and how you choose to use such opportunities. Rawls sought to respond to this criticism in *Justice as Fairness.*

Some economists have criticized Rawls' use of uncertainty and ignorance as an argument for a "maximin strategy" for choices between principles in the original position, where the disadvantaged are decisive. Among other concerns, John Harsanyi argued that uncertainty only suggests a maximin strategy for the individual if one is extremely keen to avoid risks (Harsanyi 1975). In response, T. M. Scanlon has pointed out that many of the arguments of justice as fairness can still be preserved. The contract situation must then be specified so as to rank principles not on the basis of what it would be rational to choose by self-interested choosers under a veil of ignorance, but by asking what cannot be reasonably objected against, regardless of one's social position (Scanlon 1982, 1998).

8 What are Rawls' Lasting Contributions?

Ethical theories have a function that Rawls helped remind us of: to bring order and coherence among our different moral beliefs, thus helping to settle our practical conflicts. Justification by reflective equilibrium is an important insight, which can be applied to ethical theories in general, not just to Rawls' theory of justice.

Other theories that seek to answer other questions may make use of parts of Rawls' theory, just as he built on what he saw as valuable in earlier political philosophy. For instance, many regard the idea of an original position as a fruitful tool to address other moral issues.

The theory of justice as fairness has not refuted utilitarianism or other political theories once and for all. Still, Rawls' theory is a thorough and systematic attempt to solve one of the major policy issues we disagree about. Reflective equilibrium and overlapping consensus show how values can be justified, even in a society with diverse beliefs, so that we can treat each other as free and equal human beings, in spite of all our differences.

References

Barry, B. (1989). *Theories of justice. A treatise on social justice* (Vol. 1). Berkeley: University of California Press.

Barry, B. (1995). *Justice as impartiality*. Oxford: Oxford University Press.

Buchanan, A. E. (1989). Assessing the communitarian critique of liberalism. *Ethics, 99*(4), 852–882.

Cohen, J. (1989). Deliberation and democratic legitimacy. In A. Hamlin & P. Pettit (Red.), *The good polity* (pp. 17–34). Oxford: Blackwell.

Cohen, J., & Rogers, J. (1995). *Associations and democracy*. London: Verso.
Dworkin, R. (1981a). What is equality? Part 1: Equality of welfare. *Philosophy and Public Affairs, 10*(3), 185–246.
Dworkin, R. (1981b). What is equality? Part 2: Equality of resources. *Philosophy and Public Affairs, 10*(4), 283–345.
Dworkin, R. (1987). What is equality? Part 3: The place of liberty. *Iowa Law Review, 73*, 1–54.
Elster, J. (1983). *Sour grapes: Studies in the subversion of rationality*. Paris/Cambridge: Maison des Sciences de l'Homme/Cambridge University Press.
Elster, J. (1991). The possibility of rational politics. In H. David (Red.), *Political theory today* (pp. 115–142). Oxford: Polity.
Follesdal, A. (1996). Minority rights: A liberal contractualist case. In J. Raikka (Red.), *Do we need minority rights? Conceptual issues* (Vol. 24, pp. 59–83). The Hague/London/Boston: Kluwer Academic Publisher/Kluwer Law International.
Follesdal, A. (1998). Communitarian criticisms of liberal contractualism: An account and a Defense. In B. Frank & T. Sasha (Red.), *Memory, history and critique: european identity at the millennium*. Cambridge, MA: MIT.
Freeman, S. (1990). Reason and agreement in social contract views. *Philosophy and Public Affairs, 19*, 141–147.
Gauthier, D. (1986). *Morals by agreement*. Oxford: Clarendon.
Gutmann, A. (1985). Communitarian critics of liberalism. *Philosophy and Public Affairs, 14*(3), 308–322.
Hampton, J. (1993). Contract and consent. In R. E. Goodin & P. Pettit (Red.), *A companion to contemporary political philosophy* (pp. 379–393). Oxford: Blackwell.
Harsanyi, J. C. (1975). Can the maximin principle serve as a basis for morality? A critique of John Rawls' theory. *American Political Science Review, 69*, 594–606.
Hobbes, T. (1968 [1651]). *Leviathan*. (C. B. Macpherson) (Red. and Introd.). Baltimore: Penguin.
Hume, D. (1960 [1739]). *A treatise of human nature* (L. A. Selby-Bigge & P. H. Nidditch, Red.). Oxford: Clarendon.
Hume, D. (1975 [1777]). *Enquiries concerning human understanding and concerning the principles of morals*. Oxford: Clarendon.
Kant, I. (1965 [1797]). *The metaphysical elements of justice*. Indianapolis: Bobbs-Merrill.
Kant, I. (1980 [1785]). *Grounding for the metaphysics of morals* [*Grundlegung zur metaphysik der Sitten*] (E. Ellington James, Ed.). Indianapolis: Hackett Publishing Company.
Kymlicka, W. (1991). Rethinking the family. *Philosophy and Public Affairs, 20*(1), 77–97.
Kymlicka, W. (1995). *Multicultural citizenship: A liberal theory of minority rights*. Oxford: Oxford University Press.
Locke, J. (1963 [1690]). *Two treatises of government*. (L. Peter) (Rev. and Introd.). New York: New American Library, Mentor.
March, J. G., & Olsen, J. P. (1989). *Rediscovering institutions: The organizational basis of politics*. New York: Free Press.
March, J. G., & Simon, H. A. (1993 [1958]). *Organizations* (2nd ed.). London: Blackwell.
Mulhall, S., & Swift, A. (1996). *Liberals and communitarians* (Rev. version). Oxford: Blackwell.
North, D. (1990). *Institutions, institutional change and economic performance*. Cambridge: Cambridge University Press.
Okin, S. M. (1989). *Justice, gender and the family*. New York: Basic Books.
Putnam, R. D. (1993). *Making democracy work: Civic traditions in modern Italy*. Princeton: Princeton University Press.
Rasmussen, D. (1990). *Universalism vs. communitarianism: Contemporary debates in ethics*. Cambridge, MA: MIT Press.
Rawls, J. (1971). *A theory of justice*. Cambridge, MA: Harvard University Press.
Rawls, J. (1993a [1982]). The basic liberties and their priority. In *Political liberalism* (pp. 289–371). New York: Columbia University Press.
Rawls, J. (1993b). *Political liberalism*. New York: Columbia University Press.

Rawls, J. (1997). The idea of public reason revisited. *University of Chicago Law Review, 64*(Summer): 765–807.
Rawls, J. (1999a). *Collected papers* (F. Samuel, Red.). Cambridge, MA: Harvard University Press.
Rawls, J. (1999b). *The law of peoples*. Cambridge, MA: Harvard University Press.
Rawls, J. (1999c [1982]). Social unity and primary goods. In *Collected papers* (pp. 359–387). [First in A. K. Sen & W. Bernard (Red.). (1982). *Utilitarianism and beyond* (pp. 159–185). Cambridge: Cambridge University Press]. Cambridge, MA: Harvard University Press.
Richardson, H., & Weithman, P. (Red.). (1999). *The philosophy of Rawls: A collection of essays* (Vol. 5). New York: Garland Publishing.
Rousseau, J. -J.(1978 [1762]). *On the social contract* (D. Masters Roger, Red.). New York: St. Martin's Press.
Sandel, M. J. (1982). *Liberalism and the limits of justice*. Cambridge: Cambridge University Press.
Scanlon, T. M. (1982). Contractualism and utilitarianism. In A. K. Sen & B. Williams (Red.), *Utilitarianism and beyond* (pp. 103–128). Cambridge: Cambridge University Press.
Scanlon, T. M. (1998). *What we owe to each other*. Cambridge, MA: Harvard University Press.
Sen, A. K. (1980). Equality of what? In A. K. Sen (Red.), *Choice, welfare and measurement* (pp. 353–369). Cambridge, MA: MIT Press.
Sen, A. K. (1992). *Inequality reexamined*. Cambridge, MA: Harvard University Press.
Sen, A. K. (1993). Capability and well-being. In M. Nussbaum & A. K. Sen (Red.), *The quality of life* (pp. 30–53). World Institute for Development Economics Research (WIDER) of the United Nations University. Oxford: Clarendon Press.
Wellbank, J. H., Snook, D., & Mason, D. T. (1982). *John Rawls and his critics: An annotated bibliography*. New York: Garland Publishing Company.

Love and Justice in Ricœur

Peter Kemp

One of the most important developments in ethics in our time was spearheaded by Paul Ricœur (1913–2005). In particular, he highlighted the role of the other in an ethical sense in his writings about justice and love, which must be taken as the foundation of all normativity.

He wrote about justice in his last years—particularly in his two books on *The Just* (1995 and 2001) and his last work *The Course of Recognition* from 2004. He has also written much about ethics. For example, we have what he himself called his "little ethics" in the book *Oneself as Another* from 1990 and several essays on ethics. However, he has apparently not written much about love except for his lecture on *"Amour et Justice"* ("Love and Justice"), which he gave when he received the Leopold Lucas Prize in 1989. But there are elements in what he wrote at the end of his life about friendship that have to do with love, and his analyses of forgiveness—especially in the epilogue to the book *Memory, History, Forgetting—also* concern an aspect of love that he anticipates in his short examination of the proximity of closely related persons.[1]

In a dedication to me in the first volume of *The Just,* he wrote: *"au-delà de la justice, l'amitié"* (beyond justice, friendship). Thus, justice and friendship must be situated on different levels, and I also find different levels in friendship itself. I want to analyse the other in his philosophy by describing the whole range of good human relationships in his thinking in order to scrutinize both the common features and the different forms of such relationships and, in addition, to discover the driving force behind the whole.

[1] Ricœur, Paul (2000) *La Mémoire, l'histoire, l'oubli.* Paris: Seuil, pp. 161–162; *Memory, History, Forgetting*. Chicago: University of Chicago Press, pp. 131–132.

P. Kemp (✉)
Department of Education, Aarhus University, Copenhagen Campus, Tuborgvej 164,
DK-2400 Copenhagen NV, Denmark
e-mail: kemp@edu.au.dk

G. Fløistad (ed.), *Philosophy of Justice*, Contemporary Philosophy: A New Survey 12, 329
DOI 10.1007/978-94-017-9175-5_19, © Springer Science+Business Media Dordrecht 2015

1 Love

Let us begin with his phenomenological analysis of love in "Love and Justice". He quotes Pascal, who said that charity is of a completely different order than all bodies and spirits that we can count. But how to describe this charity without exaltation or vulgarity? Ricœur thinks that there are three forms of discourse by which love expresses itself:

(a) a discourse related to praise, such as in the glorification of charity in 1 Corinthians, chap. 13, v. 4–5: "charity suffereth long, *and* is kind; charity envieth not; charity wanteth not itself, is not puffed up. Doth not behave itself unseemly, seeketh not her own, is not easily provoked, thinketh no evil", etc., and "beareth all things, believeth all things, hopeth all things, endureth all things" (v. 7), finishing with these words: "And now abideth faith, hope, charity, these three; but the greatest of these *is* charity" (v. 13),
(b) a discourse related to the command of what cannot be commanded as obligation, such as the command from the Old Testament, repeated by Jesus: "Thou shalt love thy neighbour as thyself" (Matt. 19, 19 & 22, 39). But how can a feeling be genuine if it is commanded? Normally, it cannot, but Ricœur refers to Franz Rosenzweig, who reminds us in *The Star of Redemption* that the lover says to the beloved: "Love me!". Love is expressed by the tenderness of a conjuration, Ricœur says[2]; it is expressed by a poetic use of the imperative,[3] and
(c) a discourse of metaphorical power (*la puissance de métaphorisation*) that produces a wide range of analogies in which the metaphor is more than an ornamentation and expresses power in such a way that Eros must signify Agape, i.e., other qualities than pure eroticism.

2 Justice

Let us then proceed to Ricœur's description of justice in the above-mentioned talk.

Justice belongs to quite another context than love. As a judicial concept, it belongs to a context in which a legal institution must decide between different claims of opposing interests and rights. Here is no poetry but prose by different arguments that confronts reasons for and against.

But this procedure is not without an ethical character: *audi alteram partem* (listen to the other party!) is the old norm for justice in court. And the goal of the just institution is to give everybody what is owed to him or her.

Thus, justice is originally distributive justice according to which goods and services are distributed in a fair way.

---

[2] Ricœur, Paul (1990) *Liebe und Gerechtigkeit, Amour et justice*. Tübingen: J. C. B. Mohr, p. 18.

[3] *Ibid.*, p. 20.

But this fairness is equity, a reasonable distribution according to needs and capacities based on disinterest.

3 Economy of Gift

Between justice, on the one hand, and love as charity, on the other, Ricœur calls our attention to a third phenomenon expressed in the new commandment: "Love your enemies, do good to them which hate you" (Luke, 6, 27). This is a super-ethics of a broad *economy of gift* that says that, since you have received, you must give. It is a suspension of ethics as mutuality,[4] but its aim is still very high: to protect the exercise of love and justice against pure calculation.

4 Recognition

However, according to Ricœur, the protection of justice against calculation is grounded in a profound way on a generous recognition, as the French legal philosopher Antoine Garapon has shown in his outstanding presentation of the idea of justice in Ricœur.[5] Garapon stressed that, in *The Course of Recognition,* Ricœur has demonstrated the role of recognition in the construction of a legal order between human beings and, thereby, in the creation of society.[6] And he asserts the importance of the distinction that Ricœur makes in *The Course of Recognition* between reciprocity and mutuality, two ideas that he had not clearly distinguished before.

This new distinction implies that reciprocity is a "kind of autonomous circularity",[7] i.e., a relationship between atomized individuals. Ricœur finds this reciprocity in Hobbes, where all individuals are involved in a war against all others in "the state of nature" and, in order to avoid death, agree to a covenant by which they obtain protection and "the rule of law".

Mutuality is different. It is a kind of living together that presupposes that human beings are "political beings" who can develop "political friendship" in the "economy of gift".

Thanks to this distinction between reciprocity and mutuality, Ricœur then distinguishes between two kinds of recognition: recognition built on reciprocity and recognition built on mutuality.

---

[4] *Ibid.*, p. 64.

[5] Garapon, Antoine "Justice et reconnaissance," in *Esprit*, mars-avril 2006, *La pensée Ricœur*, pp. 231–248.

[6] Ricœur, Paul (2004) *Parcours de la reconnaissance*. Paris: Stock; *The Course of Recognition*. Cambridge, Mass.: Harvard University Press, 2005.

[7] Ricœur, Paul *Parcours de la reconnaissance,* p. 320; *The Course of Recognition,* p. 219.

The first kind of recognition has its roots in Hobbes' idea of acknowledgment, wherein "each man acknowledges the other as his equal by nature" and through which he "overcomes distrust" and agrees to a "reciprocal contract"[8] that gives all rights of power to one man. This acknowledgment becomes the *Anerkennung* in Hegel's notion of the "struggle for recognition" in which the war of all against all in Hobbes is integrated into the human Spirit by the reconciliation of master and slave.

The second kind of recognition (rooted in Aristotle) can, according to Ricœur, be found in the last great work of Emmanuel Levinas: *Otherwise than Being or Beyond Essence* (first French edition in 1974). He refers to the idea in Levinas of a "comparison between incomparables".[9] Here, Levinas uses the affinity in French between the words *comparution* (appearance in a court) and *comparison* (observation of similarity) and argues that justice is constituted by a presence together before a judge.[10] Justice is founded by what he calls a synopsis of the different, a togetherness and contemporaneousness before a third part.[11] In this situation in which we are simultaneously present together before a tribunal, the judge appears as the model of all legal order, as is noted by Antoine Garapon.[12] The courtroom scene expresses our recognition of our own equality with the other and our recognition of the other as equal with us before the law. It is the same in every just institution in society: before a political institution in a just society, everyone is, in principle (that is, disregarding privileges tied to specific offices), equal with everyone else.

Antoine Garapon calls the mutual recognition that establishes the legal order *reconstructive justice* in order to distinguish it from corrective justice, which punishes crimes, and distributive justice, which allocates goods and burdens.[13] In a way, these two other forms of justice are conditioned by the reconstructive or constitutive justice that founded the legal order as such. There is, in fact, no subject of law and, thus, no law at all without this recognition of legal equality.

5 Beyond Justice

My final question is: How can friendship be beyond justice?

I would like to examine two ideas:

1. the mutual memory in close relations,
2. forgiveness that cannot be given in politics.

---

[8] Ricœur, Paul *Parcours de la reconnaissance,* p. 248; *The Course of Recognition,* p. 168.

[9] Ricœur, Paul *Parcours de la reconnaissance,* p. 237; *The Course of Recognition,* p. 161.

[10] Levinas, Emmanuel (1978, 2nd ed.) *Autrement qu'être ou au-delà de l'essence*. La Haye, p. 20, éd. Poche, Kluwer Academic, p. 33; *Otherwise than Being and Beyond*. Kluwer: Dordrecht, 1991, p. 16.

[11] *Ibid.*

[12] Article cité, *Esprit, La pensée Ricœur*, pp. 231–248.

[13] *Ibid.,* p. 231.

But let us not forget that not all forms of friendship are true love. According to Aristotle, whom Ricœur quotes in *Oneself as Another*, there are three types of friendship: for the sake of the "good", for the sake of "utility", and for the sake of "pleasure",[14] and only the first one is true care of the other as other; the two other types have other goals: the other is useful for my projects or the other is only the object of my pleasure. However, in the care for or solicitude of the other, this other is considered as another self, *an alter ego*[15] that belongs to my self-esteem in which "the self that one loves is what is best in oneself" and in which the solicitude "is based principally on the exchange of giving and receiving"[16] and endows friendship with its "mutual character".[17]

And the fact that not all friendship is love in its strongest sense also follows from the fact that we, like Aristotle and like Ricœur in his book that develops *The Course of Recognition*, can speak about a political friendship, as I mentioned above.

5.1 Mutual Memory in Close Relations

At the end of the first part of *Memory, History, Forgetting*—"On memory and recollection", Ricœur suggests that there is "an intermediate level of reference between the poles of individual memory and collective memory where concrete exchanges operate between the living memory of individual persons and the public memory of the communities to which we belong". He calls it the level of closely related persons (*"la relation aux proches"*).[18]

These people are those "who count for us, and for whom we count". They create an interplay of distanciation and rapprochement "that makes proximity a dynamic relationship ceaselessly in motion: drawing near, feeling close". And this proximity would then be, Ricœur says, "the counterpart to friendship". Indeed, these closely related persons "occupy the middle-ground between the self and the 'they'", being "others as fellow beings, privileged others".[19]

In what sense do they count? They count because, in our shared memory, two "events" that limit a human life, birth and death, are very important for us, and we celebrate or deplore them, although they only interest society in terms of public records and as a renewal of generations. Persons who are closely related are those "who approve of my existence and whose existence I approve of in the reciprocity and equality of esteem". The closely related are those who approve my existence: "that I am able to speak, act, recount, impute to myself the responsibility for my

[14] Ricœur, Paul (1990) *Soi-même comme un autre*. Paris: Seuil, p. 182; *Oneself as Another*, University of Chicago Press, p. 214.

[15] Ricœur, Paul *Soi-même comme un autre*, p. 212; *Oneself as Another*, p. 181.

[16] Ricœur, Paul *Soi-même comme un autre*, p. 220; *Oneself as Another*, p. 188.

[17] *Ibid.*

[18] Ricœur, Paul *La Mémoire, l'histoire, l'oubli*, p. 161; *Memory, History, Forgetting*, p. 131.

[19] Ricœur, Paul *La Mémoire, l'histoire, l'oubli*, p. 162; *Memory, History, Forgetting*, p. 132.

actions". But Ricœur adds: "In my turn, I include among my close relations those who disapprove of my action, but not of my existence".

And this last declaration takes us in the direction of forgiveness, which is exactly the act of approving the existence of the other without approving his or her actions.

5.2 *Forgiveness*

In the epilogue of *Memory, History, Forgetting,* Ricœur characterizes forgiveness as difficult but not impossible.[20] In that sense, no action in personal relationships is unforgivable, and it is not true that forgiveness concerns the unforgivable, as Jacques Derrida has claimed.[21]

Ricœur takes off from the question: Is forgiveness simply forgetfulness? He understands pardon in relation to guilt but not every form of guilt. If we follow the analysis of guilt in Karl Jaspers' 1946 book on *The Question of Guilt*, guilt takes on four forms: criminal, collective (political), moral, and metaphysical (survival guilt, the feeling of being guilty for having survived others).[22]

According to Ricœur, forgiveness can only respond to moral guilt, i.e., to an individual guilt corresponding to what a particular person has done and for which he or she can be held personally responsible. As such, it cannot be politically institutionalized. For example, if all punishments for certain crimes are automatically commuted to a lower sentence, this would not be forgiveness but a very dubious reduction of the penalty, which might undermine a sense of justice in society.

Even worse, according to Ricœur, is the effect of an amnesty granted by the State that is made conditional upon the crime not being mentioned to which he refers as "commanded forgetting". Moreover, such amnesty is equivalent to "commanded amnesia,"[23] a manipulation or violation of the human right to memory. It has nothing to do with real forgiveness, which is a form of love.

As purely personal, forgiveness addresses the other, saying: You are worth more than your actions. It is the power we possess to liberate the other from his or her own actions and to open up the possibility of a new life for this other person. This forgiveness is not easy to grant, because it is not simply a forgetting of the past but rather acceptance of the other despite the memory we have about the

---

[20] Ricœur, Paul *La Mémoire, l'histoire, l'oubli*, pp. 501–656; *Memory, History, Forgetting*, pp. 456–506.

[21] Derrida, Jacques "Le siècle et le pardon," in *Le Monde des débats*, December 1999, Repris dans Derrida, Jacques (2000) *Foi et Savoir*. Paris: Seuil, p. 111; Derrida criticises Vladimir Jankélévitch, see my reply to this discussion in my article "Le pardon," in *Présence de Vladimir Jankélevitch. Le Charme et l'Occasion*, sous la direction de Françoise Schwab. Paris: Beauchesne, 2010, pp. 228–230.

[22] Jaspers, Karl (1946) *Die Schuldfrage*. Munich: Piper, Taschenbuchausgabe, 1974; *The Question of German Guilt*. New York: Dial Press, 1947.

[23] Ricœur, Paul *La mémoire, l'histoire, l'oubli*, pp. 585–589; *Memory, History, Forgetting*, pp. 452–456.

person in question. If successful, however, it alleviates the memory and renders it, in the end, a "happy memory."[24]

6 Conclusion

What is beyond is, thus, a foundation that is not identical with what is founded.

The idea of Justice, which itself founds society on the principle that everyone should be treated as an equal, is founded on the idea of care or solicitude in that everyone who counts in just institutions is a person whom I take care of as "the third" in the good life. This concept of "the third" that Ricœur, like Levinas and others, uses means that this person is neither myself (the first) nor the other (the second) whom I encounter personally, but someone (the third) who simply counts as a member of the same social institutions to which I belong myself. If justice did not imply that the other is transformed into everyone in the institutions and that just institutions belong to the good life together with and for others, justice would simply be a formal system of order in society and the cry "This is unjust!" would have no meaning, cf. Ricœur's criticism in *The Just* of John Rawls' theory of justice as a purely procedural theory.[25]

But a sense of justice is not sufficient for the care of the other in personal relationships, since care concerns another person even in situations in which no legal rule protects him or her.

The idea of care, of solicitude that is not simply preoccupation with my own existence (like Heidegger's *Sorge*) is founded by Love, since I take care of the other in the same way that I take care of those who are closely related, even though there are many more of them than those with whom I have close relations. Therefore, it is true that there remains an erotic drive in all forms of agape, of communitarian love. If that were not so, there would not be any real feeling for the other "in the good life with and for others in just institutions" as it is described in *Oneself as Another,* (and the expression "good life" should not in English be put in brackets).[26]

But the practice of justice is not sufficient for love in its highest forms such as recognition as pure gift, as shared memory with others in close relations, and as forgiveness that, in very personal relations, can claim: "You are better than your actions".[27]

So if faith, hope, and love are the three greatest powers in human life, the greatest of these *is* love.

---

[24] Ricœur, Paul *La mémoire, l'histoire, l'oubli*, pp. 643 *et seq.*; *Memory, History, Forgetting*, pp. 494ff.

[25] Ricœur, Paul (1995) *Le Juste*. Paris: Éditions Esprit, pp. 71–97; *The Just*. Chicago: The University of Chicago Press, 2000, pp. 36–57.

[26] Ricœur, Paul *Soi-même comme un autre*, pp. 169 *et seq.*; *Oneself as Another,* pp. 199ff.

[27] Ricœur, Paul *La mémoire, l'histoire, l'oubli*, p. 642; *Memory, History, Forgetting*, p. 493.

Justice sociale, justice globale

Dominique Terré

La justice, comme l'être, se dit en plusieurs sens. John Rawls, en 1971, modeste, mais lucide, nous en propose une « théorie » qui porte principalement sur la justice sociale. On le suivra dans le choix de cet objet. Il s'agira ici de justice sociale, et aussi, par extension, de justice globale.[1] Une théorie, soit. Cette visée est déjà ambitieuse. Mais une philosophie ?

Qu'est-ce qu'une philosophie de la justice ? Ou plus exactement, qu'est-ce que faire de la philosophie de la justice ? C'est la question qui sera posée dans cet article en même temps que seront envisagés et interrogés deux exemples de réflexion sur la justice.

Cette étude sera organisée de la manière suivante : j'analyserai la façon dont est fabriquée ce qui me semble constituer une illustration lumineuse de ce que peut être une philosophie de la justice : il s'agit du livre, très pédagogique, d'Alain Renaut, intitulé *Un monde plus juste est-il possible ?*[2] Cet ouvrage montre qu'on ne peut pas faire de la philosophie de la justice en faisant l'impasse sur l'éthique, ce qui n'est pas étonnant, mais aussi sur l'économie. Il apparaît ainsi chez Alain Renaut que construire une philosophie de la justice revient, entre autres, à faire de l'économie.

---

[1] L'idée de justice sociale est aussi ancienne que la philosophie du Droit, rappelle Alain Supiot tout en consacrant une partie de son livre à ce qu'il appelle « l'actualité de la justice sociale », ce qui est pour le moins paradoxal. Aristote lui-même voyait dans la « réciprocité proportionnelle » une troisième forme de justice nécessaire à la vie de la Cité, à côté de la justice distributive et de la justice corrective : « la réciprocité veut qu'on rende en proportion et non selon le principe de l'égalité. [...] C'est en effet parce que l'on retourne en proportion de ce que l'on reçoit que la Cité se maintient. » Aristote, *Éthique à Nicomaque*, v, 8, commenté par Herrenschmidt, Clarisse (2007) *Les Trois Écritures. Langue, nombre, code*. Paris : Gallimard, pp. 293 sq. Supiot Alain (2010) *L'esprit de Philadelphie, la justice sociale face au marché total*. Paris : Seuil.

[2] Renaut, Alain (2013) *Un monde plus juste est-il possible ?* Paris : Stock. Ayant déjà écrit *Une société plus juste est-elle possible ?*, Alain Renaut distingue justice sociale et justice globale. Mais il me semble que ce qu'on appelle la mondialisation ou globalisation a pour effet d'estomper sensiblement cette distinction, comme on l'observe chez Alain Supiot.

D. Terré (✉)
Centre National de la Recherche Scientifique, Paris, France
e-mail: terdom@wanadoo.fr

G. Fløistad (ed.), *Philosophy of Justice*, Contemporary Philosophy: A New Survey 12, DOI 10.1007/978-94-017-9175-5_20, © Springer Science+Business Media Dordrecht 2015

C'est la raison pour laquelle je prolongerai la réflexion d'Alain Renaut en questionnant la perception que l'auteur a de l'économie, et en m'interrogeant sur la fonction qu'il concède à cette discipline. J'émettrai quelques réserves sur les conclusions qu'il apporte à son ouvrage en m'appuyant sur la mise en évidence du caractère problématique de cette science économique qu'il prend bien au sérieux. J'invoquerai ici les travaux, non plus d'un philosophe, mais d'un juriste : il s'agit d'Alain Supiot.[3]

Avec *Un monde plus juste est-il possible ?*, Alain Renaut nous livre le produit d'un travail considérable en même temps qu'une construction extraordinairement savante. Répudiant la métaphysique et les anciens systèmes, il entend faire œuvre contemporaine. Néanmoins il n'hésite pas à construire sa réflexion sur le modèle des antinomies de la raison de Kant et se réclame volontiers de la philosophie du droit de Fichte, plus réaliste que celle du philosophe de Königsberg. Ces outils philosophiques dont il rappelle le sens et l'utilité, il les applique avec virtuosité aux théories « ressourcistes » de John Rawls et Thomas Pogge ainsi qu'à celles, capabilitaires d'Amartya Sen et de Martha Nussbaum tout en prenant comme fil directeur de sa réflexion la notion de « développement humain ». Ce travail magistral, d'une exhaustivité exemplaire, constitue une véritable philosophie de la justice.

Il se situe d'emblée dans le monde contemporain où la pauvreté des pauvres et la richesse des riches provoquent un sentiment de révolte. Il part de données chiffrées, exposées dans une ample introduction. Je me bornerai à quelques exemples : « Selon le rapport de l'Organisation mondiale de la santé datant de 2008, les inégalités en la matière sont, trente ans après, largement plus grandes qu'elles ne l'étaient en 1978, quand bien même les écarts exprimés en niveau de vie (PIB par tête) seraient en voie de se réduire, au point que la différence d'espérance de vie entre les pays les plus riches et les pays les plus pauvres dépasse désormais 40 ans ».[4]

Autre paramètre irréductible au revenu par tête : l'essor des technologies de l'information et de la communication. Alors que le Vietnam totalise 80 millions d'habitants, il compte seulement 25 000 internautes.

---

[3] Supiot, Alain (2010) *L'esprit de Philadelphie, la justice sociale face au marché total.* Dans ce livre, Supiot expose comment à Philadelphie, le 10 mai 1944, est proclamée la Première Déclaration internationale à vocation universelle. Elle a la Justice sociale comme but. Un nouvel ordre mondial sera fondé, non plus sur la force, mais sur le Droit et la justice. Le lien établi entre la sécurité et la liberté est le trait commun des quatre principes fondamentaux déclinés par la Déclaration de Philadelphie. Dans cette Déclaration, l'économie et la finance sont des moyens au service des hommes.—C'est la perspective inverse qui préside à l'actuel processus de globalisation. L'objectif du livre de Supiot est d'analyser ce grand retournement qui semble avoir aboli les leçons sociales tirées de l'expérience de la période 1914–1945. Dans la première partie, Supiot montre comment se sont conjugués le communisme et le capitalisme pour faire advenir ce qu'il appelle la contre-révolution ultra libérale. Il cite Denis Kessler, appelant à « défaire méthodiquement le programme du Conseil national de la Résistance », dans *Challenge*, le 4 octobre 2007. L'appel à défaire méthodiquement cet héritage de la Résistance n'a rien qui puisse surprendre au regard de la critique beaucoup plus générale que les théoriciens néolibéraux adressent depuis trente ans à tous les textes inspirés de Philadelphie.

[4] *Op. cit.*, pp. 44 sq.

Ces chiffres impressionnants justifient le recours à l'économie : si le nom de Rawls symbolise les transformations contemporaines de la philosophie politique, celui d'Amartya Sen symbolise, pour sa part, celles de l'économie : il restaure la dimension éthique du débat économique.

Dès le début de son ample ouvrage, Renaut introduit la notion qui sera son fil conducteur tout au long de ses analyses : celle de développement. Depuis les années 1970, on a découvert que le modèle de l'industrialisation avait connu beaucoup d'échecs et s'est fait sentir un besoin de renouvellement théorique procédant de l'erreur qu'il y aurait à réduire le développement à la croissance. Les spécialistes s'accordent pour dire que si renouvellement effectif il y a eu, il a consisté dans l'émergence de la dimension « humaine » ou de la dimension de l'« humain » dans ces théories.

Comment mesurer le développement, demande Renaut ? Réalisable ou non, l'idée s'affirme avec force que la construction de nouveaux indices, plus complets et plus complexes, fourniraient des outils de gouvernement ou, au plan mondial, de gouvernance susceptibles de ménager d'autres actions publiques animées par le souci d'un « développement humain durable ». Ainsi une dimension intrinsèquement aussi qualitative du développement que la dimension culturelle devient-elle observable à travers un phénomène comme, par exemple, le degré de maîtrise de certains moyens d'expression.[5] Renaut mentionne ici, au-delà du repérage des indicateurs et de leur sélection, une autre opération décisive, à savoir la construction d'un indice de développement, qu'il s'agisse de l'indice de développement humain (1990), d'un indice multidimensionnel de pauvreté ou d'un éventuel indice de développement académique. L'enjeu de ce débat est vaste et profond. Pour évaluer dans son ensemble l'indice, qu'on appelle aussi parfois indicateur composite ou indicateur synthétique, est construit un processus qui agrège les uns aux autres les indicateurs de base. Renaut estime que le résultat obtenu n'est pas relatif puisque la combinaison de plusieurs indicateurs composites fournit une garantie importante contre ce risque. Importante est la décision d'assumer un pluralisme des indices concernant un même phénomène ; en effet le pluralisme qu'il est ainsi requis d'assumer procède aussi, indirectement, de choix de valeur (tantôt celle de la liberté, tantôt celle de l'égalité).

Renaut juge nécessaire de construire un dédoublement des approches du développement et de rechercher une antinomie de la justice globale qui s'y exprime concrètement.

Parallèlement à la manière dont les théories philosophiques de la justice en sont venues à se demander si leurs principes pouvaient s'appliquer aux relations entre pays riches et pays pauvres, les théories économiques du développement ont intégré des considérations de plus en plus normatives, éthiques ou éthico-politiques.

Nous assisterions, selon Renaut, à un renouvellement non négligeable d'une problématique classique de toute la modernité politique : cette problématique avait le plus souvent opposé et rarement réussi à combiner le réalisme politique (dicté par

[5] *Op. cit.*, p. 83.

l'intérêt) et l'idéalisme politique : « Si pourtant il n'est pas d'approche du développement qui puisse se concevoir et se pratiquer autrement qu'orienté par des valeurs, il se pourrait qu'une forme d'idéalisme ne doive plus nous apparaître incompatible avec la considération de l'intérêt bien compris. C'est là aussi un des paris que je me propose de relever dans ce livre à travers celle de ses étapes qui concernera l'éthique du développement ou, si l'on veut, l'éthique globale. »

Ce que vise Alain Renaut, c'est une théorie de la justice, non plus sociale, mais globale. Par conséquent l'interrogation se transforme : à quelles valeurs, comprises dans la justice, demande-t-il, fait référence la question sur la possibilité d'un monde juste ? À son sens, il est important d'éclairer le contenu normatif compris dans l'idée de justice.

Deux réponses sont dominantes, qui sont exposées : approche « ressourciste » et approche par les « capabilités » dont aucune, comme il l'indiquera, n'est véritablement satisfaisante. La nécessité s'imposera de les combiner ensemble par une autre interrogation. Cette autre interrogation porte sur le *welfare*, bien-être, idée trop peu présente dans l'idée de la justice. Cette question engendre deux débats engageant la valeur du développement : ils portent d'une part sur la pertinence même de la notion de développement humain ; d'autre part sur la nécessité pour le développement de mobiliser partout dans le monde les mêmes exigences normatives, c'est-à-dire la démocratie. Mais ira-t-il jusqu'au bout de son exigence de démocratie ?

Situant la justice globale entre universalisme et relativisme, Alain Renaut estime—à juste titre—nécessaire de faire le point sur l'anti-développementisme et d'en écarter le modèle au moyen d'une argumentation rigoureuse. Le développement humain, martèle-t-il, n'est pas une valeur strictement occidentale. En effet, ce n'est pas parce que la thématique du développement est née dans le contexte de la politique américaine des années 1945–1975 qu'elle devrait être tenue pour rigoureusement relative à ce contexte et vouée à exprimer les intérêts de cette politique. Tout comme la validité de l'algèbre ne se borne pas aux limites du monde arabe qui l'a vu voir le jour. Le principe de l'anti-développementisme témoigne d'une haine foncière de la modernité et de tout ce dont elle est solidaire (les valeurs de l'humanisme, les droits humains, les idéaux démocratiques). Amartya Sen répond à l'asiatisme : « la démocratie n'est pas un luxe qui peut attendre l'arrivée de la prospérité pour tous ».

Il reste difficile, selon Renaut, d'argumenter contre ceux qui relativisent les valeurs de la liberté. Sen mobilise selon lui une notion de capabilité qui est en fait bien près d'être une valeur morale. Auquel cas, précise Renaut, il faudra déterminer si l'approche du développement qui passe par les capabilités est bien de teneur politique. Ne mobilise-t-elle pas plutôt d'importants prérequis éthiques ?

Le questionnement sur les conditions d'un monde juste est, selon l'auteur, traversé par l'affrontement entre universalisme et relativisme. Dans les deux cas, Renaut estime que le débat, contre les illusions des deux formes de relativismes incarnés par l'antidéveloppementisme et l'asiatisme, devait être tranché en faveur d'un universalisme critique, c'est-à-dire conscient des limites qu'il lui faut s'imposer à lui-même pour éviter lui aussi les illusions inhérentes à sa version classiquement dogmatique.

Approche par les ressources, approche par les capabilités : ces deux approches, explique Renaut, nous mettent en présence d'un discours dédoublé sur le développement humain.

Devant « les effarants déséquilibres » pointés par les données initialement relevées par Renaut, on songera avant tout à des politiques permettant de réduire les inégalités extrêmes entre les pauvres du monde. Les défenseurs de ces politiques animées prioritairement par la valeur de l'égalité défendent une appréhension des injustices globales que l'on désigne couramment par une « approche par les ressources » ou « approche ressourciste ».

Ronald Dworkin et Thomas Pogge, représentants reconnus de cette démarche, envisagent ainsi des dispositifs de distribution ou de redistribution mondiale permettant d'améliorer le sort des « pauvres du monde » par des transferts de ressources supposés faire progresser, en corrigeant des déséquilibres criants, la cause de l'égalité. Tous deux se réfèrent à Rawls. Dans la *Théorie de la justice*, le premier principe égalise le droit aux libertés fondamentales ou « libertés de base » ; dans le second principe, l'égalité des chances s'efforce de corriger les « inégalités de naissance et de dons naturels » car une société bien ordonnée ne saurait contourner l'obligation de corriger certaines inégalités de ressources.

En incluant les ressources dans les biens premiers, Rawls pouvait en produire une liste apparemment déconcertante par son hétérogénéité, mais possédant néanmoins sa cohérence. L'étiquetage de la position comme libérale de gauche, voire comme socialiste-libérale, « m'apparaît, note Renaut, à vrai dire comme le plus adéquat ». Le paragraphe 43 de la *Théorie de la Justice* ne l'exclut pas.[6] « "Libérale" précisément parce que le respect des libertés de base ne peut jamais être sacrifié à d'autres exigences de justice ; "de gauche" ou "socialiste" parce qu'une répartition équitable ou décente des ressources (revenus et richesses) fait ainsi partie des paramètres de la justice sociale. »[7]

Selon Rawls, explique Renaut, le principe de différence exprime ou illustre, outre l'exigence d'une forme d'égalité à rechercher même dans une société stratifiée, « le principe de fraternité », qui jusqu'ici avait eu moins de place dans « la théorie de la démocratie » que les valeurs de liberté et d'égalité.

Le principe de différence, dont relève le traitement du problème de la pauvreté, apparaît ainsi mobiliser une valeur de teneur plus éthique que proprement politique. Mais selon Renaut, le ressort « fraternitaire » serait appelé à jouer, en justice globale, un rôle beaucoup plus grand qu'en justice sociale.

Après avoir précisé quels sont les critères de mesure de la pauvreté mondiale, Thomas Pogge fonde une politique de redistribution sur une critique de l'ordre injuste.[8] L'établissement de l'injustice renvoie à celui de la responsabilité : ce ne sont pas seulement les élites au pouvoir dans les pays pauvres qui sont responsables et pourraient contribuer à l'éradication de la pauvreté, ce sont aussi les citoyens privilégiés des pays riches. L'approche par les ressources contient bien dans son

---

[6] *Op. cit.*, p. 165.

[7] *Ibid.*

[8] Pogge, Thomas (2002) *World Poverty and Human Rights.* Cambridge : Polity Press.

argumentaire un « droit inaliénable à bénéficier d'un partage équitable des ressources mondiales ou d'une compensation équivalente ». La référence à Locke est, selon Renaut, à la fois légitime et habile.

Légitime puisque Locke soutenait que la terre a été donnée par Dieu en partage à tous les êtres humains : à partir du travail de chacun sur une partie de cette terre, s'accomplit un processus d'appropriation, toute personne obtenant un droit de propriété sur ce qu'elle a déjà mis en valeur.

Habile, poursuit Renaut, parce qu'il y a là un moyen de convaincre la famille libérale, en allant plus loin que Rawls, d'inclure dans sa conception de la justice une exigence d'égalisation du sort des plus défavorisés débordant le cadre national. Pogge en déduit un système d'imposition mondiale sur tous les utilisateurs de ressources naturelles. Il s'agira de mettre en place un dispositif auquel nous sommes accoutumés en interne par les politiques fiscales de redistribution, mais nouveau au plan international. Concrètement, un dividende de 1 % sur la valeur de toutes les ressources naturelles exploitées chaque année directement. À partir de quoi se constituera un fond « consacré spécialement à l'éradication de la pauvreté ».

L'approche ressourciste rencontre vite ses limites : d'une part les ressources ainsi transférées sont rapidement épuisées. D'autre part, ce type de solution risque d'instaurer une dépendance à l'infini des « pauvres du monde » à l'égard des pays nantis. En conséquence, note-t-il, si l'on adopte cette approche, importance de créer dans les pays pauvres la capacité à venir à bout de leurs difficultés. Auquel cas, nous serions bien près de basculer dans l'approche par les capabilités, théorisée par Amartya Sen.

Plus précisément, Renaut formule trois réserves à l'égard de la théorie de Pogge sur le dividende global sur les ressources (DGR). Une première réserve vise l'idée qu'un tel dividende instaurerait, pour ceux qui en sont destinataires, une relation de dépendance. Mais rien n'est moins sûr puisqu'il s'agirait d'un dispositif mécanique et impersonnel.

Une deuxième réserve consiste à observer que, construite en partie contre l'approche par les capabilités, la proposition de Pogge inclut en fait cette approche. Pogge explique en effet que les fonds collectés par le dividende, en plus d'éradiquer directement la pauvreté, pourront aussi « être redistribués afin d'encourager de meilleurs gouvernements dans les pays en développement ». Renaut suggère que la thèse ressourciste qui partage avec l'antithèse capabilitaire le rejet d'une approche par le bien-être, tend à croiser la thèse capabilitaire et, en quelque sorte, à lui rendre hommage.

Enfin Renaut formule une troisième réserve : s'agit-il en fait d'un traitement ultimement politique de la pauvreté ou d'un traitement fondamentalement éthique qui recourt à des dispositifs institutionnels (politiques) comme à autant de moyens de se rendre opératoire ? Depuis le début du XXIe siècle, cela fait une dizaine d'années que Pogge a mis en avant sa conception sans que ses réformes aient vu le moindre début d'application. L'indifférence de la communauté internationale invite à s'interroger. Trente ans plus tôt, en 1998 naissait déjà le mouvement Attac qui envisageait une taxe (Tobin) sur les transactions financières.[9]

Qu'est-ce qui bloque l'application d'une politique ressourciste passant par une vaste réforme des institutions internationales ? La démarche envisagée contient dans sa définition ce qui la rend utopique. On ne voit pas, note Renaut, « comment s'accomplit la transition de l'indignation à l'expression pure de la conscience morale qui est, dans l'optique de Pogge, le levier ultime du processus. »

Ce livre, explique alors son auteur, s'interroge lucidement sur la façon dont la solution retenue pourrait être mise à l'épreuve du réel, plutôt dans le registre de l'éthique que dans celui de la seule politique, comme la plupart des disciples de Rawls ont pourtant tenté de le faire. Il ne peut y avoir de justice globale politiquement administrée sans éthique globale. La voie à suivre, pour Renaut, consiste à se donner vraiment les moyens de construire une éthique du développement.

Après avoir exposé la démarche ressourciste, l'auteur en vient à l'approche par les capabilités, créée par Amartya Sen dans les années 1980 et développée par la philosophe américaine Martha Nussbaum.[10] Le message de Sen est le suivant : il faut approcher la pauvreté du monde en termes de capabilités, *capabilities* que Renaut explicite par l'expression de « pouvoir-faire ».

L'idée du développement humain n'était pas entièrement nouvelle lorsque Sen, puis le PNUD (Programme des Nations Unies pour le Développement) s'en sont saisis et puisque les prodromes en datent au moins du milieu des années 1950. Renaut se penche sur la discussion récurrente et impressionnante que Sen a menée avec Rawls sur la compréhension même des principes de justice. Elle éclaire en effet les choix conceptuels normatifs qui sous-tendent l'approche par les *capabilities*.

Pour expliquer ce que sont les capabilités, Renaut se réfère à la célèbre conférence donnée à Oxford par Isaiah Berlin en 1958, « Les deux concepts de la liberté ». Pour un libéral comme Berlin qui conçoit la politique avant tout comme une liberté négative, la liberté d'un citoyen serait fonction de l'étendue de l'aire d'action où il peut être assuré de ne pas se trouver entravé par l'intervention de l'État. Une telle représentation de la liberté peut être dite « négative » dans la mesure où la liberté ne consiste pas à développer telle activité plutôt que telle autre. À l'encontre de cette conception intrinsèquement libérale de la liberté (inséparable de la théorie des limites de l'État), l'autre conception évoquée par Berlin s'est incarnée historiquement dans la tradition républicaine plutôt que dans la tradition libérale.

Selon la deuxième notion, la liberté peut être dite positive puisqu'elle consiste non pas seulement à s'arracher à des entraves, mais à atteindre des fins expressément (donc positivement) poursuivies comme telle et définissant un idéal lesté d'un contenu. Les théories de la liberté positive sont conduites à définir, au-delà ou au-dessus de la liberté individuelle, un sorte d'idéal du Bien ; en conséquence, au nom de ce Bien substantiellement défini, les théories et les pratiques de la liberté positive

[9] *Op. cit.*, p. 185.

[10] Nussbaum, Martha (2012) *Capabilités. Comment créer les conditions d'un monde plus juste ?* Paris : Flammarion.

conduisent à soumettre les libertés individuelles, négatives, à d'autres limitations que celles qui sont induites par la prise en compte de la question de la coexistence.

Sen s'est fait connaître pour avoir, concernant la problématique du juste, à la fois approuvé une part importante de son traitement par Rawls et cependant modifié ce qu'était la solution rawlsienne. Le second principe de justice implique une réduction des inégalités sociales, donc la production d'une égalité plus forte : perspective que Sen partage, mais en estimant que Rawls n'a pas suffisamment clarifié ce sur quoi doit porter cette réduction des inégalités. La démarche de Sen, sur ce point, consiste très précisément à introduire ce fameux concept, présenté comme nouveau, de « capabilité ».

À considérer les « libertés et possibilités offertes » que Rawls mentionne dans sa théorie des biens premiers et dont il met au compte du second principe d'en assurer la répartition équitable, il ne s'agit pas de toute évidence de libertés négatives, mais de libertés positives. Le seul exemple qu'il en donne, celui de posséder certaines formes particulières de propriété comme des moyens de production, relève bien des libertés positives. Il correspond à une liberté employée à faire quelque chose qui apparaît comme un but ou comme une fin permettant à la personne concernée de s'accomplir (ici : faire acquisition de ce genre de propriété).

À travers sa théorie des capabilités, Sen revient sur cette question fondamentale de ce qu'il s'agit de répartir dans une société juste ou un monde juste, en mettant l'accent sur les libertés positives : un monde juste se soucie d'introduire de la légalité non seulement dans la « liberté de », mais aussi dans la « liberté à ». Les capabilités, ce dont l'homme est socialement ou globalement « capable », permettent aux yeux de Sen de mesurer concrètement si lui est ménagée, et à quel degré, la possibilité de choisir tel ou tel type de vie.

Par conséquent réaménager la théorie rawlsienne de la justice dans l'optique des capabilités consistera à compléter la doctrine des biens premiers. Selon Renaut, c'est de façon inexacte que Sen reproche à Rawls (pour l'ouvrage de 1971) d'avoir réduit les libertés à des libertés négatives, de type classiquement libéral. Selon Renaut, le débat entre Rawls et Sen a été manqué. Rawls incarne une défense rigoureuse du principe selon lequel un gouvernement libéral se doit de demeurer éthiquement neutre. Sen, d'après Renaut, surcharge de façon éthique les principes libéraux de justice. A-t-il tort, a-t-il raison de procéder à une telle surcharge ?

En argumentant au nom de la valeur d'une représentation du bien défini en termes de capabilités, Sen expose la position qu'il défend à être rejetée comme relative à des choix de valeurs que nul n'est obligé de partager ni culturellement ni éthiquement ni politiquement.

Dans sa portée pratique, l'approche par les capabilités présente des inconvénients symétriques et inverses de ceux de l'approche ressourciste. Elle répond à la difficulté du puits sans fond à laquelle l'approche ressourciste se heurtait durement. Elle prend du temps, suppose de longues années, alors que, pendant chacune d'entre elles, 18 millions de personnes meurent de dénutrition, de maladies, de pauvreté. Cette approche se heurte au problème de l'urgence.

C'est pourquoi, dans la troisième partie de son livre, Renaut opère le passage de la dimension éthique de la justice globale aux politiques de développement : de l'éthique à la politique, selon une démarche inverse que celle qu'avait pratiquée Rawls sur le terrain de la justice sociale. La sphère de la justice globale étant un véritable champ de bataille, Alain Renaut propose d'en construire une théorie plus systématique. « Pas non plus une synthèse absolue. Plutôt atteindre un point d'équilibre. »[11]

Un monde plus juste est-il possible ? est, entre autres raisons, un livre de philosophie de la justice en ce que son auteur revient, de façon réflexive, sur la forme qui lui a paru impérativement nécessaire de mettre en œuvre pour traiter son sujet.

« J'ai souhaité, précise-t-il, m'aventurer dans ce domaine sous la forme d'un unique ouvrage, plutôt que sous celle d'une myriade d'articles constituant autant d'interventions ponctuelles sur tel ou tel aspect de cette problématique. Sous ce rapport, j'avoue en effet que ce qui m'a laissé le plus insatisfait dans les travaux existants tient au moins en partie au fait que les ouvrages qui les ont promus [...] ont été le plus souvent des collections d'études ou d'articles, selon les usages des auteurs anglophones que des traités. [...] Je persiste pourtant à déplorer que la quasi-totalité des ouvrages consacrés à la justice globale aient renoncé à adopter ou n'aient pas pu adopter, si peu que ce fût, la forme de ce qu'avait été en son temps la théorie rawlsienne de la justice [...]. Ce pourquoi au demeurant je continue de penser que, en philosophie, y compris en philosophie politique et en éthique, c'est la discipline elle-même, en raison des exigences auxquelles elle nous astreint, qui impose de continuer à écrire de véritables livres. »[12]

C'est bien ce que fait l'auteur et il le prouve avec virtuosité. Il existe en philosophie, nous rappelle-t-il en invoquant la *Critique de la Raison pure*, des conflits de la raison avec elle-même : les antinomies. « Rien d'étonnant, poursuit-il, si la question du monde juste [...] expose la raison, oubliant sa finitude, à s'engouffrer dans un espace où s'affrontent deux thèses impossibles à départager. » L'approche par les ressources, renvoyant à des besoins vitaux, inscrit la démarche ressourciste dans une logique d'« impérieuse nécessité ». Quant à l'approche par les capabilités, elle désigne « un développement de l'humain en l'homme, tel du moins qu'il se représente alors l'humanité et sa dignité en termes de liberté ». Il y a une antinomie de la justice globale qui est radicale. « Nous devons, explique Alain Renaut d'une façon lumineuse, considérer l'approche par les ressources et l'approche par les capabilités comme renvoyant à deux points de vue vrais, mais unilatéraux, sur le développement humain entendu dans toute sa complexité [...]. »

La thèse qui fait référence aux pouvoirs d'agir sur sa propre vie répondrait au développement de ce que Kant désignait comme la dimension « nouménale » de

[11] C'est ici qu'il ajoute « non pas assurément au sens des anciens systèmes déductifs : le temps de ces systèmes, sublimes architectures dont la carcasse tient encore debout, mais qui ont perdu toute vie et toute fécondité, est désormais derrière nous. » *Op. cit.*, p. 220.

[12] Livre ou article ? Il me semble que l'existence d'ouvrages aussi informés et spéculatifs que celui de Renaut ménage une place pour un modeste article qui en serait comme une explication de texte. Du moins est-ce le choix que j'ai effectué ici. Il n'en reste pas moins que je suis en accord avec Alain Renaut sur l'intérêt de la forme « livre » en philosophie de la justice.

l'existence humaine, que nous désignerions plus sobrement aujourd'hui en évoquant la dimension de l'être humain en tant que liberté.

L'antithèse ressourciste répond avant tout, de son côté, au développement de ce que Kant appelait la dimension « phénoménale de l'existence humaine [...] ».

Il est probable, selon Renaut, que l'antinomie de la justice globale devrait obtenir une solution prenant pour modèle l'antinomie kantienne de la liberté.

Une fois le problème posé, Renaut aborde l'éventail des solutions. L'une d'elle passe par la justice attributive : il s'agit à nouveau du libertarianisme de gauche sur lequel je ne reviendrai pas.[13] La référence ici convoquée est celle de Philippe Van Parijs, qui défend depuis plus de vingt ans la perspective selon laquelle la « fable de Nozick »—consistant à imaginer une juste appropriation originelle des ressources naturelles—condamne son libertarianisme à n'être que formel : à quoi il faudrait opposer un libertarianisme réel. Or, pour que soit ménagé à tous les membres d'une société un tel partage d'une liberté réelle, il s'agirait de créer un revenu inconditionnellement versé à chaque citoyen, qu'il ait ou non un emploi, qu'il souhaite ou non en avoir un, quel que soit son revenu matrimonial et ses revenus d'autres sources.[14] Van Parijs (semblable en cela à Renaut) garde la conviction selon laquelle c'est le capitalisme[15] qui, en raison de son dynamisme technologique et donc des capacités à créer de la richesse, constitue économiquement l'organisation de la production qu'il faut préférer au socialisme, tant centralisé qu'autogestionnaire. Ce libertarianisme réel ou réal libertarianisme déplace de la distribution à l'attribution l'axe d'une politique juste, sur le plan national de la justice sociale comme sur celui, global ou international, de l'aide au développement.

Selon Renaut, les deux approches du libertarianisme se distribuent symétriquement par rapport à l'approche égalitariste de type rawlsien.

Qu'en est-il de la justice globale quand il s'agit, non plus d'une société, mais du monde ? Une version « attributive » de la justice globale est-elle envisageable ?[16] On pourrait s'attendre à voir le libertarianisme de gauche prendre sur ce terrain des positions assez avancées. Celles de Stéphane Chauvier se développent « à l'encontre

---

[13] Sur le libertarisme de gauche, Speranta Dumitru a rassemblé un certain nombre de contributions décisives dans la revue *Raison présente*. Dans son éditorial, elle fait état de l'argument suivant pour établir la nécessité de prendre en compte le concept de propriété de soi. « En outre, écrit-elle, il s'avère que même la critique sociale la plus puissante, y compris marxiste, ne saurait se passer de la notion de droits de propriété. C'est ce que Gerald A. Cohen, philosophe d'Oxford, que l'on qualifie de "marxiste analytique" a mis en lumière. Lorsque les marxistes protestent que les capitalistes volent leur temps de travail aux ouvriers, ils soutiennent implicitement que ce temps de travail appartient légitimement aux ouvriers. Car comment pourrait-on voler à quelqu'un quelque chose qui n'est pas sa propriété et prétendre qu'il s'agit là de la plus grave injustice ? » Cohen, Gerald A. (1995) *Self-Ownership, World Ownership and Equality*, chap. 6. Cambridge : Cambridge University Press ; la question du libertarisme de gauche fait l'objet d'une synthèse exhaustive dans *Raisons politiques*, Presses de Sciences Po, 2006/3, pp. 5–8.

[14] *Op. cit.*, p. 257.

[15] Nous verrons, dans la deuxième partie de ce travail, qu'il y a plusieurs formes et plusieurs moments du capitalisme.

[16] *Op. cit.*, p. 263. Chauvier, Stéphane (2006) *Justice et droits à l'échelle globale*. Paris : Vrin/EHESS.

d'une applicabilité de la justice en matière économique ». Il récuse l'idée selon laquelle les principes nationaux de justice distributive seraient applicables à l'échelle internationale. Chauvier est opposé à Rawls et même à Pogge. La justice seule relèverait du droit et l'humanité relèverait, elle, de la vertu. À ce titre aucune institutionnalisation des devoirs d'humanité ne lui paraît recevable.

Alain Renaut qui se présente lui-même aussi comme libéral de gauche entend prendre ses distances avec Chauvier.[17] Ce dernier envisagerait de mettre en œuvre, au plan mondial, une sorte d'allocation universelle de citoyenneté, du type de celle qu'a conçue Philippe Van Parijs sur le terrain de la justice sociale en forgeant l'idée d'une « agence cosmopolite des ressources naturelles ».

Renaut enregistre dans l'argumentaire de la gauche libertarienne sur le terrain de la justice globale une lacune, non plus seulement politique, mais éthique. Chauvier souligne que sa solution doit inévitablement mobiliser des ressorts éthiques. « Reste à se demander, note Renaut, ce qui va bien pouvoir pousser ces États à s'acquitter de cette obligation en mettant effectivement en place un tel dispositif. Au moins dans le dispositif ressourciste envisagé par Pogge, j'ai pu noter que le financement s'effectuerait mécaniquement… »

Une autre solution pour une autre justice distributive consisterait, de manière plus judicieuse, à repenser le bien-être. Qu'est-ce que le bien-être, demande Renaut ? L'utilitarisme classique, depuis Bentham, concevait, certes, l'utilité comme bien-être ou comme bonheur mais en tendant à réduire le bien-être à la somme des plaisirs et des peines. « Le welfarisme élargit pour sa part le concept du bien-être en intégrant des activités dont nous ne pouvons retirer aucun plaisir au sens de la satisfaction des désirs les plus ancrés dans notre individualité. » Sen pose la question de savoir si la capabilité d'une personne peut aller à l'encontre de son propre bien-être et invoque l'exemple de Gandhi.

C'est, note Renaut, la grandeur de l'être humain que de savoir dans quelques cas ou à quelques moments de sa vie préférer ce sommet de bien-être où réside l'être-bien aux formes de Bien être les plus fugitives et les plus interchangeables. Il se réfère à Pascal : « tous les hommes recherchent d'être heureux […] quelques différents moyens qu'ils y emploient […] jusqu'à ceux qui vont se faire pendre ». Mon propre bien-être individuel peut inclure des satisfactions qui supposent des épreuves ou des souffrances. Opposés à Bentham, les défenseurs du welfarisme ont redéfini la somme des intérêts comme intégrant certaines satisfactions liées à des préférences plus élevées que celles qui s'expriment sous forme de plaisirs, donnant ainsi naissance à ce qui s'appelle l'économie du bien-être qui, avec Arthur Cecil Pigou, remonte à l'année 1920.

D'après Renaut, même si Rawls n'a pas voulu considérer une autre dimension de la justice que la justice sociale, il n'en reste pas moins que les exigences rawlsiennes seraient également pertinentes à ce niveau : une exigence globale qui serait « sacrificielle » est à proscrire quand on s'interroge sur les conditions d'un monde juste.

[17] Qui ne voudrait être libéral de gauche ? Mais les auteurs réunis dans le numéro cité plus haut *Raison présente* ont montré que cette position était instable.

Revenant sur le bien-être, Renaut entend faire apparaître les deux thèses (ressourciste et capabilitaire) comme des points de vue vrais selon que nous nous représentons l'humain comme un être naturel (ressourcisme) ou comme un être possédant au sein de la nature une perception de lui-même qui inclut son irréductibilité au mécanisme naturel (liberté/capabilité).

Les deux approches du développement en termes de ressources et en termes de capabilités ont puisé une partie à la fois de leur inspiration et de leur désaccord dans la mémoire rawlsienne des biens premiers. « Elles ont durablement séparé ce qui avait été énuméré ensemble par Rawls ; la liste des biens primaires recensés par le paragraphe 15 de la *Théorie de la justice* reste aussi énigmatique quant à ce qui l'organise ou ne l'organise pas après plusieurs lectures attentives qu'au moment où nous l'avons découverte. »

« Dans l'ensemble, dit Rawls, on peut dire que les biens sociaux premiers sont constitués par les droits, les libertés et les possibilités offertes, les revenus et la richesse ». Rawls précise ensuite qu'il faudrait compléter une telle liste en évoquant les bases « sociales du respect de soi-même, défini comme le bien premier le plus important », ce que Renaut préfère appeler «représentation par chacun de sa dignité ».

Les êtres humains rechercheraient deux types de bien-être. Le premier correspondrait au bien-être entendu au sens physique ou naturel de la satisfaction, des besoins fondamentaux ou vitaux, auquel est dédiée une approche par les ressources. Le deuxième renverrait à cette autre source du bien-être qui s'identifie à l'être-bien. Ce dernier correspondrait à la mise en œuvre de ces capabilités sans lesquelles un individu ou un peuple ne se considère pas comme traité de façon *décente.*[18]

Premièrement, l'approche par les ressources et l'approche par les capabilités correspondent à deux points de vue sur le développement humain. Ces points de vue renvoient l'un et l'autre à la double façon dont nous nous représentons nous-mêmes et notre devenir individuel ou collectif comme inscrits sous le régime de la nécessité (besoins) et sous celui de la liberté (capabilités).

Deuxièmement, cette solution devient représentable dès lors que nous la schématisons sous la dimension multidimensionnelle du bien-être, peut-être parce que le bien-être contient en lui-même l'espace de l'être-bien. Le bien-être, pluridimensionnel, est au cœur du rapport de Joseph Stiglitz (2010) sur la mesure de la performance économique et du progrès social.

La référence à Stiglitz permet enfin à Renaut de s'installer sur le terrain des pratiques du développement humain, éthiques puis politiques. Il lui est apparu nécessaire de cerner leur dimension spécifiquement éthique, c'est-à-dire le lieu où la question se pose d'un choix de valeurs fondant des obligations. Il n'y a pas de théorie de la justice globale, notamment dans le secteur du développement humain, qui ne doive se soucier d'une éthique globale susceptible d'être partagée par la communauté des citoyens du monde. Mais cette éthique pose des problèmes encore plus

[18] C'est moi qui souligne. Le concept de décence est central dans toute philosophie de la justice, qu'elle concerne la justice sociale ou une autre forme de justice. Cf. Margalit, Avishaï (2007) *La société décente*. Paris : Flammarion.

aigus que dans les autres registres. Ainsi, que pourrait-il en être d'une éthique supranationale, laquelle apparaît comme prioritaire ? L'Union européenne n'a pas encore réussi à inscrire dans le réel l'idée d'une « paix par le droit ». Quant à l'ONU, l'OMC et le FMI, ils peinent toujours à prendre leur charge sous la forme de politiques durables et concertées. Renaut rappelle ici qu'il a déjà surmonté les illusions antidéveloppementistes et la relativisation culturaliste des principes de liberté ou d'égalité.

Un conflit entre deux types d'éthique domine aujourd'hui le champ de la réflexion morale. L'éthique de la perfection est téléologique en ce sens qu'elle situe le bien moral dans la réalisation d'une fin ultime, qui se définit par la façon dont la personne humaine atteint à l'excellence ou à la perfection tenues pour constitutives de son essence ; l'éthique de la liberté est déontologique en ceci qu'aucune conception du bien moral prédéfinie par l'attribution à l'être humain d'une essence ne précède les devoirs ou les obligations que le sujet se donne à lui-même de façon autonome.

Quelle morale peut-elle accompagner un « devenir-juste » du monde ?

Selon Renaut, l'approche par les ressources s'apparente à une éthique du devoir tandis que l'approche par les capabilités se situe du côté d'une éthique de la perfection.

Abordant en premier lieu le thème du ressourcisme et de l'éthique globale du devoir, Renaut se tourne naturellement vers les travaux de Thomas Pogge.

Pogge, remarque-t-il, est en apparence « fort attentif à ne pas confondre comme il le reproche à la démarche capabilitaire de le faire, éthique et politique. » Il récuse une réponse à la pauvreté globale en termes d'assistance à des pays encore peu développés pour des raisons dont ils seraient en partie responsables.[19] En effet, selon lui, c'est nous qui portons préjudice aux pauvres du monde et qui collaborons activement au plus grand crime contre l'humanité jamais commis.

Cependant, Pogge estime que ce serait un malentendu de classer son approche sous une rubrique prioritairement éthique. Il accorde bien qu'en portant la responsabilité (active ou passive) qui est la nôtre dans la pauvreté du monde, nous violons nos devoirs, mais, précise-t-il, il ne s'agit que de « devoirs négatifs », mais non pas des « devoirs positifs », lesquels correspondent à des obligations morales qui engagent à une « action » à l'égard des autres. Cette distinction remonte à Kant et est au cœur des débats actuels sur ce qu'il doit en être de l'éthique dans un contexte politiquement libéral. Pogge explique que, s'il n'utilise le plus souvent que cette distinction entre devoirs positifs et devoirs négatifs, c'était afin de faire « comme si les droits de l'homme des pauvres du monde n'imposaient que des devoirs négatifs ». Ceux qui refuseraient les devoirs positifs « acceptent néanmoins l'idée de devoirs négatifs contraignants tels que : ne pas torturer, ne pas violer, ne pas détruire les récoltes et les réserves de nourriture nécessaires à la survie ».[20]

---

[19] Pogge trouve cette réponse chez les « économistes du développement » de l'École de Chicago (Richard Posner, Gary Becker, Ronald Coase ou Robert Lucas) qui auraient le tort d'expliquer la persistance de la pauvreté par des facteurs locaux.

[20] *Op. cit.*, p. 317.

D'après Renaut, cette position dissimule une faiblesse philosophique. L'éthique de référence inclut de toute évidence d'autres considérations que celles de la non-nuisance, comme en témoigne l'insistance sur la responsabilité lourde des pays riches et des instances imposant un ordre mondial injuste. Il s'agit d'un kantisme classique. Renaut reproche à Pogge de dissimuler par stratégie la véritable teneur de l'éthique globale qui lui sert de référence. Renaut se réclame de Fichte (*Fondements du droit naturel*, 1796) contre Kant : fonder sur la volonté d'agir par devoir la réalisation de l'idée du juste dans le monde n'est pas réaliste.

Quelles sont alors les possibilités offertes par l'approche par les capabilités et l'éthique globale de la perfection ? Une éthique globale prenant la forme d'une éthique de la perfection consisterait à défendre qu'il existe un point de perfection collective susceptible d'être atteint par l'humanité. Renaut se réfère à la philosophe Martha Nussbaum. Sa conception consiste à nuancer la position rawlsienne selon laquelle une société démocratique est neutre ; il existe des valeurs par rapport auxquelles l'État démocratique ne peut être neutre, comme celle de dignité humaine. Pour défendre une telle option, Nussbaum se réclame d'Aristote chez lequel elle pense trouver une notion moins étroite de la dignité, incluant de façon plus complète tout ce qui fait une vie humainement accomplie.

Reprise à Sen, la notion de capabilité sert à désigner une de ces dimensions caractéristiques de la vie humaine où chacun doit être mis en mesure de pouvoir s'accomplir en toute autonomie. Dans un article intitulé « Une social-démocratie aristotélicienne », Nussbaum la déduit, à partir d'une description des caractéristiques essentielles d'une vie proprement humaine où chacun doit être mis en mesure de pouvoir s'accomplir en toute autonomie.[21]

Ces motifs issus d'Aristote parsèment la version fournie par Nussbaum d'une éthique perfectionniste du développement. À partir d'une description des caractéristiques essentielles d'une vie proprement humaine, elle déduit une liste des dix ou onze capabilités fondamentales, conditions d'une vie pleinement humaine et ouvrant sur des droits des individus aussi bien que des peuples à l'accomplissement de leur dignité.[22]

On note dans cette liste la précellence d'une conception fortement déterminée du bien sur les choix par la liberté du sujet de ses maximes d'action, essentialisme et paternalisme. Une telle version perfectionniste de l'éthique globale soulève de redoutables interrogations sur les politiques qu'elle inspirerait.

---

[21] *Op. cit.*, p. 323.

[22] (1) Pouvoir vivre autant que possible une vie humaine complète jusqu'à la fin. (2) Pouvoir jouir d'une bonne santé, d'une alimentation adéquate, avoir des opportunités de satisfaction sexuelle, etc. (3) Pouvoir éviter toute souffrance inutile et connaître l'expérience du plaisir. (4) Pouvoir utiliser nos cinq sens ; pouvoir imaginer, penser et raisonner. (5) Pouvoir aimer et éprouver douleur, désir et gratitude. (6) Pouvoir se former une conception du bien. (7) Pouvoir vivre avec les autres êtres humains. (8) Pouvoir vivre en relation avec les animaux, les plantes, le monde de la nature. (9) Pouvoir rire, jouer et nous adonner à des activités récréatives. (10) Pouvoir vivre notre propre vie et non pas celle de quelqu'un d'autre. (10b) Pouvoir vivre notre propre vie dans un environnement et un contexte de notre choix.

Amartya Sen s'est préservé contre la tentation de procéder lui-même à un tel listage des capabilités. Selon Renaut il faut identifier ici une troisième forme d'éthique globale, échappant à la réaffirmation désastreuse de ce conflit entre éthique du devoir et éthique de la perfection.

C'est alors ici qu'Alain Renaut abat ses cartes et en vient à la solution qu'il propose, c'est-à-dire une « éthique globale de l'intérêt bien compris ». La position qui lui paraît la plus défendable consiste à situer dans l'intérêt bien compris des acteurs le principal motif susceptible de les conduire effectivement à rendre accessibles aux plus démunis les conditions suffisantes de bien-être pour que des chances de survie et de vie décente leur soient plus équitablement ménagées. Pour que surgisse ainsi en nous la motivation éthique la plus réaliste de l'engagement politique, rien ne requiert donc que les citoyens et les gouvernants des pays riches soient animés par une éthique du devoir ou une éthique aristotélicienne de l'excellence.

Dans son *Projet de paix perpétuelle*, en 1795, Kant affirmait que l'objectif de la paix était réalisable « même pour un peuple de démons pourvu qu'il ait quelque intelligence ». À terme, selon Renaut, de l'injustice globale, de l'injustice entre les peuples, sortira la guerre des démunis. C'est donc par une combinatoire d'intérêts bien compris qu'adviendra la justice globale.

Alain Renaut délaisse alors les philosophes pour se réclamer de Joseph Stiglitz, auteur, en 2010, d'un rapport intitulé « Pour une vraie réforme du système monétaire et financier international ». Stiglitz estime qu'aujourd'hui, pour les pays en développement, il faut sans doute ne plus se précipiter dans le débat pour ou contre le libre-échangisme. Il convient de trouver un moyen terme. Très souvent les pays en voie de développement sont en effet confrontés pour exporter leurs produits industriels vers les pays développés à des droits de douane trois ou quatre fois supérieurs à ceux qui sont appliqués aux produits issus d'autres pays développés. Ces pays auraient à la fois intérêt à la libéralisation des échanges et intérêt à de fortes exceptions de type protectionniste pour eux-mêmes. Mais même Stiglitz contourne le problème des négociations internationales sur les questions tarifaires. S'il affirme que le monde développé doit s'engager plus nettement que par le passé à aider le monde moins avancé, il ne pose pas vraiment la question de savoir ce qui peut pousser les États riches à fournir cette aide. À vrai dire, affirme Renaut, il ne s'agit pas d'une aide par approche ressourciste ni par l'approche capabilitaire, mais « favoriser une solide culture d'analyse économique capable d'identifier les projets favorables au développement et de leur donner priorité dans les négociations [...] Tous les pays développés ont intérêt à aboutir à des accords qui seraient justes et dans l'intérêt général du monde. »

Renaut préconise ici des procédures plus justes pour un monde plus juste. Il ne s'agirait plus de justice distributive en matière de ressources ou de capabilités, mais de justice au sens juridique du terme. « Il est probable, écrit-il, qu'un accord juste sorte d'une procédure juste. »

Mais rien n'est moins sûr. Un résultat inégalitaire peut sortir d'une situation juste au départ. C'est la raison pour laquelle Rawls préfère la justice « structurelle » à la justice « historique ».

Sans doute Renaut précise-t-il en quel sens il entend ces « procédures plus justes » ; il veut dire « plus démocratiques ». Il rejoint alors l'analyse de Stiglitz plaidant pour le rapprochement entre les procédures en vigueur dans les négociations commerciales internationales et celles qui président à l'élaboration des lois dans un parlement démocratique.

Il faut postuler, selon Renaut, que les pays riches comprendront que leurs intérêts bien entendus est de fournir des fonds aux pays pauvres afin de les aider à mettre en œuvre des accords dont tout le monde reconnaîtra, s'ils sont le produit de procédures justes de délibération, qu'ils peuvent et doivent bénéficier à tous. L'intelligence de leur intérêt pourrait ainsi servir, pour tous les pays de motivation suffisante, échappant à l'alternative entre l'éthique trop « héroïque » du devoir et l'éthique trop « paternaliste » de la perfection. Il s'agit d'un « pari sur la valeur morale de l'intelligence. »

Dans cette démarche, Renaut a souhaité fuir la « grande illusion de l'idéalisme » et satisfait un besoin de réalisme politique.

Comment envisage-t-il sa politique globale de développement humain ? Il suggère de compléter les politiques de justice distributive proprement dites par des politiques de justice compensatrice ou réparatrice. Il se retourne alors encore une fois vers Pogge pour y trouver l'idée d'un processus de correction, de réparation ou de compensation. Le discours de la justice distributive peut ainsi et sans doute doit inclure dans sa logique un infléchissement vers une forme réparatrice ou compensatrice de justice.

Le trajet de Renaut va des politiques de justice globale à une reformulation de l'indice de développement humain. Il projette d'« esquisser ce qui pourrait résulter d'un bilan articulé des solutions politiques pour une reformulation d'un indice plus convaincant du développement humain que ne l'est, depuis 1990, l'IDH. »

Il entrevoit trois axes pour des politiques de justice globale.

Les orientations les plus déterminantes semblent aujourd'hui se résumer à un dispositif de justice distributive, à une orientation de ce dispositif par des exigences de justice compensatrice et à une réorganisation en termes de bien-être de ce qui fait l'objet de la distribution ou de la compensation. Le dispositif forgé par Pogge (2002) serait acceptable si l'on parvenait à y inclure la part de vérité contenue dans l'indispensable approche par les capabilités. Renaut estime tout à fait envisageable une telle inclusion des capabilités dans un dividende élargi qu'il propose d'appeler de justice globale (DJG).

Il entre dans le détail de cette réorganisation en trois moments : il préconise premièrement une aide au développement académique, étant donné l'importance de la perspective qu'on appelle aujourd'hui «économie de la connaissance ». On devrait aboutir à la construction d'un ou plusieurs indices de développement académique (IDA). Un deuxième axe des politiques de développement conduit à compenser les inégalités injustes historiquement engendrées et naturellement créées. Le but est de corriger les inégalités les plus fortes qui se trouvent avoir été produites par la loterie naturelle et par la loterie historique. Troisièmement, Alain Renaut plaide pour arracher le choix des politiques de développement au clivage des ressources et des capabilités. Il conviendrait d'inscrire dans un indice de développement humain de quoi dynamiser et orienter, grâce à des indicateurs plus multidimensionnels, des politiques concernant des secteurs jusqu'ici peu privilégiés par les pratiques de développement. Renaut appelle de ses voeux une réévaluation de l'indice de développement humain.[23]

En conclusion de cet ample ouvrage, Renaut avoue explicitement avoir privilégié le moment éthique sur le moment politique ; arguant du fait que, sans motivations éthiques claires, de quelconques politiques du développement ne seraient pas efficaces par rapport à la pauvreté. Il a décrit son éthique du développement dans les termes d'une éthique de l'intérêt bien compris ou de l'égoïsme intelligent.

Il revient alors sur les rapports de la politique et de la morale. Selon lui, en justice globale, les relations entre politique et morale gagneraient à être inversées par rapport à la façon dont elles apparaissent en général dans les théories libérales au sens rawlsien du terme.

La confusion de la morale et de la politique ne conduit-elle pas à des effets pervers, comme on l'a vu sous la Terreur ou en URSS ?

De plus, les sciences politiques se sont édifiées en se voulant, contrairement à la philosophie politique, résolument descriptives et non pas prescriptives : en affirmant l'importance du choix éthique dans la politique du développement, ne régresse-t-on pas en deçà de ce qui a permis aux disciplines touchant au politique de se constituer comme des sciences ?

Selon Supiot, dont le point de vue est ici aux antipodes de celui de Renaut, cette volonté de dépolitisation a conduit à l'abandon, par une majorité d'économistes, de la tradition savante de l'« économie politique », au profit d'une « Science économique » singeant les sciences exactes et parvenant à placer sous l'égide d'Alfred Nobel les prix d'excellence qu'elle s'attribue à elle-même. Les normes scientifiques et religieuses sont les seules à échapper au débat politique dans une société démocratique et il faut donc croire et faire croire que l'économie relève de la science pour la dépolitiser. La révolution ultralibérale renoue ainsi avec les grandes idéologies scientistes, et notamment avec le socialisme scientifique et sa foi dans l'existence de lois économiques immanentes et que la sphère politique a pour mission de mettre en œuvre et non de mettre en question.

Le premier espace est celui où l'action politique répond ou est ordonnée à la reconnaissance d'un droit. Renaut souligne ce que peut avoir d'« égarant l'affirmation, notamment chez Pogge, qu'il peut y avoir un droit des pauvres du monde : au sens strict où la notion d'un droit comprend analytiquement en elle celle d'un droit de contraindre au respect de ce droit, il n'existe pas à proprement parler de tels droits, si ce n'est au sens où on désignerait par là de nouveaux droits humains. » En fait, les droits des pauvres du monde ne sont pas des droits au sens rigoureux du terme,

[23] L'IDH actuel est actuellement tridimensionnel (niveau de vie ou revenu, santé ou espérance de vie, éducation). Il serait souhaitable, selon Renaut, que le PNUD (le programme des Nations Unies pour le développement) réaffirme solennellement que le bien-être, entendu de façon multidimensionnel, incluant la vie et les conditions de la vie, tout à la fois l'être-bien et les conditions d'une vie proprement humaine, constitue le medium à travers lequel communiquent toutes les facettes du développement que les nouvelles mesures des inégalités globales aident à cerner et à apprécier.

c'est-à-dire au sens de droits opposables à un pouvoir politique qui se trouverait contraint de les faire respecter.

Que penser de cette magistrale démonstration ? On y remarque la prédominance, certainement liée à l'influence d'Amartya Sen, de l'éthique et de l'économie. Renaut, philosophe du droit, n'aborde le droit que de façon marginale. Alain Supiot, au nom de la justice et du droit, propose une philosophie de la justice qui, selon moi, se fonde sur des analyses qui vont parfois trop loin,[24] mais n'accordent pas aux organismes internationaux et aux chiffres de la discipline—la science ?—économique une autorité aussi absolue que celle que Renaut leur accorde.

Pour Supiot il faut se méfier des mirages de la quantification et on peut être en accord avec lui sur ce point.[25] La croyance en un monde régi par le calcul d'utilité a succédé aux scientismes d'avant-guerre, qui entendaient régler le gouvernement des hommes sur les lois de l'histoire ou de la race. Se poursuit ainsi, sous une forme nouvelle, le rêve ancien de pouvoir gouverner les hommes comme on gère les choses.[26] Ce rêve procède d'une confusion, bien mise en lumière par l'historien des sciences Georges Canguilhem, entre la régulation des machines ou des organismes biologiques et celle des sociétés humaines.

Oublieux de cette distinction fondamentale, le scientisme contemporain se nourrit de la vision d'un monde débarrassé des lois—hors celles de la physique—et peuplé d'hommes devenus transparents à eux-mêmes.

Dans un tel monde, le gouvernement par les lois cède la place à la gouvernance par les nombres. Le gouvernement par les lois vise au règne de règles générales et abstraites qui garantissent l'identité, les libertés et les devoirs de chacun… Sous l'empire de la gouvernance, la normativité perd sa dimension verticale : il ne s'agit plus de se référer à une loi qui transcende les faits, mais d'inférer la norme de la mesure des faits.

Cette entreprise de réduction de la diversité des êtres et des choses à une quantité mesurable est inhérente au projet d'instauration d'un Marché total qui embrasserait tous les hommes et tous les produits de la planète, et au sein duquel chaque pays abolirait ses frontières commerciales afin de tirer parti de ses « avantages comparatifs ». L'élimination des discriminations dans les relations commerciales internationales » à laquelle œuvre l'Organisation mondiale du commerce (OMC) exige de réduire la diversité des systèmes juridiques nationaux, qui sont invités à se purger de toutes les règles susceptibles d'entraver la libre circulation des capitaux et des marchandises… C'est l'Union européenne qui, dans le contexte de l'instauration du « Marché unique » s'est la première définie juridiquement comme un « *espace* de liberté, de sécurité et de justice », ayant vocation à étendre à un nombre indéterminé et indéterminable de nouveaux pays membres, et non plus comme un *territoire* ou un ensemble de territoires aux frontières clairement identifiables. Absente du Traité

[24] Notamment lorsqu'il parle de privatisation de l'État providence et de prédation de l'État.

[25] Je l'ai montré, dans un tout autre contexte, dans *Les Sirènes de l'irrationnel*, Albin Michel, 1991 ; j'y indiquais la difficulté qu'il y avait parfois à distinguer la frontière entre le discours scientifique et le discours magique.

[26] Supiot, *op. cit.*, p. 76.

de Rome signé en 1957, la notion d'espace y a été introduite par l'Acte unique européen de 1986.[27]

Cette tentative de métamorphose de toute espèce de qualité singulière en une quantité mesurable nous engagerait, selon Supiot, dans une boucle spéculative où la croyance en des images chiffrées se substitue progressivement au contact avec les réalités que ces images sont censées représenter. Le travail de la pensée consisterait à conférer au calcul une signification, en rapportant toujours les quantités mesurées à un sens de la mesure. La nécessité d'inscrire tout calcul dans un système de références lui-même incalculable serait encore plus impérieuse lorsqu'on cherche à mesurer non des phénomènes naturels mais des faits économiques et sociaux.

Confondre la mesure et l'évaluation condamnerait à perdre le sens de la mesure : car évaluer ce n'est pas seulement mesurer, mais référer la mesure à un jugement de valeur qui lui confère un sens. Or la définition de ce sens a inévitablement une dimension dogmatique, car nos catégories de pensée ne nous sont pas données par la nature ; elles sont un moyen que nous nous donnons pour la comprendre. Les systèmes modernes d'audit sembleraient avoir complètement oublié la sage mise en garde formulée en ce sens dès la fin du XIXe siècle par James Anyon, l'un des pères de la comptabilité moderne : *« Use figures as little as you can [...] Think and act upon facts, truths and principles and regard figures only as things to express these. [...] The well trained and experienced accountant of today is not a man of figures »*.[28] Le marché, qui est une sphère du calcul, devrait être référé à une norme qui échappe au calcul pour pouvoir fonctionner convenablement. Faute de quoi, comme le montre l'implosion des marchés financiers, il est condamné à s'enfermer dans une boucle spéculative. Perdant le sens de la mesure, la finance aurait perdu contact avec la réalité jusqu'à ce que cette dernière se venge.

Cette perte de contact avec les réalités serait également à l'œuvre dans le recours aux indicateurs développés sous l'égide du *New Public Management* : selon cette doctrine managériale, les États devraient être soumis aux mêmes règles de fonctionnement que les entreprises opérant sur des marchés concurrentiels. C'est-à-dire qu'ils devraient réagir à des signaux chiffrés qui, à la manière des prix du marché, seraient une idée vraie du monde où ils opèrent. Cette doctrine aurait fortement influencé les réformes adoptées ces dix dernières années dans la sphère publique au nom de la « gouvernance ». À la différence des catégories statistiques conçues depuis Quételet, les nouveaux indicateurs ne visent pas seulement à éclairer mais à programmer surtout l'action des États et des agents publics, en leur assignant l'amélioration d'un score relativement aux performances de leurs compétiteurs.[29] Issu de la cybernétique, le concept de gouvernance porte à considérer le chiffre non comme un cadre, mais comme un but de l'action ou plus exactement comme un moteur de la réaction puisque chaque acteur privé ou public est censé, non plus agir,

---

[27] Supiot, Alain « L'inscription territoriale des lois », in *Esprit*, nov. 2008, p. 151.

[28] Cité par Boyle, David (2000) *The tyranny of Numbers*. HarperCollins, p. 38.

[29] Voir Salais, Robert « Capacités, base informationnelle et démocratie délibérative », in de Munck, Jean & Zimmermann, Bénédicte (éds) (2008) *La Liberté au prisme des capacités*. Paris : EHESS, pp. 297 *sq*.

mais rétroagir aux signaux chiffrés qui lui parviennent afin d'améliorer sa performance.

Le problème n'est pas, explique Supiot, de « réguler » les marchés comme on régule son chauffage central. Mais de les réglementer.

Cette démarche est aussi dogmatique que celle de la planification soviétique et grosse des mêmes effets : elle oriente l'action vers la satisfaction des objectifs quantitatifs, elle masque la situation réelle de l'économie et de la société à une classe dirigeante déconnectée de la réalité des dirigés. « La représentation chiffrée du monde [...] enferme les organisations internationales, les États et les entreprises dans un autisme de la quantification qui les coupe de plus en plus de la vie des peuples ».[30] Traiter les systèmes de valeur comme des choses mesurables conduirait dès lors à détraquer les instruments de mesure et à prêter à son propre système de valeurs une objectivité « scientifique » qu'il ne peut avoir.

Les indicateurs conçus par l'Union européenne ou par la Banque mondiale pour mesurer les performances des droits nationaux seraient ainsi l'image caricaturale d'une normativité qui s'ignore. L'image quantifiée qu'ils donnent à voir ne serait pas celle de la réalité, mais celle des croyances qui ont présidé à leur élaboration. Robert Salais a montré, par exemple, que l'accent mis sur l'amélioration du taux de retour à l'emploi instantané dans la Méthode ouverte de coordination suppose de tenir pour négligeable l'impact de précarisation de l'emploi sur le marché du travail. Fondés sur le concept d'employabilité, et non sur celui de capacité des personnes, ces indicateurs ne tiendraient pas davantage compte de la vulnérabilité des travailleurs exposés à un fort risque de perte de leur emploi : cécité à tout ce qui peut, en amont, prévenir le chômage.

Le dissident Alexandre Zinoviev parlait à ce sujet de « mensonge véridique », remarque Supiot.

La gouvernance par les nombres reposerait sur la croyance dans la réalité des objets que les catégories statistiques sont censées représenter et sur l'oubli des conventions d'équilibre qui ont présidé à leur construction. Ceci l'exposerait particulièrement à tomber dans les pièges de l'autoréférence, mis en évidence par la logique mathématique[31] : aucun ensemble ne peut appartenir à lui-même ni se présupposer lui-même.

Nous vivrions désormais dans l'ère de ce que l'on appelle « gouvernance ». Mais cette modalité de gestion des hommes et des choses serait loin d'être un modèle de démocratie. Les formes de représentation typique de la « gouvernance » viseraient à quantifier des faits plutôt qu'à refléter des expériences et où il ne s'agit pas de parler, mais de compter.[32] La comptabilité, les statistiques et les indicateurs seraient les trois formes principales de cette représentation chiffrée du monde. Chacune

[30] Jubé, Samuel (2011) *Droit social et normalisation comptable* [thèse (2008), Université de Nantes], préf. d'Alain Supiot et de Yannick Lemarchand. Paris: L.G.D.J./Lextenso éditions, « Droit et Économie ». Dejours, Christophe (2003) *L'Évaluation du travail à l'épreuve du réel: critique des fondements de l'évaluation*. INRA.

[31] *Op. cit.*, p. 87.

[32] *Op. cit.*, p. 125.

d'elles a sa légitimité et son domaine de validité propre. La comptabilité viserait à refléter une image fidèle du patrimoine de la situation financière et du résultat d'une entité juridique. Les statistiques, comme leur nom l'indique, viseraient à doter l'État d'une représentation scientifique de la société. Quant aux indicateurs, ils seraient en même temps des *indices* de la «physiologie du corps social » et des indications destinées à guider l'action que l'État exerce sur lui. L'essor de ces formes de représentations procéderait de l'aspiration à une gestion scientifique des affaires humaines. C'est à la fois leur force et leur danger. Force, car ils faciliteraient la réalisation d'un accord sur la règle juste à adopter. Leur danger, parce qu'ils exposeraient à l'illusion dogmatique de la scientificité de cette représentation. Or les catégories comptables ou statistiques inventeraient les catégories qu'elles décrivent, en recourant à des conventions d'équivalence, qui consisteraient à rapporter à une même quantité des situations qualitativement différentes. Le risque serait alors le « fétichisme du signe qui, prenant le nombre pour la chose même, expose aux mirages de la quantification. »

En conclusion, on ne peut que s'associer à l'ambitieux projet d'Alain Renaut de rendre plus juste le monde où nous vivons. Sa lumineuse exposition des apories de l'approche ressourciste et de l'approche capabilitaire nous convainc d'opter pour une éthique de l'intérêt bien compris. L'unique réserve, légère, consisterait à l'inciter à prendre davantage de recul par rapport aux données de l'économie et au pouvoir des organismes internationaux.

Seeing Injustice

Gülriz Uygur

What is injustice? This article is different from other views which focus on justice. It aims to determine the meaning of injustice. To focus on injustice is not a new thing. For example, Simone Weil, Judith Shklar and Amartya Sen focus on injustice. Like them, I claim that we need to look at not only at justice, but also at injustice.

> Every volume of moral philosophy contains at least one chapter about justice, and many books are devoted entirely to it. But where is injustice? To be sure, sermons, the drama, and fiction deal with little else, but art and philosophy seem to shun injustice. They take it for granted that injustice is simply the absence of justice, and that once we know what is just, we will know all we need to know. That belief may not, however, be true. One misses a great deal by looking only at justice. The sense of injustice, the difficulties of identifying the victims of injustice, and the many ways in which we all learn to live with each other's injustices tend to be ignored, as is the relation of private injustice to the public order.[1]

According to Shklar, if we only focus on justice, we miss injustice. In fact, this also causes a great gap between theory and the practical reality in which we meet many injustices. But if we focus on injustice, the distance between them may shorten.[2]

Like Shklar, Sen also states that we should focus on injustice. Sen says that what moves us is injustice, the inability to realize the just world.

> This is evident enough in our day-to-day life, with inequities or subjugations from which we may suffer and which we have good reason to resent, but it also applies to more widespread diagnoses of injustice in the wider world in which we live. It is fair to assume that Parisians would not have stormed the Bastille, Gandhi would not have challenged the empire on which the sun used not to set. Martin Luther King would not have fought white supremacy in 'the land of the free and the home of the brave', without their sense of manifest injustices that could be overcome. They were not trying to achieve a perfectly just

[1] Shklar, Judith N. (1990) *The Faces of Injustice*. New Haven: Yale University Press, p. 15.

[2] Shklar, p. 16.

G. Uygur (✉)
Law Faculty, Ankara University, Ankara, Turkey
e-mail: gulrizuygur@gmail.com

G. Fløistad (ed.), *Philosophy of Justice*, Contemporary Philosophy: A New Survey 12,
DOI 10.1007/978-94-017-9175-5_21,

> world (even if there were any agreement on what that would be like), but they did want to remove clear injustices to the extent they could.[3]

Sen also quotes from the character Pip in Charles Dickens' *Great Expectations* to show how easy it is to see injustice. Sen mentions Pip's words. In this novel, Pip says that "there is nothing so finely perceived and finely felt as injustice".[4]

In this case, we may say that there are many reasons to focus on injustice. The most important of them is that moving from justice is not enough to grasp injustices. But its meaning is not to refuse the concept of justice or conceptions of justice. They are necessary. In addition to them, however, we also need to focus on injustice.

To focus on injustice, I will, firstly, make a distinction between justice and injustice. Secondly, I will determine the meaning of injustice as a concept different from that of justice. For this, I will claim that it is necessary to focus on the concept of seeing injustice.

1 Justice and Injustice

To make a distinction between the concept of justice and injustice, we should also mention a distinction between the concept of justice and the conception of justice. Because, as we state later, the contrast between justice and injustice is generally connected with the conceptions of justice.

John Rawls makes a distinction between the concept of justice and the conception of justice. According to Rawls, the concept of justice means a proper balance between competing claims. The conception of justice includes a set of principles which identify the relevant considerations connected with determining this balance.[5]

In this regard, we may say that the conception of justice is different from injustice. Injustice is context-dependent and context-related particulars. The principles of justice are general principles. Similar to the contradiction between generalism and particularism, we may claim that there may be a contradiction between the conception of justice and injustice in some cases. Furthermore, like the Rawlsian conception of justice, a set of principles of justice does not cover all injustices. In this situation, injustice may be regarded only as departing from principles of justice. Then, the other injustices which are not covered by these principles cannot be seen. This claim may be not valid for all of the conceptions of justice. Connected with this point, we may state Sen's distinction.

Sen says that we need to focus on actual realizations and accomplishments. For this, he states a dichotomy between an arrangement-focused view of justice, and a realization-focused understanding of justice.[6]

---

[3] Sen, Amartya (2010) *The Idea of Justice*. London: Penguin Books, p. vii.

[4] Sen, p. vii.

[5] Rawls, John (1971) *A Theory of Justice*. Cambridge: Harvard University Press, p. 10.

[6] Sen, p. 10.

> The former line of thought proposes that justice should be conceptualized in terms of certain organizational arrangements—some institutions, some regulations, some behavioural rules—the active presence of which would indicate that justice is being done.[7]

For example, Rawls applies principles of justice to the basic structure of the society. But in that society, in the words of Sen, if "a big fish can freely devour a small fish",[8] we cannot say that there is no injustice. In this regard, injustice is not only seen with regard to the social institutions and general rules. For this, according to Sen, we should look at the societies themselves.[9]

Regarding conceptions of justice, I conclude that the principles of justice are not enough to see injustice. In fact, it is also possible to criticize the principles of justice in the context of distributive justice. Distributive conceptions of justice are not enough to see injustice, since they focus on how a just distribution of goods is possible in a society.

Simone Weil states that justice is not connected with the distribution of the goods.

> Justice has to do not with how things are distributed—it has nothing to do with things (property, rights, etc.) at all. It has to do with preventing harm being done to every and all human beings and with creating a social climate where every human being has the power to consent and refuse.[10]

On the other hand, connected with the language of rights there is also a problem. The principles of justice which include this language also cause invisibility. But this does not mean that injustice does not include the violation of rights.[11] Connected with rights, the problem is its abstract language. For example, in terms of abortion, one side discusses the problem regarding women's rights and the other side discusses it regarding the fetus's rights. But no side hears the voice of the woman who cries, "I am harmed".[12]

In this respect, there is a difference between the conceptions of justice and injustice. That means, we cannot define injustice according to the principles of justice. Namely, we cannot say that injustice only occurs when the principles of justice are violated. For this reason, we should insist on the relationship between the concept of justice and injustice rather than on conceptions of justice, since the concept of justice is more suitable to cover injustices.

We may claim that we can define justice away from injustice. For this, firstly, as Sen rightly stated, we cannot merely regard justice as a moral or social ideal which is sought in itself. In this regard, the concept of justice should be regarded as an

[7] Sen, p. 10.

[8] Sen, p. 20.

[9] Sen, p. 20.

[10] Bell, Richard H. (1998) *Simone Weil: The Way of Justice as Compassion*. Boston: Rowman Littlefield Publishers, p. 54.

[11] Winch, Peter (1989) *Simone Weil: The Just Balance*. Cambridge: Cambridge University Press, pp. 180–181.

[12] In this example, I follow Weil's ideas (See Winch, p. 182).

epistemological concept. To explain this point, I follow Ioanna Kuçuradi's views about the concept of justice.

Kuçuradi states that there is a difference between the concept of justice and injustice. Following Plato, she states that justice is an idea.

> By 'idea' I mean, a special kind of thought: a conception of the human mind, which, in distinction from 'knowledge'—each piece of which is related to an object independent from itself—, engenders its object; and which, in distinction from 'belief'—which also creates its object—, is not bound to those who "have" it. Ideas are brought to history, where they remain effective for a while or for good, i.e., they are added to the historical being.[13]

To conceptualize justice, Kuçuradi investigates what people say when they claim justice. According to her, people demand it in connection with a general justice aspiration or a specific case.

> The first thing we can notice is that when laymen do so in general, they express a vague aspiration; while in a special case they try to express a demand: they mean that something should be fulfilled for themselves or for somebody else, something—whatever it may be in every individual case—, that they have not just at this moment, but they think, rightly or wrongly, belongs to them; they mean that they are deprived of something which should be restored to them: they mean something due to them.[14]

According to Kuçuradi, to determine what is due to a person in a specific case, we should look at injustice regarding this case. Injustice is a fact, not an idea. In this regard there is a difference between justice and injustice. But there is also a relationship between them, since by moving away from injustice we can determine the meaning of justice.

Then, there is a relationship between the concept of justice and injustice. Injustice is related to particular situations. In this regard, to determine injustice, it is important to see injustice in that situation. Namely, the concept of the seeing has a primary role in determining injustice in the particular situation.

2 The Concept of Seeing

> It is only with the heart that one can see rightly. What's important is invisible to the eye.[15]

In this article, our aim is to define seeing in the context of justice. For this, I must try to define seeing in the ethical manner, since seeing injustice is an ethical question. As we stated earlier, injustice is connected with the human being. If so, we should define seeing as connected with the human being.

In this manner, seeing does not mean looking. To see a human being, we need some specific conditions. These are, having specific knowledge, having virtues and

---

[13] Kuçuradi, Ioanna (2013) "Justice: Social and Global," *Human Rights, Concepts and Problems*. Zurich: LIT Verlag, p. 23.

[14] Kuçuradi, p. 24.

[15] Saint-Exupéry, Antoine de *The Little Prince.*

a desire connected with realizing justice, and becoming aware of obstacles which cause us to not see injustice.

In this section, I try to explain these conditions.

2.1 Specific Knowledge

We need specific knowledge, since to see a human being requires specific knowledge of the peculiarities of the person or what is the meaning of being human. As Martha Nussbaum rightly stated, *humanity does not automatically reveal itself to strangers.*[16] She also stated that we do not live in an innocent world.[17]

> We live, [...] in a world full of bad, crude theories, self-serving passions, and tainted judgements.[18]

These are obstacles which cause the invisibility of the human. Moving from Axel Honneth, it is possible to define invisibility. There are at least two meanings to this sense of invisibility. One of them is regarding physical presence. Following Honneth, it is possible to explain the other meaning of it by looking at Ralph Ellison's *Invisible Man.*[19]

> I am an invisible man. No, I am not a spook like those who haunted Edgar Allan Poe; nor am I one of your Hollywood movie ectoplasms. I am a man of substance, of flesh and bone, fiber and liquids—and I might even be said to possess a mind. I am invisible, understand, simply because people refuse to see me. Like the bodiless heads you see sometimes in circus sideshows, it is as though I have been surrounded by mirrors of hard distorting glass. When they approach me they see only my surroundings, themselves or figments of their imagination—indeed, everything and anything except me.
>
> Nor is my invisibility exactly a matter of biochemical accident to my epidermis. That invisibility to which I refer occurs because of a peculiar disposition of the eyes of those with whom I come in contact. A matter of the construction of their inner eyes, those eyes with which they look through their physical eyes upon reality.[20]

In this passage, one can easily see the other meaning of invisibility. In Ellison's novel, the person who reports himself as invisible is a black. The others referred to in the passage are white. White people do not see him, not because his presence is not there, but because they do not see him as a true person. Although the blacks are physically present, for white people, they are invisible.[21] Honneth says that this invisibility is looking through someone.

---

[16] Nussbaum, Martha (2010) *From Disgust to Humanity.* Oxford: Oxford University Press, p. xvii.

[17] Nussbaum, Martha (2007) "Why Practice Needs Ethical Theory," *The Path of the Law and Its Influence: The Legacy of Oliver Wendell Holmes*, ed. by S. J. Burton. Cambridge: Cambridge University Press, p. 78.

[18] Nussbaum, 2007, p. 78.

[19] Honneth, Axel (2003) "Invisibility: On the Epistemology of Recognition," in Honneth, A. & Margalit, A. *Aristotelian Society Supplementary Volume*, p. 111.

[20] Ellison, Ralph (1952) *Invisible Man.* Toronto: Random House, p. 3.

[21] Honneth, p. 111.

> We possess the capacity to show our disregard to persons who are present by behaving towards them as if they were not actually there in the room. In this sense, 'looking through' someone has a performative aspect because it demands gestures or ways of behaving that make clear that the other is not seen not merely accidentally, but rather intentionally.[22]

Moving from this meaning of invisibility, I can claim that to see a human means to see a true person. For this, we need

> the knowledge of the value of certain human potentialities: those potentialities which made Edison discover the uses of electricity, Marie Skolovska Curie discover radium, Saint-Exupéry write the Little Prince and many others achieve what they have indeed achieved, the blessings of which only some of us enjoy. This is the knowledge of what a human being can become and of the significance, for humanity, of the achievements of those who have actualized such potentialities.[23]

We also need knowledge about a human's value and values, since to see a human means to see this value and values.

2.2 *Virtues*

To see injustice requires certain virtues. Firstly, one who wants to see injustice must want to realize justice. In the other words, her/his will of principle should be justice. Secondly, as a result of the first one, she/he should pay attention to the particular case for seeing.

According to Iris Murdoch, it is a duty to see the world as it is.[24] This means paying attention to a particular case which is seen. Moving from Simone Weil and Murdoch, it is possible to determine the meaning of such attention. Weil states that, in its highest form, attention is like prayer. She regards it as a method for understanding things. She says that attention means to look at a particular case till the light suddenly dawns.

> Generally speaking, a method for the exercise of the intelligence, which consists of looking. Application of this rule for the discrimination between the real and the illusory. In our sense perceptions, if we are not sure of what we see we change our position while looking, and what is real becomes evident. In the inner life, time takes the place of space. With time we are altered, and, if as we change we keep our gaze directed towards the same thing, in the end illusions are scattered and the real becomes visible. This is on condition that the attention be a looking and not an attachment.[25]

Then, attention is necessary to see things clearly. For this, according to Murdoch, it is necessary to pay attention properly. Namely, we should see the particularities of the situation. We should behave as participants, not like disinterested persons.

---

[22] Honneth, p. 112.

[23] Kuçuradi, p. 26.

[24] Murdoch, Iris (1970) *The Sovereignty of Good*. New York: Routledge, p. 91.

[25] Weil, Simone (1986) *Simone Weil: An Anthology*, ed. by Sian Miles. New York: Virago Press, p. 215.

Attention requires meeting the other as subject.[26] Attending properly also means to see things according to the idea of the Good. Murdoch moves the idea of the Good. Paying attention is connected with the application of the principle of the Good.[27]

Following Murdoch, in the context of the concept of seeing, I claim that attention means to look at a particular case in the light of a human's value and values. Namely, if we are to see the true person, we must pay attention in particular with regard to that person's value and values.[28] Thus, we can see true person, not a black or a white person.

Furthermore, paying attention properly requires particular experiences which include a way of thinking according to a human's value and values. For this, Aristotle's concept of phronesis helps us. Phronesis is the truthful habit of acting rationally in matters both good and bad for human beings. Phronesis is connected with the particulars.[29] It provides a means of making judgements according to the concrete circumstances in the light of the knowledge of value and values. Since phronesis requires particular situations, it also requires an awareness of the obstacles which block being able to see. To be aware of them, we should be open-minded. Generally, open-minded is understood as stated below:

> To be open-minded is to be aware of one's fallibility as a believer, and to acknowledge the possibility that anytime one believes something, one could be wrong. In order to see that such an attitude is epistemically valuable even to an already virtuous agent, some details of the skills and habits of the open-minded agent are elucidated.[30]

This meaning is helpful to be aware of biases and prejudices. But open-minded is also connected with the peculiarities of a situation and to others. In this meaning, to be open-minded is to be open to others and to the complexities of situations.[31] In this manner, open-minded should be regarded as a requirement of the phronesis.

In addition, imagination is also necessary to see the other as human.

2.3 *Awareness of Obstacles*

As we stated before, there are many obstacles which block the ability to see injustice. These may be the result of self-interest, biases, prejudices and disgust.

It is possible to explain other obstacles according to Iris Marion Young. Young insists on oppression which is connected to groups. Young states that the members

---

[26] Talbott, Sally E. (2000) *Partial Reason: Critical and Constructive Transformations of Ethics and Epistemology*. Greenwood Press, p. 105.

[27] Clarke, Bridget (2012) "Iris Murdoch and the Prospects for Critical Moral Perception," in *Iris Murdoch, Philosopher*, ed. by Justin Broackes. Oxford: Oxford University Press, p. 249.

[28] Uygur, Gülriz (2013) *Hukukta Adaletsizliği Görmek*. Ankara: Türkiye Felsefe Kurumu Yayını, p. 44.

[29] Uygur, p. 44.

[30] Riggs, Wayne (2010) "Open-mindedness," in *Metaphilosophy*, p. 172.

[31] Uygur, p. 73.

of groups who are under grave oppression face injustice. She states five kinds of oppression. These are exploitation, marginalization, powerlessness, cultural imperialism and violence.[32] She also states the meaning of oppression. Oppression generally is known to be connected with oppressive regimes. Young explains it differently. She explains another meaning of oppression in the context of the social movements of the 1960s and 1970s.

> In its new usage, oppression designates the disadvantage and injustice some people suffer not because a tyrannical power coerces them, but because of the everyday practices of a well-intentioned liberal society. In this new left usage, the tyranny of a ruling group over another, as in South Africa, must certainly be called oppressive. But oppression also refers to systemic constraints on groups that are not necessarily the results of the intentions of a tyrant. Oppression in this sense is structural, rather than the result of a few people's choices or policies. Its causes are embedded in unquestioned norms, habits, and symbols, in the assumptions underlying institutional rules and the collective consequences of following those rules.[33]

Moving from Young, we claim that this oppression causes invisibility of the groups which suffer injustices. This oppression is reflected in ordinary life and human practices. As well, media and cultural stereotypes cause it to reproduce.[34]

> The conscious actions of many individuals daily contribute to maintaining and reproducing oppression, but those people are usually simply doing their jobs or living their lives, and do not understand themselves as agents of oppression.[35]

For this reason, systematic oppression is connected with very deep and vast injustices. Then, we can say that structural oppression is a main example of the obstacles which block our ability to see injustice.

Obstacles also cause epistemic injustice. Epistemic injustice is explained by Miranda Fricker. Fricker distinguishes between two kinds of epistemic injustice. One of them is testimonial injustice.

> Testimonial injustice happens whenever prejudice on the part of a hearer causes them to attribute a deflated level of credibility to a speaker's world.[36]

For example, like the Invisible Man, if you cannot trust a man's words because he is black, we can say that there is a testimonial injustice. In this sense, we can claim that testimonial injustice causes another obstacle which blocks seeing another person as having the capacity of knowing.

The other kind of epistemic injustice is hermeneutical injustice. Hermeneutical injustice is connected with the interpretation of the social world in which we live.

> It happens when a certain group is hermeneutically marginalized—that is, members do not get to participate fully in those social processes of meaning-making through which shared

[32] Young, Iris Marion (2011) *Justice and the Politics of Difference*, foreword by Danielle S. Allen. New Jersey: Princeton University Press, p. 40.

[33] Young, p. 41.

[34] Young, p. 41.

[35] Young, p. 42.

[36] Fricker, Miranda (2012) "An Interview with Miranda Fricker," in Dieleman, Susan *Social Epistemology*, p. 256.

> concepts and modes of interpretation are formed for us to draw on in interpreting the social world. Members of such groups are more likely than others to be in a position where they have a certain social experience for which they do not have the concepts or interpretive tropes to be able to render it intelligible to others, or possibly even to themselves.[37]

This injustice may be regarded as a result of systematic oppression. Oppressed groups cannot share their experience and cannot participate in the interpretative processes of the social world. For example, women who suffer from sexual harassment often do not share their experiences and participate in process of meaning-making.[38]

These obstacles and injustices, then, are reasons which block seeing. For this reason, to see injustice requires being aware of it. To be aware of it, we need knowledge and virtues. As we stated before, to see injustice, knowledge is necessary. This knowledge also helps us to be aware of obstacles. Namely, one who has this knowledge makes a distinction between what obstacles one can see and what blocks seeing them. On the other hand, virtues are also important to be aware of obstacles. For example, to be open-minded it is necessary to be aware of biases, prejudices and other obstacles.

3 Conclusion

In this article, my main question is how it is possible to define injustice. For this, firstly, it is necessary to make a distinction between justice and injustice. It is also necessary to make a distinction between a concept of justice and conception of justice, since the latter may cause a person not to see injustice. Furthermore, seeing injustice requires being able to do something against injustice. Exactly what is determined according to concept of justice in the context of the particularities of a situation.

Secondly, I claim that it is possible to define injustice according to the concept of seeing. For this reason, I try to explain the concept of seeing. I consider it in the ethical manner. In this, seeing means to see another human being.

Thirdly, I claim that to see another human is possible under certain requirements. One of them is the knowledge of the human's value and values. The other is to have some virtues, like attentiveness and open-mindedness. These two requirements are related to each other. For example, we should know what is the subject of the attention. For this we need to have knowledge of humanity. Namely, it is necessary to evaluate things and to make a distinction among them, since there are some obstacles which block being able to see a human being. We should be aware of them. To be aware of them is possible together with these two requirements.

Fourthly, seeing injustice means to see the obstacles and conditions which block seeing a human as an individual being.

---

[37] Fricker, p. 257.

[38] I borrowed this example from Fricker, p. 25.

Justices : Entre les impossibilités et la sagesse tragique

Jean Godefroy Bidima

1 Introduction : Questions de mises…

« *Pouvoir ne pas parler n'est pas identique à ne pas pouvoir parler. Ceci est une privation, cela est une négation* » (Lyotard 1983 : 26).[1] La justice est justement ce qui, actuellement, se veut le baromètre et des privations et des négations de parole dans un monde où la force parodie la justice et le droit. Définitions, buts, extensions, acteurs, cadres, rendez-vous honorés ou manqués, paroles audibles ou suffoquées, secours des cultures ou fossoyeurs de celles-ci, recours des plus faibles et instrument des plus puissants, vengeance et pardon, endettement et rétribution, impératif divin et exigence humaine, parole humaine et cri inhumain, la justice qui incarne toutes ces postures pose l'une des plus grandes difficultés à la compréhension de notre humaine condition. Comment la penser aujourd'hui sans en référer à plusieurs figures et hésitations ? La question de la justice se pose souvent comme le lieu de la manifestation de la puissance et de ***l'autorité de l'État***, mais cet État qui fut et qui se décline en certains endroits comme État/Nation est aujourd'hui mis à mal par la fluidité des mouvements des populations et la globalisation des échanges culturels. La justice, qu'elle soit interne aux États, ou qu'elle s'occupe des rapports entre les États, qu'elle soit même ce qui sonde la règle et ses modalités d'application, qu'elle s'occupe des problèmes de légitimité ou de ceux de la technologie ou de la commercialisation, qu'elle se place comme un complément à la coutume ou un pendant à la théologie, qu'elle s'essouffle devant l'impossibilité de départager le règne de la force et du droit, qu'elle crie victoire après la punition des génocidaires, qu'elle hésite entre vérité, paix, devoir, égalité et équité, la justice—comme sentiment et comme institution—dit d'abord et avant tout le rapport des hommes à leur commune humanité qui regarde à la fois ses références fondatrices, ses bricolages

[1] Lyotard lui même cite Aristote, *De Interpretatione* 21 b 12–17 ; *Métaphysique* IV 1022 b 22 sq.

J.G. Bidima (✉)
Tulane University, New Orleans, USA
e-mail: jbidima@tulane.edu; jeanfomo@gmail.com

G. Fløistad (ed.), *Philosophy of Justice*, Contemporary Philosophy: A New Survey 12, DOI 10.1007/978-94-017-9175-5_22,

sociaux quotidiens et l'avenir. La justice est ainsi comme le veut Proudhon à la fois en l'homme[2] et dans la nature. Le problème que nous nous proposons de poser ici est celui du lien. La question de la justice dans un monde qui se veut sécularisé—et qui se bat encore avec le retour en force des fondamentalismes raciaux, ethniques et religieux—nous conduit, dans le cadre de l'Afrique, à sonder, à travers trois types de défis, l'application de la justice. D'une part, le défi de la prise en charge de la justice par les média (II. *Mise en scène*), et d'autre part, la question de la crédibilité de la Justice dans un monde travaillé par la méfiance et le cynisme (III. *Mise en confiance*), et enfin les différents nœuds autour de la justice pénale internationale ou la question de la propriété de la terre (IV. *Mises à mort symboliques*). Ces *trois mises en...* conduisent vers l'esquisse d'une sagesse pratique (Ricœur) qui n'est autre, dans le cas de l'Afrique, qu'une « sagesse tragique » non défaitiste.

2 Justices, media et l'industrie culturelle : le miroir de la mise en scène

La justice est à la fois une idée et une institution et, entre les deux, se trouve une mise en scène qui varie selon les cultures. Cette mise en scène est d'abord précédée par ***une mise en mots***. Le mot y est ordonné, ciselé, pesé, pris dans son propre piège et, piégeant à son tour les situations et les cas, tend la main. Qui la prendra ? La *passion* y arrive—à la hâte ou lentement selon les cas—comme pour porter secours aux mots qui, eux, exténués, n'en peuvent plus devant l'étonnement, l'indignation, la satisfaction, la vengeance et l'abattement. Les mots et les passions, dans leur course sont rattrapés par toute *une industrie culturelle* qui se saisit : *a.* de la passion et des mots, *b.* des mots de la passion, etc., de la passion des mots pour les exposer d'abord et les remettre ensuite à la juridiction de la raison et de l'efficacité. Dans sa trajectoire, la justice est ainsi soumise au regard de la société et aux diverses médiations symboliques par lesquelles toute société filtre ce qu'elle produit. La scène de la justice qui a ainsi plusieurs acteurs se déplace souvent vers les média donnant ainsi à la société l'occasion de voir l'alliance entre la justice et la publicité au sens kantien et habermasien. Cette publicité telle que nous la voyons à l'œuvre dans la manière de dire et d'exprimer les justices post-postmodernes n'est plus, dans certains cas, une étape vers l'émancipation des individus.

Populaire et populiste. Quand la justice va vers les média et quand ceux-ci s'emparent d'elle, on fait toujours croire que la justice, qui a couru le risque d'être confisquée par le clergé judiciaire, est rendue au *peuple* qui s'en emparera et en fera bon usage. Les Constitutions du monde ne se formulent-elles pas au nom du *peuple* ? Ici se joue le vieux clivage entre d'un côté les élites et derrière elles l'État et de l'autre le peuple. Cette coupure cache à l'horizon le vieux problème de l'opposition

[2] Proudhon 1858, T. III : 595. « *Le système des lois de la justice est la même chose que le système des lois du monde, agissant dans l'âme humaine non plus seulement comme idées ou notions, mais comme affections et sentiments* ».

entre une démocratie « directe » et une démocratie « représentative ». Une justice qui se fait par média interposés semble être l'un des gages de la démocratie directe. Le peuple s'y exprime et donne son opinion sur les divers problèmes qui se posent au cours de l'existence commune des hommes et femmes qui partagent un même espace politico-économico-culturel. La justice par les média semble obéir à l'exigence des Lumières dont parlait Kant. Exigence qui se décline comme la capacité de faire un usage public de la raison dans tous les domaines ; « [...] *pour répandre ces lumières, il n'est rien requis d'autre que la liberté ; et à vrai dire la plus inoffensive de toutes les manifestations qui peuvent porter ce nom, à savoir celle de faire un usage public de la raison dans tous les domaines* » (Kant 1985, T. II : 211). La deuxième justification de l'intrusion des média dans la justice concerne le souci de transparence. Dans des régimes politiques peu démocratiques, certaines affaires en matière pénale, comme les emprisonnements et les détentions arbitraires sont souvent dénoncées par la presse et, à ce titre, les média contribuent à critiquer la répression contre la liberté d'expression. Les média, en le faisant, assoient le pluralisme interprétatif au sujet des grandes préoccupations de la société comme le crime, la punition, les enquêtes criminelles, l'espionnage, la mort, les condamnations et l'emprisonnement. La publicité des média et la délocalisation de la scène de la justice—qui devient virtuelle—, la transformation du spectateur, les effets techniques utilisés par les média—couleurs, graphies et sons—, peuvent contribuer à diminuer le potentiel critique qu'une justice bien rendue peut avoir vis-à-vis de la société. Une justice qui se met au service de l'industrie culturelle transforme le spectateur ordinaire des scènes de justice en consommateur d'images et, *« pour le consommateur, il n'y a plus rien à classer, les producteurs ont déjà tout fait pour lui »* (Horkheimer & Adorno 1985 : 134). On dirait : il n'y a plus rien à juger, on a déjà jugé pour lui à travers les commentaires de ceux qui présentent et produisent ces images et textes. La justice à la radio ou à la télévision épouse ainsi les caractères et les vices de l'industrie culturelle ; la *manipulation des besoins* et la *production en série d'une justice* où l'on sait d'avance ce qu'elle veut, une justice qui ne nous montre et donne à lire l'injustice de l'affaire jugée que pour *cacher l'injustice du processus de production* qui est à la base de ce film, programme télévisuel ou journal qui nous montre/raconte l'affaire. En cachant le mode d'organisation qui est à la base de la présentation des affaires jugées, en taisant les appareils rhétorique, iconographique et « pathique » qui manipulent à la fois le regard, l'imagination et les peurs primitives, les média nous racontent et nous présentent une justice, la leur, celle qui ne doit blâmer le coupable ou plaindre la victime que pour juxtaposer à côté de cette plainte ou de cette dénonciation; la publicité, le fait divers, l'inauguration de telle entreprise qui, elle-même a été délocalisée (laissant sans emploi des milliers de gens), les résultats du football, les déclarations niaises de tel « Top-model » et le phrasé saccadé d'une rescapée à une tuerie pleurant son enfant assassiné. Prenons un journal qui nous décrirait l'affaire de la disparition du petit Gregory et les règlements de compte entre les membres de sa famille en France, ouvrons un quotidien qui relate le procès de Jodi Arias, cette jeune femme qui a tiré sur son petit ami et lui a tranché la gorge, cherchons dans les journaux de l'époque, le procès des généraux japonais qui ont provoqué le fiasco dans l'armée américaine dans l'Océan Pacifique, prêtons attention à la catastrophe écologique de l'Union Carbide à Bhopal en Inde et des procès en indemnisations qui s'en suivent, nous retrouverons ces informations, relatives aux « affaires » à côté d'autres informations qui commentent sur les bienfaits de telle pommade sur les rides, les vertus de la tenue de sport (en vente) sur la cellulite et les varices, les soupçons d'infidélité de telle Princesse, sans oublier que la publicité des produits de vente qui nous rappellent que notre commune humanité avec ses grands problèmes de justice est surveillée par le marché. Ce que les média réalisent en s'emparant des questions de justice, c'est d'introduire trois aspects qui constituent l'armature actuelle des média : *l'équivalence, l'indifférence et l'uniformité.*

En mettant côte à côte des nouvelles aux échelles dramatiques différentes, les média visent à produire dans la conscience des auditeurs, spectateurs ou lecteurs, l'idée du « tout est pareil », interchangeable : *« pour la conscience qui se laisse informer de toutes parts, tout devient problématique et tout devient égal. Un homme et une femme, deux gredins fameux, trois hommes dans un bateau, quatre points pour un alléluia* [...] *sexe au bureau, sept menaces contre la paix* [...] *neuf symphonies avec Karajan : dix petits nègres dans le dialogue Nord-Sud* [...] *»* (Sloterdijk 1987 : 382). Dans cette équivalence et cette interchangeabilité, on retrouve l'interchangeabilité des marchandises. Les situations de justice décrites et représentées par les média *ne sont après tout que des marchandises*, le procès d'un génocidaire représenté, la description d'un train qui déraille avec des boîtes de tomates à son bord, la représentation du procès d'une tentative de coup d'État dans un pays africain, le reportage sur une vedette qui rate une marche du podium pour recevoir son prix, la naissance de triplés chez un paisible chef de poste en Camargue ou la scène d'un serpent avalant la flûte d'un charmeur de serpent Bengali au moment où ce dernier voulait le charmer, tout cela est interchangeable, ravalé au même niveau. Ce nivellement joue sur les structures de l'inconscient et produit une espèce *d'indifférence* et d'anesthésie de notre capacité d'indignation et de choc. Comme le remarque Sloterdijk (*Ibid.* : 391) : *« Marx n'a-t-il pas offert dans son analyse de la marchandise une description frappante d'une logique très subtile montrant comment l'équivalence produit une indifférence qui s'exprime dans le rapport entre la marchandise et le prix ?* [...] *nous vivons dans un monde qui produit de fausses équations ; ce monde produit de fausses uniformités et de fausses équivalences* [...] *pour aboutir ainsi à une désintégration et à une indifférence intellectuelle où les hommes perdent la faculté de distinguer entre le juste et le faux, entre important et insignifiant »*. L'uniformité enfin vient du fait qu'avec l'industrie culturelle *« tout peut devenir une nouvelle, tout est disponible »* (*Ibid.* : 385). La justice comme mise en scène est le contraire de la logique des équivalences, car la justice qui a aussi pour mission d'évaluer des échelles et *des niveaux de responsabilité* ne met pas tout sur le même niveau. La justice est le contraire de l'indifférence, car il s'agit—quelque soit le fondement qu'elle se donne à travers les cultures humaines—de donner au litige ou au problème posé entre les humains une forme provisoire ou définitive, ce qui exclut l'indifférence. La logique de l'équivalence et le marché de ce flux d'informations que l'on obtient à travers les média aboutissent souvent à une perversion, ils ne donnent des informations que parce qu'ils ont renoncé à *com-prendre* le donné, c'est-à-dire à y déceler les ambiguités et les énigmes ; *« ils englobent tout parce qu'ils n'appréhendent rien ; ils parlent de tout, ne disent rien de rien. La cuisine des média nous sert quotidiennement un plat unique de la réalité avec d'innombrables ingrédients qui ont pourtant chaque jour le même goût »* (*Ibid.* : 389).

Une justice qui est—comme aux USA dite par les média—fait courir un autre grand risque : celui de dé-symboliser la justice qui est, à sa manière, *une mise en forme* (au sens où l'entend Claude Lefort) et en *sens* du social.

Les média racontent les événements de la justice de manière immédiate et prétendent donner accès à une justice libérée de la médiation procédurale. Les procès qui nous sont montrés à la télévision nous proposent une vérité immédiate. *« Cette alchimie douteuse entre justice et médias signale un dérèglement profond de la démocratie. Les médias – surtout la télévision – laminent les fondements même de l'institution judiciaire en ébranlant l'ordonnancement rituel du procès, sa mise en scène par la procédure* » (Garapon 1996b : 73).

La question du *lieu* se pose aussi. La justice se délocalise du lieu réel de la salle d'audience de la Cour vers les média, de l'espace réel avec ses interdits et vers un espace virtuel. Cette migration ne fait que suivre celle des flux financiers : *« nous assistons aujourd'hui à la délocalisation de certains procès dans les médias ; non seulement les procès ne se font plus dans les prétoires mais ils n'ont plus de lieu propre, à l'instar de certains marchés financiers, comme le fameux* off shore, *qui n'ont pas de bourse à proprement parler »* (*Ibid.* : 75). Le *rapport au temps* est aussi important dans les affaires qui touchent à la justice humaine. Le temps de la justice est normé, saccadé, lent et ponctué. Celui que nous offre les média joue sur la rapidité, l'instantané et la multiplicité et n'offre pas le loisir de la lente digestion et pérégrination entre les stimuli et les significations.

Sur un plan purement *politique*, cette intrusion des média sur la scène judiciaire est un populisme bien organisé. La justice dans les média pourrait encore donner à voir un populisme qui ne veut pas dire son nom. Comme le remarque Taguieff, le populisme a de multiples facettes car le terme *peuple* sur lequel il s'appuie, revêt de multiples significations (Taguieff 2007 : 70), mais ce que nous pouvons retenir de lui c'est qu'il oppose les citoyens entre ceux « d'en haut », les élites qui conçoivent, dictent et mettent en pratique, et le « peuple », constitué de ceux « d'en bas », qui subissent. Ce qui résulte de cette dichotomie, c'est une conception du *peuple comme victime*. Une fois cette victimologie fondée, il faut la rationaliser en mettant en marche la réduction de la distance entre le peuple et les « autres ». Cette réduction de la distance se traduit par un appel au peuple ; *« l'appel direct au peuple contre ceux d'en haut ou ceux d'en face est orienté par la double prescription de rompre avec le système politique existant et de le changer, 'en finir' avec la 'bureaucratie', la 'partitocratie', la 'ploutocratie', etc. Cet appel au changement prend souvent la forme d'un 'coup de balai' »* (Taguieff 2012 : 40). Cette descente de la justice vers les média est une sorte de populisme dans la mesure où les professionnels de l'industrie culturelle semblent dire au peuple : « l'essentiel de la justice ne doit pas être confisqué par le clergé judiciaire, mais vous (du peuple) êtes compétents pour apprécier et vous n'avez droit, ni aux médiations—qui ne sont là que pour exclure et vous cacher des choses—, ni au secret, ni enfin à la distance nécessaire pour comprendre. La justice est votre affaire et les médias sont là pour vous aider à reprendre l'initiative de la parole et du jugement ! ». Ce qui semble paradoxal dans cette exposition de la justice dans les média, c'est la manipulation du secret. Ce dernier est utile dans l'instruction des affaires et souvent dans l'établissement des preuves, mais avec les média, nous avons l'impression que le secret est aboli avec la surexposition des média. Si le secret est souvent mystificateur, toujours est-il que dans la procédure il sert doublement à retenir et à tenir. *On tient* les personnes qui sont astreintes au secret et *on retient* des informations qui ne sont pas appelées à être diffusées à tort et à travers. Il y a une discipline du dire que la justice à travers le procès met en œuvre. On ne dit pas tout et n'importe comment. Comme la justice protège, la finalité du secret, comme le dit Simmel, est la protection : « *la finalité du secret est avant tout la protection* » (Simmel 1996 : 62). Les média qui prétendent discuter de tout et éventrer tous les secrets ne disent rien de leur mise en mouvement ; « *cette volonté de 'tout dire' et de 'tout montrer' procède en réalité, d'une conception mal comprise de la transparence. La transparence dans une démocratie, ce n'est pas celle des hommes, mais celle des procédures. Elle ne consiste pas à tout savoir mais à ne savoir que ce qui a pu être légitimement établi* [...] *La procédure n'est rien d'autre que l'accord préalable sur la manière juste de savoir et également de ne pas savoir, doublier (l'amnistie) ou d'ignorer (la nullité)* » (Garapon 1996b : 84).

L'argent et le pouvoir. Aux USA, au moment où nous écrivons ces lignes, les média—la télévision surtout—nous montrent le procès de Jodi Arias, cette jeune femme, assassine de son petit ami, Travis Alexander. Durant ce procès qui a pour procureur Juan Martinez de l'État d'Arizona, les spectateurs ont eu pendant cinq mois devant la télévision les diverses épisodes de la saga Jodi Arias. La jeune femme a transpercé son petit ami de vingt-neuf (29) coups de couteau ; terrassé, ce pauvre petit ami, Travis succomba à ses blessures. La jeune Jodi Arias tira au niveau de la tête de Travis et lui trancha la gorge avant de fuir, non sans avoir filmé tout cela. Ce fait malheureux où se mêlent la compassion et l'étonnement pose le problème de la disponibilité des armes à feu dans une Amérique qui commence à ne plus être trop fière de la liberté constitutionnelle de porter des armes à feu. À côté du procès officiel, avec ses péripéties et acteurs, les diverses chaînes de télévision font des procès parallèles de Jodi Arias : un docteur spécialiste de psychologie, le Dr. Drew, fera son procès Arias en plusieurs séquences avec ses invités dans son émission « *Dr. Drew on call* ». Une ancienne procureure, Nancy Grace, fera aussi son procès Jodi Arias en allant d'ailleurs interviewer au sein de la prison d'Arias et ses codétenues et le directeur de la Prison, sans oublier que, Arias elle-même, toute prisonnière qu'elle est, ne cesse de donner des interviews en critiquant et le Procureur Juan, et l'un de ses avocats Kirck Nurmi. Dans ces mini-procès télévisuels se joue la question de la vérité dans la justice. La vérité est-elle de l'ordre de l'immédiat ou bien est-elle toujours médiatisée par des procédures et des secrets ? Quelle est la place de l'argent dans cette procédure qui parle de tout sauf du coût de la mise en scène ? Ce que le procès Arias cache, ce n'est pas le verdict dont on peut prévoir les cinq ou six possibilités, c'est la puissance de l'argent dans la production du vrai ou l'administration de la peine.

Le deuxième procès retransmis à travers les média—la télévision et l'internet—au moment où nous écrivons ces lignes se passe en Guinée-Conakry. Il s'agit de démanteler le réseau qui a été à la base de l'attaque du domicile du Président de la République de Guinée Alpha Condé. Cette attaque a eu comme conséquence immédiate la mort de plusieurs personnes et comme conséquence lointaine l'arrestation de certains membres de la hiérarchie militaire et des divers services de renseignement, des magiciens—chargés de fabriquer des protections mystiques—, des commerçantes et des fonctionnaires retraités. Le procès est donc transmis en direct à la RTG (Radio-Télévision Guinéenne). Dans ce procès, la fameuse transparence et le désir de tout montrer obéissent à la volonté des autorités politiques guinéennes de plaire à la « Communauté internationale », qui est un autre nom des bailleurs de fonds occidentaux. Ce que ce tribunal télévisé ne montre pas, c'est tout ce qu'il a eu concernant le secret de l'instruction, les circonstances des arrestations et surtout les ambiguïtés liées à la Référence : les témoins (l'exemple du Commissaire Principal de Police Aboubacar Fabou Camara), les accusés (Madame Fatou Badiar Diallo et Jean Guilavogui) et même le Procureur (Williams Fernandez) invoquent dieu, leur foi soit en l'Islam (Fabou Camara, Fatou Badiar), soit au Christianisme (Williams Fernandez), et/ou à une religion africaine traditionnelle (Jean Guilavogui), dans un pays qui se veut laïc et dont le Code de procédure pénal ne prévoit pas de prêter un quelconque serment sur Dieu. Ce type de contradictions est purement et simplement oublié quand la justice guinéenne filme et montre le procès. Cette démarche partage aussi l'illusion d'un peuple qui serait compétent—de manière immédiate—en matière de justice.

Dans ce procès, la « Justice » guinéenne ne nous a pas montré comment elle pose et résout les problèmes liés à l'adaptation tropicale et coloniale des acteurs et actes de la Justice tels que la tradition du Code Civil les a institués dans les pays africains francophones. D'abord, *le langage* : comment dit-on Procureur, Avocat général, Greffier, la saisine, en langues Sousou, Malinké, Al Puulaar et celles de la Guinée forestière ? Si ces mots n'existent pas, la fonction qu'ils remplissent dans la justice de l'État Guinéen a-t-elle une teneur symbolique ? Que vaut une justice rendue en langue française dans une Guinée où même les officiers supérieurs de l'armée n'apparaissent pas à l'aise dans cet idiome ?[3] Ensuite, *le temps de la justice*. Le Président, Monsieur Bangoura, proclame le début de l'audience, la suspension et la reprise ; « *Le Président ouvre l'audience en déclarant : 'l'audience est ouverte' ; puis avant de se retirer ; 'l'audience est levée'. Ces phrases rituelles* [...] *enserrent et délimitent le temps du procès. Elles indiquent au public que le temps est doté d'une valeur supérieure ; tout incident sera susceptible d'être acté* » (Garapon 1996a : 54). Ce que la RTG—qui nous montre le procès—ne nous montre pas, c'est bien cette valeur symbolique du temps de la justice. Elle ne nous montre que les acrobaties verbales des avocats, la rhétorique sentencieuse du Procureur et les hésitations des interprètes.

Et enfin *le décor* ou plus exactement les parures portées par les acteurs de la justice.

---

[3] Il faudrait poser le problème des langues du droit en Afrique.

Que signifient ces robes, leurs couleurs, les emblèmes et autres devises qui ornent ce lieu qu'est la cour ? La robe, nous signale le juriste Garapon, servait d'abord de protection contre une espèce de souillure ; ensuite, elle a marqué la distinction et la différenciation entre les acteurs de la justice et, enfin, ses détenteurs sont les usagers légitimes de l'agressivité quand on rend justice à la cour. « *La robe est un costume majestueux qui magnifie, non la personne mais la fonction et même au-delà l'ordre social qui l'a investie. Mais le costume juridique n'est pas réservé aux représentants de l'autorité, mais aussi aux avocats qui représentent les intérêts privés. Avocats, procureurs et présidents portent une robe quasi semblable. C'est peut-être pour cette raison que l'hostilité jouée tout au long du procès devient possible. La robe autorise l'agressivité en rappelant au-delà de la discorde l'unité. La véritable menace ne peut venir que de l'extérieur de ce cercle vestimentaire* [...] » (*Ibid.* : 85). En nous donnant dans son immédiateté le déroulement du procès, la télévision guinéenne voudrait nous persuader que le peuple a une compétence judiciaire qui lui fait apprécier immédiatement toute la procédure et le rituel de la justice avec en plus des bénéfices démocratiques. Comme le dit Garapon (1996b : 79) : « *on peut tout dire des médias à condition que ce soit dans les médias ! Les médias ne seront vraiment démocratiques que le jour où le montage de l'émission, la disposition du studio pourront être débattus, voire contestés* ».

En définitive ce que les média *couvrent*, c'est, d'une part, une réflexion comme l'a fait Marx ou Simmel sur l'argent (surtout ici dans ses rapports avec la justice), et d'autre part, les autres pouvoirs—politiques et mythologiques—qui président à la mise en scène de la justice.

2.1 Nomismos et Muthos

On spécule toujours sur la relation qu'il y a entre *Nomos* (loi) et *Nomismos* (argent). La question de justice se heurte à celle de la mondialisation du droit. La question de l'argent dans les programmes de cette mondialisation est essentielle. On évoque souvent les Droits de l'Homme comme cadre éthico-politique de la justice. Mais on exclut souvent, pour en parler, les questions économiques. Quand et pourquoi accentue-t-on dans un endroit déterminé la question des droits de l'Homme ? L'expérience montre que c'est souvent là où les enjeux économiques sont soit tus soit visibles. Delmas-Marty le note à juste titre qu'il faut cesser « *d'opposer les droits de l'homme à l'économie, et d'y voir deux modèles irréductibles l'un à l'autre. Sous prétexte que leurs finalités seraient différentes – l'un lutte contre les disparités et contre la précarité, alors que l'autre exploite les différences et impose la flexibilité –, ils engendreraient deux modèles antinomiques opposant la raison juridique qui privilégie la réglementation (interdire et sanctionner)* [...] *et la raison économique qui organise la régulation (inciter et négocier)* [...] *En réalité, les deux modèles s'enchevêtrent et le désordre vient des deux côtés* » (Delmas-Marty 1998 : 75). La question de l'argent se pose s'agissant de la Justice. Avoir un bon avocat, un bon détective dans le cadre de la Justice aux USA nécessite beaucoup d'argent. Ce paramètre est aussi à mettre à côté de « l'entreprenariat juridique » : les conseil des grandes firmes d'avocats aux entreprises et multinationales sont là pour attirer l'attention sur le fait que l'essentiel n'est plus, pour ces acteurs de la justice, la vérité, l'équité, l'impartialité et l'égalité, mais le profit et les bénéfices.

Dans le registre du mythe, cette médiatisation de la justice met en question les grands référents de l'imaginaire que sont l'espace et le temps en manipulant les peurs primitives des individus. Le résultat étant de leur barrer la voie à une véritable interrogation sur les interdits fondateurs de leurs sociétés ainsi que sur la Référence (au sens où l'entend Pierre Legendre), c'est-à-dire, ce qui dans une société *« sert de garant dans l'ordre du vrai et du faux ; structuralement la Référence a une fonction de garde-fou »* (Legendre 1988 : 121). Les média dans la justice ou bien la justice selon les média sont à explorer du côté du faire-croire.

3 Justice et crédibilité : le tiroir de la mise en confiance

Si on n'est pas au clair avec les rapports entre la justice et les média, on l'est encore moins dans la confiance que nous avons en la justice. Notre post-postmodernité, celle qui a digéré les philosophies du soupçon, se méfie de la justice. On ne sait pas très bien où la situer ; à la fois du côté des hommes et du côté des Dieux. La Grèce ancienne nous en donne l'illustration avec l'opposition de *Thémis*—qui était la justice entre les familles et dont l'objet était de régler les échanges entre les hommes—et *Dikè* qui était la justice intrafamiliale et dont les transgressions n'étaient punissables que par les dieux, les hommes se contentant de bannir le fautif. Comment faire confiance en la justice quand la victime compte souvent plus que l'offenseur *(Thémis)* ou alors l'offenseur plus que la victime *(Dikè)* ? Cette ambivalence entre justice terrestre et Justice divine ne convient pas à la compréhension analytique de nos consciences post-postmodernes habituées à distinguer et à séparer. Que faire, quand la justice repose sur la qualification des faits et situations d'une part, et d'autre part, produit des fictions ? Que choisir entre les faits et les fictions, à moins de dire que les faits construits par les justices ne sont que des fictions ? On ne fait pas aussi confiance en la justice le plus souvent à cause des problèmes *d'accès à la justice*. En Grèce ancienne, par exemple, *« le citoyen est le seul habitant de la cité grecque qui participe aux tribunaux du droit, et de la même manière, le seul théoriquement, à pouvoir se présenter comme demandeur devant les tribunaux réguliers de droit commun de sa cité »* (Cassayre 2010 : 187). L'accès à la justice est aussi rendu difficile à cause de la position particulière du juge. Celui-ci n'est-il que la simple « bouche de la loi » comme le disait Montesquieu, ou alors un bourreau dont Nietzsche haïssait le regard et le « couperet glacé » (Nietzsche 1993: 335), ou encore un « revanchard »[4] et garant des intérêts des multinationales (Salas 1998 :

[4] Denis Salas (1998 : 152) commente : *« Le thème de la revanche du juge provincial, mal payé et méprisé par la République est omniprésent* [...] *la société judiciaire est peuplée d'individus dans une profession assoiffée de revanche* [...] *où le juge devient un sheriff sans scrupules ».*

153) ? Enfin, la plurivalence de la fonction du juge pose aussi problème. Le juge est à la fois celui qui arbitre avec la Loi comme instance transcendante (Jupiter), celui qui entraîne dans le cadre des multiples fonctions qu'il doit remplir (Hercule) au sein d'un État omniprésent/interventionniste et, enfin, celui qui est l'interface des réseaux quand le Droit, l'État et l'économie se télescopent et entrent en symbiose ou en conflit (Hermès).[5] Les diverses *qualifications des infractions* rendent aussi difficile l'accès à la justice. Dans le cadre des diverses contaminations, *« les catégories du droit varient à l'infini, la contamination est-elle un crime contre l'humanité, un empoisonnement, ou une simple fraude ? Toutes ces qualification et bien d'autres ont été utilisés dans l'affaire du sang contaminé »* (Salas 1998 : 86). La difficulté de l'accès à la justice serait aussi le fait de la pluralité des sources du droit. Georges Gurvitch affirmait avec raison que : *« Le problème des sources du droit positif constitue le problème de toute réflexion juridique ; c'est le point central de la philosophie du droit, autour duquel converge toute la perplexité des problèmes »* (Gurvitch 1935 : 138). Sans oublier que, pour celui qui se mêle de penser ou d'avoir accès à la justice, il doit être fixé sur la claire distinction entre le droit et le non-droit, distinction qui n'est pas claire selon le juriste Carbonnier : *« le droit est plus grand que la règle de droit. Le droit déborde de partout la notion de règle. Il y a toute une partie du droit qui ne tient pas dans les commandements abstraits, généraux et permanents, mais qui est faite de décisions individuelles, de jugements spontanés et sans lendemain »* (Carbonnier 1988 : 20). S'agissant des pays africains, la justice suscite de la méfiance à plusieurs niveaux. 1. Elle n'a pas aidé les Africains à secouer le joug de la néo-colonisation ; au contraire, le procès de l'indemnisation des pays colonisés pour fait de colonisation n'a jamais été à l'ordre du jour et semble même une idée absurde. Comment peut-on croire à la justice, surtout sur le plan international, quand les lois qui servent à dire le droit international sont élaborées sans l'avis des peuples anciennement colonisés ? Autrement dit, la question coloniale introduit un vrai *différend* entre les nations (anciennement) colonisées et les puissances anciennement colonisatrices : le *« conflit qui les oppose se fait dans l'idiome de l'une d'elles alors que le tort dont (les) autre (s) souffre(nt) ne signifie pas dans cet idiome »* (Lyotard 1983 : 24). 2. Les Africains ne comprennent pas souvent dans ces conceptions de la justice pourquoi l'individu serait plus important que le groupe et pourquoi la vérité serait-elle au dessus de l'honneur et de la paix ? Et quand on parle de justice en se référant à la question du patrimoine, en quoi l'individu serait-il plus important que le groupe ? En effet, *« pour le droit coutumier,* [...] *l'individu ne compte guère et la volonté du testament est toujours suspecte. Pour une famille éprise d'ordre et de stabilité, la famille seule est permanente* [...]. *Dans cette vue des choses [on] n'a plus sur son patrimoine qu'un pouvoir transitoire »* (Pourliac & De Malafosse 1968 : 390). Tous ces facteurs—sans oublier le langage par lequel on rend la justice—sont aggravés par les vicissitudes et les lenteurs des bureaucraties des États dits postcoloniaux. Ces lenteurs ne peuvent qu'accentuer le manque de confiance vis-à-vis de la justice, et, au pire, de l'indifférence qui n'est plus la liaison

[5] Voir les longs et instructifs développements de François Ost (2007 : 104 et sv) sur ces trois figures du juge.

que supposeraient l'amour ou la haine de la justice mais la « *non-relation* » et «*déliaison* » (Buffault 2009 : 18).

Les théoriciens de la justice comme John Rawls ont longtemps traité du problème de la tolérance et du pluralisme mais sans toucher à celui de la confiance. Rawls (2000 : 9) dit très précisément : « *une société démocratique moderne est caractérisée par une pluralité de doctrines compréhensives, religieuses, philosophiques et morales. Pas une seule de ces doctrines n'est adoptée par les citoyens dans leur ensemble* ». Si ces doctrines ne sont pas adoptées, Rawls aurait pu se poser la question du manque de confiance. Bien sûr, Rawls ne le fait pas, car son Sujet qui demande l'équité et l'égalité est un consommateur et un calculateur, un Sujet rationnel doté de stratégies et qui, s'il ignore le mot de confiance, est encadré par des procédures. Ce Sujet coïncide pratiquement avec le type accompli de notre post-postmodernité et dont l'Amérique donne *ad nauseam* une belle illustration ; un homme cynique, sourcilleux, plaignant invétéré, amoureux des procédures en ignorant que la justice est autre chose que le gain, la punition ou la mise à mort.

Pourquoi faut-il encore parler de confiance en la justice, surtout en Afrique où elle est souvent, comme ailleurs, soit sous le poids des préjugés, soit corrompue ? La confiance met au moins trois paramètres nécessaires à l'acceptation non cynique de l'idée de justice en Afrique : la simplification, la reconnaissance et la promesse.

La simplification de la complexité. L'une des plaintes qui reviennent le plus souvent dans la manière de concevoir la justice et les institutions judiciaires, c'est la *complexité des règlements* ainsi que des réformes. Au-delà de ces difficultés, on peut noter *l'incertitude* quant à l'interprétation des normes et règlements d'une part, et sur la rencontre des types de normativités d'autre part. Mais, la multiplicité des règlements, changements et interprétations exige quand même devant les cas à résoudre une prise de décision. Et pour que celle-ci soit possible, on doit avoir une certaine confiance en l'autre et en l'avenir. Le sociologue allemand Niklas Luhmann (2006 : 27) constate que : « *malgré tous les efforts consacrés à l'organisation et à la planification rationnelle, ce ne sont pas toutes les actions qui peuvent être guidées avec certitude par une prévision de leurs effets* », d'où la nécessité d'introduire dans la gestion des institutions et des organisations une bonne dose de confiance. Quelle est la fonction de cette confiance ? Réduire la complexité. « *La confiance ouvre, au moyen d'une réduction de la complexité, des possibilités d'action qui, sans elle, demeureraient improbables et encore peu attrayantes* » (*Ibid.* : 25). Pour affronter la complexité des montages juridiques en Afrique et par conséquent agir dans ces incertitudes, il faut de la confiance.

La reconnaissance. Ce deuxième pallier de la confiance nous la montre comme ce qui assure dans un certain sens la socialisation. La confiance assure une certaine réciprocité dans la mesure où elle se veut, en tant que sentiment, la médiatrice entre le connu et l'inconnu. Dans le commerce, il faut une certaine confiance pour faire crédit, pour investir et pour acheter.

La promesse. Les latinistes traduisent la confiance par plusieurs mots (*fides* ou *fiducia*) qui ont varié selon les auteurs et les siècles. La confiance a un sens actif : « *la confiance que je donne* » (Freyburger 1986 : 37) mais aussi un sens passif, le crédit, c'est-à-dire « *la confiance que j'obtiens* » (*Ibid.* : 41). On peut aussi traduire

Fides (foi ou confiance) par loyauté.[6] Enfin, la confiance peut être une promesse, un engagement, un serment. Freyburger retrouve ce sens chez « Plaute, Frag I, 54 : 'qui data fide firmata fidentem fefellerint [...]' *Ceux qui, ayant fermement engagé leur foi, auront trompé la confiance d'autrui* » (Freyburger 1986 : 59). Une justice qui ne fait pas attention à la question de la complexité des réseaux qui la composent, une justice qui ne sait pas comment reconnaître, tenir parole et promettre est vouée à n'être au mieux qu'une technique administrative et au pire une agence de répression et de contrôle. La confiance n'est pas attachement aveugle à une institution, un objet ou un Sujet, mais distance raisonnable entre les Sujets et les Institutions entre les mots et les choses et entre les Sujets eux-mêmes. La confiance est *un pari* sur les Institutions, sur les choses et sur les Sujets.

4 Les justices internationales et mises à mort symboliques

Au moment où nous écrivons ces lignes, le Tribunal Pénal International de La Haye a initié des poursuites contre Uhuru Kenyatta et William Ruto respectivement actuels Président et Vice-président du Kenya. En son sein et parmi les détenus, nous comptons les anciens Présidents des Républiques du Libéria et de Côte d'Ivoire ainsi qu'un ancien Vice-président de la République démocratique du Congo. Il n'est pas question de revenir sur les faits qui leur sont reprochés, ni de clamer leur impunité au regard de ce dont ils se sont rendus responsables... ou non, mais il est permis de revenir sur les objectifs et le *modus operandi* de cette Cour pénale internationale.

Le premier objectif judiciaire était de mettre un terme à l'impunité et de punir les crimes de guerre, tel a été l'objectif premier du tribunal de Nuremberg qui a jugé les dignitaires Nazi et celui de Tokyo qui devait statuer sur le sort des généraux japonais. Dans le même esprit, on a jugé les responsables des crimes de Yougoslavie. Depuis les années 45, en passant par les quatre conventions de Genève du 12 août 1949 jusqu'à la création de la Cour pénale internationale[7] et des tribunaux pénaux internationaux s'agissant des cas de la Yougoslavie et du Rwanda, l'un des grands problèmes qui sous-tendait l'érection de ces tribunaux était de faire le devoir de mémoire. L'objectif n'était pas tellement de mettre l'accent sur les criminels en tant que tels que de marquer par la justice ce qui, de l'histoire passée, doit rester dans le registre de la mémoire. Ces tribunaux ont trois poumons, l'impunité, la responsabilité et la mémoire. Si tous les pays membres de l'ONU condamnent les crimes de guerre, toutefois, la création de ces Cours n'a pas reçu le soutien franc des membres importants du Conseil de sécurité des Nations Unies ; *« On peut notamment penser au fameux article 124, proposé par la France, qui permet à un État de refuser la compétence de la cour en matière de crimes de guerre pendant une durée de sept ans. On sait pourtant que cela n'empêcha pas certains États, comme les États-Unis,*

[6] Freyburger analyse ce sens chez Tite Live quand ce dernier parle de loyauté entre Porsenna et les Romains, « Vtriumque constitit fides », « des deux côtés on fit preuve de loyauté » Cf. *op. cit.* : 50.

[7] Lire pour cette évolution, Hervé Ascensio (2002 : 29–38).

de voter contre l'adoption du traité » (Ascensio 2002 : 37). La suite de l'orientation de ces tribunaux est connue ; ils ne peuvent poursuivre les ressortissants des pays membres du Conseil de Sécurité des Nations Unies. Certainement, les agissements des soldats russes en Géorgie et en Tchétchénie, le sort des opposants de la très démocratique Chine et son satellite la Corée du Nord, les pratiques très humanitaires des soldats américains à Abu Ghraib en Irak et les entraînements au tir de l'armée française installée en Côte d'Ivoire ne méritent pas d'être poursuivis par les tribunaux pénaux internationaux. Mais on pourra toujours menacer tel dirigeant politique africain de poursuites devant les juridictions du Tribunal pénal international.

Cette justice devient une nouvelle arme coloniale dans laquelle la loi est dite dans le langage des puissances commerciales et nucléaires : qui pourra traîner les USA, le Japon, la France, ses satellites du Pacifique et la Corée du Nord au Tribunal pénal international pour crime de pollution nucléaire ? Qui pourra les entendre ou les punir, qui pourra juridiquement qualifier leurs agissements en matière de délinquance nucléaire de crime ? Le Droit international—avec ces Tribunaux—peut ainsi ressembler à une arme pour contraindre les dirigeants du Tiers-Monde—encore qu'un pays asiatique comme le Cambodge a, avec ses juridictions propres, jugé les anciens Khmers rouges—à se soumettre aux ruses des Raisons d'État. Ce qui se passe avec l'arrestation des dirigeants africains—leur transfèrement à La Haye, la propension des autres dirigeants africains à accuser les membres de leurs oppositions à La Haye—est symptomatique de la crise profonde de la Souveraineté des nouveaux États africains. Avec La Haye, la justice internationale semble célébrer *la mort symbolique de la souveraineté africaine*.

Une autre *mise à mort* se trouve aujourd'hui dans le *rapport des Africains à la terre* en Afrique.

La justice vis-à-vis de la terre concerne d'abord la question de la gestion des déchets nucléaires et de leur contrôle, ensuite la vente de la terre des Africains qui s'exproprient eux-mêmes au profit des multinationales occidentales et chinoises. La question des déchets nucléaires est juridiquement encadrée par les textes et conventions juridiques concernant l'environnement, tandis que le commerce de la Nature est encadré par les règles du commerce international. Ce que nous voulons faire remarquer se situe au niveau de cette *désacralisation de leur Terre* par les Africains eux-mêmes. À quoi est due une telle désacralisation ? Elle est la résultante de *la mise à mort des alliances :* verticale entre l'Homme et la Nature, et horizontale entre nos générations et les générations futures. Le tragique de cette mise à mort se trouve dans *« l'impossibilité pour [nos générations] de schématiser [nos] rapports avec la réalité des existants au moyen d'une relation englobante »* (Descola 2005 : 542).

5 Conclusion : de la « Sagesse pratique/tragique »

On pourrait dire que la justice—qui ne se réduit pas aux seules lois – épouse les caractères de ce que le juriste Gérard Timsit (1991 : 55) dit de la loi : *« Elle est prédétermination et parole. Elle est écriture et codétermination. Elle est aussi surdétermination : je veux dire absence, silence, et dans cette absence et son silence, encore plus présente alors et plus prégnante que quand elle est présente et qu'elle trouve son expression dans la parole et l'écriture* ». En amont, dans la phase de la prédétermination, on retrouve la parole, et au moment de la surdétermination, la parole y est toujours presqu'en ellipse. Ce qui nous autorise à affirmer que la question de la justice est avant tout celle de la parole. Parole de l'innocent qui veut comprendre, parole de la victime qui suffoque, parole de l'impunité qui triomphe, parole de l'hésitant qui bégaye, parole de la vengeance qui insiste, parole dans l'incertitude qui cherche les mots, parole de la confiance qui relie et promet, parole brouillée par les réseaux bureaucratiques et médiatiques, parole rongée par la déception, le doute et le cynisme, la justice des hommes—qui, eux, ne sont pas que des consommateurs de marchandises—remet au cœur des préoccupations la question du pouvoir et de la sagesse pratique. Comme le dit Arendt, la question du pouvoir ce n'est pas seulement la question de la domination (le pouvoir sur), mais le pouvoir-ensemble, la concertation. La question de la justice nous renvoie à la manière dont la concertation en vue d'une action commune peut avoir lieu en Afrique. Dans son traitement de la Justice, Ricœur, après avoir rejeté les théories procédurales et déontologiques de la justice, propose une perspective téléologique (le souci de la vie bonne avec autrui dans des institutions à peu près justes) qui aboutit à une « sagesse pratique ». Et la conception de la justice que nous défendons pour l'Afrique devra avoir comme préalable cette « sagesse pratique ».

Ce qui est en jeu dans le traitement partial que nous faisons de la justice, c'est de faire remarquer deux choses : d'abord qu'elle est, en tant qu'*idée,* une *exigence pour lire la fragilité et la cruauté du monde,* et comme *institution,* le moyen *de sonder sa consistance,* ensuite elle nous permet de conjurer l'une des grandes menaces de notre post-postmodernité. Ce qui menace le monde n'est plus seulement le développement des techniques de manipulation génétiques, ni même les réseaux mafieux internationaux, ni même la rhétorique larmoyante et insipide des intellectuels, encore moins la prolifération des armes nucléaires et l'espionnage économique, ni même les diverses ruses des États et des religions, mais la perte de la capacité de se taire et de parler : « *ce qui est sujet à menace n'est pas un individu identifiable, mais la capacité de parler et de se taire. On menace de détruire cette capacité. Il y a deux moyens d'y parvenir : rendre impossible de parler, rendre impossible de se taire* » (Lyotard 1983 : 26). Un monde qui a mis sous tutelle une partie de l'humanité (l'Afrique), pousse aujourd'hui les Africains à vivre cette situation de double impossibilité. Cette double impossibilité de parole aura comme exigence théorique et pratique de changer ces éternels récits/pratiques—imposés aux postcoloniaux—sur l'identité, la sexualité, l'interculturalité, l'esclavage, les langues nouvelles, les Constitutions, les fondamentalismes, l'aide, la coopération, le co-développement—en récits sur l'uranium, l'or, le diamant, l'intelligence, le pétrole, les armes, l'imagination, les drones, les communications électroniques, les manipulations de la vie, la conquête spatiale, le bois, les médicaments frelatés, le sort des déchets nucléaires et la recherche scientifico-technique. La manière de « bricoler » (au sens de Lévi-Strauss) cette double impossibilité de parole sera pour les Africains une « sagesse pratique » (Ricœur) qui sera en fait une « sagesse tragique ».

Bibliographie

Ascensio, Hervé (2002) « La Justice pénale internationale de Nuremberg à la Haye », in Gaboriau, Simone & Paulat, Hélène *La justice pénale internationale.* Limoges : Presses Universitaires de Limoges.
Buffault, A. V. (2009) *L'Eclipse de la sensibilité. Éléments d'une histoire de l'indifférence.* Lyon : Parangon
Carbonnier, J. (1988) *Flexible droit.* Paris : LGDJ
Cassayre, A. (2010) *La justice dans les cités grecques. De la formation des royaumes hellénistiques au legs d'Attale.* Rennes : Presses Universitaires de Rennes.
Descola, P. (2005) *Par-delà nature et culture.* Paris : Gallimard.
Delmas-Marty, M. (1998) *Trois défis pour un droit mondial.* Paris : Éditions du Seuil.
Freyburger, G. (1986) *Fides. Étude sémantique et religieuse depuis les origines jusqu'à l'époque augustéenne.* Paris : Les Belles Lettres.
Garapon, A. (1996a) *Bien juger. Essai sur le rituel judiciaire.* Paris : Éditions Odile Jacob.
Garapon, A. (1996b) *Le gardien des promesses. Justice et démocratie.* Paris : Éditions Odile Jacob.
Gurvitch, G. (1935) *L'expérience juridique et la philosophie pluraliste du droit.* Paris : Pedone.
Horkheimer, M., & Adorno, T. W. (1974) *La dialectique de la raison.* Paris : Gallimard.
Kant, E. (1985) Qu'est-ce que les lumières ? In *Œuvres philosophiques*, T. II. Paris : Gallimard.
Legendre, P. (1988) *Le désir politique de Dieu. Essai sur les montages de l'état et du droit.* Paris : Fayard.
Luhmann, N. (2006) *La confiance. Un mécanisme de réduction de la complexité sociale.* Paris : Economica.
Lyotard, J.-F. (1983) *Le différend.* Paris : Éditions de Minuit.
Nietzsche, F. (1993) *Ainsi parlait Zarathoustra*, in *Œuvres.* Paris : Robert Laffont, « Bouquins ».
Ost, F. (2007) *Dire le juste, faire justice.* Bruxelles : Bruylant.
Pourliac, P., & De Malafosse, J. (1968) *Histoire du droit privé, III. Le droit familial.* Paris : Themis.
Proudhon, P. J. (1858) *De la justice dans la révolution et dans l'église*, T. III. Paris : Garnier.
Rawls, J. (2000) *Justice et démocratie.* Paris : Éditions du Seuil.
Salas, D. (1998) *Le tiers pouvoir. Vers une autre justice.* Paris : Hachette.
Simmel, G. (2007) *La philosophie de l'argent.* Paris : PUF.
Simmel, G. (1996) *Secret et sociétés secrètes.* Paris : Éditions Circé.
Sloterdijk, P. (1987) *Critique de la raison cynique.* Paris : Christian Bourgeois.
Taguieff, P.-A. (2007) *L'illusion populiste. Essai sur les démagogies de l'âge démocratique.* Paris : Flammarion.
Taguieff, P.-A. (2012) *Le nouveau national-populisme.* Paris : CNRS Éditions.
Timsit, G. (1991) *Les noms de la loi.* Paris : PUF.

Index

DOI 10.1007/978-94-017-9175-5, © Springer Science+Business Media Dordrecht 2015

T

U

V

MIX
Papier aus verantwortungsvollen Quellen
Paper from responsible sources
FSC® C105338

If you have any concerns about our products,
you can contact us on
ProductSafety@springernature.com

In case Publisher is established outside the EU,
the EU authorized representative is:
Springer Nature Customer Service Center GmbH
Europaplatz 3, 69115 Heidelberg, Germany

Printed by Libri Plureos GmbH
in Hamburg, Germany